A Pennant for the Twin Cities
THE 1965 MINNESOTA TWINS

Edited by Gregory H. Wolf

Associate Editors: James Forr, Len Levin, and Bill Nowlin

Society for American Baseball Research, Inc.
Phoenix, AZ

A Pennant for the Twin Cities: The 1965 Minnesota Twins
Edited by Gregory H. Wolf
Associate Editors James Forr, Len Levin, and Bill Nowlin

Copyright © 2015 Society for American Baseball Research, Inc.
All rights reserved. Reproduction in whole or in part without permission is prohibited.
ISBN 978-1-943816-09-5
(Ebook ISBN 978-1-943816-08-8)
Cover and book design: Gilly Rosenthol

Cover Photo: Bob Allison, Tony Oliva, and Harmon Killebrew (Photo courtesy of Minnesota Twins Baseball Club).

Society for American Baseball Research
Cronkite School at ASU
555 N. Central Ave. #416
Phoenix, AZ 85004
Phone: (602) 496-1460
Web: www.sabr.org
Facebook: Society for American Baseball Research
Twitter: @SABR

Table of Contents

A Pennant for the Twin Cities: The 1965 Minnesota Twins *by Gregory H. Wolf* 1

Acknowledgements 5

The Owner, Stadium, and Season

Calvin Griffith *by Kevin Hennessy* 6

The Last of the Family Owners: The Griffiths Build Their Lone
Minnesota Pennant Winner *by Daniel R. Levitt and Mark L. Armour* 15

Metropolitan Stadium *by Stew Thornley* 21

Spring Training *by Stew Thornley* 28

The 1965 Minnesota Twins Regular Season Summary *by Ben Klein* 29

The Players and Season Highlights

Bernie Allen *by Chip Greene* 55

Bob Allison *by Gregory H. Wolf* 63

Earl Battey *by Jack Herrman* 71

Dave Boswell *by Gregory H. Wolf* 76

April 12, 1965: Twins Win in Extra Innings on Opening Day *by Steve West* 83

Pete Cimino *by Jeff English* 85

Jerry Fosnow *by Greg Erion* 91

Mudcat Grant *by Joseph Wancho* 97

May 12, 1965: Killebrew Belts Two Homers,
Including Game-Winner In Eighth Inning *by Gregory H. Wolf* 103

Jimmie Hall *by Norm King* 105

Jim Kaat *by Patrick Lethert* 110

Harmon Killebrew *by Joseph Wancho* 119

May 26, 1965: Jim Perry Makes Most of His Opportunity *by Joel Rippel* 126

Jerry Kindall *by Tom Tomashek* 128

Johnny Klippstein *by Gregory H. Wolf* 133

Andy Kosco *by Norm King* 139

July 11, 1965: The Killer Clouts Walk-Off
Two-Run Round-Tripper *by Gregory H. Wolf* 143

Frank Kostro *by J.G. Preston* 146

Jim Merritt *by Gregory H. Wolf* 152

Don Mincher *by Marc Z. Aaron* 159

Mel Nelson *by Doug Skipper* 164

Minnesota and 1965 All-Star Game:
The Senior Circuit Takes Charge *by Greg Erion* 170

Joe Nossek *by Rick Schabowski* 175

Tony Oliva *by Peter C. Bjarkman* 180

Camilo Pascual *by Peter C. Bjarkman* 194

Jim Perry *by Joseph Wancho* 205

Bill Pleis *by Joel Rippel* 211

September 8 and 9, 1965: The Chicago Showdown:
The Twins Take Two at Comiskey Park *by Steve Schmitt* 216

Frank Quilici *by Norm King* 221

Rich Reese *by Chip Greene* 227

Garry Roggenburk *by Mark Armour* 234

Rich Rollins *by Rick Schabowski* 237

John Sevcik *by John Swol* 242

September 25, 1965: "Clinching a Tie is to Beer What
Winning the Championship is to Champagne" *by Alan Cohen* 247

Dwight Siebler *by Gregory H. Wolf* 250

Dick Stigman *by Tom Tomashek* 256

Cesar Tovar *by Rory Costello* 261

Ted Uhlaender *by Joseph Wancho* 268

Sandy Valdespino *by Alan Cohen* 272

Zoilo Versalles *by Peter C. Bjarkman* 277

September 26, 1965: A Pennant for the Twins *by Alan Cohen* 287

Al Worthington *by Bill Nowlin* 290

Jerry Zimmerman *by Norm King* 296

The Manager
Sam Mele *by Bill Nowlin* 300

The Coaches
Jim Lemon *by Gregory H. Wolf* 306

Billy Martin *by Jimmy Keenan and Frank Russo* 313

Hal Naragon *by Tracy J.R. Collins* 321

Johnny Sain *by Jan Finkel* 326

The Broadcasters

Herb Carneal *by Stew Thornley* 337

Halsey Hall *by Stew Thornley* 341

Ray Scott *by Stew Thornley* 347

The Sportswriters

Dick Gordon *by Steve West* 351

Max Nichols *by Steve West* 355

The World Series

The 1965 Los Angeles Dodgers *by Greg Erion* 359

The 1965 World Series Summary *by Norm King*

    Game One: Koufax's Famous Refusal to Play 363

    Game Two: Twins Beat Dodgers at Their Own Game
    to Take Commanding Series Lead 365

    Game Three: 'Well Golllly': Gomer Gets Dodgers Back in the Series 367

    Game Four: Dodger Small Ball and Twins
    Forgetting Fundamentals Tie the Series 369

    Game Five: Koufax's Clutch Hitting (!) Gives Dodgers the Series Lead 371

    Game Six: Mudcat Ties the Series with His Pitching and Hitting 373

    Game Seven: Koufax Has Nothing to Atone for
    with Classic Game Seven Performance 375

By the Numbers: Major League Baseball in 1965 *by Dan Fields* 377

A Surprising Disappointment: The Minnesota Twins
of the Late 1960s *by Daniel R. Levitt* 386

Contributors 392

A Pennant for the Twin Cities: The 1965 Minnesota Twins

BY GREGORY H. WOLF

THE ROSTER OF THE 1965 Minnesota Twins reads like an All-Star team: from Harmon Killebrew, Tony Oliva, Zoilo Versalles, and Mudcat Grant, to Bob Allison, Jim Kaat, Earl Battey, and Jim Perry. In just their fifth season in the Twin Cities, the Twins won a major-league high (and as of 2015 still a record for the franchise) 102 games to capture the American League pennant, ending the aging New York Yankees' five-year grip on the top spot.

The idea of major-league baseball in Minneapolis-St. Paul and the Upper Midwest sounded implausible, even absurd, to many in the late 1950s and early 1960s; a long, snowy winter, followed by a cold, wet spring, transitioning into a short, cool summer, and finally morphing into a frosty autumn with the prospect of snow again. But not to Minnesotans and not to Calvin Griffith, who inherited the Washington Senators from his uncle Clark Griffith in 1955 and relocated the team to the Twin Cities for the start of the 1961 season. A charter franchise of the American League in 1901, the Senators were perennial losers in the nation's capital. Syndicated sportswriter and humorist Charles Dryden wrote in 1909 following the Senators' 42-110 season, "Washington: first in war, first in peace, last in the American League." Save for a brief heyday in the 1920s and early 1930s, when they captured their only World Series title (1924) and appeared in two more fall classics (1925 and 1933), the Senators rarely proved that unflattering aphorism wrong. From their last World Series appearance to their move to Minnesota, the Senators enjoyed only four winning seasons (and one .500 season) and hadn't finished in the first division (the top four spots of a then eight-team league) since 1946. Washington's dismal teams translated into poor attendance. In each of their final six seasons in D.C., the Senators ranked last in the AL in attendance; only once in franchise history (1946) did the Senators break the million mark in attendance.

The Senators' move to Minnesota came during a 10-year period that saw major changes to the baseball landscape and reflected a shift in the demographics of the country. Following the Boston Braves' move to Milwaukee in 1953, which demonstrated that baseball could thrive in a small-market city in the Midwest, the St. Louis Browns relocated to Baltimore (1954), the Philadelphia Athletics moved to Kansas City in 1955, and the Brooklyn Dodgers turned their backs on Brooklyn and the New York Giants departed for San Francisco (both in 1958). Besides allowing the Washington franchise to become the Minnesota Twins in 1961, the American League expanded to 10 teams that season, adding the Los Angeles Angels and awarding Washington another team, aptly named the Senators. The following season, the New York Mets and Houston Astros joined the National League.

The Twins celebrate their first pennant. (Photo courtesy of Minnesota Twins Baseball Club).

A PENNANT FOR THE TWIN CITIES

TOP ROW: Jerry Zimmerman c - Frank Quilici if - Camilo Pascual p - Bill Pleis p - Rich Rollins if - Earl Battey c - Zoilo Versalles if - Joe Nossek of - Jimmie Hall of - Harmon Killebrew if - Tony Oliva of.
MIDDLE ROW: Jerry Kindall if - Dave Boswell p - Jim Merritt p - Andy Kosco of - Jim Kaat p - Don Mincher if - Dick Stigman p - Jim Perry p - Jim Grant p - Al Worthington p.
BOTTOM ROW: Ray Crump equipt manager - Sandy Valdespino of - Bob Allison of - Mel Nelson p - John Sain Coach - Hal Naragan coach - Sam Mele manager - Jim Lemon coach - Billy Martin coach - John Klippstein p - John Sevcik c - George Lentz trainer.
FRONT ROW: Batboys - John Natwick, Mark Stodghill, Dennis King.

The 1965 Minnesota Twins. (National Baseball Hall of Fame, Cooperstown, New York).

After decades of frustration in Washington, the newly christened Minnesota Twins transformed into one of baseball's most successful teams throughout the 1960s. Even though the Twins finished in usual territory in their first season (seventh place), the club set a new attendance record, drawing in excess of 1.2 million, third highest in the league. The Twins played their home games Metropolitan Stadium, located in suburban Bloomington, about 10 miles south of downtown Minneapolis. Since opening in 1956, it had been the home park for the Minneapolis Millers, a Triple-A team in the American Association. The Millers and their league rivals, the St. Paul Saints, ceased operations when the Senators relocated to Minnesota. The original seating capacity of the stadium was expanded from 18,000 to 30,637 in 1960, and expanded again to 40,000 in 1964. The Minnesota Vikings, an NFL expansion team in 1961, also played in the "Met," as the stadium was affectionately called.

At the end of the 1961 season, Sam Mele, who joined the Senators' coaching staff in 1959 after a 10-year big-league career, took over as skipper. Under Mele's guidance, the Twins battled the Yankees for the pennant in 1962, finishing in second place, just five games behind the eventual world champions. The Twins won 91 games for the second consecutive season in 1963, but finished in third, well behind the Yankees; however, they led the AL in attendance. After a disappointing sixth-place finish in 1964, the Twins seemed like a long shot to capture the pennant in 1965.

THE 1965 MINNESOTA TWINS

The Twins' success throughout the 1960s can be attributed to their excellent scouting and farm system, whose roots extended back to the final decade in Washington. The 1965 club was filled with home-grown players who developed into all-stars. Befitting the Senators' long tradition of Cuban players, two men from that island anchored the 1965 squad: 25-year-old shortstop Zoilo Versalles, who led the league in runs (126), doubles (45), triples (12), and total bases (308) to earn the AL MVP award; and 26-year-old right fielder Tony Oliva. In his second full season, the eight-time All-Star established himself as one of baseball's best pure hitters, leading the league in batting average (.321) and hits (185) for the second consecutive year. Former Rookie of the Year (1959) and vocal team leader Bob Allison was a rugged left fielder who blasted 23 round-trippers; center fielder Jimmy Hall chipped in with 20 homers and 86 runs batted in. Arguably the period's most feared slugger, 11-time All-Star Harmon Killebrew had led the AL in homers in three consecutive seasons 1962-1964, but suffered an elbow injury on August 2, 1965, that cast a shadow on the team's title aspirations. But backup first baseman Don Mincher stepped in to belt 22 homers and slug .509. Catcher Earl Battey, who had languished with the Chicago White Sox backing up perennial All-Star Sherm Lollar, was acquired in a trade prior to the 1960 season and developed into one of the best catchers in the AL. The Twins built their reputation as sluggers, smashing 225 and 221 round-trippers to lead the majors in 1963 and 1964. The 1965 squad belted 150 (to rank fourth in the league), but was an all-around team, ranking first in runs, hits, and doubles, while finishing second in triples, slugging percentage, and on-base percentage.

The Twins' pitching staff, which had been considered the club's weakness in its quest for a pennant in 1962, got a big boost from pitching coach Johnny Sain, who joined the coaching staff in 1965. Righty Mudcat Grant, acquired the previous season from the Cleveland Indians, transformed from a league-average hurler to a star, leading the AL wins (21) and shutouts (6). Southpaw Jim Kaat paced the league with 42 starts and notched 18 victories. Two graybeards, 36-year-old Al Worthington (2.13 ERA over 62 appearances) and 37-year-old journeyman Johnny Klippstein (2.24 in 56 outings), anchored a strong relief corps that helped the Twins rank third in team ERA (3.14) despite playing half their games in a hitters' park.

The Twins' 11-inning victory over the New York Yankees—in frigid weather and with the Twin Cities plagued by flooding—on Opening Day augured the team's success in 1965. Battling the Chicago White Sox, Cleveland Indians, Baltimore Orioles, and Detroit Tigers for the top spot over the first 2½ months of the season, the Twins took sole position of first place on July 5 and never looked back. By September 14 the Twins enjoyed a 10-game cushion in the pennant race and cruised to a 102-60 record, seven games in front of the White Sox. Along the way, the Twins led the AL in attendance with a franchise record 1,463,258 (since far exceeded). The Twins were a rough-and-tumble squad, feisty like their first-year third-base coach Billy Martin, who had ended his playing career with the Twins four years earlier, and enjoyed solid seasons from role players like rookie outfielder Sandy Valdespino, swingman Jim Perry (12-7, 2.63 ERA), and hard-throwing 20-year-old Dave Boswell.

The Twins, nominal underdogs against the pitching-rich Los Angeles Dodgers in the World Series, took the first two games of the fall classic, which opened at the Met. After losing three straight at Dodgers Stadium, the Twins returned to their fans in Minnesota with the Series on the line. Mudcat Grant pitched a six-hitter to win the biggest game in his career, setting up a highly anticipated Game Seven. Unfortunately the Twins had no answer for Sandy Koufax, whose otherworldly performance in Game Seven, a three-hit shutout on two days' rest, sealed the Twins' fate and gave the Dodgers their second title in three years.

The year of 1965 was a tumultuous time in American history. The war in Vietnam was escalating and news of casualties was reported on the nightly news; the civil-rights movement, led by Dr. Martin Luther King Jr., reached a critical moment with the march from Selma to Montgomery, Alabama; Malcolm X was assassinated; and the race riot in the Watts neighborhood of Los Angeles resulted in $40 million worth of damage, more than 4,000 arrests, and at least 34 deaths. Major-league baseball, by contrast, perhaps seemed trivial in light of the violence that had seemingly taken over the country. Nonetheless, as it had for decades, baseball—and sport in general—gave Americans a chance to escape, be it ever so briefly, to a place where whites, African Americans, and Latinos competed with and against each other.

This volume celebrates the 50th anniversary of the 1965 Minnesota Twins. I invite you to read the life and baseball stories of all 35 roster players, the four coaches, and the manager of that team, and relive an exciting era of baseball history. Also included are biographies of team owner Calvin Griffith; broadcasters Herb Carneal, Halsey Hall, and Ray Scott; and sportswriters Dick Gordon and Max Nichols. To provide context for the Twins' accomplishments, a comprehensive summary of the regular season, as well as meticulous essays highlighting important games and the All-Star Game played in Minnesota, an overview of the 1965 Dodgers, and thorough summaries of all seven games of the World Series are included. Feature stories about how the Griffith family built its pennant winner, the fate of the Twins after 1965, Metropolitan Stadium, and the 1965 season "by the numbers" round out this volume.

Members of the Society for American Baseball Research (SABR) researched and wrote all of the biographies and essays in this book. Their interest in baseball history and commitment to preserving its heritage have made the volume possible.

    Gregory H. Wolf, editor
    Arlington Heights, Illinois
    October 1, 2015

Acknowledgements

This book is the result of tireless work of many members of the Society for American Baseball Research (SABR). They are all volunteers united by a passion for researching and writing about baseball history. I express my gratitude to Mark Armour, chairman of SABR's BioProject, and Bill Nowlin, in charge of team projects, for their encouragement and support when I initially suggested a book about the 1965 Minnesota Twins.

I thank all of the authors for their contributions, meticulous research, cooperation through the revising and editing process, and finally their patience. I am impressed with your dedication to preserve baseball history by combing archives, interviewing players and their relatives, and telling the baseball and life stories of so many players and people associated with the 1965 Twins.

I am indebted to the associate editors and extend to them my sincerest appreciation. The second reader, Bill Nowlin, read every word of every text and made numerous corrections. This is the third book we've worked on together and it seems like we've corresponded multiple times every day for the last three or four years. James Forr served as fact-checker. His job is an arduous one, requiring him to verify every statistic and fact in every essay. I am grateful to his attention to detail. The copy editor was Len Levin, whose decades of experience as a newspaper editor have helped polish the prose of even the most seasoned writer. Thanks to each of you.

This book would not have been possible without the generous support of the staff and Board of Directors of SABR, SABR Publications Director Cecilia Tan, and designer Gilly Rosenthol (Rosenthol Design).

Special thanks to the Minnesota Twins Baseball Club and Mike Kennedy, Manager, Baseball Publications and Content, for supplying the overwhelming majority of photos for this book. The Twins' support of SABR's nonprofit mission is greatly appreciated. I also extend my thanks to John Horne of the National Baseball Hall of Fame for supplying additional photos. Stew Thornley and Joel Rippel also deserve a note of appreciation for tracking down photos, as do WCCO radio in Minneapolis and the *Minneapolis Star Tribune* for their photos.

And finally, I wish to thank my wife, Margaret, and daughter, Gabriela, for their support.

— Gregory H. Wolf

Calvin Griffith

BY KEVIN HENNESSY

WHEN CALVIN GRIFFITH SOLD the Minnesota Twins in 1984, he was the one of the last of the family owners whose franchise represented their principal business and source of wealth. Griffith spent nearly his entire life in baseball, spending his young adulthood working in one capacity or another for the Washington Senators organization that his uncle Clark owned. Upon the death of his uncle, Griffith took over the franchise and ran it from 1955 to 1984. He ran the operation as a family company, with relatives holding nearly all of the key positions. In 1961 he moved the Senators from Washington to Minnesota, and for the next ten years he oversaw one of baseball's most profitable and successful franchises. Griffith struggled during his last decade in Minnesota, however, after a couple of key family members died and baseball's changing economics undercut his operational philosophies.

Calvin Griffith was born Calvin Robertson on December 1, 1911, in Montreal, Quebec. Calvin was the second child of seven children born to Jane Davies and James Robertson, who married in 1908. His family included an older sister, Mildred (who later would marry Washington shortstop Joe Cronin), a younger sister, Thelma (who would marry Washington pitcher Joe Haynes), and younger brothers Bruce, Sherrod, Jimmy, and Billy. Jimmy and Billy were twins born in 1921. By that time the situation with his family had become a struggle due to James's alcoholism, which eventually would cut his life short in 1923 at the age of 42.

In the summer of 1922 the family was visited by James' sister Addie Robertson Griffith, wife of Clark Griffith, the owner of the Washington Senators. It was soon decided that Calvin (age 11) and his younger sister Thelma (age 9) would return to Washington, and move in with the Griffiths, who had no children of their own. From this point on Calvin and his sister were raised as members of the Griffith family. Upon the death of Calvin's father a year later, the rest of the Robertson family moved to Washington. Although Calvin and Thelma were never formally adopted, they did have their names legally changed—in Calvin's case from Calvin Griffith Robertson to Calvin Robertson Griffith.

Calvin began his involvement with baseball as the Washington batboy in 1922. This role continued through a world championship season of 1924 and the American League championship season of 1925. In 1928 the 16-year-old entered Staunton Military

Calvin Griffith inherited the Washington Senators from his uncle Clark Griffith in 1955, and moved the team to Minnesota six years later. Serving as president and general manager, he oversaw the club's transformation into one of the most successful and most profitable teams of the 1960s and early 1970s. (National Baseball Hall of Fame, Cooperstown, New York).

Academy, graduating in 1933. After Staunton, Griffith attended George Washington University for two years. During his time at Staunton and George Washington, he played baseball as a pitcher and catcher.

In the spring of 1935, Griffith left George Washington and went to work for Washington's Chattanooga farm club as secretary-treasurer, and in 1937 he took over as head man. With the team struggling in mid-season, Clark fired the manager and enlarged Calvin's duties to include field manager. In 1938 the elder Griffith moved Calvin to the same all-inclusive post with their affiliate in Charlotte. In 1941 Clark called Calvin back to Washington to take over a newly opened position with the big league club as assistant secretary, head of concessions.

Over the next 14 years, Calvin took over more and more of the responsibilities of his uncle. Specifically he began attending league meetings in place of Clark, along with taking charge of making player trades and negotiating contracts with media outlets.

Clark Griffith died on October 27, 1955, and on November 1, at age 43, Calvin was elected president of the Washington Nationals. In the reorganization, brother-in-law Joe Haynes was named roving minor league pitching instructor; brother Sherry Robertson became assistant farm director; brother Billy Robertson assumed the position of supervisor of Griffith Stadium personnel and maintenance; and brother Jimmy Robertson remained as director of concessions. Calvin and his sister Thelma had inherited 52 percent of the Nationals' essentially debt-free franchise. The ballclub and the stadium were valued at approximately $4 million.

By 1955 the Washington franchise had suffered through years of poor performance and attendance. Rumors of offers from Louisville, Los Angeles, and Minnesota's Twin Cities were confirmed by Griffith in the authorized biography written by Jon Kerr in 1990. But political difficulties in moving a franchise out of the nation's capital likely led to the delay in any transfer of the Senators. An article in the January 15, 1958 *Washington Post*, bylined by Griffith, said: "I have lived in Washington, D.C., for about 35 years. I attended school here and established many roots here. The city has been good to my family and me. This is my home. I intend that it shall remain my home for the rest of my life. As long as I have any say in the matter, and I expect that I shall for a long, long time, the Washington Senators will stay here, too. Next year. The year after that. Forever."[1]

Later that year, a Shirley Povich article in *Baseball Digest* detailed Griffith's testimony before the US Senate's Anti-Trust Committee. There Griffith tried to backpedal, explaining that what he had said in the *Post* did not mean that he would stay should the club no longer be able to financially function in Washington.[2]

With many large cities clamoring for major league baseball and baseball dragging its heels on expansion, in 1959 a New York lawyer named William Shea championed the creation of a new eight-team major league. Shea was largely interested in replacing the Brooklyn Dodgers and New York Giants, who had departed for the West Coast in 1957. The threat of Shea's Continental League sparked further talks by the American and National Leagues regarding expansion. Part of this discussion included consideration of the Minneapolis-St. Paul area as an expansion site, or alternatively, as a site for relocation of Griffith's Washington franchise. Griffith had been promised a guaranteed annual attendance of 750,000 and an estimated $430,000 media contract by the Twin Cities delegation. Part of a possible expansion plan included the addition of a new team in the nation's capital, as Griffith's possible relocation of the Senators was being challenged in the courts at the time by minority owner H. Gabriel Murphy.

The next year expansion finally became a reality. The National League voted at a meeting on October 17, 1960, to expand to New York and Houston, with those teams beginning operation for the 1962 season. In a meeting on October 26, the American League voted to expand to 10 teams for the following season (1961). Calvin Griffith would be allowed to move his franchise to Minnesota, with a new American League franchise replacing his in Washington.

The Senators were greeted warmly in Minnesota. Ticket orders rolled in for the opening of the 1961 season. Minneapolis sportswriter Sid Hartman probably put it best:

> The Senators became the Minnesota Twins, moved into Met Stadium, took over the concessions business, and there were relatives all over the place: Joe Haynes, Thelma Haynes, Sherry Robertson, Billy Robertson, Jimmy Robertson. You didn't know who was in charge of what. Your reaction was, "What is this? We didn't get a ballclub. We got a family." It was like being around the Beverly Hillbillies.
>
> And then there was this guy Howard Fox. He wasn't a relative, but he was the guy hanging out at Woodhill and Wayzata Country Clubs with Calvin. We wondered, "How does Fox fit it?"
>
> …
>
> It was an odd organization, but who cared? It was terrific to have major league baseball. The Upper Midwest went crazy, sending buses throughout the summer from every little town in Minnesota, the Dakotas, Iowa, Nebraska, and even Montana.[3]

The Twins were very successful at the gate from the beginning. From 1961 though the 1970 season Minnesota topped one million in attendance each year, including totals of over 1.4 million in four of those years: 1962, 1963, 1965, and 1967. The team also showed dramatic improvement on the field. With last-place finishes in four of their last six seasons in Washington, the Twins started with a seventh-place finish in 1961 (in the expanded 10-team American League), jumping to second in 1962 and third in 1963. After a sub-par 1964 season, the Twins won the American League pennant in 1965 and came close in 1967.

Much of the improvement was due to quality players that were signed and developed in the Senators/Twins farm system, most notably Hall of Famer Harmon Killebrew, outfielders Bob Allison, Jimmie Hall, and three-time batting champion Tony Oliva, shortstop and 1965 MVP Zoilo Versalles, and pitchers Camilo Pascual and Jim Kaat—all important members of the 1965 pennant-winning ballclub. By the end of the decade the system had also produced future Hall of Famers Rod Carew and Bert Blyleven.

Calvin was not above interjecting his opinions or directives when it came to his managers. Most fortunately, he insisted that Sam Mele stick with rookie Rod Carew during the 1967 season, when Carew was making the jump from playing Single-A ball in 1966.

In the mid-1960s, Griffith's son, Clark II, joined the organization. Joe Haynes passed away in 1967 due to a heart attack at age 49; Sherry Robertson died due to injuries suffered in an automobile crash in Houghton, South Dakota, in 1970 at the age of 51. George Brophy took over as farm director for Sherry Robertson, and Howard Fox became even closer to Griffith as a confidant/advisor.

By the end of the 1968 season, Griffith had been though three managers in Minnesota. Cookie Lavagetto, the holdover from Washington, was dismissed during the 1961 season and replaced by coach Sam Mele. Griffith let Mele go early in the 1967 season and replaced him with coach Cal Ermer, who lasted through 1968. After letting Ermer go, Griffith appointed Billy Martin as manager on October 11, 1968. Billy had played for the Twins in 1961, his final season. In 1965 the Twins brought Martin back to the major league club as third base coach—a position he held through the 1967 season. In 1968 Billy was sent to the Twins' Triple-A affiliate in Denver to manage the team, clearly grooming him for the top job.

Billy's tenure as a coach with the Twins had been controversial—most notably his physical altercation with traveling secretary Howard Fox in 1966, which had begun on a charter flight and carried over into the hotel. The two publicly made peace, but Fox would continue to dislike Martin. Another notable altercation occurred during the 1969 season when Martin fought with his own pitcher, Dave Boswell, outside a bar on

August 7. This latter event did not please Griffith, who said he had warned Martin against going to the same establishments as his players before he was hired as manager. Griffith did, however, support Martin's fine of Boswell for the incident.

The Twins won the AL West that season, the first year of divisional play, and played a best-of-five playoff series against the AL East champion Baltimore Orioles. The Orioles won the first two games in Baltimore by one run each and then beat the Twins at home 11-2. In the third game, Billy had chosen to start Bob Miller over Jim Kaat, a decision that angered Griffith.

According to Tom Mee, the Twins' public-relations director, the decision to fire Martin came at a meeting during the World Series in New York City on October 13. Everyone in the assembled group of six was asked to express his opinion about whether or not Martin, who had finished his one-year contract, should be rehired. Everyone spoke against Martin until it got to Mee. According to Mee, the "pro-Billy" people were not there–Sherry Robertson, in particular—and only Mee ended up speaking up in favor of Martin. After everyone had spoken Howard Fox called the question, saying, "Well, what are you going to do?" to Griffith, who responded, "I'm gonna fire his ass."[4]

The firing was very unpopular with fans and the media. Don Riley wrote in the *St. Paul Pioneer Press* the day before the firing:

> Just remember what I told you. Griffith may not be popular with the masses but I don't believe he's stupid. If he didn't rehire Martin, he leaves himself open to the biggest fan revolt since Gopher [University of Minnesota] fans learned there are football fields where you can see the game for five bucks.[5]

And in his column the day after:

> Griffith couldn't have done a more dastardly work of unpopularity if he turned down a reprieve for Joan of Arc — or got caught drilling holes in Washington's rowboat.[6]

Arno Goethel, the Twins' beat writer for the *St. Paul Pioneer Press*, added an analysis of the situation a couple days later. All the sources of conflict were mentioned: Martin's temperament, the Howard Fox conflict, Griffith's second-guessing of Billy's managerial style, the fact that Billy did not have complete control over the make-up of his coaching staff, and that Martin couldn't tolerate the nature of the Twins charter flights, which frequently included relatives and associates of Twins front office personnel. According to Tom Mee, the organization never fully recovered from the firing of Billy Martin as it moved into the 1970s.[7]

As Griffith searched for a replacement for Martin, he uttered one of his more memorable quotes: "I can't tell you what I intend to do, but I can tell you one thing; it won't be anything rational."[8] Griffith eventually hired Bill Rigney, and in 1970 the Twins again won AL West. Once again they lost the American League Championship Series in three straight games to the Orioles. This was to be the Twins' last championship under Griffith's ownership. Rigney survived as manager until 1972, when he was replaced in midseason by Frank Quilici.

Aging stars combined with lack of replacements led to the Twins failures of the early 1970s. As the decade wore on, the change in baseball's reserve system led to further problems for Griffith. He had been brought up in the Senators organization learning from his uncle that a baseball team was operated with a bottom line, and was concerned with making a profit, not spending money that the team didn't have. Avoiding debt and interest payments were always paramount in his management philosophy.

After 1970 the team drew over a million fans only twice (1977 and 1979) at Metropolitan Stadium. These lower attendance figures meant less revenue for salaries, which Griffith already considered too high for mere ballplayers. Griffith reacted to the new baseball economics by futilely resisting changes brought on by salary arbitration, player agents, free agency, and the increasing importance of television revenue, which gave an advantage to teams in larger markets. As time moved on, Griffith was considered a "dinosaur" or a "vestige of yesterday" relative to the new baseball owners of the late 1970s.

On the personal side, in 1974 Griffith separated from his wife and moved out of his Lake Minnetonka home. Griffith had married Natalie Morris of Charlotte, North Carolina, in 1940; the couple had three children: Clark, Corinne, and Claire. The two never did reconcile or divorce.

On Thursday, September 28, 1978, Griffith accepted an invitation to travel south to the rural town of Waseca, Minnesota, to play golf that afternoon with his friend, sportswriter Tony Sybilrud, and speak to the Waseca Lions Club that evening. Coincidentally, *Minneapolis Tribune* staff writer Nick Coleman was also in attendance that night. Coleman was not there to cover the event (Coleman lived in Rochester, Minnesota, and covered southern Minnesota for the paper) but attended as a guest of his father-in-law. It was later said that during the introduction of the audience Coleman identified himself by name only and not by vocation.

Griffith's remarks turned into a question and answer format. Griffith began to make comments about specific players and about race in general. Coleman later said, "I was wincing the whole time thinking, 'you don't want to say that.'"[9] Coleman was not there with a tape recorder or anything with which to write, so when he returned from the meeting he wrote everything down from memory. The next day he called his editors to ask if they wanted him to write a story based on what he had heard. They called back and said yes, and that it would run in the Sunday paper.

In the most damaging part of the article, Coleman detailed:

> At that point, Griffith interrupted himself, lowered his voice and asked if there were any blacks around. After he looked around the room and assured himself that his audience was white, Griffith resumed his answer.

"I'll tell you why we came to Minnesota," he said. "It was when I found out you only had 15,000 blacks here. Black people don't go to ball games, but they'll fill up a rassling ring and put up such a chant it'll scare you to death. It's unbelievable. We came here because you've got good, hardworking, white people here."[10]

A few of the comments were specifically about Griffith's star first baseman, Rod Carew. Griffith's comments are believed to have underlined his dislike for agents and multi-year player contracts but clearly also impugned Carew's intelligence:

> Carew was a damn fool to sign that contract. He only gets $170,000 and we all know damn well that he's worth a lot more than that, but that's what his agent asked for, that's what he gets. Last year, I thought I was generous and gave him an extra 100 grand, but this year I'm not making any money so he gets 170—that's it.[11]

This comment, and the comments that Griffith made about blacks, led to Carew's public response in the papers a couple of days later, which also happened to be his thirty-third birthday:

> I will not ever sign another contract with this organization. I don't care how much money or how many options Calvin Griffith offers me. I definitely will not be back next year.
>
> I will not come back and play for a bigot. I'm not going to be another nigger on his plantation.
>
> How does he expect these players to respect the thing that's across their chest—Twins—when it's coming right from the top that he doesn't care about the players?
>
> He respects nobody and expects nobody to respect him. Spit on Calvin Griffith.[12]

Prior to the 1979 season, at the end of which Carew would be a free agent, Griffith traded him to the California Angels for four players. Time, however, softened Carew's feelings for Griffith. In Bob Shower's book, *The Twins at the Met*, Carew is included as one of the narrators. He praised Griffith for sticking with him early in his career. Recalling his Hall of Fame election, Carew also said:

> When I first got the news that I was going into the Hall of Fame, he was the first person I called. It was 3 o'clock in the morning for him in Helena, Montana, and I woke him up. I called him before my mom because I owed him that much respect.[13]

From Griffith's perspective the comments from the meeting were blown out of proportion and misunderstood. Also from his perspective, comments made in a Lions Club meeting were meant to stay within the walls of the Lions Club meeting. It also had been reported that Griffith had had "a few" drinks over the course of the afternoon and evening.

The Waseca talk haunted Griffith the rest of his life. Personally, I have been working in Waseca the past three years, and it appears that even the most marginal baseball fan is aware of the story. Few obituaries for Griffith in 1999 were run without mention of the Waseca talk as the low point in Griffith's career, and his life.

In the latter years of the Griffith-owned franchise much was made of the rift that existed between Calvin and his son, Clark II. Disagreements that may have germinated when Clark did not consent to an apprenticeship in the minor leagues, as his father had done, led to the elder Griffith gradually losing trust in his son's judgment. These disagreements manifested themselves in the organization's response to the changing nature of the business: free agency, advertising, and negotiations between the players' union and the representatives of management, in which Clark II played a significant role. Calvin described his relationship with Clark in a curious comment: "This is a very close-knit family. I imagine you talked to Clark yesterday, and I imagine he may have told you that we don't talk."[14] The addition of Thelma's son Bruce Haynes to the executive mix further complicated the question of who would eventually inherit ultimate decision-making power after Calvin finally stepped down as president.

Beginning in the early 1970s, fueled by the Minnesota Vikings' desire to have a stadium with more capacity that could shelter the team from brutal Minnesota fall and winter weather, talks began regarding a new domed facility for Minnesota sports teams. By 1975, the year that the Twins' and Vikings' leases were set to expire at Metropolitan Stadium, negotiations began in earnest.

Eventually funding for the domed stadium in Minneapolis's Industry Square location on the east side of downtown made its way through the Minnesota legislature. In July of 1979 the lease agreement was worked out with the Vikings. The Twins, on the other hand, had been sending Clark Griffith II, Bruce Haynes, and lawyer Peter Dorsey to the lease meetings with no results. Eventually Calvin entered into the lease negotiations, landing some favorable clauses for the club:

1. The Twins would get 30 percent of the stadium's gross concession receipts up to an attendance of 1.4 million. After that they would receive 20 percent. In contrast, the Viking's lease was for 10 percent.

2. The lease contained an escape clause which allowed the team to be released from the contract if attendance fell below an average of 1.4 million for three successive years or if the team experienced net operating losses in three successive years.

3. If the team could produce evidence of lack of attendance due to summer heat (the architects felt that the Metrodome, being mostly underground, would make air conditioning unnecessary), then the Twins were not bound to play in the Metrodome if the commission did not install air conditioning.

4. The Twins would pay no more than $700,000 of the $1.7 million needed to build the team new offices in the Metrodome.

In 1982 the Twins moved into the Metrodome after experiencing a dismal strike-shortened 1981, both at the gate and on the field. In response Griffith unloaded five high salaried veterans—a couple of whom had just been signed to large multi-year contracts by Clark—and instead relied on a group of young, untested rookies (including Kent Hrbek, Gary Gaetti, and Tom Brunansky). The season rivaled 1981 for results: the Twins went 60-102 and drew less than a million fans—this in their first season in a new stadium. The next season the Twins' record improved to 70-92 but attendance slipped further to 858,939. The Twins were poised to test the three-year escape clause Calvin had negotiated.

Perhaps the most serious threat of relocation was to Tampa Bay. In 1983, Earle Halstead Jr., retired publisher of *The Baseball Blue Book,* took a potential ownership group from Tampa Bay to visit Calvin in Winter Park, Florida, during spring training. The group purchased the 41 percent of the Twins owned by H. Gabriel Murphy. Their plan was then to go after Calvin or Thelma's ownership in the Twins and offer Calvin an opportunity to continue to run the team. The move to Tampa Bay was to take place for the 1986 season. Calvin denied that any deal had been struck and further added that if anyone was going to move the team to Florida, it would be him.[15]

As the 1984 season proceeded, it appeared obvious that the Twins would not draw the 2.4 million fans required to bind the team to the Metrodome lease, and the community began to worry. Local businessman Harvey Mackay organized a ticket buyout that would eliminate the escape clause and force Calvin to sell to a local buyer. Calvin claimed that this attempt, in the end, was in vain, as he could still have shown net operating losses over the three seasons at the Metrodome.

Griffith contended he felt a loyalty toward Minnesota and in the end sold the club to local businessman Carl Pohlad for a price of $32 million in payments and salaries over a period of 20 years. Calvin thought Pohlad was also buying his management team, but few were held over from the Griffith ownership. After the sale Griffith had an office in the Metrodome but was never involved in any decisions. But in the end, Griffith had not only brought major league baseball to Minnesota but also allowed it to stay there.

Three years later, when the Twins won their first World Series, it was with a core of players from the 1982 team. Both 1982 and 1987 rosters included Kent Hrbek, Gary Gaetti, Tom Brunansky, Tim Laudner, Frank Viola, and Randy Bush. Twins farmhands Kirby Puckett, Greg Gagne, Gene Larkin, and Mark Davidson also played key roles on the 1987 World Champions. The new management had also reacquired former Griffith-era stars Bert Blyleven and Roy Smalley.

Griffith died October 20, 1999, at the age of 87 due to a kidney infection, 15 years after he had sold his interest in the ballclub that was his life. He is buried outside Washington, D.C.

SOURCES

BOOKS

Andelman, Bob. *Stadium for Rent: Tampa Bay's Quest for Major League Baseball* (Jefferson, North Carolina: McFarland, 1993).

Anderson, David (editor). *Quotations from Chairman Calvin* (Stillwater, Minnesota: Brick Alley Books Press, 1984).

Baseball Guide and Record Book. (St. Louis, Missouri: Charles Spink & Son, 1960.)

Brackin, Dennis and Patrick Reusse. *Minnesota Twins: The Complete Illustrated History*. (Minneapolis, Minnesota: MVP Books, 2010.)

Grow, Doug. *We're Gonna Win Twins!* (Minneapolis, Minnesota: University of Minnesota Press, 2010).

Hartman, Sid with Patrick Reusse. *Sid!* (Stillwater, Minnesota: Voyager Press, Inc. 1997).

Johnson, Charles. *The Story of How Minnesota Got Major League Baseball* (Greater Minneapolis, December, 1960), 11-13.

Kerr, Jon. *Calvin, Baseball's Last Dinosaur: An Authorized Biography* (William C. Brown Publishers, 1990).

Klobuchar, Amy. *Uncovering the Dome* (Minneapolis, Minnesota: Bolger Publications, 1982).

Leavengood, Ted. *Clark Griffith: The Old Fox of Washington Baseball* (Jefferson, North Carolina: McFarland and Company, Inc., 2011).

McCarthy, Kevin. *Baseball in Florida* (Pineapple Press, Inc., 1996).

McKenna, Brian. *Clark Griffith: Baseball Statesman* (Lulu Press, 2010).

Minnesota Twins Media Guides, 1961—1988.

Thornley, Stew. *Baseball in Minnesota: The Definitive History* (St. Paul: Minnesota Historical Society Press, 2006).

PERIODICALS

Coleman, Nick. "Griffith Spares Few Targets in Waseca Remarks." *Minneapolis Tribune*, October 1, 1978.

Goethel, Arno. "Martin Showed Foresight When Named Twins' Pilot." *St. Paul Pioneer Press*, October 14, 1969.

Goethel, Arno. "Why Did Cal Bounce Billy?" *St. Paul Pioneer Press*, October 15, 1969.

Griffith, Calvin R. "Griffith Not Happy with Armory Stadium Site." *Washington Post*, January 17, 1958.

"Griffith Nixes Report He'll Sell Twins to Tampa Bay Group." *Sarasota Herald-Tribune*. July 2, 1983.

Kahan, Oscar. "Boss of Twins Bombarded by Advance Ticket Orders." *The Sporting News*, January 11, 1961, 9.

Lenehan, Michael. "The Last Pure Men of Baseball." *Atlantic Monthly*, August, 1981.

Libman, Gary. "Angry Twins beat K.C. in 11." *Minneapolis Tribune*, October 2, 1978.

Libman, Gary. "Angry Carew vows he will not play for Griffith's Twins again." *Minneapolis Tribune*, October 2, 1978.

"Minneapolis: Big-League Town in Waiting." *Sport*. December, 1959.

Osterman, Jordan. "Griffith's Gaffe." *Waseca County News*, July 5, 2011.

Povich, Shirley. "Cal Griffith Tries to Explain." *Baseball Digest*, September, 1958, 51-52.

Riley, Don. "Sports Eye Opener." *St. Paul Pioneer Press*, October 13, 1969.

Riley, Don. "Sports Eye Opener." *St. Paul Pioneer Press*, October 14, 1969.

Ringolsby, Tracy. "Sport Interview: Calvin Griffith." *Sport*. April, 1984.

Showers, Bob. *The Twins at the Met* (Beaver's Pond Press, 2009).

Sinker, Howard. "Griffith: Talk Misunderstood." *Minneapolis Tribune*, October 2, 1978.

Smith, Gary. "A Lingering Vestige of Yesterday." *Sports Illustrated*, April 4, 1983.

Washington Post. "Clark Griffith Brings Home 5 More Children to Adopt." November 24, 1925.

INTERVIEWS

Griffith, Clark II. Interview with author, September 6, 2011.

Mee, Tom. Interview with author, September 7, 2011.

NOTES

1. Calvin Griffith, "Griffith Not Happy with Armory Stadium Site," *Washington Post*, January 17, 1958.

2. Shirley Povich, "Cal Griffith Tries to Explain," *Baseball Digest*, September, 1958, 51-52.

3. Sid Hartman with Patrick Reusse, "Sid!" (Stillwater, Minnesota: Voyager Press, Inc, 1997), 95-96.

4. Tom Mee, interview with author, September 7, 2011.

5. Don Riley, "Sports Eye Opener." *St. Paul Pioneer Press*, October 13, 1969.

6. Don Riley, "Sports Eye Opener." *St. Paul Pioneer Press*, October 14, 1969.

7. Tom Mee, interview with author, September 7, 2011.

8. John Kerr, *Calvin, Baseball's Last Dinosaur: An Authorized Biography* (William C. Brown Publishers, 1990), 88.

9. Jordan Osterman, "Griffith's Gaffe." *Waseca County News*, July 5, 2011.

10. Nick Coleman, "Griffith Spares Few Targets in Waseca Remarks." *Minneapolis Tribune*, October 1, 1978.

11. Ibid.

12 Gary Libman, "Angry Carew vows he will not play for Griffith's Twins again." *Minneapolis Tribune*, October 2, 1978.

13 Bob Showers, *The Twins at the Met* (Beaver's Pond Press, 2009), 64.

14 Michael Lenehan, "The Last Pure Men of Baseball." *Atlantic Monthly*, August, 1981.

15 Bob Andelman, *Stadium for Rent: Tampa Bay's Quest for Major League Baseball* (Jefferson, North Carolina: McFarland, 1993), 34.

The Last of the Family Owners:
The Griffiths Build Their Lone Minnesota Pennant Winner

BY DANIEL R. LEVITT AND MARK L. ARMOUR

WHEN CALVIN GRIFFITH FORmally took over the Washington Senators in late 1955 after the death of his uncle Clark, he became the last of the family owners to act as his own general manager. Earlier in the century owners like Barney Dreyfuss and Charles Comiskey had built great teams, often advised by a trusted field manager. But as wealthier, upper-crust men bought into the game, these new owners brought in professional general managers to help them assemble their squads. Money and professional management soon relegated most of the family owners to the second division.

After more than half a century, many writers have a tendency to wax nostalgic on these owner-operators. In fact, these owners, who had no outside source of income, often ran their clubs on a shoestring budget and spent much less on scouting and minor-league operations than the wealthier franchises. By the early 1950s some of these teams were spectacularly unsuccessful. Connie Mack's Philadelphia Athletics only twice finished as high as fourth in the 20 years from 1935 through 1954, the team's last year in Philadelphia, and finished last 11 times during the same period. While not quite as inept as the Athletics, the Senators rarely offered a competitive baseball product over their last 20 years in Washington. Setting aside the chaotic years of World War II, the Senators never finished higher than fourth during that period while landing in the cellar five times.

As an 11-year-old child Calvin Griffith Robertson caught a break when he and his sister Thelma left their poor subsistence lifestyle in Montreal and moved in with Uncle Clark Griffith in Washington. Clark, managing partner of the Washington Senators, introduced Robertson to a life in professional baseball. Although never formally adopted, Robertson reversed his middle and last names so that his last name would be that of his new "father," Clark. After a number of years working in the minors (as both a manager and front-office executive) to hone his craft, Calvin Griffith formally joined the Senators organization in 1942. When Clark died at age 85 after the 1955 season, Calvin assumed control of the club.

One of the Senators' few bright spots was Joe Cambria, a former minor-league player and longtime minor-league owner who became a legendary scout for the Senators. Although he signed such players as Early Wynn and Mickey Vernon, he gained most of his fame for his efforts in Cuba, which led to the signing of more than 400 players. With the help of Cambria, the Senators organization was at the forefront of signing baseball players from Latin America —particularly Cuba—a talent source that was especially attractive to the Griffiths because it was inexpensive. Cambria helped deliver several extremely talented Cuban ballplayers to the franchise.

A solid group: Rich Rollins, Harmon Killebrew, Bob Allison, Don Mincher, Jimmie Hall, and Tony Oliva. (National Baseball Hall of Fame, Cooperstown, New York).

The Cuban connection remained strong in the late 1950s. The team's top two starting pitchers during the Senators' final years in Washington, Camilo Pascual and Pedro Ramos, were both signed from Cuba, and the former had developed into one of the American League's best pitchers. Pascual led the league in strikeouts from 1961 to 1963, finished second in 1964, and won at least 20 games in both 1962 and 1963. Future reserve outfielder Sandy Valdespino came north in the mid-1950s. Cambria sent teenage shortstop Zoilo Versalles to the US in 1957.

While still in Washington, the team had also acquired a number of future Twins standouts via the more typical method of the time: signing amateur Americans. During much of the 1950s, the rules required that a player receiving a signing bonus greater than $4,000 spend his first couple of years in the major leagues. Termed a "bonus baby," this youngster typically received little playing time before being sent to the minors for more active seasoning.

In 1954 the Washington Senators signed Harmon Killebrew for $30,000, though this was partially offset as some of the bonus was earmarked against his salary. Still only 17, Killebrew turned down a multisport scholarship to the University of Oregon. As a bonus baby he played very little for the Senators before getting a chance to start his minor-league apprenticeship in 1956. After an excellent year and a half in the minors, Killebrew hoped to make the team as a regular in 1958. Manager Cookie Lavagetto, however, preferred to stay with the veteran third baseman Eddie Yost.

Griffith, who grew up in the game, was not afraid to meddle in what would generally be considered the manager's domain. In fairness, he was often correct, which paradoxically may have caused his manager even more consternation. To maneuver Killebrew into the lineup, Griffith traded Yost after the season. Nevertheless, Lavagetto still seemed unwilling to make the slugging Killebrew his regular third baseman until Griffith finally forced the decision upon his manager in the spring. Killebrew responded with 42 home runs. Cincinnati general manager Gabe Paul certainly recognized Killebrew's ability and offered Griffith $500,000—a mammoth amount for an owner-operator—for the slugging third baseman. "We knew we couldn't play the $500,000 at third base," Griffith said after turning the offer down. "And we were convinced Harmon would develop into a great box office draw."[1] Griffith wouldn't spend beyond his meager means to build a winner, but he wasn't looking to pull money out of the franchise—he wanted to win and would do everything he could within his financial wherewithal.

Griffith and his scouts signed three other key members of their pennant-winning team for exactly $4,000 in the mid-1950s, effectively skirting the bonus rule. In 1955 outfielder Bob Allison signed with the Senators after his sophomore year at the University of Kansas. Jimmie Hall, the center fielder for the 1965 club, signed in 1956 after finishing high school in North Carolina. The team signed pitcher Jim Kaat, one of the two rotation anchors on the pennant-winning club, in 1957 after his freshman year in college.

Just before the start of the 1960 season, Griffith made a great trade with the owner of the 1959 pennant-winning Chicago White Sox, Bill Veeck. He dealt 32-year-old outfielder/first baseman Roy Sievers for two young players who became key performers on the 1965 Twins, catcher Earl Battey and first baseman Don Mincher, plus $150,000. Veeck had bonded with Sievers during their days together with the Browns in the early 1950s, which possibly distorted his view.[2] Sievers had led the league in home runs in 1957, but in conjunction with his slightly diminished 1959 season, Griffith couldn't refuse this offer. Battey was only 25 years old, and though slow afoot, he was a superb athlete—when the White Sox originally signed him they had to compete with an offer from the Globetrotters for his services—and Mincher was a powerful, if raw, left-handed bat.[3] Even without the money, this trade favored Griffith.

Scout Floyd Baker landed third baseman Rich Rollins in 1960 for a $6,000 signing bonus (the previous bonus rule was no longer in effect) after he graduated from Kent State. "I signed Rollins for his hustle and determination," Baker said. "Not his ability."[4] Rollins almost didn't sign when the team told him he would be starting in a Class D league. He recognized that would strand him too far from the majors for a 22-year-old, and he successfully held out to debut in Class B. Rollins would develop into a solid regular, though by 1965 he was no longer the star he appeared to be in his first few years in the majors.

In the late 1950s, the Washington Senators finished last in American League attendance every year and usually by quite a distance. In 1956, when the Senators drew fewer than 450,000 fans, no other team was under 850,000. Thus, when Minnesota's Twin Cities of Minneapolis and St. Paul came calling on Griffith to entice a move, he was more than ready to listen, and the Senators moved to Minnesota for the 1961 season.

The franchise that Griffith moved had finally begun to show some improvement at the major-league level its last year in Washington. After three consecutive last-place finishes, in 1960 the club moved up to fifth place and a record of 73-81. That squad boasted three position players who would star for the 1965 team: Killebrew, Allison, and Battey. In addition, Versalles, Rollins, and Mincher were in the farm system, run capably by Griffith's brother, Sherry Robertson. Of the future pennant-winning pitching rotation, Pascual had established himself, and Kaat had been handed a little major-league experience as a 21-year-old.

Despite the burgeoning young talent, the team fell to a disappointing 70-90 the first year in Minnesota. Testifying to his dissatisfaction, Griffith fired manager Cookie Lavagetto with the team 23-36 and promoted coach Sam Mele. "The Mele method," wrote sportswriter Max Nichols, "was to reprimand and encourage individually, to remind players often on points to be worked on, but not to give much actual instruction. Players were expected to improve themselves."[5]

Griffith was delighted, however, with the attendance in his new home. The team drew 743,404 fans his last year in Washington, the fewest in the league. In Minnesota the club finished third in the new 10-team league, drawing 1,256,723 patrons. Griffith was not afraid to reinvest his profits in the ballclub — he would not spend more than he took in, but he wasn't using the club to fund a lavish lifestyle.

The club introduced future star Zoilo Versalles to the starting lineup in 1961. Early in his career Versalles had become known as a hot dog. Cambria had told the Twins: "He's just a baby, a hot cup of coffee. You don't light a fire under a hot cup of coffee, you cool him off a little and be nice to him then you'll find you'll love him." Nevertheless, managers Cookie Lavagetto and Sam Mele dispensed discipline and prodding.[6] And in his early years Versalles exhibited a swagger and moodiness that masked the fears of a young man in a strange country.

In early 1961 the organization added another Cuban, a man who would become one of the decade's best players. Pedro Oliva signed with Cambria in February and left for the United States six weeks later. Because he did not have a passport, he borrowed his brother Antonio's and thereafter adopted the name Tony.

After arriving in America, Oliva, along with 21 other Cubans, went straight to a tryout camp in Florida. The camp had only several days remaining, and Oliva was released after a four-game audition. Determined to get into Organized Baseball, Oliva received some help from Charlotte owner Phil Howser, then part of the Twins' minor-league system. Howser paid for Oliva's room and board, let him practice with the team, and then sent him to a rookie league in June. A player who was to become one of their greatest stars had nearly slipped away.

The team responded well to Mele in 1962, and the young talent that Griffith had accumulated finally fulfilled its potential. In a bid to improve the infield defense and support the team's young infielders, Griffith had swapped Ramos to the Indians for veteran first baseman Vic Power, renowned for his fielding prowess, and hurler Dick Stigman. To accommodate their new first sacker, the Twins moved Killebrew from first base to left field.

The Twins jumped all the way to 91 wins, the most by the franchise since 1933. Killebrew had a great year at the plate, coming in third in the MVP balloting, and both he and Allison finished in the top five in slugging. Rich Rollins joined the lineup, made the All-Star team, and came in eighth in the MVP voting. The Twins also promoted second baseman Bernie Allen to the lineup. Allen had signed the year before for a big bonus after leaving Purdue and joined the Twins' Class A farm team for the remainder of the season. In 1962 he played in 159 games and finished third in the Rookie of the Year balloting. Jim Kaat became a star, finishing second in innings pitched and sixth in ERA, and Pascual turned in another stellar season, despite missing much of August with an inflamed tendon.

For 1963 Griffith brought back essentially the same team, expecting that his young team could continue to grow. But the team started slowly, bottoming out at 11-20 on May 15. To bolster his squad, in early May Griffith swapped lefty starter Jack Kralik — the team was overloaded with left-handed starters — to Cleveland for righty Jim Perry, a terrific pitcher in 1960 who had seemingly plateaued. The team also inserted Jimmie Hall, who had been filling in for Killebrew and Allison, into the starting lineup in June. After taking over for incumbent center fielder Lenny Green, Hall validated Mele's trust. He slugged 33 home runs and finished third in the Rookie of the Year voting. The Twins bounced back after their slow start to again win 91 games, well behind the Yankees, who won 104.

This was clearly a talented squad. They hit 225 home runs, tied for the second most ever to that point, and led the league in runs scored. The pitching came through as well. Behind a rotation led by Pascual, Kaat, Stigman, and Perry, the Twins had the third best ERA in the league. Moreover, the team was likely even better than its record: its 767 runs scored and 602 allowed translated to a Pythagorean record of 98-63. Expectations were high indeed for 1964.

While Griffith was satisfied with the talent in his organization, he had a decision to make regarding one of his top farmhands. Tony Oliva had hit .304 with 23 home runs for Dallas-Fort Worth in 1963, after hitting .410 and .350 his previous two years in the minors. In Minnesota, Griffith had an outfield full of stars — Killebrew, Allison, and Hall had all finished in the top five in slugging — but Griffith smartly recognized he needed to move Oliva into the lineup. To accommodate Oliva, Griffith dictated that Mele move Allison to first, put Oliva in right, and bench the aging Power. Pushing Oliva onto the team was a brilliant move, but putting Allison at first instead of Killebrew was certainly curious.

Oliva responded to the Twins' show of confidence with one of the best rookie seasons of all time. He led the league in batting average, runs, hits, doubles, and total bases. His 374 total bases were the most in the league between Mickey Mantle in 1956 and Jim Rice in 1977. Oliva also worked extremely hard on his fielding. Although he never really became a great outfielder, he improved enough to win a Gold Glove in 1966.

Despite Oliva's performance and 221 home runs, the 1964 Twins fell all the way to sixth with a 79-83 record, and the season was viewed as a bitter disappointment. Moreover, the team lost Bernie Allen in June to a career-altering injury. He severely tore ligaments in his knee when Don Zimmer took him out at second with what Allen remembered as a "cross-body block" after a "lollipop" throw from Versalles.[7]

Griffith, ever the activist, refused to concede the season and made three key moves in June, willingly and astutely spending the money his 1963 league-leading attendance afforded him. To bolster his faltering bullpen — 1963 hero Bill Dailey suffered arm problems and couldn't repeat his outstanding performance — Griffith purchased two veteran relievers: Al Worthington from Cincinnati and Johnny Klippstein from Philadelphia. Both would excel in 1965. Griffith also picked up starter Jim "Mudcat" Grant in exchange for fifth starter Lee Stange, utilityman George Banks, and about $25,000.[8] Grant had started the season poorly, but had been a reliable, league-average pitcher over the previous several seasons.

Griffith blamed much of the season's fiasco on Mele. He felt that his manager failed to sufficiently rest his regulars. "Mele has not rested players to my satisfaction," Griffith said. "Whoever manages the Twins next year [hardly a vote of confidence for his manager] will sit down with me in the spring and discuss a general policy of resting players."[9]

Griffith also believed the team played "stupid, shabby baseball," a sentiment subscribed to by a number of sportswriters.[10] "By 1964 the Twins' mental errors had become the talk of the league," wrote Max Nichols. "Fundamental plays were beating them. Outfielders threw to the wrong bases almost daily. Infielders blew rundowns. Pitchers failed to cover first base. Infielders slept."[11] The team had once again underperformed its Pythagorean record, this time by eight games. Minnesota's run differential of 737 runs scored and 678 runs allowed would typically result in a record closer to 87-75. Whether the difference between a team's actual won-loss record and that projected by its runs scored and allowed is mostly a function of random variation or can be attributed to some fundamental team characteristic remains unresolved within the baseball analytic community. In any case, something was clearly going on with the Twins. They had underperformed their run differential by a whopping 15 games over the past two years. And at a time before baseball observers understood the direct mathematical relationship between run differential and wins and losses, there was a widespread sense that the Twins were underperforming due to mental errors and a lack of fundamentals.

Griffith decided not to fire Mele but he rearranged the team's coaching staff, bringing in two independent, strong-willed men. He signed Johnny Sain to be the pitching coach for roughly $20,000, making him one of the highest salaried coaches in baseball. Sain had been the pitching coach on the pennant-winning Yankees until he was let go after the 1963 season when he asked for a raise and a two-year contract. Sain spent 1964 working at his automobile dealership, but eagerly jumped back into baseball when Griffith came calling with an open checkbook. Whether due to Sain's influence or other factors, the Twins' ERA fell from 3.58 in 1964 to 3.14 in 1965, and the pitchers swore by Sain.

"No man alive knows more about that little baseball and how to throw it than Johnny Sain," Worthington said. Mudcat Grant told reporters: "He made a winner out of me. He's given me a second curve. It's a quick, hard pitch. He can get it out of you. He has talent. He's a great teacher."[12]

To shore up the infield defense and add some spark to the club, Griffith hired fiery Billy Martin as the infield and third-base coach. Martin's playing career had ended with the Twins when Mele released him at the end of spring training in 1962. Most recently, Martin had been a Twins scout. He immediately took an individual interest in Versalles and the two became very close. In fact, during spring training in 1965 Mele fined Versalles $300 for saying he was only leaving the field because Martin had told him to after Mele benched him for lackadaisical play.[13] This quickly blew over, and Versalles went on to the best season of his career, winning the MVP award in 1965. In Martin and Sain, Mele had a couple of great coaches, but they would require continuous monitoring and judicious handling.

Griffith also hoped to pull off at least one blockbuster trade to rearrange his talent. At the winter meetings he reportedly worked out a deal with the Mets. The Twins would receive second baseman Ron Hunt, already an All-Star at 23 (to address the uncertainty from Allen's injury rehab); catcher Chris Cannizzaro; and solid starter Al Jackson. In exchange Griffith would send the Mets Hall, Battey, Perry, and either Rollins or Allen. Luckily for the Twins, Mets president George Weiss eventually turned this deal down.[14] In a minor trade the team obtained second baseman Cesar Tovar from Cincinnati for a promising lefty, Gerry Arrigo, who never developed. Tovar went on to a number of fine seasons as a multi-position player with the Twins.

Griffith had built a great team. For 1965 Allison and Killebrew switched positions, so Harmon was now back at first and Allison was in left. Hall and Oliva rounded out a terrific outfield, at least offensively. Rollins and Versalles anchored the left side of the infield, and Battey was one of the league's best catchers.

Only at second base, manned by Jerry Kindall, did the Twins have anything less than a star-quality hitter, though Rollins had regressed significantly since his first years in the majors. Don Mincher provided a powerful left-handed bat off the bench. The rotation was anchored by Kaat, Pascual, and Grant. Sain and Mele tapped 20-year-old righty Dave Boswell, signed after high school in 1963, to be the fourth starter, leaving Perry in reserve should one of the top four falter. Worthington and Klippstein were the two key men in the bullpen.

The depth would come in handy. After a great start to the 1965 season, winning his first eight decisions, Pascual tore a muscle in his back near his shoulder. He tried to pitch through it for a month before undergoing surgery in July. Boswell missed much of the season with mononucleosis and pneumonia. To fill some of the void, Perry stepped in and pitched well enough to finish ninth in the league in ERA.

Mincher provided a valuable bat when Killebrew missed time with an elbow injury. Furthermore, to get Mincher's bat into the lineup when Killebrew was healthy, Mele experimented with a platoon in which Killebrew played third base against right-handers and Mincher played first. This cost the slumping Rollins, who also occasionally filled in at second, some playing time at third.

In his decade at the helm Griffith had masterminded the turnaround of one of baseball's most hapless franchises. While in Washington he had brought in a number of talented ballplayers on the cheap. Only Killebrew cost more than the bonus limit and many came at little or no cost through Cambria's Cuban connections. When Minnesota proved to be the financial bonanza he had hoped, Griffith spent his additional revenues on building his pennant winner. He purchased players, included money in trades, and paid top salaries to his stars.

Griffith had developed good baseball instincts at the foot of his uncle Clark, and was not shy about involving himself directly with the team. When he sensed Killebrew was ready, he forced his manager to make room for him despite a veteran incumbent blocking the position; several years later he forced the issue for another future star, Tony Oliva. When Griffith felt his team wasn't playing up to par after 1964, he revamped his on-field staff with expensive, big-name coaches, and the team responded. Under this baseball-savvy owner willing to spend his profits, the young and talented Twins appeared poised for many years of pennant contention.

NOTES

1 Dave Anderson, "The Riddle of Harmon Killebrew," *Official Baseball Annual*, 1963.

2 John Steadman, "He Made It the Hard Way," *Sports Review*, May 1958.

3 "Iron Man in an Iron Mask," *Dell Sports*, July 1962.

4 Joe Donnelly, "The Rich Rollins Surprise," *Sport*, October 1962.

5 Max Nichols, "Sam Mele: A Study in Pressure," *Sport*, April 1966.

6 Bill Libby, "Versalles in Search of Himself," *Sport*, February 1964.

7 Dean Urdahl, *Touching Base With Our Memories* (St. Cloud, Minnesota: North Star Press, 2001), 5.

8 Terry Pluto, *The Curse of Rocky Colavito* (New York: Fireside, 1995), 69.

9 Jon Kerr, *Calvin: Baseball's Last Dinosaur* (Dubuque, Iowa: Wm. C. Brown, 1990), 67.

10 Ibid.

11 Nichols, "Sam Mele."

12 Ed Rumill, "He Proves Yanks' Letting Him Go Wasn't Sain Move," *Baseball Digest*, September 1965; Pat Jordan, "In a World of Windmills," *Sports Illustrated*, May 8, 1972.

13 Francis Stann, "Erstwhile Moody Versalles Wins Acceptance," *Baseball Digest*, October-November 1965; Nichols, "Sam Mele."

14 William Leggett, "Everybody Pick Up a Drum," *Sports Illustrated*, August 23, 1965.

Metropolitan Stadium

BY STEW THORNLEY

METROPOLITAN STADIUM IN Bloomington, Minnesota, served the American League's Minnesota Twins for 21 seasons. However, it was originally the home of a minor-league team, the Minneapolis Millers of the American Association.

The drive for a new ballpark for the Millers began in the 1940s. In June of 1948, the Millers, affiliated with the parent New York Giants, and the Minneapolis Board of Park Commissioners agreed on a 17-acre tract near Theodore Wirth Park, slightly less than three miles west of downtown Minneapolis, for a new ballpark. The site was bounded on the north by Olson Memorial Highway, on the south by Glenwood Avenue, on the west by Xerxes Avenue North, and on the east by the Great Northern Railroad tracks. It was the intention of the Millers/Giants to purchase the property, reroute a stream to its natural channel, and construct a stadium with a seating capacity between 20,000 and 30,000. Home plate would be in the southwest corner, near the corner of Glenwood and Xerxes.

According to Halsey Hall in the *Minneapolis Tribune* of June 10, 1948, Minneapolis Mayor Hubert Humphrey "said flatly that the stadium would be a good thing for clean professional sport, for recreation and for a 'growing place' for young America in Minneapolis. He stressed the need for action and quickly."

However, the first action came from residents in the Glenwood-Wirth area who objected to the site and quickly formed a committee to circulate a petition that read, "This group goes on record unanimously in requesting the park commissioners not to take the contemplated action in establishing a ball park in the Wirth park area, nor to sell, transfer, or lease the property to a commercial enterprise."

One of the strategies for promoting a new stadium was to denigrate the existing one. (The strategy continued into the 21st century.) Dick Cullum, who had written for newspapers in Minneapolis and St. Paul, had his first "Cullum's Column" in the *Minneapolis Tribune* on June 14, 1948, as the new ballpark site was being debated. Cullum wrote that fans "can look forward to better things in a better park," and attacked the Millers' existing park: "That's pretty poor baseball we have to look at in Nicollet Park. We have to go to that old crate a great many times to see one well played ball game.... In Nicollet Park, where every pitcher has to work hard on every batter and where the poorest ball player in the league may upset all percentages and make a burlesque of the game of baseball, a fan does not see any fraction of the number of genuine baseball plays he would see in a standard ball park. It just isn't baseball."

A ballpark never was built at the Glenwood site. Alternate sites were studied and, in late 1949, the Minneapolis Baseball and Athletic Association went farther west, beyond the Minneapolis city limits into St. Louis Park, and purchased 33 acres of land with

Construction of Metropolitan Stadium began in June 1955. It opened ten months later in April 1956. (Photo courtesy of Minnesota Twins Baseball Club).

1,400 feet of frontage on the south side of Wayzata Boulevard (now Interstate 394), about a quarter-mile west of what is now Minnesota Highway 100.

A neighboring restaurant, McCarthy's Café, had sold the land to the association at a reduced price because of the potential business it would generate. An apparent agreement, that McCarthy's could buy back the property if no stadium emerged, was not put in writing. New York Giants owner Horace Stoneham assured the sellers and the village of plans to build an 18,000-seat stadium, with construction to start immediately and completion possibly in time for the 1950 season. Years later, a restaurant employee told reporter R.T. Rybak, "We wanted to put it in the contract that the sale would not be final unless the stadium was built, but [Giants owner Horace] Stoneham said that wasn't necessary 'because we are all men of our word.'"

However, the land remained dormant. A convenient reason given was that the outbreak of the Korean conflict in 1950 brought a halt to construction of sports facilities. Less convenient to the explanation is that Milwaukee built a new stadium in the early 1950s and the Giants and the Minneapolis Baseball and Athletic Association had plenty of time to build the ballpark before the war began. It's possible the Giants got cold feet or delayed the start of construction so long that the eventual war in Korea created material shortages and hampered plans. It's even possible that the entities only used the promise of a ballpark to get the land on the cheap.

Later in the 1950s McCarthy's Café unsuccessfully sued the Millers and Giants to get the land back. The Giants held on to the property for more than 20 years, and the empty lot eventually was called Candlestick Park, the same name of the stadium the Giants built on Candlestick Point in San Francisco after moving west. When the Giants finally sold the property, they reportedly received a price more than four times as much as they had bought it for.

As all this was happening, an itch for major-league baseball was developing in the area. The Minneapolis Chamber of Commerce asked its president, Gerald Moore, to explore the possibility. Moore appointed a committee for this purpose, and the group began meeting in March of 1953, at about the same time that the Boston Braves of the National League moved to Milwaukee, the first geographic shift in major-league baseball since 1903. Up to this point, all 16 major-league teams occupied just ten cities.

A half-century of inertia had been broken, and seeing Milwaukee, another Midwestern city approximately the same size as the Minneapolis-St. Paul area, get a team made believers not just out of the burgeoning major-league committee but of Minnesota fans in general. Milwaukee found itself in a fortunate position when a major-league team was ready to move, having just built a new stadium for the minor-league Brewers; instead it was used by the big-league Braves. No thought of major-league baseball was behind the building of this new stadium, according to Milwaukee baseball historian Bob Buege. "When ground was broken for County Stadium on October 19, 1950, the clear understanding was that the park would be used by the Brewers," Buege said. "The hope of getting major-league baseball was never even used by proponents in helping to get public funding for the ballpark."

It soon became apparent to the Minneapolis committee that a new stadium would be needed to lure a team to Minnesota. The Twin Cities joined other cities in trying to land the St. Louis Browns. The committee offered the use of an extremely spartan stadium on the park board's Parade Grounds, on the western edge of downtown Minneapolis, until a new stadium could be built. The Browns instead went to Baltimore in 1954 and became the Orioles, and the Minneapolis baseball committee set its sights on a new stadium before focusing on luring another team.

An impasse had already developed between Minneapolis and St. Paul interests over the site of the new stadium. In the fall of 1953, St. Paul voters approved a bond issue for a new ballpark in the Midway area of the city. The Minneapolis baseball committee went its own direction, picking a site outside the city limits on a 160-tract of land in suburban Bloomington, and an organization called the Minneapolis Minute Men was formed to raise money for the stadium. In the midst of the bond drive by the Minute Men, the Minnesota Legislature created the Metropolitan Sports Area Commission to operate the new stadium.

The Minneapolis Minute Men set a goal of $800,000 in bond sales through public subscription while another $3 million would be sold on the market to investors. The Minute Men organized into 16 teams, named after major-league teams, and each had a quota of $50,000 to reach the overall goal. The drive, when completed on March 31, 1955, had exceeded its goal by more than 50 percent, with $1,212,000 in bonds being sold. The Indians team, managed by Gunnar Rovick, had the top team sales, of $152,000 while Joe Duffy of the Indians was the individual champion, selling 100 bonds for a total of $50,000.

Sixty years before, Nicollet Park had been built in three weeks. Although the new Bloomington stadium didn't rise as quickly, the transformation from cornfield to baseball stadium was remarkable in its rapidity.

However, the beginning of construction—scheduled for June 20, 1955—was almost delayed because of a protest by the owners of the property on which the stadium would be built. Claiming they hadn't yet been paid, one of the owners, Paul Gerhardt, created a barricade of farm equipment along his property line, which ran directly through where the infield of the stadium would be. However, the dispute was settled in time for the groundbreaking to go forward as planned.

A large crowd of spectators joined a number of dignitaries (who included Minneapolis Mayor Eric Hoyer but not St. Paul Mayor Joseph Dillon, who had already said his city would not support this stadium site) to see the first shovelfuls of dirt being tossed. Several members of the Minneapolis Millers came out and posed for photos as pitcher Joe Margoneri tossed balls to catcher Carl Sawatski. Player-manager Bill Rigney stood in the batter's box while general manager Rosy Ryan assumed the duties of the umpire.

Kimmes Construction Company started the first work on the 160-acre site, performing grading, drainage, surfacing, sodding, sanitary sewer installation, and miscellaneous construction. The grading work involved the excavation of over 400,000 cubic yards of material. On September 15, as the earthwork continued, Johnson, Drake & Piper, Inc. of Minneapolis was awarded the general contract for the stadium on a bid of $2,949,200.

In late September Matty Schwab was brought in to oversee the laying of sod and work on the infield. Schwab was the groundskeeper at the Polo Grounds, the Giants' home in New York, and was one of the most renowned in his field. (Schwab even lived in the Polo Grounds during the season, in a small apartment beneath the left-field stands.)

The first load of structural steel, supplied by the American Bridge Division of the U.S. Steel Corporation, didn't arrive until mid-January in 1956. At the same time, Axel Ohman Company began the brick work. The structure rose quickly over the next month. Steel erection for the second and third decks began on February 10 with the placement of the first seats in the lower deck commencing a week later.

Then, on Sunday, February 26, an explosion rocked the stadium, setting off a fire on the third-base side of the grandstand that made it necessary to rebuild one section of it. The placement of the concrete had just been completed, and butane heaters were being used to warm the concrete as it cured. "Exploding tanks ripped through the concrete floor and one bomblike tank landed a few feet from the left-field fence, almost the first home run in the new stadium," said narrator Dick Enroth in a film made by WCCO Radio and Television soon after the stadium opened. Another fire struck a set of storage shacks barely three weeks later although this did not affect the stadium itself.

Despite the setbacks, construction remained on track and on April 24, 1956—barely ten months after groundbreaking ceremonies—the Minneapolis Millers opened Met Stadium with a game against the Wichita Braves. The stadium was still without an official name, which did not come until that July when

Located about ten miles south of Minneapolis, Metropolitan Stadium was the home of the Twins from 1961 through the 1981 season. (Photo courtesy of Minnesota Twins Baseball Club).

it was announced that it would be called Metropolitan Stadium. The distances down the line to right and left were 316 feet, 3 inches, and the distance to center field was 405 feet, and the outfield was surrounded by an 8-foot-high fence. A triple-decked permanent grandstand extended only to the end of each of the dugouts, although portable seating expanded the capacity and a crowd of 18,366 attended the first game.

One of the most significant components of Met Stadium was not what it had, but what it didn't have: posts to support decks or roofs above. By going to cantilever construction for the overhanging decks, architect Foster Dunwiddie of Thorshov and Cerny, Inc. had found a way to eliminate the posts, which often block the view of some fans in other stadiums. The expansion a few years earlier of Husky Stadium in Seattle, used by the University of Washington football team, had been recognized as the first use of cantilever construction in a sports facility. Met Stadium became the first baseball stadium in the country to take advantage of this principle.

The reason for the new stadium was not to provide better facilities for the minor-league Millers but to have a first-class stadium available for a major-league team to eventually occupy. The lure of the Met eventually achieved its objective. In October of 1960 Calvin Griffith announced he was moving his American League Washington Senators franchise to Minnesota, and, in 1961, the Minnesota Twins took the field for the first time.

According to James Quirk in "Stadiums and Major League Sports: The Twin Cities," a 1997 Brookings Institute publication, "For the individuals holding the revenue bonds issued to finance the Met, it [the arrival of the Twins and football's Minnesota Vikings, who also used the stadium] could not have come at a better time. Between 1956 and 1961, the Met did not earn enough to cover required interest payments on the bond, and the facility would have been in default except that certain large bondholders, civic-minded firms, and individuals agreed to wait for their money until major league sports made it to the stadium."

Met Stadium was expanded with the coming of the major-league baseball. Originally the triple-decked grandstand extended only around the infield. With the arrival of the Twins, the first two decks were extended beyond the foul pole in right field, although a similar extension was not done in left field. Bleachers filled the gap down the left-field line beyond the permanent grandstand. A new press box was built into the second deck. The previous press quarters, on top of the third deck, were converted into six "elite" boxes, an early albeit simpler version of the luxury suites that are a staple of modern stadiums.

The outfield consisted of a series of bleachers, interrupted by a batter's eye in center field and in right-center field by the scoreboard, with the bullpens in front of the scoreboard. In 1965 the bleachers in left field were replaced by a double-decked grandstand. (Work on the grandstand was continuing as the 1965 baseball season began, and one of the construction workers was able to corral a home-run ball hit into the stands by Elston Howard of the New York Yankees in the season opener.)

The new grandstand in left field was for the benefit of the National Football League's Minnesota Vikings; it allowed more fans to sit along the sidelines for football games. The Twins also benefited from the extra capacity provided by the new grandstand as they hosted two major events in 1965. The first was the All-Star Game in July. An added bonus was the World Series as Minnesota won the American League pennant. The Twins lost the World Series to the Los

Angeles Dodgers in seven games with the final game drawing 50,596, the only time a baseball crowd exceeded 50,000 at Met Stadium.

In addition to the Twins and Vikings and later the Minnesota Kicks soccer team, Met Stadium hosted events ranging from wrestling matches to a concert by the Beatles, who came to Minnesota on their second tour of the United States, on August 21, 1965.

Metropolitan Stadium was considered a good venue for baseball but not for football, even after the new grandstand was built in 1965. The gridiron ran from right field toward third base, with barely enough room to squeeze in the playing field and end zones. The space between the sidelines and the stands was vast.

From 1961 to 1970, the Twins generally had competitive teams and drew at least one million fans, then considered a benchmark for a successful season. The team dropped in the standings and also in attendance in 1971 and stayed down for many years.

This transition was coinciding with the rise of the Minnesota Vikings. An expansion team in 1961, the Vikings won their first division title in 1968. The following season, they made it to the Super Bowl, their first of four appearances in the Super Bowl in an eight-year span. The Vikings, not the Twins, were the hot item at Met Stadium.

Talks began regarding the remodeling of the Met to improve the sight lines for football or even building a brand-new stadium for just the Vikings. It was expected that, since Minneapolis interests had sold the bonds for the original stadium construction, funding for an upgrade for the Met would come once again from Minneapolis.

But this time the Minneapolis business community decided that, if it was going to foot the bill, it might as well have the stadium within its own city limits. One of the first proposals for a new stadium was a doozy: an 80,000-seat domed stadium exclusively for football on the northwest edge of downtown Minneapolis. The stadium would be surrounded by a 5,100-space parking ramp that would be uncovered on the top level to allow the tradition of pregame tailgating to continue. This stadium proposal was eventually derailed by the city's Board of Estimates and Taxation.

In 1977 the Minnesota Legislature passed a no-site stadium bill. This action by itself did not mean the end of Metropolitan Stadium, because the options included a remodeling of the Met for baseball with a new football stadium built adjacent to it. However, the new stadium commission formed with the legislation opted for a multipurpose covered facility on the eastern edge of downtown Minneapolis.

The Twins, in their final years at Met Stadium, twice more topped one million in attendance, in 1977 and 1979. The 1977 season was exciting for fans because of the play of the team, which was in the title race for much of the season, and because of Rod Carew, who finished the season with a .388 batting average and was named the American League Most Valuable Player.

The biggest day of the season came on Sunday, June 26, as the Twins played the Chicago White Sox. With first place in the West Division at stake and the fans receiving a replica Carew jersey as a giveaway, a crowd of nearly 47,000 turned out for a wild game. Glenn Adams provided the early fireworks with a grand slam en route to a team-record eight RBIs in the game. The Twins took an 8-1 lead, only to have the White Sox cut the gap with six runs in the third inning. The parade across the plate continued for both teams, unimpeded by even an alcohol-laced fan who interrupted the game in the bottom of the fourth by climbing to the top of the foul pole in left field. The Twins won the game, 19-12. Carew had four hits, scored five runs, and drove in six, capping his performance in the last of the eighth inning with a home run that raised his batting average to .403 and drew another long ovation from the fans.

In 1979 the Twins stayed in the race until the final week of the season and drew one million fans for the second time since 1970 and for the last time at Met Stadium.

The final baseball game at the Met was played on September 30, 1981 with the Kansas City Royals beating the Twins 5-2. Roy Smalley popped out to end the game as well as an era of baseball on the former cornfield. The final event at the Met was a Vikings football game against the Kansas City Chiefs on Sunday, December 20, 1981. After the game fans in search of souvenirs ravaged the stadium, taking what wasn't bolted down and many things that were.

Met Stadium remained partially dismantled for several years before being demolished, and remained a vacant site for several more years before a large shopping center, the Mall of America, was erected on the site. A plaque marking the spot of home plate was installed in an amusement-park area in the middle of the shopping center.

Metropolitan Stadium Lore

The Twins had a sunny but cold day for their season opener in 1965, the start of their run to the American League pennant. The somewhat nice weather was unusual for that spring, as the weather had been challenging, particularly with flooding. Four members of the Twins—Rich Rollins, Jim Kaat, Dick Stigman, and Bill Bethea (who was staying with Kaat before reporting to the Twins' farm club in Charlotte)—lived in Burnsville and were marooned on the other side of the swollen Minnesota River. The four were taken by helicopter to and from the Met for the opener against the Yankees. Kaat started for the Twins and would have been the winning pitcher if not for a popup dropped with two out in the ninth by Cesar Tovar, a replacement for Rollins, who had left the game in the fourth inning after twisting his knee. However, the Twins still won the game, with Tovar singling home the winning run with two out in the last of the 11th.

Weather often delayed or postponed Twins games, but a game between the Twins and Boston Red Sox at Met Stadium on the night of August 25, 1970, was interrupted for a different reason. With Tony Oliva on first base with two out in the last of the fourth and Rich Reese at bat, first-base umpire Nestor Chylak ran in toward the infield, waving his arms to call time. The interruption was explained with an announcement that the Bloomington police had been told an explosion would take place at Met Stadium at 9:30. The week before, the Old Federal Building in downtown Minneapolis had been bombed, and officials were taking no chances, although they allowed the game to start and be played until 9:15, about 45 minutes after the threat had been called in. The players congregated on the field, away from the stadium structure itself. Fans were directed to go to the parking lots. However, many of the fans, and others, found their way onto the field. The fans mingled with the players and got autographs while vendors walked through the crowd, hawking concessions. A beer vendor set his cases on second base and continued his business, quickly selling out. Few people even noticed the time when the scoreboard clock showed 9:30, the time set for the explosion, which never occurred. Twenty minutes later, fans re-entered the stadium and cleared the field, and the game resumed shortly before 10:00. The only blast of the night was from Boston's Tony Conigliaro, who homered in the eighth inning to give the Red Sox a 1-0 victory.

SOURCES

Several publications provided general information on Metropolitan Stadium and the Metrodome: *Metropolitan Sports Area Stadium: Stadium Souvenir*, published by the Metropolitan Sports Area Commission in 1956; 10: *A Decade at the Met*, by the Minneapolis Chamber of Commerce (1966); *History of the Metropolitan Stadium and Sports Center*, by Charles Johnson (Minneapolis: Midwest Federal, 1970); and *Once There Was a Ballpark*, by Joe Soucheray (Edina, Minnesota: Dorn Books, 1981).

A film, *Metropolitan Stadium*, was produced by WCCO Radio and Television shortly after the opening of Met Stadium in 1956. Narrated by Dick Enroth, this is essentially a film promoting the new stadium as well as the Twin Cities metropolitan area for the purpose of luring major-league baseball to the area. It contains footage of the final game of Nicollet Park and its demolition, the groundbreaking for the Bloomington stadium, the fire during construction in February 1956, and the first game on April 24, 1956. The film is available at the Minnesota Historical Society.

General resources on the Metrodome include T*he Hubert H. Humphrey Metrodome Souvenir Book,* compiled by Dave Mona (Minneapolis: MSP Publications, 1982) and *Uncovering the Dome,* by Amy Klobuchar (Minneapolis: Bolger Publications, 1982).

THE 1965 MINNESOTA TWINS

Additional sources of information on Metropolitan Stadium and the Metrodome include *Stadiums and Major League Sports: The Twin Cities* by James Quirk (a publication of the Brookings Institute, 1997) and *Stadium Games* by Jay Weiner (Minneapolis: University of Minnesota Press, 2000).

Other sources

Beebe, Bob, "Triple-Decked Stadium Is a Construction 'Miracle,'" *Minneapolis Tribune*, April 22, 1956, 16.

Briere, Tom, "Tovar Bats Twins to 5-4 Win in 11th: Yanks Fall in Game of 8 Errors," *Minneapolis Tribune*, April 13, 1965, 19.

Briere, Tom, "…How Many, if by Helicopter?" *Minneapolis Tribune*, April 13, 1965, 19.

Cowles, John, Jr., "City Gets Stadium Bond Go-Ahead," *Minneapolis Tribune*, July 1, 1954, 1.

Cullum, Dick, "Better Ball Park Means Better Ball," *Minneapolis Tribune*, June 14, 1948, 22.

Cullum, Dick, "First Step Taken Toward Bringing Big League Baseball to Twin Cities," *Minneapolis Tribune*, March 24, 1952, 1.

Hafrey, Danie J.l, "Property Owners Protest, Try to Halt Start on Stadium," *Minneapolis Tribune*, June 19, 1955, 1 (Upper Midwest Section).

Hafrey, Daniel J., "Dispute on Stadium Settled," *Minneapolis Tribune*, June 20, 1955, 1.

Hall, Halsey, "Glenwood-Wirth Area Picked for New Ball Park," *Minneapolis Tribune*, June 10, 1949, 16.

Hall, Halsey, "Baseball Backers Dig Up Bloomington Diamond in Rough," *Minneapolis Star*, June 20, 1955, 1.

Hertz, Will, "Stadium Drive Tops Goal by 51%," *Minneapolis Tribune*, April 1, 1955, 1.

Hertz, Will, "Work Starts on New Baseball Stadium," *Minneapolis Tribune*, June 21, 1955, 1.

Hoffbeck, Steven R., "Instamatic Memories: The Beatles in Minnesota," *Minnesota History*, Spring 2007, 191-201.

Rybak, R.T., "Bid Farewell to the St. Louis Park Giants," *St. Louis Park* (Minnesota) *Sun*, December 13, 1978.

"Millers Pick Park for Baseball Park, Will Construct All-purpose Stadium," *St. Louis Park Dispatch*, December 17, 1948, 1.

"Ballpark Location Draws Fire," *Minneapolis Tribune*, June 11, 1949, 22.

"Northwestern Bank Buys Nicollet Baseball Park," *Minneapolis Star*, June 27, 1951, 1.

"National League Moves Braves to Milwaukee," *Minneapolis Tribune*, March 19, 1953, 1.

"Fire Sweeps Stadium in Bloomington," *Minneapolis Tribune*, February 27, 1956, 1.

Stadium Damage Estimated at $50,000," *Minneapolis Star*, February 27, 1956, 1.

"2nd Fire Strikes New Stadium," *St. Paul Pioneer Press*, March 20, 1956, 1.

"You Can't Sit Behind Posts in New Stadium," *Minneapolis Tribune*, April 22, 1956, 16.

"Take Me Out to the Ball Park," *Construction Bulletin*, May 3, 1956, 52-55.

"'Metropolitan Stadium' Is Now Official Name," *Minneapolis Tribune*, July 20, 1956, 15.

"New Look in Minneapolis," *Sports Illustrated*, August 20, 1956, 36.

Correspondence with Bob Buege, February 2004.

Spring Training

BY STEW THORNLEY

ALTHOUGH THE GRAPEFRUIT League is for players to get in shape, managers to figure out rosters and rotations, and snowbirds to escape the winter and watch baseball in the sun, the Minnesota Twins didn't inspire confidence in their fans with a sputtering close to their preseason games. Coming off a second-division finish in 1964, the Twins weren't anyone's pick to win the pennant in 1965. A poll of six Minneapolis newspapermen had only one, Dwayne Netland, predicting that the team would finish as high as second.

Down in Orlando, Florida, much of the focus was on an addition to the coaching staff. Some people saw Billy Martin as a manager-in-waiting, ready to take over if the Twins started slowly and Sam Mele got fired. New York columnist Dick Young went so far as to write, "Everybody says Calvin Griffith hired Martin as coach so that Billy wouldn't have to use such a long-bladed handle." Martin handled the situation with humor; after a fishing outing in which Mele fell out of the boat, Martin said, "I threw him an anchor. It's the only thing that was handy."

A Twins press release at the time Martin was hired said he had been signed to "battle the umpires and put some life in the Twins on the field." Martin's greatest influence came with shortstop Zoilo Versalles. He flattered Zoilo, which gave him enough confidence to bring out talent that had remained largely hidden in past years. Versalles still had some rough spots and often pushed Mele's patience. A week before the season opener, Mele pulled the shortstop from a game for "lackadaisical effort" and ordered him to stay in the dugout rather than retire to the clubhouse. "I will for Billy," was Versalles's reply. Mele fined him $100 and, as Versalles goaded him on, increased the penalty to $300.

The Twins finished spring training with 11 wins and 16 losses. As usual, the record wasn't important. Improving the fundamentals while shaking out their rough spots, the Twins were ready for the season. Calvin Griffith had lamented a "lack of life" shown by the team in a loss to its Denver farm club. Martin remained upbeat and said, "This is only spring training. Wait until the season starts. They'll hustle."

He was correct.

1965 Minnesota Twins Regular Season Summary

BY BEN KLEIN

APRIL 12. MINNESOTA 5, NEW YORK 4. Predicted by *The Sporting News* to finish fifth in the American League in 1965, the Twins opened the season against the team projected to repeat as American League champions, the New York Yankees. The Yankees were not the only obstacle facing the Twins on Opening Day, as melting snow resulted in heavy floods in Minnesota. The flooding forced three Twins, including Opening Day starting pitcher Jim Kaat, to take a helicopter to Metropolitan Stadium. The rest of Sam Mele's lineup that day featured Zoilo Versalles at shortstop, Jerry Kindall at second base, Rich Rollins at third base, Tony Oliva in right field, Harmon Killebrew at first base, Jimmie Hall in center field, Bob Allison in left field, and Jerry Zimmerman behind the plate. On the mound, Kaat started hot on a cold Opening Day. Kaat not only retired the first 10 Yankees he faced, but he also helped his own cause by driving in Harmon Killebrew and Bob Allison on an RBI single in the fourth inning to give his club a 4-0 lead. Beginning with an Elston Howard homer, the Yankees clawed their way back into the game and forced extra innings after Cesar Tovar, who came in for an injured Rollins, dropped a fly ball that allowed the tying run to score. Jerry Fosnow relieved Kaat and kept the Yankees at bay through the top of the 11th inning. Seeking redemption for his costly error, Tovar drove in Allison in the bottom of the 11th to give the Twins the victory. "You could never find a better spot to make up for an error," said Tovar of his heroics.[1]

APRIL 15. DETROIT 6, MINNESOTA 4. Shrugging off a hitless performance on Opening Day, shortstop Zoilo Versalles got his MVP season on track by going 2-for-5 with a double against the Tigers. Versalles' double sparked a four-run third inning for the Twins. With the game tied 4-4 in the seventh inning, future Hall of Famer Al Kaline broke the deadlock with a two-run homer off Jerry Fosnow, giving the reliever his first loss and his second decision in as many games.

APRIL 17. MINNESOTA 3, CLEVELAND 0. Despite tallying seven hits off Minnesota ace Jim Kaat, Cleveland was unable to plate any baserunners in a shutout loss to the Twins. Zoilo Versalles got the ball rolling in the first with a leadoff double off Cleveland starter Dick Donovan. The Twins' quick start was sustained by an RBI single and RBI triple from Harmon Killebrew and Jimmie Hall, respectively. The Twins notched another run on a Bob Allison solo homer in the fourth inning. Kaat finished strong to earn the shutout win, despite failing to record a single strikeout.

APRIL 18. MINNESOTA 6, CLEVELAND 3. Although he would notch a league-leading 21 wins in 1965, Mudcat Grant's first start of the season was not one of his best. Grant gave up three runs in the third inning, including two on a Rocky Colavito double. Grant was chased in the fourth inning after walking Fred Whitfield and giving up a single to Vic Davalillo.

The backbone of Minnesota's success in the mid-to-late 1960s and early 1970s: Jim Perry, Tony Oliva, and Harmon Killebrew. (Photo courtesy of Minnesota Twins Baseball Club).

Minnesota relievers Dave Boswell and Al Worthington kept the Indians scoreless for the remainder of the game, and the Twins got Grant off the hook by taking the lead in the bottom of the fourth on Jimmie Hall's go-ahead two-run homer.

APRIL 21. MINNESOTA 7, NEW YORK 2. As the New York World's Fair opened for its second season in Queens, the Twins opened their first road trip in the Bronx, where Mickey Mantle promptly greeted Minnesota starter Camilo Pascual with a first-inning homer. Despite the shaky start, the Twins were intimidated neither by the hallowed grounds of Yankee Stadium nor by sinkerballer Mel Stottlemyre. The Twins tagged Stottlemyre for five runs in five innings, including home runs by Rich Rollins and Tony Oliva. Jimmie Hall added another home run, off Pete Mikkelsen in the eighth inning, to seal the win for the Twins.

APRIL 22. MINNESOTA 8, NEW YORK 2. The Twins followed up their three-home-run performance the day before with three more homers. Leading the Bronx bombing were Tony Oliva, who blasted two home runs, and the speedy sparkplug Zoilo Versailles, who logged an inside-the-park home run in the top of the ninth. Jim Kaat was solid once again, giving up one earned run and going the distance.

APRIL 23. MINNESOTA 8, DETROIT 6. Mudcat Grant's early-season struggle continued as the Twins rode their four-game winning streak into Tiger Stadium. Grant's travails were even more pronounced than in his first start, as he retired only one Tiger before being replaced by Bill Pleis in the first inning. Staring down the barrel of a five-run deficit, the Twins chipped away at the Tigers' lead with timely hitting and errant Detroit fielding to tie the game after nine innings. In the top of the 10th, Harmon Killebrew walked and later scored on a Jerry Zimmerman single. The Twins added an insurance run when Detroit's Jerry Lumpe committed an error on a Cesar Tovar groundball, and Minnesota improved to 6-1 with the win.

APRIL 24. DETROIT 7, MINNESOTA 4. After the Twins struck early on a two-run homer by Bob Allison in the second inning, Twins starter Dick Stigman loaded the bases with no outs in the bottom of the third. Coming in to relieve, Jim Perry limited the damage to a single run. The Twins kept the 2-1 lead into the seventh inning, until Johnny Klippstein gave up back-to-back solo homers to Don Demeter and Willie Horton. As the ninth inning unfolded, it looked as if the Twins would notch yet another comeback win when Rich Rollins and Joe Nossek scored to give the Twins a 4-3 lead. Replacing his high-school teammate Rich Reese on a double switch, Jerry Fosnow entered the game in the bottom of the ninth to save the game for the Twins. The save, however, was not in the cards for the Deshler High School product, as Fosnow gave up Willie Horton's second homer of the game. Fosnow was then tagged for the loss as the Tigers walked off on a three-run homer by Gates Brown off Al Worthington.

APRIL 27. MINNESOTA 11, CLEVELAND 1. Coming off only their second loss of the season, the Twins arrived in Cleveland to take on the Indians. Starting pitcher Camilo Pascual's masterful game began not on the mound, but at the plate, where he blasted a first-inning grand slam off Stan Williams. After giving up a leadoff double to Dick Howser, who scored on a double play, Pascual proceeded to baffle the Cleveland offense for the remainder of the game. Pascual earned the complete-game two-hitter as the Twins trounced the Indians.

APRIL 28. CLEVELAND 9, MINNESOTA 3. Costly errors were the story of this game as Birdie Tebbetts' Cleveland club scored six unearned runs in the first three innings. Starting pitcher Jim Kaat was the chief victim of his teammates' sloppiness, and was pulled in the third inning after Tony Oliva and Bob Allison failed to handle two fly balls, leading to three Cleveland runs. In addition to being the only outfielder to not make an error, Jimmie Hall added two solo home runs in the losing effort.

APRIL 30. MINNESOTA 7, CHICAGO 0. Mudcat Grant finally shook off his early-season struggles against the White Sox, who started the day a half-game ahead of the Twins atop the American League. Grant was perfect through four innings before giving up a leadoff double to Pete Ward in the bottom of the fifth. The White Sox did little more damage to Grant, who completed the shutout en route to his first win of the season. Zoilo Versalles continued to spark the Twins offense with two doubles and two runs scored, as the Twins surged to the top of the American League standings.

Team	Won	Lost	Pct	GB
Minnesota Twins	8	3	.727	-
Chicago White Sox	8	4	.667	0.5
Detroit Tigers	8	4	.667	0.5
Cleveland Indians	6	4	.600	1.5
Baltimore Orioles	7	6	.538	2.0
Boston Red Sox	5	5	.500	2.5
California Angels	6	7	.462	3.0
New York Yankees	6	7	.462	3.0
Washington Senators	4	11	.267	6.0
Kansas City Athletics	2	9	.182	6.0

MAY 1. CHICAGO 2, MINNESOTA 1. Minnesota's lead atop the standings was short-lived as the Twins continued to jostle with the White Sox for American League supremacy. Zoilo Versalles started the game with a triple off Joe Horlen, and gave the Twins the early lead by scoring on a Rich Rollins single. After the shaky start, Horlen settled down and held the Twins scoreless for the remainder of the game. Camilo Pascual did his best to keep the Twins in the game by holding the White Sox scoreless until the sixth, when Don Buford knotted the game, 1-1, with a home run. Al Worthington faced only three batters but was tagged with the loss after putting the go-ahead run, represented by Buford, on base in the eighth.

MAY 2 (GAME 1). MINNESOTA 3, CHICAGO 2. Tommy John was less than surgical against the Twins as he gave up seven hits in seven innings, but the Twins were unable to capitalize against the Chicago lefty, who was forced to leave the game after being struck in the ankle by Tony Oliva's errant bat. Jim Kaat gave up one run in six innings, and Harmon Killebrew saved his starting pitcher from the loss with a two-run eighth-inning home run off Hoyt Wilhelm to tie the game, 2-2. Killebrew then enabled lefty reliever Bill Pleis to win his first game of the season by doubling in Zoilo Versalles in the top of the 10th inning.

MAY 2 (GAME 2). CHICAGO 5, MINNESOTA 4. After playing 10 innings at Comiskey Park in the first game of a doubleheader, the Twins and White Sox took the field for the second game with the American League lead on the line. Minnesota starter Dave Boswell struggled early, giving up four runs in two-plus innings before being replaced by Dick Stigman. Stigman gave up one hit in four innings of strong relief, but the Twins hitters were unable to dig out of the early hole. The White Sox salvaged a split in the series by taking the finale, 5-4, and the Twins left Chicago exactly as they had arrived: a half-game behind the White Sox.

MAY 4. MINNESOTA 7, BALTIMORE 3. After a hard-fought series against the White Sox in Chicago, the Twins returned home to host the Orioles. The Twins erupted for five runs in the third inning, as Earl Battey and Tony Oliva went deep against Wally Bunker. Battey drove in another run in the fifth inning against Don Larsen to give the Twins a 7-1 lead. The six-run cushion was more than enough for Mudcat Grant, who earned his second consecutive complete-game win.

MAY 5. MINNESOTA 9, BALTIMORE 2. The Twins' bats struck early and often against the Orioles, starting with Tony Oliva's RBI double in the first inning. Four of the Twins' 14 hits came off the bat of Zoilo Versalles, who for the second straight game doubled and tripled against the Orioles. Versalles's 12 total bases in two games not only propelled his team to their second straight win over the Orioles, but also contributed to his campaign to lead the league in the category in 1965.

MAY 6. BALTIMORE 5, MINNESOTA 1. Future Hall of Famer Robin Roberts managed to cool down the Twins' hot bats in the series finale. Harmon

Killebrew's fourth-inning solo home run off Roberts was the only blemish for the Orioles' righty, who earned the complete-game win. Jim Kaat fell to 2-2 for the season after giving up five earned runs in seven innings.

MAY 7. CHICAGO 13, MINNESOTA 5. With the hard-fought series in Chicago fresh in their memories, the Twins welcomed the league-leading White Sox to Metropolitan Stadium for another four-game series. The series began inauspiciously for the Twins, who gave up 13 runs en route to their first back-to-back losses of the season. Minnesota starter Dick Stigman was shaky yet again, and Sam Mele was forced to go deep into his bullpen after Dave Boswell failed to contain the damage. The Minnesota defense was also off-kilter, committing seven errors in the game, which was set a franchise record since the club moved to the Twin Cities.

MAY 8. MINNESOTA 4, CHICAGO 1. Mudcat Grant went toe-to-toe with Chicago starter Gary Peters for five innings as both teams struggled to break through. Chicago's Floyd Robinson broke the deadlock in the sixth with an RBI single, but the Twins leveled the game by scrounging together a run with singles from Zoilo Versalles and Rich Rollins, and a sacrifice fly by Tony Oliva. Minnesota then pulled away with a seventh-inning RBI single by Versalles and a two-run blast by Jimmie Hall in the eighth.

MAY 9. MINNESOTA 6, CHICAGO 1. Zoilo Versalles's first-inning leadoff home run gave the Twins and Camilo Pascual an early lead. For his part, Pascual kept the White Sox scoreless through six innings and helped lead the offense with his second home run of the season. Jimmie Hall and Rich Rollins each added RBIs in the third and the fifth innings, respectively, as the Twins handed the White Sox their second consecutive defeat.

MAY 10. MINNESOTA 4, CHICAGO 3. After Mudcat Grant and Camilo Pascual turned in back-to-back complete games, Jim Kaat took the mound in the ninth inning nursing a 4-2 lead. After Kaat gave up a single to Bill Skowron, who was then driven home on a double by Pete Ward, Sam Mele turned to Al Worthington to preserve the 4-3 lead. Mele quickly reconsidered after Worthington walked Ron Hansen to put the go-ahead runner on base. Mel Nelson then answered the call by retiring three straight White Sox and earning his first save of the season. Minnesota catcher Jerry Zimmerman went 3-for-3 with a double and an RBI, as the Twins reopened a half-game lead over the White Sox.

MAY 11. MINNESOTA 3, CALIFORNIA 2. As the Twins opened a three-game series with the Angels, a big question mark emerging out of the Twins' otherwise stellar start centered on the number-four starter in the rotation. Dick Stigman, who struggled in his previous starts, could not get out of the first inning after giving up a leadoff home run to Angels center fielder Jose Cardenal and then loading the bases. Dave Boswell pitched well in relief, giving up one unearned run in 7⅓ innings, and the Twins were able to overcome Stigman's slow start with home runs from Jerry Kindall and Tony Oliva.

MAY 12. MINNESOTA 4, CALIFORNIA 3. Harmon Killebrew was the hero for the Twins as they won their second consecutive come-from-behind game against the Angels. The Minnesota slugger took California starter Rudy May deep in the sixth inning, and then clubbed a two-out, two-run homer off Bob Lee in the bottom of the eighth to put the Twins ahead by a run. Killebrew's eighth-inning blast took Mudcat Grant off the hook for the loss, and Al Worthington earned his second win of the season with two scoreless innings of relief.

MAY 13. CALIFORNIA 4, MINNESOTA 3. Scoring first proved to be disadvantageous yet again in the series with the Angels, but this time it was the Twins who could not hold onto the early lead. The Twins plated two runs in the first inning after Tony Oliva's league-leading 10th double sparked a two-out rally. Jimmie Hall added another run on a solo homer in the sixth, but the Angels clawed back against Camilo Pascual, evening the game, 3-3, on a home run by Costen Shockley. When the game moved into extra innings, the Angels beat Al Worthington and avoided the sweep when Willie Smith drove in Jose Cardenal in the top of the 10th.

MAY 14. MINNESOTA 4, KANSAS CITY 3. Coming off a 7-3 homestand, the Twins headed to Kansas City's Municipal Stadium to take on the lowly A's. Kansas City starter John O'Donoghue was less than keen on the Twins extending their winning ways as he silenced the Minnesota batters for 7⅔ innings. O'Donoghue was unable to overcome the heart of the Twins lineup in the eighth inning, however, as the Twins plated three on Bob Allison's fourth home run of the season, which knotted the game, 3-3. In the ninth inning, with Jerry Kindall at second base and a Zoilo Versalles blooper coasting through the shallow sky, the trademark derring-do of firebrand third-base coach Billy Martin came into play as he sent Kindall home to give the Twins the lead. Martin attributed his decisiveness to his old mentor, explaining that "Casey Stengel taught me to always size up the position of the outfielders before a play … [t]hen when you see the ball in the air, you can make up your mind quickly. The outfielders were deep, so I knew the ball would fall in for a hit."[2]

MAY 15. MINNESOTA 2, KANSAS CITY 0. After scoring the winning run as a pinch-runner the previous afternoon, pitcher Dave Boswell was given the start against the A's. Boswell made his case for a permanent spot in the rotation after giving up four hits in 7⅓ innings of scoreless work. Mel Nelson kept the A's scoreless for the rest of the game as the Twins coasted to a 2-0 victory on the back of second baseman Jerry Kindall, who drove in both of Minnesota's runs on a solo homer and an RBI single.

MAY 16 (GAME 1). KANSAS CITY 7, MINNESOTA 4. Just as in their first doubleheader of the season, the Twins ended up playing 19 innings on May 16. Home runs by Jimmie Hall and Tony Oliva gave the Twins a 3-2 lead heading into the eighth inning of the opener. Earl Battey's RBI double tacked on an insurance run in the eighth, but in the ninth Bill Pleis was unable to protect the lead he inherited from Mudcat Grant, giving up a home run to Dick Green and a triple to Ed Charles, who scored later in the inning. Mel Nelson then earned the loss when he gave up a three-run home run to Charles in the 10th.

MAY 16 (GAME 2). KANSAS CITY 4, MINNESOTA 2. Seeking to reverse his early-season struggles, Dick Stigman held the A's scoreless for 4⅔ innings before Kansas City first baseman Ken Harrelson tied the game, 1-1, with an RBI single. The A's took the lead in the sixth by playing some small ball, punctuated by Wayne Causey's successful squeeze bunt. The Twins answered with some small ball of their own in the seventh inning, and were able to capitalize on an error by catcher Rene Lachemann to tie the game, 2-2. In the eighth Lachemann atoned for his error at the plate by belting a go-ahead homer off Johnny Klippstein as the A's got a split in the four-game series.

MAY 17. CALIFORNIA 5, MINNESOTA 4. After dropping two to the A's in Kansas City on May 16, the Twins jetted to Los Angeles to take on the Angels. Camilo Pascual took a 3-2 lead into the eighth inning but was replaced by Jerry Fosnow after giving up a leadoff hit. Fosnow had trouble finding the strike zone and was replaced by Al Worthington, who was left to face Vic Power with two on and two out. Power came through with a hit, and gave the Angels a 4-3 lead. Pinch-hitter Don Mincher forced extra innings by homering for the Twins in the ninth inning, but the Angels walked off in the 10th on a Buck Rodgers RBI single.

MAY 18. CALIFORNIA 3, MINNESOTA 1. For the second straight game, the Twins were unable to protect a one-run lead going into the eighth inning. After shutting out the Angels for seven innings, Minnesota starter Jim Kaat ran into trouble in the eighth. The Angels tied the game on a Jim Piersall RBI single and surged ahead on a double by Joe Adcock that brought home Jim Fregosi and a very grateful Marcelino Lopez, who was awarded the win.

MAY 19 (GAME 1). MINNESOTA 3, CALIFORNIA 1. After suffering four defeats in three days, the suddenly-reeling Twins sought to right the ship in their doubleheader at Chavez Ravine. Once again the Twins found themselves in extra innings in the first game of a doubleheader. Dave Boswell got the start for the Twins and gave up one run on two hits in six innings, and Jerry Fosnow kept the Twins in the game by throwing three perfect innings of relief. Harmon Killebrew knotted the game, 1-1, in the seventh inning by doubling in Earl Battey, but neither team managed to score for the next four innings. In the top of the 12th, Tony Oliva drove home Zoilo Versalles and Sandy Valdespino to give the Twins and reliever Bill Pleis the win.

MAY 19 (GAME 2). MINNESOTA 3, CALIFORNIA 1. Mudcat Grant took the mound in the second game of the doubleheader and kept the Angels scoreless until the seventh inning when right fielder Lou Clinton scored on a Costen Shockley sacrifice fly. The Angels' lone run of the game was not enough to overcome the Twins, who enjoyed their second 3-1 victory of the day and left Los Angeles with a series split.

MAY 21. MINNESOTA 6, KANSAS CITY 4. After splitting four games with the Angels in California, the Twins returned to Metropolitan Stadium to host the visiting Athletics. In the second inning, the Twins loaded the bases for second baseman Jerry Kindall, who put the team ahead 1-0 by earning a walk from A's starter Diego Segui. Future Hall of Famer Catfish Hunter replaced Segui after the walk and got his team out of the bases-loaded jam by inducing a double play off the bat of Twins starting pitcher Camilo Pascual, who then lost the lead in the top of the third by giving up a two-run homer to A's first baseman Jim Gentile. After Moe Drabowsky replaced Hunter in the fifth inning, the Twins retook the lead on RBIs from Tony Oliva and Harmon Killebrew. Minnesota tacked onto its lead with a two-run homer by Zoilo Versalles and an RBI single by Earl Battey, as Pascual improved to 5-0 for the season and passed the .500 mark for his career with his 133rd win against 132 losses. "I think I am dreaming and I'm afraid I will wake up," said Pascual, who attributed the accomplishment to mastering his slow curve and employing his fastball more tactically.[3]

MAY 22. KANSAS CITY 6, MINNESOTA 2. Jim Kaat encountered first-inning trouble by giving up an RBI triple to Kansas City first baseman Ken Harrelson, who then scored himself on a wild pitch. Kaat ran into more trouble in the fourth inning when he made a throwing error trying to pick off Harrelson at second, which scored Dick Green. The Twins bats were unable to muster enough offense to bail out their ace, whose record went to 3-4 with the loss. Among the struggling Twins hitters was Tony Oliva, who went 0-5 and ended the day with a .227 batting average and a .261 on-base percentage, fourth worst in the American League.

MAY 25. MINNESOTA 17, BOSTON 5. There was carnage across the New England sports landscape as Muhammad Ali knocked out Sonny Liston in the first round of their rematch in Lewiston, Maine, and the Twins clobbered the Red Sox for a franchise-record 17 runs at Fenway Park. Zoilo Versalles, Tony Oliva, Bob Allison, Earl Battey, and Jerry Kindall homered, and Twins starter Mudcat Grant got in on the fun himself with a triple. The prodigious offensive output was more than enough for Grant, who collected his fifth win of the season.

MAY 26. MINNESOTA 9, BOSTON 7. In the second game of the series with the Red Sox, the Twins continued to put on an offensive show at Fenway Park. Tony Oliva and Bob Allison both homered for the second consecutive game, and Zoilo Versalles hit his league-leading 13th double. Righty reliever Jim Perry earned his first win of the season after coming on in relief for Camilo Pascual, who gave up six runs in 1⅔ innings of work.

MAY 27. BOSTON 2, MINNESOTA 0. The Twins' offensive outburst came to sudden halt against Boston starter Dave Morehead, who, together with reliever Dick Radatz, held the Twins scoreless and limited them to three hits. Despite giving up only one earned run in seven innings, Jim Kaat saw his record sink to 3-5.

MAY 28. MINNESOTA 4, WASHINGTON 1. After taking two of three from the Red Sox at Fenway Park, the Twins returned to their ancestral home in the nation's capital to play the Senators. Former Senators mainstay Bob Allison enjoyed his homecoming by belting his seventh home run of the season, off Senators starter Phil Ortega in the seventh inning. Tony Oliva added two more runs on his ninth home run of the season as the Twins cruised to a 4-1 win.

MAY 29. MINNESOTA 11, WASHINGTON 8. Mudcat Grant's perfect 5-0 record appeared to be in jeopardy after he gave up three runs on four hits in the first inning. Grant's troubles continued into the fourth inning when he gave up a home run to first baseman Bob Chance and a rare round-tripper to shortstop Ed Brinkman. The Twins surged back in the fifth and sixth innings with eight runs on eight hits, including a Rich Rollins home run and Zoilo Versalles' league-leading 14th double. Rollins tacked on another run in the ninth by doubling in Versalles as Twins reliever Jim Perry earned the win.

MAY 30. MINNESOTA 6, WASHINGTON 0. Like Mudcat Grant the day before, Camilo Pascual entered the series finale with the Senators with a perfect 5-0 record. Unlike Grant, Pascual tossed a gem. Pascual shut out the Senators on four hits and brought his strikeout total to 50, fourth best in the American League. Zoilo Versalles broke the game open in the fourth inning with a three-run home run, his fifth of the season, and Harmon Killebrew added his seventh as the Twins left their former home with an easy three-game sweep and a half-game lead in the American League.

MAY 31 (1). MINNESOTA 6, BALTIMORE 0. After sweeping the Senators in Washington, the Twins traveled up the road to Baltimore to play two against Hank Bauer's Orioles. After Camilo Pascual's four-hit shutout the day before, Jim Kaat kept the Orioles scoreless on a measly three hits to earn his fourth win of the season. The Twins scored six runs, led by Zoilo Versalles' third-inning two-run home run and a solo blast by Jimmie Hall in the sixth inning. Tony Oliva collected his 12th double of the season, which scored Sandy Valdespino.

MAY 31 (2). BALTIMORE 5, MINNESOTA 4. After doubling in his final at-bat in the first game of the doubleheader, Tony Oliva picked up where he left off by hitting an RBI double off the great Jim Palmer. Oliva's two-bagger gave the Twins the early lead, and also placed him third in the league in both RBIs and doubles. Minnesota starter Dick Stigman failed to hold the lead, though, giving up a pair of two-run home runs to Bob Johnson and Dick Brown in the second inning. The Twins battled back in the fifth by scoring three runs on two hits to knot the game, 4-4. The score remained level until Baltimore right fielder Sam Bowens hit a ninth-inning walk-off home run off Johnny Klippstein.

Team	Won	Lost	Pct	GB
Minnesota Twins	27	15	.643	-
Chicago White Sox	27	16	.628	0.5
Detroit Tigers	25	19	.568	3.0
Baltimore Orioles	25	21	.543	4.0
Cleveland Indians	21	20	.512	5.5
California Angels	24	24	.500	6.0
Boston Red Sox	21	21	.500	6.0
New York Yankees	19	26	.422	9.5
Washington Senators	20	28	.417	10.0
Kansas City Athletics	10	29	.256	15.5

JUNE 2. MINNESOTA 6, BOSTON 3. As the season entered June, the Twins found themselves atop the American League with a half-game lead over the White Sox. Mudcat Grant found himself in an early 2-0 hole and in the second inning gave way to reliever Jim Perry, who limited the Red Sox to one run in 5⅔ innings en route to the win. As for the Twins' bats, Jerry Zimmerman's leadoff triple in the bottom of the third sparked a four-run onslaught, punctuated by Harmon Killebrew's two-run home run. Jimmie Hall added another two-run homer in the fifth as the Twins took the game, 6-3.

JUNE 3. MINNESOTA 4, BOSTON 3. As NASA astronaut Edward White became the first American to perform a spacewalk high above Earth, Camilo Pascual attempted to become the second American League pitcher to win seven games this season. After Bob Allison opened the scoring in the bottom of the second with a two-run home run off Red Sox righty

Bill Monbouquette, Pascual advanced his own cause by singling in Rich Rollins. On the mound, the undefeated Pascual was solid and victorious yet again, and his victory brought him into a tie with the Tigers' Mickey Lolich for the American League lead.

JUNE 4. MINNESOTA 9, WASHINGTON 5. The Twins enjoyed a 1½-game lead atop the American League as Gil Hodges' Senators arrived in Bloomington. Although the Twins were sloppy in the field with four errors, they were prolific at the plate, scoring nine runs on 10 hits. Jimmie Hall's 10th home run came in the fourth inning and was of the inside-the-park variety. The zaniness continued in the sixth inning when pitcher Jim Kaat doubled on an infield hit to first base, driving in Jimmie Hall and Bob Allison. Kaat earned his fifth win of the season despite giving up five runs on nine hits, and Jerry Fosnow was perfect in 2⅔ innings of relief.

JUNE 6. MINNESOTA 11, WASHINGTON 2. The Twins' offensive assault on the Senators continued against starting pitcher Phil Ortega. Tony Oliva's 10th home run of the season came in the bottom of the first inning, and the Twins steadily built upon their lead by scoring in each of the first four innings. Bill Pleis came on in relief for starter Dave Boswell in the fifth inning and kept the Senators scoreless for the remainder of the game as his record improved to 3-0.

JUNE 7. CLEVELAND 2, MINNESOTA 1. Minnesota's offensive juggernaut, along with its four-game winning streak, came to a halt against Luis Tiant and the Cleveland Indians. Tiant earned the complete-game win by limiting the Twins to one run on just two hits. Don Mincher, who got the start at first base in place of Harmon Killebrew, was responsible for driving in the Twins' lone run by doubling home Tony Oliva. Despite giving up only two runs on five hits, Mudcat Grant was charged with his first loss of the year.

JUNE 8. MINNESOTA 6, CLEVELAND 2. Harmon Killebrew returned to the lineup and the Twins returned to their winning ways against the Indians. Killebrew powered the Twins in the matinee game with his ninth home run of the season, a three-run blast that came in the first inning. Catcher Earl Battey checked in with his third home run of the season in the fourth inning. Camilo Pascual not only earned a complete-game win, but he also took the league lead in both categories after the performance (8 wins, 5 CG).

JUNE 9. CLEVELAND 2, MINNESOTA 1. Jim Kaat and Cleveland starter Ralph Terry locked horns in a pitchers' duel as the former American League All-Star teammates took shutouts into the eighth inning. Terry blinked first in the bottom of the eighth as Zoilo Versalles's sacrifice fly brought home Jerry Kindall. As the Indians entered the ninth inning down a run, Cleveland manager Birdie Tebbetts employed a bit of gamesmanship to throw Kaat off his game by complaining to umpire Bill Haller about a hole in Kaat's sweatshirt. Following a confrontation between Tebbetts and Sam Mele, as well as the trimming of Kaat's shirtsleeves, Kaat got the loss by giving up a two-run homer to Cleveland third baseman Max Alvis in the top of the ninth. Tebbetts' antics riled Sam Mele, who said, "I won't forget it and I don't think our players will either."[4]

JUNE 10. CLEVELAND 4, MINNESOTA 1. Despite scattering eight hits against Cleveland starter Sam McDowell, Minnesota's only run came off the bat of pitcher Dave Boswell in the second inning. Boswell had more luck at the plate than on the mound as the Indians punished the righty for four runs in 5⅔ innings.

JUNE 11 (GAME 1). MINNESOTA 5, DETROIT 4. After dropping three of four to the Indians at home, the Twins took to the road to face the fourth-place Tigers. Tony Oliva continued to rack up doubles as he swatted his 15th of the season in the second inning. Oliva then scored on Jimmie Hall's sacrifice fly to give the Twins the early lead. Mudcat Grant let the Twins' lead slip away as the Tigers went ahead 4-3 in the sixth. The Twins tied it back up in the ninth inning when reliever Terry Fox's botched pickoff attempt allowed Don Mincher to score. Yet again the Twins were forced to play 10 innings in the first game of a doubleheader, but they made it count when Jimmie

Hall's second sacrifice fly of the game brought Sandy Valdespino home.

JUNE 11 (GAME 2). MINNESOTA 5, DETROIT 4. After using 19 players, including five pitchers, in the first game of the doubleheader, the Twins needed a strong effort from spot starter Mel Nelson. Nelson delivered by allowing two runs in 7⅔ innings, but the Twins once again found themselves in extra innings. A breakthrough came in the 12th when the Twins put together three straight singles, a sacrifice fly, and a Jimmie Hall triple to take a 5-2 lead. The lead became precarious in the bottom of the inning when Jim Perry gave up a two-run shot to pinch-hitter Jim Northrup, but Perry retired the side to earn his fourth win of the season.

JUNE 12. DETROIT 8, MINNESOTA 5. Already taxed from the 22-inning doubleheader the day before, the Twins bullpen was called to action again when Camilo Pascual was chased from the game in the second inning after giving up five runs. Pascual escaped his first loss of the season, however, as Jimmie Hall's three-run homer tied the game in the third inning. After keeping the Tigers scoreless for 3⅔ innings, Jerry Fosnow lost the game in the sixth as the Tigers plated three.

JUNE 13. DETROIT 5, MINNESOTA 4. Skipper Sam Mele was forced to turn to his tired bullpen once more after Jim Kaat lasted only three innings and gave up three runs. Sluggers Harmon Killebrew and Bob Allison made their mark on the game with their 11th and 10th home runs, respectively. Center fielder Joe Nossek went deep for the first time this season, but the Twins were unable to overcome the Tigers as they settled for a series split with Detroit.

JUNE 15. MINNESOTA 4, CHICAGO 0. The Twins pulled into Chicago nursing a half-game lead over the White Sox. Mudcat Grant closed the door on Chicago's plans to take first place as he shut out the hosts for his sixth win of the season. Chicago's Gary Peters gave up early solo home runs to Tony Oliva and Bob Allison, and Rich Rollins added a ninth-inning home run to seal the game for the Twins.

Although the Twins won the game, they lost second baseman Jerry Kindall, who was injured by a sliding Bill Skowron. The injury kept Kindall out of the lineup for most of the next two weeks.

JUNE 16. CHICAGO 3, MINNESOTA 1. Camilo Pascual cruised through his first three innings of work and took a 1-0 lead into the fourth inning. But his bid to go to 9-0 for the season came off the rails in the fourth inning when the White Sox loaded the bases. Catcher J.C. Martin and shortstop Ron Hansen each singled home a run, and then Pascual walked pinch-hitter Smoky Burgess to force Bill Skowron home for a third run. Starting pitcher John Buzhardt kept the Twins quiet into the eighth inning and then handed the ball to Eddie Fisher, who collected his 14th save of the season. Pascual fell to 8-1.

JUNE 17. MINNESOTA 3, CHICAGO 1. Jim Kaat pitched masterfully for the Twins as they set out to take the rubber game from the White Sox. The lanky lefty gave up one run on four hits, and the Twins were able to push three runs across. One of the runs came on a home run by Don Mincher, who got the start at first base as part of Sam Mele's tinkering with the infield to cope with Jerry Kindall's absence. In this game the regular third baseman, Rich Rollins, moved to second base while Harmon Killebrew moved from first to third.

JUNE 18. NEW YORK 10, MINNESOTA 2. The Twins took their road trip to New York to take on the Yankees. Although 11 games back and struggling, the Yankees reminded Minnesota starter Mel Nelson just how mighty the Bronx Bombers still could be when Mickey Mantle sent his eighth career grand slam into the seats in the first inning. Rich Rollins gave the Twins some excitement by hitting an inside-the-park home run in the fourth.

JUNE 19. NEW YORK 5, MINNESOTA 3. Second baseman Bobby Richardson set the table for the Yankees in the bottom of the first by doubling off Twins starter Mudcat Grant. The Yankees plated two in the first and scored another in the second on a Joe Pepitone home run as Grant left the game after only

Zoilo Versalles (center) receives the AL MVP Award from AL President Joe Cronin. Tony Oliva is on far left. (Photo courtesy of Minnesota Twins Baseball Club).

two innings of work. Future Hall of Famer Whitey Ford faced the minimum through three innings and took a 5-1 lead into the eighth inning. After giving up Harmon Killebrew's only triple of the season, which scored Rich Rollins and Tony Oliva, Ford gave way to Pedro Ramos. Ramos earned the save and preserved the win for Ford; Mudcat Grant picked up his second loss of the season.

JUNE 20 (GAME 1). MINNESOTA 6, NEW YORK 4. Camilo Pascual got off to a rocky start in the first inning by giving up four straight hits and two runs before recording an out. After Pascual's first-inning struggles, the Cuban righty settled down and kept the Yankees scoreless for the remainder of his outing. In the meantime, the Twins chipped away at New York's early lead. Jimmie Hall was at the center of the Twins' attack, tripling home Harmon Killebrew in the second inning and hitting a solo homer in the sixth as the Twins took a 3-2 lead into the seventh. Roger Maris's two-run home run in the seventh inning gave the Yankees the lead, but Killebrew tied the game in the eighth with a home run. In the ninth inning the New York battery handed the Twins the game when Zoilo Versalles and Sandy Valdespino scored on a passed ball and a wild pitch.

JUNE 20 (GAME 2). MINNESOTA 7, NEW YORK 4. Attempting to sweep the doubleheader and split the series, Tony Oliva and Harmon Killebrew greeted Al Downing with a triple and a double, respectively, to give the Twins a one-run lead in the first inning. Minnesota continued to pound Downing early as Zoilo Versalles's second-inning ground-rule double scored Earl Battey and Joe Nossek, each of whom later drove home a run in the third inning. Pitching before 71,245 at Yankee stadium, Dave Boswell was strong through 5⅔ innings, with his only hiccup coming in the third inning when he gave up a three-run home run to pinch-hitter Ray Barker. Harmon Killebrew put the game out of reach and secured the win for Boswell with his two-run ninth-inning home run.

JUNE 22. CLEVELAND 5, MINNESOTA 4. The Twins arrived in Cleveland just 1½ games ahead of the third-place Indians. Cleveland left fielder Chuck Hinton bookended the Indians' attack by driving in the first run of the game in the first inning, and then blasting a walk-off home run in the 10th. Hinton's home run handed Al Worthington his third loss and third blown save of the season as the Indians pulled within a half-game of the Twins. As the Twins saw their lead become more precarious, their injury troubles also mounted as Earl Battey was forced to leave the game with a dislocated finger.

JUNE 23. MINNESOTA 6, CLEVELAND 3. Minnesota relied exclusively on the long ball as two of the usual suspects, Jimmie Hall and Bob Allison, went deep in the second and fourth innings, respectively. Allison's home run plated three runs, and Sandy Valdespino gave the Twins two more insurance runs in the fifth inning with his first home run of the season. The six runs were more than enough for Mudcat Grant, who recorded his seventh win.

JUNE 24. CLEVELAND 3, MINNESOTA 1. Camilo Pascual had the opportunity to improve upon his stellar start and conclude the Twins' 14-game road trip with a win. Instead, the Twins lost both the game and Pascual, who left the game in the fifth inning after he injured his back. Harmon Killebrew drove in the Twins' only run in the seventh inning as pitcher Ralph Terry won his seventh game for the Indians. Having gone 7-7 on the road trip, the injury-riddled

Twins hobbled back to Minnesota with a razor-thin half-game cushion over the Indians and White Sox.

JUNE 25. MINNESOTA 4, DETROIT 3. With the White Sox and Indians both victorious, it looked as if the Twins would relinquish their grip on first place as they entered the bottom of the ninth trailing 3-2. Down to their last out, Harmon Killebrew and Don Mincher coaxed walks from the Tigers' starter, Dave Wickersham. The Twins capped the two-out rally with RBI hits from Bernie Allen and pinch-hitter Joe Nossek to snatch the game away from the jaws of the Tigers.

JUNE 26. DETROIT 5, MINNESOTA 2. With the Twins coping with injuries to both Camilo Pascual and Jim Kaat, Bill Pleis got the spot start against the Tigers. Although he kept the Tigers scoreless for four innings, Pleis loaded the bases with nobody out in the fifth inning before turning it over to Jim Perry. Perry almost escaped the jam by getting Don Demeter and Al Kaline on back-to-back popups, but the Tigers took a 2-0 lead on a hit by Willie Horton. Tony Oliva drove in the Twins' first run in the sixth and scored on a wild pitch in the eighth, but the Tigers cruised to a 5-2 win.

JUNE 27 (GAME 1). MINNESOTA 6, DETROIT 4. Tigers starter Joe Sparma faced eight Twins in the first inning and gave up two runs on Harmon Killebrew's RBI single. Zoilo Versalles expanded the lead to 3-0 in the second inning with his eighth home run of the season. Don Demeter's two-run homer off Mudcat Grant in the fourth inning leveled the game, but the Twins took the lead again on a Jimmie Hall groundout that scored Sandy Valdespino in the fifth. Al Worthington blew his fourth save of the season by giving up an RBI single to catcher Jackie Moore, but Worthington earned the win thanks to an eighth-inning two-run home run by Don Mincher.

JUNE 27 (GAME 2). MINNESOTA 6, DETROIT 5. With the Twins rotation decimated by injury and the bullpen taxed, Sam Mele turned to Mel Nelson to start the second game of the doubleheader against the Tigers. Nelson gave up two runs in four innings of work before handing the ball over to Jim Perry, who retired the Tigers in order in the fifth, sixth, and seventh innings. Things fell apart in the eighth, however, as Don Demeter led off with a home run. Demeter's blast ended Perry's day, but the Tigers were not finished leaving the yard in the eighth, as Willie Horton's two-run shot off Johnny Klippstein tied the game. The game stayed tied until the bottom of the 10th, when Joe Nossek singled in Rich Rollins for the win.

JUNE 28. CHICAGO 17, MINNESOTA 4. 38,405 fans packed Metropolitan Stadium to watch the first-place Twins take on the White Sox. Not only did the Twins fail to protect their half-game lead over the White Sox, but they were humiliated as Chicago scored 17 runs off starter Dave Boswell and relievers Jerry Fosnow, Dick Stigman, and Mel Nelson. Jimmie Hall's 14th home run and Tony Oliva's 19th double kept them among the league leaders in those categories, but the Twins gave up their lead in the standings as both the White Sox and the Indians surged ahead, relegating Minnesota to third place.

JUNE 29. MINNESOTA 7, CHICAGO 6. Jimmie Hall's double and Harmon Killebrew's single led to a two-run first inning for the Twins. The Twins added runs in the second and third to take a 4-0 lead into the fourth inning. The Twins continued to pile up runs, but the White Sox also began to break through against Minnesota starter Jim Kaat, who left the game in the eighth with a 6-4 lead. After Mudcat Grant made a rare relief appearance, Dick Stigman gave up a two-run ninth-inning home run to pinch-hitter Smoky Burgess to tie the game. Seeking to avoid extra innings, Bernie Allen led off the bottom of the ninth with a double and moved to third on a Joe Nossek bunt. Zoilo Versalles' sacrifice fly brought Allen home to win the game.

JUNE 30. CALIFORNIA 5, MINNESOTA 0. The Twins made a very brief trip to California to take on the Angels for one game. The visit was unproductive as the Angels tagged Minnesota starter Bill Pleis for four runs en route to a 5-0 win. The Angels' Fred Newman was masterful with a two-hit shutout win, and the Twins closed out June with a 16-13 record, trailing the Indians by a half-game.

Team	Won	Lost	Pct	GB
Cleveland Indians	43	27	.614	-
Minnesota Twins	43	28	.606	.5
Chicago White Sox	42	29	.592	1.5
Baltimore Orioles	41	32	.562	3.5
Detroit Tigers	39	31	.557	4.0
New York Yankees	36	38	.486	9.0
California Angels	33	41	.446	12.0
Boston Red Sox	29	42	.408	14.5
Washington Senators	30	45	.400	15.5
Kansas City Athletics	22	45	.328	19.5

JULY 2. MINNESOTA 3, KANSAS CITY 1. As the Twins entered July a half-game back of the Indians, catcher Earl Battey returned to the lineup after an injury. Battey made his presence felt by going 3-for-4 with a double against the last-place A's, who entered the series a dismal 22-45. Tony Oliva's July was off to a hot start as he was involved in all three of the Twins' runs by tallying his 21st double of the season, collecting two RBIs, and scoring on a Harmon Killebrew single. The three runs were more than enough for Mudcat Grant, who gave up one run in the complete-game win, his eighth of the year.

JULY 3. MINNESOTA 3, KANSAS CITY 2. Harmon Killebrew manned the hot corner and Don Mincher got the start at first base. Mele's decision to start Mincher paid dividends as the lefty slugger put the Twins on the board with a fourth-inning solo home run. The A's replied with a run of their own off Jim Kaat in the bottom of the fourth, but the Twins reclaimed the one-run lead in the fifth on an RBI single by Tony Oliva. Kaat could not keep the lead long as center fielder Jim Landis tied the game, 2-2, in the bottom of the fifth with a single that scored rookie pinch-hitter Skip Lockwood, who broke into the majors as a third baseman before converting to pitching. The game remained knotted until the top of the 11th, when Mincher went deep for his second home run to win the game for Minnesota.

JULY 4. MINNESOTA 5, KANSAS CITY 2. Returning from injury, Camilo Pascual kept Kansas City scoreless for 2⅓ innings before aggravating his bad back. Jerry Fosnow came on in relief and gave up two runs in the fourth inning. But in the sixth, with Zoilo Versalles and Sandy Valdespino on base, Tony Oliva put the Twins up 3-2 with his 12th home run of the season. Harmon Killebrew then put the game out of reach with his 14th home run, a two-run shot, in the ninth inning. With the sweep of the A's, the Twins left Kansas City tied for first place with the Indians.

JULY 5 (GAME 1). MINNESOTA 6, BOSTON 2. The Twins looked to extend their winning streak against the visiting Red Sox. Jimmie Hall got Minnesota on the right track by doubling home Tony Oliva in the first inning. Oliva scored again in the third after he tripled off Earl Wilson and came home when shortstop Eddie Bressoud threw the ball away on the relay throw trying to cut down Oliva at third. The Twins built on their lead with a three-run sixth inning, and starting pitcher Dave Boswell was strong en route to his fifth win of the season.

JULY 5 (GAME 2). MINNESOTA 2, BOSTON 0. Minnesota starter Jim Perry shut down the Red Sox in the second game of the doubleheader to earn his fifth win of the season against no losses, while bringing his ERA down to 2.59. With Earl Battey at the plate in the fourth inning, Bob Allison scored from first on a stolen base and an errant throw by Boston catcher Mike Ryan. Battey finished the at-bat with a triple, but was stranded at third. The Minnesota backstop continued to be at the center of the action when he drove home the second Minnesota run in the sixth inning. Tony Oliva's seventh-inning double tied him with Carl Yastrzemski for the American League lead with 22. In addition to winning the game, Perry won the confidence of Sam Mele, who kept Perry in the starting rotation for the remainder of the season.

JULY 6. MINNESOTA 9, BOSTON 0. Jimmie Hall devastated Boston pitchers Jerry Stephenson and Bob Heffner by mashing a pair of two-run home runs in the first and second innings to bring his season total to 16. Don Mincher added his seventh home run of the season as Mudcat Grant and the Twins shut out the Red Sox.

JULY 7. MINNESOTA 5, BOSTON 2. After outscoring the Red Sox 17-2 in the first three games of the series, Jim Kaat and the Twins completed the four-game sweep. Earl Battey's second-inning double sent Don Mincher to third base, and both Twins scored on a Bernie Allen single. Minnesota built on their lead with sacrifice flies from Jimmie Hall, Allen, and Harmon Killebrew. After completing the sweep of the Red Sox, the Twins stood alone atop the American League with a 1½-game lead over the Indians.

JULY 9. MINNESOTA 8, NEW YORK 3. The Twins jumped to a 4-0 first-inning lead against the visiting Yankees on back-to-back home runs by Harmon Killebrew and Don Mincher. The Yankees got back into the game in the fourth and fifth on a solo home run by Elston Howard and a solo inside-the-park home run by Roger Repoz. Mincher collected his second home run and second, third, and fourth RBIs of the game on his seventh-inning homer. Giving up three runs on six hits, Dave Boswell went wire-to-wire for his sixth win of the season.

JULY 10 (GAME 1). MINNESOTA 4, NEW YORK 1. With runners on second and third in the bottom of the fifth inning, Minnesota starting pitcher Jim Perry helped his own cause with a squeeze bunt that scored Jimmie Hall. The next Twins hitter, Zoilo Versalles, added to the Twins' lead with a two-run home run off Whitey Ford. Perry was solid on the mound, giving up four hits and one unearned run in eight innings, to improve to 6-0 on the season.

JULY 10 (GAME 2). NEW YORK 8, MINNESOTA 6. The Twins' torrid nine-game winning streak to start July came to a halt in the second game of their doubleheader with the Yankees. Although Jimmie Hall's RBI double in the first inning gave the Twins the early lead, Mudcat Grant gave up back-to-back home runs to outfielders Roger Repoz and Hector Lopez in the second inning. Don Mincher's bases-clearing triple in the fifth, followed by Sandy Valdespino's RBI single, put the Twins back in front until the Yankees retook the lead for good on Clete Boyer's eighth-inning grand slam off Johnny Klippstein. Despite the loss, the Twins held a four-game lead in the American League (with a record of 52-29) after 81 games, the midpoint of the season.

JULY 11. MINNESOTA 6, NEW YORK 5. After ending the Twins' nine-game winning streak, the Yankees were poised to put them on a losing streak after Jerry Fosnow's ninth-inning error gave New York a one-run lead going into the bottom of the ninth. However, with two outs and Rich Rollins on base, Harmon Killebrew slugged his 16th home run of the season to give the Twins the walk-off victory. The win sent the Twins into the All-Star Game on a high note, extending their lead to five games.

JULY 15 (GAME 1). MINNESOTA 11, KANSAS CITY 3. Tony Oliva's first-inning home run gave Jim Kaat and the Twins the early 1-0 advantage. In the second inning Jim Kaat was at the plate to oversee an expansion of his lead when Earl Battey scored on a wild pitch and Kaat drove home Sandy Valdespino on a sacrifice fly. In the bottom of the fourth inning, the A's demonstrated why they were in last place when three pitchers issued five consecutive two-out walks as part of a seven-run inning for the Twins. Tony Oliva added his second home run of the game in the fifth as the Twins routed the A's.

JULY 15 (GAME 2). KANSAS CITY 3, MINNESOTA 2. Tony Oliva continued to heat up in July as he went 2-for-4 with a double and two RBIs. Apart from Oliva's RBIs, the Twins struggled at the plate and took a precarious 2-1 lead into the ninth inning. A's left fielder Tommie Reynolds handed Al Worthington his fifth blown save and fourth loss of the year when he doubled home Ken Harrelson and pinch-runner John O'Donoghue.

JULY 16. KANSAS CITY 10, MINNESOTA 2. Mudcat Grant lasted only two-thirds of an inning, giving up four runs on five hits. Jerry Fosnow got the Twins out of the first inning, but the A's had another big inning in the third, plating three. Tony Oliva had another 2-for-4 performance, including his league-leading 26th double, but the Twins were otherwise largely silent as they were overwhelmed.

JULY 17. KANSAS CITY 5, MINNESOTA 4. Rich Rollins got the start at second base and temporarily displaced Zoilo Versalles as the Twins' leadoff hitter. Rollins went 3-for-5, including a leadoff double in the fifth inning. Bob Allison drove Rollins home on a single, and Earl Battey and Jimmie Hall followed with RBI singles to give the Twins a 4-0 lead after five. Starting pitcher Dick Stigman ran into trouble in the seventh, giving up back-to-back homers to Dick Green and Ken Harrelson. Green homered again in his next at-bat against Johnny Klippstein to tie the game, 4-4. The A's took the lead in the ninth on an Ed Charles sacrifice fly, extending the Twins' slide to three games.

JULY 18 (GAME 1). CALIFORNIA 5, MINNESOTA 3. The Angels' Jim Fregosi and the Twins' Don Mincher exchanged fourth-inning solo home runs, but the Angels added two more runs off Jim Kaat in the fifth inning to take a 3-1 lead. Replacing mononucleosis-ridden Dave Boswell and making his first appearance of the year, Dwight Siebler came on in relief of Kaat in the sixth inning. The Angels put the game out of reach against Siebler in the seventh, starting with a walk issued to the speedy Jose Cardenal, who then stole second and third, and scored on a Joe Adcock double that also brought home Tom Satriano. The game also featured a bit of drama beginning in the fifth inning when Rich Rollins and Sam Mele disputed a force-out call at second base by umpire Bill McKinley. Tempers flared again in the sixth inning between the three men, with Mele assuming what American League President Joe Cronin described as a "John L. Sullivan pose."[5] The altercation resulted in a $500 fine and a five-game suspension for the Minnesota skipper.

JULY 18 (GAME 2). MINNESOTA 5, CALIFORNIA 4. After four consecutive losses, the Twins turned to Mudcat Grant to end their slide. Grant gave up three consecutive two-out singles in the first inning, including an RBI single to Merritt Ranew that made it 1-0. In his first major-league start, second baseman Frank Quilici got the ball rolling with a leadoff double. Quilici and Tony Oliva then scored on a double by Bob Allison to give the Twins the lead. In the seventh the Twins extended their lead to 3-1 on a Jimmie Hall RBI single, but the lead slipped away in the eighth on a two-run homer by Tom Satriano and an RBI groundout by Jose Cardenal. Down a run, the Twins leveled matters in the eighth inning on a Don Mincher home run. Later in the eighth, with Bob Allison on third and Sandy Valdespino on first, Valdespino broke for second and Allison broke for home, with the latter getting caught in a rundown. Despite getting caught in the pickle, Allison scored when Jim Fregosi dropped the ball. The run put the Twins out in front for good.

JULY 19. MINNESOTA 5, CALIFORNIA 2. For the second straight game, rookie Frank Quilici led off for the Twins, and for the second straight game he reached base in the first, this time on a walk. Quilici then scored on Harmon Killebrew's 17th home run of the season. The Angels' Joe Adcock responded in the second with a solo home run, and Jim Fregosi sent another ball out of the park in the top of the fourth to tie the game, 2-2. In the bottom half, with Bob Allison on third and Rich Rollins on first, Jerry Zimmerman grounded into a double play that allowed Allison to score, giving the Twins the lead. Jimmie Hall then put the game away in the seventh by driving in Quilici and Tony Oliva with a single, his 100th hit of the season. In addition to being among the league leaders in hits and RBIs (58), Hall stood atop the American League batting race with a .321 average at day's end. Jim Perry earned the complete-game win, improving to 7-0 for the season.

JULY 20. CALIFORNIA 9, MINNESOTA 1. Frank Quilici walked again as part of the Twins' first-inning gambit, and then scored the Twins' only run of the game on a Tony Oliva groundout. The ailing Camilo Pascual, making his first start in two weeks, was unable to protect the first-inning lead, giving up five runs on seven hits in 2⅓ innings of work. All told, the Angels tallied 15 hits and plated nine runners to split the four-game series.

JULY 21 (GAME 1). MINNESOTA 8, BOSTON 6. After splitting the series with the Angels in Minnesota, the Twins were back on the road to take on the Red Sox at Fenway Park in a doubleheader. Minnesota starter Jim Kaat made himself at home, retiring the side in order in the first inning and driving in the Twins' first run in the second. The Twins sprayed 15 hits, five of which came off the bat of Tony Oliva, as they were able to overcome the Red Sox, who had six runs on 13 hits.

JULY 21 (GAME 2). MINNESOTA 11, BOSTON 8. After being treated to an offensive show in the first game of the doubleheader, the Fenway Park faithful saw even more offense in the second game. Unfortunately for the Red Sox fans, more of the offensive output came from the visiting Twins. Harmon Killebrew and Jimmie Hall both collected their 60th RBIs of the season, with Killebrew's coming on a fourth-inning two-run home run. Hall's 60th RBI came on a sacrifice fly, although he was the only starting position player on either team not to record a hit. Al Worthington collected his sixth win for the Twins.

JULY 22. MINNESOTA 11, BOSTON 5. For the second straight game the Twins scored 11 runs against the Red Sox. The Twins' three, four, and five hitters were at the center of their attack, as Tony Oliva, Harmon Killebrew, and Bob Allison were a combined 6-for-12 with 10 RBIs. Both of Allison's hits left the ballpark, and Tony Oliva collected his league-leading 28th double. Despite giving up five runs on 12 hits, Mudcat Grant earned his 10th win of the season as the Twins swept the Red Sox for the third consecutive series.

JULY 23. BALTIMORE 3, MINNESOTA 2. The Twins took their road trip to Baltimore's Memorial Stadium to take on the second-place Orioles, who entered the day 4½ games back. Baltimore starting pitcher Steve Barber kept the Twins scoreless until the eighth inning, when Bob Allison and Earl Battey tied the game, 2-2, with back-to-back home runs. Twins starter Jim Perry pitched into the ninth inning, but was replaced by Bill Pleis with runners at the corners and one out. After issuing a walk to load the bases, Pleis gave way to Johnny Klippstein, who gave up a walk-off RBI single to Brooks Robinson, and the Twins fell to the Orioles.

JULY 24. BALTIMORE 3, MINNESOTA 1. With the game knotted, 1-1, going into the bottom of the eighth, Boog Powell slugged his eighth home run of the season off Bill Pleis. Pleis was battered for another run when relief pitcher Dick Hall doubled to score second baseman Jerry Adair. With the win, the Orioles climbed to within 2½ games of the Twins for the league lead.

JULY 25. MINNESOTA 8, BALTIMORE 5. As Bob Dylan was booed for "going electric" at the Newport Folk Festival, the Twins upset the Baltimore crowd with some electric hitting in the late innings. Down 5-1 and in danger of losing three straight to the second-place Orioles, the Twins opened the eighth inning with singles by Frank Quilici, Sandy Valdespino, and Zoilo Versalles, with Versalles's hit scoring Quilici from second. Tony Oliva then cleared the bases and tied the game with a three-run homer. The Twins scored three more in the ninth inning against veteran Harvey Haddix on a two-run RBI triple by Versalles and a sacrifice fly by Oliva to give Al Worthington the win.

JULY 26. MINNESOTA 8, BALTIMORE 2. In search of a series split, first baseman Don Mincher put the Twins ahead in the first inning with a three-run homer. Although the three runs were enough for Mudcat Grant, who gave up two runs in 6⅓ innings for the win, the Twins plated five more runs, including one on Harmon Killebrew's 20th home run of the season. Making his third appearance of the year, reliever Garry Roggenburk turned in 2⅔ innings of strong relief, earning his first save of the season.

JULY 27 (GAME 1). WASHINGTON 10, MINNESOTA 7. Minnesota starter Jim Perry had trouble with the host Senators, giving up five runs on five hits in just 3⅓ innings of work. Perry's exit in favor of Johnny Klippstein did not slow down the Senators, as they posted a six-run fourth inning to take a commanding 9-0 lead. The Twins started to come alive in the sixth inning beginning with a Harmon Killebrew two-run homer, and then Earl Battey's three-run blast in the seventh inning drew the Twins within three, but Minnesota was unable to overcome the Senators.

JULY 27 (GAME 2). MINNESOTA 9, WASHINGTON 5. Zoilo Versalles, Earl Battey, and Don Mincher all went deep for Minnesota in a 12-hit, nine-run onslaught. The Twins were aided by four Washington errors, and relievers Dwight Siebler and Al Worthington combined to pitch four innings of shutout baseball, with Worthington earning the win.

JULY 28. MINNESOTA 9, WASHINGTON 1. Looking to wrap up their road trip with a win, the Senators filled out the scorecard against the Senators. The red-hot Tony Oliva went 5-for-5, raising his batting average to .308, third best in the American League. Harmon Killebrew's third-inning two-run homer put him in sole possession of the American League lead in RBIs with 69, and brought him into a tie with Detroit's Willie Horton for the lead in home runs, with 22. The only setback for the Twins was the loss of Camilo Pascual, who, after dealing with a strained back muscle for more than a month, exited the game in the fourth inning. Pascual's injury proved to be serious enough to warrant surgery, and it was projected that he could miss the remainder of the season.

JULY 30. MINNESOTA 3, BALTIMORE 2. Four days after beating the Orioles in Baltimore, Mudcat Grant went to the mound at Metropolitan Stadium to take on Hank Bauer's club again. As in his previous start, Grant allowed two runs, but unlike his last outing, he went the distance en route to his 12th win. Grant's run support came from RBIs by Tony Oliva, Rich Rollins, and Earl Battey, who broke a 2-2 deadlock in the eighth with a squeeze bunt to bring home Don Mincher.

JULY 31. MINNESOTA 2, BALTIMORE 1. Jim Perry was solid in his bid for his eighth win of the season, giving up only one run in eight innings, but the Orioles' John Miller was just as strong, keeping the Twins scoreless after eight innings. Harmon Killebrew broke through for the Twins in the nick of time, driving in pinch-runner Jim Kaat with an RBI single to force extra innings. Al Worthington kept the Orioles silent in the 10th and 11th innings, and Tony Oliva led off the bottom half of the 11th with a hit. Oliva moved to second on a bunt by Worthington. After an intentional walk to Killebrew, all eyes turned to pinch-hitter Joe Nossek. Nossek grounded to Brooks Robinson, but the Baltimore infield was unable to turn the double play, enabling the aggressive Oliva to score from second base and give Minnesota the victory. With the win, the Twins expanded their lead in the American League to six games, and improved their sterling July record to 22-9.

Team	Won	Lost	Pct	GB
Minnesota Twins	65	37	.637	-
Baltimore Orioles	58	42	.580	6.0
Cleveland Indians	58	42	.580	6.0
Detroit Tigers	56	43	.566	7.5
Chicago White Sox	54	45	.545	9.5
New York Yankees	51	54	.486	15.5
California Angels	47	55	.461	18.0
Washington Senators	44	59	.427	21.5
Boston Red Sox	38	63	.376	26.5
Kansas City Athletics	33	64	.340	29.5

AUGUST 1. BALTIMORE 7, MINNESOTA 6. Bob Allison's second-inning solo home run and fourth-inning sacrifice fly gave the Twins an early 3-1 lead over the visiting Orioles. Jim Kaat ran into trouble in the fifth inning, however, giving up a double to Dick Brown and a triple to Luis Aparicio. Later in that inning Don Mincher's error led to two more runs as the Orioles wrestled the lead away from the Twins. Jimmie Hall's fifth-inning RBI groundout brought home Kaat's replacement, Garry Roggenburk, to tie the game, 4-4. On the mound Roggenburk kept the Twins in the game by tossing 2⅓ innings of scoreless relief, and Earl Battey put the Twins out in front in the eighth with a two-run RBI double off Jim Palmer. The lead was short-lived, as Boog Powell silenced the Twins with a three-run home run in the ninth off Dick Stigman to give the Orioles the victory.

AUGUST 2. MINNESOTA 6, BALTIMORE 5. Left-hander Jim Merritt made his major-league debut when Sam Mele gave him the start against the Orioles. With Minnesota leading 2-0 in the top of the sixth inning, Merritt lost the lead and, more significantly, the Twins lost Harmon Killebrew to injury. The reigning American League home-run champion and team leader dislocated his elbow and had to be taken off the field in a stretcher after he smashed his outstretched arm into an oncoming baserunner while reaching for a wild throw. Although Minnesota would have to forge ahead without Killebrew, Mele summed up the team's persevering attitude, saying, "These guys never stop fighting. They won't now with Harmon out of the lineup."[6] True to Mele's word, the rest of the Twins kept swinging, and Minnesota retook the lead with a three-run outburst in the eighth inning. Baltimore's Dick Brown tied the game again with a three-run home run, but Jimmie Hall led off the bottom of the ninth with a solo walk-off home run.

AUGUST 3 (GAME 1). MINNESOTA 4, WASHINGTON 3. With the irreplaceable Harmon Killebrew out of the lineup until September 21, Don Mincher stepped into the role of the Twins' everyday first baseman. Mincher also filled in for Killebrew in the batter's box by slugging his 14th home run of the season to break a 1-1 deadlock in the fourth inning. Four batters later, Minnesota starter Mudcat Grant doubled his lead by doubling in Frank Quilici. Not only did Grant drive in a run, but he scored a run of his own in the seventh as the Twins held off the visiting Senators in the first game of the doubleheader.

AUGUST 3 (GAME 2). WASHINGTON 4, MINNESOTA 2. With Camilo Pascual still out of the starting rotation, Dwight Siebler started the second game of the doubleheader with the Senators. Big Frank Howard took Siebler deep in the second to give Washington a 1-0 lead, and Ken Hamlin extended the lead in the next inning with an RBI double. Zoilo Versalles put the Twins on the board and tied the game with a two-run home run in the bottom half of the third, but Don Zimmer's fifth-inning double off Mel Nelson scored two and put the Senators up for good.

AUGUST 4. MINNESOTA 4, WASHINGTON 3. Jim Perry gave up three runs in 4⅔ innings before giving way to the Minnesota bullpen. Bill Pleis, Garry Roggenburk, and Dick Stigman were all strong in relief as they kept the Senators scoreless through the ninth inning. After the trio of relief pitchers did their duty, Jerry Kindall made their efforts count by tying the game in the ninth with his fifth home run of the season. After a walk to Zoilo Versalles and a single by Tony Oliva, Jimmie Hall found himself at the plate with runners on the corners and a chance to win the game, which he did on an RBI single off Marshall Bridges.

AUGUST 5. MINNESOTA 8, WASHINGTON 5. After Earl Battey doubled in Bob Allison in the second inning, pitcher Pete Richert and the Senators were beset by a series of miscues. Jimmie Hall reached base on an error, and Battey scored on a wild pitch. The sloppiness continued as Hall scored on a passed ball with Frank Quilici at the plate. Having scored three on a series of Washington follies in the second inning, the Twins plated three more in one fell swoop in the third inning on a three-run home run by Joe Nossek. Bob Allison and Zoilo Versalles checked in later in the game with an RBI triple and home run, respectively, as the Twins took three of four from the visiting Senators.

AUGUST 6. MINNESOTA 9, BOSTON 3. The Twins had the Red Sox' number in 1965. Minnesota showcased its dominance over Boston in the bottom of the sixth when the Twins scored six runs, including two on a Bob Allison home run and three on a Zoilo Versalles blast. The offensive output carried Jim Merritt to his first career win in only his second start.

AUGUST 7. MINNESOTA 9, BOSTON 4. Zoilo Versalles and Don Mincher each collected his 15th home run of the season as the Twins cruised to victory again against the Red Sox. Despite giving up four runs, Mudcat Grant went the distance to collect his league-leading 14th win. The American League leaders in batting, Carl Yastrzemski and Felix Mantilla, both went deep for Boston, but the Twins' Jimmie Hall gained ground in the batting race by going 2-for-4, bringing his average to .306.

AUGUST 8. MINNESOTA 8, BOSTON 0. Minnesota collected yet another sweep against the Red Sox by dismantling Boston. Tony Oliva went 4-for-5 with a double and two RBIs to bring his average to .307 and thrust himself into the batting title conversation. Bob Allison and Don Mincher both tripled, and pitcher Jim Perry was stellar, improving to 8-2 with his two-hit shutout.

AUGUST 10. MINNESOTA 7, NEW YORK 3. After sweeping the Red Sox in Minnesota, the Twins embarked on a coast-to-coast road trip, beginning in New York. The Twins jumped ahead of Whitey Ford in the first inning on an RBI double by Rich Rollins and an RBI single by Tony Oliva. The Yankees tied the game, 2-2, in the seventh inning, but the Twins ran away in the eighth inning, scoring five runs on four hits and an error. Winning pitcher Jim Kaat gave up only one earned run through seven innings, but after giving up an eighth-inning home run to Mickey Mantle, Kaat gave way to Al Worthington, who recorded his 14th save of the season. It was the Twins' sixth win in a row as they improved to 73-39 and stretched their lead to 8½ games over second-place Baltimore.

AUGUST 11. NEW YORK 5, MINNESOTA 4. For the second straight game the Twins jumped ahead of the Yankees in the first inning with RBI singles coming from Earl Battey and Rich Rollins. Despite the early lead, Mudcat Grant and the Twins came apart in the fifth inning, which began with an Elston Howard base hit and a Ray Barker double. Howard scored on a wild pitch with Clete Boyer at the plate, and Boyer added to the damage by singling home Barker. Grant's nightmare inning continued when his error allowed Phil Linz to get on base. Linz and Boyer scored on a Bobby Richardson single before Grant was lifted in favor of Garry Roggenburk. The five-run fifth inning was all the Yankees needed as they ended the Twins' six-game winning streak.

AUGUST 12. MINNESOTA 8, NEW YORK 2. It was a banner day for Minnesota rookies Jim Merritt and Frank Quilici. Merritt gave up only two runs on his way to his first career complete game and Quilici collected his first career triple in the eighth inning, which produced his first two career RBIs. Don Mincher continued to contribute at the plate, taking New York starter Al Downing deep in the fourth inning. More excitement came in the ninth when Rich Rollins stole home on a double steal as the Twins took the series from the Yankees.

AUGUST 13. CLEVELAND 3, MINNESOTA 1. The next stop on the Twins' road trip was Cleveland, where they took on the Indians on Friday the 13th. Bad luck struck the Indians in the fifth inning when an error by Tony Oliva and a wild pitch from starting pitcher Jim Perry allowed the Indians to score two runs. Oliva atoned for his error with his 16th home run of the year in the seventh inning, but the Indians held off the Twins.

AUGUST 14. CLEVELAND 3, MINNESOTA 1. The Twins' bad fifth-inning luck was not limited to Friday the 13th, as Larry Brown and Chuck Hinton tagged Jim Kaat for two home runs in the fifth inning on Saturday the 14th. Cleveland hurler Sam McDowell shut down the potent Minnesota offense, limiting the Twins to one run on three hits. The lone Minnesota run came off the bat of rookie newcomer Andy Kosco, who homered in just his second major-league at-bat.

AUGUST 15 (GAME 1). MINNESOTA 4, CLEVELAND 3. Having lost two in a row to the Indians, the Twins needed to sweep Sunday's doubleheader in order to escape Cleveland with a series split. Jimmie Hall's second-inning double, followed by Earl Battey's RBI single, gave the Twins the early 1-0 lead against Luis Tiant. The Twins added three insurance runs in the top of the ninth inning on a two-RBI double by Don Mincher and an RBI single by Hall to give Mudcat Grant a comfortable 4-0 lead going into the bottom of the ninth. Leon Wagner chased Grant and made things interesting with a two-run home run in the ninth, and Chuck Hinton made reliever Al Worthington sweat with an RBI single, but the Twins managed to hold on.

AUGUST 15 (GAME 2). CLEVELAND 6, MINNESOTA 4. Tony Oliva cracked his 30th double of the season in the first inning, and was brought home on a single by Don Mincher to give the Twins the early lead. Oliva struck again in the seventh inning with an RBI single to extend the Twins' lead to 3-1. Garry Roggenburk had his first blown save of the season by giving up a game-tying two-run home run to Max Alvis with two out in the bottom of the ninth. Jerry Kindall put the Twins back out in front in the 11th inning with a solo blast, but the Indians refused to go quietly. With pinch-hitter Leon Wagner at the plate and a runner on third, Minnesota reliever Bill Pleis committed a balk to tie the game. Pleis could not shake off the miscue as Wagner tagged Pleis for a walk-off home run. Despite losing three of four to the Indians, the Twins left Cleveland with a comfortable eight-game lead over the second-place Indians.

AUGUST 17. DETROIT 7, MINNESOTA 4. The Twins continued their Midwest swing in Detroit against the Tigers, who came into the game tied with the Indians for second place. Making his fourth career start, Jim Merritt ran into a buzz saw in the third and fourth innings, giving up solo home runs to Don Wert, Al Kaline, and Willie Horton. Dave Boswell fared even worse in relief, giving up four runs, including three on Horton's second home run of the game, in the fifth inning. After being shut out by Hank Aguirre for seven innings, Minnesota rallied. Zoilo Versalles doubled to lead off the eighth inning and the Twins narrowed the seven-run deficit on RBI singles by Tony Oliva, Earl Battey, and Don Mincher. Versailles doubled again in the ninth inning and was brought home by Frank Quilici, but the Tigers held on to win.

AUGUST 19 (GAME 1). MINNESOTA 8, DETROIT 3. The Twins jumped on Tigers pitcher Dave Wickersham in the first inning, plating two. Two innings later, Minnesota did even more damage against the Detroit righty, scoring four runs on back-to-back home runs by Don Mincher and Rich Rollins to take a commanding 6-0 lead. On the mound, Mudcat Grant took a no-hitter into the fifth inning before it was broken up by a Norm Cash home run. Grant got the run back himself with an RBI double in the eighth inning, and stayed in the game to earn the complete-game win despite giving up a ninth-inning home run to Don Demeter.

AUGUST 19 (GAME 2). MINNESOTA 2, DETROIT 1. On his way to a 3-for-4 game, Zoilo Versalles hit his ninth triple of the season off Mickey Lolich before scoring the first run of the game on a Jerry Kindall squeeze bunt. Pinch-hitter Jake Wood tied the game in the seventh inning with an RBI single off Jim Kaat. The Tigers were unable to muster anything else against Kaat, and Zoilo Versalles's eighth-inning double and Sandy Valdespino's ensuing pinch-hit single handed Kaat the victory and gave the Twins the series win.

AUGUST 20 (GAME 1). CALIFORNIA 3, MINNESOTA 1. After wrapping up a doubleheader in Detroit the day before, the Twins flew to California to take on the Angels in their second doubleheader in as many days. Although the road-weary Twins managed to collect nine hits, their only run came on Jimmie Hall's sixth-inning double. In an otherwise strong start, Jim Perry gave up a two-run fourth-inning home run to Joe Adcock, which was enough to stick him with his fourth loss of the season.

AUGUST 20 (GAME 2). MINNESOTA 3, CALIFORNIA 1. Making his first start since July 9, Dave Boswell went 6⅓ innings against the Angels. Although Jose Cardenal's third-inning solo home run was the only run scored against Boswell, he left the game behind a run. The Twins were unable to crack California's George Brunet until the ninth inning when Zoilo Versalles and Rich Rollins led off with a single and a double, respectively. Taking a long lead at third, Versalles bolted for home when Tony Oliva hit a bouncing ball down the first-base line. Versalles scored when first baseman Vic Power hurried the throw home, and Rollins moved to third. Third-base coach Billy Martin hailed Versalles's aggressive baserunning, saying, "Zoilo stole that run."[7] Andy Kosco then put the Twins in the lead with a sacrifice fly.

Sandy Valdespino added an insurance run with an RBI single, and Johnny Klippstein retired the Twins in order in the bottom of the ninth on his way to his sixth win of the season.

AUGUST 21. MINNESOTA 4, CALIFORNIA 2. Jim Merritt and Angels starter Fred Newman kept the game scoreless through five innings. The Twins came alive in the sixth with three straight singles by Zoilo Versalles, Sandy Valdespino, and Tony Oliva, with Oliva's single bringing home Versalles to break the deadlock. Jimmie Hall advanced Oliva and Valdespino on a groundout, and Earl Battey brought them home on a single to give the Twins a 3-0 lead. Second baseman Bobby Knoop shaved the lead to two with an RBI double in the bottom half of the inning, but the Twins regained a three-run lead when Oliva drove in Versalles for the second time, this time on sacrifice fly in the eighth. Coming on in relief of Merritt, Al Worthington gave up a run in the bottom of the ninth but nonetheless earned his 16th save of the season as the Twins equaled their 79-win total of the previous season.

AUGUST 22. CALIFORNIA 4, MINNESOTA 1. In the first inning, Tony Oliva's league-leading 155th base hit scored Zoilo Versalles with his league-leading 98th run to put the Twins up 1-0. Unfortunately for Jim Kaat, Oliva's RBI was all that would come in the way of run support, and Kaat lost the narrow lead in the fifth inning on a two-run homer by Jim Piersall. Kaat gave up two more runs in the sixth inning on a two-run, two-out RBI single by starting pitcher Dean Chance. Kaat's record dropped to 12-10 with the loss. The defeat wrapped up Minnesota's whirlwind cross-country road trip, in which they went 7-7. They still had a comfortable 6½-game lead as they returned home.

AUGUST 23. MINNESOTA 4, NEW YORK 3. Without taking a breath, the Twins winged all the way back to Minnesota to take on the Yankees. Zoilo Versalles opened the scoring against Whitey Ford with a solo home run, his 16th of the year. Mudcat Grant kept the Yanks scoreless until Bobby Richardson doubled home Roger Repoz in the top of the sixth inning. Frank Quilici put the Twins back in front in the bottom of the sixth with a single, but Clete Boyer took Grant deep in the seventh with a two-run blast that gave New York the edge. Ford protected his one-run lead until the ninth inning, when he was chased after giving up a single to Versalles. Versalles scored on Tony Oliva's 31st double of the season, forcing extra innings. Al Worthington made the home crowd nervous by loading the bases in the 10th inning, but he struck out Elston Howard to get out of the jam. After Bob Allison and Don Mincher drew walks off Jim Bouton, the Twins walked off on Jerry Kindall's RBI single.

AUGUST 24. NEW YORK 2, MINNESOTA 1. Tony Oliva went 2-for-4 to raise his batting average to .312. One of Oliva's hits came in the sixth inning and drove home Sandy Valdespino to give the Twins a 1-0 lead. Jim Perry could not hold the lead, though, giving up a two-run home run to Tom Tresh in the eighth. The two runs were enough for Mel Stottlemyre, who earned his 16th victory for New York.

AUGUST 25. MINNESOTA 5, NEW YORK 4. The Twins' injury woes continued to grow after Tony Oliva exited in the first inning with a jammed finger. (Oliva sat out the next five games.) Bob Allison, who had recently been splitting duties with Sandy Valdespino, checked in with a home run to give the Twins and Jim Merritt the early lead. Merritt then saw his lead increase when he drew a walk and scored on Joe Nossek's fifth-inning double. In the seventh inning, the Yankees' Tom Tresh went deep for the second consecutive game, and then Hector Lopez tied the game with a sacrifice fly. The Twins struck back in the bottom of the frame, plating two on Rich Rollins's triple and adding another on Earl Battey's double. Merritt was denied the complete game after Elston Howard chased him with a ninth-inning home run, but the Minnesota rookie still earned the win after Al Worthington retired the side.

AUGUST 26. MINNESOTA 9, NEW YORK 2. With Tony Oliva out of the lineup, Bob Allison powered the Minnesota offense, hitting his second home run in as many days to bring his season total to 20, and adding two doubles. Zoilo Versalles, Jimmie

Hall, and Jerry Kindall also had multi-hit games as the Twins put up nine runs against the Yankees. Jim Kaat earned the complete-game win despite giving up 10 hits, as his record improved to 13-10.

AUGUST 27. MINNESOTA 7, CLEVELAND 0. The Indians entered the series on the ropes, losers of six of 10 games after taking three of four from Minnesota earlier in the month. Mudcat Grant was splendid as he bedeviled the Indians in a two-hit shutout performance to earn his league-leading 17th win. Grant also powered the Minnesota offense, going 2-for-4 with four RBIs. Rich Rollins, Earl Battey, and Bob Allison each collected an RBI as the Twins rolled.

AUGUST 28. CLEVELAND 6, MINNESOTA 5. Jim Perry found himself down early after giving up a two-run triple to Rocky Colavito in the top of the first inning. Not to be outdone, Sandy Valdespino responded with a first-inning triple off Luis Tiant, which scored Zoilo Versalles from second after he had doubled. Valdespino then scored on Earl Battey's sacrifice fly to tie the game. Battey's leadoff double in the fourth inning paved the way for RBI singles by Bob Allison and Jerry Kindall. The Twins continued to build on their lead in the fifth when Versalles tripled and scored on a Jimmie Hall base hit to put the Twins up 5-2. Perry's lead was not safe, however, as Cleveland tied it up on back-to-back homers by Rocky Colavito and Fred Whitfield in the eighth inning. Al Worthington was saddled with the loss, giving up a sacrifice fly to Chuck Hinton in the ninth.

AUGUST 29. CLEVELAND 3, MINNESOTA 1. Jim Merritt took the mound in the rubber game with the Indians in search of his fifth win. He had a 1-0 lead in the sixth inning, but his plans were derailed when Rocky Colavito's double tied the game and Fred Whitfield's sacrifice fly put Cleveland ahead. Whitfield struck again in the eighth inning to add an insurance run on an RBI single, and the Twins never recovered, losing the game and the series to Cleveland.

AUGUST 30. MINNESOTA 3, DETROIT 2. Left fielder Willie Horton led the charge for Detroit, driving in the first run of the game off Jim Kaat in the fourth inning. After Don Mincher's RBI single tied the game, Horton put the Tigers back in front with another RBI single and chased Kaat from the game in the process. Zoilo Versalles singled home Jerry Kindall in the seventh to put the game back on even terms, and the game remained tied after nine innings. Johnny Klippstein kept the Tigers scoreless and the Twins won the game on a walk-off RBI single by Sandy Valdespino in the 11th.

AUGUST 31. DETROIT 7, MINNESOTA 6. With the Twins leading 2-1 in the top of the fifth inning, Tigers first baseman Norm Cash mashed a three-run go-ahead home run off Mudcat Grant. The Twins loaded the bases in the bottom of the fifth inning and scored three, including two on Don Mincher's triple, to retake the lead. The back-and-forth continued as the Tigers and Twins traded RBI singles in the sixth and seventh innings, and the Twins held a 6-5 lead going into the ninth. The lead changed yet again, and this time for good, when catcher Bill Freehan blasted a two-run homer off Mel Nelson. With the loss, the Twins ended August with a 19-13 record for the month, and maintained a 7½-game lead atop the American League.

Team	Won	Lost	Pct	GB
Minnesota Twins	84	50	.627	-
Chicago White Sox	76	57	.571	7.5
Baltimore Orioles	72	57	.558	9.5
Cleveland Indians	73	58	.557	9.5
Detroit Tigers	73	59	.553	10.0
New York Yankees	66	67	.496	17.5
California Angels	61	72	.459	22.5
Washington Senators	58	75	.436	25.5
Boston Red Sox	51	83	.381	33.0
Kansas City Athletics	47	83	.362	35.0

SEPTEMBER 1. MINNESOTA 5, DETROIT 2. Entering the home stretch, the Twins entered September with a 7½-game lead in the American League. Minnesota's prospects for capturing the pennant were bolstered by the return of Tony Oliva to the lineup. Oliva went 3-for-4 and initiated the scoring in the first inning by giving the Twins the lead on an RBI double. Oliva scored on a passed ball with Earl Battey at the plate, and then Battey drove home

Bob Allison to give the Twins a 3-0 lead. Jim Perry gave up a two-run second-inning homer to light-hitting shortstop Ray Oyler, but otherwise shut down the Detroit offense as he captured his ninth win of the season.

SEPTEMBER 2. DETROIT 5, MINNESOTA 4. Detroit third baseman Don Wert had a field day against Jim Merritt, tagging the Twins starter for a two-run single and a two-run homer, the latter of which gave the Tigers a 4-2 lead in the fifth inning. The Twins loaded the bases in the bottom of the inning but were able to plate only one run when Cesar Tovar drew a walk off Joe Sparma. With the Twins down two going into the bottom of the ninth, Don Mincher gave his team hope by leading off with a home run, but Detroit reliever Terry Fox was able to save the game for the Tigers.

SEPTEMBER 3. MINNESOTA 6, CHICAGO 4. Trailing the Twins by 6½ games with only 27 left to play, the second-place White Sox rolled into Minnesota needing to make a statement. Instead, it was the Twins' Tony Oliva who did the talking, going 3-for-4 with four RBIs and a stolen base. Don Mincher added two more runs for Minnesota on his 19th home run of the season. With six runs of support, Jim Kaat earned the win despite giving up four runs in 5⅓ innings, and Al Worthington collected his 19th save of the season.

SEPTEMBER 4. CHICAGO 5, MINNESOTA 4. Chicago shortstop Ron Hansen had a nightmare first inning, making errors on two straight plays, allowing Zoilo Versalles and Sandy Valdespino to reach base to lead off the game. Both scored on RBI groundouts by Tony Oliva and Don Mincher as the Twins took a 2-1 lead without recording a hit. With an RBI single in the fourth, Earl Battey gave Mudcat Grant a two-run cushion. The White Sox clawed back with two runs in the fifth, and then center fielder Ken Berry put Grant behind with a solo home run in the sixth. The White Sox added one more in the eighth when Don Buford stole home, and Hoyt Wilhelm held off the Twins to earn his 16th save of the season.

SEPTEMBER 5. CHICAGO 2, MINNESOTA 0. Chicago's Joe Horlen gave up only three hits in a shutout performance. Jim Perry gave up only one earned run in 7⅔ innings, but was stuck with the loss as the White Sox left Minnesota having gained some ground on the league-leading Twins.

SEPTEMBER 6 (GAME 1). MINNESOTA 8, KANSAS CITY 6. Making his first appearance since aggravating his back on July 28, Camilo Pascual was given the start as the Twins traveled to Kansas City for a quick doubleheader. Pascual ran into trouble in the second inning, giving up five runs to the A's before making way for Dave Boswell. The Twins quickly got back into the game with a two-run third inning and a three-run fourth. Jerry Kindall was at the center of the attack in both innings, collecting two hits and scoring twice. Rich Rollins put the Twins ahead in the fifth inning with a single, and Earl Battey and Don Mincher added insurance runs in the eighth. Despite getting roughed up in his return, Pascual remained confident, saying, "my back is okay. It will take me two or three more times out. Then give me the ball."[8]

SEPTEMBER 6 (GAME 2). KANSAS CITY 4, MINNESOTA 3. The Twins gave Jim Merritt the early lead by plating two in the second inning. Although Merritt gave up a run in the second, his fourth-inning RBI single got the run back, and he took a 3-1 lead into the eighth inning. Mike Hershberger led off the eighth with a double, moved to third on a passed ball, and then scored on a groundout. Dick Green and Jose Tartabull had back-to-back doubles, which tied the game and caused Sam Mele to turn to Al Worthington. Worthington lost the game in the ninth on a sacrifice fly by Santiago Rosario.

SEPTEMBER 8. MINNESOTA 3, CHICAGO 2. After splitting the doubleheader in Kansas City, the Twins headed to Chicago with their lead over the White Sox narrowed to five games. After giving up two runs in the first inning, Mudcat Grant settled down and blanked the White Sox for the remainder of the game. Zoilo Versalles brought the Twins within one by bringing home Rich Rollins on a sacrifice fly in the third inning. With his two-run home run in the seventh inning, Jimmie Hall put the Twins up for good as they extended their lead to six games.

SEPTEMBER 9. MINNESOTA 10, CHICAGO 4. After eking out a win the day before, the Twins exploded against the White Sox at Comiskey Park. Giving up four runs on six hits in just 1⅔ innings, Chicago starter Joe Horlen was replaced by Bob Locker. Horlen's counterpart, Jim Kaat, was strong enough, giving up three runs in 6⅔ innings. Al Worthington gave up one run in 2⅓ innings of relief, and Jimmie Hall went deep for the second straight game as the Twins cruised to victory.

SEPTEMBER 10. MINNESOTA 8, BOSTON 5. After stretching their lead back to seven games in Chicago, the Twins headed to Fenway Park to take on the ninth-place Red Sox. With the bases loaded in the second inning, Zoilo Versalles cleared them with his 40th double of the season. Sloppy fielding by third baseman Rich Rollins and a wild pitch by Jim Perry put the Red Sox on the board in the bottom of the second, but the Twins extended their lead in the third on an RBI double by Don Mincher and a sacrifice fly by Earl Battey. The Twins pulled away with hits by Jerry Kindall and Jimmie Hall in the sixth inning, as Jim Perry earned his 10th win of the season and the Twins crossed the 90-win threshold.

SEPTEMBER 11. MINNESOTA 8, BOSTON 4. For the second straight game, the Twins plated eight against the Red Sox. Every Twins position player got a hit and the top three men in the order—Zoilo Versalles, Jimmie Hall, and Tony Oliva—went a combined 10-for-15 with three doubles, four stolen bases, and five RBIs. Camilo Pascual also returned to form, going 7⅓ innings and giving up a respectable three runs on five hits to earn his ninth win of the season.

SEPTEMBER 12. MINNESOTA 2, BOSTON 0. The final game of the season between the Twins and the Red Sox could not have come soon enough for Boston. Mudcat Grant put the Red Sox out of their misery by shutting them out on four hits. With his fifth triple of the season, Tony Oliva (.318) edged closer to Carl Yastrzemski (.323) in the American League batting race, and RBIs from Bob Allison and Don Mincher gave the Twins the victory. With the win, the Twins' domination of the Red Sox was complete, as they ended the season with an incredible 17-1 record against Boston.

SEPTEMBER 14. MINNESOTA 4, KANSAS CITY 3. The Twins returned home to Minnesota to play the A's, having gone 6-1 on their road trip to open a nine-game lead in the American League with 16 games left to play. After the A's Mike Hershberger put Kansas City on top in the second inning, Earl Battey struck back for the Twins by doubling home Bob Allison. With the game tied, 2-2, in the bottom of the seventh, the hot-hitting Jimmie Hall drove in Zoilo Versalles and Rich Rollins to hand Jim Kaat his 16th win of the season.

SEPTEMBER 15. MINNESOTA 7, KANSAS CITY 5. Jim Perry squared off against Catfish Hunter, but neither starter recorded a decision. Hunter's subpar day came to a close in the fifth inning after he gave up RBI singles to Zoilo Versalles and Bob Allison. Perry was not far behind Hunter, as he was chased in the sixth inning after giving up home runs to Ken Harrelson and Larry Stahl. With the game tied, 5-5, going into the bottom of the ninth, rookie pinch-hitter Ted Uhlaender recorded his first career RBI by singling home Don Mincher. Joe Nossek, also coming in as a pinch-hitter, added an insurance run by driving in Rich Rollins as the Twins won their seventh straight.

SEPTEMBER 17. WASHINGTON 2, MINNESOTA 1. Camilo Pascual had another strong outing off the disabled list, giving up only one run on five hits in nine innings. Unfortunately for Pascual, his counterpart, Pete Richert, put up the exact same line and the game entered the 10th inning tied, 1-1. Making his third relief appearance since going to the bullpen to make room for Pascual, Jim Merritt gave up a go-ahead single to Don Lock as the Twins' winning streak came to an end.

SEPTEMBER 18. MINNESOTA 4, WASHINGTON 2. Rookies Ted Uhlaender and Frank Quilici started the game for Minnesota in left field and at second base, respectively, and ended up playing central roles in the victory. Uhlaender reached base on an error in the first inning, stole second, and scored on a single by Earl Battey. Quilici walked in the next inning and scored on Zoilo Versalles's 17th home run of the season. Jim Kaat walked six, and left the game in the fifth inning with a 4-2 lead, so he was ineligible for the win. That distinction went to Johnny Klippstein, who pitched 2⅓ innings of scoreless relief.

SEPTEMBER 19. MINNESOTA 8, WASHINGTON 1. Minnesota jumped on Washington in the first inning, as Joe Nossek doubled and stole third. Although Nossek was thrown out trying to score on a fielder's choice, the Minnesota attack was undeterred as Bob Allison doubled home Andy Kosco and Earl Battey. Don Mincher kept the line moving by driving in Allison, as the Twins took an early 3-0 lead. Although the three runs were more than enough for Jim Perry, who went the distance and allowed only one run, the Twins added five more on RBIs by Frank Quilici, Zoilo Versalles, and two from Perry himself.

SEPTEMBER 20. KANSAS CITY 8, MINNESOTA 2. Don Mincher clubbed two home runs for Minnesota to bring his season total to 21; however, the Twins were able to muster little else against 19-year-old rookie Catfish Hunter and the A's. Mudcat Grant was handed his sixth loss in 25 decisions, and Garry Roggenburk was roughed up in relief, giving up three runs on two hits and two walks without retiring a batter.

SEPTEMBER 21. BALTIMORE 6, MINNESOTA 4. The Twins welcomed Harmon Killebrew back to the lineup as they closed in on the American League pennant, but the second-place Orioles arrived in Minnesota to keep their own remote pennant hopes alive. Boog Powell buoyed Baltimore's hopes with a first-inning RBI single off Camilo Pascual, and Paul Blair's fourth-inning blast extended Baltimore's lead. With the Twins down 4-2 in the bottom of the eighth, Andy Kosco's sacrifice fly and Zoilo Versalles's league-leading 44th double pulled the Twins even. The Twins came apart, though, in the 10th inning, when Luis Aparicio singled home Jerry Adair and Boog Powell walked with the bases loaded as the Orioles took the game.

SEPTEMBER 22. BALTIMORE 5, MINNESOTA 2. The Orioles again refused to go quietly in their final visit to Minnesota. Jerry Adair's two-run second-inning homer off Jim Kaat put Baltimore ahead, and the Orioles added three more runs in the fifth inning. Other than allowing RBI singles to Tony Oliva and Bob Allison, the Orioles' Dave McNally shut down the Twins, who saw their loss-column lead over Baltimore shrink to six games, with eight remaining.

SEPTEMBER 25 (GAME 1). MINNESOTA 5, WASHINGTON 0. After being idle for two days, the Twins played two against the Senators in Washington. Zoilo Versalles broke the 0-0 tie in the fifth inning with a two-run homer, his 18th of the year. The Twins added three more in the seventh on Tony Oliva's double and Sandy Valdespino's two-run RBI single. Mudcat Grant earned his league-leading 20th win in style, shutting out the Senators with a one-hitter.

SEPTEMBER 25 (GAME 2). MINNESOTA 5, WASHINGTON 3. The Twins made two errors and Camilo Pascual gave up two hits in the second inning, leading to three Senators runs. The Twins earned one run on two singles and a sacrifice fly by Jimmie Hall in the fourth, and they added another run on a Don Mincher homer in the seventh, but they still trailed 3-2 going into the eighth inning. With two out and runners on first and second, Joe Nossek doubled to tie the game. Two batters later, Frank Quilici drove home two more runs with a single as the Twins wrested the game from the Senators. However, with Baltimore sweeping a doubleheader from California, the Twins would have to wait another day to celebrate.

SEPTEMBER 26. MINNESOTA 2, WASHINGTON 1. Just as he had in his previous start against the Twins, nine days earlier, Senators pitcher Pete Richert made life difficult for Minnesota. Fortunately for the Twins, Jim Kaat kept his club in the game by giving up only one run in nine innings, but the Twins trailed 1-0 going into the sixth. Zoilo Versalles cracked Richert by legging out his league-leading 12th triple of the season. A passed ball allowed Versalles to score to tie the game. Two innings later, Frank Quilici led off the eighth with a double and moved to third on a wild pitch by Richert. With one out and Quilici on third, Versalles hit a fly ball to center field that allowed Quilici to tag up and give the Twins the lead. Kaat stayed in the game and kept the Senators scoreless in the eighth and ninth innings to earn the victory. With the win, the Twins clinched the American League pennant, bringing the World Series to the fans of Minnesota for the first time. Kaat's reward for clinching the pennant was a spot in Minnesota's World Series rotation, which had been less than a certainty given his recent struggles in closing out games. "I had plenty of incentive. I wanted to show them what I could do," said the triumphant lefty.

SEPTEMBER 28. BALTIMORE 4, MINNESOTA 2. With the pennant in hand, the Twins traveled to Baltimore to take on the Orioles, whose late-season surge had come up short. Jim Perry gave up two runs on six hits in four innings before being replaced by Al Worthington. Worthington encountered some control problems, loading the bases on two walks and a hit batsman before walking home two runs. In an encouraging sign for Minnesota, Harmon Killebrew hit his first home run since returning to the lineup, a two-run shot that brought the Twins within two, but Minnesota fell to Baltimore.

SEPTEMBER 29. MINNESOTA 3, BALTIMORE 2. Mudcat Grant went to the mound in search of his 21st win. Although he gave up only two runs in eight innings, Grant looked as if he might instead get his seventh loss, with the Twins down 2-1 going into the eighth inning. With Cesar Tovar on second after a double, Bob Allison carried Grant and the Twins to the lead with his 22nd home run of the season. After Grant loaded the bases in the ninth, Jim Merritt and Johnny Klippstein combined to hold the Orioles hitless for the remainder of the inning, with Klippstein earning his fourth save of the season.

SEPTEMBER 30. MINNESOTA 7, BALTIMORE 6. He did not have his best stuff on the mound, but Jim Kaat did better at the plate, hitting his only home run of the season, off Milt Pappas. Kaat was not the only one to save a first for the end of the season; Zoilo Versalles clubbed his first career grand slam, off Pappas in the fifth inning. Jimmie Hall added two more runs on a single in the seventh. Hall's insurance runs turned out to be crucial when Baltimore plated four in the bottom of the seventh to make it a 7-5 game. Baltimore's Curt Blefary cut the Twins' lead to one by scoring on an error by Jerry Kindall (who was filling in at shortstop) in the eighth, but Al Worthington was able to save the game for Minnesota.

OCTOBER 2. CALIFORNIA 5, MINNESOTA 4. The Twins returned home for the first time since clinching the pennant to take on the Angels. Camilo Pascual got the start and gave up two runs in five innings before turning the ball over to Mudcat Grant. Perhaps uncomfortable coming out of the bullpen, Grant did something he rarely did in 1965: he lost, giving up three runs in two innings. Harmon Killebrew and Bob Allison both went deep for Minnesota, but it was not enough to overcome the Angels.

OCTOBER 3. MINNESOTA 3, CALIFORNIA 2. Jim Kaat got the start in the Twins' final regular-season game, but Sam Mele distributed the day's pitching load among Kaat, Dave Boswell, Al Worthington, Jim Perry, and Johnny Klippstein, with all but Klippstein getting two full innings of work. The pitchers combined to give up two runs on 12 hits, and Jim Perry was awarded his 12th win of the season. Although he would not repeat as home-run champion, Harmon Killebrew clubbed his 25th home run in the first inning. Don Mincher's third-inning RBI single extended the Twins' lead, and Minnesota concluded its stellar 1965 campaign with a record of 102-60.

Team	Won	Lost	Pct	GB
Minnesota Twins	102	60	.630	-
Chicago White Sox	95	67	.586	7.0
Baltimore Orioles	94	68	.580	8.0
Detroit Tigers	89	73	.549	13.0
Cleveland Indians	87	75	.537	15.0
New York Yankees	77	85	.475	25.0
California Angels	75	87	.463	27.0
Washington Senators	70	92	.432	32.0
Boston Red Sox	62	100	.383	40.0
Kansas City Athletics	59	103	.364	43.0

SOURCES:

BaseballReference.com

Retrosheet.org

NOTES

1 "Tovar Sheds Goat's Horns With Winning Smash in 11th," *The Sporting News*, May 1, 1965.

2 Max Nichols, "Twins Run, Ignore Base-Line Caution," *The Sporting News*, June 5, 1965.

3 Max Nichols, "Pascual, After 11 Long Years, Finally Passes .500," *The Sporting News*, June 5, 1965.

4 Max Nichols, "Victory Escapes Through Small Hole in Kaat's Sleeve," *The Sporting News*, June 26, 1965.

5 Max Nichols, "No Valentine for Mele—$500 Fine, Five-Day Ban," *The Sporting News*, July 31, 1965.

6 Max Nichols, "Injuries? They Just Spur Fighting Twins," *The Sporting News*, August 14, 1965.

7 Max Nichols, "With Zoilo on Base, Look for Dust Cloud Around Home Plate," *The Sporting News*, September 4, 1965.

8 Max Nichols, "Camilo's Fast Ball Crackles—Back Surgery a Huge Success," *The Sporting News*, October 2, 1965.

Bernie Allen

BY CHIP GREENE

ALTHOUGH THE PURDUE University Boilermakers football team ended the 1960 season with a mediocre 4-4-1 record (despite which they still finished the season ranked 19th in the Associated Press poll), they nevertheless snared two signature victories. On October 15 Purdue hosted then-unbeaten and third-ranked Ohio State University and upset the Buckeyes, 24-21. The following month they scored an even bigger upset when they traveled to Minnesota and upended the number one-ranked Gophers, 23-14.

As Purdue's starting quarterback, senior Bernie Allen played a prominent role in both wins. Many years later, long after his professional baseball career was ended, Allen recalled, "What I am most proud of in regards to my football career at Purdue was that I never lost to Notre Dame or Indiana. Those two in-state schools were, and still are, big rivals for Purdue."[1] In particular, one game he most enjoyed "was when I kicked a field goal to beat Ohio State, 24-21. Woody Hayes [the legendary Ohio State coach] had said I was too small to play football in the Big Ten, so I was happy to prove him wrong face to face."[2] In the end, whether or not Allen was too small to play football never really mattered, because all he ever wanted to be was a baseball player.

Born on April 16, 1939, in East Liverpool, Ohio, Bernard Keith Allen was one of the greatest all-around athletes in the history of East Liverpool High School. A star in baseball, football, and basketball (in which he was named a High School All-American), Allen was inducted into the school's Athletic Hall of Fame as a member of the inaugural class of 1982. One of five children born to Thurman and Fern Allen, Bernie no doubt emulated the athletic prowess of his father, who played baseball and was an avid golfer. Thurm, as he was known, spent 47 years employed by the Smith and Phillips Furniture Company, from which he retired in 1981 as vice president and general manager.

When Bernie graduated from high school in 1957, his athletic skills were in high demand at the collegiate level, but he had also drawn notice in major-league baseball. Ultimately, Purdue proved largely an afterthought. "Previously," Allen told *Sports Collectors Digest*, "I had visited Ohio State and met with coach Woody Hayes [following which he received Hayes's rebuff that he was too small to play Big Ten football]. I was only 6-foot, 180 pounds. I was planning on going to Colgate, but the August after I graduated from high school, Billy Elias, who was a Purdue assistant football coach, came down and watched me play in a summer baseball tournament. He convinced me to [at] least

Minnesota's starting second baseman in 1962 and 1963, Allen played in only 19 games in 1965, spending much of the year in Triple-A. The infielder fashioned a 12-year career (1962-1973). (Photo courtesy of Minnesota Twins Baseball Club).

visit the campus. My mom, dad, and I visited Purdue and we really liked the campus."

"I made it clear that baseball was my number-one sport. The scholarship was for football, as there weren't many full baseball scholarships in those days. I was intent upon playing pro baseball, but I wanted to get an education first." Additionally, "The Yankees were very interested in me at that time." Nonetheless, Allen enrolled at Purdue University.

At the time, freshmen didn't play varsity athletics, so Allen became the sixth of nine quarterbacks on the freshman team's depth chart, a circumstance that worked in his favor. "The freshman team was actually cannon fodder for the varsity," he recalled. "The quarterbacks above me … kept getting hurt as they went up against the varsity. … By the time I got to play against them late in the year, I was getting comfortable with the system. I completed some passes against the varsity and caught the attention of the coaching staff [which included future New York Yankees owner, and Allen's future boss, George Steinbrenner, whom Allen recalled as 'an excellent recruiter']. At the end of the season, the freshman team had a big intrasquad game, and I was named MVP of the game." The following season, Allen joined the varsity.

In that first varsity season, Allen was a starting defensive back on the best defensive team in the country; during the season's last several games, he also saw action at quarterback. Yet Allen also was a standout on the varsity baseball team, for whom he was named the season's MVP, and that drew the consternation of football coach Jack Mollenkopf, who, Allen said, "kept telling me I wouldn't even make the baseball team. He wanted me to give up baseball and concentrate on football." Thus began yearly battles with the pugnacious football coach.

As his junior season got under way in 1959, Allen was slated to be the second-string quarterback behind Ross Fichtner, who went on to become a successful defensive back with the Cleveland Browns. While Allen continued to pursue his dream of playing major-league baseball, Coach Mollenkopf demanded his presence at football practice. "In the spring of my junior year," Allen recalled, "I agreed to leave baseball practice early to go to football practice. Mollenkopf claimed we were supposedly putting in a new offense. After a couple of days," however, "I realized that the offense wasn't new, only the terminology." Nevertheless, Mollenkopf's needling paid dividends to the football program, for in the season's second game Fichtner broke his collarbone, and Allen assumed the starting position. He remained the starter for the remainder of that season and all of the next.

By his senior season, Allen was firmly entrenched as Purdue's starting quarterback. His availability for that role, however, wasn't a certainty. "I almost packed it in after my junior year," Allen reflected, "as I wanted to put my brother through college." For the final time, Mollenkopf railed against Allen's lack of commitment to football; but to pursue his passion, Allen again weathered Mollenkopf's wrath, in exchange for a singular moment.

"I missed the first two days of football practice as I was playing [baseball] in the NABC tournament in Wichita." There, "I got to face Satchel Paige. … Admittedly, he was at the end of the line, but still, it was Satchel Paige."

Returning to Purdue, Allen faced his tormentor. "My punishment for missing two days of practice was that Mollenkopf was only going to let me play defense in our first game of the season, against UCLA. It was real hot, so I didn't mind only getting to play defense. We were down eight points when we got the ball back for the final time, with about a minute to go in the game. As I came off the field with the defense, Mollenkopf told me to get back in there and throw the ball. … We ended up scoring a touchdown. We went for two and scored. It ended up 27-27. As I came off the field, Mollenkopf said, 'You'll start next week versus Notre Dame.' I remarked, 'Don't do me any favors.' The next week, we went out and beat Notre Dame 51-19."

That season Allen was named the football team's MVP. In an era of run-dominated football, he completed 59 percent of his passes, threw for 765 yards, and tossed five touchdowns. Allen's 54 points led the team in scoring, as he rushed for four touchdowns and kicked 21 points after touchdown and three field goals. He also punted 38 times for a 34.9-yard average. In his three varsity football seasons, Allen completed 49 percent of his passes for 1,200 yards, threw for 10 touchdowns, and tossed 11 interceptions.

With his collegiate football career over, there was never a question of playing the sport professionally. "I never had any desire to play football after college," Allen later recalled. "In fact, I played football only to get an education. I never really enjoyed it." And of Allen's availability for National Football League teams, he said, "There never was any doubt in my mind at that time. I received many phone calls from pro grid teams, but I told them not to waste a draft pick because I wanted to play baseball."[3]

The turning point in Allen's future professional baseball career came the afternoon of the football team's upset victory over the Minnesota Gophers. "After the game at Minnesota, as we made our way out of the locker room and onto the bus, the Minnesota fans came up and congratulated us on how well we had played. I remembered those gracious fans a few months later when I was trying to decide whom to sign with. It came down to the Twins and the New York Mets. I took half as much money to sign with the Twins. … The Mets weren't really even in existence at that point. They were just out signing players. The Tigers had wanted to sign me as a catcher, but I knew they had just signed Bill Freehan, whom I had played against in college [Freehan attended the University of Michigan]. I knew how good of a catcher he was." So Allen signed with the Minnesota Twins, and began what became a 10-year career in the major leagues. (Allen, who batted .360 in three varsity seasons at Purdue, was signed by Twins scout Dick Wiencek.)

Allen played just 80 minor-league games before reaching the majors. After signing in 1961, he spent two weeks with the Twins before they sent him to the Charlotte (North Carolina) Hornets, in the Class A South Atlantic League, where he finished the season.

Over that span, Allen was mediocre at the plate, .241/.324/.320, but proved a major-league-caliber fielder. The following spring, Allen made the Twins roster, spent the entire season with the team, and took over as the starting second baseman. With the exception of 41 Triple-A games four years later while he was recovering from an injury, Allen never again played in the minor leagues.

On Opening Day 1962, Allen took his place as the Twins' starting second baseman. He replaced one of baseball's most enigmatic personalities. The previous fall, Billy Martin, in his lone season as a player with the Twins, had ended his 11-year playing career. Outplayed by Allen during spring training of '62, Martin was subsequently released by Minnesota. Allen always remained grateful to Martin for the veteran's mentoring, in spite of their competition.

"Even though Billy knew that I was trying to replace him, he taught me to truly play second base," Allen later explained. "Billy emphasized that it was important for the older players to help the younger players learn how to be major leaguers. … Billy also taught me to be serious on the field. It's okay to have fun off the field, but you have to play like a pro on the field. It's a business."

Indeed, Allen never forgot Martin's advice. Years later, after he'd been traded to the Washington Senators, Allen developed "my own little entourage—Toby Harrah, Jeff Burroughs, Tom Grieve, and Jim Mason. They followed me around all season. I was glad to help them."

(After he retired, Allen often accepted invitations to play in Martin's golf tournament. "[Martin] would take me around the room, telling people that I was the player who forced him to retire as a player. That made me feel great, but actually it was Father Time who made Billy retire.")

On the field Allen never enjoyed a finer season than his rookie year of 1962. In fact, he rarely again even approached the offensive numbers he posted that season. With a slash line of .269/.338/.403, Allen, who

Bernie Allen (Photo courtesy of Minnesota Twins Baseball Club).

typically batted seventh, ahead of shortstop Zoilo Versalles, set career highs in almost every offensive category, including impressive power totals of 27 doubles, 7 triples, 12 home runs, and 64 RBIs. Defensively, too, Allen was stellar. Only once after that season did he produce a better fielding percentage over a full season than that year's .983, the fifth best average in the league among second basemen; and in 158 games he turned the league's third highest number of double plays. Allen received one first-place vote in the Rookie of the Year balloting (the Yankees' Tom Tresh won the award), and was named to the Topps All-Rookie team. It was a heady season; yet it marked the pinnacle of Allen's career.

If Allen's rookie season announced him as one of baseball's rising stars, the next two years frustratingly quieted any acclaim. In 1963, as the Twins, under manager Sam Mele, looked to improve on 91 wins and a second-place finish, Allen inexplicably got off to a dreadful start. After an 0-for-4 performance on June 21 that left his batting average at just .197, Allen was temporarily benched in favor of Johnny Goryl, before recovering his stroke to finish the season with a .240 average. Years later, Allen blamed his poor performance that season on a change in stances, explaining, "I was a spray hitter that first season. The following spring they told me I couldn't hit with my stance, so they changed me to become a pull hitter. I figured they knew more than I did, but maybe they didn't."[4] Allen's defense suffered too, as his fielding percentage dropped to .976. That year, he started only 110 games. (Ironically, in April 1964, Mele stated, "I want [Allen] to learn to become more of a punch hitter, something like Nellie Fox. He [Allen] hit well to left field two years ago. When Bernie tries to pull the ball, he has trouble."[5])

Things got even worse in 1964, although for a moment Allen seemed to regain his footing. For all intents and purposes, that season effectively marked the end of his tenure as a full-time player. It began in the spring, as Allen engaged with Goryl in a hard-fought battle to retain the second-base job. After working extremely hard at all facets of his game, Allen won the Opening Day start, yet began the season with just one hit in his first nine at-bats, before he exploded with four hits in his next seven, including a two-homer game on April 18 at Washington. By the next afternoon his average stood at .313, and it appeared that his 1963 season had been an aberration.

"We moved Bernie up closer to the plate so he would be more aggressive with the bat," Mele remarked about coaching the left-handed hitter. "He had to swing hard or get jammed. It worked. He's been swinging well ever since."[6]

Likewise, Allen's defense returned to his rookie-year heights, as Twins owner Calvin Griffith attested. "Bernie's looking sharp in the field," Griffith said, "much like he did two years ago. He has made several good plays going far to his left. I think he's improving his range."[7]

As with his hitting, coaches offered Allen much advice on ways to improve his defense. "One coach," he said, "had me standing on my toes with my arms hanging down low. I almost fall on my face when I try that. When I was a quarterback, I used to get a good start moving laterally. But I was bent over just enough to get my hands under center.

"That's the way I like it in baseball—bend over just enough to put my hands on my knees. Then I get lower as I move left or right. When I start too low, I usually stand up and then move, which slows me down."[8]

After his impressive start, Allen tailed off significantly; his batting average bottomed out at .149 on May 13. By June 13, however, Allen had raised it to .220, and his fielding had regained its efficiency. Then it all fell apart on the infield dirt in Washington. On the 13th the Twins led, 2-1, in the bottom of the fifth. Leading off for the Senators, Don Zimmer drew a walk, and left fielder Chuck Hinton came to the plate. As Allen recalled, "It was a hit-and-run play. Chuck Hinton hit the ball to Zoilo Versalles at short. The grass was tall, so the ball was slow in getting to him. Zoilo made a soft toss which I had to wait on. ..."[9] The runner and ball got to me at the same time, Don Zimmer giving me a cross body check that tore up the ligaments in my left knee."[10]

It was a devastating injury, the kind that in those days typically ended careers. After missing almost two months, Allen returned on August 4, played 10 games, then missed a week before returning on August 21. With a batting average of just .214, he saw his season end prematurely on September 1. Allen wasn't operated on until October, and then only because he sought medical advice on his own from the Minnesota Vikings' orthopedic surgeon, who diagnosed tears in both medial collateral and anterior cruciate ligaments.

"By the time they operated," Allen recalled, "the ligaments had shriveled up."

Surgeons took part of the hamstring from Allen's left leg and used it on his knee. "The doctor said I had a 50-50 chance of ever being able to play any type of sport again, and zero percent chance of ever playing baseball. ... The average career at that time was four years. You had to play five years back then to get a pension. The rehab was very painful. I had to wear an iron boot everywhere I went, to build up the strength in my leg."

Allen was disappointed in the team's reaction to his injury. "What really upset me was that I didn't receive a card or a call from anyone in the Twins front office. Then, to top it off, they wanted to cut my salary from $12,000 to $10,000 in 1965."

Allen would never again be the same player he was as a rookie.

As luck would have it, the Twins went to the World Series in 1965. In the aftermath of his injury, Allen missed the chance to participate. Still rehabbing his knee, he was on the disabled list from the beginning of the season until June 4. He returned on June 22 and played 19 games, but was eventually sent to Denver in the Pacific Coast League.

"They had told me I would be called up before the rosters were expanded in September," Allen said. "That way I would be eligible for the World Series. Right before I was to go back up," though, "I dove for a ball and broke my thumb. That ended my year right then."

Much to Allen's disappointment, he failed to receive a World Series ring. "I got seven-eighths of a share [of the Series winnings], but I didn't get a ring. That's what I really wanted. Mudcat Grant, Jim Kaat, and others went to the front office on my behalf. I've never forgotten that slight. A few years later, Johnny Klippstein dropped his ring and the diamond broke. That must have been some fine diamond," he said with sarcasm. As things turned out, Allen's time in Minnesota was almost through.

Throughout Allen's time with the Twins, likely motivated by his injury and undoubtedly with a thought to his post-playing career, he displayed an interest in business matters both in and outside the sport. In 1962 infielder Rich Rollins had joined the Twins, and Allen and Rollins forged a friendship; both were from Ohio, shared the same birthday (although born a year apart), were roommates on the road, and had adjoining lockers during home games. Following Allen's injury, pitching coach Johnny Sain gave him a book called *Think and Grow Rich*, a treatise on positive thinking written by 83-year-old Dr. Napoleon Hill, who had been teaching his principles since 1908. Allen read the book during a two-week stint in the Army Reserve and asked Rollins to read the book. The two took Dr. Hill's course and together opened a Napoleon Hill Academy franchise in Minneapolis. A year later, after Allen was traded, they sold the franchise, and then opened an agency in St. Paul, Minnesota, for the Wayne National Life Insurance Company (partly owned by Al Kaline). Although they were then playing for different teams, Rollins handled PR for the firm, while Allen did some selling.[11] Theirs was a friendship that lasted beyond their playing days.

The year 1966 was Allen's final season with the Twins. On December 3, after a season in which he split time at second base with Cesar Tovar, Allen and pitcher Camilo Pascual were traded to the Washington Senators in exchange for reliever Ron Kline. Announcing the trade in its December 17, 1966, edition, *The Sporting News* reported that "Allen was a play-me-or-trade me malcontent" who had batted just .238, but was playing well until June, when he reinjured his knee. In contrast, Allen later contended, "I got traded for a very simple reason. I was the players' rep on the Twins. Being a players' rep in those days was a surefire way of getting yourself traded."

Having endured a pay cut with Minnesota, to $10,500, Allen was anxious for a pay raise with his new team. "George Selkirk, who was a former Yankee player, was the Washington GM," Allen remembered. "He and I had a tough time negotiating. We negotiated through the mail." In the end, Selkirk increased Allen's salary to $15,000. His teammates quickly voted in Allen as the Senators' player rep.

Over the next five full seasons with mediocre to poor Senators teams, Allen evolved into the role of a part-time second baseman, splitting time with such players as Bob Saverine, Frank Coggins, and Tim Cullen; he also saw some action at third base. Still able to generate some occasional pop in his bat (in 1969 he produced the second highest home run and RBI totals of his career 9 and 45), Allen's batting average with the Senators was .237. During his first year with the team, in which he batted a dismal .193, Allen was diagnosed with astigmatism in his right eye, particularly hampering to a left-handed hitter. As a result, Allen tried wearing glasses at the plate, but later remembered, "I could never adjust to wearing glasses, but I found it possible to wear a contact lens in my right eye. My left eye was fine, so I decided to wear only the necessary lens."[12] Ultimately, he added, "the eye didn't hamper me as much as the knee injury, which still bothers me in cold weather."[13]

By his final season in Washington, Allen was being used only sparingly by manager Ted Williams. Although the team had finished 10 games over .500 and in fourth place in the American League East during Williams's first season, 1969, two years later they had fallen to 63-96 and fifth place. That year Allen started just 24 games at second base, and he later recalled Williams as "the most egotistical man I've ever met in my life."[14]

"The first year he managed he wasn't bad at all, but he lost communication with the players last season [in 1971]."[15]

One day in late July 1971, Williams asked Allen, "How are you?" and Allen responded, "I'd be better if I were playing more"; after that "he never said hello to me the rest of the year. I don't know what I did to him, but he just refused to play me."[16]

"When you have six hits in your last seven times at bat and can't start against a right-handed pitcher the next day, I don't know what I'm supposed to think of him."[17]

By then Allen knew he was no longer in the Senators' plans. After the 1971 season the team moved to Texas and became the Rangers, and on December 2, 1971, the Rangers traded Allen to the New York Yankees for two left-handed relievers, Gary Jones and Terry Ley.

Allen was cheered by the move, "chiefly because I had always admired Ralph Houk."[18] Acquired as a backup to second baseman Horace Clarke, Allen initially thought he might be a candidate to play third base, but when the Yankees acquired Rich McKinney, Allen understood what his role would be.

"I never got a chance to talk to Ralph until spring training," Allen said. "He told me exactly what job he had planned for me, then didn't deviate. The whole Yankee organization has treated me better than any I've ever been with."[19]

In all, Allen played 84 games for the Yankees in 1972, splitting time equally between second and third base. In May the Yankees traded their player rep, Jack Aker, to the Cubs, and as with his two previous teams, Allen was elected to replace him.

The next season was Allen's last. In August the Yankees sold his contract to the Montreal Expos, for whom he played his final 16 games. In November the Expos asked waivers on Allen and gave him his unconditional release, at which point he chose to retire.

"I knew I was going to hang it up at the end of that year," Allen recalled 25 years later, "even before I was traded. The Expos wanted me to come back, but I knew it was time to call it quits."

In retirement, Allen became a successful businessman, yet also took an opportunity to keep his ties with the game. An old college classmate owned a sporting-goods store in West Palm Beach, Florida, so Allen relocated with his first wife, Sharon, and four children to become the store manager. Coincidentally, at the same time the Expos had a Class A team in town, the West Palm Beach Expos of the Florida State League. The owner of the store purchased the team when it came up for sale. Jim Fanning, the Expos' GM, approached Allen and asked his opinion regarding a manager, and after assessing the candidates, Allen suggested Felipe Alou. During the team's homestands, Allen coached first base and instructed the infielders.

Allen also kept tabs on old friends from his playing days, such as Roy Sievers, with whom Allen often played in golf tournaments, and who stood in as best man at Allen's wedding to his second wife, also named Sharon.

In 1982 Allen became Midwest representative for the Ferro Corporation, a performance materials company based in the Cleveland suburbs. His territory covered western Kentucky, Indiana, Illinois, Missouri, Iowa, Minnesota, and Wisconsin. Allen and his second wife (his first marriage ended in 1987) had two sons, four daughters, and seven grandchildren, and lived in Carmel, Indiana.

As of 2015, Allen still resided in Carmel.

SOURCES

The author attempted to interview Bernie Allen for this biography, but was unsuccessful.

Sincerest appreciation to SABR member Bill Mortell for his research contribution.

Bernie Allen player file from the National Baseball Hall of Fame, Cooperstown, New York

baseball-reference.com

NewspaperArchive.com

retrosheet.org

The Sporting News

sports-reference.com

NOTES

1 *Sports Collectors Digest*, November 20, 1998. Unless otherwise noted, all of the Allen quotes in this biography are taken from this article.

2 *The Sporting News*, July 15, 1972. Note: Allen's field goal came in the third quarter, and put Purdue ahead 17-14. After a subsequent touchdown that put Ohio State ahead, 21-17, Allen led Purdue on a drive that culminated in the game-winning touchdown, after which he kicked the extra point.

3 Ibid.

4 Ibid.

5 *The Sporting News*, April 18, 1964.

6 Ibid.

7 Ibid.

8 Ibid.

9 *Sports Collectors Digest*, November 20, 1998.
10 *The Sporting News*, July 15, 1972.
11 *The Sporting News*, February 4, 1967.
12 *The Sporting News*, July 15, 1972.
13 Ibid.
14 Unidentified clipping dated March 9, 1972, in Allen's Hall of Fame file.
15 Ibid.
16 Ibid.
17 Ibid.
18 *The Sporting News*, July 15, 1972.
19 Ibid.

Bob Allison

BY GREGORY H. WOLF

THREE-TIME ALL-STAR AND 1959 Rookie of the Year Bob Allison was a feared slugger, an aggressive, daring baserunner, a versatile outfielder and first baseman with a powerful arm, and, above all, a competitive team player. He played his entire 13-year career (1958-1970) with the Washington Senators/Minnesota Twins, helping transform a moribund franchise into a consistent winner and pennant contender. "Anyone can be successful in baseball if he follows the path of Bob Allison," wrote Leonard Schechter in *Sport* in 1964. "All you have to do is be 6'4", strong as a weightlifter, handsome as a shirt model, have the personality of an honor graduate of Dale Carnegie, and also work your head off."[1]

William Robert Allison was born on July 11, 1934, in Raytown, Missouri, located about 10 miles southeast of Kansas City. His parents, Robert "Lou" and Frances (Witte) Allison, were hard-working, industrious people who provided Bob and his two younger siblings, Jim and Frances (known as Frankie), a solid, middle-class life. Bob got his first lesson in baseball from his father, a construction worker and former semipro catcher. He began playing organized baseball by the time he was 11 years old and attending Chapel Elementary School. He was a big, rugged, and agile youth, and his favorite sport was football. At Raytown High School he was a standout in multiple sports, starring at quarterback and fullback on the gridiron, playing in the front court in basketball, and running track. He was "something of a legend around Raytown," read one report.[2] Although his school did not have a baseball team, Bob played in the highly competitive Ban Johnson League in the Kansas City metro area.

After graduating from high school in 1952, Allison enrolled on a football scholarship at the University of Kansas, about 50 miles from home in Lawrence. He was a fullback on the Jayhawks football team in 1952 and 1953, and played baseball in 1954 for legendary coach, Floyd Temple, in his first of 28 years guiding Kansas. At 6-feet-3 and weighing 200 pounds, the right-handed Allison might have had the prototypical build for a professional fullback, but he garnered more attention as a hard-hitting, rough-and-tumble infielder-outfielder for Milgram in the Ban Johnson League in the summers of 1952-1954. "At 18, he could out throw most big leaguers I saw," said one of his former coaches.[3] Scouts from the New York Yankees, Chicago White Sox, St. Louis Cardinals, Milwaukee Braves, New York Giants, Cleveland Indians, and Washington Senators were on his trail in Kansas City and Lawrence. "Tom Greenwade, who discovered Mickey Mantle, came to the university to see me," said Allison. "He gave me all the sweet talk about the Yankees, and I must admit that I was surprised. [Senators scout] Ray

Three-time All-Star and 1959 AL Rookie of the Year, Allison was an acknowledged club house leader. An overlooked slugger, Allison averaged 28 homers and 88 RBIs from 1959 to 1965 and finished with 256 round-trippers in his 13-year career (1958-1970). (National Baseball Hall of Fame, Cooperstown, New York).

Baker had told me that it was easier to make it in the Washington organization than with some of the richer clubs."[4] The decision to pursue a career in baseball became more immediate when Allison lost his athletic eligibility for the fall of 1954 due to poor grades. According to the Associated Press, the Senators signed Allison on Baker's recommendation on January 24, 1955.[5]

With a bonus of $4,000 in hand, the 20-year-old Allison reported to the Class B Hagerstown (Maryland) Packets of the Piedmont League in 1955. He batted .256, but showed little power, slugging just .332. The Senators invited him to spring training in 1956 for a look-see. Although Washington sportswriter Shirley Povich praised him for his "big swing and determination,"[6] Allison was over his head and was subsequently assigned to the Charlotte (North Carolina) Hornets in the Class A South Atlantic League, where his average dipped to .233.

In Charlotte Allison roomed with 20-year-old Harmon Killebrew, in his first year in the minors. Killebrew had signed with the Senators two years earlier for a reported $30,000 bonus; because of the bonus rule in effect at the time, he was required to spend his first two (agonizing) seasons on the big-league squad. The two prospects became lifelong friends and accompanied each other on their arduous journey to the big leagues. The following season, with the Double-A Chattanooga Lookouts, Killebrew developed into a slugging sensation, belting 29 home runs to lead the Southern Association, while Allison batted just .246 and hit only two home runs, though his 11 triples tied for the league lead. Despite his weak hitting, Allison had established a reputation as good center fielder with excellent range and a rifle arm.

Back with Chattanooga in 1958 after another trial with Washington in spring training, Allison blossomed, batting .307 and slugging .446, and earned a call-up to the Senators when the rosters expanded in September. On September 16 he made his major-league debut, playing center field and batting leadoff, and going 1-for-4 in a loss to the Cleveland Indians. Allison appeared overmatched at the plate (7-for-35), but according to *The Sporting News* "can handle centerfield."[7] Allison honed his skills in the Cuban Winter League, leading Almendares to the league championship and earning a berth on the all-star team while experiencing a front-row view of the Cuban Revolution.[8]

Allison's rookie season with the Senators in 1959 defied all expectations. His size, speed, strength, and athleticism inspired awe. Team trainer George "Doc" Lentz, who had worked for the Senators for 31 years and also for the Washington Redskins, called the now 220-pound, muscular Allison "the strongest man I ever handled."[9] Club owner Calvin Griffith praised him as having "the best arm that has come to our outfield since Jackie Jensen."[10] Said coach Ellis Clary, "I know he'll scare the daylights out of the opposition. Man, when he runs down the line from home plate I can hear the ground shake."[11] But despite this praise, many felt that Allison would not even make the team because of his poor hitting. Boston sportswriter Hy Hurwitz wrote that Allison "should be shipped out" during camp while Senators beat reporter Bob Addie noted that "none of the scribes covering the team in training camp thought much of Allison."[12] Shirley Povich cautioned, "[Allison's] not a power hitter."[13] His manager, Cookie Lavagetto, was even more direct in his evaluation, "He was the worst you ever saw at the plate. He chopped at the ball like he had an axe in his hand."[14]

Dubbed the "hardest worker in camp," Allison recognized that his future in the big leagues rested on improved hitting.[15] Roy Sievers, renowned for his graceful swing, proved to be most influential on the youngster. "He had me move closer to the plate so I could reach the pitches," said Allison. "He also taught me not to lunge."[16] A classic line-drive hitter, Allison's new approach helped him temper the tendency to pull the ball. He impressed Lavagetto with his work ethic, "He's a curious kid. If he makes a mistake, he'll talk about it. Bob studies pitchers," said his skipper.[17]

Allison made an immediate impression on fans with his energetic style of play. He opened the 1959 season with a nine-game hitting streak, including his first home run. He began in right field, moved to left, and then took over center field in the 12th game of the season, making Albie Pearson, the 1958 Rookie of the Year, expendable. (He was traded on May 26.)

With only 28 home runs in four years in the minors, no one expected Allison to develop into a home-run threat. But he surprised everyone. On June 5 Allison collected a career-best five hits (in five at-bats) and walloped two home runs for the first of 16 times in his career, yet the Senators lost to the Detroit Tigers, 7-6. By the end of July, Allison had clouted 27 round-trippers, and was named to the AL All-Star team for the second of two games scheduled that season, although did not play. "He can run, he can throw, he swings a good bat," wrote Bob Addie.[18] Allison intimidated baserunners with his accurate arm, but also tested Lavagetto's patience for occasionally showboating and overthrowing the cutoff man to show off his arm strength, thereby permitting runners to advance.

Despite slumping the final two months of the season, Allison finished with 30 home runs and batted .261; he also knocked in 85 runs despite hitting in the two-hole for just over half of his at-bats. More than a slugger, he led the AL in triples (9) and finished fifth in stolen bases (13). He topped off the season by winning the Rookie of the Year award. The Senators were accustomed to losing, and finished in last place in 1959, but they treated their fans to a home-run barrage. En route to a new team-record 163 home runs, Allison, Killebrew (42), and Jim Lemon (33) became just the seventh trio of teammates to blast 30 round-trippers in one season, and the first in the AL since the 1941 New York Yankees with Joe DiMaggio, Charlie Keller, and Tommy Henrich.

After another offseason playing winter ball in Cuba, Allison reported to spring training in 1960 with high expectations. Calvin Griffith, the perpetually cash-strapped owner of the club, pronounced him an untouchable and rebuffed offers to sell the young star. Moved to right field, Allison got off to a torrid start. In his first seven games he collected 17 hits in 30 at-bats and drove in 12 runs. He caught President Dwight Eisenhower's pitch on what turned out to be the last home opener for the Senators in Washington. Batting primarily in the third spot, usually in front of Lemon, Allison hit .328, scored 35 runs and knocked in 33 through the first 50 games, and seemed destined for stardom. But just as the Senators were putting together a winning record for three consecutive months (June, July, and August) for the first time since 1952 to begin September with a winning record, Allison commenced a prolonged sophomore slump, batting just .205 in his last 95 games. More disconcerting to the Senators was Allison's loss of power—just 15 home runs for the season. One of those, however, was a dramatic two-run walk-off blast in the 10th inning to defeat the New York Yankees on July 5. While the Senators floundered in September to finish in fifth place, Griffith became willing to listen to trade offers for Allison.

It was not a surprise when the Senators moved to Minnesota in the offseason. Griffith, the adopted son of former owner Clark Griffith, had begun exploring relocation options soon after taking control of the team in 1955. Since breaking the one-million mark in 1946, the club had struggled mightily at the gate, finishing last in attendance every year since 1955. Griffith, whose primary source of income was the baseball club, also complained that the location of Griffith Stadium, in the historically black neighborhood of Shaw, kept fans from the games. In the Minneapolis-St. Paul metropolitan area, he hoped to reap the same kinds of financial rewards that the Boston Braves, Brooklyn Dodgers, and New York Giants did after relocating in the 1950s.

Ignoring trade rumors, Allison got off to another hot start in 1961 as the Minnesota Twins played their first six games on the road. In their season opener, he walloped the first home run in Twins history, a deep line-drive blast to left field off Whitey Ford in the club's convincing 6-0 victory over the New York Yankees. Three games later, he blasted two round-trippers and drove in a career-high seven runs in a Twins' victory over the Baltimore Orioles. Two more games of two home runs followed in mid-May at Metropolitan Stadium, located in Bloomington, about 11 miles due south of downtown Minneapolis. Though

Bob Allison (Photo courtesy of Minnesota Twins Baseball Club).

the Twins finished in seventh place (70-90) in the year the AL expanded to 10 teams, the club finished third in attendance, proving that major-league baseball could succeed in the Upper Midwest where cool, indeed cold, temperatures in April, May, and September were the norm. Allison placed seventh in home runs (29) and RBIs (105) while drawing a career-high 103 free passes (fifth best in the AL).

Allison was an immediate favorite in Minnesota. As the first player to establish year-round, permanent residence in Minnesota, he helped Minnesotans forge a strong bond with their recently relocated team. He, his wife (his high-school sweetheart, Betty Shearer, whom he had married in 1956), and their three children, Mark, Kirk, and Kyle, were fixtures at the ballpark and in the community. Allison had matinee-idol good looks — tall, dark, and handsome with brownish black hair and hazel-green eyes — and played with an ethos that endeared him to fans and the media. He had all sorts of nicknames, from Paul Bunyan and Mr. America to Muscles, all which played on his Herculean physique. "He plays hard and he plays every second of every game," commented *The Sporting News*.[19] Called a "throw back to the old times," Allison was "Old School" when it meant playing an all-out style like the 1920s or 1930s.[20] He crashed into outfield fences going after balls and made daring, diving catches. Though not conventionally fast like Mickey Mantle or a great basestealer like Luis Aparicio, Allison was an excellent and fearless baserunner. His specialty was breaking up double plays, barreling over shortstops, many of whom he outweighed by 50 to 60 pounds.

In 1962 the Twins were the youngest team in the AL and had assembled a nucleus of players who helped transform the club to a pennant winner in 1965, and laid the foundations for the team's success throughout the decade. Killebrew (age 26) and Allison (27) in the outfield, Zoilo Versalles (22) at shortstop, Rich Rollins (24) at third base, and catcher Earl Battey (27) were All-Star selections in the 1960s. The Twins farm system produced other future All-Stars who joined them: outfielders Jimmie Hall in 1963 and Tony Oliva in 1964, and second baseman Rod Carew in 1967.

Allison was hampered by several early-season injuries in 1962, including a pulled rib muscle and spiked fingers, and experienced a drop in his power numbers through early June. Nonetheless, the Twins briefly took over the top spot in the AL that month. "I've never seen the kind of spirit we've got on the club," said Allison.[21] Manager Sam Mele, who had replaced Cookie Lavagetto during the previous season, relied on the long ball; all eight position players swatted at least 11 home runs as the club set a new team record with 185. Allison regained his power in June and put together one of the most productive stretches in his career, hitting 27 round-trippers and knocking in 86 runs in 108 games from June 9 through the end of the season. On July 18 Allison and Killebrew became the first set of teammates in big-league history to wallop grand slams in the same inning when they accomplished the feat in the first frame of a 14-3 laugher against the Cleveland Indians at the Met. Minnesota finished with 91 victories, five behind the New York Yankees. In an era when high batting averages and low strikeout totals were the signs of good hitters, Allison — who struck out a lot and seldom hit for a high average — did not receive as much credit for his production as he probably should have. He finished third in runs (102) and seventh in RBIs (102), joining Norm Siebern of the Kansas City Athletics as the only AL players in triple digits in both departments;

he also finished eighth in home runs (29) and fifth in slugging (.511).

Sluggers Killebrew and Allison were affectionately known as "Mr. Upstairs and Mr. Downstairs." Whereas the "Killer" clouted legendary arcing homers, Allison ripped bullets that cleared the fences. The ever modest Allison claimed, "I've never been much of a long-ball hitter," and added, "I swing down at the ball and I'm more of a line-drive hitter."[22]

Using a wider batting stance and a heavier bat, Allison enjoyed arguably his best season in 1963 in an offensively depressed era. He was named Player of the Month by Fleer in April (five home runs and 18 RBIs in 19 games) while his teammates struggled and the club dropped into last place. "Allison is only doing what comes naturally when he plays Paul Bunyan so it is no surprise that he's trying singlehandedly to carry the Twins," wrote UPI after the slugger connected for three home runs for the first and only time in his career, against the Indians on May 17.[23] On the strength of his league-leading 21 home runs, Allison was named a backup on the AL All-Star squad. (He struck out against Houston's Hal Woodeshick in his only at-bat.) Despite being briefly sidelined in August when a pitch from Dean Chance of the Los Angeles Angels broke a bone in his right hand, Allison finished third in the AL in home runs (a career-best 35), fourth in RBIs (91), third in walks (90), and second in slugging (.533). He paced the circuit with 99 runs scored, marking the first time that the AL leader failed to reach 100 in a full season since Elmer Flick in 1906. The Twins proved to be a streaky team, winning 91 games, but finishing in a distant third place, 13 games behind the Yankees. They also established a new team record with 225 home runs—113 of them from Allison, Killebrew (45), and Hall (33).

Twins beat reporter Arno Goethel once referred to Allison as the "unknown outfielder."[24] Soft-spoken off the field, yet articulate, Allison shunned the spotlight, played in the shadows of Killebrew and Oliva, and was rarely mentioned in discussions about the best outfielders in the early to mid-1960s. He played any position the team asked, moving from center field to right field, to first base in 1964, and then to left field in 1965 to accommodate younger players or improve the team. "I don't care where I play," he told sportswriter Dick Gordon. "I don't think moving around affects my play and I like being able to play more than one position."[25] On the field Allison exhibited a completely different persona. Managers and teammates acknowledged him as the vocal team leader. Minneapolis sports reporter Max Nichols praised his "take charge instincts" and noted that he's the "holler guy" on a team filled with "silent types."[26]

The Twins fell to sixth place in 1964 with a 79-83 record despite a league-leading 221 home runs. Four of those home runs came consecutively against the Kansas City A's when Oliva, Allison, Hall, and Killebrew connected in the 11th inning of a 7-3 victory. Allison was a jack-of-all-trades, starting 90 games at first base and 45 in the outfield (at all three positions). He was a starter in his third and final All-Star appearance (he went 0-for-3 with a walk). Allison's season ended about a week early when he was hit by a pitch from Lew Krausse of the Kansas City A's and broke a knuckle. With 32 home runs, 86 RBIs, and a career-best .287 average, Allison set career-best marks in slugging (.553) and on-base percentage (.404).

The 1965 Twins were an unusually deep team, with seven legitimate All-Star position players, and two more on the pitching staff. Three new coaches, Johnny Sain, Jim Lemon, and Billy Martin, helped forge them into a mentally tough and fundamentally sound team. In first place for the overwhelming majority of the season, the Twins overcame injuries to key players to pull away from the pack in August and September and cruise to their first pennant, seven games ahead of the Chicago White Sox, with a record of 102-60.

Allison started out the 1965 season in left field, his third different position in as many years. He put up typical numbers (.267, 12 HRs, 34 RBIs) until he was hit on the right wrist by a pitch from Boston's Jerry Stephenson on July 6. Diagnosed with a fractured wrist, Allison missed 10 days. He struggled after his return (batting just .199, though he hit 11 homers and knocked in 44 runs in 68 games) and was often platooned with Sandy Valdespino, a speedy, left-handed-hitting rookie. About four weeks after Allison's injury, Killebrew suffered what appeared to be a season-ending elbow injury in a collision at first base with Baltimore's Russ Snyder on August 2.

The Twins' pennant was a testimony to the team's depth and team-oriented attitude. "We find a different way to win every day," said Allison. "This team is a bunch of fighters."[27] With Allison bothered by a sore wrist and Killebrew out seven weeks, the Twins relied on a collective effort. "No player on this club has dominated the clutch hitting role," wrote Max Nichols.[28] Don Mincher belted 22 home runs and replaced Killebrew at first base, Oliva batted .321 to capture his second successive batting crown, and Versalles led the league in runs scored (126) and extra-base hits (76) and won the AL MVP award.

The Twins lost the 1965 World Series to the Los Angeles Dodgers, whose other-worldly ace, Sandy Koufax, hurled shutouts in Game Five and Game Seven (on two days' rest), but Allison's remarkable catch in Game Two has endured as one of the most memorable in Series history. In the fifth inning of a scoreless game, with a man on first and no one out, Allison made a diving backhanded grab of Jim Lefebvre's sinking line drive to left field. He caught the ball with his glove just off the ground in fair territory and skidded on the soggy field across the foul line. "It was the greatest catch I've ever seen," said Killebrew.[29] The Twins went on to win the game, 5-1, to take a two-games-to-none lead in the Series. Like his teammates, Allison struggled against Dodgers pitching. In five games (he did not start Games One or Four against Don Drysdale), Allison went 2-for-16. One of those hits was a two-run homer in Game Six off Claude Osteen. The last of his nine strikeouts accounted for the final out in Game Seven.

In 1966, Allison, now 31 years old, lost his position in left field to Valdespino and saw only limited action in an injury-plagued season. On July 23 he suffered his fourth hand/wrist injury in as many years when a pitch from Boston's Jim Lonborg fractured his left wrist. "You can't blame the pitchers for pitching me tight," said a philosophical Allison. "That's part of the game."[30]

In light of a miserable campaign (8 homers and 19 RBIs) Allison endured an offseason filled with trade rumors, but the Twins had no viable options in left field. Two of his supposed replacements, Valdespino and Andy Kosco, had failed to lived up to their hype. Allison reclaimed his position as the everyday left fielder, though he was often replaced for defensive purposes late in games. With the Twins floundering in sixth place (25-25), Cal Ermer replaced Mele as skipper and ignited the team. They won 24 of their next 36 games, culminating in a doubleheader sweep of the California Angels on July 16 to pull to within a half-game of first place. In that twin bill, Allison went 3-for-5 with two home runs (one as a pinch-hitter) with five RBIs and three runs scored. Throughout August and September, Minnesota battled Boston, Chicago, and Detroit in one of the most exciting pennant races in league history. In first place entering the final weekend of the season and with just 1½ games separating four teams, the Twins were swept by Boston in a two-game series to finish in second place. Allison finished with a .258/24/75 line.

Collectively, the Twins struggled in 1968, the "Year of the Pitcher," and fell to seventh place, their worst finish since their inaugural season in Minnesota. The players failed to respond to skipper Cal Ermer, whose authority players openly challenged, leading to some high-profile confrontations, such as one with Carew. Owner Calvin Griffith conceded that Ermer had lost control of the club. Allison, who had hurt his right knee the previous season, needed regular cortisone shots to play in the field. In his last season as an everyday starter, Allison was still an offensive threat, clouting 22 home runs (tied for eighth in the AL) and slugging .456 (sixth).

Although he was reduced to a role player in 1969, Allison looked forward to playing for Billy Martin, whose aggressive, daring style he appreciated. Martin considered Allison excellent coaching material (Allison turned down Martin's offer to join his staff in Detroit in 1971). In his autobiography (with Peter Golenbock),

Number 1, Martin called Allison "my leader behind the leader on the bench."³¹

En route to the AL West crown in the first year of realignment, Allison was involved in an ugly scene with Martin and pitcher Dave Boswell in August. At a local watering hole in Detroit, the Lindell Athletic Club, Boswell began arguing with pitching coach Art Fowler. Allison intervened as peacemaker and took Boswell outside to cool off. Boswell took out his frustration on Allison, knocking him out (with a sucker punch, according to some reports), whereupon Martin rushed outside. In the now infamous fight, Martin beat up his pitcher, who was subsequently hospitalized.³²

Allison was placed on waivers during spring training in 1970, but there were no claims on the 35-year-old with creaky knees. Relegated to an occasional start and pinch-hitting duties, Allison saw sporadic action for manager Bill Rigney, who had replaced Martin and led the Twins to their second consecutive AL West crown. For the second year in a row, the club lost to the Baltimore Orioles in the ALCS and Allison went hitless in a combined 10 at-bats, both series sweeps. At the conclusion of the season, he announced his retirement. In his 13 years with the Senators-Twins, Allison hit 256 home runs, knocked in 756 runs, and batted .255.

On September 9, 1971, the Twins celebrated B.A.T. Day (Bob Allison Tribute Day), marking the first time a professional athlete had ever been feted with his own day in Minneapolis-St. Paul. The broad-shouldered, down-to-earth Allison was wildly popular as much for what he did off the field as for his accomplishments on the diamond. "[Allison] has been unmatched in the team's history as a tireless good-will ambassador in Twinsland," wrote Arno Goethel.³³ Long associated with the Easter Seals, Allison worked tirelessly on behalf of sick children, visiting hospitals and raising money.

Allison was well positioned for his post-baseball career. Since his early days in Minnesota, he had worked in the offseason for Coca-Cola, and began working for the company full-time in 1971, moving into sales. His association with the soft-drink company gave rise to one of his funniest monikers, "Bubble-Up." Allison maintained close ties to the Twins and former teammates, and participated in reunions and special events with the club. In 1989 he retired with his wife to a resort community north of Fountain Hills, in the desert of Arizona. An avid outdoorsman, Allison anticipated playing golf, hunting, hiking, and traveling.

Not long after retiring from Coca-Cola, Allison was tragically diagnosed with ataxia, a rare, incurable disease that affects nerve cells in the brain and gradually impairs coordination. As the disease progressed and his health began to fail, Allison and his family established the Bob Allison Ataxia Research Center at the University of Minnesota.

Bob Allison died at the age of 60 on April 9, 1995, from the effects of ataxia. He was buried in Rio Verde Memorial Gardens, in Rio Verde, Arizona. Said close friend Jim Kaat, "This guy had the ideal body. Very durable. He was a hard-nosed player, and played every day. He was always so fit. Everyone marveled at his condition."³⁴ "When I think of Bob Allison," remarked former Twins owner Calvin Griffith upon learning of Allison's death, "I think of brute strength."³⁵

SOURCES

Bob Allison player file at the National Baseball Hall of Fame, Cooperstown, New York.

Ancestry.com

BaseballLibrary.com

Baseball-Reference.com

Retrosheet.com

SABR.org

The Sporting News

NOTES

1 Leonard Shechter, "A Hitter Has to Have a Killing Desire," in *Sport*, September 1964, quoted from Bill James, *The New Bill James Historical Abstract* (New York: Free Press, 2001), 825.

2 *The Sporting News*, September 23, 1959, 3.

3 Ibid.

4   Ibid.

5   Associated Press, "A Boy Here to the Senators," *Kansas City Times*, January 25, 1955, 16.

6   *The Sporting News*, March 14, 1956, 4.

7   *The Sporting News*, October 8, 1958, 26.

8   *The Sporting News*, January 28, 1959, 8.

9   *The Sporting News*, September 23, 1959, 3.

10 *The Sporting News*, April 1, 1959, 18.

11 *The Sporting News*, November 25, 1959, 3.

12 *The Sporting News*, February 3, 1960, 6; *The Sporting News*, September 23, 1959, 3.

13 *The Sporting News*, April 1, 1959, 18.

14 Whitney Shoemaker (Associated Press), "Bob Allison Crowds Ted's Frosh Record," *Gastonia* (North Carolina) *Gazette*, August 5, 1959, 24.

15 *The Sporting News*, April 8, 1959, 32.

16 *The Sporting News*, November 25, 1959, 3.

17 *The Sporting News*, September 23, 1959, 3.

18 Ibid.

19 *The Sporting News*, June 29, 1960, 21.

20 Ibid.

21 *The Sporting News*, June 16, 1962, 16.

22 *The Sporting News*, August 29, 1964, 3.

23 United Press International, "Bob Allison's Three Homers Spark Twins," *Pittsburgh Post-Gazette*, May 18, 1963, 6.

24 *The Sporting News*, January 22, 1965, 8.

25 *The Sporting News*, January 16, 1965, 20.

26 *The Sporting News*, July 11, 1964, 11.

27 *The Sporting News*, August 21, 1965, 13.

28 Ibid.

29 *The Sporting News*, October 23, 1965, 6.

30 *The Sporting News*, January 21, 1967, 25.

31 Billy Martin with Peter Golenbock, *Number 1. Billy Martin* (New York: Dell, 1981), quoted in Bill James, 826.

32 Myron Cope, "A Little Love, A Few Lunches, Make a Team," *Life*, September 19, 1969, 79-82.

33 Arno Goethel, "The Citizen Who Never Whiffs," *St. Paul* (Minnesota) *Pioneer Press*, August 2, 1970.

34 Bob Cohn, "Rare Illness dims life for ex-Twins slugger," *Arizona Republic* (Phoenix), October 27, 1991. articles.chicagotribune.com/1991-10-27/sports/9104070130_1_earl-battey-mudcat-grant-watches.

35 Phil Pepe, "Star-Crossed Twin," *New York Daily News,* October, 14, 1990, C46.

Earl Battey

BY JACK HERRMAN

EARL JESSE BATTEY, JR. WAS ONE of the top defensive catchers in the American League in the early 1960s. His Twins teams were in contention for the pennant in 1962 and 1967, and won the pennant in 1965, losing the World Series to Sandy Koufax and the Los Angeles Dodgers in seven games. Battey was also a part-time player for the pennant-winning 1959 White Sox, though he did not appear in the World Series.

Battey was born in Los Angeles on January 5, 1935, to Earl and Esther Battey. In his own words, "I was the oldest of three brothers and seven sisters. My father was a construction foreman in Whittier, just outside metropolitan Los Angeles. He pitched for the Seventh-Day Adventist Church, and my mother, believe it or not, caught for the Nine-O ladies team that played at church outings."[1] Battey attended Jordan High School in the Watts neighborhood of Los Angeles.[2] There he was scouted by the White Sox. According to Bob Vanderberg, *Chicago Tribune* assistant sports editor, "Billy Pierce told me the story that when the Sox were in California training, Paul Richards after practice asked Billy to go with him to see a high-school game. When Billy asked why, Richards told him about a great young catcher [Battey] who supposedly was the best in the country."[3] White Sox scout Hollis Thurston signed Battey to a $3,999 contract. His mother was ill and his family needed the money.[4] At that time, a player signing for a bonus of $4,000 or more had to be kept on the major-league roster for at least two years.

After high school the White Sox sent Battey to play for Colorado Springs in the Western League in 1953, and then to Waterloo in the Three-I League in 1954, where he hit .292, played in 129 of Waterloo's 135 games and was the league's rookie of the year.[5] He spent most of 1955 in Triple-A, with Charleston, West Virginia, of the American Association. In a 1964 book that Jackie Robinson put together concerning integration in baseball, Battey said he encountered segregation for the first time playing in the minors. His Los Angeles neighborhood had a mix of races and no segregation. In the minors there was no problem at the ballpark, but he was forced to eat and sleep apart from his white teammates in some of the road cities, including Wichita and Louisville, as well as at home during the year he played for Charleston.[6] He was a late-season call-up to the White Sox when the roster expanded and made his first appearance in September of 1955. He also played in Chicago briefly at the beginning and end of 1956, but spent most of that year with Toronto of the International League, where he hit .178 in 101 at-bats. Of that season, Battey explained: "I was knocked out in a play at home plate. I suffered

Battey, a four-time All-Star, was a dependable catcher in the 1960s, starting at least 113 games every season from 1960 to 1966. He led big-league backstops with a robust .297 batting average in 1965. (National Baseball Hall of Fame, Cooperstown, New York).

a knee injury that kept bothering me when I finally got back in the lineup."[7]

Healthier, Battey hit .331 in winter ball in Venezuela and impressed new manager and former catcher Al Lopez during spring training with the White Sox in 1957.[8] When the major-league roster was cut to 28 on Opening Day and then 25 a month into the season, Battey stayed with the team.[9] He continued to impress defensively as a fill-in when regular catcher Sherman Lollar needed a rest. On June 4 the White Sox were in first place with a five-game lead, and Battey was one of a number of bright spots. Manager Lopez said, "I've tried to rest Sherman Lollar as often as possible. Having a good young catcher like Earl Battey gives us the chance to rest Sherman, of course. The development of Battey has been one of my pleasant surprises."[10] Battey's hitting didn't hold up, however. Later in June Lollar broke his wrist in a game against the Orioles and Battey and Les Moss shared the catching duties as Lollar missed 41 games.[11] Lopez said: "Neither can measure up to Lollar. Lollar would have won one more game against the Yankees. Battey was up with the bases loaded and he struck out. We went on to lose, 6-5."[12] Battey hit only .174 in 48 games with the White Sox that year and in August he was optioned to the Los Angeles Angels of the Pacific Coast League. His hitting improved at that level and in winter ball in Venezuela he again hit over .300. He hit well in spring training of 1958 ("I now have the confidence that I can hit major-league pitching."[13]) and made the major-league roster again. He showed more power (eight home runs in 68 games) and spent the whole season in the majors for the first time, but still hit only .226.

The 1959 season was catcher John Romano's first full season with the White Sox, and his presence limited Battey's playing time. In a preseason article, the *Chicago Tribune* speculated about moving Lollar to first if Battey or Romano began to hit with power.[14] Romano did, and caught 38 games while hitting .294. Battey appeared in only 26 games, catching in 20, as he hit .219. Lollar won his third consecutive Gold Glove as the No. 1 backstop. Battey made the White Sox World Series roster in 1959, but saw no action as Lopez relied on the veteran Lollar to start all six games. (John Romano didn't do much better; he got one at-bat in the Series.)

The 1959 team had been built on pitching, speed, and defense. Before the 1960 season began, the White Sox traded some of their young players in order to get some established power. The management wanted 1957 American League home-run champion Roy Sievers from the Washington Senators. The Senators asked for Battey and infielder Sammy Esposito, but Lopez opposed that trade, saying he was "reluctant to give up 'two players who figure to be regulars for the Senators.'"[15] In early April 1960, however, the White Sox offered Battey, minor-league first baseman Don Mincher, and cash for Sievers, and the Senators accepted.[16]

Lopez was right; Battey became a regular for the Senators in 1960. No longer in the shadow of Sherm Lollar, he blossomed into an American League star. He led the league in games caught by a catcher (136), putouts, and assists, but also in errors and passed balls, and he won the first of three consecutive Gold Gloves. Washington won more than 70 games for the first time since 1953 and Battey was voted the team MVP. The right-handed batter drove in 60 runs and hit .270. He finished eighth in AL MVP voting.[17]

The Senators moved to Minnesota and were renamed the Twins for the 1961 campaign. Battey hit over .300 for the only time in his career (.302) and hit 17 homers as he caught in 131 games. He asked for a $1,300 raise from the Twins' owner, Calvin Griffith, but Griffith was noted for being tight with a dollar.[18] "I was quite elated with my season," Battey recalled. "I had never hit over .300 in the majors. But he said, 'We finished in seventh even with you hitting .302,' and he didn't see any reason for a raise."[19]

Metropolitan Stadium was an exciting place for the Twins in the next couple of years. Both the Twins and the Los Angeles Angels challenged the Yankees in 1962 before falling back. The Twins finished second by five games. Battey made the All-Star team for the first time, getting 150 votes from the players and coaches to Romano's 84.[20] Both the AP and UPI postseason polls voted him the best catcher in baseball.[21] He had 17 home runs at the All-Star break the next year and was again voted the starter for the American League, outpolling eventual league MVP Elston Howard, 196 to 70, in the vote among players and coaches. Despite 26 homers, he was fourth in homers for the power-laden Twins. Harmon Killebrew had 45, Bob Allison, 35, and rookie Jimmie Hall, 33. Killebrew finished fourth in league MVP voting and Battey was seventh. The Twins led the league in homers (225), runs (767), and batting average (.255), but were eighth in defense. They won 91 games, but finished third behind the Yankees and White Sox.

The Twins dropped below .500 in 1964 for the first time since 1961. Battey was injured several times, but still caught 125 games. His most spectacular injury occurred when he was knocked out hitting his head against a chair after making a diving catch over a railing on May 10.[22] He had reported to spring training at 260 pounds, a fact that caused the Twins to make $1,000 of his salary dependent on reporting at no more than 230 pounds the following spring. He also reinjured his right knee and was batting .220 at the end of June, but rallied to finish with .272.[23] He did not make the All-Star team in 1964.

In 1965 the Twins, behind great pitching from starters Jim Grant, Jim Kaat, and Jim Perry, excellent relief work from veteran Al Worthington, and an excellent offense led by batting champion Tony Oliva, won 102 games and took the American League pennant by seven games over the White Sox. Always known for his great arm, Battey threw out 26 of the 54 runners who attempted to steal with him behind the plate that year, according to Retrosheet data.[24] Earl hit .297 and was selected to start the All-Star Game. Though he struck out only 23 times all season, he fanned five times in the World Series against the Dodgers, including twice against Koufax, with two runners on in the first inning and with one runner on in the ninth inning of Sandy's three-hit shutout in Game Seven.[25] A factor in Battey's .120 hitting performance in the Series was

Earl Battey (Photo courtesy of Minnesota Twins Baseball Club)

an injury he sustained in the seventh inning of Game Three. He hit his throat against a dugout railing in Dodger Stadium while chasing a foul pop hit by Willie Davis.[26] He left the game, but returned to start every game in the Series. Nonetheless, the Dodgers stole nine bases in winning the three games played in Los Angeles after losing the first two in Minneapolis.[27]

The Twins kept essentially the same lineup in the following year, 1966, and won 89 games, but couldn't keep pace with the Baltimore Orioles and finished in second place, nine games out. Battey's batting average dropped to .255, but he made the All-Star team as a reserve after Bill Freehan outpointed him among votes from the players and coaches, 111 to 95. Over the first six years of the Twins' residence in Minneapolis, Battey had, despite frequent injuries, played in 805 of the Twins' 972 games.[28]

The 1967 season was Battey's last as a player. It was the year of the exciting four-team race for the pennant among the Twins, White Sox, Tigers, and Red Sox, but Earl was frequently injured and lost his starting job to Jerry Zimmerman. On May 18, after Jim Kaat was knocked out of the box for his eighth consecutive start, manager Sam Mele sent Kaat to the bullpen temporarily and benched Battey.[29] Zimmerman injured his finger on July 17 and Battey played for a while, but then he was placed on the 21-day disabled list on August 9 after a foul ball dislocated his thumb.[30] He ended up playing in only 48 games that year, catching in 41, and hitting .165. The Twins finished in a tie for second place, one game out. He announced his retirement on November 3 after a season "plagued by injuries."[31]

In April of 1968, Battey "accepted a job as baseball consultant to Consolidated Edison … to help run the [NYC] power company's part of a baseball-community relations program."[32] It was known as the Con-Ed Answer Man program. Con-Ed would buy Yankees tickets and give them free to inner-city kids. The youngsters attended the game with Battey, "combination chaperone and the Con-Ed Answer Man (He answered their baseball questions)."[33]

In 1980 Battey enrolled at Bethune-Cookman University in Daytona Beach, Florida. He finished his undergraduate studies in 2½ years. After graduating he taught high school and coached baseball in Ocala, Florida.[34]

Battey was named the catcher on the Twins' 40th-anniversary all-time team in 2000, and attended a reunion ceremony.[35] He died of cancer on November 15, 2003. He and his wife, Sonia, had five children (Earl, Corey, Darren, Brenda, and Barbara) and, at the time of his death, four grandchildren.[36]

Since his death a number of Twins teammates have recognized Battey's contribution during the 1960s. "Earl was a great storyteller, and he could tell them both in Spanish and English," second baseman Frank Quilici said. "He had the biggest personality on the team. That was as close a group of players as I've been around, and Earl was probably the main reason." Harmon Killebrew said, "Earl had two very important things going for him. He was a fun guy in the clubhouse. More importantly, he had everyone's respect, because he had sore knees, sore hands, sore everything, but he stayed in the lineup. I didn't realize how good of a catcher Earl was until he was gone."[37] Sam Mele, his manager from midway through 1961 to midway through 1967, said, "He was one of the best catchers I had in my life. He ran the pitching staff, I don't mind telling you: He was the leader of my ballclub."[38]

Earl had a great career with the Twins, and one can only wonder if the White Sox would have been better off keeping him. As one White Sox blogger has noted, the Sox came close in 1964, and if they had kept one or two their young nucleus of future All-Stars—Battey, Johnny Callison, Norm Cash, Barry Latman, or John Romano—they might have won a pennant in the 1960s.[39] In an interview with the *Chicago Tribune* in 1968, farm director Glen Miller shook his head, "as if to say 'never again,'when he [thought] of John Callison, Earl Battey, and Norm Cash, all of whom were Sox property."[40]

This article originally appeared in the book *Go-Go To Glory—The 1959 Chicago White Sox* (Acta, 2009), edited by Don Zminda.

NOTES

1   Jack R. Robinson and Charles Dexter, *Baseball Has Done It* (New York: J.P. Lippincott Company, 1964), 183.

2   Russ J. Cowens, "Russ' Corner: Minnie, Doby & Battey," *Chicago Defender*, June 15, 1957.

3   Mark Liptak, "Remembering Earl Battey," Whitesoxintereactive.com aka FlyingSock.com, 2004.

4   David Condon, "Battey Looms in Sox's Plans," *Chicago Daily Tribune*, March 19, 1957.

5   *Chicago Daily Tribune*, February 1, 1955.

6   Robinson and Dexter, 184.

7   "Battey to Stay with White Sox," *Chicago Defender*, April 27, 1957.

8   David Condon, "Battey Looms in Sox's Plans."

9   Edward Prell, *Chicago Daily Tribune*, February 24, 1957.

10 David Condon, "In the Wake of the News," June 4, 1957.

11 Edward Prell, *Chicago Daily Tribune*, August 2, 1957.

12 Bob Glass, "Lollar Injury Hinders Sox," *Chicago Defender*, July 9, 1957.

13 Russ J. Cowens, "Lopez Lauds Battey," *Chicago Defender*, March 18, 1958.

14 Edward Prell, *Chicago Daily Tribune*, January 20, 1959.

15 Edward Prell, "Lopez Opposes Sox Deal for Sievers," *Chicago Daily Tribune*, March 30, 1960.

16 *Chicago Defender*, April 5, 1960.

17 *Chicago Daily Tribune*, November 10, 1960.

18 Jon Roe, LaVelle E. Neal III, and John Millea, "Memories of Calvin," *Minneapolis Star Tribune*, October 21, 1999.

19 Ibid.

20 "Voting for All-Stars," *New York Times*, July 1, 1962.

21 "2 Baseball Polls Agree on 8 All-Star Berths," *New York Times*, October 18, 1962.

22 "A Smashing Catch," UPI Telephoto, *Chicago Tribune*, May 11, 1964.

23 Edward Prell, "Twins Set to be 'Revved' Up," *Chicago Tribune*, February 11, 1965.

24 1965 daily logs, retrosheet.org.

25 Edward Prell, "Johnson Homer Off Kaat Aids 2-0 Victory; Dodgers Win Series Finale, 2-0," *Chicago Tribune*, October 15, 1965.

26 "Calamity in Chavez," AP Wirephoto, *Chicago Tribune*, October 10, 1965.

27 Richard Dozer, "A.L. Blushes over Twins," *Chicago Tribune*, October 13, 1965.

28 Tony McClean, "Remembering Catcher Earl Battey," *Black Athlete Sports Network* website, blackathlete.com/Baseball/031304.shtml, posted March 13, 2004.

29 "Twins Assign Pitcher Kaat to Bullpen," *Chicago Tribune*, May 19, 1967.

30 *Chicago Tribune*, August 10, 1967.

31 *Chicago Tribune*, November 4, 1967.

32 *Chicago Tribune*, April 23, 1968.

33 Blog posted by "Tim" on March 21, 2007, in response to "Absence of African-Americans in Baseball: Crisis or Fact of Life?", "Extra Bases" section of *108 magazine*, 108mag.typepad.com/extra_bases/2007/03/absence_of_afri.html.

34 Tony McClean, "Remembering Catcher Earl Battey."

35 "Twins All-Time Teammates Love Reunion," *Minneapolis Star Tribune*, August 13, 2000.

36 "Earl Battey, 68, 4-Time All-Star Catcher for Minnesota Twins," obituary, *New York Times*, November 19, 2003.

37 Patrick Reusse, "'65 in 05: A Twins Reunion," *Minneapolis Star Tribune*, August 19, 2005.

38 Jim Souhan, "Twins Notes: Battey joins team Hall," *Minneapolis Star Tribune*, June 6, 2004.

39 Mark Liptak, "Remembering Earl Battey."

40 Richard Dozer, "Meetings May Determine 'Untouchables,'" *Chicago Tribune*, September 19, 1968.

Dave Boswell

BY GREGORY H. WOLF

HARD-THROWING RIGHT-HANDER Dave Boswell debuted with the Minnesota Twins in 1964 at the age of 19, and was a valuable contributor to the Twins' pennant-winning team the following season. Despite chronic blisters on his pitching hand, and arm, shoulder, and back miseries, Boswell averaged 14 wins and 210 innings over a four-year stretch with the Twins (1966-1969) and established a reputation as one of the most competitive pitchers in baseball. "He would do anything to win a ballgame," said his longtime roommate, infielder Frank Quilici. "On the field, you loved playing behind him because you knew he was taking care of his guys. If anybody threw at somebody or something like that, well, there was going to be a response, believe me. He wasn't afraid to get it done."[1] En route to winning a career-high 20 games in 1969, Boswell was involved in a legendary fight in which he was knocked out cold by his manager, Billy Martin. The two patched up their differences and Minnesota captured the first AL West crown. After blowing out his arm in a frustrating 1-0 loss to the Baltimore Orioles in Game Two of the 1969 American League Championship Series, Boswell won only four more games and was out of the major leagues by the age of 26 with a 68-56 record.

David Wilson Boswell was born on January 20, 1945, in Baltimore to Grover W. "Buck" and Marceline Boswell. Raised in a tight-knit, working-class community on the east side of the city, Dave began playing baseball by the age of 8 or 9, and was taught by his father, a pit crane operator at a local steel mill and a former amateur heavyweight boxer. Baltimore was a hotbed for amateur baseball, and Boswell learned from some of the city's renowned coaches. At the age of 14, he pitched and played outfield for coach Sterling "Sheriff" Fowble, whose team, Gordon's Stores, counted Al Kaline as an alumnus.[2] Boswell amassed an impressive 28-2 record at Calvert Hall College High School, in nearby Towson; however, he gained he gained national exposure hurling for a sandlot team, Leone's, coached by Baltimore Orioles scout Walter Youse, who fed players to big-league clubs.[3]

Boswell's exploits on the mound and the plate drew scouts from all 20 major-league teams. A child prodigy, Boswell tossed batting practice for the Orioles at 14, had a tryout with the Pittsburgh Pirates at 15, and learned to throw a forkball from Pirates reliever Elroy Face. Said then Orioles president Lee McPhail, "We ranked [Boswell] and Wally Bunker as the best pitching prospects in the country."[4] By Boswell's senior year, rumors swirled that he might be the next $100,000 bonus baby, but the prep phenom suffered an arm injury that scared away scouts. Though he had an opportunity to sign as an outfielder, Boswell returned to Leone's after graduating in 1963 to prove that his arm was healthy. In late summer, the 18-year-old signed with the Minnesota Twins on the recommendation of scout Ed Dunn for a reported $15,000 to 20,000 bonus.[5] In 2014 Boswell was named to the 1960-2009 All-Baltimore Amateur Team.[6]

Boswell's meteoric rise to the big leagues began in the Florida Instructional League, where he struck out 37 batters in 21 innings in the fall of 1963, thereby earning an invitation to the Twins' spring-training camp in Orlando the following spring. Hailed as one of Minnesota's "hottest prospects," but not expected to make the team, the 19-year-old was a late cut and assigned to the Bismarck-Mandan (North Dakota) Pards in the Class A Northern League.[7] He got off to a rough start (1-6), but turned his first year in professional ball around and was named to the league's midseason all-star team. After posting a 7-11 record and 3.88 ERA in 160 innings for the league's worst team, Boswell was promoted in August to the Charlotte Hornets of the Double-A Southern League. His four wins in six starts and a stellar 2.85 ERA earned him a mid-September call-up to the big-league club.

On September 18, 1964, just about 15 months after graduating from high school, Boswell made his big-league debut by starting against the Boston Red Sox at Fenway Park. "My first pitch . . . was to Felix Mantilla," recalled Boswell with a chuckle in an interview with John Swol, "and it was a home run, the next batter was a rookie named Tony Conigliaro and on the first pitch he hit a double off the wall that would have been a home run in most parks."[8] Despite surrendering four hits, five walks, and three runs in three innings, Boswell escaped with a no-decision. Five days later he limited the Kansas City Athletics to five hits over eight innings and whiffed nine to pick up his first victory, 2-1. His 2-0 record and 25 strikeouts in 23⅓ innings in four starts with the Twins suggested a promising future. Boswell was back in the Florida Instructional League in the fall, but a broken ring finger on his pitching hand (the first of what seemed to be annual injuries he suffered while in the Twins organization) cut his season short.[9]

With higher personal and organizational expectations in 1965, Boswell joined a deep Twins staff, led by Mudcat Grant and Jim Kaat and mentored by Johnny Sain, in his first year as manager Sam Mele's pitching coach. Slatted for middle relief to start the season, Boswell tossed 9⅓ scoreless innings over his first three appearances to earn a start. He was pummeled (four runs in two innings) and picked up first big-league loss, but was undeterred. "Sain really gives you confidence," Boswell once said.[10] Equipped with an arsenal of fastballs, sliders, curves, and slow curves (the latter two he learned from Sain), Boswell flashed moments of brilliance in his final four appearances in May (including three starts) by yielding just one earned run and 11 hits in 26⅓ innings (0.34 ERA) while punching out 24 batters. Despite his success, Boswell was criticized for not going deep in games; however, he suffered from blisters on the middle finger of his right hand throughout his career. Boswell claimed that the painful blisters, which developed around the fourth inning, were caused from gripping the ball too tightly, and often required him to take extra days of rest between starts.[11] Following two commanding victories (10 strikeouts against the Boston Red Sox and his first big-league complete game, a six-hitter against the New York Yankees on July 9), Boswell seemed to reach his stride. Sandy Padwe of the Newspaper Enterprise Association praised him as "one of the Twins' biggest surprises," but the promising righty was diagnosed with mononucleosis before his next start.[12]

Expected to be out about four weeks, Boswell suffered a bruised shoulder in a car wreck and missed almost 40 days. Not the same pitcher when he returned on August 17, Boswell did not win another game, and

Best known for his fight with manager Billy Martin in 1969, Boswell was hard-throwing rookie for the Twins in 1965. From 1966 to 1969 he won 56 games before blowing out his shoulder in the 1969 ALCS. He posted a 68-56 record in eight seasons (1964-1971). (Photo courtesy of Minnesota Twins Baseball Club).

finished with a 6-5 record with a 3.40 ERA in 106 innings for the pennant-winning Twins. In Minnesota's disappointing seven-game loss to the Los Angeles Dodgers in the World Series, Boswell saw action only once. In Game Five, he relieved Kaat in the third inning and tossed 2⅔ innings, yielding three hits and a run in the Twins' 7-0 loss to Sandy Koufax.

Splitting his time between starts and relief outings to start the 1966 season, Boswell was only 0-4 on June 1 despite a sturdy 3.07 ERA. He then commenced the best stretch in his big-league career, winning 12 of 13 decisions. Over those 15 starts, Bos, as his teammates called him, completed seven games, struck out 112 batters in 111⅔ innings, including 10 or more four times. On July 30 at Metropolitan Stadium he tossed the best game of his career, a one-hitter, and whiffed 11 Baltimore Orioles to record the first of his six career shutouts.

Among the hottest pitchers in the majors, Boswell was paid arguably the highest compliment to a power pitcher when the Associated Press tabbed him the "Koufax of the AL" after his nifty four-hit complete-game victory with 10 strikeouts over the Boston Red Sox on August 3.[13] Notwithstanding his success, Boswell was suffering from an aching shoulder, the result of getting hit by a line drive on July 26, and had difficulty throwing his heater. "He can get by on his breaking stuff when he hasn't got his good fastball," said Sain.[14] He was diagnosed with bursitis after his winning his eighth consecutive decision on August 7 to tie a Twins team record. Bothered by pain the rest of the season, Boswell started just one more time among his four appearances. He finished with an impressive 12-5 record to lead the AL with a .706 winning percentage, and posted a 3.14 ERA in 169⅓ innings.

Boswell was a fun-loving teammate, often described in various press reports as "colorful," "a free spirit," or even a "flake." In response, Boswell once said, "I'm not goofy, I am loose."[15] He had a good sense of humor, and loved to joke with his teammates and go out for beers. He was also known for his malapropisms and impressions, especially of animals. "It was the most fun I've ever had in baseball," said Quilici about the years together as roommates. "That character was a lot of fun on and off the field."[16] Boswell was known to have pet baby alligators at one time, carried a revolver during spring training, and shot snakes from his room. "You gotta have a little bit of boy in you to play this game for a living," he said.[17]

But the 6-foot-3, 185-pound pitcher was also fiercely competitive, had a low boiling point, often argued strikes and balls with umpires, and chewed out teammates for fielding errors. His temper led to several highly publicized off-the-field fights with alcohol lurking in the background. Though teammates praised Boswell's winning, gung-ho spirit, syndicated sportswriter Joe Falls offered a different view in the aftermath of the pitcher's fight with Billy Martin. Falls tabbed him one of the "Awful All-Stars" and a player he would not want on his team.[18]

During spring training in 1967, Boswell abandoned his three-quarters motion in favor of an overhand delivery in order to overcome nagging pain. The result was disastrous. He yielded 16 runs (14 earned) and walked 16 in just 12⅔ innings in his first four starts and was relegated to the bullpen. He worked closely with new pitching coach, Early Wynn, to refine his mechanics. "Wynn has a theory that if you throw until you are tired enough, you will revert to your natural form," said Boswell.[19]

He returned to the starting rotation on May 21 and tossed a complete game and fanned 11 to defeat the California Angels for his first victory of the season. This commenced a dominant stretch during which he won eight of 12 decisions, struck out 104 batters in 98 innings, and posted a stellar 2.66 ERA. Boswell's surge coincided with the Twins' struggles which culminated in Mele's dismissal after 50 games with the team in sixth place at 25-25. While the team squabbled and endured a fight between outfielders Tony Oliva and Ted Uhlaender (which Twins beat reporter Arno Goethel and the AP claimed Boswell provoked by refusing to put away a gun he was playing with),[20] the squad caught fire under mild-mannered manager Cal Ermer and battled the Boston Red Sox, Detroit Tigers, and Chicago White Sox in a tense four-team pennant race.

As if following a well-rehearsed script, Boswell developed tendinitis in his elbow in mid-July and was bothered by pain the rest of the season.[21] He had his moments of brilliance (such as his three-hit shutout of the New York Yankees on August 19 and a six-hit shutout against the Tigers on September 2 to put the Twins into first place), but struggled with his fastball.

With a one-game lead over the Red Sox and the Tigers and just two games to play, the Twins lost both games in Fenway Park in Boston's "Impossible Dream" season to finish in second place. After the team's collapse (they lost five of their last seven games, five of which were started by Jim Kaat and Dean Chance), Boswell voiced his displeasure with Ermer for skipping his last scheduled start. "I feel like our club's talent is being surpassed because of personal differences between the players and manager," said Boswell ominously.[22] He finished with a 14-12 record, struck out a career-high 204 (in 222⅔ innings), posted a 3.27 ERA, and was the second most difficult pitcher to hit (6.5 hits per nine innings) in the AL for the second consecutive season.

In 1968 the Twins were decimated by injuries (most notably to Harmon Killebrew, who tore his hamstring in the All-Star Game, as well as to Rod Carew and Oliva) and experienced their first losing season since relocating from Washington. Echoing Boswell's insights from the offseason, Arno Goethel reported that Ermer had lost the respect of the team by his failure to discipline players and halt the incessant in-fighting.[23] Boswell got off to a good albeit inconsistent start to the season. On May 29 he tossed a three-hit shutout with 10 strikeouts to defeat the Cleveland Indians, 1-0. Always adept at the plate, Boswell knocked in the game's only run on a sacrifice fly.

Throughout his career, Boswell fashioned himself as a hitter, and raised the eyebrows (and sometimes the ire) of teammates by claiming he could hit .260 if he played in the field. For his career, he batted .202 (74-for-367) with four home runs and 22 runs batted in.

In 1968 Boswell hit at a .233 clip, three points above the AL cumulative average in the "Year of the Pitcher." But for the fourth consecutive season, he suffered an injury that hampered his effectiveness the rest of the season. On July 18 against the Red Sox, Boswell collided violently with catcher Russ Nixon while tagging him out at home plate. "It feels like I broke my back," said Boswell after the game.[24] To his credit, Boswell, who suffered strained ligaments in his sacroiliac area, returned to the mound and retired Mike Andrews to record the complete game and even his record at 8-8. After a stint on the disabled list, he returned three weeks later but notched only two victories (both complete games) and finished with his first losing season in the majors, 10-13, while posting a 3.32 ERA in 190 innings.

Boswell looked forward to the chance to play for manager Billy Martin, who, after four years as a Twins coach, took the reins of the team in 1969 and promised to build an aggressive, fundamentally sound ballclub. The 24-year-old pitcher got a scare in spring training when he sliced two tendons on his left hand while cleaning a fish, but was ready for the beginning of the first season of realignment. In seemingly the best health of his career, Boswell logged a career-high 12 innings in a no-decision against the Chicago White Sox on July 14, and sported an 11-9 record at the All-Star break, helping the Twins to a four-game lead in the AL West.

On August 6 Boswell was involved an infamous brawl that overshadowed much of his success in 1969 and unfortunately has served as his most enduring legacy. The event was hushed up for four days until Billy Martin held a press conference to explain why his pitcher was not with the team on its road trip. Though many versions of the story exist, the final results were clear. According to *Minneapolis Star* reporter Mike Lamey, Boswell confronted coach Art Fowler at a Detroit watering hole, the Lindell Athletic Club, after Fowler threatened to inform Martin that the short-fused pitcher had refused to run wind sprints earlier in the day.[25] After a heated argument ensued, teammate Bob Allison pulled Boswell outside to calm him down.

Dave Boswell (Photo courtesy of Minnesota Twins Baseball Club).

The course of the subsequent events is still murky and disputed. Boswell flattened Allison (by one account even kicked him when he was on the ground), after which Martin supposedly came rushing out of the bar. The alcohol-infused brouhaha ended with Boswell lying unconscious on the ground. Boswell denied claims that he attacked his manager. "He really mauled me," said Boswell of Martin. "He isn't telling the truth if he said I went after him."[26] Martin assessed the situation unapologetically, "I started to hit him in the stomach. I worked up and hit him in the mouth, nose, and eyes. He bounced off the wall and I hit him again and he was out cold before he hit the ground."[27] Boswell was hospitalized and reportedly required 20 stitches in his face. Said Quilici about his roommate, "He was beaten to a pulp."[28]

The fracas cast doubts on Boswell's future with the team. The battered pitcher ultimately met with team owner Calvin Griffith, who fined him an undisclosed amount, but did not suspend him. "In no way will this hurt the team," said Martin about the fight.[29]

Boswell returned to the mound on August 18 and in the words of Dick Couch of the AP enjoyed a "remarkable late season surge."[30] In his final 11 starts (from August 22 to October 1), Boswell went 8-3 with a 2.81 ERA. The stretch was highlighted by an overpowering, career-high 14-strikeout performance in a complete-game victory over the Seattle Pilots on September 19. After notching his 20th and final victory of the season, against the Pilots on September 28, the contrite Boswell commented, "Give the credit to Billy."[31] Despite missing almost three weeks recovering from his brawl, Boswell set career high in wins, starts (38), and innings (256⅓). He finished with a robust 3.23 ERA despite not registering a shutout among his 10 complete games for the division winners.

Boswell's career came crashing down in Game Two of the ALCS versus the Baltimore Orioles on October 2 in Memorial Stadium. Through 10 innings, Boswell and Orioles southpaw Dave McNally were locked in a scoreless duel. Lacking his best stuff, Boswell escaped a bases-loaded jam in the second inning with no outs. When he struck out Frank Robinson to end the 10th, he felt an excruciating pain in his arm. "I threw him a slider and it was a rocket," he told John Swol. "He didn't even swing at it. By the time I got back to the first-base line going back to the dugout, my arm felt like it was going in to my jaw. Then I went out and still tried to pitch."[32] Boswell issued walks to two of the first four hitters he faced in the 11th before yielding to reliever Ron Perranoski with two men on. The next batter, pinch-hitter Curt Motton, lined a walk-off single to right field for a dramatic, 1-0 victory and collared Boswell with loss. The Twins were swept in the best-of-five series.

Boswell endured trade rumors during the offseason, but was back with the club in spring training, unlike Martin, who was replaced by Bill Rigney. In an attempt to overcompensate for his ailing arm, Boswell developed back problems in camp. Lacking his fastball and unable to extend in his follow-through, Boswell was ineffective. He lost his first five starts and was finally put on the disabled list in early August with a 3-7 record and an unsightly 6.42 ERA in 68⅔ innings.

During the Twins' celebration after clinching their second consecutive AL West crown, Boswell was involved in another fight with a teammate, catcher Paul Ratliff, at the team hotel, and required medical attention.[33]

A shell of his former self, Boswell spent 1971, his final full season in baseball, on an odyssey. After the Twins released him in spring training, he signed with the Detroit Tigers, and was reunited with manager Billy Martin. Their reunion lasted less than two months (and just 4⅓ ineffective innings). Released again, Boswell finished the season with his hometown Orioles, including a demotion to their Triple-A farm club, the Rochester Red Wings.

Following his release by the Orioles in 1972 and an abbreviated comeback attempt in 1973, Boswell retired from baseball. In eight big-league seasons, he won 68 games and lost 56, logged 1,065⅓ innings, and posted a 3.52 ERA. He completed 37 of his 151 starts. "I would have pitched until my arm fell off," Boswell once said about his approach to pitching. "I never want to quit when I'm out there. No matter what the situation—you're tired but you push yourself."[34]

According to his obituary, Boswell worked for the Carling-National brewery in Baltimore, as well as a beer distributor after his baseball career.[35] A lifelong baseball fan, he also served as a pitching coach for Grand Slam USA baseball.

On June 11, 2012, Boswell died at the age of 67 from a heart attack at his home in Joppatown, Maryland. He was buried at Moreland Memorial Park, in Parkville. He was survived by his wife of 47 years, Eleanor "Lou" (nee Smith), sons Dan and Jason, and daughter Christina.

SOURCES

Dave Boswell player file at the National Baseball Hall of Fame, Cooperstown, New York

Ancestry.com

BaseballLibrary.com

Baseball-Reference.com

Retrosheet.com

SABR.org

The Sporting News

NOTES

1. "Shooter News: Minnesota Twins 'Character' Dave Boswell Dies," *TwinsCities.com*, June 12, 2012.
2. Doug Brown, "Fowble, coach 46 years on sandlots, dies at 76," (Baltimore) *Sun*, December 10, 1991.
3. "Leone's and Ijamsville to Play Thursday," *The News* (Frederick, Maryland), July 5, 1961, 14.
4. Jacques Kelly, "Dave Boswell, major league pitcher," (Baltimore) *Sun*, June 13, 2012.
5. *The Sporting News*, March 21, 1964, 25.
6. Keith Mills, "1960-2009 All-Baltimore Amateur Team," *Pressbox*, July 15, 2014. pressboxonline.com/2014/07/12/1960-2009-all-baltimore-amateur-baseball-team
7. *The Sporting News*, March 21, 1964, 25.
8. John Swol, "Dave Boswell interview," *Twins Trivia*. twinstrivia.com/interview-archives/dave-boswell-interview/.
9. *The Sporting News*, December 5, 1964, 27.
10. *The Sporting News*, November 20, 1965, 13.
11. *The Sporting News*, September 23, 1967, 11.
12. Sandy Padwe, "For Mele and the Twins," *The Index-Journal* (Greenwood, South Carolina), July 10, 1965, 6.
13. Associated Press, "Dave Boswell Is Koufax of AL," *Janesville* (Wisconsin) *Daily Gazette*, August 4, 1966, 12.
14. *The Sporting News*, October 1, 1966, 12.
15. *The Sporting News*, August 19, 1967, 26.
16. "Shooter News: Minnesota Twins 'Character' Dave Boswell Dies," *TwinsCities.com*, June 12, 2012.
17. *The Sporting News*, December 10, 1966, 29.
18. *The Sporting News*, August 30, 1969, 35.
19. *The Sporting News*, June 10, 1967, 1.
20. *The Sporting News*, January 6, 1968, 45; Associated Press, "Ermer Won't Discuss Oliva-Uhlaender Tiff," *Kansas City Times*, June 22, 1967, 2D.
21. *The Sporting News*, July 29, 1967, 9.
22. *The Sporting News*, January 6, 1968, 45. To be fair to Ermer, Boswell was clobbered in his last start, a loss to the New York Yankees on September 23 (yielding four hits, six walks and four runs in just 2⅓ innings) and again in his last appearance of the season (surrendering three runs in one-third inning of relief) in a loss to the California Angels two days later.
23. *The Sporting News*, August 24, 1968, 12.

24 United Press, "Twins Rake Bell, Bosox in 7-2 Rout," *Winona (Minnesota) Daily News*, July 18, 1968, 14.

25 *The Sporting News*, August 23, 1969, 31.

26 Associated Press, "Dave Boswell Sits Out Unofficial Suspension," *Cumberland* (Maryland) *News*, August 12, 1969, 12.

27 *The Sporting News*, August 23, 1969, 31.

28 Patrick Reusse, "Site of Boswell-Martin fracas closes up shop," *knoxnews.com*, December 12, 2002.

29 UPI, "Fighting Twins Minus 'One Weakness,'" *San Bernardino County* (California) *Sun*, August 12, 1969, 21.

30 Dick Couch (Associated Press), ""Stottlemyre, Boswell Become 20 Game Winners in American League," *The Daily Republic* (Mitchell, South Dakota), September 29, 1969, 12.

31 Ibid.

32 John Swol, "Dave Boswell interview," *Twins Trivia*. twinstrivia.com/interview-archives/dave-boswell-interview/

33 *The Sporting News,* October 17, 1970, 29.

34 Jacques Kelly, "Dave Boswell, major league pitcher," (Baltimore) *Sun*, June 13, 2012.

35 Ibid.

Twins Win in Extra Innings on Opening Day

April 12, 1965: Minnesota Twins 5, New York Yankees 4

at Metropolitan Stadium, Bloomington, Minnesota

BY STEVE WEST

A COLD, WET WINTER IS NORMALLY brightened by the approach of Opening Day, but in 1965 Opening Day was the last thing on most people's minds in Minnesota. A very cold winter was followed by deep snow in the northern part of the state during March, and when rain came in early April, the snow melted, causing a rapid rise in the Minnesota and Mississippi Rivers.[1] By Opening Day, Monday, April 12, Minnesota was suffering through what as of 2015 was still the worst flooding on record, with numerous areas across the state dealing with more than 20 feet of water. (Chaska, just southwest of the Twin Cities, reported a high of 34.5 feet.)

The previous day President Johnson had declared a "major disaster" in 39 counties across the state. The Minnesota National Guard had been mobilized and was working side-by-side with thousands of people to sandbag towns along the rivers, desperately trying to save lives and property. The eventual toll would include several deaths and more than $200 million in property damage, plus many thousands of people displaced from their homes.

On Sunday night the Twins held their annual "welcome home" baseball dinner, with several players unable to make it because of flooding near their homes in Burnsville, on the south side of the Minnesota River. On Monday the high water made it impossible for those players—including starting pitcher Jim Kaat—to make it from their homes to Metropolitan Stadium. A call to the team's traveling secretary, Howard Fox, was necessary, and he was able to make arrangements with local radio station WCCO to pick up the players in a helicopter—two at a time—and carry them to the parking lot outside the ballpark.[2]

Once the players, and a crowd of just 15,388, made it to the game, they sat in cold and windy conditions, with a temperature of 44 degrees at first pitch. The stadium was undergoing expansion, with the NFL Vikings building a $1.2 million double-deck grandstand in left field, meaning that section of the park was closed to spectators.[3] The grounds crew had worked miracles to get the field ready for play, removing 40 inches of snow and ice from the field in the week prior to the game.[4] The weather was bad enough that the Twins announced the cancellation of Tuesday's game before Monday's game began (with the visiting New York Yankees complaining that they did that only because they would get a much bigger gate during the summer).

The Yankees came in as defending American League champions, having won the flag five years in a row, and were favorites for another pennant, although they were aging and going through several personnel changes. After the Yankees lost the World Series in 1964 to the St. Louis Cardinals, they had fired manager Yogi Berra and surprisingly appointed former Cardinals manager Johnny Keane to take his place. Mickey Mantle was also making the full-time move from center to left field to try to give some rest to his aching legs.

The Twins were picked to finish in the first division, although they were not considered serious contenders for the pennant. A couple of years with 91 wins had been followed by a slump to 79 wins and sixth place in 1964, and there were questions about whether they could bounce back. Even manager Sam Mele wasn't sure: "I think the Twins have to be better but I can't say how much."[5]

When the game began, Yankees starter Jim Bouton walked a couple of Twins batters in the bottom of the first, allowing one to score on a groundout. Then an error by new Yankees center fielder Tom Tresh gave the Twins a 2-0 lead in the second. That was the first of many errors this cold day, as the Yankees ended with five and the Twins with three. Meanwhile Kaat retired the first 10 batters he faced, and helped his own cause with a two-run single in the fourth. He gave up a solo home run to Elston Howard in the fifth inning (caught by one of the construction workers in the bleachers), and two more runs on a groundout and sacrifice fly in the seventh, but went to the ninth with a 4-3 lead.

Twins third baseman Rich Rollins had to leave the game early after wrenching his knee, and was replaced by Cesar Tovar, who was making his major-league debut. With two out in the ninth, Tovar dropped a Joe Pepitone pop fly, allowing Art Lopez (also making his debut, pinch-running for Mantle, who had singled to center) to score from second (he had advanced on a groundout) and tie the game. The game went into extra innings. Jerry Fosnow took over pitching duties for the Twins, after Don Mincher had pinch-hit for Kaat in the bottom of the ninth. Pedro Ramos entered the game to pitch for the Yankees in the bottom of the 10th.

Lopez returned the error in the bottom of the 11th, losing a fly ball in the wind in left field that let Twins leadoff hitter Bobby Allison go all the way to third. The Yankees intentionally walked the next two hitters, and then secured two outs on a pop fly and strikeout. Next, Tovar came to bat. He made amends for his earlier error, stroking a single to center — the umpire ruled that a diving Tresh trapped the ball, although many thought it was caught[6] — to bring home the winning run and send the small crowd home happy. "I had to get a base hit," said Tovar. "You could never find a better spot to make up for an error."[7]

So the season was off to a winning start for the Twins, and for Jim Kaat the day ended with another helicopter ride, returning him and the other players across the rising floodwaters to their homes that evening.

NOTES

1   Jeff Boyne, "Mississippi River Flood of 1965," crh.noaa.gov/arx/?n=flood1965.

2   Max Nichols, "Marooned By Flood, Three Twins Reach Game in Helicopter," *The Sporting News,* April 24, 1965, 22.

3   "Stadium Expansion OKed," *Fergus Falls* (Minnesota) *Journal,* December 16, 1964, 8.

4   Dick Gordon, "Twins' Field Crew Chases Away Winter," *The Sporting News*, April 24, 1965, 19.

5   Jack Hand, "Managers See 6-Team NL Race, 3-Team AL Chase," *Clearfield* (Pennsylvania) *Progress*, April 12, 1965, 10.

6   Tom Yuzer, "Twins' Opener an Exciting One," *Fergus Falls* (Minnesota) *Daily Journal*, April 13, 1965, 12.

7   "Tovar Sheds Goat's Horns With Winning Smash in 11th," *The Sporting News*, May 1, 1965, 18.

Pete Cimino

BY JEFF ENGLISH

IN THE SPRING OF 1960 FEW HIGH-school athletes in the country were more highly sought after than Pete Cimino. As a 17-year-old senior pitcher at Bristol (Pennsylvania) High School, he followed up a 14-strikeout perfect game on May 16 with a no-hitter four days later. His exploits on the diamond were overshadowed only by the numbers he had turned in as a forward on the school's basketball team. As a senior he averaged 29 points and 17 rebounds per game on his way to being named First-Team All-State. At 6-feet-2 and 195 pounds, Cimino looked like every coach's dream, regardless of the sport.

Peter William Cimino was born on October 17, 1942, in Philadelphia. His parents, Peter and Philomena, first met at St. Ann School in Philadelphia as teenagers. They were married in 1941 and had two children, Pete and another son, David

Both parents were extremely supportive of Pete's athletic endeavors and seldom missed an opportunity to see their son play. He enrolled at Bristol High as a freshman in the fall of 1956. It was not long before he began to garner notice for his all-around athletic ability. On August 2, 1957, he registered six strikeouts in a complete-game 8-4 victory over Phoenixville to capture Bristol's first Babe Ruth League state championship. In April 1958, as a member of the Bristol High Warriors, he hurled a one-hit shutout with eight strikeouts in a 7-0 victory over William Tennent. As a member of the basketball team, he scored 30 points in a 107-62 victory over Palisades High on December 16, 1958. Bristol finished the regular season with a 20-2 record, and Cimino scored 16 points in an 85-54 victory over Upper Dublin to advance to the District 1 Class B championship. Bristol lost the title game to Darby, 71-69, in a matchup that featured multiple overtimes. Among Cimino's 20 points was a last-second shot to tie the game and force the second overtime.

And so it went. Cimino was back on the mound for his junior season the following spring, tossing a complete-game win with nine strikeouts against William Tennent on May 14. Between his performance on the diamond and his prowess on the hard court, expectations were high for his senior year. Before the year was out, Pete Cimino more than exceeded even the highest of them.

Starting a contest against visiting Palisades on January 22, 1960, Cimino was averaging 23 points per game for the season. He scored 20 points in the first quarter alone. "It was halfway through the first quarter and Pete had quite a few points, and Coach [Chic] D'Angelo said we were going to go for the league record for Pete," recalled Jack Wichser, a Bristol team-

Cimino made only one appearance for the Twins in 1965, but it was a memorable one: his big-league debut. The right-handed reliever made 86 appearances in parts of four seasons in the majors. (Photo courtesy of Minnesota Twins Baseball Club).

mate, in a 2012 interview.¹ He added 24 more in the second quarter, leaving him just 18 points shy of the single-game Lower Bucks County League record of 62 points held by Lou Klein of Delhaas. He pumped in 32 more in the third quarter to easily surpass the record and then finished strong with 38 points in the fourth quarter for a game-high total of 114. Bristol won the game 134-86. Cimino shot 44 of 79 from the field and 26 of 29 from the foul line, and his 114-point total was only 6 shy of the then national scholastic scoring record of 120 points in a game. As of 2014 the total was tied for fourth all-time and remained the Pennsylvania state record.² Cimino was more than willing to share the spotlight for the accomplishment, stating, "I can't begin to give the other fellows enough credit. The way they got the rebounds and passed off to me is what made it possible."³ Looking back on the game many years later, Cimino recalled that his mother was not there to see it. "My father telephoned her at halftime and she was visiting my grandmother and he told her she better come up to the game because I was scoring a lot of points. She said she wasn't coming up because the other team wasn't very good—and I think that was the only game she missed."⁴ News of Cimino's game made national headlines and earned a mention in *The Sporting News*.⁵

Cimino contributed 25 points in a season-ending, losing effort to Columbia in the Pennsylvania state basketball playoffs. He shared First-Team All-State honors with Richard "Dick" Allen of Wampum, who would go on to a productive 15-year career with 351 home runs in major-league baseball. With the basketball season drawing to a close, it was time for Cimino to turn his attention back to the pitcher's mound.

Cimino's perfect game and no-hitter in May certified him as a prospect in the eyes of several scouts, but on May 20 it was reported that he had accepted a scholarship to play basketball at Rider College.⁶ Three weeks later, the Associated Press reported that the Washington Senators had signed Cimino for a $12,000 bonus. He was signed by club vice president Joe Haynes. He was assigned to the Senators' Wytheville, Virginia, farm team in the Class D Appalachian League. Of his signing, Cimino said, "I passed up several basketball scholarships to play baseball. School wasn't for me."⁷

Cimino was more or less a one-pitch pitcher, relying almost exclusively on a hard, rising fastball. He had some control issues. In his first professional season, at Wytheville, he finished with a 6-2 record and a 3.43 ERA for the league's first-place team. After the season he spent the winter playing in the Florida Instructional League before finding himself with the Wilson Tobs of the Carolina League in 1961. The Tobs had the best record in the league, but Cimino struggled to a modest won-loss mark of 4-5 and a 5.61 ERA.

In 1962 Cimino was invited to participate in spring training with the major-league club, now in Minnesota. Although he was not expected to make the club, it was a sign of the high regard in which the Minnesota Twins held him. According to club president Calvin Griffith, "Often, just the spring-training association with major leaguers in camp helps some of these youngsters to mature more quickly. They realize they go first-class in the majors and it develops a greater desire to attain big-league status."⁸ The Twins once again assigned Cimino to Wilson in the Carolina League. While his record for the season was just 12-13, he managed 190 strikeouts in as many innings, and frequently overpowered the opposition. On April 30 he tied a 17-year old Carolina League record by striking out 20 batters in a 7-3 win over the Burlington Indians. He struck out the side in the second, third, sixth, and eighth innings, as well as the final two batters in the ninth to tie the record. On July 1 he tossed a no-hitter against the Winston-Salem Red Sox, striking out eight and walking one while retiring the first 22 batters he faced. Nine days later, he recorded 14 strikeouts in a 5-1 win over the Kinston Eagles.

Cimino returned to the Florida Instructional League in October, and after pitching a three-hit shutout against the Reds on November 16, he was mentioned in *The Sporting News* along with several other young Twins pitchers as showing "great promise."⁹ The Twins promoted Cimino to the Dallas-Fort Worth Rangers of the Triple-A Pacific Coast League to begin the

1963 season. In May he was optioned to the Charlotte Hornets of the Double-A South Atlantic League. On July 19 he hurled 13 shutout innings before allowing two runs in a 4-3 loss to the Chattanooga Lookouts in an 18-inning contest. By the end of July Cimino was ninth in the league with a 2.80 ERA and 81 strikeouts in 103 innings of work. On August 22, he tossed a three-hit, 3-0 shutout over Nashville to lower his ERA to 2.50 in 127 innings. His performance earned him a recall to Dallas-Fort Worth, where he picked up a win in three scoreless innings of relief work against Oklahoma City on August 27.

After once again pitching in the Florida Instructional League, Cimino entered the spring of 1964 as one of the Twins' top pitching prospects. In April he was sent to minor-league camp for reassignment and ended up with the Triple-A Atlanta Crackers. On May 14 his wife, Barbara, gave birth to their second child, Michael, while visiting her husband during a Crackers stay in Rochester. The couple already had a daughter, Darlene.

The Crackers were easily the worst team in the International League, and from time to time the players and coaches had to do what they could to keep things loose. On June 4, while visiting the Columbus Jets, Cimino and fellow pitcher Jim Merritt bought a four-foot rubber snake in an effort to scare catcher Chuck Weatherspoon, who was known for his fear of snakes. The June 20, 1964, edition of *The Sporting News* detailed what happened next:

"They put it under a pillow and tried to lure Weatherspoon to their room, but he was intent on more sleep. Their plot foiled, Merritt and Cimino left for breakfast. While they were gone, a maid came in to tidy up the room. You guessed it: When she saw the snake, her screams woke everyone on the floor. She insisted she had been bitten and only after the calming effects of a sedative and a long rest was she ready to return to work."[10]

Once again Cimino's overall numbers for Atlanta were not overwhelming, but from time to time he still dominated his opponents. On July 7 he allowed just one hit and an unearned run in a 1-0 loss to Jacksonville. Four days later he tossed a five-hitter to beat Columbus, 6-2. He contributed a grand slam to his own cause.

Although Cimino began the 1965 season with the Triple-A Denver Bears in the Pacific Coast League, many expected that a solid performance would earn him a shot with the big-league Twins before the end of the season. His 9-7 record, 3.70 ERA, and 91 strikeouts in 90 innings of work warranted a September call-up. Unfortunately for Cimino, when the call came, he was on the disabled list with a fractured pitching hand. The result is that he appeared in only one game for a 1965 Twins team that won the American League pennant and faced the Los Angeles Dodgers in the World Series. On September 22, 1965, Cimino retired Paul Blair, Boog Powell, and Brooks Robinson with three straight fly outs in a perfect ninth inning of a 5-2 loss to the Orioles. Of his first and only big-league appearance that year, Cimino later recalled, "I got through it without allowing a hit. So I have the lowest ERA in the majors—0.00. Boy was I shaking after I finished that inning! I sat on the bench and couldn't stop shaking."[11]

Cimino spent that winter pitching for the Ponce Lions in the Puerto Rican League. He eagerly anticipated the start of the 1966 season and his chances to stick with the Twins as a reliever. He reported to spring training in Orlando a week before the February 21 start date. "… I'm going early so I can get a jump on things. And I'm 215 pounds and want to get down to 205," he said.[12] With only a few open roster spots, Cimino expected stiff competition, adding, "And they'll be a few fighting for them. It will be a tough struggle but I'm confident."[13]

Cimino performed well in the spring and claimed one of only two open spots on the pitching staff. Manager Sam Mele called him and right-hander Dwight Siebler "the most improved pitchers in our camp."[14] On April 5 Cimino received word that he had made the club, after which he called his parents in Bristol to share the good news.

The 1966 Twins finished a distant second behind the Baltimore Orioles. For his part, Cimino proved a useful member of the bullpen. Initially he did not see much action, but generally he pitched well when the opportunities came. He earned his first big-league victory on June 9 against the Kansas City Athletics with two scoreless innings of relief. The game was notable because Minnesota tied a major-league record by hitting five homers in a single inning in the seventh, Cimino's final frame.

By August Cimino's quality work was sparking speculation that he was the heir-apparent to the 37-year-old Al Worthington as the ace of the Minnesota bullpen. He worked hard to develop a curveball, taught to him by Twins pitching coach Johnny Sain. "Before Sain taught me this, I was never able to throw a curve in my life," Cimino remarked.[15] Mele envisioned Cimino offering the club some flexibility in the future, commenting, "He still gets a little wild sometimes. He needs experience. But he can become a good reliever. And he can become a starter too, if we get in a jam and I need one. He's strong and can pitch a lot of innings."[16] But as the season wound down, Cimino grew less and less effective. He took his fourth loss, against the Boston Red Sox, on August 21, surrendering two runs in two-thirds of an inning. Three days later he blew a save opportunity in the ninth inning in a long relief appearance in Washington. On August 28 against the White Sox, he allowed three hits and walked three in 2⅔ innings while taking his fifth loss of the season. On October 2 he made his final appearance of the season, tossing two scoreless innings in the first game of a doubleheader against the Orioles. He wrapped up his rookie season with a disappointing record of 2-5, but despite some control trouble, his ERA was a very healthy 2.92.

By mid-October, it became clear that club officials did not necessarily view Cimino as the future savior of the Minnesota bullpen. The October 15, 1966, issue of *The Sporting News* included an article discussing club president Calvin Griffith's desire to bolster the bullpen in the offseason, stating, "Griffith wants help in the relief pitching department. Griffith felt Pete Cimino did not show that he was quite ready to take over the lead." In late October the Twins hired 300-game winner Early Wynn to replace Johnny Sain as the club's pitching coach. Among his expected tasks was to further the development of young pitchers Jim Roland and Cimino.

Cimino spent a portion of the offseason traveling with teammates Tony Oliva, Sandy Valdespino, and Earl Battey as part of the Twins winter banquet tour. They were scheduled to appear at over 90 dinners across the Midwest. But before the tour was over, Cimino found himself traded to another team.

On December 2, 1966, Minnesota sent Cimino, outfielder Jimmie Hall, and first baseman Don Mincher to the California Angels for former Cy Young Award winner Dean Chance and a player to be named later. Cimino acknowledged shock over the deal, telling reporters, "I had no idea they were thinking of trading me since I thought I'd be here several years to help them. But maybe it'll work out since I'll have more opportunities to pitch with the Angels."[17] In the weeks that followed, statements from Angels officials made it clear that they considered Cimino a priority in the deal. Angels manager Bill Rigney acknowledged, "We did not make the trade until Pete was included."[18] In assessing the trade, *The Sporting News* noted that after observing Cimino in the Pacific Coast League, Angels pitching coach Bob Lemon was impressed, and that "initially, Cimino will be provided a starting opportunity, but he will likely go on to relief."[19]

In March 1967 a minor controversy occurred when new Angels first baseman Don Mincher said he thought the Twins gave away too much to acquire Chance. He told reporter Ross Newhan, "I firmly believe the Twins gave up too much. I could see the Twins giving up one or two of us, but not all three. … I am especially high on Cimino. He's going to be a great pitcher."[20] The comments garnered a diplomatic response from Chance, who offered, "And that Pete Cimino could be a good pitcher. That is quite a bit of talent to give up."[21]

The 1967 California Angels finished with a winning record of 84-77, in fifth place in the American League. Cimino was optimistic about his prospects for the season, and after 14 appearances, he boasted a 2-1 record and a solid 2.81 ERA. Against the White Sox on May 26 he entered in the second inning and went the rest of the way for the win, striking out seven in 7⅔ scoreless innings. He began working with Lemon on a new curveball to increase his effectiveness and prolong his career. But in August he hit a rough patch in which he allowed nine earned runs in five appearances totaling 9⅓ innings, pushing his ERA from 2.70 to 3.40. He finished the season with a modest 3-3 record, 80 strikeouts, and an uninspiring 3.26 ERA in a career-high 88⅓ innings of work. Of the trade that brought Cimino from the Twins, Angels general manager Fred Haney said bluntly, "Mincher has done a fine job. Hall has been adequate. Cimino has been less than expected."[22] Having failed to meet the club's lofty expectations, Cimino looked to sharpen his skills as a member of the San Juan club in the Puerto Rican league over the winter.

In 1968 Cimino made only four early-season appearances with the Angels, allowing two earned runs in a total of seven innings. His final appearance in the major leagues came on May 7 against the White Sox. He allowed three hits and one earned run in 1⅔ innings of relief. Shortly thereafter the Angels sent him to Seattle in the Pacific Coast League. His demotion was one of many over the course of the 1968 season as the Angels struggled to a disappointing 67-95 record and an eighth-place finish. He pitched well in Seattle, posting a 3-0 record and a 2.57 ERA in 21 innings. He ended the season with the El Paso Sun Kings in the Double-A Texas League. The team won the Texas League title but Cimino pitched in only two games. They were the final innings of his career.

Cimino held a job driving a truck for a beverage company for 19 years, and then worked for a chemical company for two years before retiring. On May 23, 1992, Pete married Linda, a woman with whom he had reconnected after initially meeting in Virginia when they were both 17 years old. In a 2010 letter to the website Kentucky Baseball, he wrote, "We really liked each other but got separated for 30 years. Then we found each other again, got married, and have lived happily for 18 years."[23] In retirement, he spent time with his wife, his two children, and his three grandchildren.

Looking back on his time in the big leagues, Cimino said he had fond memories and few regrets:

"I always wanted to play pro ball. I realized my dream. Unfortunately, it didn't last as long as I would have liked. But nevertheless, I was there. In the majors everything was first class all the way. In the minors you had to put up with those long bus rides through the South — maybe 10 or 14 hours on a bus. And they only gave us a few dollars for meals. So you had to eat at a greasy spoon. It was the best you could do. But it still seems worth it."[24]

NOTES

1. articles.philly.com/2012-03-02/sports/31117286_1_bristol-area-jack-wichser-bristol-high-school.

2. en.wikipedia.org/wiki/List_of_basketball_players_who_have_scored_100_points_in_a_single_game.

3. "Prep Basketeer Rips Cords For Total of 114 Points," *Hutchinson* (Kansas) *News*, January 24, 1960.

4. articles.philly.com/2012-03-02/sports/31117286_1_bristol-area-jack-wichser-bristol-high-school

5. James Enright, "Big O' on Edge? Fans Wondering," *The Sporting News*, February 3, 1960.

6. "Land Prep Star," *Sandusky* (Ohio) *Register*, May 20, 1960.

7. "Twins' Rookie Turned Down Hoop Offers to Try Mound," *The Sporting News*, March 8, 1961.

8. Tom Briere, "Twins Invite Farm-Club Pilots to Join Huddles at Orlando Base," *The Sporting News*, January 24, 1962.

9. Fed Lieb, "Hall, Oliva and McCabe Spark Twins' Six-Game Win Splurge," *The Sporting News*, December 1, 1962.

10. "Lowly Crax' Hijinks Liven Dull Situation in Columbus," *The Sporting News*, June 20, 1964.

11. Max Nichols, "Twin Problem Kids Roland, Nieson and Cimino Eye Hill Jobs," *The Sporting News*, March 26, 1966.

12. Dick Dougherty, "Pete Cimino Heads South To Get Jump On Training," *Bucks County Courier Times*, February 15, 1966.

13. Ibid.

14 Max Nichols, "Great Cesar's Ghost, Twins Find Zoilo's Sub in Wraith-Like Tovar," *The Sporting News*, April 16, 1966.

15 Max Nichols, "Twins Making Bow to Cimino As Crown Prince of Bull Pen," *The Sporting News*, September 10, 1966.

16 Ibid.

17 Ray Di Lissio, "Trade Comes as Shock to Pete Cimino," *Bucks County Courier Times*, December 3, 1966.

18 Ross Newhan, "Rubio Choice Gem in Jewel Kit of Angels," *The Sporting News*, December 24, 1966.

19 Ibid.

20 Ross Newhan, "Slugger Mincher Sees Deal As Real Calamity for Twins," *The Sporting News*, March 11, 1967.

21 Max Nichols, "Dean Holds His Fire In War With Angels," *The Sporting News*, March 25, 1967.

22 Ross Newhan, "It's Official—Angels Will Rehire Rigney," *The Sporting News*, October, 1967.

23 kentuckybaseball.blogspot.com/2010/02/pete-cimino-1965-1968-major-leaguer.html.

24 Ibid.

Jerry Fosnow

BY GREG ERION

A GOAL OF EVERY MAJOR LEAGUER is to play on a team destined for the World Series. While individuals are in the game for money and personal achievement, being part of a team going to the fall classic is a treasured experience. Nearly 50 years after Minnesota took the 1965 championship, Jerry Fosnow—who gained credit for the first of their 102 victories in the season—continued to savor memories of being part of that team. He was especially aware that for one whose career spanned just a few games in 1964 and half the season in 1965, his timing was perfect. Many whose careers extended over 20 years never had a like opportunity. For every Derek Jeter who played on multiple pennant winning teams there are dozens like Hall of Famer Ted Lyons who played 21 years without being part of a championship squad.

Gerald Eugene Fosnow, born on September 21, 1940, in Deshler, near Toledo in northwestern Ohio, was the second of two children born to Harry and Dorothy Fosnow. He and his sister, Joan, grew up on their parents' 400-acre farm. Fosnow recalled his earliest memory of wanting to be a big-league pitcher.[1] To that end, he pitched countless hours to his father. A bellwether day came when his father could no longer catch his pitches. Gerald's cousin became the new receiver. Speed, then accuracy, became the goal; later hitting a tire nailed to the barn helped him develop consistency in the strike zone. Small for his age, Fosnow was undistinguished until his senior year at Deshler High School. Sprouting seven inches between junior and senior years, he became a dominant pitcher who helped his team to a district championship in 1959 and gained him the attention of several scouts.

Detroit and Cleveland showed the most interest. Indians scout Charles LeCrone arranged for Fosnow to come to Cleveland Stadium for a tryout. In a simulated game against college and semipro players, he struck out six in three innings, impressing the Indians, who offered a $500 signing bonus. Fosnow wanted to try out with the Tigers, who had offered to look at him in Toledo. However, his father, a devoted Indians fan, persuaded him, after some arguing, to sign with Cleveland.

Cleveland assigned Fosnow to the Selma Cloverleafs of the Class D Alabama-Florida League in 1959. At 18, he was the youngest player on the team, where he played with future major leaguers Max Alvis, Larry Brown, and Doc Edwards. He got off to a fast start, winning his first nine games. *The Sporting News* carried almost weekly notice of Fosnow's exploits, which included pitching Selma's first shutout of the year, defeating Panama City 2-0, then later beating Pensacola 7-4 while striking out 14.[2] Subsequently, *The Sporting News* reported Fosnow winning his eighth

A southpaw reliever, Fosnow appeared in 29 games and logged 46 2/3 innings for the Twins in 1965, his second and last season in the majors. (Photo courtesy of Minnesota Twins Baseball Club).

straight game.³ His performance continued to impress, leading Fosnow to consider that perhaps he ought to receive a raise. He was underpaid, like most rookies, earning $150 per month. Writing the Cleveland head office, he requested a $25-a-month increase.

Indians general manager Frank Lane had a reputation for his epic — and acrimonious — salary battles with such major leaguers as Rocky Colavito and Roger Maris. One has to wonder how the front office viewed an 18-year-old rookie's request for a pay raise in midseason. If Lane was going to haggle with Colavito over $1,500, a Class D player would receive scant — and disdainful — attention.⁴ The Indians denied Fosnow's request; if he continued to do well he would see an increase the following year.

Fosnow was 9-0 when he lost his first game in late June; he went on to compile a 15-4 record.⁵ His 3.42 ERA was well under the league average of 3.97.⁶ Selma finished second. In the best-of-five semifinal playoffs, Fosnow pitched a no-hitter against Pensacola, walking just one batter.⁷ Selma went on beat the Dothan Cardinals for the league championship.

The next season the Indians promoted Fosnow to the Minot Mallards of the Class C Northern League, where he posted a 13-9 record and tied for the league lead in shutouts. He pitched in 40 games, starting 21. Then Fosnow's career took a curious turn. In 1961 Cleveland assigned him to Dubuque of the Class D Midwest League, seemingly a demotion. In an interview Fosnow said he did not recall why he was demoted, but Cleveland had cut its eight affiliate teams in 1960 to five in 1961.⁸ After pitching in seven games for Dubuque, and despite a 3-1 record, Fosnow was released. He recalled going to the ballpark and finding someone else wearing his uniform number. He confronted manager Pinky May, who could not adequately explain Cleveland's decision to let him go. After offering May a few choice words, he vowed, "I will make it to the majors." Fosnow did not pitch the rest of 1961.

Fosnow signed with the Minnesota Twins before the 1962 season after he impressed scout Dick Wiencek while pitching in a tournament.⁹ The Twins placed Fosnow at Wilson of the Class B Carolina League, where he went 12-12, striking out 187 batters in 209 innings and posting a 2.84 ERA. Next year, the Wilson Tobs — and Fosnow — moved up to Class A. He went 13-9 and pitched in the league all-star game.

Fosnow's performance earned him a promotion to Triple-A Atlanta in 1964. Manager Jack McKeon made him a short reliever. Fosnow did well in his new role. In late June, he became particularly effective. Called on to make an infrequent start, he threw a complete game to snap the Crackers' 10-game losing streak. The next day Fosnow won in relief, and just two days later he relieved again for another victory. He pitched 16 innings during these three appearances, giving up just six hits.¹⁰ While Fosnow was proving particularly effective, the Twins needed help.

Minnesota was in the pennant race as the American League season neared the halfway point. The Twins had an explosive offense; they would lead the league in runs scored thanks to the power of Harmon Killebrew and Bob Allison and the hitting of rookie sensation Tony Oliva. What they did not have was pitching, especially in the bullpen. Bill Dailey and Bill Fischer, counted on to be mainstay relievers, had disappointed. (Dailey was released and after Fischer injured his ankle, he was placed on the voluntary retired list and became a scout.¹¹) The Twins purchased Johnny Klippstein and Al Worthington from the Philadelphia Phillies and the minor-league San Diego Padres respectively. They also decided to bring up Fosnow as well.

Fosnow pitched in a losing effort for the Crackers on June 26. Three days later he appeared in his first major-league game, facing Baltimore at Memorial Stadium. He came into the game in the seventh inning with the Twins down 4-1 and walked Jackie Brandt, the first batter he faced. After getting two outs (the second, Boog Powell, on strikes), he gave up a home run to Norm Siebern. The Orioles eventually won 6-3.

Fosnow next pitched three weeks later against the California Angels, throwing two scoreless innings in a blowout game. His performance the rest of the season was subpar, as he appeared in just five more games. Fosnow recalled asking Twins manager Sam Mele for more opportunities to pitch, arguing that he would do better if allowed to pitch more. "Give me a chance; let me get my feet wet," Fosnow urged the manager.[12]

Among the factors working against Fosnow at the time was the combined effectiveness of Klippstein (1.97 ERA) and Worthington (1.37). Fosnow finished the year with a 0-1 record and a 10.97 ERA in seven games. The Twins finished sixth.

Fosnow had not pitched well, but he had redeemed his pledge to Pinky May that he would pitch in the majors some day. Sadly, his making the majors came too late for his father to enjoy it. The elder Fosnow had died in 1962 never having had the opportunity to see him pitch in the majors.[13]

Fosnow's substandard performance for Minnesota made his position on the roster tenuous. Mele liked his potential, but was concerned about a lack of control, saying, "He's got the stuff if he gets it over the plate."[14] Fosnow had his work cut out for him in the offseason. He did have a few factors working in his favor. As solid as Klippstein and Worthington's performance had been, they were 37 and 36 respectively. Fosnow was 24 and he was a left-hander—always a plus on a pitching staff.

Assigned to the Florida Instructional League at season's end, Fosnow did well. Then he pitched for San Juan in the Puerto Rican winter league, also impressing with his performance.[15] While pitching in Florida, he came under the tutelage of Johnny Sain, the Twins' new pitching coach, who went to work on his technique and pitch repertoire. In a subsequent article in *The Sporting News*, Fosnow's description of how Sain worked with him illustrated why Sain was one of the most respected pitching coaches in the game. "For the first time, I can throw a curve ball and change of pace and know I will get them over the plate," Fosnow said. "I throw everything side arm and my curve always was flat. Sain watched me a while, them he asked if I ever had a dip in my curve. I told him no one had ever taught me how to do it. So he showed me how to bend my wrist and hold the ball farther back in my hand. Now it dips."[16]

During spring training, Fosnow made his mark; at one point he had given up one hit in 12 innings over five appearances. Mele added to his earlier comments, "I need a left-hander for late-inning relief. We've been trying to get Fosnow ready for that job."[17] His strong performances continued, enabling him to make the Opening Day roster.

Fosnow joined a team not expected to do well; the Baseball Writers Association of America picked them to finish fifth. The consensus was that while the Twins' offense was peerless, lack of pitching and defensive limitations would consign them to the list of also-rans.[18] There was a more serious problem—a sense of lethargy. They had finished second and third before tumbling to sixth in 1964. With the team's disappointing performance, owner Calvin Griffith publicly questioned their apathetic play and lack of commitment, suggesting that Mele fine players when the occasion warranted it. During spring training, Mele did just that, pulling shortstop Zoilo Versalles out of an exhibition game for indifferent effort. It turned the team around, generating a new attitude and paying immediate dividends.[19]

On Opening Day, it was apparent that Mele had gained a higher opinion of Fosnow's abilities. With the score tied 4-4 in the top of the 10th at Metropolitan Stadium, Mele called on Fosnow to relieve Jim Kaat who after pitching solidly, gave way to a pinch-hitter in the ninth inning. Fosnow held the New York Yankees scoreless in the 10th and 11th. Nearly 50 years later, he recalled the thrill of striking out Roger Maris to end a Yankees scoring threat. In the bottom of the 11th, Cesar Tovar singled Bob Allison home to win the game. For Tovar, winning the game was redemptive—he had committed an error in the ninth that allowed New York to tie the score.

It was the first of the Twins' 102 victories for the season. It was Fosnow's first major-league win. He later joked that he was only 19 wins from his 20th victory of the season.[20] The win had significance beyond winning on Opening Day: It came at the expense of the Yankees, who had won five straight pennants and were favored to win a sixth by the same writers who saw the Twins finishing fifth.

Fosnow was Mele's go-to hurler in the Twins' next game. Entering in relief of Camilo Pascual against Detroit with the score tied 4-4 in the sixth; he soon faced future Hall of Famer Al Kaline with a runner on first. Trying to keep the ball down, he missed high and Kaline hit what turned out to be a game-winning home run. Not found in the box score was that before Kaline batted, Dick McAuliffe had hit a line drive off Fosnow's hand. *The Sporting News* noted approvingly, "Fosnow pitched three more innings, striking out four after that"—a performance that demonstrated to his teammates Fosnow's grittiness.[21]

A little over a week later Fosnow faced New York again, this time at Yankee Stadium, a daunting experience for most young players. Fosnow entered the game with Minnesota leading 7-2 in the eighth. Facing the likes of Mickey Mantle and Maris, he held the Yankees scoreless to gain (retroactively) his first save. The victory provided a further psychological boost for Minnesota—vanquishing the favorite team, this time in their backyard.

By the end of April the Twins were in first. As the season progressed, they melded into a team that believed in itself, and believed that something special was developing. Mele felt that the win on Opening Day was in a game they would have lost the year before after allowing the Yankees to tie it.[22] Fosnow reminisced that everyone was pulling for one another and that the clubhouse was loose.[23] Oliva felt the same: "There was no jealousy on this team. If you failed, there was always someone there to pick you up. I was happy for everybody."[24] Jimmie Hall's observation was more succinct, "We're together and we're winning."[25]

Mele continued using Fosnow regularly. Catcher Earl Battey appreciated his ability, telling him he was the most difficult pitcher of the Twins to catch because of how his pitches moved. Fosnow threw a pitch described as a "heavy ball," a fastball that as it neared the plate dropped several inches. He became more effective as the season progressed.

On July 4 the Twins and Cleveland were tied for the American League lead. The next day Minnesota took sole possession of first place, sweeping a doubleheader from Boston as Cleveland lost to Chicago. Less than a week later the Twins had opened their lead over the Indians to four games as they hosted the Yankees. New York was 13½ games behind as the last game before the All-Star break took place. Despite their substandard record, many still felt the Yankees a viable contender, fully capable of making a run for the pennant.

The July 11 game went into the last inning tied 4-4. Two Twins errors contributed to the tie, offsetting a home run by Versalles. Mele called Fosnow in to hold New York. With two outs and Yankees at first and third, Roger Repoz hit a high bouncing ball down the first-base line. Running down the baseline, he made contact with Fosnow as the ball dropped to the ground. Repoz was called out for interfering with Fosnow, apparently ending New York's scoring opportunity. But Yankees manager Johnny Keane protested the call, contending Fosnow had possession of the ball but dropped it, thus negating the interference call. The umpires reversed their call. Repoz was safe at first and a Yankee runner scored, giving them a 5-4 lead. Mele argued but could not get the umpires to go back to their original call. He notified the umpires he was playing the game under protest.

Lurking in the back of everyone's mind was that this was the sort of break the Yankees had been capitalizing on over the years, the type that opened the gates for them to get back in the race. Keane brought Pete Mikkelsen in to save the game. With two outs and a runner on first, Killebrew slammed a 3-and-2 fastball over the left-field fence to turn what would have been a disheartening loss into a rousing victory. The win erased the last vestige of hope New York had for a comeback and essentially determined that this was to be Minnesota's year. The victory was Fosnow's third of the season—and his last in the majors.

Sometime before pitching against New York, Fosnow had hurt his arm. He told the writer it happened in Kansas City a week earlier. He woke up the morning after pitching against the Athletics feeling as if a knife had been stuck into his arm.

After the All-Star break, Fosnow was called in to relieve Jim Grant, who being pummeled in the first inning by the Royals. Fosnow didn't do much better, giving up three runs in 1⅓ innings before leaving the game. It proved to be Fosnow's last major-league appearance. With his arm rendering him ineffective, Minnesota had no choice but to replace him on the roster. He was optioned to Denver and replaced by Garry Roggenburk. In 36 major-league games, all in relief, Fosnow had a record of 3-4 with two saves and a 5.65 ERA.

Fosnow's arm miseries did not go away. He went 3-3 with a 5.14 ERA in Denver while watching from afar as Minnesota took the pennant by seven games over the White Sox, then lost the World Series to the Dodgers in seven games. Several weeks after the Series ended, Fosnow got a check for $4,422.90, two-thirds of a Twins player's share of the World Series revenue.[26]

When Fosnow was hurt, pitchers faced the stark choice of "pitching through" their ailment, resting with hope that the pain might disappear, retiring, or trying a new method of treatment, cortisone shots. (Sandy Koufax's career was extended in part because of cortisone.) After the season Fosnow saw a physician who took x-rays and determined that he had not torn any muscles, but had pulled a tendon. The physician recommended cortisone injections. Fosnow agreed. The doctor admonished him to refrain from throwing for 24 hours after the procedure. The treatment worked; he was pain-free.

Invited to spring training in 1966, Fosnow pitched well in exhibition games; however, he was dropped when the Twins made their final cuts.[27] Fosnow's name came up in a potential trade that would have sent him to Boston in exchange for catcher Bob Tillman. Mele advised Calvin Griffith to make the transaction if possible, but it never came about.[28] Optioned to the Charlotte Hornets in the Southern League, Fosnow went 5-9 for the sixth-place club. He struck out 93 batters in 98 innings, the best strikeout rate of his professional career.

Fosnow was invited to spring training in 1967, only to be optioned out again. Convinced he was not going anywhere with the Twins organization, he asked for an opportunity elsewhere. The Twins obliged and Fosnow joined the Spokane Indians for the 1967 season. He pitched well, posting a 4-1 record with a 2.51 ERA as Spokane won the western division championship. Manager Roy Hartsfield, in his end-of-season report, acknowledged Fosnow's solid work, but concluded that he was no longer major-league material.[29] Furious with Hartsfield, Fosnow sought out the advice of his friend Tommy Lasorda, then managing the Ogden Dodgers in the Pioneer League. Lasorda, a realist, essentially told Fosnow there were not many options available to him.

When Fosnow was with the Twins, he became acquainted with several officials of Gulf Oil who were fans. Several times he left tickets for them to attend games when the Twins played the White Sox at Comiskey Park. His new friends advised him to look them up should he need a job after his baseball career ended.

Fosnow, 27 years old with a family and only a high-school education, decided it was time to get out of baseball, and called to see if the offer still held. An interview a few days later consisted entirely of a discussion about baseball. His interviewer eventually told him there was an opening in Anderson, Indiana, with Gulf in marketing. Fosnow took the job and began a long association with Gulf and later Chevron, which took over Gulf. He was employed at various locations in the Northwest. Later he joined American Personnel Services supervising the advertising, buying, and merchandising for more than 100 stores. Eventually he moved to Florida, where he retired.

As of 2014, Fosnow and his wife, Diane, lived in DeBary, Florida. Their marriage was the second for both; there are. three children and four grandchildren.

Fosnow gives time to the MLB Alumni Association, participating in clinics it runs for young players, offering tips on how to play the game and advice on how to conduct themselves off the field.[30]

In *The Cool of the Evening*, Jim Thielman described how the 1965 Twins kept in contact with one another over the years the way a close-knit high-school class might. Celebrity golf tournaments, local events, and travel plans were coordinated to get together. Fosnow eagerly joined in. Ticking off a list of how several teammates were doing, he specifically described keeping in touch with Jim Grant on a regular basis. As teammate Frank Kostro said, "You just cannot believe how these friendships were such a genuine part of the deal.[31]

Summing up, the farmer's son who wanted to pitch ever since he could remember did fairly well. He made the major leagues and pitched on a pennant-winning team. If you doubt it, just ask Jerry Fosnow. He'll show you his ring for being a member of the 1965 American League champions.

NOTES

1 Phone interview with Jerry Fosnow, May 18, 2014 (hereafter cited as Fosnow interview).

2 "Minor League Highlights: Alabama-Florida League," *The Sporting News*, May 27, 1959, 38.

3 Minor League Highlights: Alabama-Florida League, *The Sporting News*, June 24, 1959, 38.

4 Bob Vanderberg, *Frantic Frank Lane, Baseball's Ultimate Wheeler-Dealer*, (Jefferson, North Carolina: McFarland & Company, Inc., Publishers, 2013), 83, 90-91.

5 Unless otherwise noted, all records are from baseball-reference.com/ or retrosheet.org/.

6 J.G. Taylor Spink, ed., in collaboration with Paul Rickart and Cliff Kachline, *1960 Baseball Guide* (St. Louis: The Sporting News, 1960), 316.

7 "Indian Farmhand at Selma Posts Gem in Playoff Game," *The Sporting News*, September 2, 1959, 39.

8 Fosnow interview; Baseball Reference.com.

9 Max Nichols, "Ex-High School Pals Fosnow, Reese Together as Twins," unidentified publication dated April 24, 1965, in Fosnow's file at the Baseball Hall of Fame, Cooperstown, New York.

10 "International Items," *The Sporting News*, July 4, 1964, 36.

11 Jim Thielman, *Cool of the Evening: The 1965 Minnesota Twins*, (Minneapolis: Karl House Publishers, 2005), 110-111; "Rest Cure Working Wonders—Killer Goes on Homer Rampage, *The Sporting News*, June 13, 1964, 11.

12 Fosnow interview.

13 Ancestry.com.

14 Max Nichols, "Ex-High School Pals."

15 "Torrid Boswell Temper Chilled By 5-Day Ban," *The Sporting News*, November 14, 1964, 26; "Crabbers Tip Their Caps to Hurler Talbot," *The Sporting News*, December 19, 1964, 27.

16 "Twin Hurlers Salute Sain—Master Tutor," *The Sporting News*, March 13, 1964, 25.

17 Max Nichols, "Eight Rookies to Dot Twin Roster," unidentified, undated publication I Fosnow's Hall of Fame file.

18 "Yanks, Phils Picked by Writers, Fans," *The Sporting News*, April 17, 1965, 1.

19 Thielman, 2-3.

20 Ibid, 75.

21 "Injury Wave Claims Five Twins In First Two Games of Campaign," *The Sporting News*, May 1, 1963, 18.

22 Thielman, 74.

23 Fosnow interview.

24 Thielman, 215.

25 Thielman, 116.

26 "Dodgers' Series Slice: $10,297 each," *Chicago Tribune*, October 28, 1965, E1.

27 "Great Cesar's Ghost, Twins Find Zoilo's Sub in Wraith-Like Sub," *The Sporting News*, April 16, 1966, 22.

28 "Red Sox Seek Twins Fosnow," *Boston Globe*, February 1, 1966, 17.

29 Fosnow interview.

30 Fosnow interview.

31 Thielman, 239.

Mudcat Grant

BY JOSEPH WANCHO

THE 1965 WORLD SERIES MOVED to Metropolitan Stadium for Game Six. The Los Angeles Dodgers were holding a 3-2 series lead, and Walter Alston's crew was looking to close out the Twins. Standing in the way of the championship was Minnesota ace Jim "Mudcat" Grant. Claude Osteen took the hill for the Dodgers. Grant, who had been suffering from a cold for weeks, was pitching on two days' rest and felt much older than his 30 years. If there was any question about Grant's ability while under the weather and working on short rest, those doubts were answered rather quickly, as Grant faced the minimum through four innings.

With the Twins leading 2-0 in the bottom of the sixth, second baseman Frank Quilici was intentionally walked to bring Mudcat to the plate. Grant drilled a home run to left-center to give the Twins a 5-0 lead. He became just the second American League pitcher to hit a home run in a World Series. Mudcat forced a Game Seven by beating the Dodgers with his pitching and hitting. He went the distance, giving up one run on six hits, striking out five batters and walking none. "I really didn't know how long I would go," said Grant. "I just figured I'd go as long as I could for as hard as I could."[1] Mudcat got the Twins to the seventh game, but they fell short against Sandy Koufax, 2-0.

James Timothy Grant was born on August 13, 1935, in Lacoochee, Florida. Lacoochee, then a lumber town, is about 40 miles north of Tampa. He was one of seven children born to James and Viola Grant. Like many of the residents of Lacoochee, James Grant, Sr. worked at the lumber mill, but he died when Mudcat was 2 and the responsibility fell to Viola to provide for the family. She worked during the day at a citrus canning factory and took in domestic work as well.

Jim was a three-sport star (football, basketball, baseball) at Moore Academy in Dade City, Florida. He also competed on the semipro sandlots for the Lacoochee Nine Devils. Grant was mostly stationed at third base in those days because he had such a strong arm. He earned an athletic scholarship to Florida A&M University to play football and baseball.

Grant left Florida A&M during his sophomore year because of financial constraints on his family. He sought work to help out at home, saying, "Somebody had to start earning money and sacrifice."[2]

Grant relocated to New Smyrna Beach, Florida, and found work as a carpenter's helper while he lived with relatives. It was the keen eye of Cleveland Indians bird-dog scout Fred Merkle that started Grant on his way to life as a professional baseball player. Merkle worked the State Negro Baseball Tournament at Daytona Beach when Grant was a senior in high

Mudcat Grant led the AL with 21 victories and six shutouts in 1965. The combative righty fashioned a 145-119 record and logged 2,442 innings in a 14-year big-league career (1958-1971). (Photo courtesy of Minnesota Twins Baseball Club).

school, but Grant was only 17, too young to sign a contract. When Merkle heard that Grant had left Florida A&M, he tracked Mudcat down in Daytona Beach to sign him up with Cleveland.

The Indians held their minor-league camp in Daytona Beach and offered Grant a tryout. It was here that his moniker was bestowed upon him. "A guy named Leroy Bartow Irby saw me, decided I was from Mississippi and called me 'Mudcat,'" recalled Grant. "I didn't know him very well, and I didn't pay attention to what he called me. The old Yankee pitcher Red Ruffing was the coach in charge of making the minor-league assignments. He read off names and the fields where the players were to report. The first day I heard him say 'Mudcat Grant, field number two.' I thought there was another Grant in camp, that I would be the last one standing there. I wouldn't hear my name so I would just float around the different diamonds."[3]

Grant straightened out the name confusion, but he would forever be known as Mudcat, a nickname that he came to embrace. He left Florida for the first time in his life, traveling to North Dakota to pitch for Cleveland's Class C affiliate, Fargo-Moorhead of the Northern League. There were many cultural differences between Lacoochee and Fargo, most notably an absence of blacks living in Fargo. Although Fargo was not the segregated South, Grant still found racial bias.

But he didn't let his new surroundings affect his pitching ability. After losing his first game of the season, Grant won 12 in a row. He was the league's Rookie Pitcher of the Year, completing the season with a record of 21-5 and an ERA of 3.40. After a brilliant season at Class B Keokuk (Iowa) of the Three I (Illinois-Indiana-Iowa) League in 1955, he landed at Reading of the Class A Eastern League, where he endured his first losing season in pro ball (12-13). That winter Grant played winter ball for the Willard Blues of the Colombian League, where he was voted unanimously as Player of the Year. His record was 9-7 including a no-hitter against Vanytor. Manager Don Heffner also played Grant at second base and the outfield between his starting assignments. Mudcat hit nine home runs to finish second in the league.

Grant was assigned to San Diego of the Pacific Coast League in 1957 and went 18-7 with a spectacular ERA of 2.32 and 178 strikeouts. "I've never seen a young pitcher come along as fast as he has," said San Diego general manager Ralph Kiner. "He wants to learn and is willing to take advice. That is a big point in his favor." Mudcat directed the credit to Padres pitching coach Vic Lombardi. "When I joined the Padres, Vic Lombardi took me in hand and taught me a lot," he said. "When I make a mistake out there on the mound, Vic tells me so I won't repeat it."

Grant reached the major leagues with the Indians at the start of the 1958 season. Larry Doby was reacquired during the offseason from Baltimore, giving Grant an older black player to lean on, and Doby took him under his wing. "You figured because you made the majors, you now were on equal terms with the other guys. But that wasn't the case," said Grant.[4] He started the third game of the year, winning his debut 3-2 over Kansas City. He went the distance, striking out five batters. He won two of his next three starts, sporting a 3-0 record with a 1.85 ERA, but leveled off and finished the year at 10-11. He struck out 111 batters, but walked 104. Grant's lack of control would be a burden during his early years in Cleveland. After Joe Gordon took over as manager when Bobby Bragan was fired, Grant spent as much time relieving as starting. Cleveland finished in fourth place with a record of 77-76, closing out the year winning 13 of its final 18 contests.

Spurred on by such a strong finish, Indians fans greeted the 1959 season with high hopes. The Indians finished second in the AL behind the Go-Go White Sox, and Mudcat finished the year at 10-7 with an ERA of 4.14. Six of his 10 wins came against the Senators (he won all six decisions against Washington and was 11-0 all-time at Griffith Stadium), but he started less frequently than he did in 1958.

The next season was one to forget for Grant. For the second year in a row, he took the hill for 19 starts in 1969, posting a 9-8 record with a 4.40 ERA. He walked 78 batters and struck out 75. On September 5 Grant started in Detroit, pitched seven innings and struck out 10, but lost, 4-3. It was his career high for punchouts; he equaled it three more times.

The 1960 season ended early for Grant, and with a loud thud, the result of an ugly incident. On September 16 the Indians were at home getting ready to play the Kansas City Athletics. Before the game, as the National Anthem was being played, Grant got into an argument with bullpen coach (and Texas resident) Ted Wilks. "I was standing in the bullpen, singing along with the National Anthem as I always do," Mudcat said. "When it got to that part 'home of the brave and land of the free' I sang something like 'this land is not so free. I can't even go to Mississippi.' It was something like that and I sang it in fun. Wilks heard me and called me a (racial) name. I got so mad I couldn't hold myself back. I told him that Texas is worse than Russia. Then I walked straight into the clubhouse."[5]

Grant dressed and left the park without telling manager Jimmy Dykes, who had no idea what had happened. Dykes suspended Grant for the rest of the season without pay, which Grant accepted. "Jim called me after the game and told me he had made a big mistake," said Dykes. "I said, 'Yes you did and there's nothing I can do about it now. The suspension sticks.'" Wilks apologized for his remarks, which Grant refused to acknowledge. "I'm sick of hearing remarks about colored people. I don't have to stand there and take it," said Grant.[6] Wilks left the organization after the season.

With Dykes in charge, Grant finally found some stability in his career in 1961. Rather than shuttling him between the starting rotation and the bullpen, Dykes used Grant exclusively as a starter. Mudcat started 35 games and responded with his best season to date, leading the team in wins (15), complete games (11), innings pitched (244⅔), and shutouts (3), and was second in strikeouts (146). He won six straight starts from May 15 to June 7. "I figured this was my fourth year with the team and if I was going to have a good season, this should be it," he said. "When did I realize that I had won a steady job? I still haven't come to the point of saying to myself 'I'm a starting pitcher.' We fellows who are starting now can take nothing for granted. Some of those fellows in the bullpen can replace us."[7]

"Grant is an entirely different pitcher now," said his former manager, Joe Gordon, who managed Kansas City in 1961. "He concentrates on every pitch. He had to grow up. But not everybody grows up as fast as Mud did. Some of them have to reach 27 or so. What's Grant, 25?"[8]

Just when things were going Grant's way, he was told to report to active duty in the US Army on November 2, 1961. Grant reported for a year of duty at Fort Belvoir, Virginia, where he pitched for and managed the base's team. Grant was able to pitch on weekends with the Indians. He received a 30-day furlough and beat the Yankees, 7-1, on May 11, but developed a sore arm during that period. Grant was discharged from the Army early and rejoined the Indians for good in mid-July. He managed two 10-strikeout efforts in September, one a loss to Baltimore, the other a win against Los Angeles. He finished the season with a 7-10 record and a 4.27 ERA.

For the Indians, 1963 was a long season as they finished in fourth place, 25½ games behind New York. Mudcat finished with a record of 13-14 and an ERA of 3.69. He achieved his career high in strikeouts with 157, walked 87 and pitched 10 complete games.

For several offseasons, Grant had worked in the Indians ticket office. Now he was part of the Community Relations team, and he was in demand to speak at churches, businesses, and colleges. He made more than 100 public appearances in the offseason between 1963 and '64. He also started a nightclub act, "Mudcat and the Kittens." Grant, who was an accomplished singer with a voice he described as "somewhere between a baritone and a tenor," fronted the group, which played in jazz clubs all over Cleveland and once appeared on *The Tonight Show* with Johnny Carson.

A bright spot for Jim and his wife, Lucile, known by most as Tiny, was the birth of their first son, James Timothy III. They later adopted another son, Rusty.

Jim "Mudcat" Grant (Photo courtesy of Minnesota Twins Baseball Club).

After getting got off to a rocky start in 1964, Grant found himself shipped to Minnesota for pitcher Lee Stange and infielder George Banks on June 15. "I'm sure this trade will help both ballclubs," said Minnesota manager Sam Mele. "Grant is a good all-around man and we'll use him as a starter. He's been having his troubles and we hope he can straighten himself out."[9] Turn it around he did. With the Twins, Mudcat posted a record of 11-9 with a 2.82 ERA. He struck out more than twice as many as he walked and threw 10 complete games. He started July on a four-game winning streak, lowering his ERA from 3.86 to 2.62. The Indians and Twins finished the year with identical 79-83 records, 20 games off the pace.

In 1965 the Twins were embarking on their fifth season since relocating from Washington, and everything came together for them as they made their first appearance in the World Series. Trailing Cleveland by a half-game on June 30, the Twins went on a 22-9 run in July and never looked back, finishing with a record of 102-60, seven games ahead of Chicago.

Grant enjoyed his best season in the majors. His name was all over the AL statistical leader board at the end of the season as he led the league in wins (21) and shutouts (six), was second in complete games (14), and third in innings pitched (270⅓). He pitched in the All-Star Game on July 13 at Metropolitan Stadium. (Grant was on the 1963 squad but didn't pitch.) The only downside was that Grant led the league with 34 home runs allowed. He was the leader of a pennant-winning staff in which no starter had an ERA over 3.50 (Grant 21-7, 3.30 ERA, Jim Kaat 18-11, 2.83, Jim Perry 12-7, 2.63, Camilo Pascual 9-3, 3.35). Mudcat was named *The Sporting News* American League Pitcher of the Year, and was the first black pitcher in the American League to win 20 games in a season, as well as the first black AL pitcher to win a game in the World Series.

What was the cause of Mudcat's fine season? He claimed that he was the same pitcher in Minnesota as he had been in Cleveland, except that the Twins had the potential to score more runs to back him. But Mudcat also was quick to give credit to his new pitching coach, Johnny Sain. Sain, a great pitcher with the Boston Braves, taught Grant a new pitch. "It's a fast curve," said Grant. "Johnny Sain is teaching it to several of the guys. I've never had a real good fast curve before. I've always had a good fastball, a change of pace and a slow curve. They said I needed to change speeds. I've always been able to change off my fastball, throw a straight slow ball up there. But until this year, I never thought in terms of spinning the ball. That's where Sain helped me." Grant's former batterymate in Cleveland, John Romano, noticed the difference, saying, "This isn't the same Grant that I used to catch. He never had a curve when I caught him."[10]

In 1966 the Twins were enthusiastic as they reported to spring training at Tinker Field in Orlando. Grant initially held out for a bigger contract, but eventually signed and reported to camp. He started the season poorly, posting a 5-12 record at the All-Star break with an ERA of 3.28. "Last year I pitched well enough in tough games until the late innings," Mudcat said. "Then a lot of times our guys would come along and score. This year I've been pitching well until late innings and losing. I haven't pitched as bad as my 5-12 record in the first half indicated. But maybe I can make it better by pitching better. I'm going to try."[11]

After meeting with Mele and Sain at the break, Grant did turn himself around, going 8-1 the rest of the way. Despite his turnaround and Kaat's 25 wins, the Twins could not catch Baltimore for the pennant. Kaat, who won the Gold Glove for a fifth time, said, "I've always had the reputation as a good fielder, but I think it's a lot of publicity. I got a couple of Gold Glove Awards as the best-fielding pitcher in the major leagues, but in my mind, the award should go to Mudcat Grant, who is a much better fielder then I am."[12]

It should have been an omen to Grant when he started the 1967 season on the shelf. He was struck in the forearm during the last week of spring training, and missed the first two weeks of the season. Mele had fired Sain at the end of the 1966 season, and he himself was let go when the Twins got out of the gate playing at .500. Cal Ermer, who was the skipper at Triple-A Denver, took over the reins. Many of the current Twins had come through the minors under Ermer's watch and supported the change. Due in part to injury, Grant made only 14 starts, and did much of his work out of the pen. He finished with a 5-6 record and a 4.72 ERA. The Twins narrowly lost the pennant in a final-weekend showdown with the Red Sox.

Because of Ermer's erratic use of Grant and his injuries, Grant was looking for a fresh start and an exit from Minnesota. He got his wish when he and shortstop Zoilo Versalles were shipped to Los Angeles for catcher John Roseboro and pitchers Ron Perranoski and Bob Miller. Grant was elated to be joining the Dodgers. "During last season I felt so terrible, I couldn't be happy," remarked the right-hander. "It was a problem between the Minnesota manager and management and myself. Some of it was racial, too. They made me feel as though I wasn't even a man. I'd pitched only 95 innings and it isn't because of my knees, either. I have lived with the knee trouble for years. But I told them I couldn't remain with them and wanted to be traded."[13] Dodgers manager Walter Alston used Grant out of the bullpen. Indeed, he made only four starts in 37 appearances, going 6-4 with a 2.08 ERA. "I tell you, he's working his tail off for us," said Alston.[14]

Before the 1969 season, Grant was selected by the Montreal Expos in the expansion draft. He made 10 starts with a record of 1-6 before being dealt to St. Louis for pitcher Gary Waslewski on June 3. Pitching in long relief, Grant went 7-5 for the Cardinals. At the end of the year, St. Louis sold Grant to Oakland. Pitching exclusively out of the bullpen, the 34-year-old Grant showed he had plenty left in the tank as he had 24 saves, a 6-2 record, and a sparkling 1.83 ERA. From May 17 to June 16, Grant pitched 28 innings and allowed one earned run, lowering his ERA to a minuscule 0.79. Oakland sold Grant to Pittsburgh in mid-September. He pitched in eight games, all in relief, for the Pirates.

The 1971 season was Grant's last. He started the season in Pittsburgh but was sold back to Oakland on August 10. He saved 10 games for the two teams. Grant appeared in the League Championship Series against Baltimore and pitched two scoreless innings in Game Three. Released after the season, he was unable to make the Indians out of spring training in 1972 and pitched in 49 games with the Iowa Oaks of the American Association before retiring.

In retirement, Grant tried his hand at many jobs in and out of baseball. He worked in the Indians community relations office and was the analyst on Indians TV broadcasts. He later worked on broadcasts for the Athletics. At the request of Hank Aaron, the Atlanta Braves' director of player personnel, Grant was a pitching coach for the Durham Bulls of the Class A Carolina League in the mid-1980s.

Grant later worked for an Anheuser-Busch distributor and for Nationwide Advertising in Cleveland, and was the spokesman for many sponsors. He wrote a book in 2005 called *The 12 Black Aces*, which detailed the lives of 12 black major-league pitchers who had won 20 games in a season.

Grant moved to Los Angeles, where he became a community activist and public speaker. As the number of black players has dwindled in the major leagues, Grant worked to counter the downward trend. Part of the problem, he said, is that former major leaguers need to take the responsibility to spread the word about baseball. "We just gotta motivate them to play and we've got to be around," Grant said in 2008. "We haven't been around enough. Now, part of that is the African-American ex-players' fault, too, because we haven't been there. Even though we see tons of children, we haven't been in the inner city like we should."[15] Grant may have had something to do with that very issue right within his own family. His nephew, Domonic Brown, was drafted by the Phillies in the 20th round in 2006 and made his big-league debut in 2010 for the Phillies.

SOURCES

Pluto, Terry, *The Curse of Rocky Colavito* (New York: Simon and Schuster, 1994).

Thielman, Jim, *The Cool of the Evening* (Minneapolis: Kirk House Publishing, 2005).

The Sporting News

Sports Illustrated

Baseball Digest

National Baseball Hall of Fame Archives

minors.sabrwebs.com/cgi-bin/index.php

retrosheet.org

sabr.org

NOTES

1 Article, publication unknown, in Grant's file at the Baseball Hall of Fame Library, Cooperstown, New York.
2 Ibid.
3 Terry Pluto, *The Curse of Rocky Colavito*, 66-67.
4 Pluto, 68.
5 *Cleveland Plain Dealer*, September 18, 1960
6 Ibid.
7 *Baseball Digest*, August 1961, 5-7.
8 Ibid.
9 *Cleveland Plain Dealer*, June 16, 1964.
10 Jim Thielman, *The Cool of the Evening*, 55.
11 *The Sporting News*, July 30, 1965, 9.
12 *The Sporting News*, October 23, 1966, 14.
13 *Los Angeles Times*, March 9, 1968.
14 *Sports Illustrated*, April 28, 1968.
15 *Cleveland Plain Dealer*, April 15, 2008.

Killebrew Belts Two Homers, Including Game-Winner In Eighth Inning

May 12, 1965: Minnesota Twins 4, Los Angeles Angels 3 at Metropolitan Stadium, Bloomington, Minnesota

BY GREGORY H. WOLF

WHEN THE MINNESOTA TWINS headed to Metropolitan Stadium to play the Los Angeles Angels on Wednesday, May 12, they had reason to be excited. The previous night, in the first contest of a three-game set with the visitors from Southern California, the Twins won in exciting fashion. With one out in the bottom of the ninth inning and the score tied 2-2, slugging first baseman Harmon Killebrew sent a bullet back to the mound that ricocheted off the leg of Angels starter Dean Chance into center field. His walk-off hit drove in Tony Oliva and gave the Twins their fourth consecutive win. More importantly, manager Sam Mele's squad improved its record to 15-7, one game in front of the Chicago White Sox and 1½ games ahead of the Angels.

Despite the loss, the Los Angeles Angels (the club officially changed its name to the California Angels on September 2, 1965, in anticipation of its move into the newly constructed Anaheim Stadium) had been playing their best ball of the season. After a slow start, they had won 11 of 15 games for skipper Bill Rigney, who had guided the club since its admission to the AL during the expansion year of 1961.

A sparse crowd of 10,711 showed up on a beautiful, 64-degree evening at Metropolitan Stadium, located in Bloomington, about 11 miles due south of downtown Minneapolis. The Twins' faithful were treated to another exciting come-from-behind victory.

The game got under way when Jim "Mudcat" Grant took the mound. The hard-throwing 29-year-old right-hander had thrived since the Twins acquired him from the Cleveland Indians the previous season at the trading deadline, winning 14 of 23 decisions, including a clean 3-0 slate in '65. The Angels' light-hitting right fielder and former Rookie of the Year Award winner (1958), Albie Pearson, put LA on the board first against Grant with a home run in the first inning. Grant struggled with the gopher ball in 1965, surrendering a league-high 34; however, he still managed to lead the circuit in wins (21) and shutouts (6). The Angels increased their lead to 2-0 in the third inning on Jose

Over a 12-year stretch (1959-1970) Harmon Killebrew averaged 40 homers and 103 RBIs per season. (National Baseball Hall of Fame, Cooperstown, New York).

Cardenal's sacrifice fly which scored Bobby Knoop, who had doubled and stolen third.

The Twins' home-run-bashing offense (they led the AL with 221 round-trippers in 1964) did not intimidate the Angels' 20-year-old rookie southpaw, Rudy May, making just his fifth career start. A hard thrower who suffered from control problems, May had whiffed 10 in his major-league debut just about three weeks earlier, and sported an impressive 2-1 record and a 1.73 ERA. He retired the first seven batters he faced before yielding a walk and two singles, including one off the bat of second baseman Jerry Kindall that drove in catcher Jerry Zimmerman for the Twins' first run.

The Angels maintained a 2-1 lead until the sixth inning, when first baseman Joe Adcock lined a two-out single to left field, scoring Cardenal. Still an offensive threat despite his bum knees, the 37-year-old Adcock had led the Angels in round-trippers with the 21 the previous year (even though he played home games in a pitcher's paradise, Dodger Stadium) and became just the 23rd big leaguer to hit 300 home runs. Killebrew blasted a home run, his fourth of the season, in the bottom of the sixth to pull Minnesota back to within one. The "Killer's" smash was music to the Twins' ears. The 28-year-old slugger had clouted 48, 45, and 49 home runs in the three prior seasons to lead the AL in that department each year. However, he had an unexpected power outage to start the 1965 season, going homerless in his first 12 games. "When Harmon Killebrew's bulging forearms snapped his bat through the strike zone and made full contact," wrote the *Star-Tribune* years later, "there was nothing else like it in baseball."[1] Standing just 5-feet-11, Killebrew generated his power from a short, compact swing.

The Twins entered the bottom of the eighth inning trailing 3-2. Pinch-hitter Frank Kostro drew a one-out walk from reliever Bob Lee, who had taken over from May to start the seventh. Lee was no slouch; as a rookie in 1964, the hard-throwing righty posted a 1.51 ERA in 137 innings. He went on to earn a berth on the AL All-Star team in 1965, and posted similar numbers (1.92 ERA in 131 innings). Lee registered the second out by striking out Oliva, who had led the AL in batting as a rookie the previous season with a .323 average but had been mired in a slump thus far in 1965, entering the game batting only .267. Next up was Killebrew, who lived for these situations. The stocky Idahoan with a rapidly receding hairline launched an estimated 450-foot blast that cleared the center-field fence and gave the Twins the lead, 4-3. "That was no pop-gun Harmon Killebrew used on the Angels," wrote Dick Couch of the AP.[2]

Righty Al "Red" Worthington, a 36-year-old journeyman, relieved Grant to start the eighth inning and held the Angels scoreless in the final two frames to pick up the victory. The game, which was finished in 2 hours and 15 minutes, was typical for the mid-1960s — good pitching and low scoring. Each team managed just seven hits, three of which were home runs. There were no double plays and no errors.

The Twins are "going like gangbusters," wrote George C. Langford of UPI.[3] Minnesota won its fifth consecutive game, but the club's lead in the standings shrank by a half-game in light of the Chicago White Sox' doubleheader sweep of the Kansas City A's.

SOURCES

BaseballReference.com

Retrosheet.org

SABR.org

NOTES

1 La Velle E. Neal, III, "Killebrew was 'Paul Bunyan with a uniform on,'" (Minneapolis) *StarTribune*, May 18, 2011. startribune.com/sports/twins/122004519.html.

2 Dick Couch, Associated Press, "Killebrew Swings Hot Bat for Twins," *The Daily Reporter* (Dover, Ohio), May 13, 1965, 19.

3 George C. Langford, United Press International, "Killebrew's Muscle Returns to Form; Bosox Keep Yanks Sinking," *The Daily Register* (Harrisburg, Illinois), May 13, 1965, 14.

Jimmie Hall

BY NORM KING

IT'S AN OLD STORY. A PLAYER COMES on the scene, dazzles in his rookie year, and is gone seemingly as fast as he came. Then there's Jimmie Hall.

Hall burst on the scene with a bang with the Minnesota Twins in 1963. Actually, he had 33 of them, which broke Ted Williams's AL record for home runs by a first-year player who had never batted in his rookie year. Yes, THAT Ted Williams! But after five seasons that ranged from respectable to excellent, Hall hit seven home runs in his last three campaigns, and then disappeared from the game.

Hall was born on March 17, 1938, in Mount Holly, North Carolina to James R. and Velma (Williamson) Hall. He was one of 11 children, three of whom died in childhood. His father was a farmer and his mother a housekeeper.

As a youngster Hall batted .564 in his senior year at Belmont High School in Belmont, North Carolina. His father advised him not to imitate anyone else's batting style but to develop his own. James (Jimmie's legal name is Jimmie, not James Jr.) also persuaded his son to stay with baseball instead of working in a cotton mill.

"In my last year of high school, I wanted to go work in the cotton mill or a service station," said Hall. "I wanted to make money to buy a car like most kids. But dad wanted me to play [American] Legion ball."[1]

That extra playing time led to a minor bidding war among the Cleveland Indians, Pittsburgh Pirates, New York Yankees, Chicago Cubs, Baltimore Orioles, and Washington Senators. Senators scout Chick Suggs signed Hall for $4,000 in 1956, although the club was much more impressed with his hitting capabilities than his fielding.

"The only thing they liked about him was that whiplash batting stroke he could generate with his skinny 175 pounds," wrote Shirley Povich. "He butchered every infield job they tried him at."[2]

The 18-year-old Hall began a long, circuitous journey to the majors that was interrupted by injury, illness, and military service. His first stop was with the Superior Senators of the Class D Nebraska State League as a second baseman. He showed some of the batting stroke that he displayed more consistently later on, hitting .385 with 15 home runs in only 226 at-bats.

Those numbers impressed the Senators enough for them to bump Hall up two levels to Class B for 1957 with the Kinston Eagles of the Carolina League, which moved to Wilson, North Carolina, early in the season and were renamed the Tobs.[3] By Hall's own admission,

Centerfielder Jimmie Hall burst on the scene by walloping a career-high 33 homers as a rookie in 1963. In 1965 he smashed 20 round-trippers and set career highs in RBIs (86), batting average (.285). (Photo courtesy of Minnesota Twins Baseball Club).

that move proved a bit hasty as his offensive numbers showed he wasn't ready to face the pitching at that level. In 128 games he batted only .233 and hit just six home runs in 404 at-bats. He also was adjusting to a new position. He was originally signed as a second baseman, but because Wilson was short on outfielders, Hall volunteered to go out there so he could get some playing time.

"I was a year out of high school. The [Washington] Senators were hard up for players, and they sent me here," said Hall when visiting Wilson in 2005. "The Carolina League was good baseball. I was so overmatched. I was fighting for my life all summer."[4]

Although he was "overmatched," as he put it, Hall began the 1958 season with a promotion to the Charlotte Hornets of the Class A South Atlantic League. He played in only nine games there before he required a tonsillectomy. After he recovered the Senators sent him to the Fox City Foxes of the Class B Illinois-Indiana-Iowa (Three-I) League. He was better equipped to handle Class B pitching this time, as his average rose to .267 with 15 home runs and 38 RBIs in only 255 at-bats.

Despite the limited playing time in Class A, Hall choo-chooed off to the Chattanooga Lookouts of the Double-A Southern Association in 1959, where he played in 133 games, 78 of them at shortstop. He also spent some time at second base and the outfield. At the plate he complemented a .245 batting average with 11 home runs and 57 RBIs. In 1960, Hall played for the Charleston Senators of the Triple-A International League. His numbers weren't overly impressive there either: a .227 average, 9 home runs and 30 RBIs in 336 at-bats.

Hall also married his wife, Judy, in 1960. They went on to have two daughters, Donna and Kimberly, and two sons, Michael and Jeffrey.

None of Hall's totals left the Twins thinking they had a budding star on their hands. Uncle Sam didn't help his case either. In 1961 Hall missed some time due to a hernia operation, after which he did a six-month hitch with the Army, followed by a 10-month stretch as a grunt in 1962. For the two seasons combined (1961 with the International League's Toronto Maple Leafs and Syracuse Chiefs and 1962 with the Triple-A Pacific Coast League's Vancouver Mounties) he had 141 at-bats in 54 games, and batted .234 with three home runs. These numbers were hardly a harbinger for what happened next.

The Minnesota Twins were a team on the rise in 1963. After they went 70-90 in 1961, manager Sam Mele guided them to a 91-71 record in 1962, just five games behind the World Series champion New York Yankees. They were loaded with young, quality players like Jim Kaat, Harmon Killebrew, and Zoilo Versalles. In fact, the 1962 squad was the youngest team in the American League.

Hall faced a rather daunting challenge when he went to the Twins' 1963 spring-training camp. To get a job on the major-league roster, he would have to crack a well-established outfield that had great numbers in 1962. It included Killebrew (an All-Star who had led the league with 48 home runs and 126 RBIs in 1962), Lenny Green (.271 batting average, 14 home runs, and 63 runs batted in), and Bob Allison (who had hit .266 with 29 home runs and 102 RBIs).

"And I read a lot during the winter about Tony Oliva, too," said Hall.[5] "I knew it was going to be tough to stick with the club. But I figured it was now or never."[6]

Two things went Hall's way that spring training. First, he did all he could do, which was hit .293 in 22 exhibition games. Then he got a lucky wrench, er, break, when Killebrew wrenched his left knee, which allowed Hall to make the team, but even then that was a last-minute decision on the part of the Twins. They offered him a contract for the major-league minimum of $6,000 at 11:00 P.M. on the last day of spring-training cuts, just an hour before rosters had to be finalized. He started the season well, hitting a double and triple with four runs scored in seven plate appearances in his first start, an 11-10 win over Los Angeles on April 16. By mid-May, however, Hall was hitting only .167 and Mele soon relegated him to the bench.

That may have been the best thing for Hall, because he started showing signs of improvement when he got the opportunity. He hit his first major-league home run on May 19 in Cleveland. On May 24 his walk-off home run against the Chicago White Sox gave the Twins an 8-6 victory and kept alive a winning streak that eventually reached 10 games. These feats were just a tuneup for the hot streak that began June 1. Between that date and July 15, Hall batted .303 with 8 doubles, 3 triples, 10 homers, and 25 RBIs. As if they needed it, the Twins suddenly had another power bat in their lineup.

The streak continued throughout the summer. Hall hit five homers between June 30 and July 4. He homered in four consecutive games starting July 31 in games against the Red Sox and Kansas City Athletics. He hit 13 dingers in the month of August. All of a sudden he was a home-run hitter. No one was more confounded by the turn of events than Hall himself.

"I feel stronger in the majors," he said. "I've surprised myself. I hit only three in Vancouver in 1962 and all were to dead left field."[7]

A lot of that improvement could be attributed to the time Hall spent in the Florida Instructional League the previous winter. Del Wilber, who was Hall's manager in Charleston, managed the Twins' club in the FIL and spent a lot of time working with Hall. The result was a hitter who learned to spray the ball to all fields, and with power. His final totals were a .260 batting average with 33 home runs and 80 RBIs and a third-place finish in Rookie of the Year voting, behind Gary Peters and Pete Ward, both of the White Sox.

The Twins had a down year in 1964. After two consecutive 91-win seasons, they went 79-83, tied for sixth with Cleveland. No one could blame Hall for the team's decline, as his average shot up to .282, with 25 home runs and 75 RBIs. He played in his first All-Star Game, at Shea Stadium in New York; he didn't bat, but replaced Mickey Mantle in center field in the bottom of the ninth of a 7-4 National League win.

The All-Star Game was just about the only action Hall saw in early July, as he was benched for the first two weeks of the month after a poor performance at the plate in June. The slump came after he was hit in the cheek by a pitch from Bo Belinsky of the Los Angeles Angels on May 27. He was out for only a week, but he lost weight and strength during that time and was slow in getting his timing back. The rest did Hall good, for he soon embarked on a 15-game hitting streak that lifted his average 28 points.

Before the beaning Hall reached a milestone when he hit the major leagues' 75,000th home run since 1900, a solo shot in the second game of a May 3 doubleheader at Kansas City that the Twins lost 8-7.

After the disappointing 1964 season, Twins owner/general manager Calvin Griffith attended the winter meetings intent on making a big trade. And after two days of negotiations he almost made a blockbuster deal with Mets general manager George Weiss—Hall, catcher Earl Battey, pitcher Jim Perry, and either second baseman Bernie Allen or third baseman Rich Rollins in exchange for second baseman Ron Hunt (an All-Star in 1964), catcher Chris Cannizzaro and pitcher Alvin Jackson. Fortunately for the Twins, Weiss ended up nixing the trade. Minnesota went on to win the American League pennant and Griffith was pleased that the Mets deal, as well as another one with the Athletics, had fallen through.

"I can't trade Hall now," he said. "We might get something to help us but it would sure hurt us to give him up."[8]

It turned out to be a career year for Hall; although his home-run total dipped to 20, he set career highs in hits (149), RBIs (86), and stolen bases (14). He played in the 1965 All-Star Game in front of the hometown fans in Bloomington, Minnesota, going 0-for-2 with a walk and a run scored as the American League lost again to the National League, 6-5.

But for all of Griffith's praise and Hall's career-high numbers, he was primarily a spectator as the Twins reached the World Series. Hall, a left-handed hitter,

Jimmie Hall (Photo courtesy of Minnesota Twins Baseball Club).

could not hit left-handed pitching very well (only four of his 121 career home runs came against left-handers), and Mele felt that he would struggle against Dodger left-handers Sandy Koufax and Claude Osteen. Hall appeared in only two games and had one single in seven at-bats with five strikeouts as the Twins lost to the Dodgers in seven games.

The 1966 Twins got off to a rough start and were 38-43 at the halfway point in the season. Mele began platooning Hall in June. He finished the season, and his career with the Twins as it turned out, with a .239 batting average, 20 home runs, and only 47 RBIs.

In December 1966 Griffith pulled off the big trade that he didn't make prior to the 1965 season, sending Hall, pitcher Pete Cimino, and first baseman Don Mincher to the California Angels for 1964 Cy Young Award winner Dean Chance and infielder Jackie Hernandez. Hall's average improved slightly to .249 in California, but with only 16 home runs and 55 RBIs.

While Hall's numbers diminished in 1966 and 1967, they hit rock bottom in the last three years of his career. From 1968 to 1970 he played for the Angels, Indians, Yankees, Cubs, and Braves, hitting a total of seven home runs as a part-time player, with 69 RBIs. The Atlanta Braves released him after the 1970 season. He signed on with the Hawaii Islanders of the Pacific Coast League for 1971 but was released in June after appearing in 21 games with no home runs and only five RBIs.

The cause of Hall's precipitous decline is a mystery. Sportswriter Jim Murray speculated that he never fully recovered from the beaning he suffered in 1964.

"Some lefthanders got the idea Jimmie may have developed an instinct for survival in the rest of his anatomy, too [in addition to his right cheek, which he protected at the plate with an earflap before they were common]," wrote Murray, "and from that day they tend to try a route to the catcher with a curveball that will orbit his right ear on the way."[9]

That explanation isn't likely, as Hall was an All-Star in both 1964 and 1965, and he was still reaching double figures in home runs as late as 1967.

Another possibility mentioned in the BR Bullpen section about Hall in baseball-reference.com was that he, like all other hitters, was victimized by the increasing domination of pitchers in the late 1960s.[10] That is doubtful because Hall's statistics didn't improve even after the pitching mound was lowered from 15 inches to 10 inches in 1969, when Hall was still young enough at 31 to produce solid numbers.

Little is known about Hall's life after his baseball career ended. He returned to Elm City, North Carolina, and made his living as both a woodworker and long-haul truck driver. When he wasn't working, he was an outdoorsman who liked to hunt and fish. He also enjoyed spending time with his children and grandchildren.

Hall stayed away from the game entirely, even refusing to return to Minneapolis in 2005 for a 40th-anniversary reunion of the 1965 team. When he heard that Hall wasn't attending the reunion, former teammate Jim Kaat responded with a remark that perhaps gave insight into why Hall never reached his full potential as a player.

"That sounds like Jimmie," Kaat said. "He was so talented, but the glass always seemed to be half empty for him."[11]

SOURCES

Ancestry.com

St. Petersburg Times

The Pantagraph (Bloomington, Illinois)

Baseball-reference.com

The Sporting News

Urbandictionary.com

Sports Illustrated

Florence (Alabama) *Times*

Milwaukee Sentinel

Cooloftheevening.com

NOTES

1 "Jimmie's Dad, Red-Hot Fan, Gave Son Sound Batting Tip," *The Sporting News*, September 14, 1963.

2 Shirley Povich, "Twins Hope Jimmie Hallmark of Victory," *St. Petersburg Times*, March 19, 1964.

3 Tobs is short for tobacco.

4 " Patrick Reusse, "Keeping his distance; Jimmie Hall was a sweet-swinging outfielder, one of the Twins' early heroes. But he won't be back for a reunion of the 1965 American League champs," *Minneapolis Star-Tribune*, July 17, 2005.

5 Tony Oliva was a hot prospect who went on to a 15-year career with the Twins that included eight All-Star selections.

6 Arno Goethel, "Wasp-Waisted Frosh Hall Ads Big Stinger to Twins' RBI Punch," *The Sporting News*, July 27, 1963.

7 Goethel, "Quiet Rookie Hall Carries Cannon to Plate," *The Sporting News*, September 14, 1963.

8 Murray Chass, "Twins' Jimmie Hall Is On Real Slugging Binge," *Florence* (Alabama) *Times*, July 7, 1965.

9 Jim Murray, "Angels Hope Jimmie Hall Bounces Back," *Milwaukee Sentinel*, March 23, 1967.

10 baseball-reference.com/bullpen/Jimmie_Hall.

11 Reusse.

Jim Kaat

BY PATRICK LETHERT

THE MINDS AND MEMORIES OF casual baseball fans often recall the names and exploits of pitchers who have performed brilliantly during a career peak or even a single shining season. Hall of Fame careers have been built around a few great years in succession and the awards and buzz that accompany these successes. At the other end of the spectrum are those pitchers whose consistency, longevity, and less than perfect timing leave many observers to forget too quickly how effective they were over their careers. Jim Kaat may epitomize the consistent, underappreciated hurler. According to Bill James, Kaat might be a Hall of Famer if only his best years had come closer together.[1]

Jim Kaat was born on November 7, 1938, and grew up in Zeeland, Michigan, a small Dutch community in the western part of the state. His father, Hans, known to locals as John, was a shopkeeper. John Kaat was a baseball fanatic who passed his love of the game and his passion for the Philadelphia Athletics on to his youngest son.[2] Always a good athlete, Jim starred in baseball and basketball in high school, although he would say that he wanted to be a pitcher from the age of 8.[3]

In high school Kaat was small enough to earn the nickname Little Jimmy, but learned early how to retire hitters without throwing hard.[4] By his senior year he was still only 5-feet-10, 170 pounds, and unable to secure an athletic scholarship for college. As a result, he enrolled at Hope College in nearby Holland, Michigan.

After high school, Jim began to grow quickly, ultimately reaching 6-feet-4 and filling out to more than 200 pounds.[5] During his year at Hope, Kaat was invited to work out for the Washington Senators before a game in Chicago. The Senators were impressed and offered him a $4,000 signing bonus. Later, the White Sox offered Kaat $25,000, but Jim's father advised him to turn down the larger offer, which would make him a "bonus baby" and require him to start his career on a major-league roster.[6] He signed with the Senators in June 1957 and spent the summer at Superior in the Class D Nebraska State League. In 1958 Kaat was assigned to the Class B Fox City Foxes, but was convinced by player-manager Jack McKeon to pitch for the Class C Missoula Timberjacks (Pioneer League) instead. McKeon was a catcher and convinced Kaat that he would take a special interest in making him a better pitcher.[7] Kaat had a very strong season in Missoula, going 16-9 with a 2.99 ERA in 223 innings as a 19-year-old lefty. Based on his strong showing, he jumped to the Double-A Chattanooga Lookouts (Southern Association) as a 20-year-old.[8]

Southpaw "Kitty" Kaat won 18 games and led the AL with 42 starts in 1965. A three-time 20-game winner, Kaat compiled a 283-237 record in 25 seasons, and won 16 consecutive Gold Glove Awards (1962-1977), yet as of 2015 was not a member of the Hall of Fame. (Photo courtesy of Minnesota Twins Baseball Club).

Kaat spent most of 1959 pitching for Chattanooga. His 8-8 record as the youngest player on the team earned him three major-league appearances with the Senators that season. His first major-league start was, in a word, inauspicious. On August 2 Kaat started for the last-place Senators in the second game of a road doubleheader against the AL-leading White Sox. Heading into the game, Chicago was riding a five-game winning streak while Washington was enduring a 15-game losing streak. Kaat surrendered just one earned run in 2⅓ innings, but the Senators bullpen allowed six runs to assure that his first decision was a loss.[9] In three appearances that season, Kaat went 0-2 with a 12.60 ERA in just five innings.

In 1960, Kaat moved up to Triple-A Charleston, where he went 7-10 with a 3.82 ERA, again as the youngest member of the pitching staff. He was rewarded with nine major-league starts and four relief appearances, going 1-5 with a 5.58 ERA in 50 innings. His 48 hits allowed was respectable, especially for a 21-year-old, but 31 walks and five hit batters did not help him. Kaat never pitched in the minors again, nor did he pitch again for the Senators, who left Washington to become the Minnesota Twins in 1961.

The 1961 Twins were a promising young team that led the American League through much of April. Kaat began his career in Minnesota with a solid 7⅓-inning win at Boston to get the club to a 5-1 start. The Twins fell to the middle of the pack by the end of May, and a 13-game losing streak dropped them to last place by June 7. They went 51-58 the rest of the way and finished seventh, with Kaat going 9-17, 3.90 in 200⅔ innings as the club's youngest starter.

In June of 1961 the Twins fired manager Cookie Lavagetto and replaced him with Sam Mele, who would lead the young club's ascension to prominence. Jim Kaat was a centerpiece of the 1960s Twins. A big, solid left-hander with bright red hair and outstanding athletic ability, Kaat was one of the fastest workers in the game. Firing each pitch just seconds after getting the ball back from the catcher, he confounded umpires and angered opposing hitters, but kept his defense on its toes.[10]

In 1962 the Twins emerged as one of the best teams in the American League for the next decade. Minnesota registered just two losing seasons from 1962 through 1970 with Kaat winning 146 games during those years. The 1962 Twins finished a strong second with a 91-71 record, just five games behind the Yankees. Kaat was a big part of their emergence, finishing 18-14 with a 3.14 ERA in 269 innings. He was named to his first All-Star Game in 1962 and finished among the league's top 10 pitchers in wins, ERA, WHIP (walks and hits per inning pitched), strikeouts, complete games, and strikeout/walk ratio, and he tied for the league lead with five shutouts while logging more innings than anyone but the Yankees' Ralph Terry. He also earned his first Gold Glove, as writers voted him the best fielding pitcher in the American League.

Kaat's fielding prowess was recognized annually for the next 16 years, the longest streak ever by a pitcher. By his retirement he and third baseman Brooks Robinson were tied as the all-time leaders in Gold Glove awards, each winning 16 in succession. While Hall of Famer Greg Maddux holds the record (as of 2014) for total Gold Gloves during his career (18), Kaat and Robinson remain the all-time leaders in consecutive Gold Gloves.

In 1963 the Twins again won 91 games but finished a distant third in the AL. With 767 runs scored and only 602 allowed, the Twins' 91-70 record was well below what it might have been. For Kaat, 1963 was also a tough year. He started 31 games in 1963, managing only 178⅓ innings, a 10-10 record, and a 4.19 ERA, worst among Twins starters. The next season, 1964, was a season of underachievement for the Twins, who finished 79-83. For Kaat, however, it was a return to form as he went 17-11 with a solid 3.22 ERA in 243 innings.

Heading into 1965, New York had won five consecutive American League pennants and 15 of 18 flags since 1947. But with the Yankees aging, a changing of the guard was inevitable. The Orioles, White Sox, Tigers, and Twins all had reason to believe they might overcome the Yankees. In their difficult 1964 campaign, the Twins had led the American League in runs scored but struggled on the mound and on defense. However, with the bats of Harmon Killebrew, Tony Oliva, and Bob Allison and the arms of Camilo Pascual, Jim "Mudcat" Grant, and Jim Kaat, there was a solid foundation set for a return to contention.

By 1965 Kaat had emerged as one of the faces of the Minnesota franchise. His teammates described him in glowing terms. They heralded him as smart, outgoing, a "wonderful guy," and a natural leader who "could do anything."[11] He and his teammates had rather quickly transformed a hapless franchise into one of the best teams in the league after the move from Washington.

The fall of the Yankees was much more dramatic than imagined. In 1965 New York went 77-85 and finished sixth. The Twins battled the White Sox, Indians, and Orioles through the first half. By the end of July their lead was six games. Leading by 4½ games on September 6, they won seven in a row and never looked back. Kaat won two of those seven, including the second of a two-game sweep at Chicago. After pitching near .500 through mid-August, he won six of his last seven decisions to finish 18-11 (third in the AL in wins) with a 2.83 ERA and 154 strikeouts in 264⅓ innings.

The Twins faced the Los Angeles Dodgers in the World Series. Minnesota was led by powerful Harmon Killebrew, All-Star right fielder Tony Oliva, center fielder Jimmie Hall, and AL MVP shortstop Zoilo Versalles. On the mound, Kaat joined 21-game-winner Mudcat Grant and Jim Perry at the top of the rotation while aging relievers Al Worthington and Johnny Klippstein both logged sub-2.25 ERAs. Los Angeles had a no-name offense led by Jim Gilliam and Ron Fairly but had one of the game's most feared rotations anchored by three-time Cy Young Award winner Sandy Koufax and fireballer Don Drysdale.

The Twins opened the Series in spectacular fashion. Grant pitched a complete game in the Twins' 8-2 win in Game One at Metropolitan Stadium. Kaat started Game Two, battling Koufax through five scoreless innings. The Twins took a 2-0 lead in the sixth, chasing Koufax. Kaat surrendered a run in the seventh but his offense added three runs for a 5-1 win and a 2-0 Series lead. In his first postseason game, Kaat had notched a complete-game victory over Koufax, the best pitcher in the game.

In Los Angeles, the Dodgers were a different team, winning Games Three and Four in convincing fashion and setting up a rematch of lefties Koufax and Kaat in Game Five. This time Koufax was at his best. Kaat struggled from the outset, allowing two runs in the first with one coming in on an error by second baseman Frank Quilici. Trailing 2-0 in the third, he surrendered three more hits and two more runs and was relieved by Boswell, trailing 4-0. With Koufax on his game, the rest of the game was academic as the Dodgers won 7-0 and took a 3-2 Series lead.

The Series returned to Minnesota for its conclusion. Grant bested Claude Osteen, 5-1, in Game Six, setting up a deciding seventh game. Kaat and Koufax battled for a third time, each on just two days of rest. For three innings, both Kaat and Koufax held the opponent scoreless, each allowing three baserunners. In the fourth inning left fielder Lou Johnson homered to give the Dodgers a 1-0 lead. A double by Fairly and a single by Wes Parker made it 2-0 and Kaat was relieved by Worthington. Four Twins pitchers held the Dodgers the rest of the way but Koufax was brilliant, allowing just three hits and three walks while striking out 10. Koufax's masterpiece propelled the Dodgers to their second title in three years. The Twins' first World Series appearance was spoiled by an all-time pitching performance but Kaat remained part of a core that believed it would be back.

The 1966 Twins came out of the gate slowly and never contended with the powerful Orioles. The Twins fell as low as seventh place and as many as 19 games back but finished strongly enough to take second place to the Orioles with a record of 89-73. While the team struggled, Kaat had an exceptional season, finishing 25-13 with a 2.75 ERA and 205 strikeouts. With five more wins than any other AL hurler, league bests in innings pitched, complete games, and walks per nine innings, and a second-place finish in strikeouts, Kaat was clearly the best pitcher in the AL. However, in

1966 there was just one Cy Young given for the major leagues and Sandy Koufax won the award unanimously.

During 1966, manager Mele became embroiled in tensions with outspoken pitching coach Johnny Sain that led to Sain's firing. During the management struggle, Kaat sided publicly with Sain, the former major-league pitcher, against Mele, the former outfielder. After Sain was fired, Kaat penned a letter in support of him to the *Minneapolis Star*. His letter did not sit well with Mele or coach Billy Martin.[12]

Kaat's Twins were involved in one of the most storied pennant races ever in 1967. Assumed by many to be the favorite for a second pennant in three seasons, the Twins stumbled out to a 25-25 start that led to Mele's firing. A 12-3 run into the All-Star break vaulted the Twins into a four-team race that remained unsettled until the season's final day. As fate would have it, the Twins faced the Red Sox at Fenway Park in the final two games of the season with Minnesota leading by one game. Even a split would net the Twins the pennant.

Kaat started the first game. After an awful 1-7 start, he had won seven straight games, stood 16-13, and was the Twins' best pitcher as the season wound down. Leading 1-0 in the third inning, Kaat felt "something pop" in his left arm.[13] He was pulled from the game and later diagnosed with a torn muscle. Twins relievers allowed six runs, four of which were driven in by Carl Yastrzemski, resulting in a Boston win and a final-day showdown in which Yastrzemski drove in two more and scored another run as Boston's "Impossible Dream" spoiled the Twins' hopes of returning to the World Series.

In 1968 the Twins fall hard, finishing seventh with a 79-83 mark. Pitching for a team that was out of contention by early June, Kaat posted a respectable 14-12 record, with a 2.94 ERA, and won his seventh consecutive Gold Glove.

In addition to his abilities as a fielder, Kaat was considered one of the best hitting pitchers of his generation. Over the course of his 25 seasons, Kaat recorded a .185 batting average, a .227 on-base percentage, and a .267 slugging percentage as a left-handed hitter, recording 65 extra-base hits, including 16 home runs. In 1972, his best season at the plate, Kaat batted .289/.304/.489 with five extra-base hits, including two home runs, in 47 plate appearances. Over his career, he scored 117 runs and drove in 106. Few pitchers have done as much in the field and at the plate to advance their chances of winning ballgames.

Twins ownership attempted to inject some fire into the talented team in 1969 by promoting Billy Martin to manager. Martin, Minnesota's third-base coach from 1965 to 1968, had most notably been a member of the 1950s Yankee dynasty and was well known as someone who liked to have fun off the field and who had a temper. Martin was known to be fiercely loyal to "his guys" and to hold grudges against anyone who he perceived had slighted him. Although Kaat was an established clubhouse leader for the Twins, Martin kept the lefty at arm's length as Kaat had sided with Johnny Sain in his feud with Mele. Martin, who had been loyal to Mele, felt Kaat was partly to blame for Mele's firing in 1968.[14]

The 1969 Twins were an offensive powerhouse, leading the league in runs scored. Killebrew was named the AL's Most Valuable Player as he enjoyed the finest season of his Hall of Fame career. Oliva, first baseman Rich Reese, and second baseman Rod Carew all had outstanding seasons and hit over .300. Jim Perry and

Jim Kaat receives the Gold Glove Award (Photo courtesy of Minnesota Twins Baseball Club).

Dave Boswell each won 20 games and bullpen ace Ron Perranoski was outstanding. For his part, Kaat was solid, finishing 14-13/3.49 in 242 innings. He completed 10 games and was clearly the team's third best starter.

The Twins took possession of first place after 11 games and battled the young Oakland Athletics through early June. A sweep of the A's at Metropolitan Stadium in July gave them a lead that they would not relinquish. After a series win at Oakland in early September expanded their lead to 8½ games, they cruised to a nine-game divisional win. The 97-65 Twins met the powerful Baltimore Orioles (109-53) in the first American League Championship series.

The first two games were tightly contested, but the Orioles won both of their home games in extra innings. Heading into Game Three, Twins owner Calvin Griffith directed Martin to start Kaat at home. Based on his mistrust of Kaat, Martin started swingman Bob Miller instead. Miller lasted only 1⅔ innings. Martin used six relievers, including starters Dean Chance and Tom Hall, but did not use Kaat, his best remaining arm. The Orioles battered the Twins' bullpen and clinched the AL pennant with an 11-2 win. Martin was fired after one season. Despite his off-field issues, including a fistfight with pitcher Dave Boswell, Twins owner Calvin Griffith said that Martin's dismissal was a result of his unwillingness to follow instructions from above.[15]

After the 1969 playoff disaster, the Twins made a number of changes heading into 1970. The two most significant moves were an overhaul to the on-field management and a major trade aimed at improving the starting pitching. Martin was replaced with the calmer Bill Rigney, who had managed the Angels throughout the 1960s. In addition, the Twins dealt Chance, Miller, center fielder Ted Uhlaender, and utilityman Graig Nettles to Cleveland for 20-game-winner Luis Tiant and reliever Stan Williams.

The 1970 Twins rotation looked formidable heading into the season, but did not perform close to expectations. While Jim Perry won 24 games and the AL Cy Young Award, Tiant and Boswell were beset with injuries. For his part, Kaat was inconsistent, starting 34 times, going 14-10 with a mediocre 3.56 ERA. Offensively, the 1970 Twins also faced challenges, most notably a season-ending injury to defending batting champion Rod Carew in June. Despite the struggles of some key players, the 1970 Twins won the American League West by nine games over Oakland. After several rough patches, a 21-10 September locked up a second AL West title and the desired rematch with Baltimore.

Kaat's 1970 performance was streaky, but saw him peak as the season wound down. Through May Kaat was 5-1, but he went just 5-9 from June 4 through August 28. However, his 4-0 record in September saw him rounding into form as the playoffs loomed. Pitching both as a starter and reliever, Kaat saw his ERA creep to 4.01 on July 5, but he pitched well enough to bring it to 3.56 by season's end.

For the Twins, the 1970 ALCS was even worse than the 1969 sweep. Baltimore's Game Three blowout in 1969 came only after two one-run victories. In 1970 the three Orioles wins lacked any drama or real hope for the West Division Champs. In the first two games at Met Stadium, visiting Baltimore took early leads and coasted to 10-6 and 11-3 wins.

Unlike 1969, Kaat was called upon to start Game Three in 1970. Facing Jim Palmer, he would need to be strong to get the Twins back into the series. Palmer was brilliant in Game Three, scattering seven hits over nine innings, striking out 12, and surrendering just one run. Kaat was no match for Palmer, giving up a scratch run in the first, an unearned run in the second, and two hits to open the third inning. Bert Blyleven entered the game in relief and allowed both runners to score before giving up a run of his own. The Orioles led 5-0 after three innings and completed their second consecutive ALCS sweep over Minnesota with a 6-1 win. They went on to win the 1970 World Series in five games over Cincinnati.

After several years in the upper echelon of the American League, the 1971 Twins began the club's decline into more than a decade of mediocrity. Kaat's 1971 season was statistically similar to his 1970 campaign. He finished with a 13-14 record and a respectable 3.32 ERA. Unlike 1970, the 1971 Twins finished 74-86, dropping to fifth place in the AL West.

In 1972 Kaat had a fantastic half-season but had his outstanding campaign cut short by injury. Through July 2 he started 15 games, compiling a 10-2 record with a 2.06 ERA and surrendering two or fewer runs in each of his first seven outings. In the midst of perhaps his finest season, the 33-year-old lefty broke a bone in his pitching hand while sliding at Comiskey Park and was done for the season.[16] Just days after Kaat's injury, Rigney was fired and replaced with former utility infielder Frank Quilici in an attempt to breathe fire into the team, but the Twins played nearly .500 baseball under each. Perhaps robbed of a chance for a Cy Young Award, Kaat settled for his 11th straight Gold Glove.

As in 1972, the 1973 Twins were a .500 team, finishing 81-81. After his outstanding season in 1972, Kaat had used his leverage to push penny-pinching owner Calvin Griffith to raise his salary back to its previous high of $60,000. The negotiations were drawn out and acrimonious but eventually the pitcher prevailed.[17] In early August the Twins lost seven straight games and fell to 10 games behind the AL West-leading Royals. Griffith took the opportunity to get the last word and placed Kaat on waivers. Claimed by the White Sox, Kaat went 4-1 for Chicago to finish 15-13 and avoid his second losing season since 1961.

Kaat's two seasons in Chicago saw him return to the upper echelon of American League pitchers. As a 35-year-old in 1974, he logged 277⅓ innings, going 21-13 with a 2.92 ERA and 15 complete games. With only six starters getting Cy Young votes, Kaat was one of three 20-game winners left off all ballots. In 1975 Kaat went 20-14 with a 3.11 ERA in 303⅔ innings and finished fourth in the Cy Young voting. He was selected for the 1975 All-Star Game and added two more Gold Gloves while in Chicago. While the White Sox were never contenders while Kaat was with them, his performance was a bright spot for otherwise forgettable teams.

In December of 1975 the White Sox dealt Kaat to Philadelphia. Kaat spent three seasons with the Phillies, which may have felt like the same story repeating itself. The Phillies won three straight NL East titles from 1976-1978. The core of those teams included Hall of Famers Mike Schmidt and Steve Carlton, Gold Glove center fielder Garry Maddox, and All-Stars Bob Boone, Larry Bowa, and Tug McGraw. However, Philadelphia's postseason results were little better than the two ALCS defeats Kaat endured in Minnesota. The Phillies were swept 3-0 by the Reds in 1976 and lost back-to-back series to the Dodgers in the 1977 and '78 NLCS, both ending three games to one.

Kaat's role declined over his three seasons in Philadelphia. In 1976 he started 35 games, going 12-14 with a 3.48 ERA. As in 1970, he started Game Three of the League Championship Series for a team that had lost the first two games at home. After six scoreless innings, he allowed the first two men in the seventh to reach safely. He left with the lead, but the Phillies bullpen collapsed in a 7-6 walk-off defeat. Kaat started 27 games in 1977 but performed well below expectations. He rebounded in 1978, going 8-5, 4.10 in 24 starts, but was not used in either the 1977 or 1978 NLCS.

Kaat was sold to the Yankees early in 1979 and proved to be a solid left-handed bullpen arm. He was granted free agency after 1979 but re-signed with the Yankees for $150,000, a healthy contract for a 40-year-old at the time. Less than a month into the 1980 season the Yankees sold him to St. Louis.

The 1980 season was the last in which Kaat started more than two games. He was 41. As a swingman he started 14 times and made 49 total appearances. In strike-shortened 1981 he threw 53 innings in 41 games, starting just once.

After second-place finishes in both halves of 1981, St. Louis rose to the top in 1982. The Cardinals were managed by Whitey Herzog and led offensively by first baseman Keith Hernandez, speedy outfielder Lonnie Smith, catcher Darrell Porter, and Hall of Fame shortstop Ozzie Smith. The pitching staff, though lacking star power, used spacious Busch Stadium to allow the fewest runs per game in the National League. Kaat was used as a left-handed bullpen arm and appeared in 62 games at the age of 43.

The 1982 NL East was a tight, if not overly dramatic race. The Cardinals took over first place on April 15 and remained there through early July. They fell behind the Phillies several times but took over the division lead for good in early September, ultimately winning the division by three games.

St. Louis swept the NL West champion Atlanta Braves 3-0 in the NLCS. Kaat did not pitch in an NLCS in which the Cardinals needed only one relief inning by a pitcher other than closer Bruce Sutter.

The 1982 World Series pitted the Cardinals against the Milwaukee Brewers, who were led by future Hall of Famers Robin Yount, Paul Molitor, and closer Rollie Fingers. The Brewers were known as Harvey's Wallbangers in honor of manager Harvey Kuenn and a lineup loaded with productive bats. The Brewers boasted the American League's most potent offense, scoring nearly 5½ runs per game.

Unlike in the NLCS, Kaat was used regularly in the World Series. In Game One, he pitched 1⅓ scoreless innings in a 10-0 Brewer blowout. In Game Two Herzog brought him on to relieve starter John Stuper, who left in the fifth inning trailing 3-2. Kaat surrendered an RBI single to Cecil Cooper that increased the Brewers' lead to 4-2 but retired the next two hitters before exiting. The Cardinals battled back for a 5-4 win to tie the Series. In Game Three Kaat entered with a 5-0 lead and retired one of two batters, as St. Louis took the Series lead with a 6-2 victory. He appeared in a fourth straight World Series game in Game Four but gave up an RBI single to Cooper and delivered a wild pitch before exiting. In four appearances, he allowed four hits and one earned run in 2⅓ innings, for an ERA of 3.86.

The Brewers and Cardinals traded victories in Games Five and Six before St. Louis won the deciding game, 6-3, behind Joaquin Andujar and Bruce Sutter. Although the results over his four appearances were mixed, the 43-year-old Kaat called the Series win the greatest moment of his career.

In 1983 Kaat made 24 appearances out of the bullpen with a 3.89 ERA for the fourth-place Cardinals. He was released by the Cardinals on July 6. Kaat felt that an adversary in the Cardinals' front office had been behind the decision but was hurt that he received no personal communication from Herzog.[18] After speaking to a few clubs that fall and going to spring training with the Pirates in 1984, Kaat found himself without a pitching job for the first time in a quarter-century. In August 1984 Kaat joined the Cincinnati Reds as their pitching coach. The Reds were then managed by Pete Rose, a teammate of Kaat's in Philadelphia. During his one full season as a pitching coach, the Reds staff improved its ERA from 4.16 to 3.71 but Kaat chose not to return to coaching in 1986.

After his brief coaching tenure, Kaat turned to broadcasting and became one of the most respected analysts in the game. His move into the booth was no surprise as he had held various broadcasting positions dating back to his playing days in Minnesota. His most notable broadcasting job was as a television announcer for the Yankees. In between two stints as a Yankees broadcaster (1986 and 1995-2006), Kaat was a member of the Minnesota Twins broadcast team from 1988 to 1993.

Kaat was considered a knowledgeable and candid baseball analyst and was highly sought after for baseball assignments beyond his team duties. In addition to his years with the Yankees' and Twins' broadcast teams, he provided play-by-play, analysis, and on-field reporting for virtually every television baseball outlet. Between 1986 and 2009, Kaat worked baseball broadcasts for CBS, NBC, ESPN, ABC, the MLB Network, and TBS. In addition to regular major-league telecasts, he worked the American League Championship Series, the World Series, the College World Series, the 1988 Summer Olympics, and the 2009 World

Baseball Classic. He provided baseball analysis for ABC's *Good Morning America* for two seasons. He won seven Emmy Awards for sports broadcasting from 1996 through 2005 for baseball commentary, announcing, and feature presentations.

Kaat's candor was an enduring element of his analysis. His willingness to assess baseball strategy and player abilities ran afoul of several high-profile players, including Wade Boggs and Rickey Henderson. However, he was always willing to face players and explain his comments and clear the air. His preference for objectivity contributed to his not taking an announcing job with the Chicago Cubs after his first stint in New York. When the Cubs asked him if he could root for the team during broadcasts, Kaat told them that he could not.[19]

In 2012 Kaat received coverage for an open letter he wrote to pitching phenom Stephen Strasburg. In the letter Kaat noted that his greatest moments had been his appearances in the World Series and urged the young pitcher to take an active role in deciding whether he agreed with the Nationals' decision to "shut down" his arm during the final weeks of the season. A known fitness buff, Kaat decried the notion that it was more important to rest than play for a chance at ultimate victory.[20] This position seemed to sum up a career that spanned a quarter-century and saw his teams come close many times before he earned a World Series ring.

In his 70s Kaat remained active in baseball and in life. Married four times, he has four children (all with his third wife, MaryAnn) and six grandchildren. He maintained low handicaps as both a right-handed and left-handed golfer. In 2013 *Golf Digest* noted that he had played full rounds in fewer strokes than his age as both a righty and as a lefty, perhaps the first player to have done so.[21] He also maintained an active blog at mlb.com entitled Kaat's Korner.[22]

Kaat received 87 votes (19 percent) for the Hall of Fame in his first year on the writers' ballot, 1989.[23] He was among the top 10 candidates in nearly all of his years on the BBWAA ballot, peaking at 29 percent in 1993. His candidacy moved to the Veterans Committee and then the Golden Era Committee, for which voting is conducted by current Hall of Famers. In 2012 Kaat was the second leading vote-getter among Golden Era candidates, falling just two votes shy of election. Former teammate Rod Carew has openly offered to join the committee and is an open supporter of both Kaat and Tony Oliva as worthy additions to the Hall of Fame.

NOTES

1 Bill James, *The Politics of Glory. How Baseball's Hall of Fame Really Works* (New York: Macmillan Publishing Company, 1994), 335.

2 Jim Kaat, *Still Pitching, Musings From the Mound and the Microphone* (Chicago, Triumph Books, 2003), 10-12.

3 Jim Kaat open letter to Stephen Strasburg, 2012. jimkaat.mlblogs.com/2012/09/08/if-i-could-have-a-conversation-with-stephen-strasburg/.

4 Kaat, 16.

5 Wayne Anderson, *Harmon Killebrew, Baseball's Superstar* (Salt Lake City: Deseret Book Company, 1971), 315.

6 Kaat, 18-23.

7 Kaat, 30-33.

8 All season statistics from the minor leagues are from BaseballReference.com, baseball.reference.com/minors/.

9 All statistics from individual games are from BaseballReference.com, baseballreference.com.

10 Kaat, 196.

11 Quotes from Johnny Klippstein and Vic Power included in Danny Peary, ed., *We Played the Game. Memories of Baseball's Greatest Era* (New York: Black Dog and Leventhal, 1994).

12 Kaat, 54-55.

13 *The Sporting News Baseball Guide, 1968* (St. Louis: The Sporting News, 1968).

14 Peter Golenbock, *Wild, High and Tight: The Life and Death of Billy Martin* (New York: St. Martin's Press, 1994), 173.

15 Anderson, 315, 319.

16 *The Sporting News Baseball Guide, 1973* (St. Louis: The Sporting News, 1973).

17 Kaat, 98-99.

18 Kaat, 95-96.

19 Kaat, 150-155.

20 Kaat letter to Strasburg.

21 Is Jim Kaat the first golfer to shoot his age as a switch-hitter?, golfdigest.com/blogs/the-loop/2013/12/is-jim-kaat-the-first-golfer-to-shoot-his-age-as-a-switch-hi.html.

22 jimkaat.mlbblogs.com.

23 Hall of Fame vote totals are from Baseball-Reference.com,

Harmon Killebrew

BY JOSEPH WANCHO

IT MAY HAVE SEEMED LIKE AN ETERnity. As in many cases when a player is on the verge of breaking a record or accomplishing a milestone, the waiting can be interminable. Such was the case with Minnesota Twins slugger Harmon Killebrew, who had set his sights on 500 home runs. But the epic homer was elusive, keeping Killebrew from joining an exclusive club. Entering the 1971 season, Killebrew had blasted 487 homers. On June 22 "Killer" clubbed number 498 off Oakland's Daryl Patterson. The Twins' promotion department had commemorative mugs made to celebrate the achievement. The mugs were to be distributed at a game on July 6. Certainly he would break through by then. But Killebrew was still sitting at 498 as the day came and went.

A sprained right toe curtailed Killebrew's at-bats. But in the All-Star Game at Tiger Stadium on July 13, Killebrew knocked one out against Ferguson Jenkins. Then on July 25, he inched closer to his goal when he connected for number 499 against Luis Tiant of Boston.

Finally, on August 10, 1971, Killebrew smacked the monumental blast, in the first inning of a home game against Baltimore. He drilled a Mike Cuellar curveball into the left-field seats. The sparse crowd of 15,881 cheered with joy as Killer rounded the bases, all of the tension washed away. He became the 10th member of the 500 home-run club. "I didn't feel much pressure, if that's what you want to call it, until they passed out those mugs," Harmon said. "Then it seemed everyone started asking about it and talking about it and I tried a little harder to hit it."[1] The Twins lost, 4-3 in extra innings, and Killebrew was the true team player. "It means a little less since the team lost. It's hard to be too happy when you lose," he observed.[2]

"He didn't say much when he came back to the dugout," said Twins manager Bill Rigney. "But you could tell he was happy. You could see it on his face."[3] Rigney told Harmon, "Don't let it be so long between 500 and 501."[4] Killebrew acquiesced as he connected for number 501 in the sixth inning off Baltimore southpaw Cuellar.

Henry Aaron, who set milestones through his illustrious career, knew what Killebrew was going through. "When you get it, you are relieved," said Aaron. "You know you can hit, you know you will get it, but everybody wants to know when. If you have a couple of bad days, you just wish you could get it over so everyone would leave you alone."[5]

Harmon Clayton Killebrew, Jr. was born on June 29, 1936, in Payette, Idaho. He was the youngest of five children (Eugene, Eula, Patricia, Robert) born to Harmon and Katherine Killebrew. Harmon Sr., who preferred to be called Clay, had a big, burly type of

One of the most feared sluggers in baseball history, Killebrew belted 573 homers in his 22-year career, leading the AL six times. The 11-time All-Star and 1969 AL MVP award winner, "the Killer" dislocated his elbow in 1965 and was limited to 113 games. (National Baseball Hall of Fame, Cooperstown, New York).

build and was a fine athlete. He was a bruising fullback at West Virginia Wesleyan University. (The head coach there was Earle "Greasy" Neale, who was an outfielder for eight years, 1916-1924, primarily with the Cincinnati Reds. Later he went on to coach the NFL champion Philadelphia Eagles in 1948 and 1949, and was elected to the Pro Football Hall of Fame in 1969.)

Clay went on to play professional football for a couple of years with the Wheeling Steelers. He and Katherine then moved out west in search of better opportunities for their family, settling in Portland, Oregon. Eventually the Killebrew clan settled in Payette, where Clay was a sheriff, and eventually started a house-painting business.

Harmon had the same build as his father, and as a freshman at Payette High School was much bigger than his brother Bob, who was a senior. Harmon lettered for four years in baseball, basketball, football, and track. His boyhood friend Ron Manser recalled, "Harmon was the only person that I recall who graduated from Payette High with four letters in all four years. Heck, that's all we had. He was just an ordinary hard-working kid. And from the time I'd known him as a little kid until he passed away, he hadn't changed any. He was just the same person all his life."[6]

When Harmon was 16, his father died one evening at home as the result of a heart attack. Clay had worked with Harmon and Bob molding their athletic skills as young men. His death left a big void in Harmon's life. However, by the time Killebrew reached his senior year at Payette, his athletic accomplishments had spread outside of Idaho. He was a quarterback for the Payette Pirates and possessed a rifle arm. His intentions were to attend the University of Oregon on a football scholarship and play baseball there in the spring.

Killebrew was recommended to Washington Senators owner Clark Griffith by Senator Herman Welker (R-Idaho), who had seen him perform on the diamond. (Welker was a regular at Senators home games.) Griffith, either to pacify the Senator or to find out just how good Killebrew was, dispatched Ossie Bluege, head of the Senators' scouting department, to take a look at the youngster. Bluege, who had been a fine third baseman for the Senators in the 1920s and '30s, waited out a rainstorm to see Killebrew play, and then saw the strength of the 17-year old as he clouted a home run some 435 feet into a beet field. Bluege left a contract for Killebrew to look over, and hopefully sign. "The team I wanted to sign with was Boston," said Killebrew. "For a couple of years, I had spoken to Earl Johnson, who was a former Red Sox player who was now their scout in the Northwest. He said that when I got an offer from another team I should call him to see if he could better it. However, when I got an offer from Washington, he said the Red Sox couldn't match it. I wish I could have seen myself in Fenway Park for my career."[7]

Killebrew signed with the Senators at a salary of $6,000 for each of the next three years and a $4,000 signing bonus. The size of his bonus made him a "bonus baby," and accordingly was to be placed on the Senators' roster for two years. It was quite a whirlwind for a 17-year-old from Payette, Idaho. "I joined the team on the road in Comiskey Park. I didn't know what to expect in the majors," Killebrew said. "I had never even seen a major league stadium, and all of a sudden I am playing in them with and against major league players I had read about. So everything was strange."[8]

Killebrew was a third baseman, but he was not about to unseat Eddie Yost at the hot corner on manager Bucky Harris's club. He made his major-league debut as a pinch-runner on June 23, 1954, at Comiskey Park. He played in only nine games, and at times was stationed at second base. He started 17 games in 1955, but like many bonus-baby players placed on big-league rosters, he could have benefited from some seasoning in the minor leagues. After playing sparingly for three seasons with the Senators, Killebrew made his way through Washington's minor-league chain. He started with Charlotte of the Class A South Atlantic League and worked his way up to Indianapolis of the Triple-A American Association. Each year he also found his way back to the Nats, receiving varying amounts of playing time with the parent club.

In 1956 Harmon married the former Elaine Roberts, his high-school sweetheart. They had five children: Kenneth, Kathy, Erin, Shawn, and Cameron.

After the 1958 season, Yost was traded to Detroit, and Washington skipper Cookie Lavagetto gave Killebrew the opportunity to earn his way into the starting lineup. Although Killebrew had showed power in the minor leagues (29 home runs at Double-A Chattanooga in 1957), no one could have predicted the breakout year he had in 1959. Killebrew tied Cleveland's Rocky Colavito for the league lead in home runs with 42. He finished third in RBIs with 105. Lavagetto, who had been a second baseman and third baseman for the Pirates and Dodgers, helped Killebrew with the nuances of playing third base — specifically his throwing. Killebrew threw a baseball much like a football, with a stiff wrist, which seemed to be curtailing his arm strength.

But there was no doubting Killebrew's ability to swing the lumber, as he enjoyed a spectacular month of May in 1959, hitting 15 home runs and driving in 28 runs. He was selected to play in the All-Star Game. It was the first of 11 appearances for Killebrew. "People have been comparing me to Joe Hardy, the hero of the musical *Damn Yankees*," he said. "You might be interested to know what (sportswriter) Bob Addie told me the other night after I struck out against the Yankees to end the game. 'You may look like Joe Hardy to some,' said Addie, 'but today you were more like Andy Hardy.'"[9]

There were many who thought Killebrew's defense was suspect. At times teams would bunt down the third-base line to test him. In some ways the 1960 season was frustrating for Killebrew. A leg injury caused him to miss some time, but also Lavagetto moved him across the diamond to first base. "When I played third, left-handed hitters Julio Becquer and rookie Don Mincher played first, and when I played first, Reno Bertoia played third. Shifting back and forth was hard mostly because it was hard to use different gloves."[10] Lavagetto said of Killebrew, "He pays his way with his bat."[11]

Like many power hitters, Killebrew had holes in his swing. Early in his career he struck out more often than he walked. He worked hard to reverse the trend and led the league in walks four times as he became more disciplined at the plate. Also, teams began to use shifts against Killebrew. "Lou Boudreau was the first to do that to me when he was managing Kansas City in the mid-'50s. I think I could have been a .300 hitter, but I decided early on that I was helping the club more driving in a lot of runs than going for a high average," Killebrew said.[12]

During the emergence of Killebrew, along with Bob Allison, Earl Battey, and Jim Lemon, the Senators often remained American League cellar dwellers. As a result, attendance was in a steady decline at Griffith Stadium. This and competition for fans with the Baltimore Orioles caused Senators owner Calvin Griffith to look to relocate the club. Major League Baseball was entering its first expansion period. Many burgeoning cities were vying for an expansion franchise, or one that was relocating. Dallas, Houston, Minneapolis, Seattle, and Louisville were looking to land a team. The league was also considering second clubs in Los Angeles and New York, which left a lot of cities and ownership groups jockeying for position. Recent moves by the Dodgers, Giants, Athletics, Braves, and Browns/Orioles, seemed to make relocation a grand solution for some owners.

In the end Griffith chose Minneapolis as his club's new home. Minneapolis was a growing city. The Twin Cities were granted an expansion franchise in the NFL in 1960, and played their first schedule in 1961. The Twins had the potential of drawing people from the Dakotas and Iowa as a secondary fan base. The choice for Griffith was clear. Killebrew was fond of playing in Washington. He liked that ballpark, with fans close to the field. He felt that the Nats' faithful supported the team in spite of its losing ways.

As the club moved to Minnesota, Washington and Los Angeles were granted American League expansion franchises. (The New York Mets and Houston would join the National League the following season.) Killebrew benefited from the move to Minnesota

Harmon Killebrew (Photo courtesy of Minnesota Twins Baseball Club).

because Metropolitan Stadium was a hitter-friendly park. In the Twins' first season, 1961, he batted a career-high .288, smacked 46 homers, drove in 122 runs, and had a slugging average of .606.

Killebrew began working at WTCN-TV during the season, hosting a pregame show when the Twins were at home. He did interviews with the Twins and opposing players. The show lasted 12 years. He hosted a radio show in the offseason. The jobs helped Killebrew reshape himself from a quiet, reserved type to a more outgoing person.

The transformation in Minneapolis began with the 1962 season. Sam Mele had replaced Lavagetto the previous year. The Twins went from a 70-90 record in 1961 to 91-71 in 1962. They finished second to the New York Yankees by five games. The 21-game swing was amazing. Camilo Pascual and Jim Kaat led the '62 pitching staff with 20 and 18 wins respectively. The smooth-fielding Vic Power took over at first base and Rich Rollins was the new third baseman. Killebrew, now patrolling left field, led the league with 48 home runs and 126 RBIs. Bob Allison had 29 round-trippers and drove in 102 runs. On July 18 against Cleveland,

Killebrew and Allison each hit a grand slam in the first inning. The Twins scored 11 runs in the inning on their way to a 14-3 thumping of the Indians.

Killebrew led the league in homers again in 1963 (45) and 1964 (49(. For the most part they weren't cheapies either. He hit a homer off Jim Bunning that soared above the double-decked stands and cleared the left-field roof at Tiger Stadium. "The homers he hit against us would be homers in any park—including Yellowstone," quipped Baltimore manager Paul Richards.[13]

The Twins put it altogether in 1965 to win the American League pennant by seven games over the Chicago White Sox. Jim Grant led the league in wins with 21 and Kaat won 18. Jim Perry was inserted into the rotation in the middle of the season and posted 12 wins. The team also had offense, with Tony Oliva leading the league in batting (.321) and Zoilo Versalles in doubles (45) and triples (12). Killebrew was on his way to another tremendous season when misfortune came his way. In the sixth inning of a game against Baltimore on August 2, the Orioles' Russ Snyder bunted down the third-base line. Third baseman Rollins made an errant throw to Killebrew at first base. Killebrew reached back to stab the throw and tag Snyder in the same motion, but his left arm collided with Snyder's body. It was said that the snapping of his elbow could be heard in the Twins dugout. Medical personnel ran out to tend to Killebrew as swelling occurred instantly. "You could hear everyone's heart go 'bump, bump, bump' on the bench," said Grant.[14] Killebrew was out of the lineup for seven weeks, returning in late September.

The Twins' faced the Los Angeles Dodgers in the World Series. Through Game Six, each team had won three games in its home park. Game Seven was played at Metropolitan Stadium, but Sandy Koufax proved to be too much, shutting out Minnesota 2-0 on three hits. Killebrew batted .286 in the Series, hit one homer, and drove in two runs.

In succeeding seasons Killebrew kept up his home-run pace. In 1966 he hit 39. He led the league in 1967 with

44, tied with the Red Sox' Carl Yastrzemski. Killebrew was selected to *The Sporting News* AL All-Star Team in 1967 as a first baseman. But there was another part to his game that came to the forefront: his ability to draw walks. From 1966 through 1971 Killebrew led the league in walks four times and in intentional walks three times. Opposing teams respected his ability to wreak havoc, and issuing a free pass began to be the road most traveled. Some pitchers went against logic. "I was 2-and-0 on him one night and I threw him a fastball," said pitcher Dean Chance. "The home run he hit on that pitch was hit so hard that no one in the stands even yelled."[15]

In 1967 Sam Mele was let go after posting a 25-25 record. He was replaced by Carl Ermer. Under Ermer the Twins the Twins went 66-46. On September 26 they held a one-game lead with three games to play. But they dropped the three games, including two to the Red Sox at Fenway Park. Boston squeaked by to grab the pennant.

It was truly the last "pennant race" in the major leagues. The Tigers breezed through the American League in 1968. In 1969 both leagues expanded by two more teams and went to a two-division format. This created a round of playoffs before the World Series. No longer was the team with the best record guaranteed a spot in the fall classic.

Killebrew suffered a serious hamstring injury in the third inning of the 1968 All-Star Game. The first player to be voted a starter at three positions (left field, first base, and third base), he stretched to catch a throw from shortstop Jim Fregosi. But the soil around first base in the Astrodome did not give, his lead foot gave way, and Killebrew folded over his left leg. His hamstring was torn and a bone tore away from his pelvis. He returned to the Twins in September, but was of little value, hitting .257 in 35 at-bats.

Perhaps that was the incentive that made the 1969 season Killebrew's best. He led the league in games played (162), home runs (49), RBIs (140), on-base percentage (.427), walks (145), and intentional walks (20). He was voted the Most Valuable Player by both the Baseball Writers Association of America and *The Sporting News*. He surprised some people with his defense as well. New skipper Billy Martin had moved Killebrew back to third base. "Everybody told me not to play Harmon at third," said Martin. "Well, he's done a hell of a job there. Admittedly, there is only one Brooks Robinson and Harmon's no Brooks. But then, who is?"[16]

"If Harmon Killebrew isn't the league's number-one player, I have never seen one," said Oakland's Reggie Jackson. "He's one of the greatest of all time."[17] Killebrew, never one to draw attention to himself, accepted the MVP with his usual aplomb. "What I'm really happy about is that I played every game. That had to mean I was healthy. I had no real slumps, but yet I like to feel that I could have done better. You should never be satisfied. "[18]

The "Big Man" carried the Twins to their first American League West Division championship in 1969. He had plenty of help, as Rod Carew won the first of his seven batting crowns with a .332 batting average, and Tony Oliva led the league in hits (197) and doubles (39). Jim Perry and Dave Boswell each won 20 games and Ron Perranoski led the league with 31 saves. But the Twins were swept by Baltimore in three games in the ALCS.

Killebrew again captured *The Sporting News* MVP honors in 1970, hitting 41 home runs and driving in 113 runs. He was named as third baseman on *The Sporting News* AL All-Star team for the second consecutive year. Bill Rigney replaced Billy Martin in 1970. The team won the West Division again, despite missing Carew to a knee injury for a good chunk of the season. But their fate was a carbon copy of the previous season; they were swept by the Orioles in three games.

The 1970 season was the eighth and final one in which Killebrew would exceed 40 home runs. He hit them at a dizzying pace. Through his career, comparisons would be made to Babe Ruth. There would be much conversation about whether Killebrew could eclipse Ruth as the home-run king. Harmon would dismiss such talk as nonsense. "Forget it, I'm just taking them one season at a time," he said. "I'm not thinking of any records. I just want to stay healthy and keep on playing."[19]

Killebrew belted his 500th career home run in August 1971, but as he reached the age of 35, his production sank. He hit 28 home runs and led the league in RBIs (119) that season, but in 1972, though he hit 26 homers, his RBIs were down to 74. Sidelined by a knee injury for almost three months in 1973, he played in only 35 games and hit five home runs. He was healthier in 1974, but hit only 13 home runs and drove in 54 runs. For 1975 the Twins offered Killebrew a contract to be a player-coach or possibly manage Tacoma, the Twins' Triple-A affiliate. But Killebrew still wanted to play and rejected the offer. Owner Calvin Griffith replied, "Well, that's fine if you would like to do that. You're welcome to call any other club or talk to any other ballclub that you'd like to."[20]

Elaine Killebrew, Harmon's wife, said he strived to please everyone, and never wanted to let anyone down. By all accounts, he was a wonderful person, but at times his good-natured behavior could be taken for granted. He could even let himself be used. He was Mr. Nice Guy. When contract came, Killebrew didn't quibble too much with Griffith. He was paid well, but not overpaid. Jim Kaat told Killebrew that when he stopped hitting home runs over the fence, the front office would forget how to spell his name. Killebrew was beginning to see that Kaat was right. "The Cardinals made a vice president out of (Stan) Musial and the Twins wanted to send you to Triple-A," Kaat told Killebrew during spring training in 1975.[21]

Killebrew signed a one-year deal with Kansas City to be the Royals' designated hitter in 1975. The Twins, seeking to squeeze all they could out of him, announced a Harmon Killebrew Day for May 4. The attendance was dismal, 14,805 paid, but Killebrew smacked a homer in the first inning. Perhaps it was a swan song for the Twins fans. Killebrew retired at the end of the season. He had homered 573 times, and amassed 1,584 RBIs. He walked 1,559 times and his lifetime batting average was .256. He drove in 100 or more runs nine times. In eight seasons he hit 40 or more home runs, trailing only Babe Ruth who had 11 such seasons. When he retired, Killebrew was fifth in career home runs.

In retirement Killebrew took to broadcasting, working for the Twins, the Oakland A's, and the California Angels. Outside of baseball, his life was on a downward spiral. He and Elaine divorced after more than 30 years of marriage. His car dealership in Ontario, Oregon, and his car leasing company in Bloomington, Minnesota, both failed, pushing him to bankruptcy. He owed money to banks, to Griffith, and to Reggie Jackson. "It's been a living hell," Killebrew said. "You have a lot of those days when you feel you're at the bottom. You get to feeling that sometimes you're out on an island by yourself. I don't feel anger, more sometimes frustration, sadness is another, loneliness is another one. Stressful? That's an understatement."[22]

Killebrew appeared at sports memorabilia shows, sometimes collecting up to $5,000 for an appearance. But he could never make back what he owed. He filed for bankruptcy in 1993.

Meanwhile, in 1984 Cooperstown came calling, enshrining Killebrew in the National Baseball Hall of Fame. "It's the biggest thrill I've had in baseball, although the full impact of it probably won't hit me until I go to Cooperstown next summer," he said.[23] Killebrew was the first Twin to be inducted into the Hall. He was elected to the Minnesota Twins Hall of Fame in 2000, and the club retired his number 3.

Harmon "Killer" Killebrew died of esophageal cancer on May 17, 2011, at his home in Scottsdale, Arizona. He was surrounded by his family, including his second wife, Nita. If ever a nickname was an aberration, it was Killer. Killebrew influenced younger players, passing on his knowledge of the game. The saying "he would do anything for you" was not idle chatter when it came to Killebrew. He lived it for all.

An example: In 1964 Johnny Guiney was hospitalized in New York Hospital with burns over 50 percent of his body. The 8-year-old's robes caught fire as he lit candles at his parish church. Killebrew was the boy's favorite baseball player, as the magazines and baseball cards at home featuring Harmon's likeness could attest to. Johnny's father phoned the *New York Daily News* to see if they could arrange a visit by Killebrew, who was in town to play the Yankees. Told that Johnny's doctor said a visit "would be the best medicine the kid could have," Killebrew went to see him. Killebrew gave him an autographed baseball and a signed photo to "My pal John," signed his baseball glove, said when he left, "Maybe I'll hit you a couple."[24]

Killebrew kept his word. He homered in the first and eighth innings of the Twins' victory. Harmon couldn't let Johnny down now, could he? That was Harmon Killebrew; he would do anything for you.

SOURCES

sabr.org/

baseball-reference.com/

retrosheet.org/

baseball-almanac.com/

minnesota.twins.mlb.com/index.jsp?c_id=min&tcid=mm_cle_sitelist

US Census Bureau

NOTES

1 *The Sporting News*, August 28, 1971, 7.
2 Ibid.
3 Ibid.
4 Ibid.
5 Steve Aschburner, *Harmon Killebrew: Ultimate Slugger* (Chicago: Triumph Books, 2012), 130-131.
6 Aschburner, 20.
7 Danny Peary, *We Played the Game* (New York: Hyperion Books, 1994), 276.
8 Ibid.
9 *Sports Illustrated*, June 1, 1959, 49-53.
10 Peary, 486.
11 *Sports Illustrated*, June 1, 1959, 49-53.
12 Peary, 485.
13 Aschburner, 75
14 Jim Thielman, *Cool of the Evening* (Minneapolis: Kirk House Publishers, 2005),170 .
15 Aschburner, 122.
16 *The Sporting News*, October 25, 1969, 3.
17 Ibid.
18 Ibid.
19 *The Sporting News*, May 15, 1971, 16.
20 Aschburner, 149.
21 Aschburner, 150.
22 Aschburner, 172.
23 *St. Paul Dispatch*, January 11, 1984, 1A.
24 *New York Daily News*, May 27, 1964.

Jim Perry Makes Most of His Opportunity

May 26, 1965: Minnesota Twins 9, Boston Red Sox 7 at Fenway Park, Boston, Massachusetts

BY JOEL RIPPEL

SOMETIMES THE BEST DEAL FOR A major-league team is the one it doesn't make.

In the first six weeks of the 1965 American League season, pitcher Jim Perry was given little opportunity to show the Minnesota Twins the truth in that adage.

From the start of spring training through the first 35 games of the regular season, the right-handed Perry tossed just 10⅔ innings: 7 in three spring-training appearances and 3⅔ innings in four regular-season appearances. Uninjured, but relegated to far end of the bullpen, Perry had been mentioned in trade rumors since the start of spring training.

At the start of the game against the Red Sox in Boston on May 26, it didn't seem likely anything would change for the little-used right-hander, who had been mentioned in numerous trade rumors since the end of the 1964 season.

Twins workhorse Camilo Pascual was scheduled to start for the 22-13 Twins, who went into the game in second place, one game behind the league-leading Chicago White Sox. The Red Sox were in seventh place with a 17-19 record.

Pascual, who had averaged 256 innings a season in the Twins' first four seasons in Minnesota, took a 5-0 record and a reputation as a warm-weather pitcher into the game, played on a day when the high temperature in Boston was 92.

The Twins, who had collected 20 hits in a 17-5 victory over the Red Sox the previous night, came out swinging. They scored four runs in the first inning—three on a two-out home run by Bob Allison off Earl Wilson—to stake Pascual to a 4-0 lead. But Pascual didn't make it out of the second inning.

The Red Sox scored one run in the first, then erupted for five in the second to take a 6-4 lead. The scoring all came after Pascual had gotten two outs. Carl Yastrzemski's bases-loaded double cleared the bases and chased the hard-throwing Cuban.

Perry, who was in his seventh big-league season, replaced Pascual. The first batter to face him was Felix Mantilla, who lifted a popup in front of home plate.[1] Catcher Earl Battey dropped the ball and Yastrzemski, running with two outs, scored the fifth run of the inning before Mantilla was thrown out trying to advance to second on the play. While Perry was holding the Red Sox scoreless over the next three innings, the Twins made it 6-5 on a solo home run by Harmon Killebrew in the third and then regained the lead with four runs in the fifth. The Red Sox got one run back in the sixth to cut the Twins' lead to 9-7, but also had a runner thrown out at the plate. Tony Conigliaro opened the inning by reaching first on an error. Eddie Bressoud followed with a double, with Conigliaro stopping at third. Bob Tillman singled to score Conigliaro, but Bressoud was tagged out at home by Battey (on a throw by center fielder Jimmie Hall). Left-hander Bill Pleis relieved Perry and went on to pitch 3⅓ scoreless innings before giving way to Al Worthington with two out in the ninth. Worthington got the final out to save Perry's first victory of the season.

Perry had pitched 3⅔ innings (matching his season total to that point), allowing three hits and an unearned run.

"Perry pitched very well, especially when you consider he has not had much work," said Twins manager Sam Mele. "His control might have been bad with so little work. He had good control and threw hard."[2]

The victory, just their fifth in 10 games, moved the Twins (23-13) into first place in the AL standings by percentage points over the White Sox (24-14), who lost to Cleveland, 3-1, in Chicago.

Perry said the speculation about his job security and the trade rumors didn't distract him.

"I figured I would get my chance," Perry remembered years later. "I just kept in shape. I worked in the bullpen. I threw all the time. I'd throw a lot of b.p. (batting practice). Hal Naragon, our bullpen coach, would say, 'You can't throw that much.'"[3]

The opportunity was a steppingstone for Perry, who was a valuable member of the Twins pitching staff in the second half of the season.

"After I got the chance to pitch [May 26] I won seven straight," said Perry. "Camilo got hurt and I started [19 games] in the second half of the season. I always pitched the same. I pitched like I had a one-run lead, even if I had a six-run lead."

During the stretch in which Perry won seven straight, the Twins went 34-20 to open a 3½-game lead over Cleveland on July 19.

Perry gave credit to Johnny Sain, who was in his first season as the Twins pitching coach. "Johnny Sain was great. He stressed control. He really built confidence in you. He always said, 'Don't talk [bad] about my pitchers.'"

SOURCES

Author's phone interview with Jim Perry, August 2014

Minnesota Twins 1965 media guide

Minneapolis Tribune

Minneapolis Star

NOTES

1 According to the game report in the *Minneapolis Tribune* of May 27, 1965, "Yastrzemski scored from second when catcher Battey dropped Mantilla's pop in front of the plate." However, BaseballReference.com has the play scored as Battey's error on a ground ball.

2 *Minneapolis Star*, May 27, 1965.

3 Phone interview with Jim Perry, August 2014. All subsequent quotes from Perry are from the interview.

Jerry Kindall

BY TOM TOMASHEK

JERRY KINDALL HAD NO TROUBLE making it to the major leagues. All the 21-year-old University of Minnesota 1956 All-American infielder had to do was sign on the dotted line, and the next day he was in Chicago wearing a Cubs uniform.

For Kindall, one of 59 major-league "bonus babies" signed from 1953 through 1957, the bonus rule then in effect had its downside. The rule, initiated in 1947, rescinded in 1952, then revised and restored in 1953, required that any player signed for $4,000 or more had to be retained on the team's major-league roster for two calendar years or be subject to the postseason draft. The rule made it difficult, if not impossible, for a player to get enough experience to succeed in the majors.

Gerald Donald Kindall, the son of Harold "Butch" Kindall and Alfield Kindall, wasn't looking for instant gratification. He was just coming off a College World Series championship and had a basketball scholarship at the University of Minnesota, but he did want to see how he would fare in professional baseball, and the bonus money, reported to be $50,000, was extremely appealing in light of his family's financial situation.

"My dad was working two jobs, 70 hours a week. My mom was in a wheelchair, I had two younger brothers, and my grandfather was living with us," Kindall said in a telephone conversation. "It was a handsome offer so I signed, but not before I made a promise to my parents that I would complete my education." True to his word, Kindall went back to school during the offseasons, completing his bachelor's degree early in his big-league career and then pursuing and completing his master's degree.

Kindall signed on June, 30, 1956, and the next morning was on a plane to Chicago, where the Cubs were completing a homestand. The Cubs had one other bonus baby, Don Kaiser, and a couple of weeks later signed a third, Moe Drabowsky. All three were required to be on the 25-man roster. Some of the older players who had struggled their way up to the majors and were paid poorly in the minors were resentful of youngsters coming in with a pocketful of money and taking a major-league spot.

"So, here I come walking in, a college guy and All-American with what they think is a pocketful of money. …They didn't know I left that money at home," Kindall said. "And what I didn't realize was that to make room for me, they had to send down a popular utility player, Ed Winceniak, who was a real nice guy."

In his final of nine years in the big-leagues, Kindall started 101 games at second base for the Twins in 1965. He later served as head baseball coach at the University of Arizona (1973-1996), leading the Wildcats to three College World Series titles. (Photo courtesy of Minnesota Twins Baseball Club).

Kindall was limited to pinch-running opportunities for several weeks, one of them leading to his first at-bat in Pittsburgh, against Elroy Face. He entered the game as a pinch-runner, scored, and returned to the dugout. Oblivious to the fact that the Cubs had batted around, he was shaken out of his reverie when someone hollered, "Hey kid, get a bat, you're up." He quickly grabbed a bat, rushed to the on-deck circle, and took a couple of rapid swings before stepping to the plate.

"Someone told me before I went up to watch for his forkball," Kindall said lightly. "So I went up looking for the forkball, but he threw three fastballs. I watched two pitches and swung at the third for strike three."

The 6-foot-2, 175-pound infielder, nicknamed Slim, made his first start, at shortstop, when Ernie Banks was sidelined by an infected hand, and he remained in the lineup for a couple of weeks. Kindall didn't hit well but made enough defensive plays to validate Chicago's substantial investment. Overall in 1956, he played in 32 games, hitting a scant .164 but making only four errors in 90 chances. In 1957 he played in 72 games and started 36, again struggling offensively and making 15 errors in 197 chances.

Although Kindall was an excellent hitter in college ball—he batted .381 with 18 home runs and 48 runs batted in as a senior—he struggled offensively in his first two seasons in the big leagues, hitting .164 and .160 in limited duty.

Whatever hardships were imposed by his premature inaugural, Kindall coped with them through his devout Christian beliefs and the friendship and guidance of several men, including Pepper Martin, the former Cardinals great and then the Cubs' third-base coach, who took him under his wing on road trips. The Cubs management was impressed by Kindall's glove and after the 1957 season, when the bonus rule was changed to read that a season and any part of another season counted as two, they sent their promising bonus baby to Fort Worth, hopeful that full-time duty would enhance his batting skills.

"I was grateful for the major-league experience, but I was glad when they sent me down," Kindall said of his two seasons in Fort Worth. "That was my apprenticeship. It was an excellent experience, although it did come a year and a half late."

Kindall played second base and hit .229 in 1958 with 16 home runs and 65 RBIs in 1958, when Fort Worth played in the Double-A Texas League. Fort Worth joined the Triple-A American Association in 1959, and Kindall went along. He slipped in home runs (7) and RBIs (42), but his 1960 spring training was impressive enough to earn him a return to the Cubs.

"I got a lot of help from the manager, Lou Klein, a former major-league infielder who was among those players who had jumped to the Mexican League in the 1940s," Kindall said. "I played almost every inning with him while I was in Fort Worth."

Kindall frequently started at second base in the next two seasons. He had exceptional defensive skills and range and occasionally hit for power but was unable to sustain any overall offensive consistency. Lou Boudreau, who in 1960 replaced Charlie Grimm as the Cubs manager, worked with Kindall, attempting to make him a slap hitter by getting him to abandon his long stride and uppercut swing, but even a Hall of Famer's attention failed to get the promising big-league infielder on track offensively. Kindall was hitting .303 in early July of 1960 and hovered around .275 in mid-July of 1961, but each season he faltered late and finished at .240 and 242, respectively. Before heading back to Minnesota after the 1961 season, however, he got a vote of confidence when the Cubs informed him that Ernie Banks might be moved to first base and that he was the heir apparent at shortstop.

Kindall was ecstatic and had reason for greater optimism when he read an article in *The Sporting News* with the headline, "Banks to First Base, Kindall to Short." When he completed a graduate class, he rushed home to tell his wife, Georgia, who had news for her husband. "She told me, 'Gabe Paul called from Cleveland, and here's the number, he wants you to call him back.'" Paul was the Indians' general manager.

"I called him and was told that I had been traded to Cleveland." The Cubs did move Banks to first, but Andre Rodgers became Chicago's regular shortstop and Ken Hubbs, impressive in late 1961, took charge at second base.

Cleveland, however, quickly made Kindall feel at home and made him the regular second baseman. He started 154 of the team's 162 games. He made nearly all the defensive plays and demonstrated some offensive promise, hitting as high as .289 on May 11. In what Kindall called his finest hour offensively, he played an integral role in a four-game sweep of the New York Yankees in June, a surge that hoisted the Indians into the American League lead. Kindall went 8-for-14 with two home runs, the first a two-run blast in the bottom of the ninth for a 10-9 victory and the second coming in the first game of a Sunday doubleheader played before nearly 71,000 frenzied fans in Municipal Stadium.

"I was living on a cloud," said Kindall, "but the next day Boston came to town and I came back to ground in a hurry. I went 0-for-4."

He struggled after this and finished the season with a lackluster .232 batting average, albeit an average underscored by 13 home runs and 55 RBIs. But despite further offensive advice from the Indians coaching staff, he continued to struggle at the plate. "I was a project every season," Kindall said. "It was always, 'If we could get Kindall to hit .260, he could be a regular.' Maybe I got confused trying so many different things, and I struck out too much to hit for average."

Besides his outburst against the Yanks, Kindall's other claim to fame with the bat was his success against future Hall of Fame right-hander Robin Roberts, against whom he hit .269 and stroked four homers, the most he hit off any pitcher. "One time (Roberts) said, 'Hey kid, how do you hit so well against me?'" Kindall said. "I told him at first that I didn't know but then explained that he gave me good fastballs below the belt. From that point on I got nothing but belt-high fastballs and curves. I don't know why I said that."

Kindall started more than half of Cleveland's games in 1963, switching between shortstop and second base, and the lanky infielder once again had another season of good-field, no-hit, finishing with a .205 average. So when manager Birdie Tebbetts had a heart attack in early April of 1964, Indians interim manager George Strickland and Gabe Paul had a different plan. Larry Brown became the starting second baseman, with Kindall catching an occasional start until he was sent to Minnesota in a three-way deal on June 11, just before the trading deadline.

At Minnesota it became a case of "Who's on second?" with Kindall sharing the job with more than a half-dozen other infielders. Kindall played in 85 games in 1964, 41 as a starter, and occasionally filled in for Zoilo Versalles at shortstop, but once again he was unable to hit and between the Indians and Twins, he batted .183. He did, however, survive the next spring training and wound up playing in 125 games (102 starts).

In late June of 1965, Kindall tore a muscle just above his hamstring, missed more than a week, and, shortly after getting back in the lineup, reinjured the muscle while running out a base hit down the line. Frank Quilici, a 26-year-old rookie and, like Kindall, a former All-American shortstop, was called up from the minors in July and shared time with Kindall at second. Although Kindall started more than 100 games during the regular season, Quilici played every inning in the World Series against the Los Angeles Dodgers.

"It was a disappointment, but while I was healthy in time for the World Series, Quilici was doing such a good job there was no reason to take him out," Kindall said. "There is one thing that rankles me to this day and that was an article written in the [Minneapolis] *Tribune.* A reporter said that I had never gotten a hit off Sandy Koufax [who pitched three games in the Series], but that wasn't true.

"I faced Koufax at least 30 times while I was in the National League and I confess that I struck out most of the time, but I did have at least four hits against him. But I think that maybe affected [manager Sam Mele's] thinking. I'd grab a bat and walk around hoping he'd see me, but that didn't work." Actually, Kindall had more trouble than he thought against Koufax: 28 at-bats, 2 singles, 1 walk, and 18 strikeouts.

When the Twins broke camp after spring training in 1966, Kindall was beckoned to owner Calvin Griffith's trailer and told he was being released, that he still might have time to catch on with another team. "Cal, never one known for his diplomacy, told me, 'I've got you and Quilici, and neither one of you can hit,'" Kindall said, laughing. "'So, I'm giving you a chance to make a deal for yourself.' I was shocked and surprised. I know my leg was bothering me and that I hadn't played well in exhibition games. After the injury I couldn't cover the ground I did before.

"But I figured I'd done some important things for the Twins. He did ask me if I'd go to the minors, but I told him that I wouldn't."

So Kindall cleaned out his locker, joined the recently traded Dick Stigman, who had been dealt to the Boston Red Sox, and went back to their spring quarters to wait for their wives, who had taken their children to the zoo. Kindall did check with several teams to see if they had an opening, but when he realized that all the rosters were set, he began looking for a job. Fortunately, he had a great reputation with the University of Minnesota, and athletic director Marsh Ryman patched a job together for him, one that included assisting in baseball and basketball, directing a fundraising program, and selling advertisements for the football program.

Eventually Kindall settled into a full-time assistant's job on the baseball team with his former coach, Dick Siebert, and in February of 1972 became the University of Arizona's head baseball coach in waiting (taking over the position the following year).

Life was good until 1984, when Georgia, a registered nurse, was diagnosed with Lou Gehrig's Disease; she died on June 29, 1987. "I had been teaching and coaching at the time, but the university relieved me of my teaching duties," Kindall said. "It wasn't baseball that helped me get through it, it was my faith in the Lord, but I continued to coach. Georgia insisted that I keep coaching."

In July of 1988 Kindall met Diane, a widow, and they became engaged in September. They were married on Thanksgiving weekend. Kindall continued to coach until he retired in 1996 after having won 861 games and three College World Series titles. As of 2014 he was the only man ever to have played on and coached College World Series championship teams, and in an ironic twist, the man with a .213 major-league batting average was the only player ever to have hit for the cycle in the College World Series.

The disappointing conclusion to Kindall's professional playing career also didn't diminish his appreciation for the major-league opportunity; in fact, he credited the experience for opening the door to arguably the greatest phase of baseball life. "If I had any success as a college coach, it's because of the many good things I saw and learned in professional baseball … the struggles it presented," Kindall said. "As spotty as my career was, it opened the door for me to get the best college coaching job in the world. There were three men interviewed for the job [at Arizona], Bobby Richardson, Steve Hamilton, and me.

"Bobby withdrew and so they asked him if he would recommend one of us. He said, 'Jerry Kindall is a close friend and Steve Hamilton named his son, Robert, after me. I don't know what to tell you.' I really think they wound up flipping a coin."

Kindall's atypical power for an infielder raised this question: Did he ever consider that playing the outfield might have enhanced his major-league career? He responded instantly and emphatically. "No, I belonged in the infield … as a middle infielder," he said. "Others may have considered the possibility, but I never did."

It goes without saying that Jerry Kindall also belonged in baseball from the day he entered St. Paul's Washington High School, where he was named the 1953 State High School Baseball Tournament's Most Valuable Player, until the day he retired from Arizona.

Note

A version of this biography appeared in the book *Minnesotans in Baseball*, edited by Stew Thornley (Nodin, 2009).

SOURCES

The *Baseball Encyclopedia*, the Baseball Cube and several other Google sites to validate Baseball Cube information, Baseball Old-Timers Data Base, the University of Minnesota Media Relations department, the University of Arizona database, Wikipedia, and more than two hours interviewing Kindall by telephone.

Johnny Klippstein

BY GREGORY H. WOLF

ON MAY 26, 1956, THE CINCINNATI Redlegs and Milwaukee Braves faced off in the second game of a three-game series in Milwaukee. The result was one of the most unusual and memorable games in the history of each franchise.

On the mound for the Redlegs was Johnny Klippstein, a hard-throwing right-hander in his seventh season in the major leagues with an undistinguished career record at the time of 43-63. After a 1-2-3 first inning, Klippstein found himself in trouble in the second. He loaded the bases by hitting Hank Aaron and walking Bobby Thomson and Bill Bruton. Aaron scored on Frank Torre's fly ball to left field, but Klippstein avoided more trouble by striking out the next two batters. After six innings, the Redlegs were losing 1-0, but Klippstein was working on a no-hitter.

His counterpart for the Braves, 24-year-old Ray Crone, in his third season and sporting a career record of 13-10, was pitching a three-hitter. Klippstein walked three more in the seventh, but was again able to work out of the jam. In the eighth inning with the Redlegs' Smoky Burgess on second base and one out, Klippstein was due to bat, and the unthinkable happened: Shunning tradition and sentimentality, Redlegs manager Birdie Tebbetts pinch-hit for Klippstein despite his no-hitter through seven innings.

Klippstein was relieved by Hersh Freeman, and Joe Black, who each pitched a hitless frame, thus completing an unprecedented three-man no-hitter through nine innings. The Redlegs tied the game in the top of the ninth inning. The Braves finally got a hit in the tenth, and won the game with two more hits and a run in the bottom of the 11th. Though the Braves were held hitless for nine innings, Major League Baseball removed the game from the official list of no-hitters in 1991 when it decided that a game in which a team didn't get a hit until extra innings would no longer be considered a no-hitter. Still, the game was still a thrilling one.

"We all would have made history if I could have gotten the Reds out in the ninth," said Ray Crone, who gave up the tying run to the Redlegs in the ninth inning.[1] (The Braves would have won even though they were held hitless.) "I wasn't even aware that Klippstein had a no-hitter at the time," said Crone. "Klippstein was a hard thrower. We were just glad to win the game and didn't know the game was anything special."

Klippstein's performance (seven no-hit innings with seven walks, a hit batsman, and four strikeouts) could be seen as a microcosm for his entire career: great potential, with flashes of dominance tempered by poor

At the age of 37, right-hander Klippstein was a dependable reliever, winning nine times and posting a stellar 2.24 ERA in 76 1/3 innings over 56 appearances for the pennant-winners. In 18 years in the majors (1950-1967), Klippstein went 101-118, appeared in 711 games, and logged 1,967 2/3 innings. (Photo courtesy of Minnesota Twins Baseball Club).

control, which resulted in his fine performances often being overlooked.

John Calvin Klippstein was born in Washington, D.C., on October 17, 1927, to August and Mamie Klippstein. August was born in Stettin, Germany, in 1883 and immigrated to the United States with his parents in 1894, settling in Wisconsin. He joined the US Army and while stationed in Washington he met Mamie Groves from Virginia. They married in 1913 and had three children, Katherine, George, and John, the youngest.

An athletic youngster, John played baseball and basketball at Montgomery Blair High School in Silver Spring, Maryland, a Washington suburb. By all accounts he was a good student, was president of his junior class and president of the student council his senior year, and graduated in 1945. His passion was baseball, which he indulged as an usher in the Washington Senators' Griffith Stadium while in high school. When he was just 15 years old, he had an opportunity to show big-league scouts his ability. "I was visiting an uncle in Appleton, Wisconsin, in the fall of 1943," Klippstein recalled. "As fate would have it, the Cardinals were conducting a tryout camp there and I enrolled because I thought I was a pretty hot article after one year of high-school ball."[2] Former pitcher Tony Kaufmann, a Cardinals scout, ran the camp. "The following spring I was signed" by longtime Cardinals scout Pop Kelchner, Klippstein said.[3]

Now a professional, Klippstein was no longer eligible to play high-school baseball. When the school year ended in the spring of 1944, Klippstein, just 16 years old, reported to Allentown of the Class B Interstate League. Against players averaging about 22 years old, he pitched in six games, and won his first game, but with a lofty 10.50 earned-run average, he was sent to Lima of the Class D Ohio State League. He went 3-2 with a 4.75 ERA. After graduating from high school in 1945, he pitched briefly for Allentown and then for Winston-Salem in the Class C Carolina League, where he finally exhibited the promise the Cardinals' organization had envisioned. In 23 games, including 15 starts, he posted an 8-7 record and a 2.48 ERA, which ranked second in the league.

Klippstein was drafted into the Army in 1946 and missed the entire baseball season. When he returned to the mound in 1947 with the Omaha Cardinals of the Class A Western League, he complained of arm troubles and struggled to regain his form, posting an unseemly 5.37 ERA.[4] He was demoted to Lynchburg in the Class B Piedmont League where he didn't fare much better, then finished the season with two brief relief appearances in Triple-A with Columbus of the American Association. He was wild; for his three teams in 1947 he walked 90 batters in 127 innings. Save for one relief outing with Columbus, Klippstein pitched the entire 1948 season with Lynchburg. Used as a starter and reliever, he was plagued by wildness, walking 119 in 155 innings– while still complaining of arm and shoulder pains. Just 20 years old, Klippstein was still considered a top prospect, and the Cardinals lost him to the Brooklyn Dodgers in the November 1948 draft; that proved to be Klippstein's big break.

The Dodgers assigned Klippstein to Mobile in the Double-A Southern Association for the 1949 season, and he excelled. He won 15 games, posted a 2.95 ERA, second best among starters in the league, and appeared ready for the major leagues. The Dodgers hoped to hide Klippstein from other teams in the 1949 draft by assigning him to their top Triple-A affiliate, the Montreal Royals, but the Chicago Cubs drafted him, paying an estimated $10,000 for his rights.[5] "The Dodgers lost a good man in the draft," said *The Sporting News*.[6]

In March 1950 Klippstein reported to his first major-league spring training, at the Cubs' facility on Catalina Island, off the Southern California coast. Manager Frankie Frisch was impressed with Klippstein, calling him "the fastest fellow in camp," but he also noticed that Klippstein was still raw: "He's just a baby. He needs some experience."[7] Cubs coach Spud Davis, a former big-league catcher, said he thought he detected the flaw that caused Klippstein's wildness: " … (H)e looked down to the ground and not the plate when he was going into his windup."[8]

Klippstein stuck with the Cubs and his major-league debut, on May 3 was inauspicious. He lost in a start against the Phillies, lasting just four innings and surrendering nine hits and four runs. Used as a starter and reliever during the season, Klippstein had trouble finding his rhythm. His first major-league win came on July 19, a complete game against the Boston Braves in which he gave up 11 hits but only three runs. He followed that up with two consecutive complete-game losses, underscoring his potential as a starter. He finished his rookie campaign with an unsightly 2-9 record, and a 5.25 ERA.

Klippstein pitched for the Cubs through the 1954 season but he never established himself as the effective starter the team expected him to be. By the middle of 1951, Klippstein's second season, the buzz around him began to fade and he was considered a "borderline hope" and not an imminent star.[9] A masterful performance like his six-hit shutout of Pittsburgh in his first start of the 1951 season was countered by several poor outings with "flights of wildness" eroding Frisch's confidence in him. He finished 1951 with six wins and six losses.

In 1952, Phil Cavarretta, who replaced Frisch at midseason in 1951, slotted Klippstein for the bullpen. He fought his way back into the starting rotation after shutting out the Dodgers in early May and then completed three of his next four starts. "Johnny has a world of stuff," said pitching coach Charlie Root. "Johnny was pitching out in the open, far away from his body. The batter could follow the ball too easily. We got him to change his windup so now he brings the ball down just below his belt and then pivots before delivery."[10] Klippstein had a losing record (9 wins and 14 losses) while compiling a 4.44 ERA. Fighting wildness, he hit six batters and uncorked a league-leading 12 wild pitches.

Described as a "gangling loose-jointed fellow with an unruly mop of curly black hair outlining a baby face," Klippstein married Mary Ann Artac in 1952.[11] She was a niece of Cubs pitcher Dutch Leonard, whom Klippstein considered one of his biggest influences in his early career. The Klippsteins lived in Chicago, where Mary Ann was a nurse. They had two daughters, Mary Jo, and Barbara, and a son, John Jr. In the off-season Klippstein had a series of jobs, among them working for sporting-goods stores and selling insurance.

Klippstein's nickname, "The Wild Man of Borneo" (the title of a 1941 film), was reinforced by his erratic campaign in 1953. He reached double-digit victories for the first time (10) but lost 11, and walked 107 batters. By 1954 the Cubs disclosed that they had been actively shopping him since the previous spring. In '54 Stan Hack, Klippstein's third manager in five years, gave him another opportunity to prove himself as a starter, but Klippstein struggled all year and at one point lost eight consecutive decisions on his way to a miserable 4-11 season. His ERA ballooned to 5.29 and he walked almost six batters per nine innings.

After the season Klippstein was traded to Cincinnati in a five-player deal. Manager Birdie Tebbetts tabbed him for middle relief, to which Klippstein responded, "Either starting or relief pitcher is all right with me, but not both. That's the way it was in Chicago."[12] An impressive seven-inning start in early May moved Tebbetts, who was seduced by Klippstein's hard throwing. Despite not being used consistently as a starter, Klippstein pitched better as the season progressed. He always possessed a strong overhand fastball, but his slider and curveball were inconsistent. Klippstein credited Reds pitching coach Tom Ferrick with helping him develop a slider thrown at three-quarters. "That way the ball breaks in the same plane instead of down and away," Klippstein said. "It's mistaken for a fastball when coming plateward."[13] He finished 1955 with a 9-10 record and a 3.39 ERA, but pitched one of his two career one-hitters, beating the Dodgers 9-0 in early September, his fourth victory of the year against Brooklyn.

Klippstein began 1956 with an impressive 10⅓-inning complete-game loss to the Cubs, and completed seven of his first 12 starts, including his seven innings of no-hit ball and another tough 10⅓-inning complete-game loss. He finished the season with career highs in several categories, including wins (12), innings pitched (211), starts (29), and complete games (11). Klippstein's inconsistencies confounded manager Tebbetts, who thought he experimented with too many different pitches and had problems pacing himself as a starter. "I don't know what's holding back Johnny Klippstein," Tebbetts said. "He throws harder… than almost anybody we've got. Johnny has everything a pitcher needs to win."[14] Given the Opening Day start in 1957, Klippstein expected great success, but the season devolved into a complete disappointment as he was hit hard almost all season and shuttled unceremoniously between relief and occasional starts. If anything, Klippstein was exasperating. After not starting for almost two months, he pitched two consecutive complete-game victories, including a ten-inning gem, to close out the season, but still finished with an atrocious 5.05 ERA and just eight wins (11 defeats).

The turning point in Klippstein's career came in 1958. Lost in the Redlegs' bullpen, he was traded hours before the deadline to the Los Angeles Dodgers, along with first baseman Steve Bilko and pitchers Art Fowler and Charlie Rabe for pitcher Don Newcombe. "Johnny Klippstein's got good stuff," Dodgers manager Walter Alston said. "I am planning to use him as a middle man in relief."[15] Pitching exclusively out of the bullpen for the first time in his life, Klippstein seemed more relaxed, had better command of his pitches, and was arguably the Dodgers' most effective reliever.

Over the next nine seasons, Klippstein breathed new life into his career by establishing himself as an effective relief specialist. "By pitching more often in relief," Klippstein said, "it sharpened my control and gave me more confidence." In 1959, he was on pace to pitch in more than 50 games, but he developed back problems in mid-June and was ineffective the rest of the season.[16] The Dodgers won the NL pennant on the strength of their pitching and Alston decided to carry Klippstein on the World Series roster despite his having had just two appearances in the last two months. Johnny saw mop-up duty in the White Sox' 11-0 victory in Game One, pitching two scoreless innings, his only appearance in the Dodgers' World Series victory.

Klippstein's age, health, and poor outings during spring training in 1960 concerned the Dodgers, and they sold him to the Cleveland Indians in April 1960 for a reported $25,000. Indians general manager Frank Lane was undeterred by Klippstein's back problems, and desperately wanted an experienced relief pitcher to shore up his very young starting rotation. Pitching in the American League for the first time, Klippstein assured the Indians that he felt fine. "The doctors told me to rest all winter," he said. "They told me I couldn't make my back any worse by pitching."[17] This information seemed to remove a psychological barrier, and Klippstein pitched well enough to be awarded the closer's role for the first time in his career. He pitched extremely well all season, led the league with 14 saves, posted his first sub-3.00 ERA, and was one of the most effective closers in baseball.

Despite Klippstein's success, the Indians made him available for the American League expansion draft conducted in December 1960. The Washington Senators grabbed him, and Senators general manager Ed Doherty said Klippstein "would be a strong relief pitcher on any club" and pronounced his bullpen as one of the best relief corps in the league.[18] While the Nats limped to a 61-100 record, Klippstein struggled with his control all season, his ERA ballooned to 6.78, and he led the league with ten wild pitches. Not surprisingly, he was traded at the end of the season back to Cincinnati. He pitched better for the reigning National League pennant winners, and even started seven games. In one of the most memorable games of his career, Klippstein relieved Bob Purkey to start the 11th inning in a 0-0 game against the Houston Colt .45's at Colt Stadium. In the top of the 13th, Klippstein hit his fifth career home run, a solo shot, and then pitched his third consecutive scoreless inning to give the Reds a 1-0 victory, the first time a National League pitcher had won a 1-0 game in extra innings with a home run.[19] Circling the bases, Klippstein said, "I looked to Bob Aspromonte who was playing third base, I said, 'If you think you're surprised, imagine how I feel?'"[20]

Klippstein joined his sixth team in six years when the Philadelphia Phillies purchased his contract from the Reds during spring training in 1963. "He can still throw hard," Phillies manager Gene Mauch said of the 35-year-old pitcher. Other than one start, Klippstein was used exclusively out of the bullpen and responded with his best year as a professional. He pitched in 49 games, threw 112 innings, and posted a microscopic 1.93 ERA. In five of his relief appearances he pitched at least six innings. "If I had known that I could have thrown so often as I did, I would have liked to have started relieving earlier because I really had a [lot of] luck relieving," he said. The Phillies finished in fourth place with 87 wins, the team's most since 1952.[21]

The Phillies were poised for even more success in 1964 but Klippstein's prospects soured. When the team acquired reliever Ed Roebuck from the Senators on April 21, to set up closer Jack Baldschun, Klippstein was marginalized. He lost favor with manager Gene Mauch, and pitched just 11 times totaling 22⅓ innings in the Phillies' first 61 games. When injured starter Cal McLish, a personal friend of Mauch's, returned to the club in late June, Klippstein was waived. At the time, the Phillies were in first place with a 38-23 record. Klippstein was claimed by the Minnesota Twins, and impressed Twins manager Sam Mele by pitching in 33 games in three months and posting a 1.97 ERA. Neither Baldschun nor Roebuck pitched as well for the Phillies as Klippstein did for the Twins. One can only wonder if Klippstein would have helped the Phillies avoid their epic collapse.

In 1965 Johnny Sain was named pitching coach for the Twins and began to work his wonders on Klippstein by teaching him a quick-pitch curve. "It's sort of a slider that drops," Klippstein said. "It is thrown with the motion of a curve, but you throw it fast."[22] With closer Al Worthington, Klippstein as the most effective relief duo in the American League, the Twins won the pennant. In early July, Klippstein threw 8⅔ consecutive hitless innings over three appearances. "If I am loose and throwing," The 37-year-old Klippstein said of his ability to pitch so often, "I can get ready to pitch in ten pitches in the bullpen and eight more on the mound."[23] He finished the season with a sparkling 2.24 ERA in 56 appearances. In the World Series, he pitched a scoreless inning in Game Three when Claude Osteen shut out the Twins, and pitched another 1⅔ scoreless innings in Game Seven when Sandy Koufax tossed his three-hit gem to clinch the title for Los Angeles. Klippstein capped off a stretch of 23 consecutive appearances dating from August 1 in which he did not give up a single run.

Klippstein lost some of his effectiveness in 1966, and pitched in just 26 games. "I believe that [manager] Sam Mele has lost confidence in me," he lamented after the season. "I didn't pitch much and that bothered me."[24] When he was released after the season, it was the first time in 23 years that he was out of work. Klippstein wanted one last chance to pitch. The Detroit Tigers invited him to work out during spring training in 1967. He pitched well enough to earn a contract, but was released in late May after just five appearances.

An easy-going man, Klippstein retired after playing 18 years for eight major-league teams. He finished with a 101-118 career record and a 4.24 ERA. He had a wry sense of humor about his career. "For years, people used to ask me, 'When did you have your best season?' And I always answered, 'I've never had what I call a good one.'"[25] Asked what he could have done differently to enjoy the success so many predicted for him, Klippstein responded, "I don't know the answers. I think I fooled around with too many offbeat pitches, the knuckle scrooge and slider when I should have known the fastball was my bread and butter."[26] With his effective fastball with natural movement, and ability to warm up quickly, Klippstein might have been perfectly suited to be a closer in today's game.

After his playing career ended, Klippstein resided with his wife in Chicago, and northwest Cook County. He scouted for the Tigers until the mid-1970s and then worked for a corrugated box company until he was past 70. An avid golfer and a reader of mysteries, he followed the Cubs closely and was a longtime Cubs season ticket-holder, president of the Chicago Old-Timers Association, and past president of the Pitch and Hit Club. After a protracted illness, Klippstein died on October 10, 2003, at the age of 76 and was buried at St. Mary's cemetery in Huntley, Illinois. Jerome Holtzman, former official historian of Major League Baseball, offered the most succinct testimony to Klippstein's career: "He was one of the most-liked players of his time."

NOTES

1. The author would like to express his gratitude to Ray Crone, who was interviewed on April 23, 2012.
2. *The Sporting News*, March 22, 1950, 13.
3. Ibid.
4. Ibid.
5. *The Sporting News*, November 30, 1949, 7.
6. *The Sporting News*, December 7, 1949, 26.
7. *The Sporting News*, March 22, 1950, 17.
8. Ibid.
9. *The Sporting News*, June 13, 1951, 8.
10. *The Sporting News*, May 21, 1952, 4.
11. *The Sporting News*, February 23, 1955, 25.
12. Ibid.
13. *The Sporting News*, September 21, 1955, 19.
14. *The Sporting News*, February 20, 1957, 21.
15. The Sporting News, June 25, 1958, 11.
16. *The Sporting News*, August 5, 1959, 9.
17. *The Sporting News*, May 25, 1960, 8.
18. *The Sporting News*, February 15, 1961, 10.
19. *The Sporting News*, August 18, 1962, 9.
20. *The Sporting News*, May 25, 1960, 8.
21. Ibid.
22. *The Sporting News*, March 20, 1965, 21.
23. *The Sporting News*, June 24, 1965, 7.
24. *The Sporting News*, November 5, 1966, 31.
25. *The Sporting News*, April 23, 1966, 35.
26. Sandy Grady, "Modern Marco Polo. Johnny Klippstein's a man on the go," *Baseball Digest*, September, 1964, 56.

Andy Kosco

BY NORM KING

IF ANDY KOSCO'S BASEBALL CAREER could be described in a song, it might be the old Hank Snow classic "I've Been Everywhere." Australian country music artist Geoff Mack wrote the song; in the original version a man hitches a ride with a truck driver and proceeds to tell him that he has visited every town, hamlet, and billabong in Australia.[1] Snow adapted the song by incorporating the names of North American locales, and it seems that Kosco, who wore the uniforms of 19 teams in the major and minor leagues during his professional career, played in every one of them.

Andrew John Kosco, IV was born on October 5, 1941, in Youngstown, Ohio. He was the third of four children of Andrew Kosco, III and Minnie (Rotz) Kosco. Andrew III ran a newsstand with his brother while Minnie stayed at home to raise the children.

Kosco excelled at every sport as a youngster. By the time he was a senior at Struthers High School, he was a strapping 6-feet-3 and 210 pounds, and excelled in football, basketball, and baseball. He received 44 scholarship offers for football, including ones from powers such as Michigan State and Ohio State, and 27 offers for basketball. "I think I was blessed with a lot of size," said Kosco. "I ran well and threw well."[2]

Kosco was also blessed with a lot of baseball ability, which really manifested itself in his senior year, when he batted over .700 in 11 high-school games with eight home runs, and averaged 14 strikeouts a game as a pitcher. Those numbers attracted interest from all 16 major-league teams.

One scout who spent a lot of time tracking Kosco's progress was Edwin "Cy" Williams of the Detroit Tigers.[3] Williams began watching Kosco play baseball, football, and basketball around the Youngstown area when Andy was a high-school sophomore and followed him for the next couple of years. Eventually, Williams signed him right out of high school in June 1959 for what at that time was an enormous bonus of $62,500.

Of course, sometimes it's not the money that's the deciding factor in what sport you decide to play or whom you sign with. Kosco's father influenced him to go with baseball because that was his favorite sport. His mother's respect for Williams also had a role in Kosco's ending up with the Tigers.

"My mom took a real liking to the fellow," said Kosco. "He was a religious, dedicated fellow and my mom said that (Williams) was her favorite, so that's the reason why I ended up signing with Detroit."

As soon as he signed, Kosco began working out with the major-league club, but it was apparent that actually

After knocking in 116 runs in 119 games in the PCL in 1965, Kosco was called up in August and saw limited action in right field and first base. He played ten years in the majors, and belted 19 homers for the Los Angeles Dodgers in 1969. (Photo courtesy of Minnesota Twins Baseball Club).

playing was better for Kosco's development than just working out with the major leaguers, so they sent him to the Decatur (Illinois) Commodores of the Class D Midwest League. Except for one 18-year-old who played in six games with the Commodores, Kosco, at 17, was at least two years younger than anyone else on the team. The transition was not easy.

"It was the first time I had ever been away from home (other) than visiting some colleges," he said. "We had never been on a vacation or left town, really."

Kosco also had to adapt to superior competition. Even Class D pitchers threw better curveballs than high schoolers and they also threw them when they were behind in the count. In addition, he had never seen a slider before he reached the pro level, and he also had to get used to the inside knockdown pitch. The result of making all those adjustments was a low batting average (.237), but Kosco did show some power, hitting nine home runs in 232 at-bats.

The Tigers were impressed enough with those numbers to move Kosco up two levels to Class B with the Durham Bulls of the Carolina League. He had impressive statistics there, with a .273 average and 22 home runs. The Tigers promoted him again, but he quickly showed he couldn't hit A ball. Or Double-A or Triple-A for that matter. In 1961 he hit nine home runs, in 1962 he hit six and in 1963 he hit zero.

Kosco began the 1964 season with the Duluth-Superior (Duluth, Minnesota/Superior, Wisconsin) Dukes, a Tigers affiliate in the Class A Northern League. But the Tigers, convinced Kosco was regressing, cut him on June 3.

Being let go by the Tigers could be classified under the "blessing in disguise" category, because just as Kosco was getting ready to return home to Ohio, he got a call from Vern Morgan, manager of the Northern League's Bismarck-Mandan (North Dakota) Pards, a Twins affiliate. Morgan signed Kosco, and then spent hours working with him on his hitting, including having him stop switch-hitting and bat exclusively from the right side. Suddenly the can't-miss guy who was missing everything revived his power stroke. He won the league's Triple Crown, hitting .346 with 28 home runs and 97 RBIs and earned an invitation to the Twins' spring training in 1965.

An invitation doesn't mean you'll make the team, and although Kosco had a good spring, and even went north with Minnesota, he had the misfortune of being an outfielder on a team that sported the likes of Tony Oliva, Jimmie Hall, and Bob Allison. The Twins sent him back to Triple-A Denver, where he tore up the Pacific Coast League, batting .327 with 27 home runs and 116 RBIs in only 119 games. He made it difficult for the Twins to keep him down on the farm. They finally called him up in August 1965.

Kosco made his first appearance in a major-league game on August 13 at Cleveland. He grounded out pinch-hitting for pitcher Garry Roggenburk. He got his first start, first hit and first home run the next day, going 1-for-4 and playing right field.

At that point in the 1965 season, the Twins held a comfortable eight-game lead over second-place Cleveland. The winning continued as the Twins went on to capture the American League pennant. Kosco got into 23 games and hit .236 with that one home run to his credit. He did not play in the World Series even though he was with the team prior to the August 31 cutoff date. He was dropped when Commissioner Ford Frick allowed Minnesota to include pitcher Camilo Pascual, who was injured at the deadline, on its World Series roster.

"It was exciting being with the team through the excitement of winning," said Kosco. "But I probably would have been better off getting more at-bats down (in the minors)."

Kosco was with the Twins again in 1966, but the team's strong roster meant playing time was at a premium, and he got into only 57 games with two home runs and 13 RBIs. He spent most of the 1967 season back in Denver, where he hit a respectable .297 with 13 home runs and 67 RBIs in 108 games. After that season, the Oakland A's purchased his contract, and then allowed the New York Yankees to obtain him in the Rule 5 draft.

The 1968 Yankees weren't the Bronx Bombers of old, as they finished fifth with an 83-79 record (the Twins finished seventh with a 79-83 mark). The Yankees gave Kosco playing time and he responded with a .240 average, 16 home runs, and 59 RBIs in 131 games, all the while loving every minute he wore the pinstripes.

"You cannot imagine the thrill it is to put on a Yankee uniform and play in Yankee Stadium," he said. "And you have to be around [Mickey] Mantle every day to appreciate what he is — the most courageous man I have ever seen."[4]

The thrill was short-lived. The Yankees traded Kosco to the Los Angeles Dodgers for pitcher Mike Kekich after the season, but they claimed they did it for his sake. The old Yankee Stadium had a vast outfield (it was 463 feet to straightaway center and 457 feet to left-center), and Yankees manager Ralph Houk felt that the warning-track drives Kosco hit in New York would go over the fence in another home park.

"At one time [Yankees broadcaster] Jerry Coleman told me that I had hit 24 balls on the warning track in left center by the All-Star break," said Kosco. "Ralph called me during the winter and said we have a chance, for your sake, of trading you to the Dodgers, which would [have] a more conducive ball park for you."

Houk was right, at least for 1969. Kosco played in 109 games in the Dodgers outfield (74 in right and 40 in left) and batted .248 with 19 home runs and 74 RBIs.[5] In 1970, however, he lost his outfield spot to Willie Crawford, got into only 74 games and batted .228 with 8 home runs and 27 RBIs. The Dodgers began a youth movement after that season, bringing up some of the talent they were nurturing on the farm. Kosco became expendable, and was traded to the Milwaukee Brewers for pitcher Al Downing.

After playing 98 games for Milwaukee in 1971, Kosco went on to the California Angels and Boston Red Sox in 1972, then spent two seasons with the Cincinnati Reds. From 1971 to 1974, he played in 244 games and batted .237 with 28 home runs and 84 RBIs. His stint with the Reds gave him his only taste of postseason experience when they appeared in the 1973 National League Championship Series against the New York Mets, a best-of-five affair, which the Mets won, three games to two. Kosco got three singles in ten at-bats.

He also spent some time in the minors during that period, and finished his career in 1975 by playing 48 games with the Toledo Mud Hens, the Philadelphia Phillies' Triple-A affiliate in the International League. He batted .235 in his final year of professional ball with six home runs and 22 RBIs. He broke his wrist that year, and that injury, along with the death of his father, caused him to lose interest in baseball and motivated him to move on.

Having played for seven major-league teams, Kosco became very proficient at adapting to new surroundings. "I think you make an adjustment," he said. "[With fewer teams at that time] you got to know a lot of the players on the opposition, so you would kind of fit in a little bit easier. As long as you're playing in the major leagues, to me at that time it was immaterial who I played with or for."

After his playing career ended, Kosco combined working with education. By showing the same persistence in the classroom that he did on the field, he got a bachelor's degree at Youngstown State University after 15 years as a part-time student. He also worked in admissions at his alma mater.

In the 1980s Kosco got into the insurance business with former major leaguer Nick Goulish, who played with the Phillies in 1944-1945. Goulish was suffering from ALS and died in 1984, but the company remained the Goulish-Kosco Insurance Agency. As of 2014 Kosco ran the agency with his sons Bryn and Dru, both of whom reached the Triple-A level in the minors.[6]

Kosco's wife, Cathy, was his high-school sweetheart. They married in 1962. Besides Bryn and Dru, they had three daughters. When not working, Kosco took part in charity golf tournaments around the United States with former teammates. All in all, he sadi, he has had a very rewarding life. "I was blessed to play as long as I did and have such a wonderful family and that's what it's all about."

SOURCES

Amherst (New York) *Bee* amherstbee.com/news)

Tuscaloosa (Alabama) *News*

Winona (Minnesota) *Daily News*

ballparks.com

geoffmack.25ox.com

metrolyrics.com/ive-been-everywhere-lyrics-hank-snow.html

seamheads.com/ballparks/

Special thanks to Andy Kosco for generously donating his time and agreeing to an interview.

NOTES

1. The writer's real name was Geoffrey Mackay, but perhaps his stage name was Geoff Mack.
2. Unless otherwise noted, all quotes are from a telephone interview conducted by the author on April 10, 2014.
3. During his career Williams signed 45 players who made it to the major leagues.
4. John Wiebusch, "Once Written Off, Kosco Has a Chance," *Tuscaloosa News*, March 16, 1969.
5. The numbers for the games Kosco played in each position do not add up to 109 because he sometimes played both positions in the same game.
6. Dru Kosco played three games for the Calgary Cannons, the Seattle Mariners' affiliate in the Pacific Coast League, in 1989. Bryn Kosco played for the Iowa Cubs of the American Association in 1995-1996.

The Killer Clouts Walk-Off Two-Run Round-Tripper

July 11, 1965: Minnesota Twins 6, New York Yankees 5 at Metropolitan Stadium, Bloomington, Minnesota

BY GREGORY H. WOLF

HARMON KILLEBREW CLOUTED 573 home runs in his 22-year big-league career, but few were more dramatic than his walk-off, two-run smash with two outs in the ninth inning to give the Minnesota Twins an exciting victory over the New York Yankees, 6-5, on Sunday, July 11, 1965, at Metropolitan Stadium. "The scene could have been set in Hollywood," wrote Fred Down of the UPI. "[Killebrew's home run] was the most devastating blow struck against the Yankees all season."[1]

Heading into the game, the last before the three-day All-Star break, the Twins were hitting on all cylinders. Sitting atop the AL standings (52-29) by four games over the Cleveland Indians and 4½ games over the Baltimore Orioles, the Twins had played mediocre ball in June (16-13), and had slipped briefly out of first place. But manager Sam Mele's resilient club responded by reeling off nine consecutive victories in July before losing to the Yankees in the second game of a doubleheader, on July 10. One concern to the club was the loss of slugging left fielder and inspirational leader Bob Allison, who had fractured his wrist when he was hit by a pitch from Jerry Stephenson of the Boston Red Sox on July 6, and was expected to miss three weeks.

Winners of the last five AL pennants, the New York Yankees were trudging through a season their fans had not seen in two generations. Manager Johnny Keane, the former St. Louis Cardinals skipper whom the Yankees had hired after their stunning seven-game loss to the Redbirds in the World Series the previous year, inherited an aged squad. In sixth place (41-45), New York was en route to its first losing season since 1925.

Both teams received good news prior to the game. The AL announced that Killebrew would start at first base in place of the injured Moose Skowron of the Chicago White Sox in the All-Star Game, to be played at Metropolitan Stadium in two days. Meanwhile, the Yankees' gregarious 24-year-old star, Joe Pepitone, was added to the AL roster.[2]

On a beautiful, 74-degree summer afternoon, 35,263 fans packed the "Met" expecting to see a well-pitched game featuring two of the brightest young southpaws in the league. Minnesota's 26-year-old Jim Kaat had established himself as one of the best young hurlers in the AL, as well as the premier fielding pitcher in baseball. He had led the team with 17 wins the previous season; his 42 starts would pace the league in 1965. New York's hard-throwing 24-year-old Al Downing had struck out a league-leading 217 in 1964 and was set to replace Whitey Ford as the club's left-handed ace. He was also the first African American pitcher to start consistently for the Yankees.

The Yankees came out swinging in the first inning. Four of the first five batters managed a hit but produced just one (unearned) run. After leadoff batter Bobby Richardson was erased on a 5-4-3 double play, Mickey Mantle and Elston Howard singled. Mantle, who had been out of the lineup since June 22 because of a leg injury, raced toward home on Hector Lopez's single to right field. Tony Oliva's throw was in time, but Mantle scored when Twins backstop Earl Battey misplayed the ball at the plate for an error.

Shortstop Zoilo Versalles put the Twins on the board in the third inning when he belted his 10th home run of the season, a solo shot with two outs, to tie the game at 1-1. Oliva and Killebrew led off the fourth inning with consecutive singles. Oliva, who had been on a tear in his previous 14 games, batting .375 (21-for-56), scampered home on Jimmie Hall's sacrifice fly; Battey drove in Killebrew on a line-drive single to left field to give the Twins a 3-1 lead. "This club is a bunch of fighters," Bob Allison told Minneapolis sportswriter Max Nichols about his club's relentless attack.[3]

Kaat encountered problems in the fifth inning when he yielded a one-out single to Phil Linz and walked Mantle. He had the Commerce Comet picked off at first base, but his errant throw to Killebrew enabled both runners to move into scoring position. Both scored on Howard's long double to center field as the Yankees tied the game at 3-3, and sent Kaat to the showers. With the run, Mantle became the 34th major leaguer to score 1,500 runs. In the bottom half of the frame, the Twins took a one-run lead on Rich Rollins's double, which scored Versalles.

Coming on in in relief of righty Al Worthington with one out and two on in the seventh, Twins southpaw Bill Pleis fielded Pepitone's grounder and threw to first for the second out. Playing the odds, he intentionally walked Clete Boyer to load the bases and faced rookie left-handed center fielder Roger Repoz. The plan backfired as Pleis uncorked a wild pitch, enabling Howard to score as the Yankees tied the game yet again, 4-4.

The stage was set for an exciting, controversial ninth inning. Jerry Fosnow, the Twins' fifth pitcher of the day, surrendered a leadoff single to Howard. Pepitone hit what appeared to be an inning-ending double-play grounder, but third baseman Rollins muffed the ball. After Howard moved to third on a line out to right field by Boyer, Pleis fielded Repoz's grounder down the first-base line. As he applied the tag to Repoz, he dropped the ball; Howard romped home.

At first, home-plate umpire Ed Hurley ruled Repoz out on interference, and skipper Johnny Keane burst onto the field. After a heated exchange with Keane, Hurley consulted first-base umpire Red Flaherty, and reversed his call. Fosnow was charged with an error (the Twins' fourth of the game), the run counted, and the Yankees led, 5-4. Now it was Mele's turn to storm onto the field. With AL President Joe Cronin in attendance, Hurley stood by his call. Mele announced that the Twins would play the game under protest.

The Yankees brought in righty Pete Mikkelsen, the game's 10th pitcher, to face the top of the Twins' order, stacked with right-handers. With two outs and Rollins on first via a walk, Mikkelsen faced Killebrew. According to Joesph Durso of the *New York Times*, Killebrew fouled off two pitches with a 3-and-2 count, before he "ripped a fastball" that traveled an estimated 360 feet into the left-field bleachers, giving the Twins a dramatic 6-5 win.[4]

"The New York Yankees wear the scars today to prove that Harmon Killebrew belongs among the stars," wrote Fred Down.[5] The "Killer's" 16th home run made a winner out of Fosnow and saddled Mikkelsen with the loss. He finished with three hits in four at-bats, scored twice, knocked in two runs, and walked once; coincidentally, that was the same batting line for Elston Howard, who had integrated the New York Yankees in 1955.

Twins skipper Mele maintained a level head in spite of the thrilling victory. Told that his club was in its best position since 1933, when the Washington Senators (the team relocated to Minnesota for the 1961 season) won the pennant, Mele responded cautiously, "It's a long season and it's going to be a struggle. There are a lot of good teams."[6] Mele reminded the reporter that the Twins lost 18 of 22 games shortly after the All-Star Game the previous summer to fall out of contention by late July.

THE 1965 MINNESOTA TWINS

SOURCES

BaseballReference.com

Retrosheet.org

SABR.org

The Sporting News

NOTES

1. Fred Down (UPI), "Killebrew Convinces Yanks," *Cumberland (Maryland) Evening Times*, July 12, 1965, 10.
2. Associated Press, "Pepitone an All-Star; Killebrew Will Start," *New York Times*, July 12, 1965, 32.
3. *The Sporting News*, August 21, 1965, 13.
4. Joseph Durso, "Twins Beat Yanks, 6-5, on Killebrew's Homer in 9th," *New York Times*, July 12, 1965, 32.
5. Down.
6. Associated Press, "Twins Open Up 5-Game Lead," *Kansas City Star*, July 12, 1965, 13.

Frank Kostro

BY J.G. PRESTON

FRANK KOSTRO PLAYED PARTS OF seven seasons in the major leagues in the 1960s but never advanced beyond roles as a right-handed-hitting pinch-hitter and utilityman. He started only 80 games in the big leagues (at five different positions) and never had more than 151 at-bats in a season. But he earned a World Series ring as a member of the 1965 Twins, even though he was sent to the minors in June and was not on the World Series roster, and he finished his professional career with a .303 minor-league average in nearly 1,200 games.[1]

Kostro was born on August 4, 1937, in Windber, Pennsylvania, the same southwestern Pennsylvania town just outside Johnstown where his father, also named Frank, had been born 21 years earlier. (While some newspaper stories over the years have referred to them as "Frank Sr." and "Frank Jr.," that's not technically true; the father's name was Frank Adam Kostro, while the son is Frank Jerry Kostro.) The senior Kostro was one of 11 children and, like his father (a Polish immigrant also named Frank), worked in the coal mines.[2]

Athletic prowess kept the younger Frank Kostro from following his father and grandfather into the mines. He grew up in the small coal-mining community of Blough and earned 11 varsity letters in three sports at Forbes High School in nearby Kantner.[3] As a senior in 1954-55, he was named Somerset County's most valuable player in football and averaged 27 points a game in basketball.[4] Asked what his favorite sport was, Kostro said, "As far as the games were concerned, football," then added with a chuckle, "I didn't particularly care for the practices." He earned a combined football-basketball scholarship from the University of Michigan.

But Kostro never played a varsity game in either sport for the Wolverines, leaving school after one semester when his father was injured in a coal mining accident.[5] He then turned to his other sport—baseball—to earn money, by signing with the Detroit Tigers. Tigers scouts Ed Katalinas and Cy Williams had tried to sign Kostro when he finished high school, only to have him turn them down to accept the Michigan scholarship.[6]

"I started playing in the Somerset County League when I was 12," Kostro said, "but I was playing with men who were working in the coal mines. My dad convinced me that I should start playing against guys my own age."[7] But to do that he had to go to Johnstown, which he was afraid to do, "since I thought that it was such a huge city."[8]

Kostro went to Johnstown and starred in the Johnstown Junior League, which he said was "without a doubt... the biggest break for me."[9] In both 1954 and 1955 he

A versatile utilityman, Kostro made 36 plate appearances with the Twins in 1965 before he was optioned to Triple-A Denver in late June. (Photo courtesy of Minnesota Twins Baseball Club).

played for Johnstown teams in the All-American Amateur Baseball Association national tournament, an event attended by major-league scouts.[10] "He was a special player with some real physical ability," said Ken Keiper, who coached Kostro in Johnstown. "He had a tremendous desire to succeed."[11]

"I learned one important thing from my dad," Kostro said. "I just learned that you had to put forth the effort for whatever you did. If you do that, things will work out."[12]

Kostro started his professional career in 1956, as an 18-year-old in the Class D Pennsylvania-Ontario-New York (PONY) league. He hit .332 for Jamestown (New York), was fourth in the league in runs scored with 97 and led the league's shortstops in putouts. That earned him a promotion for 1957 to the Class B Carolina League, where he was named the league's all-star shortstop playing for the pennant-winning Durham Bulls.[13] Kostro batted .290 and led the league in hits, doubles, and triples.

The Tigers bumped the 20-year-old Kostro to Birmingham of the Double-A Southern Association to start the 1958 season, but when he struggled they demoted him to Augusta of the Class A South Atlantic League in May. A .288 batting average in 65 games there earned Kostro another trip to Birmingham at the end of July, and in a total of 44 games for the Barons he hit .255. Both Augusta and Birmingham won their league pennants.

It was back to the South Atlantic League in 1959, as the Tigers' affiliate moved to Knoxville, and Kostro was the shortstop on the league's all-star team that took on Gastonia on July 20.[14] A week later he was promoted to Charleston (West Virginia) of the Triple-A American Association.[15] Kostro hit .300 at Knoxville (only two players who spent the full season in the South Atlantic League topped that mark) and hit .310 at Charleston At the end of the season the Tigers added him to their 40-man roster.

Detroit general manager Rick Ferrell said, "In appearance and in his performance at the plate, [Kostro] reminds you of Harvey Kuenn [who had been with the Tigers since 1952 and led the American League in hits four times]. I say he's like Kuenn because he knows where the strike zone is, seldom fans, and when he connects, it's a good sharp line drive. He sprays 'em all over, too, just the way Harvey does. We have plenty of confidence in his hitting. The question has been whether we can use him at shortstop."[16]

Kostro went to spring training in 1960 with at least an outside shot to stick with the Tigers. "If 22-year-old Frank Kostro could field half as well as he can hit, he would be the team's No. 1 shortstop on opening day," the Associated Press's Dave Diles wrote, after Kostro drove in four runs in an exhibition game.[17] "The kid's going to be great some day," said Detroit manager Jimmy Dykes. "He has a good bat and a great arm."[18]

But Kostro's glove prevented him from beating out Chico Fernandez at short (Kostro made at least 47 errors in each of his first four minor-league seasons), and Dykes elected to send him to the Tigers' new Denver affiliate in the Triple-A American Association so he could play every day. "It's good to know I can recall him whenever I need him," Dykes said.[19]

It turned out the Tigers didn't need Kostro in 1960. It turned out Denver didn't need him, either. He hit .277 for the Bears, but when he made 14 errors in 21 games at shortstop he was sent down to Double-A to try some other positions, playing third base for Birmingham of the Southern Association and left field for Victoria of the Texas League. He would spend the rest of his career looking for a home in the field.

Kostro found a home off the field in 1961 after spending the season at Denver. In October he married a Colorado woman, Janet Baker, and took up residence in Denver. The Kostros were married nearly 50 years before Jan died on August 28, 2011. They had three children: Frank T. (who died in 1997 at age 35), John, and Greg.

Kostro spent the 1961 season as a utility player and pinch-hitter in Denver, with just 184 at-bats in 73 games, including 34 in the outfield and 15 at short. It wasn't clear that he would be asked to return to Denver in 1962, but "there wasn't a more determined, hustling player in the Bears' [spring training] camp," according to *The Sporting News*, and he made the club.[20] He cemented a spot in the lineup after getting off to a blazing start, with nine home runs in his first 27 games. It was an uncharacteristic power burst for Kostro; he hit only four home runs the rest of the year and never hit more than 10 home runs in any other season.

Even after the home runs stopped coming, Kostro kept hitting and had his best season as a pro. His .321 batting average ranked third in the American Association, just behind Tom McCraw of Indianapolis and Dave Roberts of Oklahoma City, and his career-high 97 RBIs were second in the league, behind Indianapolis's Jim Koranda. Kostro was named to the postseason all-star team as a utility player after playing six different positions, with 57 games in the outfield, 45 at shortstop, and 36 at first base. An article in *The Sporting News* said, "Frank Kostro is in his seventh year of Organized Ball and still hasn't found his best position. Unless you consider 'hitter' a position. ... [I]t's a good bet that some big league club, needing the hard-to-find utility type, will find him useful."[21]

The Tigers gave Kostro his first taste of major-league ball that September. He made his debut on September 2, striking out as a pinch-hitter against Eddie Fisher of the White Sox ("The slider that he threw me to strike me out was about a foot outside," Kostro later recalled). His first hit, also as a pinch-hitter, was a double off Minnesota's Jim Kaat on September 7. Later in the month Kostro started 10 games at third base and wound up with a .268 batting average for the Tigers, with three doubles among his 11 hits.

Kostro made the Tigers' Opening Day roster for the first time in 1963 after hitting .458 in spring training,[22] but once the regular season started, playing time was hard to come by. He started just eight games (four at third base, two at first, and one each in left field and right field) and was 5-for-20 as a pinch-hitter, with a .231 overall batting average, before being traded to the Los Angeles Angels on June 15 with pitcher Paul Foytack for outfielder George Thomas. "[Third baseman] Felix Torres is swinging a hot bat right now," said Angels manager Bill Rigney, "so I imagine I'll use Kostro primarily as a pinch-hitter until Felix cools off or a crisis develops at another position."[23]

Kostro got just four at-bats, going hitless, before the Angels sent him to their Hawaii farm club in the Triple-A Pacific Coast League on July 8. But he quickly earned a return trip to the majors, hitting .415 with two home runs in 10 games for the Islanders, and was put in Torres' spot at third base to face his old teammates, the Tigers, on July 19. The next day he hit his first major-league home run, off Jim Bunning, to help the Angels to an 11-2 win.

From the time of his return through September 6, Kostro started 23 of the Angels' 47 games, which would turn out to be his most extensive experience as a starter in the major leagues, playing first base, third base, left field, and right field. But including pinch-hitting appearances, he hit just .220 during that time, and Rigney seemed to have been satisfied that Kostro was not the answer to any of his problems. For the season, combining his numbers with the Tigers and the Angels, Kostro hit .225 in 74 games, and in December the Angels sold him to Hawaii and took him off their 40-man roster.

Back in the PCL, Kostro got off to another hot start in 1964 and was batting .344 when he was traded and made his return to the big leagues. On June 11 the Angels sent him to the Twins as part of a three-team deal that also included the Cleveland Indians; the Twins acquired Jerry Kindall from the Indians, and sent Vic Power and Lenny Green to Los Angeles. (Cleveland got Billy Moran from the Angels.)

"That was probably the best thing that happened to me," Kostro said of the trade. "The Twins just had a lot of great guys on that ballclub."

At the time of the trade, Twins pinch-hitters were just 6-for-62, and Kostro was seen as a potential improvement on that weakness. "I made these deals to beef up our pinch-hitting," Twins owner Calvin Griffith said.[24]

Twins manager Sam Mele didn't wait long to see what his new player could contribute. Kostro got a pinch-single in his Minnesota debut on June 13; three days later, with Mele giving Harmon Killebrew a rare day off in left field, Kostro got his first Twins start and banged out a single, double, and home run against Cleveland lefty Jack Kralick. But that wasn't enough to keep Kostro in the Twins' star-studded lineup, and he started just one game over the next five weeks. He went just 2-for-12 as a pinch-hitter during that time.

Later in the season Kostro became a reliable option off the bench, getting hits seven times in nine pinch-hit appearances from late August into September, including four consecutive opportunities (September 3, 12, 15, and 18). Kostro finished the season with a .286 pinch-hitting average (10-for-35) and tied for fourth in the American League in pinch hits.

"I remember Mele as one of my favorite managers," Kostro said. "He was the kind of guy who would come up to you an inning before and say, okay, if this is the situation you're going to hit. I felt because of that it gave you a chance to get ready in your mind. He was all around just a good manager."

In 59 games with the Twins in 1964, Kostro hit .272 with three home runs and 12 RBIs in what was his most productive major-league season. He started 19 games (10 at third base, seven at second, and one each at first base and left field) and hit .281 in those games, with all three of his homers.

Kostro went north with the Twins to start the 1965 season, but playing time was hard to come by. He didn't get his first hit of the season until the team's 36th game, on May 26, and started only three games, two at third base, and one at second. His pinch-hitting success of 1964 did not carry over, as he was hitless in eight plate appearances as a pinch-hitter. When second baseman Bernie Allen was deemed sufficiently recovered from knee surgery to rejoin the team on June 21, the Twins sent Kostro to Denver, which had become a Minnesota farm club.[25]

Kostro had just five hits in 31 at-bats with the 1965 Twins, for a .161 average, and committed five errors in just 61 innings in the field. But after the Twins won the American League pennant, his teammates recognized his contributions during his two months with the team by voting him a two-fifths share of the team's postseason money, good for $2,653.74.[26]

Kostro didn't play for Denver after leaving the Twins; the Bears sent him to PCL rival Seattle in exchange for pitcher Ron Piche,[27] and he hit .282 for the Angels, playing 53 games at third base and 21 in the outfield. But in 1966 Kostro returned to Denver and spent the entire season there, batting .300 with 10 home runs and 78 RBIs in 140 games, primarily in the outfield. His batting average ranked 10th in the league, and he was fourth in the league in doubles with 32.

Back in Denver again in 1967, Kostro continued to hammer PCL pitching and was leading the league with a .369 batting average (and an active 17-game hitting streak) when he was summoned to return to the Twins on June 16 to replace injured rookie infielder Ron Clark.[28] He started in left field in his first two games, but although he spent the rest of the season in the majors, he did not start another game, making just two late-game appearances in the field. But he rekindled the pinch-hitting magic he had in 1964, with nine hits and three walks in 26 pinch-hit appearances for a .462 on-base percentage. His .391 batting average in the pinch was the highest in the major leagues for anyone who had more than 20 pinch-hit opportunities.[29]

In 1968 Kostro hit .343 in spring training and made the Twins' Opening Day roster.[30] "So far I've played right, left and first base, and I'm Polish," he told reporters at the end of training camp. "Does that make me a utility Pole?"[31] Again his spring success didn't lead to a lot of playing time in the regular season, but for the first (and only) time, Kostro spent the entire year in the major leagues. His appearances in the field were again limited, just 29 games including 15 starts (eight in left field, six in right, and one at first base). He finished the season with a .241 average in 108 at-bats, including a 7-for-35 mark as a pinch-hitter.

After a disappointing season in '68, the Twins went into 1969 with a new manager: Billy Martin, who was getting his first chance to run a major-league team. Martin sent Kostro back to Denver late in spring training. (Asked in 2011 what he thought about Martin as a manager, Kostro replied, "To be truthful with you, I would just as soon not answer that question. If you can't say something good about somebody, you gotta just pass on it.") As always, Kostro hit for the Bears, batting .311 (he had 516 hits during his years in Denver, the most of any player during Denver's years as a Triple-A franchise from 1955 to 1992).[32] But he played in just 57 games before he was hospitalized with severe pain in his right foot on June 26.[33]

When the major-league rosters expanded in September and the Twins had a comfortable lead in the American League West, the club called Kostro back to the majors in order to give him enough service time to qualify for a five-year pension.[34] In his first appearance, as a pinch-hitter on September 8 at Anaheim, he was retired on a groundball. "It should have been a base hit," Kostro remembered in 2011, "but I took two or three steps out of the batter's box and fell down. My foot never did come back."

He made just one more appearance in a major-league game, striking out as a pinch-hitter against the Seattle Pilots on September 21 at Minnesota's Metropolitan Stadium. Shortly thereafter, he underwent surgery to remove a bone spur from his foot.[35] He finished his major-league career with a .244 average and five home runs in 266 games. His career pinch-hitting average was .241 (34-for-141).

Because of his foot injury, Kostro decided he was through playing at the end of the season, but to his surprise he was contacted by the Hankyu Braves of Japan's Pacific League. "The Japanese knew more about the American ballplayer than we did here," Kostro said. "They knew all about my foot and all about the injury. They flew me to Los Angeles to have their own doctor check my foot out, and evidently he sent a report that they could sign me and I could still play."

Hankyu purchased Kostro's contract from the Twins, and he and his family went to Japan for the 1970 season. "My foot really was still bothering me, but they seemed to think I could play," he said. "Here in the States I think the most I made [in a season] was $16,000; they offered me $30,000 tax-free. I wanted to start a business in Denver and I had no money, so that was hard to turn down."

The 32-year-old Kostro played only 37 games in Japan, mostly as a pinch-hitter, and batted .200 in 45 at-bats. He said it was difficult for his family there, as they did not have an interpreter (he did when he was with the ballclub). However, he had nothing but praise for his Japanese hosts.

"I played winter ball a number of years," he said, "and in winter ball, if you're supposed to make $1,000 they'd try to give you $800. So I expected that in Japan, but it was just the opposite, they'd do everything to make you happy. They wanted me to stay there another year, but I had enough money saved to start my business so I didn't want to. I thought they'd be upset with me when I left, but they me met at the airport and gave my wife a pearl necklace and me a pearl ring and tie clasp."

Kostro returned to Denver and had a successful insurance business, providing extended warranties to car dealers.[36] He kept in touch with former teammates as a member of the board of directors of the Harmon Killebrew Foundation and became active with the Major League Baseball Players Alumni Association. He is a member of three Halls of Fame: the All-American Amateur Baseball Association Hall of Fame (inducted in 1997), the Somerset County (Pennsylvania) Oldtimers Baseball Association Hall of Fame (2000); and the Cambria County (Pennsylvania) Sports Hall of Fame (2004). Despite his foot injury, and later Tommy John surgery, he was an active handball player into his 70s.[37]

SOURCES

Unless otherwise indicated, all Kostro's quotes are from an interview conducted in January 2011 available online at twinstrivia.com/

interview-archives/frank-kostro-interview/. Minor-league statistics are taken from the appropriate annual *Sporting News Official Baseball Guide*.

NOTES

1 In his January 2011 interview, Kostro said he received a ring.

2 Frank A. Kostro's obituary appears in the *Johnstown* (Pennsylvania) *Tribune-Democrat*, January 12, 2006, A9; his middle name is confirmed in the Social Security Death Index accessed via Ancestry.com. His father's birthplace is listed in the 1940 US Census and his occupation is listed on his World War II draft registration card, both accessed via Ancestry.com.

3 Hugh Conrad, "Kostro went from Blough to the big leagues," *Johnstown Tribune-Democrat*, July 18, 2004, C2.

4 "Frank Kostro Named Somerset's Most Valuable Gridder," *Connellsville* (Pennsylvania) *Daily Courier*, November 26, 1954, 12; "Hornets, Kantner In District Playoff," *Cumberland* (Maryland) *Evening Times*, March 7, 1955, 9.

5 Kostro mentioned his father's accident in his January 2011 interview. The fact that he was enrolled at Michigan for only one semester was confirmed by University of Michigan associate athletic director David Ablauf in an email on August 11, 2014, citing records in the school registrar's office. "I do not have a complete roster for the 1955 freshman football team, but if he was out for the team, he did not win a freshman numeral in football," Ablauf wrote. Kostro is in a group photo of students who lived in the Cooley Hall dormitory that appears in the 1956 Michigan yearbook, accessed via Ancestry.com. Another photo of Cooley residents on the same page includes another future major leaguer, Steve Boros.

6 Hal Middlesworth, "Kid Clouter Kostro May Plug Big Gap as Tiger Shortstop," *The Sporting News*, February 3, 1960, 19.

7 Hugh Conrad, "Kostro went from Blough to the big leagues."

8 Ibid. The population of Johnston according to the 1950 US census was 63,232; its population is about 20,000 today.

9 Ibid.

10 Mike Mastovich, "Home-grown talent," *Johnstown Tribune-Democrat*, December 7, 2003. For more on the history of the AAABA Tournament, which has featured hundreds of future major leaguers over the years, go to johnstownbaseball.com/

11 Hugh Conrad, "Ex-manager spotted talent at young age," *Johnstown Tribune-Democrat*, July 18, 2004, C2. Keiper also managed the Johnstown team that finished second in the 1956 AAABA tournament, after Kostro had turned professional. "The guys from that team always said if we had Frank that year, we would have won the whole thing," he told Conrad. AAABA tournament results can be found at aaabatournament.com/archives/archive.html.

12 Hugh Conrad, "Kostro went from Blough to the big leagues."

13 The Carolina League all-star team is listed in "Caught on the Fly," *The Sporting News*, November 6, 1957, 26.

14 The all-star team is listed in the South Atlantic League notes in *The Sporting News*, July 22, 1959, 40.

15 *Morgantown* (West Virginia) *Post*, July 29, 1959.

16 Hal Middlesworth, "Kid Clouter Kostro May Plug Big Gap as Tiger Shortstop," *The Sporting News*, February 3, 1960, 19.

17 Dave Diles, "Detroit Tigers Defeat Philadelphia," *Ludington* (Michigan) *Daily News*, March 25, 1960, 6.

18 Joe Reichler, "Jimmy Dykes Blows Smoke Rings, Sees Bengals On Rampage If He Finds 5th Pitcher," *Findlay* (Ohio) *Republican-Courier*, April 1, 1960, 23.

19 Ibid.

20 "Kostro's Bat Sounds Warning to Twirlers," *The Sporting News*, June 2, 1962, 37.

21 Ibid.

22 Watson Spoelstra, "Aguirre Makes Early Grab to Hold Onto ERA Laurels," *The Sporting News*, April 20, 1963, 24.

23 Ross Newhan, "Angels Open Stand Against Pesky A's," *Long Beach* (California) *Press-Telegram*, June 18, 1963, C-1.

24 Max Nichols, "Opportunity Knocks—Kindall Opens Twin Door," *The Sporting News*, June 27, 1964, 17.

25 "Twins Invade Atlanta After Double Win Over Yankees," *Fergus Falls* (Minnesota) *Journal*, June 21, 1965, 8. The Twins were in Atlanta for an exhibition game against the Milwaukee Braves, who would move to Atlanta the next year.

26 Clifford Kachline, "A Ten-Grand Payoff In Series Becoming Habit With Dodgers," *The Sporting News*, November 6, 1965, 6.

27 Max Nichols, "Spindly Nossek: A Light Eater, Heavy Swinger," *The Sporting News*, July 10, 1965, 11.

28 "Frank Kostro Rejoins Twins," *Mitchell* (South Dakota) *Daily Republic*, June 16, 1967, 10.

29 *The Sporting News Official Baseball Guide for 1968*, 253.

30 Arno Goethel, "Hernandez Clear Winner In Twins' Shortstop Derby," *The Sporting News*, April 20, 1968, 22.

31 Arno Goethel, "Twins Have a Fine Chance With Dean Setting an Example," *The Sporting News*, April 27, 1968, 12.

32 Irv Moss, "The '60s: Turning up minor-league hits," *Denver Post*, June 17, 2008, available at denverpost.com/classics/ci_9606702

33 "Kostro Ailing," *The Sporting News*, July 12, 1969, 42.

34 Mike Lamey, "If You Win Big Like Twins, Fun Is Part of the Picture," *The Sporting News*, October 11, 1969, 12.

35 Ibid.

36 "Oldtimers to induct nine new members," *Somerset* (Pennsylvania) *Daily American*, September 13, 2003, available at articles.dailyamerican.com/2003-09-13/sports/26344237_1_guest-speaker-new-members-pitcher-and-catcher

37 Coloradohandball.com/main/Default.aspx?tabid=274

Jim Merritt

BY GREGORY H. WOLF

AN ALL-STAR AND 20-GAME WINNER in 1970, Jim Merritt was a crafty southpaw who went 81-86 during an 11-year big-league career spent most notably with the Minnesota Twins and the Cincinnati Reds. "Aggressiveness," replied Merritt when asked about the key to his success. (He won 62 games over the four-year period 1967-70 before arm injuries derailed his career at the age of 31 in 1975.) "The first pitch is the most important one…get the hitters out."[1] With impeccable control, Merritt kept hitters off balance with breaking balls, especially sliders and curves, and caught batters sleeping with a sneaky heater. "You're looking for the slow stuff," Henry Aaron once said about Merritt, "and you get the fastball in a good spot."[2]

James Joseph Merritt was born on December 9, 1943, at St. Luke's Hospital in Altadena, California, a few miles north of Pasadena in Los Angeles County. His father was Ephraim Merritt, a World War II veteran originally from Colorado, who worked in Southern California as an engineer and draftsman. Jim's mother, Edna Lenora (McNulty) Merritt, was a native of Detroit. The couple married in 1939 and raised two children, Jim and Bruce, in a middle-class family in the San Gabriel Valley, about 20 miles east of LA.

Tall and lanky, Jim progressed through Little League and Babe Ruth baseball, and starred as a pitcher for West Covina High School and then for nearby Edgewood High School, where he reportedly went 14-2 as a junior in 1960.[3] An unabashed Dodgers fan after the team relocated from Brooklyn, Jim fulfilled every boy's dream when the Dodgers hired him as batboy and clubhouse attendant. Though the job forced him to forgo his senior year of baseball, he enjoyed some added perks. "I used to listen [to pitchers] all I could when I worked for the Dodgers," Merritt told Minnesota sportswriter Max Nichols.[4] He had up-close and personal conversations about pitching with hurlers like fellow lefties Sandy Koufax and Ron Perranoski, as well as Don Drysdale, each of whom was only about eight or nine years older than the big-league wannabe. Tutoring from the pros paid off. When Merritt graduated from high school in 1961, the Dodgers signed him on the recommendation of well-respected team scout Kenny Myers, for a reported bonus of $8,000.[5]

Before Merritt's career in the Dodgers' farm system got under way, he was chosen by the Minnesota Twins on November 27, 1961, in the first-year player draft. The Dodgers had not assigned the 17-year-old to a minor-league team after signing him. Rather, the southpaw had pitched for the Los Angeles Dodgers Rookies, who were instructed by coaches in the

Merritt won five games for the Twins as a 21-year-old rookie in 1965. After averaging 16 wins and 238 innings over a four-year stretch (1967-1970) with the Twins and Cincinnati Reds, the crafty southpaw was plagued by arm problems. He retired in 1975 with an 81-86 record. (Photo courtesy of Minnesota Twins Baseball Club).

Dodgers organization and played exhibition games throughout Southern California.⁶

Merritt made a commanding debut in Organized Baseball in 1962 leading the Class D New York-Penn League in wins (19), innings (223), and strikeouts (249) as a member of the Erie Sailors. The 18-year-old turned heads with an overpowering 18-strikeout performance in June, and was named to the league's all-star team. Sent to the Florida Instructional League in the fall, the green hurler who "shows great promise" won eight more contests.⁷

Described by Twins beat reporter Arno Goethel as having an "outside chance" to make the big-league squad, Merritt was invited to the Twins' spring training in 1963. "He's not overpowering," said an impressed Joe Haynes, team VP, "but he changes speed well and has good control and poise."⁸ The youngster was bumped up to the Double-A Charlotte (North Carolina) Hornets in the South Atlantic League. He initially struggled against more seasoned competition, losing his first four decisions, and finished the season with a 9-12 record for a poor team (58-82). The Twins added him to the 40-man roster after another encouraging showing in the Florida Instructional League.

Merritt was once again a long shot to make the Twins club in spring training in 1964. Minnesota boasted two sturdy southpaw starters, Jim Kaat and Dick Stigman, as well as lefty Bill Pleis in the bullpen. The Californian was ultimately assigned to Triple-A Atlanta. Praised by Crackers beat writer Lee Walburn as the "hottest pitcher in the Twins' farm system," Merritt was the shining star on the International League's worst club (55-93).⁹ Joining Richmond's Mel Stottlemyre (13-3, 1.42 ERA) on the league's all-star team, Merritt paced the circuit in innings pitched (200) and strikeouts (174) and won 13 games, but also tied for the league lead with 17 losses, despite a low ERA (2.74). Playing for bad teams had an upside, according to Merritt. "When you're with a club that does not score a lot of runs and makes a lot of errors, you learn how to pitch."¹⁰

The Twins' inconsistent pitching staff contributed to the club's disappointing sixth-place finish in 1964 (79-83). Manager Sam Mele hired pitching guru Johnny Sain, out of baseball since his resignation as New York Yankees pitching coach in 1963, to mold a young but promising staff. Considered a lock to land a spot, Merritt possessed five legitimate pitches (fastball, curve, slider, changeup, and screwball) as well as an excellent, quick pickoff move that Mele thought was as good as Whitey Ford's.¹¹ It was a "surprise," confessed sportswriter Max Nichols, when Merritt was assigned to the Denver Bears of the PCL.¹² Pitching for Cal Ermer, Merritt was named to his third all-star team in four years, won 13 of 21 decisions, and etched out a robust 3.13 ERA in 190 innings.

By the end of July 1965, the Twins were cruising to their first pennant since 1933, when they were called the Senators and played in Washington, D.C., but their pitching staff was in trouble. Righty Camilo Pascual, who had won 56 games the previous three seasons, landed on the disabled list after his outing on July 28; hard-throwing 20-year-old Dave Boswell, who had moved into the rotation in mid-May, had been out since early July with mono and then was involved in a car wreck. In need of a starter, the Twins recalled Merritt on July 31. Two days later, the 21-year-old made his big-league debut against the Baltimore Orioles at Metropolitan Stadium, located about 11 miles south of Minneapolis in Bloomington. Merritt cruised through eight innings, yielding just five hits and two runs (one earned), before surrendering three hits, including Dick Brown's two-out, three-run shot which tied the score, 5-5, in the ninth. Johnny Klippstein came on in relief and whiffed reliever Jim Palmer. Jimmie Hall, Minnesota's first batter in the ninth, probably wondered why skipper Hank Bauer had let 19-year-old rookie Palmer bat, but was glad he did. Hall clouted a walk-off game-winner off him. But it was a costly victory. In the sixth inning, slugger Harmon Killebrew injured his left arm in a collision at first base, and missed almost seven weeks.

Merritt picked up victories in his next two starts; the latter was his first complete game, with eight punchouts (but also 10 hits) at Yankee Stadium on August 12. "I started pitching with my arm higher, more overhand," replied Merritt when asked about the reason for his success. "Now my fastball is moving better and my curve is breaking."[13] He posted a respectable 4-3 record and 3.55 ERA while averaging just over seven innings in his nine starts through September 6 before he was moved into the bullpen to accommodate Pascual's return. The young lefty proved his value as a fireman in the final month, posting a 1.35 ERA while striking out 17 over seven appearances and 13⅓ innings for the AL champions.

The Twins got off to a fast start in the 1965 World Series by taking the first two games from the Los Angeles Dodgers in front of roaring Midwestern fans at the Met. In Game Three, Merritt relieved starter Pascual to start the sixth inning, down 3-0. After Maury Wills smashed a two-out double to drive in Wes Parker, who had singled, Merritt demonstrated his deceptive pickoff move by catching the stolen-base champ sleeping at second. Merritt tossed a 1-2-3 seventh before he was removed for a pinch-hitter in the eighth inning of Claude Osteen's momentum-changing five-hit shutout. Merritt retired all four batters he faced in the decisive Game Seven, one of the most famous clinching games in World Series history, when Sandy Koufax tossed his second shutout on two days' rest to give the Dodgers their second title in three years. Despite his being with the team for just over two months, the players voted Merritt a two-thirds World Series share, worth $4,422.90.

Merritt endured a frustrating season in 1966. The Twins had a deep rotation with southpaw Kaat and righties Pascual, Boswell, Mudcat Grant, and Jim Perry. After pitching primarily out of the bullpen for the first 2½ months of the season, Merritt moved into the starting rotation in early July. On July 21 at Griffith Stadium in Washington, he tossed the first of his nine big-league shutouts, a nifty three-hitter against the Senators, during which he tied a then AL record with seven consecutive strikeouts and finished with 12. But Merritt was often the victim of poor run support (in his 11 losses as a starter, the Twins managed only 15 runs). He lost his first six decisions and boasted a dismal 2-12 record in mid-August despite a 3.65 ERA. Merritt took Sain's suggestion and began pitching from a full windup, instead of from the set position. "It gives more rhythm on my curve," said Merritt, "and more momentum on my fastball."[14] The change paid dividends as Merritt won five of his final seven starts to conclude the season with a 7-14 record and a 3.38 ERA with 124 strikeouts in 144 innings for the second-place club.

Despite his success late in the previous season, Merritt began the 1967 campaign lost in the Twins bullpen and made only six appearances in the first five weeks of the campaign. But injuries and inconsistencies gave the 23-year-old another shot. On May 26 and May 30, he tossed consecutive shutouts, the latter a sparkling two-hitter with 11 strikeouts against the Yankees in New York.

Mired in sixth place with a 25-25 record, the Twins replaced Mele with Carl Ermer. Merritt proved to be the Twins' most consistent hurler all season. In the second game of a doubleheader on July 26, he tossed a career-high 13 innings at Yankee Stadium, but received a no-decision as the Twins beat the Yankees 3-2 in 18 innings. Minnesota clawed its way back into the pennant race by winning 24 of its first 36 games under Ermer. Affectionately called "Bones" by his teammates for his 6-foot-3 frame which carried at most 175 pounds, Merritt tossed a seven-hitter to defeat the Chicago White Sox at the Met on August 13 to move the club into first place for the first time all season. "This was the most important victory in my life," said an exuberant Merritt, who had issued just two walks (one was intentional) in his previous 68⅔ innings. "Merritt throws his curve and slider for strikes so efficiently," said batterymate Jerry Zimmerman, "that hitters can't get ready for his fastball."[15]

Poised to capture their second pennant in three years, the Twins lost four of their final five games. On the last day of the season, the Boston Red Sox defeated them, 5-3, at Fenway Park to complete the "Impossible Dream." By one modern metric (WAR), Merritt was the best pitcher in the AL.[16] He finished with 13-7 record and a career-best 2.53 ERA in 227⅔ innings, including four shutouts and 11 complete games in 28 starts. His 1.2 walks per nine innings and 5.37 strikeouts per walk were the best marks in the major leagues. "I'm no junk pitcher," said Merritt, who also recorded 161 punchouts. "My strikeout pitch is a fastball about belly high."[17] Merritt attributed much of his success to Sain, who helped him develop impeccable control of his breaking balls. "Sain showed me 10 variations of the slider," Merritt once said. "It's all a matter of how much you turn the ball over."[18]

Widely hailed as a possible 20-game winner in 1968, Merritt was described by Arno Goethel as a candidate for "flop of the year" toward the end of that season.[19] However, that comment seems out of place, and may be more indicative of the entire team, which fell to seventh place. The Twins were consumed by infighting, and players openly challenged Ermer, who club owner Calvin Griffith admitted had lost the team. By the end of July Merritt's record was a dismal 6-12, but he won six of his last 10 decisions, including a masterful four-hitter with 11 strikeouts to beat the Yankees in the Bronx, 3-2, on August 10, and finished the season with a 12-16 record. Merritt also suffered from bad luck. The Twins scored three runs or fewer in 14 of his losses. His ERA rose to 3.25 in the "Year of the Pitcher," even though he set a career high in strikeouts (181 in 238⅓ innings) while his opponents' batting average and homers allowed were almost identical to the year before.

On November 21, 1968, the Cincinnati Reds acquired Merritt in a trade for veteran All-Star shortstop Leo Cardenas. The slugging Reds already had the nucleus of what became known as the "Big Red Machine" (Johnny Bench, Tony Perez, and Pete Rose, among others), but their young pitching staff was injury-plagued and finished dead last in the NL in ERA in '68 (3.56). Gary Nolan, a 20-year-old righty who had burst on the scene as a teenage rookie in 1967, winning 14 and striking out 206, had been limited to 22 starts; another fastballer, Jim Maloney, who had gone 105-55 and whiffed 1,273 in the previous six seasons, was battling arm and shoulder pain; and Tony Cloninger, who had won 24 games for the Braves in their last season in Milwaukee, had not fully recovered from elbow problems that bothered him the previous two seasons. Much was expected of Merritt. Cincinnati beat writers suggested he would lead the Reds to the division crown in the newly created NL West — as long as the staff remained healthy, which it did not.

Merritt had a reputation for attacking the strike zone, being willing to give up hits, and letting his defense do its job. "I try to throw nothing but strikes," he told Cincinnati sportswriter Earl Lawson in spring training.[20] After acclimating himself to pitching in the cramped quarters of Crosley Field, Merritt won four consecutive decisions in May and emerged as the most consistent starter for Dave Bristol, in his fourth year as Reds pilot. On August 16 Merritt tossed a complete game to defeat the Pittsburgh Pirates. It was his third of six consecutive victories in the month, and more importantly gave the Reds a 1½-game lead in the standings. But the Reds played just a nick above .500 the rest of the way (25-23) to finish in third place (89-73). Despite losing four of five decisions in September, the 25-year-old Merritt won 17, and set career bests in starts (36), appearances (42), and innings (251), but also yielded a NL-high 33 homers, 122 earned runs, and 9.6 hits per nine innings. Merritt was not fazed by the long ball or by his high ERA (4.37). "The home runs I give up will go out of municipal airports," he said jokingly while pointing to his win total as a sign of his effectiveness.[21] "When a team gets you some runs," said Merritt about the high-octane Reds offense, which led the NL with 798 runs, "you pitch differently than if you were in a close game."[22]

Merritt gave the Reds' brass a scare when he showed up in spring training with his left arm in a cast after supposedly injuring it when he fell attempting to retrieve his son's kite at their home in Southern California.[23] He recovered in time to be named the starter on Opening Day, and tossed an impressive three-hitter to defeat the Montreal Expos in the NL's traditional first game of the season. By the end of May he owned a stellar 10-3 record as the Reds, under new

Jim Merritt (Photo courtesy of Minnesota Twins Baseball Club).

skipper Sparky Anderson, got off to a torrid start, pulling away from the competition. On July 6 Merritt blanked the San Diego Padres on six hits to notch his NL-leading 14th victory.

Eight days later he appeared in his only All-Star Game, tossing two scoreless innings, yielding only a single to former teammate Killebrew in the NL's 5-4 victory.

Often hailed as a "thinking pitcher," Merritt rolled through August, winning five consecutive decisions, including an overpowering five-hit complete game with a career-best 13 strikeouts to defeat the New York Mets. That streak concluded with his 20th victory, as he became the first Reds left-hander to reach that coveted mark since Eppa Rixey in 1925. But while the Reds clobbered their opponents, Merritt was hurting. He had developed tendinitis in his elbow, and made only three disastrous starts in September, yielding eight earned runs in seven innings. Merritt finished the season with a 20-12 record and a 4.08 ERA in 234 innings and was named the left-handed starter on *The Sporting News* All-Star team. He placed fourth in voting for the Cy Young Award, and also picked up a handful of votes for the NL MVP Award (21st place). The Reds took the NL West crown with a league-best 102 victories, but entered the postseason with question marks surrounding Merritt and 21-year-old rookie Wayne Simpson, who had posted a 14-3 record in 26 starts, but had made just two starts since the end of July.

In a surprise move, Merritt started Game Two of the NLCS on October 4 against the Pirates. (The Reds had won Game One.) Merritt tossed 5⅓ innings, yielding just three hits and a run, to earn the win, 3-1. "It isn't the pain that bothers me," he said. "It's the swelling. When it's swollen I can't raise my arm to touch my shoulder."[24] Merritt took the mound again 11 days later in the deciding Game Five of the World Series against the Baltimore Orioles. He was roughed up for three hits and four runs in 1⅔ innings and was saddled with the loss.

Offseason rest did not help Merritt's tendinitis, which quickly resurfaced in spring training in 1971. Ineffective, he remained in Florida as the Reds broke camp and flew to Cincinnati. Joining the club in the second week of the season, Merritt tossed four innings of scoreless ball on April 18 against the Expos in his first start of the season. Then his season took a disastrous turn. He lost his next seven starts and his spot in the rotation. "I don't know how [Anderson] can keep going with me," said a dejected Merritt. "I wouldn't if I were him."[25] Unable to throw his fastball, Merritt could no longer keep hitters off balance. "Opposing batters are just sitting on his breaking stuff," said catcher Johnny Bench. Relegated to the bullpen and given an occasional spot start, Merritt's record dropped to 0-11 and his losing streak reached 13 games before he picked up a win in long relief. In light of his 1-11 record and limited to 107 innings, Merritt confided to sportswriter Earl Lawson that he did not anticipate being back with the Reds, who had fallen to 79-83.[26]

The Reds actively shopped Merritt in the offseason but found no takers. His tenure with Cincinnati came to an unceremonious close in May 1972 when he was optioned to the Triple-A Indianapolis Indians (American Association). "I can't believe I'm through at the age of 28," said a dejected Merritt upon learning that not one big-league team claimed him. Merritt had also served as the Reds' player representative during the strike at the beginning of the 1972 season, and had been booed badly during his few outings in the Queen City.[27] Dividing his time among starts and relief appearances for Indianapolis, Merritt posted unspectacular numbers (4-8, 4.33). In the offseason the Reds sent him to the Texas Rangers in exchange for utilityman Jim Driscoll and backstop Hal King.

Merritt threatened retirement, but ultimately accepted the Rangers' offer to attend spring training as a nonroster player. He surprised manager Whitey Herzog by posting a stellar 2.46 ERA during camp and earning a spot of the staff.[28] On a squad that lost 105 games, Merritt moved into the starting rotation in June and experienced a renaissance in July, completing five of his six starts and winning three of them. Merritt garnered national attention on August 26 when he tossed a glittering three-hit shutout to defeat Gaylord Perry and the Cleveland Indians, 9-0, in Ohio. After the game Merritt admitted in an interview that he threw 25 to 30 percent spitballs, which he called "Gaylord Perry fastballs."[29] "Heck, there are a lot of guys around the league who are throwing them," said Merritt. "I'm going to continue until they stop it."[30] Joe Cronin, AL president, subsequently fined and suspended the hurler. The brouhaha preceded an almost identical incident about a week later when Billy Martin, skipper of the Detroit Tigers, supposedly ordered pitchers Joe Coleman and Fred Scherman to throw spitballs in a game against Perry and the Indians. That episode led to Martin's dismissal as manager; in an ironic twist, the Rangers hired him just days later, on September 8, to pilot the club. Merritt finished the season with a 5-13 record, but logged 160 innings, second most on the club, and posted a 4.05 ERA.

Given the unglamorous role of mop-up man in 1974, Merritt was used sparingly by the Rangers, who surprised baseball by winning 84 games and finishing in second place. He appeared in 26 games and logged only 32⅔ innings. His big-league career came to a conclusion the next season when he was given his outright release in July after making only five appearances.

Over the course of 11 seasons in the major leagues, Merritt posted an 81-86 record, logged 1,483 innings, and carved out a 3.65 ERA. He enjoyed great success against Rick Monday (2-for-21, .095), Boog Powell (4-for-34, .118), and Elston Howard (4-for-30, .133), but had difficulties with Felipe Alou (10-for-21, .476), Al Kaline (12-for-26, .462), and Manny Mota (13-for-29, .448). As a member of the Reds, he was especially tough on the slugging Pirates (7-1, 3.52 ERA), yet was hit hard by the Detroit Tigers (2-10, 5.47) while hurling for the Twins and Rangers.

Merritt retired to the Los Angeles area with his wife, Jean (Daniel) Merritt, whom he met in high school and married in 1962 after his first year in Organized Baseball. They raised three boys, Randy, Ron, and Rod. During his playing career, Merritt had begun working for the Walton Publishing Company in LA, and was well prepared professionally and financially to embark on a business career away from baseball.

In 2011 he was inducted into the West Covina Walk of Fame, located at the Big League Dreams Sportsplex.[31] In November 2013, Jean, his wife of 51 years, passed away. As of 2015, Merritt resided in Southern California.

SOURCES

In addition to the sources listed in the notes, the author consulted:

Jim Merritt player file at the National Baseball Hall of Fame, Cooperstown, New York

Ancestry.com

BaseballLibrary.com

Baseball-Reference.com

Retrosheet.com

SABR.org

The Sporting News

Johnson, Lloyd, and Miles Wolff, eds. *The Encyclopedia of Minor League Baseball*. 2nd edition. (Durham, North Carolina: Baseball America, 1997).

NOTES

1. *The Sporting News*, June 20, 1970, 3.
2. Stu Camen (United Press International), "Jim Merritt Gets 13th Win," *Bennington* (Vermont) *Banner Voice*, July 3, 1970, 10.
3. UPI, "Dodgers Sign Bonus Players," *Redlands* (California) *Daily Facts*, June 23, 1961, 6.
4. *The Sporting News*, April 10, 1965, 24.
5. *The Sporting News*, June 20, 1970, 3.
6. "Aroused S.B. Braves Deadlock Dodgers Rookies in 7-7 Thriller," *San Bernardino* (California) *County Sun*, July 6, 1961, 3.
7. *The Sporting News*, October 13, 1962, 28, and December 1, 1965, 39.
8. *The Sporting News*, March 2, 1963, 9.
9. *The Sporting News*, September 19, 1964, 29.
10. *The Sporting News*, June 20, 1970, 3.
11. *The Sporting News*, May 7, 1965, 25.
12. *The Sporting News*, April 17, 1965, 26.
13. *The Sporting News*, August 21, 1965, 13.
14. *The Sporting News*, August 6, 1966, 13.
15. *The Sporting News*, August 26, 1967, 11.
16. WAR stands for "Wins Above Replacement" and attempts to assign a number to the wins the player added to the team above those of a replacement player. Merritt's 6.5 WAR led all AL pitchers.
17. *The Sporting News*, August 26, 1967, 11.
18. *The Sporting News*, June 20, 1970, 3.
19. *The Sporting News*, August 24, 1968, 21.
20. *The Sporting News*, March 22, 1969, 9.
21. Ibid.
22. *The Sporting News*, June 20, 1970, 3.
23. *The Sporting News*, March 7, 1970, 28.
24. *The Sporting News*, October 31, 1970, 39.
25. D. Byron Yake (Associated Press), "Clemente Homers, Bucs Bop Reds," *Indiana* (Pennsylvania) *Gazette*, May 28, 1971, 18.
26. *The Sporting News*, October 2, 1971, 20.
27. Mark Stallard, ed., *Echoes of Cincinnati Reds Baseball* (Chicago: Triumph, 20007).
28. *The Sporting News*, April 21, 1973, 22.
29. *The Sporting News*, September 15, 1973, 8.
30. UPI, "Texas Pitcher Jim Merritt Threw 25-30% Spitter," *Van Nuys* (California) *News*, August 28, 1973, 32.
31. West Covina Big League Dreams. westcovina.org/home/showdocument?id=1317.

Don Mincher

BY MARC Z. AARON

DONALD RAY MINCHER WAS A TWO-time member of the Oakland Athletics. In 1970 he was the team leader in home runs with 27. Before being traded for the second time to the Athletics on July 20, 1972, Mincher homered off Joe Coleman at Detroit on July 10. It was a personal career milestone, his 200th home run. It was also to be his last.

Minch,[1] as he was often called, "is the only man who played for both the original Twins and the original Rangers, 11 seasons apart. And, for that matter, he was the only player to see the end of both Senators' runs in Washington."[2]

Born on June 24, 1938, in Huntsville, Alabama, Mincher was of German-Irish-Indian descent. At Butler High School (Class of 1956) he played baseball, basketball, and football. In his senior year he captained both the baseball and football teams. He was a good enough football player to make both All-State and High School All-American. Mincher turned down a football scholarship at the University of Alabama to pursue his love of baseball.[3] At 6-feet-3 and 205 pounds, he was built for the sport. An American Legion baseball player, Mincher was signed by former major leaguer Zack Taylor to a Chicago White Sox contract for $4,000 after high school and was sent to Duluth-Superior of the Class C Northern League.[4] That year he married his high-school sweetheart, Patsy Ann Payne.[5] Mincher returned to Duluth-Superior in 1957 and led Northern League first basemen in putouts, assists, and double plays. In 1958, playing for Davenport in the Class B three-I League, he finished fourth in batting (.330) and was named to the league All-Star team.[6]

After spending the 1959 season at Charleston of the Class A Sally League (.272, 22 home runs), Mincher was sent on April 4, 1960, with Earl Battey and $150,000 to the Washington Senators for Roy Sievers.

On the 18th, Mincher was in the Opening Day lineup at first base, going hitless in front of the home crowd against the Boston Red Sox. In his third game, at Baltimore on the 20th, Mincher got his first two major-league hits. On the 25th, at home against Baltimore, he hit his first major-league home run, off Milt Pappas, to deep right field. In mid-May, batting .230 with 2 home runs, Mincher was sent to Charleston in the American Association. Recalled in late September, he had two hits in five pinch-hitting appearances.

Before the 1961 season the Senators franchise was moved to Minneapolis-St. Paul, to play as the Minnesota Twins. Mincher hit five home runs for the Twins but spent most of the season at Triple-A Buffalo. In 1962 he was back with the Twins. On April 28, playing at Cleveland, he hit a pinch-hit home run off

An overlooked slugger from the 1960s, Mincher smashed 22 home runs for the Twins in 1965 and filled in brilliantly for the injured Killebrew at first base. A 13-year veteran (1960-1972), the two-time All-Star finished with 200 round-trippers. (Photo courtesy of Minnesota Twins Baseball Club).

Ron Taylor, then, remaining in the game at first base, he homered for a second time, off Frank Funk. (Mincher was to finish his career with ten pinch-hit home runs, four of them in 1964.) Mincher had another two-home-run game on July 20, 1963, at Minnesota's Metro Stadium, taking starter Steve Ridzik of the expansion Senators deep twice as the Twins won 11-3. The next day he did it again, homering twice off Senators starter Don Rudolph as the Twins won 3-2. (Mincher, a left-handed batter, had no problem that day off the lefty Rudolph. However, throughout his career he always fared better against right-handers, and was often out of the starting lineup against left-handed starters.) Four days later, on July 24 at Cleveland Stadium, Mincher again hit two home runs, off Pedro Ramos and Jerry Walker.

Mincher made Ridzik a particular target. On August 26, 1963, he homered off the right-hander again, at D.C. Stadium, and on August 18, 1964, homered twice in consecutive at-bats off Ridzik, again in Washington.

Mincher settled in as the Twins' first baseman. He told an interviewer in 2010 that his biggest thrill in baseball came in the first game of the 1965 World Series when he hit a home run of the Los Angeles Dodgers' Don Drysdale. "To bat against Koufax and Drysdale when it really meant something," Mincher said. "I didn't realize what a big thrill it was until I got older and started thinking back on these things."[7] His wife, Patsy, knew Mincher was slightly nervous as he was extremely quiet as she drove him to the ballpark. Usually he was talkative.[8] In the bottom of the second inning, in his first Series at-bat, Mincher homered to deep right field off Drysdale. Mincher spoke of the feat often, his wife said.[9] In Game Two, Mincher tied a World Series record with four assists at first base. (Three of the assists were on groundballs by lefty Willie Davis.)

On June 9, 1966, Mincher was part of baseball history again when he was one of five Twins who hit home runs in one inning, an American League record. The Kansas City Athletics were the victims; the others besides Mincher to go deep in the seventh inning that day were Rich Rollins, Tony Oliva, Zoilo Versalles, and Harmon Killebrew.[10]

After the 1966 season Mincher was traded by the Twins with pitcher Peter Cimino and outfielder Jimmie Hall to the California Angels for infielder Jackie Hernandez and pitcher Dean Chance. With the Angels Mincher had his best major league season in 1967. He hit 25 home runs and was selected to the All-Star team for the first time.

On April 11, 1968, in the second game of the season, Mincher was hit on the cheek by a fastball thrown by the Cleveland Indians' Sam McDowell. The blow was a glancing one and Mincher missed only nine games, but he was plagued by headaches and dizziness and struggled at the plate for the rest of the season.[11] On September 4, after he reeled backward while swinging at a pitch, he was removed from the game. X-rays and tests were inconclusive, but Mincher was given the rest of the season off.[12] Mincher's average for 1968 was .236, down from .273 in 1967; his home run and RBI production suffered likewise.

Though Mincher was cleared after tests at the Mayo Clinic, Angels manager Bill Rigney considered him damaged goods after his struggles during the season, and did not feel that the reports provided positive assurance as to Mincher's full recovery.[13] The Angels left Mincher unprotected in the expansion draft after the season and Mincher was selected as the Seattle Pilots number-one pick. He played in 140 games for the Pilots hit 25 home runs, and was named to the American League All-Star squad. Mincher was the Pilots player representative.[14]

On January 15, 1970, as the Pilots were becoming the Milwaukee Brewers, Mincher was traded to the Athletics with infielder Ron Clark for outfielder Mike Hershberger, pitchers Lew Krausse and Ken Sanders, and catcher Phil Roof. With Oakland he hit 27 home runs, his career high. His walk-off home run on August 2 off Horacio Pina of Washington with two outs in the ninth inning of a scoreless game in Oakland was one of 27 he hit that season — a career high.

The following season, on May 8, 1971, Mincher was traded by the Athletics along with catcher-outfielder Frank Fernandez, pitcher Paul Lindblad, and cash to the Washington Senators for first baseman Mike Epstein and pitcher Darold Knowles. On July 17 at RFK Stadium in Washington, Mincher, not in the lineup that day against the Twins, was in the outfield bullpen when in the fourth inning home-plate umpire Hank Soar motioned him to move away from the bullpen fence in center field, where he could pick up Minnesota's signs. Mincher's gesture in response 410 feet away was not to Soar's liking. In what could be a distance record for an ejection in baseball, Soar ejected Mincher without hesitation.[15] Patsy Mincher said that her husband was only motioning back to mean, "What do you want?," but it was taken differently by Soar.[16]

After the 1971 season the Senators moved to Texas to become the Rangers. On July 20, 1972, Mincher was traded back to Oakland with infielder Ted Kubiak for utilityman Vic Harris, infielder Marty Martinez, and pitcher Steve Lawson. Mincher was not too happy. "I'm not ready to sit on the bench," he said, noting that Athletics first baseman Mike Epstein was hitting well.[17] "I've been around a long time and I've learned to expect almost anything, but this trade knocked me off my feet," Mincher said.[18] But Epstein went out with an eye infection, and Mincher was placed at first base and in the cleanup spot. He got off to a poor start, going 2-for-22 with no home runs or RBIs. When Epstein returned, Mincher was relegated to pinch-hitting for the balance of the season.[19] He did contribute in the World Series; his pinch-single in Game Four drove in the tying run in the ninth inning against Cincinnati. The next batter, pinch-hitter Angel Manguel, singled home the game-winning run.

With little hope for his role to change in 1973, Mincher decided to retire. "I just have no desire to play the role I did last year," he said. "I don't care to be that kind of player. I enjoyed being on a world championships club, but I didn't want to sit on the bench watching my more mature years slip by."[20] (Patsy Mincher said in 2013 that Don's shoulder at this time hurt so much

Don Mincher (Photo courtesy of Minnesota Twins Baseball Club).

that he could hardly comb his hair without being in pain.[21]

During Mincher's two stints with the Athletics he played in 210 games, hit 29 home runs (27 of them in 1970 that led the club), knocked in 87 runs and batted .236. Described by one sportswriter as "intense and introverted,"[22] Mincher may have been his own worst enemy. He admitted in 1968 to putting too much pressure on himself both when he was doing well (worrying about keeping it going) and when he was not (staying in the slump). He applauded his supportive wife, Patsy, for spending long nights listening to him spilling his guts out.[23]

After 13 seasons Mincher's retirement allowed him to spend more time with his wife and three children at home in Huntsville. It also provided Mincher with time to pursue his hobbies, which included fishing and hunting.

Mincher ran a sporting-goods store, specializing in trophies and awards for about ten years before returning to baseball in 1985 as the general manager of the Huntsville Stars of the Southern League.[24] The Stars were an Athletics affiliate from 1985 to 1998. When there was a chance in 1994 that the franchise might be moved out of the city, Mincher put together a group of investors to buy the team from owner Larry Schmittou. After the 1998 season the Stars and Athletics parted ways and the Milwaukee Brewers became the Stars affiliate. During Mincher's time with the Stars they won two Southern League championships. During all these years Patsy worked with him at the ballpark. In October 2000 Mincher was elected interim president of the Southern League when Arnold Fielkow left for the NFL. His interim position was made permanent before the start of the 2001 season. Later Mincher and his group sold the Stars to a New York attorney. During his time with the Stars, Mincher was twice elected Executive of the Year and in 2008 was inducted into the Alabama Sports Hall of Fame.

Mincher had a deep interest in the development side of baseball. He made it the mission of the Southern League to promote minor-league baseball as wholesome family fun and entertainment at a reasonable cost.[25]

In October 2011 Mincher stepped down as president of the Southern League. In January 2012 he felt pain in both arms that proved to be symptoms of serious heart problems. He underwent surgery to take care of blockages. Then pneumonia kicked in. He died on March 4, 2012.[26] He is buried in Maple Hill Cemetery, Huntsville, Alabama.

Mincher was preceded in death by his parents, George and Lillian. He was survived by his wife, Patsy; and three children, Mark (head baseball coach for almost 30 years at Huntsville High before becoming principal), Lori Lumpkin, and Mincherna Hopper; and many grandchildren and great-grandchildren. At the 2012 Winter Meetings Patsy was honored as "The First Lady of Southern League Baseball." Not only had she worked at the ballpark during Mincher's tenure with the Huntsville Stars but she also handled the logistics and much of the child-rearing during Mincher's major-league career.[27]

NOTES

1. 1974 player file fact sheet contained in Mincher's Hall of Fame Library Player file. (Hereafter cited as HOF file).
2. John Branch, "A Twin, a Ranger and, Most of All, a Senator," *New York Times*, October 6, 2010.
3. Telephone interview with Pat Mincher on December 10, 2013. (Hereafter cited as Pat Mincher interview.)
4. Maury Allen, "Mincher Enjoys HR and Series Chance," *New York Post*, October 7, 1965.
5. Pat Mincher interview.
6. 1974 player file fact sheet.
7. John Branch, "A Twin, a Ranger and, Most of All, a Senator."
8. Pat Mincher interview.
9. Pat Mincher interview; Oakland Athletics Press Release; HOF file.
10. Max Nichols, "Mele's Maulers Tie Mark, Clout Five HRs in Inning," *The Sporting News*, June 25, 1966.
11. John Branch, "A Twin, a Ranger and, Most of All, a Senator"; Hy Zimmerman, "Pilots Looking Toward Mincher to Get Em over *The Sporting News*, Choppy Seas," *The Sporting News*, February 1, 1969; Hy Zimmerman, "Mincher Fired Up to Clip Angel Wings," April 19, 1969.
12. "Mincher Goes to Hospital, Suffers from Dizzy Spells," *The Sporting News*, September 21, 1968; John Wiebusch, "Mincher Dismayed, Excited on Leaving Angels for Pilots," *The Sporting News*, November 2, 1968.
13. John Wiebusch, "Mincher Dismayed."
14. Hy Zimmerman, "Krausse Wants to be Starter ... Pilots Will Give him a Chance," *The Sporting News*, January 31, 1970.
15. "Soar's Vision Sharp," *The Sporting News*, August 7, 1971.
16. Pat Mincher interview.
17. Randy Galloway, "Critics Fault Ranger 'Suicide' Youth Drive," *The Sporting News*, August 5, 1972.
18. Ibid.
19. Ron Bergman, "Mincher Weary of Bench Duty, Retires as 200-Homer Belter," *The Sporting News*, January 13, 1973.
20. Ron Bergman, "Mincher Weary of Bench Duty."
21. Pat Mincher interview.
22. Ross Newhan, "Mincher Sings Happy Tune With Long Bow to Rigney," *The Sporting News*, March 30, 1968.
23. Ibid.

THE 1965 MINNESOTA TWINS

24 John Branch, "A Twin, a Ranger and, Most of All, a Senator"; Pat Mincher interview.

25 Southern League website.

26 Mark McCarter, April 13, 2011: al.com/sports/index.sst/2011/04/opening_night_remains_special.html.

27 Mark McCarter, December 5, 2012: al.com/sports/index.ssf/2012/as/pat_mincher_proclaimed_first_1.html

Mel Nelson

BY DOUG SKIPPER

MEL NELSON ENTERED PROFESsional baseball as a right-handed-hitting outfielder, spent parts of six seasons in the major leagues as a left-handed pitcher, and when his playing days were over served as a scout for several teams.

He spent more than half a century in professional baseball, including 17 years as a player.

Although he didn't pitch in the 1965 World Series after 28 regular-season appearances for the American League champion Minnesota Twins, Nelson did hurl a scoreless inning in the 1968 fall classic for the St. Louis Cardinals. It was his second stint with the Cardinals; he also pitched for the Los Angeles Angels.

The 6-foot-tall, 185-pounder posted a 4-10 record in the majors, with an earned-run average of 4.40. He started 11 games, tossed one complete game, and appeared in 82 games in relief. He finished 31 of those games, and recorded five scattered saves. His defense was perfect; he handled 40 career chances flawlessly.

Melvin Frederick Nelson was born on May 30, 1936, in San Diego, California, the older of Melvin and Kay (Martin) Nelson's two children. The elder Melvin Nelson (the family did not use the senior or junior designations) was a civilian engineer employed by the US Navy. His expertise in radial aircraft engines was in high demand, and he was posted to short stints at military air depots in Sacramento, California; Alameda, California; and Pensacola, Florida. After the United States entered World War II in December 1941, Melvin was commissioned into the Navy, and assigned in 1942 to the Army Air Force's air depot at San Bernardino, California. After six nomadic years, the family, which included younger brother Ken, settled down to stay in San Bernardino, located in the Inland Empire region east of Los Angeles. After the war ended, the elder Nelson returned to civilian life and managed the engine shop for Norton Aircraft Maintenance Services.

The younger Nelson was a blossoming athlete who led San Bernardino High School to a Citrus Belt League title as a power-hitting center fielder and also a hard-throwing pitcher, and earned all-California Interscholastic Federation honors.

"Mel Nelson was King Kong at San Bernardino High," former classmate Jack Brown said years later. "Mel was the purest baseball player that I've seen, and I saw Kenny Hubbs."[1]

In 1954 Nelson was scouted by the St. Louis Cardinals, and was invited to Wrigley Field in Los Angeles, about a 60-mile drive from his home, where he participated in an infield practice before a Cardinals exhibition game against the Cubs.

A left-handed reliever, Nelson was winless in four decisions with the Twins in 1965. In parts of six seasons in the big-leagues, he appeared in 93 games and logged 173 2/3 innings. (Photo courtesy of Minnesota Twins Baseball Club).

Later that summer, the organization invited Nelson and his father to St. Louis, where he worked out in right field with Stan Musial. Cardinals chief scout Joe Mathes and minor league personnel director Walter Shannon met Musial in his restaurant that evening. "Is the kid coming out again tomorrow?" asked Stan the Man. They said he was. "Then put him in left field," said Musial. "Don't let him show my arm up."[2]

Soon after, Ken Penner, the Cardinals' West Coast scout, signed Nelson to a contract, and the youngster joined the organization where Musial was in the midst of a Hall of Fame career.

"I was lucky enough to spend six or seven spring trainings with Stan Musial," Nelson remembered after Musial died in 2013. "The Cardinals held their camp in St. Petersburg, Florida. Stan didn't offer anyone pointers on how to be better. If you asked, he would help. You just watched him play and you try to let it rub off. When he did talk, I would listen. He lived a long life. I guess you can't ask for much more if you make it to 92."[3]

After he signed, Nelson was assigned to Fresno of the Class C California League, where he batted .228 with three doubles and a triple in 39 late-season games as an 18-year-old in 1954.

He returned to Fresno in 1955 and batted .296 with 185 hits, 27 of them homers, to help the Cardinals cruise to the California League pennant. He scored 151 runs, drove in 112, and stole 29 bases. In July he tripled to lead the South to a win in the loop's All-Star Game. It was an impressive offensive showing for the 19-year-old Nelson, but he also struck out 152 times. "After my dad saw me hit in the minor leagues, he told me I'd be pitching in the big leagues in five years; he was right," Nelson said later.[4]

After the season Nelson was invited to the Cardinals' spring-training camp in St. Petersburg. Manager Fred Hutchinson said that he had the potential to develop into a good hitter, but that the strikeouts were a concern and Nelson needed to eliminate a hitch in his swing. Hutchinson was also bluntly opinionated about a lefty thrower hitting right-handed—for some reason considered taboo at the time. "If I were an owner, I'd give $100,000 for Nelson right now—if he batted left-handed," Hutchinson said, still excited about Nelson's potential. "He struck out more than 140 times, so you can imagine what he is going to do when he cuts that down."[5]

One sportswriter summed up the Cardinals' confidence in their young slugger. "The numerous old heads coaching fledgling Cardinals here are confident, however, that Nelson, not yet 20 … will turn out to be an exception to the rule that left-handed throwers can't hit right handed," Harry Grayson wrote. "The ball explodes when Nelson hits it."[6]

After an extended spring training, Nelson was promoted to Triple-A Rochester (New York) in the International League, where he batted .244 with 4 home runs and 35 runs batted in 427 at-bats. He also made the first seven appearances of his pitching career, without a decision, for manager Dixie Walker.

Nelson struggled to hit at the Triple-A level again in 1957, batting just .133 in 17 games for Rochester, and just .156 in 24 games for the Columbus (Georgia) Foxes of the Class A South Atlantic (Sally) League, before landing with the Billings (Montana) Mustangs, where he batted .280 with 11 home runs in 68 games for the Class C Pioneer League champions. Nelson also finished with a 4-3 record and a 4.33 ERA in seven starts and four relief appearances.

In spring training in 1958, the Cardinals persisted in their efforts to see Nelson on the other side of the plate. "I was 22 years old, and they asked me to try switch-hitting, but I had enough problems hitting right-handed, and now they are trying to get me to hit left-handed. It didn't go very well and I gave it up."[7]

He spent the majority of his time on the mound that season, posting an 8-5 record and a 4.08 ERA in 30 appearances, including 18 starts for the York (Pennsylvania) White Roses in the Class A Eastern League, and a 4-1 record with a 1.29 ERA in eight games for the Houston (Texas) Buffaloes of the

Double-A Texas League. He appeared in 24 games as an outfielder in York, but was used exclusively as a pitcher by Dixie Walker's brother, Harry, at Houston.

The Cardinals moved their Texas League affiliation to Tulsa in 1959, and Nelson posted a 9-9 record and a 3.02 record for the Oilers, completing 10 of 19 starts, with three shutouts. He advanced to the Omaha Cardinals of the Triple-A American Association, where he was used primarily in relief, compiling a 2-0 record and a 4.43 ERA in 25 appearances. He was also an offensive weapon, posting a .353 batting average with 18 hits, including a pair of homers.

Though still property of the Cardinals in 1960, Nelson posted a 13-7 record, with a 3.69 ERA in 33 appearances, including 22 starts, to help the Triple-A Spokane Indians, a Dodgers affiliate, capture the Pacific Coast League title.

After the season he was promoted to St. Louis, and made his major-league debut on September 27, 1960, at the age of 24, against the Los Angeles Dodgers. He replaced Bob Gibson in the bottom of the eighth and struck out the first two batters he faced, Maury Wills and Charlie Neal. After giving up a single to former minor-league teammate Willie Davis, he induced a groundout from Gil Hodges. After the game he and his father celebrated at Musial's St. Louis restaurant, Stan and Biggie's, with a steak dinner.

Nelson made one more appearance for manager Solly Hemus, a start against San Francisco on the final day of the season. He took the loss despite pitching seven strong innings, and finished the campaign with a 3.38 ERA and seven strikeouts, while walking just two and surrendering a home run to Willie Mays. He also collected the first hit of his career and drove in a run in two plate appearances.

Nelson failed to stick with the Cardinals in 1961, and returned to the Pacific Coast League, this time with the Cardinals' Triple-A affiliate, the Portland Beavers, where he was briefly a teammate of legendary 54-year-old pitcher Satchel Paige. "He was 55 when they signed him and only pitched on weekends to increase attendance," recalled Nelson. "He had a dry sense of humor, very funny. I can imagine how good he was at 22 or 23 years old."[8] Nelson posted a 9-12 record, with a 4.65 ERA.

After a brief stint in the Army that ended in August, Nelson appeared in just eight games as a 26-year-old, winning once, with the Cardinals' new affiliate, the Atlanta Crackers, champions of the Triple-A International League. On October 15, 1962, the Cardinals sold his contract to the Los Angeles Angels of the American League for $25,000.

While a member of Bill Rigney's staff, which also included Bo Belinsky and Dean Chance, Nelson developed a screwball, and appeared in a career-high 36 games, posting a 2-3 record and a single save, with a 5.30 ERA over 52⅔ innings. He surrendered 55 hits, seven of them home runs, walked 42, and struck out 41, in an up-and-down year.

In July, days before he was to be honored at San Bernardino-Colton Day at Chavez Ravine, where the Angels were temporary tenants of the Dodgers, the Angels sent Nelson back to the PCL, this time to the Hawaii Islanders, where he posted a 4-4 record with a 6.19 ERA. While he was there, Nelson and Jeanne Barr of Riverside, California, were married on August 12, 1963 in Honolulu.

After the season, Nelson and six other Angels played in the Venezuelan Professional Baseball League, where he posted a 3-2 record and a 2.18 ERA in 10 appearances for Estrellas Orientales (Eastern Stars), representing the tourist-friendly Anzoátegui region. He completed three of six starts, and hurled the second no-hitter in the league's history, shutting down the Caracas Lions.

Nelson started the 1964 season with the Islanders, suffered from a sore arm, and made nine appearances before the Angels sold his contract to the Minnesota Twins. The Twins sent him to their Triple-A affiliate, the Atlanta Crackers of the International League, where he posted a 9-12 record and a 2.96 ERA, starting 23 of the 24 games in which he appeared.

Nelson earned a spot on Sam Mele's staff with the Twins in 1965, at the age of 28, and Johnny Sain served as pitching coach. "When I made the team, Johnny Sain said that I had made my team on my ability, and he didn't want me to change how I pitched; he wanted me to improve," Nelson said. It was great to have him as a pitching instructor."[9]

In 28 appearances, including three starts, Nelson posted an 0-4 record with three saves and a 4.12 ERA (the league average ERA was 3.46). He gave up 57 hits and 29 runs in 54⅔ innings, walked 23, and struck out 31. He collected a single and a sacrifice bunt in 10 plate appearances.

Nelson was a part of Minnesota's first-ever pennant-winning team, and became a lifelong fan of slugger Harmon Killebrew. After the Twins legend died in 2011, Nelson remembered him first as a great teammate, saying, "He always made time for people no matter who you were. He represented nothing but the best. He was a fun guy on the club. There is no doubt that Harmon ranks up there with the best. He didn't hit for an average like Ted Williams, yet as a person he was near the top. He was strong and had arms like big irons. He could catch the ball"[10]

"It was fun to have Harmon as a teammate. It wasn't fun to pitch against him. When he hit the ball it would go. You could watch it go far into the night," said Nelson. "It took him a while to get his career going. Once he got going, he was consistent."[11]

When the Twins met the Los Angeles Dodgers in the World Series, Nelson was a spectator. "Going to the World Series was a thrill," he remembered. "There were four of us who didn't get into a game. That's the way it is." He was more disappointed that the Twins weren't able to beat a team that included many of his minor-league teammates and rivals, and one that was played so close to his hometown. "If we could have won one of the games at Dodger Stadium, maybe it would have been different … but pitching overshadowed hitting at that time," Nelson said. "The Dodgers had a great team, but if we had played a week later, maybe we would have won."[12]

Nelson was back in the minors the next year, and after an early-season appendectomy, posted a 5-11 record and a 6.21 ERA for the Twins' Triple-A farm club in the Pacific Coast League, the Denver Bears, as a 30-year old in 1966.

Nelson was much better the following year, sporting a 10-3 record and a 2.67 ERA at Denver, making one start in 54 appearances. At the end of the PCL season, he was recalled by the Twins, who were a part of a four-team race for the American League pennant. He offered little help, making one relief appearance and giving up three hits, including a homer, and two runs in just one-third of an inning for manager Cal Ermer.

The Twins returned Nelson's contract to Denver, and in December the Bears traded him to the Jacksonville Suns of the International League for pitcher Joe Grzenda. Nelson absorbed a loss in three appearances for the New York Mets' Triple-A farm team, and was released in May.

At first contemplating a return to San Bernardino and a full-time job at the local Sears store, Nelson averted retirement when he signed a free-agent contract with St. Louis. Bing Devine, who had regained his position as general manager of the Cardinals after a four-year exile, remembered Nelson from his previous stint. After he posted a 1-2 record and a 2.52 ERA in 13 games for the Triple-A Tulsa, Nelson was called up to St. Louis, and in his first appearance, on June 23, hurled the only complete game of his career, a six-hitter against the Atlanta Braves, retiring Hank Aaron four straight times. He made 14 relief appearances, finished eight games, and posted one save. He gave up 49 hits and 17 earned runs, walked 9 and struck out 16. Nelson finished the season with a 2-1 record with a sparkling 2.91 ERA over 52⅓ innings for Red Schoendienst's pennant winners. This time he played in the World Series, pitching a perfect ninth inning in Game Six, a 13-1 Detroit win. "Someone told me I was the only one that was able to get them out that day," Nelson remembered. "I told them that their guys were just tired from running around the bases all day."[13]

Later Nelson remembered his time with the Cards fondly: "Bob Gibson was the team leader and Roger Maris was the prankster. Both were very good to me."[14]

The veteran hurler started the 1969 season with the Cardinals, gave up four runs in his first appearance, made five scoreless appearances, and then gave up three runs in his next outing. On June 2, 1969, at the age of 33, Nelson appeared in the major leagues for the final time, walking the only batter he faced in a 6-3 loss.

Sent to the minors, Nelson posted a 6-6 combined record for two American Association teams, Tulsa, a Cardinals farm club, and Denver, back in the Twins' organization

He found work again in 1970. In his final minor-league season, at the age of 34, Nelson posted a 6-8 record with a 4.55 ERA in 37 appearances with the Richmond of the International League, the Atlanta Braves' top farm club.

After his playing career ended, Nelson scouted for the Cleveland Indians (1973), Los Angeles Dodgers (1974-1976), Chicago White Sox (1978-1980), and the Oakland A's (1982-1989), was a scouting supervisor for the St. Louis Cardinals (1990-1992), a major-league scout for the Colorado Rockies (1994-1995), a scouting supervisor for the New York Yankees (1996), and a scout for the Houston Astros (1998-2005). Among his signings were Dmitri Young for the Cardinals and Ron Coomer for the Athletics. His organizations made five World Series appearances, the Dodgers in 1974, the A's in 1988 and 1989, the Yankees in 1996, and the Astros in 2005.

After the Astros "forced me out due to economic reasons" in 2006, Nelson was hired by Jack Brown, his old San Bernardino High School teammate, to work in construction, building and development for Stater Brothers Markets. "Stater Brothers is lucky to have someone of Mel's stature," Brown told a local newspaper. "He encourages kids and is a leader. Wherever Mel Nelson goes you can expect a win."[15]

Nelson was employed there for 3½ years. In retirement, he worked in his yard, attended California League and California Winter League games, and visited a nearby baseball camp. Outgoing and affable, he attended the 40th anniversary celebration of the Minnesota Twins 1965 AL pennant in 2005. "It was great to get together with all of the guys. They were all good players and great guys; Killebrew, Allison, Grant, Oliva, Kaat, Rollins, Sam Mele. I hope they do it again sometime," Nelson said in a 2014 interview. "We might be able to see each other and sit down and sign a few pictures."[16]

Nelson is one of several hundred living former major-league players who finished their careers prior to the establishment of the players union, and is not eligible for a pension. "The current Major League Baseball agreement does not include us old guys. Players now can receive $10,000 per month. We get nothing. There's only 900 (as of 2009) of us pre-union guys still alive. We didn't make anything in our day and it's the old guys who need the help. They only care about the young guys," he said.[17]

Nevertheless, in a phone conversation he looked back on his career and many teammates fondly. "I was very fortunate," Nelson said. "I played on some great teams and some bad teams, but all of the guys were really great guys."[18]

As of 2014 Nelson and his wife, Jeanne, reside in Highland, California, not far from San Bernardino. They had three children—Lance, a member of the 1980 Cal Poly Pomona Division II national championship team, Brigg, and Shannon—and four grandchildren.

SOURCES

Grayson, Harry, "Success Isn't in the Cards for 'Big Rookie' Nelson," Grayson's Scorecard, *Pittston* (Pennsylvania) *Gazette*, March 7, 1956, 7.

Kahn, Harvey M., "Former SBHS Great Mel Nelson Was a Baseball Associate of Musial," *Inland Empire Community Newspapers*, January 24, 2013, A5.

Kahn, Harvey M., "Former SBHS Star Remembers Teammate Killebrew," *El Chicano Weekly*, May 26, 2011.

Kahn, Harvey M., "Jackie Robinson: One of America's Greats to Be Subject of Warner Brothers Release," *El Chicano Weekly*, 2013.

Kahn, Harvey M., "Mel Nelson Ends Long Championship Baseball Career," *El Chicano Weekly*, June 25, 2009.

Thielman, Jim, *Cool of the Evening: The 1965 Minnesota Twins* (Minneapolis: Kirk House Publishing, 2005).

"Cherubs Up in Air Over Missing Part in Mound Machine," *The Sporting News*, December 15, 1962, 15.

"Longshot Nelson Supplies Cards With Quick Lift," *The Sporting News*, July 6, 1968, 7.

"Tutor Marv Hones Seraph Slab Corps to Razor-Fine Edge," *The Sporting News*, May 4, 1963, 15.

"1955 Fresno Cardinals," Bill Weiss and Marshall Wright, MiLB.com.

San Bernardino County Sun

The Sporting News

minors.sabrwebs.com (Society for American Baseball Research minor leagues database).

bioproj.sabr.org/bioproj.com

scouts.baseballhall.org (Diamond Mines, the National Baseball Hall of Fame scouts database).

retrosheet.org

baseball-almanac.com

baseball-reference.com

denverpost.com.

purapelota.com

milb.com

Telephone interview with Mel Nelson, September 24, 2014.

NOTES

1. Harvey M. Kahn, "Mel Nelson Ends Long Championship Baseball Career," *El Chicano Weekly*, June 25, 2009. Hubbs, an infielder from nearby Colton, California, was the National League Rookie of the Year in 1962, but died in a plane crash in 1964.
2. Harry Grayson, "Success Isn't in the Cards for 'Big Rookie' Nelson," Grayson's Scorecard, *Pittston* (Pennsylvania) *Gazette*, March 7, 1956, 7.
3. Harvey M. Kahn, "Former SBHS Great Mel Nelson Was a Baseball Associate of Musial," *Inland Empire Community Newspapers*, January 24, 2013, A5.
4. Kahn, "Mel Nelson Ends Long Championship Baseball Career."
5. Ibid.
6. Grayson, "Success Isn't in the Cards."
7. Telephone interview with Mel Nelson, September 24, 2014.
8. Kahn, "Mel Nelson Ends Long Championship Baseball Career."
9. Nelson interview.
10. Harvey M. Kahn, "Former SBHS Star Remembers Teammate Killebrew," *El Chicano Weekly*, May 26, 2011.
11. Ibid.
12. Nelson, September 24, 2014.
13. Ibid.
14. Kahn, "Mel Nelson Ends Long Championship Baseball Career."
15. Ibid.
16. Nelson interview.
17. Kahn, "Mel Nelson Ends Long Championship Baseball Career."
18. Nelson interview.

Minnesota and 1965 All-Star Game: The Senior Circuit Takes Charge

National League 6, American League 5
July 13, 1965, Metropolitan Stadium, Bloomington, Minnesota

BY GREG ERION

SEVERAL THEMES WERE EVIDENT for All-Star games played in the 1960s. First was the National League's crushing superiority during the midsummer classics. Of the 13 games played (two games were played from 1960 through 1962) the National League took 11; the American League won only once (the second game in 1962 was a tie).

Toward the end of the decade another development, the overwhelming dominance of pitching, manifested itself. Successive scores of 2-1, 2-1, and 1-0 from 1966 through 1968 reflected regular-season play where the equilibrium between hitting and pitching had gone out of balance.[1]

Another factor, born of expansion, was that new facilities and venues influenced the selection of where games took place. While venerated ballparks such as Fenway Park and Wrigley Field hosted contests, baseball's hierarchy determined it prudent to showcase recently built stadiums, too. New facilities for the expansion Houston Astros, New York Mets, Los Angeles Angels, and Washington Senators were the site of All-Star contests.[2] Older franchises with new stadiums were chosen as well: San Francisco's Candlestick Park in 1961 and Busch Stadium in 1966. A true anomaly took place in 1965 when the Minnesota Twins' Metropolitan Stadium became the site for the 36th contest. Neither the franchise nor the ballpark was new.

Metropolitan Stadium ("The Met") was nine years old, originally built for the minor-league Minneapolis Millers of the American Association. The Minnesota Twins franchise had shifted from Washington after the 1960 season, after being in the nation's capital since 1901. That Minneapolis was a new location for the majors helped lure the All-Star Game to the Twin Cities. Twins president Calvin Griffith's determination to make sure his club was duly recognized ensured that the game would take place in Minnesota. He had campaigned for Minnesota to host the game almost as soon as his team moved west. According to *The Sporting News*, Griffith was almost successful in 1963, when at the last moment Cleveland gained selection.[3] Undeterred, Griffith continued his quest and because of that persistence he gained approval for the game to take place in Minnesota in 1965.

Griffith had several tasks before him. The seating capacity of the Met was substandard. Construction of double-deck bleachers down the left-field line increased the capacity from 40,000 to 45,000.[4] The Minnesota Vikings of the NFL paid the bill and received terms for lower rent in return.[5] The seats would be completed mere days before the All-Star Game.[6] Griffith also undertook another enterprise, working with Twin City officials and business interests to ensure that visiting baseball fans and officials would get a favorable impression of the Twin Cities. This endeavor took on a life of its own, requiring a great deal of effort in the area of public relations.

The team itself unexpectedly boosted local interest in the All-Star Game. Pegged by many to finish fifth in 1965, the Twins got off to a quick start and by the end of April they and the Cleveland Indians were tied for first.[7] Starting pitcher Jim "Mudcat" Grant and veteran relievers Johnny Klippstein and Al Worthington, acquired at midseason the previous year, bolstered the staff. Future Hall of Famer Harmon Killebrew and the 1964 batting champion, Tony Oliva, led a potent offense. (Oliva would repeat in 1965.) Two off-field acquisitions also proved key to the team's success. Johnny Sain, perhaps the best pitching coach in the game, joined the club, as did Billy Martin. Martin's fiery style contributed toward a more aggressive baserunning game. Manager Sam Mele ably molded the players into a cohesive unit that played to its full potential.

On July 5, after being near the top of the standings all season, the Twins climbed back into first place and held the lead from then on. The following Sunday, July 11, Minnesota faced the New York Yankees, their last game before the All-Star break. The Yankees were in sixth place, 13½ games out, but their reputation (they had won the pennant the five previous seasons) was such that many felt they still had the ability to charge back into contention. Playing at the Met, where Griffith's project to add bleacher seats had been completed just two days before, Minnesota went into the bottom of the ninth down 5-4. With a runner on, two outs, and two strikes on Killebrew, he blasted a game-winning home run into the left-field seats. The blow proved fatal to New York, and confirmed the Twins as the team to beat. Two days later the 36th All-Star Game took place.

Griffith not only got the bleachers completed on time, his efforts to engage Minnesotans in the process of welcoming baseball to the state also came to fruition. Governor Karl Rolvaag and fellow citizens went out of their way to make visitors to the state feel welcomed. Local businessmen donated golf shirts, dinnerware and briefcases to guests and newsmen. Women received Betty Crocker cookbooks.[8] A smorgasbord was scheduled at the Met on the day of the game featuring over 120 local delicacies, including mooseburgers and roast pheasant.[9] Griffith had the pool at baseball's lodging headquarters stocked with fish and made sure visiting officials were provided with poles to catch them.[10]

Fans began gathering outside the stadium the night before the game hoping to obtain standing-room tickets, which would go on sale noon. Their wait included weathering a passing rainstorm that gradually gave way to morning clouds, which cleared just before game time.[11] Griffith's efforts to generate enthusiasm worked; an over-capacity crowd of 46,709 fans showed up to watch the game.

An underlying drama of the game was that after 35 contests (including the 1961 tie) each league had won 17 games. This development would have been largely unimagined after the 1949 All-Star Game, at which point the American League held a 12-4 advantage over the senior circuit. The tide began to turn in 1950 when the Cardinals' Red Schoendienst hit a 14th-inning home run for a 4-3 come-from-behind NL victory. The momentum carried forward as the National League proceeded to win 12 of the next 18 contests.

Of key importance in this surge of victories was the National League's early embrace of black players. Aaron, Banks, Campanella, Clemente, Marichal, Mays, Newcombe, Robinson (Frank and Jackie), and others more than outnumbered their American League counterparts, who for much of the 1950s largely consisted of Larry Doby and Minnie Minoso, only gradually increasing as the 1960s began.[12] This imbalance of black talent at the All-Star Game in favor of the National League would prove telling in the game at Minnesota.

Managers for each league did not come to their selection through the traditional process, that of having led the previous year's World Series representatives. Johnny Keane, manager of the World Series champion St. Louis Cardinals, had resigned after winning the Series. The Yankees at season's end had fired his counterpart, Yogi Berra. In their place, Philadelphia's Gene Mauch and White Sox skipper Al Lopez, who had guided their teams to second-place finishes in 1964, led the squads.

Twins fans not only boasted of their first-place club but also crowed that Minnesota had more players on the squad than any other American League team as Lopez added Jim Grant, Jimmie Hall, Harmon Killebrew Tony Oliva, and Zoilo Versalles to the roster. Twins catcher Earl Battey started at catcher; he was selected by a poll of players, managers, and coaches for that honor. Minnesota's Mele and coach Hal Naragon were members of the coaching staff. Twins reliever Bill Pleis was called on to throw batting practice on a field where the infield foul lines were colored red, white, and blue, and then white to the fences. Bases were red, white, and blue and the fungo-hitting circles contained red, white, and blue stars.[13]

Charley Johnson, sports editor of the *Minnesota Star and Tribune*, threw out the first pitch. He was a significant force in drumming up support to build Metropolitan Stadium and then later succeed in bringing major-league baseball to Minnesota. Johnson and the rest of the folks at the game did not have to wait long for the fireworks to begin.

A major attraction of the game for Minnesotans besides having a chance to see their local favorites play was the opportunity to view the National League stars, none of whom shined brighter than San Francisco Giant Willie Mays. Mays had played for the Millers in 1951. He was hitting a torrid .477 when called up to the Giants, much to the unhappiness of resident fans. The outcry at his being taken from the Millers was so great that Giants owner Horace Stoneham found it necessary to buy ads in Minneapolis newspapers apologizing for taking the gifted outfielder from their midst.

Mays, as usual, was having a great season. Leading the majors in home runs with 23 and batting at .339, he had just passed Stan Musial in career home runs with his 476th, placing him sixth on the all-time list. In the last game before the All-Star break, however, he and catcher Pat Corrales of the Phillies had collided in a bone-jarring play at the plate, and both players had to be from the game. There was legitimate concern that Mays might not be able to play.[14]

Mays did indeed play, and batting leadoff, promptly reminded Minnesotans why Stoneham had brought him to the majors 14 years earlier. On the second pitch of the game from Orioles starter Milt Pappas, Mays ripped a 415-foot home run into the left-field pavilion.[15] Musial was dinged once again; Mays's homer was his 21st hit in All-Star Game competition, breaking a tie with the St. Louis Cardinals great.

Mays's homer was just the initial blow. With two outs and Pittsburgh's Willie Stargell on first, the Braves' Joe Torre launched a home run, barely fair, into the left-field pavilion to make the score 3-0 against a stunned American League. Pappas gave way in the second to Minnesota's Jim Grant, who at 9-2 was in the midst of his best season. Grant was as unsuccessful at holding the National League at bay as Pappas. Willie Stargell came to bat with a runner on third and homered into the right-field bullpen, making the score 5-0.

Meanwhile, the almost effortless pitching of San Francisco's Juan Marichal shut down the American League through the first three innings. He faced the minimum nine batters; Cleveland's Vic Davalillo's single in the third was erased when Battey grounded into a double play. Marichal, having pitched the maximum three innings allowed in the All-Star Game, gave way to Cincinnati's Jim Maloney to start the bottom of the fourth.

Maloney gave up one run that inning and was on the verge of getting through the fifth when disaster struck. With two outs, he walked Hall. Detroit's Dick McAuliffe homered over the center-field fence. Mays injured his hip when he slammed into the fence in an unsuccessful attempt to catch McAuliffe's drive but stayed in the game, a key development as it turned out. Brooks Robinson beat out an infield hit, which brought Killebrew to the plate. Having thrilled Twins fans with his game-winning homer over the Yankees two days before, he brought them out of their seats again, connecting off Maloney for a game-tying homer into the left-field pavilion. Maloney departed after allowing five runs in 1⅔ innings. It proved the only All-Star Game appearance of his career.

The game remained tied until the top of the seventh. Once again Mays proved to be the catalyst. Leading off, he drew a walk off Cleveland's Sam McDowell and advanced to third on Hank Aaron's single. Cubs third baseman Ron Santo came to bat and chopped the ball up the middle. Shortstop Versalles corralled the high chopper but there was no chance to get Mays at home or Santo at first. It proved to be the game-winning hit. (Santo had joked just the day before, "As a .258 hitter, I felt I was pretty much on the squad on a rain check."[16]) Mays's 17th run, the most in All-Star Game competition, merely extended a record he already held.[17]

There would be one more moment of drama. Versalles walked with two outs in the bottom of the eighth and moved to third on a single by Tigers catcher Bill Freehan, who took second on Mays's throw to third. Hall came to bat, Twins fans willing him to win the game. He flied to deep center, where Mays would normally have caught the ball with little effort, except that on contact Mays appeared to misjudge the ball. Recovering, he leaped to make a backhand catch, ending the inning. After the game he said, "I slipped as I started to go back. I was scared to death."[18]

Tony Oliva doubled to lead off the ninth, giving Twins fans hope for a rally, but Bob Gibson finished off the inning, getting the last two outs on strikeouts.

Sandy Koufax, who was pitching when Santo drove in the deciding run, got the win. Marichal edged out Mays for the Most Valuable Player of the game with his three innings of shutout ball, but the big news was that the National League had edged ahead of the American League in wins for the first time since the games began in 1933. As of 2014, their lead remains intact.

Killebrew's home run represented a consolation prize of sorts for Twins fans; however, an even greater reward awaited them on September 26, when the Twins beat the Washington Senators, 2-1, to clinch the pennant.

The All-Star Game represented Minnesota's ability to support major-league baseball; the Twins' triumph represented their ability to play better than anyone else did in the American League that year. Twenty years later the All-Star Game took place at the Metrodome and in 2014, the 85th summer classic (including two ties) took place at Target Field. Minnesota subsequently won two pennants and two World Series championships after their encounter with the Dodgers. While these contests generated tremendous excitement, they could not recapture the first-time thrill of watching baseball's finest in July 1965 or the continuing pleasure of the locals achieving an unexpected pennant.

NOTES

1 Which it was. After the 1968 season, which saw a combined major-league batting average of .237, the pitching mound was lowered and the strike zone reduced in size, restoring a semblance of offense to the game.

2 Washington hosted the All Star Game twice in the 1960s—first in 1963 then in 1969, the latter driven in part by the celebration of professional baseball's centennial.

3 "Minnesota Has Reason to Be Proud," *The Sporting News*, July 17, 1965, 14.

4 Minnesota.twins.mlb.com/min/ballpark/min_ballpark_metropolitan_stadium.jsp

5 Jim Thielman, *Cool of the Evening, The 1965 Minnesota Twins* (Minneapolis: Karl House Publishers, 2005), 73.

6 "Twin Bleachers Completion Now Scheduled for July 9," *The Sporting News*, July 17, 1965, 20.

7 "Yanks, Phils Picked By Writers, Fans," *The Sporting News*, April 17, 1965, 1.

8 "Twin Cities Twinkles," *The Sporting News*, July 24, 1965, 8.

9 "Hungry for Mooseburger? It Was on All-Star Menu," *The Sporting News*, July 24, 1965, 5.

10 Thielman, 207.

11 "Twin Cities Twinkles," 8; "Juan 'n' Willie Set N.L. Stars Winking," *The Sporting News*, July 24, 1965, 5.

12 The Boston Red Sox and Detroit Tigers did not even integrate their teams until the late 1950s and even then only with marginal utility players.

13 "Twin Cities Twinkles," 6.

14 James Hirsch, *Willie Mays: The Life, The Legend* (New York: Scribner, 2010), 430-431.

15 "Juan 'n' Willie." In a move designed to give Mays and Hank Aaron more at-bats, Mauch unconventionally placed them first and second in the batting order.

16 "Twin Cities Twinkles," 8.

17 "Juan 'n' Willie."

18 "Juan 'n' Willie."

Joe Nossek

BY RICK SCHABOWSKI

JOSEPH RUDOLPH NOSSEK SPENT 43 years in professional baseball as a player, manager, and coach. Seven of those years were as a player with a high point being his season with the 1965 American League champion Minnesota Twins.

Nossek was born in Cleveland on November 8, 1940. He loved baseball and enjoyed listening to Jimmy Dudley, the Cleveland Indians broadcaster. His father, Joe Sr., was a standout pitcher in the Cleveland sandlot leagues, and an uncle, Jim Stepp, helped cultivate the youth's interest in baseball. Nossek began as a pitcher, but he played outfield in high school, making the All-Ohio team at that position and helping lead his Euclid High School team to a spot in the state championship tournament in 1958, his senior year. Nossek recalled, "I worked out with the Washington Senators after I graduated from high school. I went to Washington for a couple of days and they said, 'We'll keep an eye on you, but we think you should go to college for a couple of years,' which I ended up doing, and it turned out to be the right thing to do."[1]

Nossek attended Ohio University, where as a junior in 1961 he was named to All-American, and All-Mid-American Conference first teams, which drew attention to him from a number of major-league scouts. "When it was time to make a decision to sign, our college coach and my dad were in the room with the scout (Floyd Baker), and Minnesota was the first team in, and I ended up signing with them," he remembered. "I didn't even talk to the other teams."[2] Sure enough, the Senators/Twins organization had kept its word, and kept its eyes on Nossek.

After signing with the Twins for a $45,000 signing bonus, Nossek was sent on June 12, 1961, to their Charlotte (North Carolina) team in the Class A South Atlantic (Sally) League. He ended up batting .274, and he had a big day against Charleston on August 9, when he went 4-for-4 and belted a bases-loaded single that gave the Hornets a 6-5 victory.

While in Charlotte, the Caucasian Nossek witnessed racism on a scale he had never experienced before. "The Jim Crow laws were in effect back then so that was a new experience for me, to see how they treated the black players," he said. "That was a culture shock! My wife came to visit and there were separate restrooms and drinking fountains at the ballpark. And my black teammates had to stay in a different part of town and they had to go to the back of the kitchens to get served (at restaurants). It really stunk, but unfortunately that's the way it was."[3]

In 1962 Nossek was placed on the Twins' 40-man roster and took part in spring training until he was sent back to Charlotte on March 26. He played in 134 games for the Hornets, batting .276. One of the highlights

Nossek was a valuable utilityman as a rookie for the Twins in 1965, seeing action at all three outfield positions and third base. He played in 295 games in parts of six big-league seasons (1964-1970). (Photo courtesy of Minnesota Twins Baseball Club).

of his season was getting five consecutive singles in a 9-0 victory over Norfolk-Portsmouth on May 30.

Nossek was moved up to Triple-A in 1963, playing in the Pacific Coast League with the Dallas-Fort Worth Rangers, managed by Jack McKeon. Not noted as a power hitter, he still won two games with home runs. in 128 games, he batted .293.

Nossek began the 1964 season with the Twins. His first major-league appearance came on April 18, when he entered the game as a defensive replacement for Harmon Killebrew, with Bob Allison moving from center field to left. In his only at-bat for the Twins that season, pinch-hitting on April 24 against the Tigers' Mickey Lolich, he popped out to second base. Shortly thereafter, Nossek was sent to the Twins' Triple-A farm team in Atlanta (International League). Nossek had an offyear for Atlanta, batting only .238, but a broken thumb was a big factor. However, he had developed into an excellent defensive outfielder. In a 1965 interview he said, "The big step was when I learned to turn my back on the ball hit over my head. I started learning that in 1961 with the help of [Minnesota center fielder] Lenny Green. Last summer it really helped me."[4]

After the 1964 season, Nossek played in the Florida Instructional League and led the league with a .350 batting average. Nossek's path to the Twins outfield was blocked by solid players like Killebrew, Allison, Jimmie Hall, and Tony Oliva, so Nossek played third base in Florida. Twins' assistant farm director George Brophy observed, "Nossek needs experience at third base, of course, but he has the ability. I saw him make good plays on the slow-hit ball, and he has good range at third. He handles those sharply hit grounders."[5]

How much did the Twins value Nossek? Before the 1965 season, they tried to trade for Red Sox second baseman Chuck Schilling. Twins' president Calvin Griffith said, "The last time I talked to them, they wanted Joe Nossek. I consider Nossek too good a young prospect to give up on right now."[6] Great performances in the Florida Instructional League and at spring training earned Nossek a spot on the Twins' 1965 roster. The team planned to use him as a utility outfielder, and to platoon him with Jimmie Hall against left-handers.

On June 27 Nossek singled home the winning run in the 10th inning off Larry Sherry, giving the Twins a 6-5 victory. The hit raised his average to .315. After the game Nossek said, "Sometimes I go for a week and don't eat much. I just don't feel like eating sometimes, but I have a good Italian wife who likes me to eat. So I eat better when I am at home."[7] This habit of light eating led to his nickname, "Coffee and Juice" which fit well for the slender 6-foot-1, 175-pounder.

Nossek hit his first major-league home run off Hank Aguirre at Tiger Stadium on June 13. Over the course of the season Nossek's batting average plunged to its final .218 in 170 at-bats. Nossek started in center field in five games of the Twins' seven-game World Series loss to the Los Angeles Dodgers. In Game Two he had a fourth-inning single off Sandy Koufax, the first Twins hit of the game en route to a 5-1 victory that gave the Twins a 2-0 series lead. Nossek singled off Claude Osteen in Game Three, and added a pinch-hit single off Don Drysdale in Game Four. He went 4-for-20 in the Series. Reflecting on his performance, Nossek said, "I think my biggest accomplishment was only striking out once in that Series, and that was against Howie Reed, a right-handed curveballer. Koufax didn't get me and neither did Drysdale or Osteen."[8]

Nossek was involved in a controversial play in Game Seven. In the third inning, Zolio Versalles singled with one out and tried to steal second base. As Nossek swung, Versalles broke and had the base stolen easily, but umpire Ed Hurley ruled that Nossek had interfered with catcher John Roseboro's throw, ordered Versalles return to first base, and called Nossek out for interference. Nossek denied that he interfered: "I just went for an outside pitch. I tried to duck when I heard Roseboro coming."[9] The Dodgers, behind Koufax's three-hit, 10-strikeout performance, defeated the Twins 2-0 to win the Series.

Nossek spent the offseason in the Florida Instructional League learning yet another position, second base. "… I am always happy to learn a new position," he said. "I feel it makes me more valuable. If I don't make it at second, the experience should make me a better all-around utility man."[10]

Nonetheless, on May 11, 1966, Minnesota placed Nossek on waivers, and the Kansas City Athletics claimed him. Nossek was optimistic, "Coming to Kansas City may be a break in more ways than getting a shot at playing regularly. For one thing, the park is one that I should do my best in. I'm not a home-run hitter anyway and I'm not going to be tempted to try here."[11] But he was upset with the Twins. "I was really disappointed by that," he said of their placing him on waivers. "They talked about what a great bench they had and I had won a few games for them pinch-hitting.[12]

After the Athletics' Jose Tartabull suffered an ankle injury, Nossek replaced him and played so well he accumulated a lot of playing time. Nossek enjoyed playing for A's manager Alvin Dark. "Dark is a fine handler of men," Nossek said. "He has given me the opportunity to play every day and he has also helped me with my batting."[13] Dark said, "He's the kind of player you like to have for defensive purposes."[14]

Nossek played in 87 games with the '66 Athletics, batting .261. Among the highlights were an inside-the-park home run off the Indians' Sam McDowell on July 10, and a streak of 87 plate appearances without a strike out. Nossek will never forget a nice surprise he received after the season bonus after the season. He was pleasantly surprised at 11:30 P.M. on Christmas Eve. "I get a call at 11:30 at night, and it's Charlie Finley wanting to talk contract. He gave me a nice raise to $10,500, and that was a great Christmas present."[15]

Nossek played in 87 games for the A's in 1967 and batted .205. He had an unusual experience during spring training. The Twins and A's were playing in Caracas, Venezuela, on the campus of Central University. Neither team knew why so many armed soldiers were at the stadium. It turned out that students were rioting outside the ballpark. The music and cheering at the game muffled the sound of gunfire, but one policeman and two students were injured. After hearing about the disturbance, Nossek commented, "The soldiers in the dugout didn't look so bad after all."[16] Before spring training he spent the offseason employed by a St. Paul brokerage company.

The A's sent Nossek to Triple-A Vancouver in 1968. He played every game of the Mounties' PCL schedule and batted .247. He was named the team's MVP and most popular player. He ranked a game on September 7 against the Hawaii Islanders as one of his most memorable. "Mickey Vernon was our manager in Vancouver and I talked him into letting me pitch the second-last game of the season. It was a doubleheader that day, so it was only seven innings, but I ended up pitching a complete game and we won 5-1. I remember I struck out two guys in the first inning and then I couldn't lift my arm when I went out for the second inning. But I did make it through the game, [and] I got a whole new appreciation for pitchers and what it takes them to get in shape."[17]

In 1969 the Kansas City A's were the Oakland A's. Nossek was with the team in spring training, He faced a tough fight to make the major-league roster in the face of competition from Reggie Jackson, Mike Hershberger, and a hot prospect named Joe Rudi, but Nossek cherished the opportunity. "All I want to do is stick, then I'll worry about the rest. I need one more year for my pension," he said.[18] In a spring game against the San Francisco Giants, he had four hits, scored two runs, drove in two, and made a fine defensive play on a ball hit by Willie Mays. Nossek made the A's roster and appeared in 13 games with six at-bats before being sent to Triple-A Iowa. On July 12 Oakland traded him to the St. Louis Cardinals for infielder Bob Johnson. Nossek was assigned to Triple-A Tulsa, and was a September call-up to St. Louis, where he recorded a single in five at-bats.

Although he was on the bench frequently, Nossek still focused on the game and what was happening and developed a reputation as one of the game's best sign stealers. He recalled one incident of many. "When I played for Hank Bauer, out in Oakland in 1969. I was sitting on the bench a lot, so I started to watch the [opposing] manager and the third-base coach interact. I was sitting there one game and thought, 'Gee whiz, I think they did this yesterday and I think it's going to be a hit-and-run.' So I went up to Hank, who could be quite gruff, and I said, 'Hank, I think the hit-and-run is on here.' And he just looked at me and gave me that stare and looked away and didn't do anything about it, so I went back and sat down and sure enough, the hit-and-run was on. The following day I'm sitting there, not playing again, and I see the same signs and so I walked over to Bauer again—a little fearful of what he might do—and I said, 'Hank, I think the hit-and-run is on again.' And he says, 'You think?' And I said, 'Yes, sir.' And so Hank pitched out and we get the guy and I got hooked [on stealing signs]."[19] Word of Nossek's uncanny skill spread quickly. "I built up a reputation that I think was deserved for the first half of my career, but I think a lot of it was psychological later in my coaching days, but psychologically it turned out to be a good weapon."[20]

Nossek spent most of the 1970 season at Tulsa, batting .228 in 396 at-bats. He was a September call-up and had one at-bat on September 13, his last as a major leaguer. He grounded out against the New York Mets' Tug McGraw.

In February 1971, Nossek was sold to the Milwaukee Brewers and spent the season with Triple-A Evansville. He batted .223 in 174 at-bats, and also was a coach assisting manager Del Crandall.

With his playing days behind him, Nossek in 1972 managed the Danville Warriors, the Brewers farm team in the Class A Midwest League to the league championship. Del Crandall became the Brewers' manager in 1973 and named Nossek his third-base coach. Nossek had the job for three seasons, until Crandall was fired after the 1975 season.

Nossek returned to the Twins as third-base coach in 1976. Released after the season he wasn't out of work for long; the Cleveland Indians hired him to be the third-base coach. He remained on the Indians' coaching staff until the end of the 1981 season, when he and pitching coach Dave Duncan left over a salary dispute. (They were making $30,000 and sought raises to $36,000, but the Indians offered $33,000.) Players were upset with the potential loss of the two coaches—Duane Kuiper and Mike Hargrove even offered to chip in to pay the pair. Commenting on the impasse, Nossek said, "I have been a big league coach for nine years, I spent the last five in Cleveland. The Indians gave me a job when I needed one a few years ago, but now I think it's time for me to find out what I am worth on the open market and make the best living I can for my family."[21] Duncan became the pitching coach for Seattle, while Nossek agreed to a two-year, $75,000 deal with Kansas City.

Nossek played a role in the George Brett pine tar incident on July 24, 1983 at Yankee Stadium. Nossek attempted to restrain an angry Brett, and when the game was resumed on August 18, Nossek was as the Royals manager, replacing the ejected Dick Howser.

The Royals let Nossek go after the 1983 season, and again it didn't take him long to find a new job. The Brewers offered him a contract for $38,000, but the White Sox won out with a $50,000 offer. Nossek's salary led White Sox board chairman Jerry Reisdorf to comment, "We just don't sign coaches, we hire instructors."[22] Nossek remained with the White Sox until the middle of the 1986 season, serving as a coach and advance scout, and left to work as advance scout for the Houston Astros. After the 1989 season, the Astros gave the White Sox permission to talk to Nossek about a job, which Nossek took. Astros manager Art Howe commenting on the departure of Nossek said, 'That's a key job and Joe was one of the best. We're really going to miss him, but he had a great opportunity and couldn't pass it up."[23] Nossek rejoined the White Sox coaching staff as an outfield coach, and also served as an eye-in-the sky defensive coordinator.

Nossek served as the eye-in-the-sky coordinator in 1990. In May of that season the Baltimore Orioles filed a complaint with the American League charging

Nossek with illegally stealing signs. League rules permitted a coach to position defenses from an agreed-upon high perch, but the Orioles claimed Nossek sat in the stands facing the Baltimore dugout, and relayed the information to manager Jeff Torborg. It got to the point that Orioles general manager Roland Hemond sat with Nossek to watch him. Nossek brushed off the incident, saying, "Why don't they just change their signs? It's that simple. They put coaches in the dugout. What's the difference? But I'm glad they're worried."[24]

Nossek became the White Sox' bench coach in 1991. Before the 2004 season he stepped down because of his physical condition. "Unfortunately, my aches and pains have reached a point where I don't want to jeopardize being able to fulfill my responsibilities in uniform," he said. "I have had a knee replaced, a shoulder is next and my back continues to be a problem. It just has gotten tougher to be at the ballpark each day, and I wanted to make this decision now so that it is not a distraction to [manager] Ozzie [Guillen] or the team."[25] White Sox general manager Ken Williams said, "We cannot say enough about Joe Nossek and what he has meant to the White Sox organization over the past two decades. His loyalty, skills, and baseball knowledge are unmatched in this game. We understand how being in uniform each day has become more difficult for Joe, but we are going to make sure he remains a valuable resource for this organization in some capacity."[26]

As of 2014 Nossek and his wife, Jean, lived in Amherst, Ohio, enjoying their four children, 11 grandchildren, and one great-grandchild.

NOTES

1 "Joe Nossek recalls special night in Vancouver in 1968," Cooperstowners in Canada, November 7, 2013. http://cooperstownersincanada.com/2013/11/07/joe-nossek-recalls-special-night-in-vancouver-in-1968/

2 Ibid.

3 Ibid.

4 Max Nichols, "Spindly Nossek: A Light Eater, Heavy Swinger," *The Sporting News*, July 10, 1965.

5 Max Nichols, "Twins Infield Tussle Takes on Added Starters, Nossek, Quilici," *The Sporting News*, December 5, 1964.

6 Max Nichols, "Griffith Expects Trouble Signing Reluctant Twins," *The Sporting News*, January 23, 1965.

7 *The Sporting News*, July 10, 1965.

8 Cooperstowners in Canada

9 Lowell Reidenbach, "Dodgers Never Forget—Follow '55 Script," *The Sporting News*, October 23, 1965.

10 Max Nichols, "Nossek and Kosco Earn Passing Grades in Twins' Florida Book," *The Sporting News*, December 18, 1965.

11 Major Flashes, American League, *The Sporting News*, June 11, 1966.

12 *The Sporting News*, June 25, 1966.

13 Ibid.

14 Ibid.

15 Cooperstowners in Canada.

16 "A's, Twins Play In Caracas—Machine Guns in Dugouts," *The Sporting News*, April 1, 1967.

17 Cooperstowners in Canada.

18 *The Sporting News*, March 22, 1969.

19 Cooperstownes in Canada.

20 Ibid.

21 Terry Pluto, "Two Tribe Tutors Unhappy With Pay," *The Sporting News*, October 24, 1981.

22 Stan Isle, "Footnotes," *The Sporting News*, November 14, 1983.

23 N.L. West, *The Sporting News*, November 13, 1989.

24 Alan Solomon, "O's Charge Sox Cheated," *Chicago Tribune*, May 26, 1990.

25 "Joe Nossek Steps Down as Bench Coach," chicago.whitesox.mlb.com, March 19, 2004.

26 Ibid.

Tony Oliva

BY PETER C. BJARKMAN

TONY OLIVA STANDS AT THE FOREfront of an exceedingly select group — one that also includes Tany (Atanasio) Pérez, Rafael Palmeiro and Orestes "Minnie" Miñoso. These are the few unrivaled candidates for recognition as the greatest major league hitter ever to emigrate to the professional big time from the baseball-rich island nation of Cuba. Palmeiro (with 569 long balls in 2,831 games) and Pérez (379 in 2,777 games) far outstripped Oliva (220 in 1,676 games) in big league career homers; Miñoso (playing 159 more games) also would register a marginally more lofty career base hit total (1,963 to 1,917). But Oliva was the only one of the stellar quartet to claim a league batting title (which he did on three occasions); five different times Oliva also paced a big league circuit in base hits, a feat never achieved by Pérez and accomplished only once by Miñoso and Palmeiro. And only Oliva retired with a lifetime batting average still above the .300 high-water mark.

If raw career power numbers amassed by the other three (and also by José Canseco, with 462 homers and 1,407 RBI) notably outstrip those in Oliva's resume, an easy explanation is found in the significant differences in total seasons and total games logged on the big league diamond. Reduce the career of each Cuban star to a single 162-game lifetime average, and the differences between them become rather too close to adequately distinguish one from the other. Oliva leads the pack in two categories (185 hits and a .304 BA); his average of 21 home runs nearly matches Pérez (at 22) and is outdistanced only by Palmeiro (at 33); his 92 yearly RBI average total edges Miñoso (90), essentially equals Pérez (96), and lags behind only Palmeiro (105).

But such thumbnail comparisons somewhat blunt the true significance of Tony Oliva's near-Hall-of-Fame-stature career. While the Pinar del Río native may remain without an official plaque hung in Cooperstown, his place in diamond history will nonetheless always be easily assured by a memorable collection of early-1960s pioneering awards and achievements. He was the first among his fellow Cuban countrymen to win a big league batting title and perhaps even more significantly the first big leaguer (Latino or otherwise) ever to capture batting crowns in his initial two seasons. To add some further luster, Oliva was also the first Cuban to earn Rookie of the Year plaudits in the majors. Among the long list of stellar Latin American imports, only Venezuela's Luis Aparicio (1956) and Puerto Rico's Orlando Cepeda (1958) preceded Oliva in claiming the big league top rookie award. And before 1964 (when Oliva topped the junior circuit and Puerto Rico's Roberto Clemente also paced the senior

One of the great pure hitters of his generation, Oliva (Zoilo Versalles on right) captured his second consecutive AL batting crown in 1965 (.321) and led the club with 98 RBIs. The eight-time All-Star led the AL in hits five times, batting three times, and finished with a .304 career average in his 15-year career, all spent with the Twins (1962-1976). (Photo courtesy of Minnesota Twins Baseball Club).

circuit), only Mexico's Roberto Avila (1954) and Clemente (1961) among Latinos stars had ever walked off with either an American League or National League batting crown.

If statistics go a long way toward explaining baseball's endless fascination for some fans, mere numbers always fall far short of elucidating the sport's unparalleled beauty for true devotees. Thus in the end neither the raw numbers nor celebrated honors quite do sufficient justice to the aesthetics of Pedro "Tony" Oliva's image as a complete big league ballplayer. The flashy Cuban could simply do it all—hit for superior average, slug with eye-popping power, run like a svelte gazelle, and throw accurately and powerfully from the outfield with the best of them.

Unfortunately, his one great flaw proved to be a set of weak knees that repeatedly folded under the immense stresses of the lengthy summer baseball wars. A series of painful knee injuries that began less than a half-dozen seasons into his American League sojourn with the Minnesota Twins would soon cut short a potentially unparalleled career, steal away what might have been some of his prime seasons, and rob him of almost certain Hall of Fame status. In the end the only thing that Cuba's Tony Oliva lacked on a baseball diamond were healthy legs and thus a measure of reasonable career longevity.

It was the original "Cuban Comet" Orestes "Minnie" Miñoso who a dozen years before Oliva's arrival paved the way for dark-skinned Latinos on big league diamonds. Oliva would ironically not only compile a career resume highly similar to that of his pioneering countryman but would also share with Miñoso many of the debilitating misconceptions and misunderstandings—both intentional and unintentional—that plagued the careers of a dozen or more groundbreaking Latin American imports of Fifties and Sixties-era "golden age" baseball. Both played on the big stage under falsely assigned monikers that were not their natural given or family names (a fate also shared by Felipe Alou and his two big-league brothers, as well as by Puerto Rico's Vic Power).[1] And while Tony Oliva lost his possible shot at Cooperstown by not hanging around long enough, Miñoso squandered his by remaining on the scene just a little too long.[2] Both were victims of reigning stereotypes, and both were clearly undervalued by racially insensitive writers and fans, as were so many Latinos of their pioneering generation.

A decade into his own 15-season big league sojourn Oliva would comment with astute awareness but surprisingly little apparent anger about the second-class status he shared with his countrymen as a Spanish-speaking Latino ballplayer. In his late-career autobiography (penned with the assistance of St. Paul baseball beat writer Bob Fowler while still an active player) he spoke of the lack of commercial opportunities as merely a considerable annoyance. During 1971 spring training the veteran Twins hero had filmed his first television spot (alongside Cincinnati Reds star Pete Rose) promoting Gillette razor blades. Speaking of his personal excitement surrounding that rare opportunity, Oliva could not avoid observing that despite his elevated status as a hometown hero local businesses had always skipped over him for (often less prominent) white athletes to push their commercial products. He had for a long time dismissed such oversights as a simple result of his broken English, but was eventually disabused of that illusion when he began noticing French Canadian hockey stars gracing the local airwaves with just as little English fluency as his own.[3]

Oliva chose to relate his own plight to a broader discomfort share by all athletes of his race during that immediate post-baseball integration era: "Blacks and Latins must realize that they don't get nearly as many chances to do commercials or make endorsements as the white players. That's why when the Gillette people contacted me in March I was shocked; I was flattered, too, that they would think of me. But I don't know if my commercial with Rose was good or not; I never saw it." The observation (as polished by co-writer Fowler) reveals Oliva's quiet reserve as much as his underlying resentments. Unlike contemporary Latino stars Roberto Clemente and Felipe Alou, the humble and respectful Oliva never turned such dissatisfactions into a personal crusade and never sought out a visible stage with local baseball beat writers for outspoken advocacy against the abuses of Latino ballplayers. Far less outspoken than Clemente, Oliva remained far less controversial and thus often also far more easily overlooked and undervalued both on and off the diamond.

The future Minnesota Twins star grew up during the pastoral 1940s on a family farm in Cuba's rural Pinar del Río Province, the lush tobacco-growing region that also produced star pitcher Pedro Ramos for the same Griffith-family-owned American League franchise. Born on July 20, 1938, Pedro (Pedro Oliva II, his given birth name) was the oldest of four boys and the third of ten children in the family of Pedro and Maria López. Of three younger brothers, named Antonio, Reynaldo and Juan Carlos, the latter two would also prove to be talented ballplayers on their native island. Of five sisters, Maria Antonio and Gricelia were the oldest of the brood, while Irene, Adelia and Felicia were all younger than the first-born son. The elder Pedro harvested tobacco, oranges, mangos, potatoes and corn on his one-mile square plot located outside the hamlet of Entrongue de Herradura and approximately forty kilometers distant from the provincial capital also labeled Pinar del Río. Pedro senior also possessed local fame as an expert cigar roller and during his youth had enjoyed a successful stint as a semi-professional ballplayer on local and regional diamonds.

Baseball ran deep in the Oliva family blood (as it did and still does in the blood of most rural Cuban families), and the oldest Oliva son learned the finer points of the game early on from his once-talented father. Pedro senior built a crude diamond on the family farm for a local squad that played area opponents on Sunday afternoons. Tony took up the sport by the time he was seven and was finally able to crack the lineup of the neighborhood ball club (which also included his father as the catcher and sometimes outfielder) for a single summer when he was fifteen. Tony would later credit his father in the pages of his autobiography for providing hours of invaluable evening practice on the family diamond, but more even specifically for long lectures about the subtle art of hitting.[4]

The soon-promising young athlete was inked to a professional contract by Minnesota scout Joe Cambria in February 1961, several months before his twenty-third birthday.[5] Cambria was at the tail end of his own legendary scouting career in pre-Castro Cuba that had produced dozens upon dozens of prospects (and a handful of eventual big leaguers, including stars Pedro Ramos and Camilo Pascual) for the Griffith-family franchise in Washington. Cambria had been alerted to the hard-hitting prospect by former Washington Senators journeyman minor leaguer Roberto Fernández. Also a Pinar del Río native, Fernández had been playing alongside Oliva during the winter season on the Los Palacios village ball club that competed in a strong provincial league in western Cuba. Fernández had contacted Cambria who was then based in Havana and alerted him to a raw but promising youngster who "could hit all pitches to all fields and had a strong arm" and who thus merited immediate signing.[6]

It is unclear if Cambria knew Oliva's actual age at the time of extending that first contract offer, but the experienced birddog was impressed enough with the judgments of Fernández to orchestrate Oliva's transfer as a largely untested prospect to the Minnesota farm system. As Oliva himself recounts the events, his February signing allowed only a few short weeks before a scheduled departure for spring training in the United States. The cramped time frame created a significant problem because he lacked a passport. But since his brother Antonio (older by Oliva's telling) did possess proper documentation, a switch was hurriedly arranged and the hopeful ballplayer was cleared to leave his homeland with obviously illegitimate paperwork. The Twins' timely offer and the availability of his brother's passport papers enabled an escape from Cuba in the immediate aftermath of the 1959 Castro-led revolution and thus at the precise time of worsening Cuba-USA relations. One fateful consequence for the future was that the youngster would become known by a brother's name and not his own, a fate he could never shake despite later legally changing his name in U.S. courts to Pedro Oliva Jr. (actually his rightful given name in Cuba). An equally devastating consequence was the fact that worsening relations between Washington and the newly installed Castro regime would soon block any possibilities of returning to his beloved homeland and his family homestead for decades into the future.

There has been considerable controversy surrounding Oliva's actual birth date, with 1938, 1940 and 1941 all appearing as alternative choices in standard baseball reference works and various on-line sources. [7] The ballplayer's own account in his autobiography attests that he was the second son, born in 1941 and preceded by older sibling Antonio. Oliva retells the familiar tale of how after his signing with Cambria his departure from Cuba necessitated the use of his brother's Cuban papers.

"The problem was that I didn't have a birth certificate and couldn't get a passport without one. It would take time to get a birth certificate. My older brother, Antonio, had one but I don't remember why. People get them for passports, to get married, for a lot of reasons, and he had one so I borrowed it. That seemed like the thing to do; he didn't need it, and I did. We were born on the same day, July 20, but he was born in 1938 and I was born in 1941."[8]

In short, the true Antonio Oliva had a birth certificate (not a passport), and it was this that brother Pedro borrowed; the passport was indeed issued to the ballplayer, but the papers needed to acquire it were his brother's and not his own. All this led to "Tony" Oliva's arrival in the United States with a false name (but not a false age, as it turns out) that then immediately became part of his lasting legacy. Oliva's own account was later contradicted by his wife in a 2011 newspaper interview which seems to clarify the issue. Gordette Oliva explains that Tony was indeed the elder (the one born in 1938) and being already 23 when he inked with the Twins he (likely on the advice of Cambria) assumed that he might stand a better chance of making the grade if the ball club thought him younger than he actually was. This was a standard practice with Latino ballplayers in the 1950s and 1960s (and has also been known to occur in more recent decades).

One of course might think that any individual would have the final word on his own birthdate.[9] But Gordette's explanation goes far toward explaining why Tony might well manipulate the facts for an autobiography written while he was still an active player. He would not have wished in 1973 to admit publicly that he had lied to the Twins a dozen years earlier. And there is yet a stronger argument that Oliva had fudged the story about his own age and that of his brother. It is far more plausible that the oldest son in the family would have been a "junior" in accord with the popular Hispanic tradition of first-borns being their father's namesakes. It would hardly seem logical that Pedro Oliva would have dubbed his first son Antonio and his second male child (the eventual major leaguer) Pedro; it should have been (and seemingly was) the other way around.

Complex circumstances surrounding Pedro (now renamed "Tony") Oliva's departure from his homeland almost cancelled out a promising career before it even got started. First off, there were visa-related delays upon his arrival in Mexico City, where Tony and a contingent of fellow Cuban-born Minnesota Twins rookie prospects (reportedly numbering more than 20) sat marooned in a hotel for eleven days awaiting the proper papers permitting their entry into Miami. Upon their eventual arrival at the Minnesota rookie camp in Fernandina Beach (Florida) a half-dozen of the darker-skinned Cubans (Oliva included) were turned away from the assigned local hotel and forced into cramped lodgings in private Negro homes. For the young and racially naïve Cuban import this was his first disturbing brush with a brand of racial prejudice still rampant in the American South of the early 1960s. But an even greater setback was the fact that a late arrival had cut short Oliva's limited time to impress scouts, coaches and minor league managers working at the Minnesota rookie camp.

Appearing in four inter-squad contests in the mere five remaining days of camp tryouts Oliva collected seven hits in ten trips to the plate. His outfield play was rough and unpolished, however, and despite the brief hitting spree he was one of a handful of island

Tony Oliva (National Baseball Hall of Fame, Cooperstown, New York).

imports given a quick release and told to pack his bags for shipment back home. Tony's own recollection of the disastrous first tryout (as reported in his autobiography) was that his chances were severely limited not only by such limited exposure but also by racial politics. Of the two remaining clubs in the lower-level Minnesota farm system with open roster slots, only Erie (located in Pennsylvania) was able to use black-skinned ballplayers. And Erie had already grabbed one of the earlier-arriving black Cuban hopefuls and therefore had no opening left either.

A rare break that would save Oliva's career from an immediate dead end came when sympathetic Joe Cambria decided to intervene on behalf of Oliva and two young countrymen by contacting Phil Howser, general manager of the organization's Class A club in Charlotte, North Carolina. Cambria lobbied for assistance in placing the desperate hopefuls with any team that might have them. In retrospect the phone call was probably the most significant service that Cambria (signer of so many journeymen Cubans who filled the Washington rosters in the Fifties) ever provided for the Griffith family and their basement-dwelling ball club. Howser fortuitously agreed to take the Spanish-speaking trio under his wing for a few days in Charlotte while he attempted to find openings on a number of Class D squads then operating throughout the Carolinas. After six weeks of desperate waiting in Charlotte (and only a month after the April 1961 Bay of Pigs invasion had set in motion events that would soon begin isolating stateside Cuban ballplayers from their families back on the native island), Howser was finally able to find Tony a vacant roster assignment with a short-season rookie league ball club located in rural Wytheville, Virginia.

Oliva—already almost 23—thus began his soon-stellar career in the Class D Appalachian League and again encountered immediate problems of linguistic and cultural adaptation. Since Wytheville did have hotel space for blacks, the Spanish monolingual prospect was lodged in a Negro rooming house with two black American teammates. He walked daily to and from the ballpark, and his dining was restricted to the single eatery serving local blacks.[10] He had equally as much trouble communicating on the field as he did ordering food when away from the park. Already a weak fielder, he particularly struggled with fly balls during night games since he had never played under lights back home in Cuba. Teammate Frank Quilici (a teammate and one of his future managers with the Twins) provided a much-needed assist in aiding Tony with English lessons, and easy-going manager Red Norwood displayed considerable patience with his raw "good hit, no field" prospect. But it was another encouraging visit by Cambria that finally eased the initial pressures and convinced the increasingly depressed Cuban prospect to put up with such rough times and growing homesickness until things took a turn for the better.

The turnaround was not long in coming. Despite some pronounced defensive shortcomings in right field, Oliva simply tore up the league with his hot bat and productive offense during that debut professional season in Wytheville. Spraying the ball to all fields during a short 68-game schedule, the promising Cuban's .410 average was that summer's best in all of

Organized Baseball. Even his fielding showed some improvement under the tutelage of Norwood, and although he committed 14 errors (second worst in the circuit among outfielders), to go with a fielding percentage of .854, his strong arm allowed him to pace the league in outfield assists. Since a return to Cuba for the winter was now out of the question because of mounting tensions between Washington politicians and the Castro government, Tony was rewarded for his strong debut showing with an invitation to spend September in Minneapolis working out with the parent big league club. The Twins then assigned him to the wintertime instructional league in St. Petersburg, Florida for further polishing.

A fast start in 1961 (after so many initial delays) only accelerated at breakneck speed during the summer of 1962. Realizing they had a true prospect on their hands—one they had almost let get away—Twins management decided to protect Oliva in early 1962 by elevating him to the 40-man roster and thus also extending a spring training invitation with the big club. Surprisingly promoted to the top of the system with the AAA Vancouver club at the end of the spring, Tony was quickly reassigned to the Class A Sally League where he opened his second campaign with Phil Howser's Charlotte Hornets. Here the rapidly developing phenom was even more impressive than he had been as a rookie league upstart, again posting big numbers on offense with an average of .350, plus 17 round trippers and 93 RBI in 127 games. While Charlotte finished in the league basement, Tony was a league all-star selection (alongside Macon second baseman Pete Rose and Savannah third sacker Don Buford) and also tabbed as circuit MVP. His .350 BA virtually tied league-leader Elmo Plaskett (but his 469 ABs missed the cutoff for the official league crown). It was all enough to earn a brief nine-game September trial with the American League Minnesota Twins after fewer than 200 minor league games.

After a second winter season with the Florida Instructional League club in St. Petersburg, Tony continued a torrid hitting pace during his second spring training tour with the Twins and headed north with the club when the team broke camp at the end of March 1963. The brief dream of a leap to the majors in only his third pro season quickly crashed, however, when the Twins promptly reassigned him to AAA Dallas-Ft. Worth of the Pacific Coast League on the eve of the new campaign. Fortunately, he overcame an immediate impulse to reject the demotion and return to Cuba thanks to some sage advice from veteran Twins teammates Vic Power and Zoilo Versalles. Tony himself would soon enough readily admit that the further minor league seasoning was far more of an advantage than a career setback. A third strong campaign at the plate (this time under the guidance of future big-league manager Jack McKeon) featured a .304 average (sixth best in the league), 23 homers, and a solid 74 RBIs. The reward was another September return to Minnesota and a second fall "cup of coffee" visit to the American League (this time with seven plate appearances, all in a pinch-hitting role). Having now obviously outgrown the instructional league, Tony made his first visit to a Caribbean island circuit that December and January, starring for Arecibo in the Puerto Rican Winter League and slugging the ball at a .365 pace (losing the batting race to San Francisco Giants all-star Orlando Cepeda by a slim three-point margin).

Tony received two especially pleasant surprises upon reporting to a third spring training session in Orlando on the heels of his winter league campaign. He found his name emblazoned above his clubhouse locker stall, and that locker also contained a uniform bearing the low number "six"—both telling signs that the club and manager Sam Mele had every intention of keeping him this time around. The uniform number (the same as the one worn by Al Kaline in Detroit) held a special significance for Tony since in his first brief stay with the Twins two seasons earlier he had been immediately awed on a first visit to Tiger Stadium by Kaline's eye-catching talent and smooth style. The impressionable rookie quickly decided that Kaline was the one player he most wanted to pattern himself after.[11]

If he had not been all that highly touted by the Twins organization only two springs before his permanent arrival in Minnesota in April 1964, the now-suddenly-impressive Cuban slugger was soon enjoying one of the most remarkable and productive rookie campaigns in big league annals.[12] Lodged in the second slot in an impressive Twins batting order (ahead of Harmon Killebrew, Bob Allison and Jimmie Hall) Oliva enjoyed a 2-for-5 opening day performance in Cleveland against veteran Indians hurler Jim "Mudcat" Grant. In the season's second game in Washington a warning-track fly-out in the ninth prevented the rookie from hitting for the cycle in only his second big league start. By mid-May it was already apparent that Tony was a strong Rookie of the Year candidate as he still boasted a .400-plus average and seven homers. Despite a painful late-May sliding injury and an increasing role as the target of enemy bean balls, the pace slowed only moderately and the young Twins star was honored by fellow players (who then did the voting) as the American League's youngest All-Star Game selection. By season's end Oliva had established a handful of new league records for a first-year player. He also had become the first rookie in big league history ever to capture both a league batting crown plus the circuit's top newcomer award.[13]

Oliva's complete statistical line has never been matched by another big league rookie campaign before or since. His league-best .323 BA led the AL; his league-leading 374 total bases outdistanced runner-up and league MVP Brooks Robinson by a whopping 55; he trailed only Boog Powell and Mickey Mantle in slugging percentage; he paced the league in five additional offensive categories (hits, doubles, extra base hits, runs scored, and runs created); his 217 hits were the only league total above 200. At the ballot box he was a near-unanimous Rookie of the Year selection—with one sole renegade vote cast for Baltimore pitcher Wally Bunker. It was perhaps a bit surprising that such an unprecedented display by a league newcomer left him only in fourth place when it came to the American League MVP selection. In that vote he trailed only Robinson, Mantle and Elston Howard.

The breakout onslaught from the Twins' hottest new prospect certainly didn't sag any during Oliva's second campaign. Few big league batsmen have done a better job of avoiding the legendary sophomore slump. Tony once again reigned as junior circuit batting champion, this time outstripping Boston's Carl Yastrzemski (only Oliva at .321, Yaz at .312 and Vic Davalillo of Cleveland at .301 topped .300). Oliva again paced the circuit in an additional major batting category—base hits (185) and ranked in the top four in five more: runs scored (second to teammate Versalles), doubles (third), total bases (third), RBIs (third), and on-base percentage (fourth). The second batting title made him the first big leaguer ever to debut with two straight hitting crowns. And while again failing to capture an MVP award (this time thanks only to teammate and fellow Cuban Zoilo Versalles—league leader in runs, triples and total bases), Tony was nonetheless named AL Player of the Year by *The Sporting News* and was a serious Gold Glove candidate in right field for good measure. Perhaps as important as any of the individual plaudits, Oliva was the key factor (alongside Versalles) as the Minnesota Twins captured their first-ever American League pennant.

That autumn's Fall Classic provided a much anticipated matchup between vaunted Minnesota hitting (Oliva, Versalles, Killebrew, Allison, Earl Battey and Jimmie Hall) and exceptional Los Angeles Dodgers pitching (Sandy Koufax, Don Drysdale, Claude Osteen, Ron Perranoski, Jim Brewer). Many anticipated a Dodgers four-game sweep, but the more likely stalemate between American League offense and National League defense held up, and the result was a dramatic tussle that went the distance with Koufax's brilliant Game Seven three-hit shutout proving the slim difference. Despite hanging in for seven games, the Twins' batsmen were largely stymied by the Dodger aces; the AL champs hit only .195 collectively, and Killebrew and Versalles were the only big guns offering much productivity. Tony for his part collected only five base knocks (a .192 average); his one homer came off Drysdale during a Game Four losing effort in Los Angeles. Outside of the injuries that would eventually shorten his career, Oliva's uncharacteristically weak offensive performance during his only shot at a World Series ring was his biggest on-field disappointment.

So many numerous personal athletic milestones during those early big league years were also sweetened by triumph and happiness away from the diamond. Above all else the star ballplayer's storybook courtship and later marriage to South Dakota native Gordette DuBois in January 1968 indeed seemed like something scripted in Hollywood for the silver screen. In point of fact the real-life romance between the dark-skinned Cuban athlete and Caucasian Midwest teenager bore an eerie resemblance to a popular late-Sixties Hollywood film starring Spencer Tracy, Katherine Hepburn, and Sydney Poitier. *Guess Who's Coming to Dinner*—an Academy-Award-winning classic that openly tackled the subject of inter-racial marriage still so controversial at the time—would debut in American theaters less than a month before Tony's and Gordette's wedding. The couple's first meeting actually came early in his rookie season and was of the most unlikely sort. Gordette, who was only 17, crossed paths with the shy Spanish-speaking ballplayer while on a senior class trip to Minneapolis. She and two dozen companions were staying in the very hotel where Oliva was living during his first month as a big leaguer. An autograph request led to postal correspondence, frequent telephone conversations, and eventual dating once Gordette moved to the big city in mid-summer to begin her first semester of business school classes.

Tony and Gordette's first date came when the shy ballplayer escorted her and her parents (who had driven their daughter down to Minneapolis to begin her planned classes) out on the town for a formal get-acquainted dinner. (The event anticipated by several years the later eerily parallel Tracy-Hepburn film.) The couple's match was improbable not only because of their differing racial and cultural backgrounds but also because neither spoke more than a few words of the other's language. Gordette's decision to carry a Spanish dictionary on their outings and also frequent dates with couples (like teammate Sandy Valdespino and his wife) who spoke both Spanish and English helped warm an early friendship which soon blossomed as a full-fledged fairytale romance.

Season number three was yet another brilliant one even if Oliva's string of batting titles would finally run out (he was runner-up to Triple Crown winner and American League MVP Frank Robinson of Baltimore). The failure to overtake Robinson down the stretch prevented the Minnesota star from becoming the first junior circuit batter to capture three straight batting crowns since the immortal Ty Cobb did it in 1917-1919. The Twins also finished in the runner-up slot, trailing the Orioles by nine full lengths. Tony again led the club in most offensive categories (BA, hits, runs, doubles, and triples) and was again selected to the AL squad for the mid-summer All-Star Game. An odd entry in the record books came on June 9 when Tony was part of a single-inning five-homer outburst by the Twins against Kansas City—the first such explosion in league history. There were additional personal batting milestones including a third straight season registering the top American League hits total. Most significant perhaps was a Gold Glove at season's end. The latter honor showed just how far Tony had progressed toward becoming a complete ballplayer by drastically improving the once weak defensive side of his game.

One of the most poetic descriptions of Oliva's offensive brilliance came from the pen of *Christian Science Monitor* columnist Phil Elderkin in a freelance piece written for the pages of *Baseball Digest*. Elderkin opened his hyperbolic 1974 essay devoted to Oliva's late-career resurrection as a pioneering designated hitter with the clever trope that "Watching Tony Oliva hit a baseball is like hearing Caruso sing, Paderewski play the piano, or Heifetz draw a string across a bow."[14] According to Elderkin (extending the clever musical metaphor) "That Old Bat Magic comes through as loud and clear as if Oliva's swing had been orchestrated." It is admittedly a rather strained piece of hyperbolic sports writing but also probably not a bad characterization of the lefty-swinger's artistry with a bat.

But if he possessed a near-perfect and aesthetically pleasing swing, Oliva was made all the more dangerous (and thus all the more feared by junior circuit hurlers) by his reputation as a notorious "bad ball" hitter. In this regard he mirrored his fellow Latino and National League counterpart Roberto Clemente. In his 1974 article Elderkin quoted Oliva's observations on an unbreakable habit of hacking away at pitches outside the strike zone. "There is no such theeng as a bad peetch. If you like the peetch, you swing. Batting a lot of luck anyway. You no locky you no get base heets. I no look at strike zone much, because even if peetch is six inches inside or outside I can still heet it."[15] Despite a politically incorrect rendering of Oliva's words that was so fashionable for the times, the general message here is clear. Oliva was confident in his abilities to make contact at the plate, and his aggressiveness in the batter's box always paid large dividends,

Gordette and Tony were finally married in her childhood hometown of Hitchcock, South Dakota, on January 6, 1968, and the union would produce a first daughter Anita a year later and then a son (Pedro Jr.) in January 1970. After more than four decades the couple remains together in the Minneapolis suburb of Bloomington. All three Oliva children (there was a later son Ricardo and now also four grandchildren) today reside within a dozen miles of the Oliva home base in Bloomington. On the occasion of the recent dedication of a life-sized Target Field Tony Oliva statute, Gordette granted a rare interview to the *Minneapolis Star-Tribune* in which she revealed numerous details about the family's post-baseball life and their annual pilgrimages back to Havana to visit Tony's remaining family still residing in their native communist-ruled Cuba.

In the late Sixties there were several short stints of winter ball play, first with the Dominican Republic's Aguilas (Eagles) Cibaeñas club in 1968-69, and then with the Mexican Pacific League Los Mochis team the following two winters. The original motivation for playing in Mexico had quite a bit to do with Tony's growing feelings of isolation from his parents and siblings back in Cuba. When Twins teammate Sandy Valdespino had first suggested joining Los Mochis (where Valdespino also played in the off-season) Tony's first inquiry was about the possibilities of the Mexican club obtaining visas that might permit a long overdue reunion with his estranged Cuban family. While the first effort at obtaining those visas failed during Oliva's first month-long stint with the Mexican club in December 1969, a second effort yielded more happy results in the winter of 1970-71.[16] Tony's mother and youngest sister Felicia visited for more than a month in Los Mochis, and the joyous reunion provided a first opportunity for his aging mother to meet her two grandchildren—Anita and Pedro—and also her newly acquired American daughter-in-law Gordette.

Oliva continued his remarkable hitting barrage for a half-dozen campaigns after his sensational debut summer. He averaged 20 dingers a year and only dipped below .300 twice during that early career stretch (hitting at a .289 clip in both 1967 and 1968). He paced the American League in base hits four more times after his rookie campaign and also led the circuit in doubles on three additional occasions. But his career was clearly a ticking time bomb sabotaged by an inherited physical deformity in his knees. Oliva would eventually endure seven painful surgeries in the same number of seasons and undergo an arduous physical rehabilitation regimen on a half-dozen separate occasions. The ballplayer's single serious and debilitating flaw was something the Twins training staff had noticed early-on. Minnesota Twins trainer George "Doc" Lentz was quoted in Oliva's 1973 biography as having already assessed Tony's questionable future during an initial late-season September 1962 "cup of coffee" with the parent big-league club.[17]

It was in the early 1970s that that Twins star suffered his first truly debilitating setback. There had already been two surgeries in 1966 and 1967 for torn ligaments, and during the winter following the Twins' World Series appearance surgeons removed bothersome bone chips from Tony's right knee. But on June 29, 1971 a major career turn came when he dove for a ball off the bat of Oakland's Joe Rudi. Trailing the A's by 14 games and desperate to get back in the pennant race, Minnesota was facing a must-win situation during a mid-season road trip clash with the division leaders. With a 5-2 Twins lead in the home ninth Oliva went all-out to haul in the smash by Rudi into the right field corner. The result was significant damage to the already fragile right knee. That injury kept Tony out of nearly 30 mid- and late-season games and forced eventual September surgery to remove the torn knee cartilage; it also forced him to remain on the sidelines for the Mid-Summer Classic after his eighth-straight (and final) selection to the American League All-Star squad. But it was not enough to slow a charge to a third league batting crown that made Oliva only the 14th big leaguer and sixth American Leaguer to claim three league hitting titles. His .337 average was at the time the best in Minnesota club history. To put the icing on a mixed-blessings season Tony also led the league in slugging percentage and was tabbed American League Player of the Year by *The Sporting News*.

It was on the heels of his third batting crown and that career-threatening injury that Tony Oliva finally took the major step of becoming an official United States citizen. His wife and children were of course natural American citizens by birth, and Tony himself had now been residing in North America for eleven years since he departed his homeland to seek his fortune as a 22-year-old baseball hopeful. Two years after the citizenship ceremonies he would speak of the event with pride but also with a dose of practicality. Traveling to Mexico was decidedly easier with an American passport and citizenship papers, and another family reunion in Los Mochis was now in the works for January 1972. If Oliva was now proud to be a naturalized American, he also strongly emphasized his unshakeable Cuban identity.[18]

The pride in newly achieved citizenship was soon overshadowed by the joy of a long awaited reunion between the junior and senior Pedro Olivas. Tony flew to Mexico City in early January 1972 to greet his father and sister Felicia, who were arriving for an extended stay. Oliva's father would eventually come north for several months after the winter league season ended in Los Mochis; Pedro Sr. would experience a snowy winter in Minneapolis with Tony's clan, and also make a lengthy automobile road trip with his son to Orlando for spring training. It was indeed one of the happiest times of the young ballplayer's life, and Tony's autobiography highlights those brief visits with his long-separated father. A truly special moment came for Tony when he cracked a homer in front of his father during a spring training contest, although as later related the event did not have quite the expected outcome the proud son had hoped for. Slowed by his knee surgery of the previous fall, Tony made few exhibition game appearances that spring. But he was able to take advantage of one rare opportunity and blast a fifth-inning homer against Chicago. The elated son was nevertheless dismayed when he rounded third base, glanced into the stands, and saw his father sitting placidly amidst other cheering fans. When Harmon Killebrew smashed another homer a few pitches later, the elder Oliva rose to his feet with loud applause. When a puzzled Tony asked his father about cheering more for Killebrew than for his own son, the baseball-wise elder merely responded that Killebrew's homer was far more important because it came with a runner aboard and not with the bases empty like Tony's.

The 1972 season would turn out to be a complete loss due to the previous summer's injury. The defending batting champion was hobbled during spring training by pain and severe swelling in the recently repaired knee that simply didn't seem to be heeling properly. An April players' strike delayed the season briefly and allowed a couple extra weeks of fruitless rehab at the Twins minor league camp in Melbourne. When Tony eventually rejoined the parent club he remained on the disabled list until mid-June. When he finally cracked the starting lineup for the first time in Cleveland, he found himself in a strange environment — left field, a position he had almost never played before. Manager Bill Rigney wanted Oliva's bat back in lineup and opted for the new outfield slot since he thought it would demand less running from his crippled slugger. But the experiment proved fruitless, and after ten games (and despite a .321 batting mark in his mere 30 plate appearances) Oliva was back on the DL and scheduled for still another mid-season surgery. During a second major operation on July 5th, doctors removed 100 cartilaginous fragments from the knee in an effort to save Oliva's now severely threatened career.

On the heels of his frustrating lost campaign Tony journeyed to Caracas, Venezuela, to watch his younger brother Juan Carlos star for the Cuban national team during a September international junior-level baseball tournament. Juan Carlos had been only six at the time of his older brother's departure for the United States a decade earlier and now was a top 17-year-old right-handed pitching prospect who would eventually log 11 stellar Cuban League seasons. Tony reports in the final pages of his autobiography that his brother had pitched his league team to the Cuban amateur league championship in 1971 and was now pitching on a Cuban national team that would win the 1972 Pan American Games tournament with a perfect 12-0 mark. None of these claims are entirely accurate since the Pan American Games (played in odd-numbered years) had been held in Cali, Colombia, during July of 1971 (where Cuba did win with an 8-0 record), and Juan Carlos would not make his rookie debut in the top Cuban League until the 1972-73 winter season (and then with a Pinar del Río team that was a basement-dwelling club during that era).[19]

Oliva's own late career was partially saved—at least temporarily—when the American League introduced its controversial Designated Hitter rule for the 1973 campaign. Few players ever benefited more substantially or more immediately from a rule change. In the new role Oliva quickly earned a rare spot in the annals of baseball trivia by stroking the first-ever homer by a DH; the historic smash came off Oakland's Catfish Hunter in the first inning of the April 7th season opener. Earlier the same afternoon New York's Ron Blomberg had entered the record books as the actual first-ever DH to step into an American League batter's box. The Opening Day smash was Oliva's first since late in the 1971 campaign and the first of 16 he would slug that summer in his newly assigned role. On July 3rd in Kansas City Tony would also tie a club record by smacking a career-high three round trippers and matching another career best with 12 total bases. By season's end he also paced the Twins with 92 RBIs for what was by any measure a remarkable (if rule aided) comeback season.

Oliva hung on for three more campaigns before his bad knees finally forced him to retire during the mid-Seventies. In 1974 he logged 127 game appearances, enjoyed four 4-hit games, earned American League Player of the Week honors in early July, and managed to lead the majors in pinch-hitting (7 for 13 for a .538 average). When he smacked career home run number 200 off Stan Bahnsen in Chicago's Comiskey Park on June 27, he became only the 89th big leaguer to reach that milestone. A year later he tied Don Baylor for the major league lead in the hit-by-pitch category (13) and upped his career pinch-hitting mark above .400. A final highlight of that penultimate 1975 season was his 27th career 4-hit-plus game on July 10 in New York. But season's end also brought with it two additional October knee surgeries (his sixth and seventh) for the removal of painful bone spurs.

Tony's swan song campaign in 1976 included a dual role as player-coach and was limited to a mere 67 games of mostly late-inning pinch-hitting duty. There was one final four-hit outing in late July against Detroit and a final homer to nudge his career total to 220. The winter months included a stint managing the Los Mochis "Cañeros" ball club to a second-place finish in the Mexican Pacific League (his club finished the regular campaign in third place with 35-31 ledger but reached the postseason finals before dropping four of the five title games to Mazatlan).

After his playing days ended, Oliva extended his lengthy and loyal service to a Minnesota franchise that had provided his only big league home; there were various and repeated stints as a first base coach (1977-1978 and 1985), big league hitting coach (1977-1978 and again in 1986-1991), and roving minor league hitting instructor (1979-1984). It was while serving a second term in the role of batting instructor with the big league club that Tony played a major role in the development of his protégé and future Hall of Fame outfielder Kirby Puckett. The latter duty may in some respects have been something of a bittersweet triumph for the Cuban slugger who still remains outside the doors of baseball's Valhalla. One can certainly argue that Chicago-born Puckett's Cooperstown credentials (12 seasons, 207 homers, 1085 RBIs, .318 BA) are essentially equal to those of his never-enshrined mentor.[20]

If Cooperstown has yet to come knocking, there have been a couple of rarely paralleled post-career honors for one of Minnesota's most cherished big league stars. The franchise officially retired Tony's uniform number 6 on July 14, 1991, almost exactly thirty years after his first appearance as an unpromising Appalachian League rookie refugee from revolution-torn Cuba. He was only the third such honoree in club history (after Harmon Killebrew and Rod Carew) and has since been joined by four others (Kent Hrbek, Kirby Puckett, Bert Blyleven, and Tom Kelly). A prouder moment, perhaps, transpired for the 73-year-old Oliva in April 2011 when the Minnesota Twins unveiled an impressive larger-than-life-size bronze statue of their franchise great at the entrance to newly opened Target Field, the ballclub's state-of-the-art twenty-first-century stadium.

Over the past two decades Tony Oliva has made numerous unpublicized sojourns back to the nation of his birth to visit with still-living family members in Pinar del Río Province. He has also held forth with crowds at Havana's renowned Central Park *esquina caliente* ("hot corner") on several occasions and delighted small clusters of island fans with colorful tales of his storied years in the big leagues. Oliva remains a larger-than-life hero on his home island even though he has been repeatedly overlooked for several decades now by a generation of Cooperstown voters.

SOURCES

Bjarkman, Peter C. *A History of Cuban Baseball, 1864-2006* (Jefferson, North Carolina: McFarland & Company Publishers, 2007), Chapter 3.

Bjarkman, Peter C. *Diamonds around the Globe: The Encyclopedia of International Baseball* (Westport, Connecticut: Greenwood Press, 2005), 76-77.

Bjarkman, Peter C. *Baseball with a Latin Beat: A History of the Latin American Game* (Jefferson, North Carolina: McFarland & Company Publishers, 1994).

Elderkin, Phil, "The DH Rule Saved Tony Oliva from Oblivion," *Baseball Digest*, Volume 33, No. 9, September 1974.

Oliva, Tony (with Bob Fowler), *Tony O! The Trials and Triumphs of Tony Oliva* (New York: Hawthorn Books, 1973).

Pietrusza, David et. al. *Baseball: The Biographical Encyclopedia* (Kingston, New York: Total Sports Illustrated, 2000), 846-847.

Reusse, Patrick, "Oliva a legend rooted in Minnesota," *Minneapolis Star Tribune*, April 8, 2011 (http://www.startribune.com/sports/twins/119448294.html)

Simons, Herb, "Scouting Reports of 345 Major League Rookies," *Baseball Digest*, Volume 23, No. 2, March 1964.

The Official Tony Oliva Web Site at http://www.tonyoliva.com/

Thielman, Jim, *Cool of the Evening: The 1965 Minnesota Twins* (Minneapolis: Kirk House Publishers, 2005).

NOTES

1. In his Biography Project essays on Felipe and Matty Alou, Mark Armour has pointed out that both have been long misnamed: the brothers shared the surnames Rojas Alou, the first being the father's surname and the second the mother's family name. Following Latin American custom Felipe, Mateo (deceased) and Jesús were all known in their native Dominican Republic as the brothers Rojas. American sportswriters and baseball officials improperly used the mother's name because it came last in the sequence (family names are last and not penultimate in English). Armour also correctly points out that the name ALOU in Spanish rhymes with LOW and not (as incorrectly pronounced in English) with LOU. Tany Pérez would be refashioned as Tony Perez in the USA (with his first name "Americanized" and his last name improperly stressed on the final syllable). It is an often repeated story of how Saturnino Orestes Armas Arrieta (Miñoso) was falsely assigned the last name belonging to two stepbrothers who were also ballplayers, and also how he earned the somewhat condescending (and feminizing) moniker of "Minnie" (see Bjarkman, A History of Cuban Baseball, 1864-2006, Chapter 3 for details). And Vic Power (nee Victor Pellot Pove) also became "Power" through a complex set of linguistic errors during his minor league playing days in Drummondville, Canada (for details see Bjarkman, Diamonds around the Globe, p. 76-77).

2. Miñoso's overall career was negatively impacted by a series of publicity stunts mostly orchestrated by Chicago White Sox ownership and especially Bill Veeck. He was inked to sham contracts which allowed him to make token appearances with Veeck's Chicago club at ages 53 and 55 and thus join Nick Altrock as baseball's only five-decade player. Then in 1993 and 2003 he made further "staged" and circus-like one-at-bat appearances with the minor league St. Paul Saints (owned by Veeck's son Mike) to establish a claim as baseball's only six- and then seven-decade player. Such distasteful stunts have only diminished what had originally been a near Hall-of-Fame status career and done Miñoso more harm than good with some Cooperstown old-

timers committee voters. And racial prejudice may also have hurt Miñoso in subtle ways long after his playing days had ended. For years popular Go-Go Chisox second baseman Nellie Fox benefitted from a grass roots induction lobbying campaign that somehow never attached itself to such popular Latino stars as Miñoso (or Tony Oliva and Luis Tiant).

3   This account is related in Oliva and Fowler, p. 187

4   "I owe much to my father because he helped me with baseball as soon as I started playing the game. It wasn't that he pitched to me or hit a lot of grounders and fly balls. He did those things sometimes, but not often. Mostly he would talk to me and give me advice about playing the game and especially hitting." (Oliva and Fowler, p. 4)

5   There are inconsistencies surrounding the date of Oliva's signing, just as there are mysteries involving his true birthdate. The official Minnesota Twins website (the page on Oliva in the section devoted to retired numbers) provides a July 24, 1961, signing date, also crediting the signing to Joe Cambria and the original birddogging to Roberto Fernández. But since Oliva reported to spring camp with the Twins in March 1961 — already supposedly inked by Cambria in Havana — the July date cannot be correct. The only explanation here is that the July date refers to a re-signing after Oliva was initially released in spring camp and then hooked on with the short-season Appalachian League club in Wytheville.

6   Oliva and Fowler, p. 6.

7   Most standard encyclopedias, including Total Baseball (Sixth Edition) and Baseball: The Biographical Encyclopedia (Total Sports Illustrated) both opt for July 20, 1940. That year is also found in Jim Thielman's volume on the 1965 champion Twins. The 1938 date is not only used by Baseball-Reference.com and Oliva's Wikipedia entry, but also by the Official Tony Oliva website. The latter site is not maintained by the ballplayer himself but approved by Oliva who is therefore most likely aware of its contents. Oliva's 1973 autobiography is not the only source of the July 20, 1941, date; it also appears on the official Minnesota Twins website in the section dedicated to ball club retired numbers (http:/Minnesota.twns.mlb.com/min/history/oliva.jsp).

8   Oliva and Fowler, p. 7.

9   Oliva is not the only renowned Cuban ballplayer to provide false testimony regarding his date of birth. Take the case of Connie Marrero. Despite a number of competing and inaccurate birthdates in various encyclopedias and on the back sides of his several Topps ball cards, the date now agreed on for centenarian Conrado Marrero is April 25, 1911 (see the discussion in my own Biography Project essay on Marrero). This is the date on the ballplayer's Cuban passport and the one that is honored each year in Havana with official government-sponsored celebrations. But during my recent visit to Havana in January 2012 the 100-year-old Marrero repeated the tale that he uttered to this author on several earlier occasions — that he was actually born in August 1911 but that an error in family record keeping caused the April date. Outside of Marrero's own now-questionable memory, there is no firm documentation for an August birthdate.

10 "Because I didn't know English, I was afraid to take a chance and point at something on the menu. Once I saw a nice chocolate candy bar in a drug store, and I pointed at it and bought it. I took it back to my room to eat that night before I went to bed. Later I unwrapped it and took a bite — and gagged. It was a hunk of chewing tobacco." Oliva and Fowler, p. 17.

11 Tony's early desire to pattern himself after Al Kaline of course ignored the fact that they batted from different sides of the plate. Oliva remembers that it was fellow Cuban teammate Camilo Pascual that first suggested he pay attention to Kaline if he was looking for models to demonstrate the proper way to play right field. Clearly it was the defensive side of Kaline's smooth game that first caught the raw rookie's attention. (Oliva and Fowler, p. 37)

12 If the Twins organization may have been slow initially to warm up to Oliva's potential, some outside the organization seemed to be even less impressed with his rookie prospects. The March 1964 issue of Baseball Digest carried the following capsule evaluation of Oliva (penned by Herb Simons) as part of their popular annual rookie forecast feature: "Real good arm. Fast runner. Fair hitter. Can make somebody a real good utility outfielder." (p. 104)

13 "Shoeless" Joe Jackson owns the highest-ever rookie batting mark of .408 for Cleveland in 1911 and yet didn't win the league crown that year, thanks to Ty Cobb, who punished the ball at a .420 clip (during the first of his own two .400-plus seasons).

14 Elderkin, p. 49. The same poetic description is also quoted in Pietrusza et. al., p. 846.

15 This is the same kind of unfortunate and clearly condescending interpretation of Latino ballplayer speech that was almost always attached to the utterances of Conrado Marrero and Orestes Miñoso in the 1950s, and Roberto Clemente, Felipe Alou, and Orlando Cepeda among other Hispanic stars throughout the 1960s. Elderkin's article vividly demonstrates that the practice was still very much with us in the popular sports writing of the seventies.

16 Tony reports in his autobiography (p.145) that the initial abortive effort was first delayed due to a late start with the complex visa paper work. It was then further complicated when he was duped by a dishonest local Los Mochis resident who promised to arrange the final details but in the end absconded with the $400 the overly trusting ballplayer had given him as a good-faith initial payment.

17 "Doc" Lentz was quoted by Oliva and co-author Fowler (pp. 25-26) as follows: "I had been associated with athletic teams since 1930 and I had never seen an athlete with a body like his. From the hips up, he had a build as good as anyone, although he was skinny. From the hips down, well, his legs looked like those of a newborn colt. He had a deformity in his right leg; his leg from the knee down was bent at a forty-five degree angle. He was knock-kneed, but especially in that right knee. I remember

18 In his own words (as shaped by co-author Bob Fowler) Oliva assessed his new-found dual identity: "I'm proud to be an American citizen, but I believe I'm a Cuban-American. You can't be a citizen of two countries, but you can't take an oath and give up what you are inside either, and inside I'm Cuban." It is a rare Cuban-born big leaguer (including especially a majority of Cuban League "defectors" of the past two decades) who has not stressed his deep dedication to his native identity in almost identical phrasing.

19 Juan Carlos Oliva pitched for Pinar del Río in the Cuban League for 11 seasons between 1973 and 1983 and compiled an impressive career mark of 101-57 with a 2.46 career ERA. He would indeed make one appearance with the Cuban national team in the Pan American Games, but that was in 1979 in Puerto Rico where he would win his only decision. He would also pitch on the gold medal Cuban team in the Central American Games in Medellín (Colombia) in 1978 where his 3-0 mark left him undefeated in international games. Tony's brother Reynaldo (three years old than Juan Carlos) also logged four Cuban League seasons as a sparsely used Pinar del Río outfielder (he had an anemic .175 career batting mark with no home runs). The squad Juan Carlos played for in Caracas in 1971 was a national junior team and why Tony would have billed the event as the Pan American Games in his 1973 autobiography is not at all obvious. But as has already been pointed out, there are a number of even more glaring biographical inconsistencies in the volume coauthored with Bob Fowler.

20 Cooperstown enshrinement of Puckett and the ignoring of Oliva might well be taken as one of the best arguments for a popular notion that Latin American ballplayers still suffer from undervaluation and often blatant prejudice. Oliva and Puckett boast very similar career numbers and if Puckett's stats are marginally higher they also came in an era of greater overall offensive production league wide. Both might have had more substantial Cooperstown credentials had Tony Oliva's career not but cut short by bum knees and Puckett's interrupted by the sudden appearance of glaucoma. Oliva was always viewed by press and fans as a model citizen off the field while Puckett's revered early career positive image was unfortunately heavily blemished by several post-career scandals and an eventual court trial involving sexual harassment charges.

Camilo Pascual

BY PETER C. BJARKMAN

"FIRST IN WAR, FIRST IN PEACE, AND last in the American League"[1]—Charles Dryden's memorable line was certainly one of the most fitting epigrams ever penned to capture just about any inept big-league baseball team from just about any epoch. Authors Brendan C. Boyd and Fred C. Harris went one hilarious step further when they chose to describe rail-thin Washington infielder Wayne Terwilliger as "the perfect utility man … he played with some of the worst Washington Senator teams of the early fifties, teams consisting of entire rosters of utility men."[2] Of course the Boyd and Harris portrait (like the famed "first in peace" aphorism) was a shade over the top, a bit unfair, and chock full of delicious hyperbole. Yet the Washington Senators outfit of the post-World War II era was indeed one of the most lamentable also-ran ballclubs in the sport's long history. The midcentury lackluster "Nats" of penurious owner Clark Griffith indeed perfectly fit the bill of loveable losers and altogether forgettable tail-enders from baseball's reputed "Golden Era."

The team Griffith assembled on a self-imposed shoestring budget during the decade immediately following the war was one that lent itself to such limiting stereotypes, never climbing out of the junior circuit second division between 1947 and 1960, peaking with four fifth-place finishes over that stretch, losing more than 90 games on nine occasions, and only once (1952) finishing fewer than 20 games off the winning pace. The '50s-era Washington club seemingly drew attention for only a single day each year with its traditional role of hosting the American League season opener complete with the presidential first-ball tossing.

And no stereotype belittling the franchise was more exact and defining than the one involving the lengthy roster of Cuban recruits compiled through the scouting efforts of Papa Joe Cambria.[3] Most were merely cup-of-coffee fill-ins who didn't hang around very long; Oliverio Ortiz, Moín García, Angel Fleitas, and Armando Roche are four examples from the late 1940s who all lasted but part of a single season and none of whom appeared in more than 15 games. A few were curiosities like ancient rookie hurler Conrad Marrero (39 when he broke in in 1950) who was talented enough to make the 1951 American League All-Star squad and twice won in double figures. And a few more were destined to eventually blossom as league mainstays if not league stars once they shed their Washington uniforms and found more supportive surroundings. The latter group featured Camilo Pascual and Pedro Ramos, a pair of ill-starred hurlers who were among

A durable, overlooked workhorse in the late 1950s and 1960s, Pascual led the AL in complete games, shutouts, and strikeouts three times, and won 20-games twice. Plagued by arm problems in 1965, Pascual went 9-3 in 27 starts for the Twins. He won 174 games and logged 2,930 2/3 innings in his 18-year career (1954-1971). (Photo courtesy of Minnesota Twins Baseball Club).

the best ever produced by their baseball-crazed homeland and yet were destined to ring up records for futility throughout their early American League years under Griffith's club ownership.

The Washington ball club of the '50s wasn't exactly a true train wreck despite its string of basement finishes and overload of colorless diamond personalities. At least by decade's end Griffith had assembled a handful of solid, capable big-leaguers. Outfielders Jim Lemon (who twice topped 30 homers, in 1959 and 1960, and led the league in triples in 1956) and Bob Allison (30 home runs and a league-best nine three-baggers in 1959) made some noise in the slugging department, even if they didn't contribute much to pennant races.

And two players in particular stood among the most coveted by other owners around both leagues. It was widely reported in December 1959 that Cincinnati GM Gabe Paul had offered Griffith the then-startling sum of $1 million in cash ($500,000 each) for promising slugger Harmon Killebrew (league home-run pacesetter in his just-completed official rookie campaign) and crafty right-hander Camilo Pascual (fresh off his first season of double figures in the victory column). According to one source, Paul unequivocally stated that he viewed Pascual as the best pitcher in the majors, even if the then 25-year-old had posted but one winning mark in his half-dozen big-league campaigns.[4] But Griffith apparently wasn't cash-conscious enough to risk gutting his slowly improving franchise (whose brightening prospects would be confirmed by a jump in the standings from eighth to fifth the following summer) by accepting such a major financial windfall.

By the end of a barren 1950s decade that had produced only two non-losing seasons, Pascual was the best of the crew still residing in Griffith's camp, although that fact didn't become clear exactly overnight. From his rookie season of 1954 onward, Pascual was recognized around the junior circuit as a considerable natural talent who possessed one of the most devastating curveballs ever seen on the professional diamond. By only his third season (as a 22-year-old) he had worked his way into the starting rotation alongside Chuck Stobbs (15-15), Dean Stone (5-7 and Bob Wiesler (3-12). But the understaffed Senators (losers of 99 games) offered little support and Pascual, the team's only right-handed starter, had little to show for his efforts beyond a league second-worst total of 18 losses.

Early on (before 1959), fellow Cuban Pedro Ramos seemed to have the upper hand and offer the greatest promise, winning in double figures on four occasions and outstripping Pascual in the victory column by a wide margin (between 1955 and 1958 Ramos went 43-55, Pascual 24-59). But the long haul would favor Pascual with his tricky curves, more than Ramos with his blazing heater. Ramos would enjoy a short dance with glory a decade later when he donned a Yankees jersey. But it was Pascual who would eventually blossom in new surroundings away from the nation's capital into one of the most dominant hurlers in the junior circuit.

Resituated in Minneapolis in 1961 as one of the biggest beneficiaries of big-league baseball's first major flirtation with coast-to-coast expansion, Camilo Pascual would miraculously transition from one of the league's biggest losers to one of its proudest and most proficient winners. Of course, this all had very much to do with the slowly developing talent on Griffith's roster and not merely with the change in venue from the East Coast to America's northern frontier. But once in Minnesota and surrounded by an upgraded supporting cast—including not only rapidly improving sluggers Killebrew and Allison but also a pair of additional talented Cuban imports named Tony Oliva and Zoilo Versalles—Pascual would enjoy an all-too-brief but not unsubstantial career peak that, had it only started a bit earlier, might have landed him at the doors of Cooperstown.

Pascual's six years on the hill in Minnesota would elevate his victory total substantially, as he won 88 games over that stretch (measured against the seven initial Washington campaigns (where he claimed 57 victories but lost 84). He twice led the league in complete games and twice in shutouts (compared with once each in the nation's capital). He posted a winning record every year he labored for the transplanted Twins with the single exception of his first summer (when he fell a game shy at 15-16), and he twice reached the coveted 20-win mark (1962, 1963). And for four years running he also topped the milepost plateau of 200 strikeouts, reigning for the first three summers as the league leader in that category.

It all makes a casual observer puzzle over what might have transpired if Camilo Pascual hadn't been forced to labor with such lamentable also-ran ball clubs during his first half-dozen major-league campaigns. The Cuban curveball specialist doesn't stand alone in that department, of course. One also ponders what his contemporary Ned Garver might have accomplished in a Yankees jersey during the century's middle decade; stuck for almost five seasons in St. Louis with the faltering Browns, Garver accomplished the miraculous feat of posting 20 wins on a 1951 team that itself won only 52. Or what accolades might have attached to Virgil "Fire" Trucks had he labored in Cleveland or Chicago at career's height instead of in Detroit, where in 1952 (with a 50-game-winning basement dweller) he won but five and yet tossed two no-hit gems. But Pascual—even with company in this department—can easily stand as the number one poster boy for the archetype of the ill-starred ace saddled with nearly worthless supporting casts.

Yet to measure Pascual's schizophrenic career by only those years in Washington across the latter half of the 1950s and Minneapolis in the first segment of the 1960s is also to miss the full arc of a lengthy and much-accomplished baseball life. After the handful of highlight years falling between 1962 and 1966 there would unfold five more less notable campaigns as a slow-fading journeyman who collected an American League pennant ring for his efforts, made a nostalgic return trip to an expansion club back in Washington where his career had started, enjoyed two short layovers in the National League (where he never collected a single victory), and finally culminated with a final "tip of the cap" in Cleveland. More significant still was the lengthy winter-league career back on his home island of Cuba that stretched out for nearly a full decade. And once he hung up his spikes as an active player, Pascual would hang on to the game that was his very lifeblood for another half-century, serving as pitching coach under Gene Mauch for a few years back in Minnesota before laboring as a highly successful international scout almost until he turned 80.

The future ace big-league pitcher was born in the city of Havana on January 20, 1934, the middle of three children (including an older brother and younger sister) of Camilo Pascual Lopez and Maria Lus. As with several other past and future Cuban-born big leaguers (from Marsans at one end of the twentieth century to Palmeiro at the other), his family name would reveal a Spanish Galician heritage. Baseball was a central passion for the senior Camilo, who regularly took his two sons to La Tropical Stadium to watch games of his favorite Almendares Alacranes and also encouraged their early sandlot play in the capital city's San Miguel del Padrón neighborhood where they were raised. Both youngsters displayed considerable talent when it came to tossing a baseball and the older brother, Carlos, would also eventually make it to the big leagues for a short cup of coffee with the Senators.[5]

One curiosity early attached to the ballplaying siblings was the odd nicknames they carried along with them to North America and their early professional baseball days in Washington. Numerous standard baseball references would for years refer to them as "Potato" and "Little Potato" and the online source Baseball-Reference.com still repeats this error. The colorful labels (originating from a slang Cuban term loosely equivalent to "Shorty") in fact had a quite different meaning in Havana and the error is the result of a sloppy translation of the Spanish.[6]

Camilo began his destined baseball career as a teenager with the Club Ferroviario ("Railway Workers") amateur-league club playing in the Havana neighborhood of Lawton. He debuted in the professional Cuban winter league as an 18-year-old with the Marianao team during the 1952-53 winter season and impressed in limited duty, pitching 15 innings of relief in 10 games and winning his only decision. But he was promptly traded to the Cienfuegos Elephants by club owner Alfredo Pequeño at the outset of the following campaign in an exchange that would generate some interesting future press. Journalist Angel Torres would later opine that it was a "ridiculous" exchange of a promising prospect for a handful of bats, while historian Roberto González Echevarría (a youngster in Havana at the time who recalled watching hitters flail hopelessly at the rookie's biting curve) would label the deal "the biggest gaffe of the season."[7] The folly of the trade might have also been signaled by the fact that the young right-hander had already posted a solid 18-12 ledger over the previous two summers in combined duty with the Tampa Smokers and Havana Cubans of the Class B Florida International League. The bottom line, however, was that the fateful exchange altered league history throughout much of the following decade as Pascual would quickly emerge as the Cienfuegos ace and would lead the club to a trio of championships in coming winters (1956, 1960, 1961). It was on the Cienfuegos roster of the mid- and late-'50s that Camilo also teamed with Washington big-league teammate Pedro Ramos to form one of the most dominant pitching duos of the final years in professional Cuban League history.

Pascual's half-dozen full seasons with Cienfuegos led to a number of distinctions in the Cuban league record books. He eventually ranked fifth all-time in winning percentage (58-32, .644) in a circuit that lasted in various forms for more than eight decades. His best season was arguably 1956-57 (15-5, 16 complete games), although he also precisely matched that year's ledger four campaigns later (1959-60). A year preceding his initial 15-win season, he was crowned the league MVP with a 12-5 mark and twice he paced the circuit in strikeouts (1959, 1960), in victories (1957, 1960), in winning percentage (also 1957, 1960), and in complete games (the same two seasons). Only Ramos (66-45 over the same stretch and also a two-time league pacesetter in victories, winning percentage, and strikeouts) could rival Pascual when it came to being the most dominant pitching ace of the league's final dozen seasons.

Pascual and Ramos teamed to lead the Elephants to a runaway league title in 1955-56, the first for the team in a decade and only the second in club history. The latter paced the league in victories (13) but the former (with his 12 victories and minuscule 1.91 ERA) earned the MVP plaudits. Between them the two aces walked off with 25 of the club's 40 wins and combined with Sandalio Consuegra to provide manager Oscar Rodríguez with the league's only trio of native-born big-league hurlers. The uptick in the ballclub's fortunes that year had resulted largely from the return of Pascual, who had been held out of winter action a year earlier by the Senators on the heels of his rookie big-league campaign, and the sudden surge by Ramos, who was previously winless in only three league starts.[8] The following winter brought more of the same with Camilo sweeping individual pitching honors in seven major categories (including wins, won-lost percentage, strikeouts, and shutouts). But Ramos (8-6) slumped off the pace and the defending champs lost out to Marianao (fronted by its own pair of big-league aces in Cuban Mike Fornieles and American Jim Bunning) in the down-to-the-wire pennant race.

Cuba lost one of its true baseball icons between the 1956-57 and 1957-58 winter seasons with the death of legendary pitcher and manager Adolfo Luque, Cuba's most successful big-league hurler before the arrival of Pascual. It had been Luque—briefly his manager during his initial league season with Marianao—whom Camilo would years later credit for developing his marvelous curveball. Luque remained Pascual's manager for only a few months before being fired by the Marianao club in midstream 1953-54 during a dispute over an American pitcher (Red Barrett) whom the volatile skipper wished to release. But if Luque's career influence as Pascual's mentor was altogether brief it was nonetheless highly significant.[9]

The grandest "offseason" baseball stage for Camilo Pascual would turn out to be the annual Caribbean Series, launched in 1949 in Havana and traditionally matching the winners of the four wintertime Caribbean Basin circuits. It was an annual affair that Cuban League teams would initially dominate with seven victories across a dozen-year first stage brought to a close by the Castro revolutionary takeover. Camilo appeared on three occasions, twice (1956, 1960) with his own Cienfuegos club and once (1959) as a reinforcement selection with the league champion Almendares team. On all three occasions he claimed victory in both his pitching appearances, tossing five complete games and yielding only 11 earned runs over 52-plus innings. The perfect record in six outings stands to this day as a Caribbean Series record while Pascual's victory total of six has been matched only twice (by Puerto Rico's Rubén Gómez and Venezeula's José "Carracho" Bracho) in the half-century that has followed.[10]

More than a full year before Camilo made his late-autumn 1952 debut in the Cuban winter circuit, he had already pocketed experience during the summer of 1951 as a 17-year-old minor-league free agent toiling with the Class D Chickasha (Oklahoma) Chicks of the Sooner State League. He also appeared that same year with an additional pair of Class C teams in the Longhorn League and the Border League in New York State and in the process managed to capture five games (and lose four) before summer's end. It was something of a rare irony that Camilo would first pitch professionally outside his homeland before getting his initial crack at domestic league play. He had been inked that previous spring of 1951 to an initial contract by legendary Senators Havana-based bird dog Papa Joe Cambria along with a host of other raw countrymen who would make up a good portion of the 1951 Border League Geneva Robins roster.[11] Despite Pascual's moderate stats that first summer, Cambria re-signed him to an amateur free agent contract for Washington in the spring of 1952. The Senators assigned him to the Tampa Smokers and later the Havana Cubans in the Class B Florida International League. Over the course of that split-team 1952 campaign he appeared in 24 games (10 complete-game affairs), logged more than 100 innings, and claimed eight victories. A summer later (his third as a pro) at the ripe age of 20 he worked full time with the Havana Cubans, logging a team second-best 10 victories while his brother Carlos was the club's biggest loser (12).

Pascual quickly made the parent club's roster in spring 1954 and would debut as a largely untested big leaguer on April 15. The initial outing consisted of three innings of mop-up relief at Fenway Park during a 6-1 Washington loss to Boston in the season's third game.[12] Two initial American League campaigns with under-staffed second-division clubs under managers Bucky Harris and Chuck Dressen didn't involve many boasting points—6 victories, 19 losses, and an ERA over 6.00 in his 12-loss sophomore campaign. By his third season the rapidly improving Cuban was posting impressive strikeout numbers (162, the club's best by a wide margin and the second best league mark per nine innings behind Cleveland's Herb Score) and also drastically improving his walk-to-strikeout ratio which had been a rookie-year Achilles' heel. But the losses continued to mount—mostly a reflection of lack of offensive support on a league tail-ender—peaking with 18 in 1956 and then 17 a year later. The breakthrough finally came in 1959, the next to last Washington season, when a first-ever winning ledger (17-10) put him among the league's top five in victories despite still laboring for the circuit's most consistent loser. Pascual would later remark that the 1959 campaign was, in his own mind, the best he ever enjoyed in the big leagues.[13]

A peak career moment in Washington came on Opening Day (April 18) of the 1960 American League season, a 10-1 drubbing of Boston that witnessed the Cuban ace eclipse a pair of long-standing strikeout records. What was fated to be the very last Opening Day in the nation's capital for the original Washington franchise also turned out to be one of the most noteworthy as Pascual mowed down 15 Red Sox batters, surpassing both the single-game franchise mark (14 by Walter Johnson in 1910) and also the league record for an inaugural game. Only months after Griffith had turned down the $500,000 offered tendered by Cincinnati for his top hurler, Pascual validated his owner's decision with arguably the single best outing of his blossoming career. And the performance came on the heels of workmanlike efforts during the previous summer and winter league seasons which saw the Cuban log a remarkable combined 12-month workload of over 400 total innings pitched. The Opening Day record still stood more than a half-century later despite two close challenges (14 Ks twice) by Randy Johnson.

It was the final two Washington campaigns that launched Pascual's five-year peak, a stretch in which he won at a .612 (85-54) clip and laid claim to his ranking among the league's two or three best. He racked up top numbers each year in complete games (a league leader three times) and strikeouts (also a trio of league bests), plus shutouts (again a league pacesetter on three occasions). It can perhaps be argued on numbers alone that his best effort came in 1962—a 20-11 final mark and the top spot in the league in all three of the above categories. Only Ralph Terry of the world champion Yankees won more that year and Camilo shared the shutout lead (at five) with teammate Jim Kaat and Cleveland's Dick Donovan. Behind Pascual and Kaat (18-14), the transplanted Twins raced home as second-place finishers—five games off the Yankees' pennant-winning pace—the highest franchise finish in 17 years. Camilo was also named to four consecutive All-Star Game rosters over that same stretch, actually appearing in the midsummer classic twice.[14]

One of the great ironies of Pascual's career would be the overlapping joys and disappointments of the 1965 American League championship season. The previous year had been frustrating enough as the club slipped from third to sixth in the standings and a shoddy supporting cast likely cost the Twins ace a third consecutive 20-win season. Falling five wins short of the coveted 20-win circle, Camilo allowed under three earned runs on 15 different occasions, but a shoddy defense and weak offensive support meant that he would lose five of those stellar outings. But the course was radically reversed a year later as the Twins finally reached paydirt, rolled to 102 victories, and walked off with a runaway league championship. Pascual himself began the year strong enough at 8-2 (winning his first eight decisions). But then the worst dry spell of his career set in during June and July and during the nearly three-month-long winless streak the struggling Cuban had to abandon the hill early on several occasions due to shoulder tightness. He made only nine largely unsuccessful starts during the season's second half and was temporarily shut down in early August for minor surgery to correct a painful torn shoulder muscle. Miraculously, Pascual would recover in time for the stretch run and the pennant celebrations, but the bulk of the championship load had been carried by newcomer Jim "Mudcat" Grant (21-7), Jim Kaat (18-11), and Jim Perry (12-7). And to add to the disappointments spliced between the highs of a stellar team performance, Pascual lost his lone World Series appearance. Starting Game Three at Dodger Stadium, he struggled with a suddenly ineffective curveball and went down to an inglorious 4-0 defeat, allowing three tallies and departing after five innings.

A year later the arm problems continued to plague the fading star. Relegated to the number two starting role behind Grant, he again started well in 1966 with six wins in his first seven outings before the shoulder soreness and a resulting extended slump again threatened to sabotage his summer. He appeared in only 21 games and logged only 103 innings during a second straight frustrating campaign as the ballclub as a whole also slid off the previous year's torrid pace. By July 7 Camilo was back on the disabled list after developing elbow tendinitis during a June 28 outing that turned out to be his final victory of the year. Returning to the active roster before year's end he saw mostly limited bullpen duty and quietly seethed over what he perceived as manager Sam Mele's loss of faith in his abilities. It was the beginning of the end, at least in Minnesota, and in December Pascual—now a liability with only eight wins and only 103 innings of work the entire year—was traded away along with failed prospect Bernie Allen to the new version of the Washington Senators for 35-year-old relief specialist Ron Kline.

There was a brief renaissance of sorts over the next couple of campaigns as Camilo's trusty arm seemed to heal enough for the then only 33-year-old former ace to lead the new-version Senators in wins (while finishing second in strikeouts and innings pitched) each of the next two summers. Of course the numbers were much more modest on a second-division ballclub—12 wins in 1967 and 13 a year later. The clock was clearly ticking and to make matters worse, the second-edition Senators teams he labored for under managers Gil Hodges and Jim Lemon were near reprises of the mediocre Washington teams he had been saddled with a decade earlier. On April 7, 1969, Camilo made his fifth and final Opening Day start and departed early as an 8-4 loser to the Yankees. Over the season's first three months, he managed to eke out only a pair of victories and after 13 starts his ERA was only a shade below 7.00. The disastrous 1969 start brought a quick trade to Cincinnati in the Senior Circuit where the rapid slide continued with only five appearances and a single start and an ERA of 8.59 in the closing months of the campaign. Failing to make the Reds roster the following spring, he was peddled off to the Los Angeles Dodgers and fared no better there (10 relief outings without a decision). Another trial in Cleveland in 1971 proved conclusively that Pascual's career had run its course and after a meager 19 appearances that final summer, he was finally forced into retirement long before the campaign rolled to a close.

Away from the playing field the most personally satisfying moments for Camilo came more than five years apart in 1959 and in 1964. On the eve of the 1959 baseball season he married his longtime sweetheart Rachel Ferrero. The couple eventually had four children (sons Camilo III and Adalberto, and daughters Maria Isabela and Sandra), and as of 2015 the marriage had stretched well beyond 50 years. Added joy arose in August 1964 when—with the aid of Minnesota Senator Hubert Humphrey—arrangements were finally made for the exit of his parents and sister from Fidel Castro's Cuba. The trio of long-estranged family members traveled to Mexico City and then arrived in Minnesota barely in time for the birth of Camilo's fourth child, daughter Sandra. That same winter he purchased a house for his clan in Minneapolis before eventually relocating the entire entourage to Miami, where he and his wife still resided in 2015

By the time Camilo Pascual's career had finally wrapped up, his greatest legacy would remain his impressive strikeout totals rather than any numbers in the victory column. Heading into the 2015 big-league season, he still stood number 57 on the all-time list with 2,167 strikeouts—only a handful behind such Hall of Fame luminaries as Pete Alexander and Jim Palmer. At the time of his retirement he was lodged in the Top 20, and among those ahead of him only a few were not already enshrined in Cooperstown. But he also had ranked in the league's Top 10 on four separate occasions in the less laudatory categories of walks and home runs allowed, and at the end of the 2014 season he still ranked in or near the all-time Top 100 for both free passes (85th) and gopher balls 101st).

The Pascual family had been residing in the offseasons in Miami during his waning days with the original Senators in Washington, and it was to South Florida that Pascual relocated after his final release in early summer 1971 by the Cleveland Indians. But the retirement as such lasted only a half-dozen years and by 1978 he was back in uniform as the Twins pitching coach under fiery skipper Gene Mauch. It was a tenure that lasted merely three seasons as the Minnesota club struggled in the middle of the AL West Division pack. Pascual did tutor a few star pupils during the brief tenure including 20-game-winner Jerry Koosman, 30-saves closer Mike Marshall, and durable starters Dave Goltz and Geoff Zahn. After another hiatus from the game, lasting only a handful of months, Pascual signed on as an international scout, first with the Oakland Athletics and later with the Los Angeles Dodgers, where for a number of years he covered the amateur baseball scene in Venezuela. As of early 2014 Pascual was still actively working as a bird dog with the Los Angeles club although his previously extensive international travels had recently been significantly curtailed.

Pascual's scouting activities over the years (1982-1988 with Oakland and since 1989 with the Dodgers) have led to a number of noteworthy signings, the most significant being Cuban-born "bad boy" José Canseco, whom he inked in June 1982. Other noteworthy signings credited to Pascual (all with Los Angeles and all eventual big leaguers) include Puerto Rican infielder

Alex Cora (1996), Venezuelan pitcher Omar Daal (1990), Venezuelan infielder Miguel Cairo (1990), and Venezuelan outfielder Franklin Gutiérrez (2000). Brother Carlos Pascual also served briefly as a professional scout with the Yankees, Orioles, and Mets and claimed one jackpot signing (1982) in the person of celebrated Mets hurler Dwight "Doc" Gooden.[15]

In July 2013 Pascual was still beating the scouting trail for the Dodgers in Omaha, Des Moines, and Durham as he tracked the Cuban national team during its "Friendly Series" with the USA Baseball College All-Stars. The Omaha layover was occasion for a lengthy conversation between the former hurler and this writer in which Camilo asked most of the questions. He was curious about my own experiences and discoveries in Cuba, where I have been traveling and covering the island's national pastime for nearly two decades. It was obvious that his native Havana still held a strong attraction for an estranged exile who had not set foot in his native country in more than a half-century. But like so many who had fled the changing political and social environment of their island home in the early 1960s, Camilo also spoke eloquently about precisely why he had never returned and in fact never would revisit his childhood home without the disappearance of Cuba's long-standing communist government.

Long overdue enshrinement in the Cuban Hall of Fame first loomed on the horizon in 1983 when Pascual was inducted alongside 1950s-era big-league contemporary Orestes Miñoso at a gala banquet ceremony staged in Miami and not in his native Havana. But this was something of tainted honor since the original Cuban shrine had been shut down with the 1961 demise of professional baseball on the island. A replacement had been reactivated on North American shores in 1962 by a Miami exile group known formally as The Federation of Professional Cuban Ballplayers in Exile and carried with it the heavy overtones of anti-Castro Miami politics. The new group had already inducted such lesser postwar-era island stars as Sandy Amoros (1978), Willie Miranda (1979), Zoilo Versalles (1980), Pedro Ramos and Tony Taylor (1981), and Tony Oliva and Cookie Rojas (1982). It was a point of pride of sorts, but it wasn't Cooperstown or even the now moribund original institution once lodged in pre-Castro Havana, and it was a recognition that went largely unrecognized anywhere outside of Miami's "Little Havana" neighborhood.[16]

Pascual's most recent highly active decades have been spiced with a handful of other prestigious honors as well as filled with endless road trips in search of elusive future big-league stars. In 1996 he was honored more significantly as an inaugural member (alongside Dominican big leaguer Rico Carty, Mexico's Héctor Espino, and American Blackball star Willard Brown) of a newly formed Caribbean Baseball Hall of Fame. In part that latter honor was renewed recognition of his still-standing record as the winningest hurler in Caribbean Series history. When a Latino Baseball Hall of Fame was established in the Dominican Republic in May 2010, the ex-Twin and ex-Senator was again an inaugural class honoree. And two years later (July 2012) he also became only the 24th former Minnesota Twin to be inducted into that big-league club's Hall of Fame.

In the end Pascual's baseball fate would be the exact polar opposite of former teammate and Havana winter league sidekick "Pistol Pete" Ramos. Both were launched on professional careers under quite similar circumstances and both suffered similar record-sapping handicaps during early playing years with the woeful 1950s-era Washington Senators. In the earliest going Ramos seemed to hold the upper hand and enjoy the greatest initial promise. But the switch to Minneapolis which paid such lofty career dividends for Pascual never quite panned out for Ramos, who was the club's biggest loser that first year in the Midwest (dropping a career-high 20 games) and was then promptly dumped off to Cleveland. Ramos would eventually be remembered for his failures (a double-figure loser his first eight big-league seasons) and his post-career debacles (which included a series of arrests and imprisonments). Pistol Pete's MLB career was also marked not by strikeout records but by the penchant for delivering gopher balls in record numbers and of record distances. His run-ins with the law and eventual emigration to Nicaragua would leave him a largely forgotten figure.

Pascual, in stark contrast, flourished in Minnesota as a star hurler and then in later decades as a model baseball citizen. As Roberto González Echevarría emphasizes, Camilo Pascual was the last player to star in both the Cuban winter league and also in the major leagues.[17] His long scouting career kept him actively employed in the sport for four additional decades. Few half-century-tenured scouting legends also played the game quite so well in their own youth, or left quite so indelible a mark in the game's record books.

Few men have enjoyed a longer and more fruitful connection with America's national pastime than has Cuban-born Camilo Pascual. Among his island countrymen, only four (Tiant, Luque, Cuéllar, and Liván Hernández) have won more big-league games. No Cuban hurler (with the two possible exceptions of Conrad Marrero and Orlando Hernández) enjoyed a more successful domestic baseball career back on his native Caribbean island. That fact was formally recognized in November of 2014 when the 80-year-old Pascual was selected as one of 10 initial inductees into the newly resurrected Cuban Baseball Hall of Fame in Havana.[18] If Pascual had long ago chosen to turn his back on his homeland, he was nonetheless never quite forgotten nor ever unappreciated in the baseball-crazy island nation that has itself so long lived outside the realms of Major League Baseball.

SOURCES

Bealle, Morris A. *The Washington Senators: The Story of an Incurable Fandom* (Washington, D.C.: Columbia Publishing Company, 1947).

Bjarkman, Peter C. *A History of Cuban Baseball, 1864-2006* (Jefferson, North Carolina: McFarland & Company Publishers, 2007).

Bjarkman, Peter C. *Diamonds Around the Globe: The Encyclopedia of International Baseball* (Westport, Connecticut: Greenwood press, 2005).

Boyd, Brendan C., and Fred C. Harris. *The Great American Baseball Card Flipping, Trading and Bubble Gum Book* (Boston: Little, Brown and Company, 1973).

Figueredo, Jorge S. *Who's Who in Cuban Baseball, 1878-1961* (Jefferson, North Carolina: McFarland & Company Publishers, 2003).

Figueredo, Jorge S. *Cuban Baseball, A Statistical History, 1878-1961* (Jefferson, North Carolina: McFarland & Company Publishers, 2003).

Figueredo, Jorge S. *Béisbol Cubano: Un Paso de las Grandes Ligas, 1878-1961* (Jefferson, North Carolina: McFarland & Company Publishers, 2005).

González Echevarría, Roberto. *The Pride of Havana: A History of Cuban Baseball* (New York: Oxford University Press, 1999).

Hernandez, Lou. *Baseball's Great Hispanic Pitchers: Seventeen Aces from the Major, Negro and Latin American Leagues* (Jefferson, North Carolina: McFarland & Company Publishers, 2014).

Rucker, Mark, and Peter C. Bjarkman. *Smoke: The Romance and Lore of Cuban Baseball* (New York: Total Sports Illustrated, 1999).

Torres, Angel. *Tres Siglos del Béisbol Cubano, 1878-2006* (Miami: Review Printers [self-published], 1996).

Torres, Angel. *La Leyenda del Béisbol Cubano, 1878-1997* (Pico Rivera, California: Best Litho Printers [self-published], 2005).

Walters, Charley. "Shooter Now: Camilo Pascual's Road to Minnesota Twins Hall Filled With Curves," online at twinscities.com (July 10, 2012).

NOTES

1 One of the most celebrated scribes of baseball history, Charles Dryden (1860-1931) was the fourth man selected for Cooperstown by the Baseball Writers Association of America and is reputed to have originated such standard baseball terms as "pinch hit," "ball yard," and "old horsehide." He is credited by numerous sources as providing the popular labels for some of the sport's most colorful figures of the first half of the twentieth century: e.g., Charles "The Old Roman" Comiskey, Frank "the Peerless Leader" Chance, Fred "Bonehead" Merkle, and the "Hitless Wonders" 1906 Chicago White Sox. His infamous label for the Washington American League franchise was penned on the occasion of the team posting a 42-110 record (56 games off the championship pace set by Detroit) during the 1909 American League pennant chase. The disdainful sobriquet was therefore nearly a half-century old before it was widely reattached to the Washington club during its last decade of its residence in the nation's capital. Clark Griffith did not take ownership of the franchise until a decade (1920) after Dryden's playful slur.

2 Terwilliger is the very first player profiled by Boyd and Harris in their classic and delightfully humorous portrait of baseball cards and baseball culture of the mid-twentieth century decades. Players from the inept Senators of those decades were a frequent target for Boyd and Harris, to wit Cuban Carlos Paula ("Paula's ability to hit a baseball could never quite make up for his inability to catch it"), Clyde Kluttz ("there has never been, nor could there ever be, a major league ballplayer named Clyde Kluttz"), Herb Plews ("there was something almost heroic about the stupefying mediocrity of his play"), Hal Griggs ("Griggs

was to pitching what Wayne Causey was to hitting. That is to say—nothing."), Dick Brodowski (who "should never, under any circumstance, be allowed out of the house without his mother"), and Clint Courtney ("who tried to make up for his playing deficiencies with generous doses of what the hard rock disciplinarians in the athletic realm like to refer to as 'leadership qualities'").

3   Of the 56 Cubans to put on big-league uniforms between Roberto Estalella in 1935 and Ossie Alvarez in 1958, 33 of them (almost all signed by Griffith's Havana-based superscout Papa Joe Cambria) debuted with the Washington club. Writing in 1947 in advance of the arrival of more talented imports like Marrero, Pascual, Ramos and Julio Bécquer, club historian Morris Bealle (*The Washington Senators*, 162-163) compared Washington's "Latin Era" to the Brooklyn Dodgers "Daffiness Era" of the 1930s and suggested that Cambria would serve his employer much better if he only "could get over his predilection for Cubanolas."

4   Shirley Povich, "Reds' Million Offer for Pair Nixed by Nats," *The Sporting News*, December 23, 1959.

5   Older brother Carlos was born three years earlier (March 13, 1931) and debuted as a pitcher with the same Washington Senators on September 24, 1950. Also signed by Cambria, Carlos also possessed apparent talent and apparently threw harder than his younger sibling before slowed by an arm injury (this being related to Robert González Echevarría—*The Pride of Havana*, 320—by Camilo himself. But the pint-sized Carlos only enjoyed the proverbial big-league "cup of coffee" while appearing in a mere two starts (1-1) during his one-month big-league tenure. Carlos pitched seven seasons in the Cuban winter league (mostly with the Havana team), amassed a respectable career 14-5 ledger, and appeared twice in the Caribbean Series, where he won one of three decisions in 1953. He died in Miami on May 12, 2011, at the age of 80. .

6   The colloquial nickname "*patato*" (Shorty or Runt) was attached to Carlos apparently because of his diminutive stature (5-feet-6 by the time he reached the majors). Thus his more renowned brother would pick un the handle "Patato Pequeño" not so much as an indication of physical stature (he was 5-feet-11 as a big leaguer) but as indication of his junior status. As with so many such linguistics distortions involving Latino ballplayers of the era (e.g., Clemente labeled as Bob instead of Roberto) Americans misheard the name, failed to grasp its colloquial content, and began calling Carlos "Potato" and Camilo "Little Potato."

7   Torres, *La Leyenda del Béisbol Cubano*, 182; González Echevarría, *The Pride of Havana*, 320. Pascual immediately moved into the starting rotation for second-place Cienfuegos under American manager Al Campanis, winning four, losing five, hurling four complete games, and posting a club-best 1.95 ERA (second best in the league).

8   Three other Cubans were denied permission to play winter-league games by their big-league owners and the move proved highly unpopular and controversial in Havana, where attendance had recently waned for games at Gran Stadium. The others held out of play (all by the Chicago White Sox) were Orestes "Minnie" Miñoso, Miguel "Mike" Fornieles, and Sandalio "Sandy" Consuegra (who had just posted the American League's best winning percentage). The Senators also attempted to bar Pascual from winter-league action in 1957-58 (citing the need to rest a sore arm) but since the MLB regulation allowing such actions had expired, Commissioner Ford Frick ruled against Washington's effort and cleared the player for the Cienfuegos roster. But after only three games Pascual decided himself to remain on the sidelines, attributing his actions to a weakened physical condition and high blood pressure. Details are reported by Lou Hernandez in *Baseball's Great Hispanic Pitchers*, 87.

9   *The Pride of Havana*, 320, 329. A reputedly great teacher and mentor (as well as highly skilled pitcher and manager), Luque is also credited with having taught Sal "The Barber" Maglie how to "shave" hitters with his devastating knockdown pitchers during their time together in the Mexican League (where Luque managed the Puebla club in 1946 and 1947), Cuba (where Luque managed Maglie with Cienfuegos in 1945-46), and the New York Giants (where Luque was Maglie's pitching coach in 1945). In a 2012 interview with twincities.com columnist Charley Walters, Pascual would explain how Luque early on convinced him to abandon his practice of side-arm deliveries and throw "straight over the top" to get full value out of his natural curve. Camilo also admitted in that interview that he suffered control problems with the new delivery initially but eventually so thoroughly mastered the art of "a fast curve with a sharp break" that he had sufficient confidence to throw it with any ball-and-strike count (cf. "Shooter Now: Camilo Pascual's Road to Minnesota Twins Hall Filled with Curves.")

10 cf. *Diamonds Around the Globe*, Chapter 11 (for full Caribbean Series details) and pages 520-521 (for Pascual's Caribbean Series record summary).

11 Of a dozen Cubans on the 1951 Geneva roster (baseballreference.com/minors/team.cgi?id=59caa2b5) Pascual was the only one to eventually make it to the major leagues. Stressing the Geneva-Cuba pipeline connection, a Class D club in that city playing under the name of the Geneva Redlegs in the New York-Penn League and affiliated with the Cincinnati Reds would boast a lineup in 1960 featuring rookie-league prospects Pete Rose and Cuban Tony (Tany) Perez playing alongside the son (Martin Jr.) of Cuban Negro league legend and Cooperstown Hall of Famer Martin Dihigo.

12 Pascual was the 58th Cuban native to debut in the big leagues and one of only two (along with Washington's Carlos Paula) to break into the big time in 1954.

13 Personal conversation with the author at Werner Park (Omaha, Nebraska) on July 19, 2013.

14 The major leagues staged two separate All-Star Games during the four-year 1959-1962 stretch and Pascual was named to American League rosters in 1959 (second game), 1960 (both), 1961 (second), and 1962 (both). He was also tabbed again in 1964.

His first appearance came on July 31, 1961, in Fenway Park when he hurled the final three hitless innings of a 1-1 deadlock; he suffered the loss in the opening 1962 game at Washington, surrendering four hits and two runs over the middle three frames. In 1964 at Shea Stadium, he worked two additional innings without a decision. When Pascual took the All-Star Game field in 1961 at Fenway Park, he became the fifth Cuban to do so, after Miñoso (eight previous appearances), Consuegra (1954), Tony Taylor (both games in 1960), and Fornieles (1961 first game).

15 Scouting records for Camilo and Carlos Pascual were provided by Rod Nelson of the SABR Scouts Committee.

16 The exile-community Hall of Fame reached its zenith in the mid-1980s and unveiled a small but impressive museum building known as "La Casa del Béisbol Cubano" in 1985. One of the group's central activities was the annual staging throughout most of the 1990s of a Miami-based Cuban "old-timers" game featuring many of the expatriate former Cuban winter league stars. The institution began to experience dwindling financial support that same decade as the original exile community aged and Miami anti-Castro politics began to somewhat erode. As early as the mid-1980s (beginning the year following Pascual induction) the institution began mass inductions of just about every player still living in South Florida (or with surviving family in Miami) with the barely concealed (and illegitimating) purpose of selling hundreds of banquet tickets and raising desperately needed cash. The result was 13 inductees in 1984, 11 in 1985, 12 in 1986, and (after a decade of dormancy) a whopping 60 in 1997 (about half of them not ballplayers but club executives, radio announcers, sportswriters, and even team masseuses). By that time there was virtually no one left to induct and the institution suffered a quiet and barely noticed demise.

17 González Echevarría (The Pride of Havana, 358-59) makes the debatable but not indefensible claim that Pascual was actually better than Luis Tiant Jr., despite the fact that Tiant (often pitching for much better teams) won 55 more big-league games. But the claim of course covers only the pre-Castro "professional" winter league affiliated with Organized Baseball. More recently at least three pitchers were top stars in the contemporary Cuban circuit before defecting to the States and starting in the big leagues. That trio would include Orlando Hernández, Liván Hernández, and José Ariel Contreras; all three compiled significant victory totals despite their late arrivals in the majors and the Hernández half-brothers were both postseason MVP award winners.

18 After 54 years of dormancy, decades of debate over a proper location, and constant setbacks due to lack of financial resources, the Cuban Hall of Fame was formally re-established during a heavily publicized early November weekend convention of Cuban Federation baseball officials and 30-plus specially selected baseball journalists and historians (including this author as the only non-Cuban). The new institution will have a permanent museum location in Havana at the historic site of the original Vedado Tennis Club in what is now known as The Social Club José Antonia Echevarría. The special induction panel (chosen from among the colloquium participants) named 10 new inductees, five from the pre-1961 "professional" era (Estebán Bellán, Camilo Pascual, Orestes Miñoso, umpire Amado Maestri, Conrado Marrero) and five from the post-1961 "Revolutionary Baseball" era (Omar Linares, Luis Giraldo Casanova, Orestés Kindelán, Braudilio Vinent, Antonio Muñoz). This group was formally enshrined alongside the original 68 members at elaborate induction ceremonies held in conjunction with the Cuban League All-Star Game on December 28, 2014, in Granma Province.

Jim Perry

BY JOSEPH WANCHO

NEW YORK FANS HAD TO BE pleased at the scene that was unfolding before their eyes on May 12, 1959. Their Bronx heroes trailed the league-leading Indians 7-6 heading into the bottom of the eighth inning. Cleveland starter Cal McLish, who was attempting to raise his record to 5-0, was lifted by manager Joe Gordon for Jim Perry. Jim Perry? Surely Gordon could turn to a more experienced arm in the bullpen. Why go with a green rookie in such a tight game? In his previous outing, in Chicago three days earlier, Perry faced four batters in the third inning, walked three, and gave up a hit to the other; all four players scored. When told that Gordon favored Perry because he threw hard and liked Perry's guts, a New York scribe commented that perhaps "Gordon had more guts than his pitcher." Gordon Cobbledick, sports editor of the *Cleveland Plain Dealer*, was watching the game on television back home. "That Gordon is crazy!" he remarked to his wife.[1]

Young Perry was visiting Yankee Stadium for the first time. Certainly the crowd of 36,000-plus would intimidate the young hurler. Gordon had simple advice for the rookie: "Joe told me to go in there and start firing and that's just what I did," said Perry afterward.[2]

Jerry Lumpe grounded out to first base, and pinch-hitters Enos Slaughter and Andy Carey struck out. Gordon left Perry in for the ninth inning, with the meat of the Yankees' order coming to the dish. Tony Kubek led off by stroking a double down the third-base line, sending the crowd into a frenzy. But Perry bore down and got Mickey Mantle on strikes for the first out. Yogi Berra popped out to second base, and Elston Howard struck out to end the game. Four punchouts for young Perry in two innings. "We knew before that Jim was pretty good," Gordon said. "Now we know for sure he can come in and throw his blazer over the plate and past the hitters. From now on he's my No. 1 tough-spot pitcher—early, late, or any time. A game like this can make a young pitcher."[3]

When the game ended, Mrs. Cobbledick turned to her husband and asked, "Which Gordon is crazy, dear?"[4] Jim Perry made believers out of many fans that day. And for the next 17 years, he continued to prove himself.

James Evan Perry, Jr. was born on October 30, 1935, in Williamston, North Carolina. He was the oldest of three children born to James Perry, Sr. and Ruby Perry. Gaylord Perry, three years younger than Jim, went on to a Hall of Fame career. Sister Carolyn

Perry posted a stingy 2.63 ERA in 167 2/3 innings and won 12 games for the Twins in 1965. A two-time 20-game winner, he won the AL Cy Young Award in 1970 by leading the circuit with 24 victories. He compiled a 215-174 record and logged 3,285 2/3 innings in 17 big-league seasons (1959-1975). (Photo courtesy of Minnesota Twins Baseball Club).

completed the family. Jim Sr. was a sharecropper, with tobacco being his major crop.

Jim pitched on the Williamston High School baseball team, while younger brother Gaylord played third base. "We won the state championship that year," said teammate Gerald Griffin. "When one of the Perry boys pitched, the other played third, and they switched off the next game." Jim Perry recalled that he and his younger brother "had nine shutouts in a row."[5]

Jim was attending Campbell College when he was signed by Cleveland scout Jim Gruzdis. His first stop in the minor leagues landed him in North Platte of the Class D Nebraska State League in 1956. In a victory over McCook, Perry limited the Braves to three hits, struck out 16, and set down 21 batters in a row. He rose through Cleveland's minor-league chain, making stops in Fargo-Moorhead (North Dakota) of the Class C Northern League in 1957 and then Reading (Pennsylvania) of the Class A Eastern League in 1958.

In 1959 the Indians invited Perry to the big-league spring camp in Tucson based on his 16-8 record at Reading. He came to camp with a determined attitude that some took as being brash. "I'm here to make the team," Perry proclaimed as he arrived. Although he was earmarked to pitch in Double-A in 1959, Gordon stuck with Perry. "He doesn't care who he is pitching against — he can throw strikes," said Tribe pitching coach Mel Harder. "I don't think his inexperience necessarily counts against him because you cannot judge pitchers by any rule. A man who can throw a strike with confidence may make it in three years instead of seven."[6]

The starting rotation for Cleveland was pretty much set in 1959 with Cal McLish, Herb Score, Gary Bell, and Mudcat Grant. Perry began the year throwing mostly out of the pen. Score was recovering from his eye injury two years earlier, and pitched sparingly in the second half of the season. Perry posted a 12-10 record his rookie season, with six of those wins as a starter after he took Score's spot in the rotation. He posted an ERA of 2.65.

Cleveland was in the race for much of the year, but after closing the gap on first-place Chicago to one game, the Tribe dropped a four-game set to the White Sox at home in late August and never recovered. Perry went up against Dick Donovan in the second game of that series and lost a tight game, 2-0.

Perhaps the way the Indians played down the stretch prompted general manager Frank Lane to make some major trades. In December he sent McLish, who had led the team with 19 wins, to Cincinnati. Two days before the 1960 season opened, Rocky Colavito was dealt to Detroit for Harvey Kuenn. Cleveland traded the home run king (Colavito) for the batting champion (Kuenn). Lane was vilified by the fans for trading Colavito, the team's most popular player. The next day Score was sent packing to the White Sox for Barry Latman. It was not enough for Lane, as he and his counterpart in Detroit, Bill DeWitt, pulled off an unprecedented trade in August. They swapped managers, Gordon going to Detroit for Tigers skipper Jimmy Dykes.

Through all this, it appeared that Jim Perry found his stride in 1960. He tied Chuck Estrada of Baltimore for the league lead in wins with 18. He won six in a row from May 21 through June 15, lowering his ERA from 4.14 to 2.63 during the streak. Unfortunately for Perry he also led the league in giving up home runs, 35 in 261⅓ innings. He gave up a round-tripper every 7½ innings.

In the offseason, Perry married Daphne Snell of Raleigh, North Carolina. They had three children: Chris, Michelle, and Pam.

Over the next two years Perry was inconsistent. His ERA jumped to over 4.00 in each season, and he was still giving up the long ball. He served up a combined 49 home runs in 1961 and 1962. On May 10, 1962, in Minnesota, Perry surrendered a home run to the first two Twins hitters, Lenny Green and Vic Power. He was the 12th major-league pitcher to accomplish the dubious feat. The irony was not lost on many when Perry took a job between seasons selling bomb shelters.

After Dykes piloted Cleveland in 1961, Mel McGaha managed the team in 1962. Now the Indians would hear from another voice in 1963; Birdie Tebbetts was hired to manage Cleveland. Perry found himself in the bullpen at the start of the season. He was the odd man out of a starting rotation made up of Latman, Grant, Donovan, and Pedro Ramos. On May 2 Perry was dealt to the Twins for pitcher Jack Kralick. Cleveland, needing a left-handed starter for its predominantly right-handed staff, had its sights set on Kralick for some time. Minnesota manager Sam Mele seemed unexcited by the deal. "We would like to have got Bell [Indians right-hander Gary Bell], but he just wasn't available," said Mele.[7] Many years later, Cleveland pitcher Mike Paul had a different view of the deal. "Perry had more lives than a cat," said Paul. "It was hard to know he would have a career like that."[8]

Perry had plenty of hard luck in his first two starts for the Twins. In the first, against the Los Angeles Angels, he gave up just three hits, but lost 2-0. In his next start, against Kansas City, he surrendered one unearned run in a 2-1 defeat. Over 16 innings, he gave up 10 hits and 3 earned runs, but his record stood at 0-2. He quickly rebounded, winning four games in a row in June, and finishing the season with a record of 9-9 for the third-place Twins.

In 1965 former Boston Braves great Johnny Sain joined Mele's staff as pitching coach. Sain had a tremendous effect on the pitching corps. Under his tutelage, Perry learned to throw a sharp breaking curveball, and to turn over his fastball so it would break in on right-handed batters. Perry got his chance after injuries or illness sidelined Dave Boswell, Mudcat Grant, and Camilo Pascual. He became a stalwart of the rotation and helped propel the Twins to first place. "I've never seen a man work so hard on his own," said Sain. "The coaches and manager have been getting the credit for the team leading the league, but it's effort like Perry's that put us there."[9]

After picking up four wins as a reliever, Perry got his first starting assignment against Boston on July 5. He responded with a seven-hit shutout, fanning eight. He went 7-7 as a starter and posted an ERA of 2.63 for the season.

The Twins pulled ahead of Cleveland when Perry won his first start, and coasted to the pennant, finishing a comfortable seven games ahead of second-place Chicago. They met the Los Angeles Dodgers in the World Series, but lost in seven games. Jim Kaat and Grant each started three games for the Twins, and Perry went back to pitching relief. In two games he pitched four innings, giving up two earned runs.

Used primarily as a starter the next season, Perry went 11-7. His ERA was 2.54 and he struck out 122 hitters while walking 53. He w eight games after the All-Star break. "Perry has shown me too much," said Mele after the season. "He can do too many things and you need pitchers like that. He can start regularly, he can spot-start, he can relieve. When injuries start popping up, a man who can do all of those things can really help. Twice Jim started with two days of rest. And I haven't forgotten it."[10]

Mele may not have forgotten Perry's efforts, but Cal Ermer may not have been aware of them. Ermer managed Triple-A Denver and was promoted to replace Mele 50 games into the 1967 season. Another major change was Sain leaving the Twin Cities after 1966 to become Detroit's pitching coach. Under Ermer, Perry again bounced between starting and relieving. But in 1969, Billy Martin succeeded Ermer after serving as a Twins coach since 1965. Martin and Perry had been teammates at Cleveland in 1959, and Martin immediately inserted Perry into the rotation and, for the most part, let him be.

Perry made Martin seem like a genius, going 20-6 with a 2.82 ERA. Two of his wins came on the same day. On July 19 the Twins and Seattle Pilots battled to a 7-7 tie through 16 innings. The teams used 41 players in the game. After 16 innings, the game was suspended and completed the next day. Perry pitched the final two innings for the victory. He started the winning rally with a one-out double and scored the go-ahead run. In the regularly scheduled matchup, Perry started and blanked the Pilots 4-0, scattering

Jim Perry (Photo courtesy of Minnesota Twins Baseball Club).

nine hits. (Ironically, Perry could have been pitching for the other side; he had been left unprotected by the Twins in the expansion draft before the season, and Seattle could have claimed him.)

Over his first 10 years in the big leagues, Perry was considered an above-average hitter for a pitcher. His deftness with the bat was on display on June 22 in the second game of a twin bill in Oakland. With the score tied, 3-3, Tony Oliva led off the top of the 13th inning with a double and advanced to third base on a groundout by Graig Nettles. The Athletics walked Charlie Manuel in order to face Perry. But Perry laid down a suicide squeeze bunt to score Oliva with the eventual winning run. "Oliva waited for just the right moment to break for home-when the pitcher [Rollie Fingers] was at the top of his motion, and Perry did the rest," said Martin.[11]

Perry captured victory number 20 against the Pilots on September 20. His strikeout of Danny Walton in the first inning was the 1,000th of his career.

The Twins breezed through the newly formed American League West Division. They finished ahead of second-place Oakland by nine games while the rest of the division trailed the Twins by at least 26 games. Perry started Game One of the American League Championship Series in Baltimore, giving up three runs in eight innings, and received a no-decision as the Orioles won 4-3 in 12 innings. Baltimore went on to sweep Minnesota in three games in the best-of-five series. It was not enough to save Martin's job; he was fired shortly thereafter. The front office received backlash from fans who supported Martin. Although Martin later won at almost every stop in his 16 years of managing, many of his problems in the Twin Cities were self-inflicted. He refused to adhere to the club's policies, ripped the organization over the farm system, and fought with pitcher Dave Boswell. Most fans, and many players, saw wins and a division championship and opposed Martin's firing by team president Cal Griffith. "I owe Martin a lot," said Perry. "He gave me a chance to prove what I could do. I'm grateful for that. I know some players don't like the way some things were handled, but you can't satisfy 25 players."[12]

Minnesota hired Bill Rigney as its skipper for the 1970 campaign. Rigney, a former infielder for the New York Giants, had managed the Angels the previous nine seasons. In his first season guiding the Twins, Perry led the American League with 24 wins and 40 starts. Perry was without question the ace of the Twins' staff. He pitched in the All-Star Game at Riverfront Stadium in Cincinnati, giving up one run in two innings of relief. Meanwhile, his brother Gaylord tied Bob Gibson with 23 wins for most in the National League. They were the first brother combination to both win 20 games in the same season. "Jim is a hard man to keep up with," said Gaylord. "I've been watching his progress closely. We always knew he'd be an outstanding pitcher."[13] The Baseball Writers Association of America Association agreed, selecting Jim as the AL Cy Young Award winner. He beat a stellar group of pitchers, including Sam McDowell, Mike Cuellar, and Dave McNally; 11 points separated the top four vote-getters. Perry was also named to *The Sporting News* All-Star Team.

The next two years were subpar for Perry. In 1971 he gave up 39 round-trippers, almost doubling his total from the previous season (20). At the end of spring training, Perry was dealt to Detroit for pitcher Danny Fife. The move reunited Jim with Billy Martin, the skipper in Detroit. "I think he can help us win the pennant," said Martin. "I think he'll win over 15 games. We got the noncheating Perry [a reference to allegations that Gaylord threw a spitball]. We've been scouting him, we think he can win."[14]

Jim finished the year 14-13, one win short of Martin's prediction. Martin, meanwhile, was fired in August and was replaced by Joe Schultz. Before that, on July 3, Jim took the mound against Gaylord, who was now pitching for Cleveland. It was the first time in the American League that two brothers had pitched against each other in a regular-season game. Neither pitcher was around at the end; Jim got a no-decision and Gaylord was tagged with the loss in a 5-4 Tigers win. A disputed three-run homer down the right field line by Cleveland outfielder Charlie Spikes gave the Indians a slim 3-2 lead, but by the time the Tigers mounted a comeback, Jim had hit the showers. "I should've won and I would've if the umpire (Merlyn Anthony) didn't call the ball wrong," Perry said of Spikes' homer. "There's no way that ball is fair, and you can ask anybody who was in our bullpen. They were right there and saw it."[15]

In two of Perry's defeats in 1973, he was the victim of a no-hitter, by Steve Busby of Kansas City on April 27, and by Nolan Ryan of California on July 15. Perry had earlier been victimized by a no-hitter by Oakland's Vida Blue in 1970 when he was with the Twins.

As in the previous spring, Perry was dealt again in March 1974. This time he was part of a three-team deal with the New York Yankees that sent him back to Cleveland. He was going to be teamed with Gaylord. The trade was made with much anticipation, both for the Perry brothers and for Indians fans. "I'm looking forward to putting on a Cleveland uniform," Jim said. "I know I'll get a chance to pitch. You [Cleveland] have a good (defense) and you can score runs. I hope the brother combination can do a good job and get fans back to the park the way they used to come."[16]

The brother combination won 38 games for the Indians. Gaylord went 21-13 with a 2.51 ERA and Jim 17-12 with a 2.96 ERA. But the rest of the staff fell flat; no other pitcher posted double-digit wins. Their 38 wins were almost half of the team's total of 77.

For 1975 Cleveland replaced manager Ken Aspromonte with Frank Robinson, who became the first black manager in the big leagues. Robinson ran a tight ship and demanded that all of his players adhere to his regulations. Gaylord Perry fought him at almost every turn. Both Perrys had dismal starts to the season. It was only a matter of time before the sibling reunion came to an end, and on May 20 the Indians dispatched Jim to Oakland with Dick Bosman for Blue Moon Odom. Gaylord was dealt to Texas three weeks later.

Perry made 11 starts for Oakland. One was a one-hitter against Baltimore, a 3-0 win on June 10. Al Bumbry's single in the sixth inning ruined Perry's no-hit bid. "I'm not a no-hit pitcher," said Perry. "I'm just trying to win. I've been struggling, and I can't worry about that no-hit stuff."[17]

The A's released Perry on August 13, and he retired as a player shortly thereafter and became a scout for Oakland. His top signee was catcher Terry Steinbach, who was a core player for the dominant Athletics teams in the late 1980s. Perry eventually relocated to Sioux Falls, South Dakota, where he worked for DialNet, a long-distance telephone service. Campbell University named its baseball field in Perry's honor in 2012. His son, Chris, became a professional golfer, and had a successful career on the PGA tour.

SOURCES

Baseball Digest

Cleveland Plain Dealer

Cleveland Press

minors.sabrwebs.com/cgi-bin/index.php

retrosheet.org

sabr.org

National Baseball Hall of Fame archives.

Pluto, Terry, *The Curse of Rocky Colavito* (New York: Simon and Schuster, 1994).

The Sporting News.

Thielman, Jim, *The Cool of the Evening* (Edina, Minnesota: Kirk House Publishers, 2005).

NOTES

1. *Baseball Digest*, September, 1960, 27-32.
2. Ibid.
3. Ibid.
4. Ibid.
5. *Cleveland Plain Dealer*, July 22, 1991.
6. *New York World-Telegram*, May 13, 1959.
7. *Cleveland Plain Dealer*, May 3, 1963.
8. Terry Pluto, *The Curse of Rocky Colavito*, 174.
9. *The Sporting News*, August 14, 1965.
10. *The Sporting News*, December 31, 1966.
11. *The Sporting News*, July 5, 1969.
12. *The Sporting News*, October 3, 1970.
13. *The Sporting News*, September 26, 1970.
14. Perry's file, National Baseball Hall of Fame.
15. *Cleveland Plain Dealer*, July 4, 1973.
16. *Cleveland Plain Dealer*, March 20, 1974.
17. Perry's file, National Baseball Hall of Fame.

Bill Pleis

BY JOEL RIPPEL

THE 13-YEAR PROFESSIONAL baseball career of Bill Pleis almost ended before it even got started.

Pleis, a St. Louis native, was signed after a tryout camp in late August of 1955, several weeks after his 18th birthday and several months after graduating from Kirkwood High School.

Scout Danny Menendez signed the left-handed pitcher to a contract with the Charleston (West Virginia) Senators, an independent team in the American Association. In December Charleston assigned Pleis outright to the Memphis (Tennessee) Chickasaws, a Chicago White Sox affiliate in the Southern Association.

In March of 1956, Pleis reported to the Memphis spring-training camp in Hollywood, Florida. "I didn't pitch (for Memphis) the whole spring," said Pleis. "I didn't even throw b.p. (batting practice). I was young and naïve. I had no clue what was going on."[1] Near the end of the training camp, Pleis was informed he had been traded. "It was almost time to break camp," said Pleis. "I was told, 'Bill you've been traded, along with a shortstop, to Orlando.'"

On April 10, 1956, Pleis joined the Orlando Seratomas of the Class D Florida State League. "I got over there and I hadn't pitched at all," said Pleis. "The same thing happened over there. And after a couple of days, I'm sitting there and I'm wondering what's going on." Finally, Pleis got an opportunity.

"(Orlando manager) Taft Wright came over and said, 'Throw some b.p.'" Pleis said. "I was so naïve and had no clue. As I walked to the mound I decided I wasn't going to throw b.p. I was going to treat it like a game situation.

"So the first hitter steps and in and I throw a fastball on the outside corner. Then I throw a curveball and he yells at me. The next pitch I throw inside. The next hitter comes up and I do the same thing. He started yelling at me.

"Taffy comes over and asks me, 'What's going on?' And I said, 'To tell you the truth, I just wanted to show you what I could do.' He said I 'looked good from the outfield.' Then he said 'Opening Day is in two days. Our best pitcher is starting that game. Are you ready to pitch the next day?'"

About a month into the season, Pleis was explained the circumstances around his spring-training experience. "Taft took me out to lunch," said Pleis. "He said, 'I bet you wonder what happened (with Memphis). We wanted the shortstop. The White Sox said, 'We'll give you the shortstop, but you have to take this kid

A solid reliever for the Twins in 1965, the southpaw Pleis appeared in 41 games and carved out a 2.98 ERA. In his six-year big-league career (1961-1966), he appeared in 190 games and won 21 times. (Photo courtesy of Minnesota Twins Baseball Club).

(Pleis) too. He seems like a nice kid. We're too embarrassed to release him when he hasn't pitched all spring.'"

William Pleis, III was born on August 5, 1937, in St. Louis to William Pleis, Jr. and Celeste Pleis. William Jr., who served in World War II, was a millwright for General Motors. His mother worked for McDonnell-Douglas. "One of my earliest memories is when my father came home from World War II," said Pleis, who had a sister. Pleis didn't go out for baseball at Kirkwood High School until his junior year (1954). "I loved baseball, but I was very shy," he said. "I was too shy to go out. I played a little football when I was young, but I wasn't very good."

As a senior in 1955, Pleis helped Kirkwood reach the Missouri state tournament. In two playoff victories, Pleis pitched a 1-0 two-hit shutout with eight strikeouts in against Brentwood and then pitched five shutout innings in Kirkwood's 8-0 victory over Festus.

Pleis showed potential in his first professional season. At age 18, he was the second youngest player on the Orlando roster (which included infielder Lou Marchegiano, the brother of heavyweight boxing champion Rocky Marciano). His rookie season took another unexpected turn on August 15, just 10 days after his 19th birthday, when he was sold by Orlando, the only independent team in the eight-team league, to the Louisville Colonels of the Triple-A American Association. *The Sporting News* detailed the transaction: "The (Louisville) Colonels added a new player Aug. 15, when personnel director Joe Cambria announced that Bill Pleis had been purchased from Orlando (Florida State League) for $250 and two players (catcher Rafael Enoa and pitcher Sergio Hebra) already on option with Orlando. Oddly, Cambria, in addition to his position with Louisville, is owner of the Orlando club."[2]

Pleis had pitched well in 26 appearances for Orlando, which was headed for a last-place finish after winning the Florida State League title in 1955. Pleis was 11-12 with a 2.75 ERA for Orlando, which would win just 55 games. He allowed just 170 hits in 193 innings.

In the final two weeks of the American Association season, Pleis made four appearances for the Colonels. The second youngest player to appear in the American Association in 1956, he was 0-0 with an 8.25 ERA in 12 innings for the Colonels, who finished last with a 60-93 record.

His sophomore professional season was as eventful as his first. After the 1956 season, Louisville assigned Pleis outright to the Toronto Maple Leafs of the International League. Before spring training, Toronto, an independent team, assigned him to Memphis, which was now a Chicago Cubs farm team.

On April 11 Pleis was optioned to Lafayette (Louisiana) of the Class C Evangeline League. He pitched well for Lafayette, going 7-3 with a 2.79 ERA in 22 appearances. But two months into the season, there was another unexpected change.

Through the games of June 19, Lafayette was leading the six-team league with a 36-20 record. But despite being in first place, the franchise was struggling at the gate, and (along with the Baton Rouge franchise) it folded on June 20. Pleis and five teammates were assigned to the Magic Valley (Twin Falls, Idaho) Cowboys of the Pioneer League.

The Lafayette contingent joined a Magic Valley team that was mired in last place and helped the Cowboys put together a solid second half of the season. Over the final two months of the season, Pleis went 6-3 for the Cowboys to finish the season with a combined 13-6 record in 44 appearances.

After the season Pleis was reserved on the Memphis roster, but in early April of 1958, he was assigned outright to the Allentown (Pennsylvania) Red Sox, Boston's affiliate in the Double-A Eastern League. It turned out to be another tumultuous season. Allentown, managed by Eddie Popowski, got off to a slow start in 1958, winning just six of its first 22 games. Pleis pitched adequately, going 1-2 with a 3.09 ERA in 32 innings over seven appearances. With Allentown struggling, Boston decided to send help. On May 28 the Red Sox assigned bonus-baby shortstop Al Moran and pitchers Roy Tinney and Ron Jirsa to Allentown. To make room on the Allentown roster, the Red Sox wanted to send Pleis to Magic Valley. When he told the Red Sox he didn't want to go back to the lower-level Pioneer League they placed him on the suspended list.

"They told me they wanted to send me back to the Pioneer League," said Pleis. "And I said no. I just drove home (to Missouri). I got hold of an uncle who had a construction company. I worked for him as a hod carrier. It's an awful, tough job. I dug ditches. The only good thing about the work was that it kept me good shape." Another positive thing came out of his time back home in St. Louis as Pleis began dating the woman who became his wife. "She (Sue) is such a wonderful person," said Pleis. "She didn't know I played baseball."

After the season the Red Sox reinstated Pleis and assigned him to Memphis. He spent the entire 1959 season with Memphis, which was an independent team managed by future Hall of Famer Luke Appling.

On June 27, 1959, in the second game of a doubleheader in Chattanooga, Pleis showed his feisty side. Pitching against future Minnesota Twin Jack Kralick, Pleis didn't allow a hit in the first four innings as Memphis took a 1-0 lead into the bottom of the fifth inning. In the fifth, Chattanooga's first two hitters singled and then a double (by future Twin Dan Dobbek) put runners at second and third with nobody out. After getting an out on a groundball with the infield drawn in, Pleis walked a hitter to load the bases. Appling brought in right-hander Bill Slack, who struck out the next two hitters to get out of the jam. Memphis went on to win, 2-1.

"I was all over the place and we were clinging to a one-run lead," said Pleis. "Luke came out to talk to me and I told him I could get out of it. After I walked the guy, he started to come out again and I said to him, 'Don't cross that line. I'm fine. I'm staying in.' But he took me out. I was angry. I drop-kicked my glove into the stands. I went up to the clubhouse and got dressed and went back to hotel before the game was over. It was totally stupid. I just messed up. I called my mother and told her I was coming home because I thought was going to get released for my actions."

After Appling got back to the hotel, he talked to Pleis. "He was the nicest man I ever met and he treated me like a son," said Pleis. "He said he liked my competitiveness, but what I did was wrong. I said I was sorry."

Appling didn't hold the outburst against Pleis. On July 2 Pleis was outdueled by Nashville's Cholly Naranjo, 1-0. On July 11 he pitched a three-hit shutout with nine strikeouts in a 6-0 victory over New Orleans.

For the 1959 season, Pleis was 8-8 with a 3.28 ERA. After the season, the Red Sox assigned him to Minneapolis of the American Association. Pleis, who was married on October 16, was placed on the service list on November 7, when he went on six months' active duty.

On May 17, 1960, Pleis was reinstated from the service list, but the Boston organization had no room for him on the Minneapolis roster. He was released. Two weeks later the Washington Senators signed Pleis and assigned him to Charlotte of the South Atlantic League. "I was in good shape, but I hadn't pitched in six months," said Pleis. "(Scout) Bill Messmann convinced the team to sign me."

After a 10-4 season with a career-best 2.73 ERA (third best in the league), Pleis joined the Senators' Florida (Winter) Instructional League team, which included Jim Kaat and Don Mincher and was managed by Del Wilber. In late October Calvin Griffith announced he was moving the Washington franchise to Minnesota.

Pleis had a solid instructional league season. He was 4-1 and pitched in the league's all-star game. That performance earned Pleis an invitation to his first big-league spring-training camp. On March 1 Pleis and 16 other pitchers reported to Orlando. In the Twins' first 20 exhibition games, Pleis pitched one inning — the fewest on the team. But in the final week of the exhibition schedule, he made three appearances and allowed just one run in six innings. That won him a spot on the Twins' Opening Day roster.

On April 16, 1961, in the second game of a doubleheader in Baltimore, Pleis made his major-league debut. He entered the game in the bottom of the ninth with the score tied and the potential winning run at third. He got Dave Philley to pop out to short for the third out of the inning. Pleis retired the Orioles (Dick Williams, Earl Robinson, and Brooks Robinson) in order in the 10th inning. He was lifted for a pinch-hitter in the 11th and the Twins scored two runs on Zoilo Versalles' home run to give Pleis his first major-league victory.

Two days later Pleis earned his first save when he closed out a 3-2 victory over the Red Sox for Jim Kaat. On April 22 he was the winning pitcher in the Twins' first victory in Minnesota — a 5-4 decision in 10 innings over the Washington Senators.

The Twins sent Pleis to Syracuse of the International League in May but recalled him in June. Pleis was 4-2 with two saves and a 4.95 ERA in 37 appearances in his rookie campaign with the Twins.

Pleis began the 1962 season with Vancouver of the Pacific Coast League, but returned to the Twins on June 25. He was a fixture in the Minnesota bullpen for the next 3½ seasons. In 21 appearances (which included four starts) with the Twins in 1962, he was 2-5 with three saves and a 4.40 ERA.

Over the next two seasons, Pleis was 10-3 (6-2 in 1963 and 4-1 with four saves in 1964) with a 4.17 ERA. Among his 83 appearances in 1963 and 1964, Pleis made four starts, including the only complete game of his career, an eight-hitter with one walk and six strikeouts in an 11-4 victory over the Senators in Washington, on June 28, 1963. Another highlight for Pleis was being selected to throw batting practice at the 1964 All-Star Game at New York's Shea Stadium.

In the Twins' championship season in 1965, Pleis was 4-4 with four saves and a 2.98 ERA in 41 appearances. He appeared in one game in the 1965 World Series, pitching one inning and allowing a run by the Dodgers in Game Four (a 7-2 Dodgers victory in Los Angeles). For the second year in a row, Pleis threw batting practice at an All-Star Game. (The 1965 game was in Minnesota.)

Pleis spent the first three months of the 1966 season with Denver of the Pacific Coast League before being recalled by the Twins on July 8. He made just eight appearances with Minnesota, going 1-2 with a 1.93 ERA in 9⅓ innings. In his final major-league appearance, on September 15, 1966, Pleis was the losing pitcher in an 8-5 loss in Detroit, allowing four unearned runs in his one inning.

In February of 1967, the Twins traded Pleis, who was just short of qualifying for his major-league pension, to the Washington Senators in exchange for infielder Ken Hamlin. The Senators assigned Pleis to their Hawaii farm team in the Pacific Coast League.

Pleis struggled for the Islanders, going 1-9 with a 5.02 ERA in 44 appearances. But after the Islanders' season ended, he got a pleasant surprise. On September 18, 1967, the Twins purchased his contract from the Senators. *The Sporting News* wrote, "Who says baseball has no heart? With two weeks remaining in their four-way battle for the pennant, the Twins brought back their former relief pitcher, Bill Pleis, for the 13 days necessary to qualify him for a five-year pension."[3]

"That's the nicest thing that ever happened to me in baseball," said Pleis. "I couldn't get anybody out in Hawaii. I think Jim Kaat and a couple of the guys went to Calvin and said, 'We want Shorty back.'" Pleis said the only disappointing thing was that the Twins fell one game short of the American League title and the chance to play the St. Louis Cardinals in the World Series.

After the season the Twins returned Pleis to the Senators organization. He began the 1968 season as a coach with the Senators' Buffalo farm team in the International League but was released in June so he could pursue playing opportunities. On June 13 Pleis signed with Louisville (Boston's farm team in the International League). He went 3-5 with an 8.27 ERA in 23 appearances with the Colonels, his final appearances as a professional player.

At age 30, Pleis's playing career was over, but his association with professional baseball wasn't. In 1969 he went to work for the Houston Astros and began a nearly 40-year career as a scout.

One of the first players Pleis signed for the Astros was Minnesotan Paul Siebert. Siebert, the son of University of Minnesota coach and former major leaguer Dick Siebert, was the Astros' third-round pick in the 1971 amateur draft. He spent parts of the five seasons in the major leagues.

In 1976 Pleis joined the scouting staff of the Los Angeles Dodgers. He started as an area scout in the Midwest for the Dodgers and then became the Dodgers' Florida scout in 1987. In 1989 the Dodgers drafted two players in the first round who were scouted by Pleis—Kiki Jones and Jamie McAndrew.

Pleis retired in 2006 but his connection to major-league baseball continues with his son. Scott Pleis, who was born in Minneapolis while his father pitched for the Twins, is the director of amateur scouting for the Detroit Tigers.

"I was a 5-foot-10 left-hander who didn't throw very hard," Pleis said. "It was a great thing to get to play for the Twins. The '65 Twins were a great bunch of guys, who really pulled for each other. My wife (Sue) is the most wonderful person. I don't know what I would have done without her."

SOURCES

Author's telephone interview with Bill Pleis, August 2014.

Bill Pleis player file, National Baseball Hall of Fame Library.

1963 Minnesota Twins yearbook.

1965 Minnesota Twins press, radio, TV guide.

Allentown (Pennsylvania) *Morning Call*

Chattanooga (Tennessee) *Sunday Times*

Deseret News, Salt Lake City.

Minneapolis Star.

Minneapolis Tribune.

Palm Beach (Florida) *Post.*

Reading (Pennsylvania) *Eagle.*

The Sporting News.

NOTES

1. Author's phone interview with Bill Pleis, August 2014. All subsequent quotes from Pleis are from the August 2014 interview.
2. *The Sporting News*, August 29, 1956.
3. *The Sporting News*, October 7, 1967.

The Chicago Showdown: The Twins Take Two at Comiskey Park

September 8 and 9, 1965: Minnesota Twins 3, Chicago White Sox 2; Minnesota Twins 10 Chicago White Sox 4 at Comiskey Park, Chicago, Illinois

BY STEVE SCHMITT

THEY CALLED IT THE CHICAGO showdown. The Minnesota Twins, in first place in the American League since May 30, held a five-game lead over the Chicago White Sox, winners of 26 of 39 games leading up to a crucial two-game series between the two Midwestern contenders on September 8 and 9 at venerable Comiskey Park.

Minnesota had built a seemingly comfortable lead with a record of 61wins and 40 losses after Camilo Pascual blanked the Washington Senators, 6-0, on May 30. Throughout the campaign, the Twins picked up for each other when slumps or injuries required it. In critical series against their hottest pursuers, the White Sox and the Baltimore Orioles, they had a knack for winning by one run or in their last at-bat. They won three of four games against the Orioles July 30-August 2, each victory by one run. Jimmie Hall's August 2 walk-off homer off rookie Jim Palmer punctuated the series and occurred on the same day that Harmon Killebrew dislocated an elbow that kept him out of the lineup until September 21.

A major change from the previous years was a new approach that combined the Twins' traditional home-run slugging with sound fundamentals—hitting the cutoff man, taking the extra base and stealing bases to create more scoring chances. Shortstop Zoilo Versalles became a star and won the American League Most Valuable Player award, fulfilling manager Sam Mele's prediction after the showdown series.[1] Pitcher Jim "Mudcat" Grant learned how to make his fastball and curveball spin and won 21 games. Southpaw Jim Kaat led the league with 42 starts, won 18 games, and beat the White Sox four times without a loss in 1965. Relief pitcher Al Worthington, a National League castoff with 10 seasons in the big leagues and a few minor league stops along the way, saved 21 games. Injuries to Killebrew, Pascual, right fielder Tony Oliva, catcher Earl Battey, and left fielder Bob Allison meant that youngsters had to step up, too. Rich Rollins took over at third base, Don Mincher started at first with Killebrew out, and left fielder Sandy Valdespino, signed in 1956 when the Twins were the Washington Senators, made some dazzling catches in the outfield and got key hits during the stretch drive. Twenty-year-old Dave Boswell and 21-year-old Jim Merritt combined to win 11 games in their rookie seasons while Pascual nursed an injured back.

By September it was clear that the White Sox employed the same team-oriented formula that had worked for Minnesota. They won 26 of 39 games from July 29 to September 2, including a 10-game winning streak from August 14 to August 22 during which seven different pitchers got credit for victories and knuckleball relievers Hoyt Wilhelm and Eddie Fisher combined for five saves. On September 2 Chicago swept a doubleheader from Baltimore to pull within 6½ games of the leaders. "My pitching is right again, we've got the balance I like," said Chicago manager

Al Lopez, who had three starters with 60 or more RBIs going into the showdown series and four others with between 40 and 52 RBIs. "Early-season injuries killed us," general manager Ed Short said. "I'm amazed we still have a shot but we do have a shot. The thing I like best is the balance. It's not a one-man deal. … Everybody is taking a turn at picking somebody else up." The "ex-cripples, zombies, and also-rans" who once trailed by 11½ games were breathing down the Twins' necks.[2]

The White Sox had invaded Metropolitan Stadium on Labor Day weekend and beat the league leaders two games out of three. The Twins won the Friday night opener, 6-4. On Saturday, September 4, journeyman John Buzhardt—having his best season (13-8, 3.01)—beat Grant, 5-4, before 27,078 fans. The next day, Joe Horlen pitched a three-hit shutout to beat Jim Perry with 39,136 fans on hand. "The Twins have been out in front too long," said White Sox relief specialist Eddie Fisher, who made 82 appearances in 1965, winning 15 and saving 24 with his signature knuckleball. "Nobody has really challenged them. Now that we're closing in, let's see if they can take it."[3]

They took it. On Wednesday night, September 8, Mudcat Grant again took the mound against Buzhardt and struggled from the start. Don Buford walked and Floyd Robinson reached on second baseman Jerry Kindall's error. Buford moved to third on Earl Battey's errant pickoff throw and then scored when John Romano lofted a deep fly ball to Sandy Valdespino in left, with Robinson taking second. The Sox led, 1-0. Pete Ward's single to center scored Robinson with an unearned second run before Moose Skowron, the White Sox' RBI leader at the time, bounced into a 6-4-3 double play to end the inning. The Twins trailed, 2-0.

Minnesota's first scoring threat came when Rich Rollins, starting at third base with Killebrew still nursing a dislocated elbow, opened the third inning with a single to center. Kindall's poke to left put the tying runs aboard for Grant, who batted .155 that season but had five extra-base hits and would stroke a homer in the World Series. Grant whiffed but Zoilo Versalles brought Rollins home from third with a fly ball to left fielder Tom McCraw to slice the White Sox' edge to 2-1.

In the fourth Grant pitched his first perfect inning and kept the White Sox off the scoreboard for the rest of the night, though he had to retire Ron Hansen on a comebacker with Skowron and McCraw on base in the sixth. Minnesota failed to provide any offensive help through the sixth inning. It would take another come-from-behind victory. So far, the Twins had won 20 games in the seventh inning or later, not including an 11-5 record in extra-inning games.

Mincher led off the seventh. A large, bespectacled man (6-feet-3, 205 pounds) with deadly left-handed power who originally signed with the White Sox in 1956, he had one thought in mind: Tie the game. Instead, he bounced easily to Skowron at first base. But Battey singled to center. Jimmie Hall, who had portside power similar to Mincher's and had hit 76 home runs for the Twins in nearly three seasons, drove a hanging curve from Buzhardt over the wall for his 19th home run and 75th and 76th RBIs—his first round-tripper since August 2. It gave the Twins a 3-2 lead. For nearly a month, Hall had complained of a "tired bat," with 21 hits in 77 at-bats during one stretch but no home runs. Flirting with .300 for much of the season, Hall said, "I don't really care about the average. I just want to bat in some runs and help the club. That's what we need right now—runs."[4]

With one out in the bottom of the seventh, Grant faced pinch-hitter Smoky Burgess, a master at the craft who in 1965 led the majors with 20 pinch hits in 65 at-bats, a .308 average. He had been in baseball since 1944, when Grant was 9 years old. Burgess "whirled like a merry-go-round in fishing for the first pitch," *Chicago Tribune* columnist Dave Condon reported. Eventually Smoky met the ball and it carried to the opposite field but right into the glove of Valdespino for the second out. Lopez's decision to use Burgess was all about Grant. "Well, if I didn't use him at that opportunity, I might not have had the chance to use him at all," the skipper said.[5] Next, Buford—a former football player at the University of Southern

California and the White Sox leadoff hitter — bounced to Kindall and Grant got ready to lead off the eighth inning.

Hoyt Wilhelm, on in relief of Buzhardt, struck out Grant, who took a dazzling knuckler for a third strike. The V&V Boys — Versalles and Valdespino — went down easily and Grant took the hill for the eighth with a 3-2 lead. Romano walked with one out, and with two out, Grant faced Skowron with pinch-runner Al Weis on second. A .205 lifetime hitter against Grant with 3 home runs and 7 RBIs, Skowron flied out to Oliva to bring yet another one-run game into the ninth inning, fertile ground for late-season Twins victories.

Oliva and Mincher both popped out on Wilhelm's fingertip specialties. Battey singled to left but Hall grounded out to Buford, leaving it up to Grant and the defense to give the Twins a six-game lead. McCraw bounced to Kindall and Hansen flied out to Valdespino. With one out left, Lopez sent Danny Cater up to hit for Ken Berry, despite the light-hitting center fielder's recent tear of four home runs in seven games. Cater popped to Kindall, who squeezed the baseball with his glove to preserve the 3-2 victory. Minnesota led by six games.

"We were lucky to get even two runs," Lopez lamented. "That Grant can sure turn over the ball."[6] Grant had learned from pitching coach Johnny Sain to add spin to his pitches. On the occasion of his 18th victory of the season, Grant said, "I don't throw the fastball any harder but the spin does something for it."[7]

Joe Horlen, who had shut out the Twins just four days earlier, got the starting call the next day for the White Sox against Jim Kaat, who had beaten Chicago three times in '65 and was seeking his 15th win. A small Thursday afternoon gathering of 5,786 would witness perhaps the most important game of the pennant race.

The Twins "cannonaded their pursuers with a 10-4 drubbing," wrote Condon.[8] Oliva delivered a sacrifice fly to center field in the first inning for a 1-0 lead. Versalles had singled, moved to second on Valdespino's sacrifice bunt, gone to third on a wild pitch, and scored on Oliva's drive. Maximum efficiency; whatever it took to win. Kaat set Buford, Robinson, and Danny Cater down in order.

In the second inning the Twins broke the game open against a beleaguered Horlen. Battey and Hall singled to center and Rollins — a .249 hitter for the season — singled to left, scoring Battey and sending Hall to third. Kindall went the other way on Horlen and his sacrifice fly to Floyd Robinson in right field was his sixth and final one of the season to make it 3-0. Kaat grounded out to shortstop Hansen, sending Rollins to second, and then Versalles delivered a single to center for a 4-0 lead. Valdespino's opposite-field single sent Horlen to the showers.

What was different from Horlen's shutout just four days before? Sam Mele observed that his hitters were pounding Horlen's low curves into easy outs in the first encounter. "I told my players to move up to the front of the plate on him," Mele said. "His ball was higher down here in Chicago."[9]

The White Sox finally scored on Kaat in the bottom of the fifth. Romano walked and Skowron singled to right. Ward forced Skowron at second. On Hansen's bouncer to the mound, Kaat's Gold Glove flicked the ball to Kindall, who nailed Hansen at first. Romano scored Chicago's first run and Ward reached second. With a chance to cut the Twins' lead in half, Berry popped out to Rollins.

Typical of that season, Minnesota responded with two more runs in the sixth. With two down, Rollins singled, Kindall walked, and Kaat helped himself with his second hit of the game, off Buford's glove. The runners scored when Buford made a wild throw. It was 6-1 when White Sox pinch-hitter Jim Hicks led off the White Sox sixth with a double to right field and scored on Robinson's sacrifice fly after Buford beat out a dribbler to the mound. Kaat bore down, retired Cater on a fly to right and caught Romano looking at strike three.

The cannonading continued in the seventh inning. Valdespino and Oliva hit back-to-back doubles off Fisher. The slugging cleanup hitter Mincher then shocked the baseball world with a sacrifice bunt. Oliva moved to third and, yes, scored on Battey's single, an opposite-field hit to right. Hall's single sent Battey to third. With second base open, Hall stole. Rollins got fooled on a knuckler and Kindall flied out. It was now 8-2.

When Hansen and Berry singled to put runners on the corners with two outs in the bottom of the seventh, Mele summoned Al Worthington to wrap up the sweep. Gene Freese, purchased to platoon with Ward at third base, was due to pinch-hit against Kaat but Burgess, a lifetime .455 hitter against Worthington, got the call instead. Lopez must have known about his veteran catcher's track record against the Twins' closer. Burgess smoked a double to center field, scoring Hansen, making it 8-3, and sending Berry to third. Worthington took it as another day against Smoky Burgess and calmly struck out Don Buford, leaving Burgess at second. The White Sox threatened again in the bottom of the eighth when Floyd Robinson pulled a singled to right and Skowron singled to left two outs later. Now Worthington had to face Pete Ward, tough in the clutch despite a .249 average and a 2-for-10 career record against the Twins closer. Ward smacked a line drive toward right but Kindall speared it for the third out.

Greg Bollo, who made his major-league debut on May 9 against the Twins, retired five batters in a row before backup catcher Jerry Zimmerman walked and Hall hit his second home run of the series, his 20th (and last) of the season, and the lowest total of his three-year career.

Closing out the game continued to be a struggle for Worthington, Minnesota's gray-flecked redhead who had pitched briefly for the White Sox in 1960. Versalles booted a grounder to start the ninth but Worthington recovered and struck out Berry. Marv Staehle, called up in September and with one official major-league at-bat, singled to right field as Hansen went to third. Buford's fly ball to center field scored Hansen to make it 10-4. Robinson hit a line drive right at Worthington, who gloved it for the final out. The Twins led by seven with 19 games to play.

"We're not in," said Mele. "We're still in it," said Lopez.[10]

Mele enjoyed the attention the Chicago showdown received and hoped to reach his first World Series after missing his opportunity as a player for the 1948 Boston Red Sox, who lost a one-game playoff to the eventual world champion Cleveland Indians. "It's different when you're a winner," he said. "You walk down the main streets and they call you Mister."[11] Mele not only dealt with injuries and the repeated question of whether the Twins would win the pennant. His wife, Connie, was expecting her fifth child. "She's got more on her mind than I have," Mele said from the shower in Comiskey Park's visiting locker room. "They'd better reserve a bed for me at a Minnesota hospital," a confident Connie said from the couple's nine-room home in Quincy, Massachusetts, "because I'm not going to miss [the World Series] for anything."[12]

The two victories at Chicago started a seven-game winning streak and the Twins clinched the pennant on September 25. They won two of three games at Baltimore on September 28-30 that no longer mattered. The White Sox dropped their next two games but won 11 of their last 13, including an anticipated three-game sweep of the Kansas City Athletics that some thought would give Chicago a pennant. As it was, they finished seven games out and failed to gain any ground in the standings after those back-to-back losses to Minnesota.

The Chicago showdown was a culmination of the Twins' consistent play throughout the season. They had a winning record every month and winning records in extra-inning games, one-run games, and against both right-handed and left-handed pitchers. They also did not care where they played: The Twins won 51 games at home and 51 games on the road, and had winning records against seven of nine teams while outscoring their opponents more on the road than at home. The home-run total dropped from 221 in 1964 to 150 but the Twins scored 37 more runs and allowed

78 fewer runs than in 1964 while stealing 92 bases in 125 attempts (.736). The 1965 pitching staff had 12 shutouts to 3 for opponents, compared with 1964 when the Twins were blanked 14 times and recorded only 4 shutouts. The 1965 team did whatever it took and took everything it could get. And it gave the Twins and their fans, who led the league in attendance, their first pennant.

The night of Kaat's victory in Chicago, the Dodgers' Sandy Koufax pitched a perfect game against the Chicago Cubs. The Twins, focused on winning the franchise's first pennant in 32 years, probably paid little attention but they would witness the same pitching dominance a month later with a World Series championship on the line.

SOURCES

The Sporting News

Baseball-Reference.com

ProQuest Historical Newspapers

NOTES

1. Dave Condon, "In the Wake of the News," *Chicago Tribune*, September 10, 1965, C1.
2. John Hall, "Chicago Showdown," *Los Angeles Times*, September 8, 1965, B3. .
3. Jerome Holtzman, 'Who Says Pennant Race Is Over?' White Sox Ask, *The Sporting News*, September 18, 1965, 6.
4. Max Nichols, "Hall's 'Tired Bat' Pumps New Life Into Twins," *The Sporting News*, September 25, 1965, 13.
5. Dave Condon, "In the Wake of the News," *Chicago Tribune*, September 9, 1965, F1.
6. Ibid.
7. Ibid.
8. Condon, September 10, 1965.
9. Ibid.
10. Edward Prell, "Minnesota Leads by 7; 19 to Play," *Chicago Tribune*, September 10, 1965, C1, 2.
11. Condon, September 10, 1965.
12. Ibid.

Frank Quilici

BY NORM KING

FRANK QUILICI MUST HAVE BEEN a milliner in a previous life because he's worn so many hats with the Minnesota Twins. From player to coach to manager to broadcaster, Quilici came up from working-class roots in Chicago to become a baseball lifer with the Twins' logo tattooed on his heart. He is also the only person in Twins history to hold all those positions with the franchise.

Francis Ralph Quilici (QUILL-iss-ee) was born in Chicago on May 11, 1939, the son of Guido Quilici and the former Laura Domanowska, who met while working at a bakery. Quilici and his sister, Rose-Marie grew up in an area of southwest Chicago that by his own admission wasn't the ritziest neighborhood, but he loved it nonetheless.

"At the time it was tough, but we didn't realize it and I wouldn't change it if I could," he recalled.[1]

Growing up, Quilici was active in sports and developed his baseball skills by playing softball with his father in a league where gloves were not an option, even though the ball was "soft" in name only. He began playing baseball in Chicago area parks at the age of 12 with the encouragement of Pete Klein, a longtime instructor and supervisor in the Chicago parks system, and progressed through the ranks until he was old enough to go to college.

Quilici entered to Loras College in Dubuque, Iowa, but quit after one semester because of financial difficulties. He returned to Chicago and got a job in a brewery bottle shop, while continuing to play in the Chicago area. One day former Detroit Tiger, National League umpire, and scout George Moriarty approached him between games of a doubleheader and told Quilici he could get him onto the team at Western Michigan University as a walk-on. Good to his word, Moriarty got Quilici his chance.

Quilici was a good player on some good college teams at Western Michigan, where Jim Bouton was his roommate during his freshman year. Quilici was a second-team all-American in 1960, when he hit .400, and a first-team all-American as a senior in 1961, with a .369 average. His teams made it to the College World Series in 1959 and 1961, finishing fifth both times.

Even people playing in Charlie Brown's league attract attention from major-league teams when they hit .400. In Quilici's case that attention came from the New York Yankees in the form of a $28,000 signing bonus, but in an action rare and gutsy for the time, Quilici turned the offer down.

"I had always promised my dad and myself that I would finish college," Quilici said. "I told (Yankee

A midseason call-up, Quilici made 39 starts at second base for the Twins in 1965, batting .208. He played five seasons in the majors, all with the Twins. (Photo courtesy of Minnesota Twins Baseball Club).

scout) Pat Patterson, I know if I don't finish and get a taste of baseball, I'll never go back."[2]

The Yankees weren't interested after Quilici hit "only" .369 in his senior year, but the Minnesota Twins were. Kalamazoo, Michigan, home of Western Michigan University, was the territory of Twins scout Dick Wiencek, who signed Bert Blyleven and Graig Nettles among others. Wiencek signed Quilici in to a contract containing a $15,000 signing bonus in June 1961 after he graduated. Quilici immediately joined the Wytheville Twins of the Class D- Appalachian League. After 40 games there he moved up to the Erie Sailors of the Class D New York-Pennsylvania League for another 27 games.[3] Between the two teams, Quilici hit a respectable .276 with eight home runs.

If someone asked Quilici, "Where were you in '62?" he would say "North Carolina," with the Wilson Tobs of the Class B Carolina League for 117 games, then for another 25 with the Charlotte Hornets of the Class A South Atlantic League.[4] Quilici had a tougher time with the pitching in these circuits, batting a combined .210 with seven home runs (all with Wilson) and 51 RBIs.

He also changed positions that season. Quilici played shortstop prior to 1962, but with the emergence of Zoilo Versalles at short with the parent club, Quilici's only hope of reaching the majors was at second base, so he switched.

Quilici found himself playing in Wilson and Charlotte again in 1963, but in the alchemy that one finds in the minor leagues, the Carolina League was bumped up to Class A, while the South Atlantic League became a Double-A circuit. Quilici handled A-level pitching better that season, batting .279 with eight home runs in 110 games; but advancing to the next level again proved difficult, as he hit only .148 in 17 games in Double-A.

After another year with Charlotte in 1964, during which he batted .261 and drove in a career-high 60 runs, Quilici was promoted to the Denver Bears of the Triple-A Pacific Coast League. He had played 83 games and was hitting .277 when the call he had waited for his entire career finally came in July 1965.

The Twins held a slim lead over Baltimore, Cleveland, and the Chicago White Sox when the club chose to improve its depth by sending infielder Bernie Allen to Denver and calling up Quilici. Manager Sam Mele decided to go the baptism-by-fire route, immediately inserting Quilici into the ninth spot in the lineup during the late innings of the first game of a doubleheader against the California Angels (he fouled out to the first baseman in his first major-league at-bat) on July 18. Quilici started the second game, going 1-for-3 with a double and a run scored.

As everyone knows, there's nothing like a good first impression with the boss, and that's exactly what Quilici achieved with Mele. "I was impressed with the second-base play of Quilici," Mele said after the Twins swept a doubleheader from the Red Sox on July 21. "He looked very good. … He took away a couple of hits and did a fine job with the double play."[5]

Overall, Quilici appeared in 56 of the Twins' final 76 games at second base and shortstop, including 42 starts. He hit only .208 in 149 at-bats, but acquitted himself well in the field, committing only two errors in 218 chances.

The Twins won the 1965 American League pennant going away, compiling a 102-60 record. Their closest pursuer was the White Sox, who finished seven games back. Minnesota reached the World Series for the first time since the franchise moved from Washington in 1961; the Senators' last visit to the fall classic had come in 1933.

Quilici and the Twins caught a break in Game One, on October 6, when Dodgers pitcher Sandy Koufax famously refused to pitch that day because it was Yom Kippur, the most solemn date in the Jewish religion. Instead, the Twins faced Don Drysdale, and Quilici made history by getting two hits in one inning in the World Series. Drysdale was off that day, and the Twins unloaded on him for six runs in the bottom of the third inning. Quilici led the inning off with a double and scored on a three-run homer by Zoilo Versalles. Then he singled and drove in Don Mincher for the frame's sixth run. Dodgers manager Walter Alston lifted Drysdale after Quilici's second hit.[6] Those two safeties represented half of Quilici's hit total for the Series; he had four hits in 20 at-bats, and played in every game as the Twins lost to the Dodgers in seven.

Twins president Calvin Griffith said in a March 24, 1966, article that if the season were to start that day, manager Mele would alternate Quilici and Bernie Allen at second base.[7] Unfortunately for Quilici, the season did not start that day. He was demoted just before the season began and spent the entire year in the minors with Denver, where he hit .256 with eight home runs. He was called up when teams were allowed to expand their rosters, but he did not see any action.

Quilici managed to land a spot on the Twins' roster for 1967; playing time, on the other hand, was at a premium because Minnesota also brought up future Hall of Famer Rod Carew, who took over the second-base job and went on to win Rookie of the Year honors. Quilici played in only 23 games with the Twins (.105 batting average in 19 at-bats) and another 11 at Triple-A (.265 batting average in 34 at-bats).

Spending so much time on the bench gave Quilici time to think, and he realized that he needed to be a lot more like the famous stripper Gypsy Rose Lee to get more playing time—very versatile.[8] He played all over the infield in 1968, including 48 games at second base, 40 at third, and six at shortstop; he even played one inning at first base. That versatility helped his career take off—he played in 97 games, a career high to that point. His hitting also improved, thanks to a tip from Twins coach Billy Martin during spring training that resulted in a career-best .245 batting average. Quilici also hit his first major-league home run, a solo shot off the Oakland A's Jim Nash in a 4-3 Twins victory on the last day of the season.

"(Martin) suggested I bring the bat closer to my body on the swing," said Quilici. I used to extend my arms, but I'm making better contact with Martin's method.[9]

Martin became the manager in 1969. The team had had finished 79-83 the previous season, but Martin took it to first place in the newly minted American League West with a 97-65 record. Quilici was again a utility infielder, coming in primarily as a defensive replacement at second and third. He had only 144 at-bats in 118 games, with only 30 starts, and hit an anemic .174 with two home runs. He did not appear in the American League Championship Series, which the Twins lost in three straight games to the Baltimore Orioles.

The Twins retained their American League West title in 1970. Quilici was again used primarily for his defensive prowess, with only 141 at-bats in 111 games. He hit .227 with two home runs. The Orioles duplicated their three-game sweep from the previous season, but Quilici played in all three games, going 0-for-2.

Quilici didn't know it at the time, but his days as a major-league player ended with the last out of the 1970 ALCS. What followed when spring training for 1971 rolled around was another example of how cruelly owners treated players before the Players Association gathered strength. The Twins had a problem because they saw Quilici as an extra infielder and didn't want to give him a roster spot at the expense of a promising younger player. At the same time, they didn't want to lose a positive clubhouse influence. Their solution was to make the 32-year-old a coach without portfolio, which meant that he had no responsibilities and was described by one team official as little more than a cheerleader. In fact, the only time he did any coaching was when first-base coach Vern Morgan became ill toward the end of the season.

"He's in charge of team spirit," the official said. "He's our morale coach."[10]

It's hard to be the "sis boom bah" guy when your boss keeps kicking you in the pom-poms. For example, the team didn't activate Quilici to replace injured infielders Danny Thompson and Rick Renick, and instead went through the season with a 24-man roster. As well, only four team coaches could take part in the pension plan at that time, and Quilici, was coach number five.[11]

Quilici celebrates with skipper Sam Mele (Photo courtesy of Minnesota Twins Baseball Club).

Griffith's treatment of Quilici stemmed from Quilici's relationship with Billy Martin. Martin had been fired after the 1969 season for ignoring club policies. Apparently it was against club policy to deck a pitcher, which Martin did to Dave Boswell, or to punch a team vice president, which Martin did to Howard Fox. Martin became the Detroit Tigers' manager for the 1971 season and wanted Quilici to join him on his coaching staff.

"Back when Calvin was jacking around with my career, he didn't want me to go to Detroit with Billy," Quilici said. "He felt Billy was tampering, and I said no, he just wants me to go over there and do the same thing for him I did in '69. ... I said, 'Calvin, he isn't tampering.'"[12]

All these shenanigans were going on at a time when Twins attendance was declining and the team was no longer competitive (the firing of Martin had a lot to do with the state of affairs because the fans were furious at the move). The decline continued into 1972, with Quilici signing a contract that called for a $5,000 pay cut and still no clear definition of his duties.

That all changed on July 5, 1972. That's the date on which Griffith fired manager Bill Rigney after the Twins lost eight games out of 11 and named Quilici as his replacement. The Twins were in third place at the time with a 36-34 record, 9½ games behind the division-leading Oakland A's. Rigney told reporters that he was fired because of poor ticket sales, while Griffith said that Rigney wasn't tough enough with the players. "Too many of them (the players) were nonchalant," said Griffith.[13]

The Twins actually fared a bit worse under Quilici (41-43). However, it would be unfair to blame him for the Twins' performance because they suffered injuries that would have devastated any club. Among the casualties were reigning batting champion Tony Oliva, who played only ten games all season, and pitching ace Jim Kaat, who was lost for the year with a broken wrist after a blazing 10-2 start.

Quilici's first full year at the helm, 1973, proved there was no fortune in being .500. The Twins finished 81-81, 13 games behind Oakland. Leading slugger Harmon Killebrew had an injury-riddled season and only hit five home runs in 69 games. The team was also dumping the salaries of players who were no longer effective. Jim Perry, 36, was traded to Detroit along with his $61,000 salary. Kaat and his $60,000 salary were placed on waivers on August 15 when his record was 11-12.

Griffith's holy parsimony wasn't restricted to players. In his interview with John Swol, Quilici recalled arguing with Griffith to get more money for pitching coach Al Worthington. Quilici lost both the argument and Worthington, who left after the 1973 season to become the baseball coach (and later athletic director) at Liberty Baptist College in Lynchburg, Virginia.

"Al had five kids, and he was only making $16,500 or $17,000," recalled Quilici. "I said, 'Cripes, Calvin, he's got to support his family.' He said, 'Just stay out of that end of it.' Al had to quit after the season."[14]

Worthington's worth wasn't worth as much as Quilici thought it was if one uses team ERA as a measurement.

Under pitching coach Bob Rodgers, Twins pitchers had a collective 3.64 ERA in 1974, slightly lower than the 1973 team total of 3.77; both numbers ranked sixth in the 12-team American League. This middle-of-the-road pitching contributed to a mediocre 82-80 record in 1974, one game better than the previous year. That mark was actually pretty good when one considers Griffith's continual cost-cutting. Besides Rodgers, Quilici had only two other coaches, Vern Morgan and Ralph Rowe. Quilici and Rodgers had to throw batting practice. The Twins' record looks even better when other factors are thrown into the mix.

"Those who want Quilici rehired point out that he can't perform for the players, that he has had a virtual 22-man roster with the part-time status of Killebrew, Oliva, and Randy Hundley, and that he hasn't had the benefit of an established pitching rotation (only Joe Decker hasn't missed at least one turn) for various reasons," wrote Bob Fowler in *The Sporting News*.[15]

Despite the speculation to the contrary, Griffith brought Quilici back for 1975. The gum and spit Quilici used to hold the team together and drag it toward .500 the previous two seasons no longer worked as the Twins limped to a 76-83 record, 20½ games behind Oakland. The pitching staff was a perfect ten — tenth in team ERA (4.05), runs allowed (736), earned runs (640), home runs allowed (137), and bases on balls (617).

Not surprisingly, Quilici was fired at the end of the 1975 season and was replaced by former Montreal Expos manager Gene Mauch, but he stayed with the organization as a broadcaster in 1976. Quilici had three stints behind the mike, 1976-77, 1980-82, and again in 1987.

Upon leaving baseball, Quilici found success in business and was active in the community. He partnered with a fraternity brother in a company that took over finance offices for car companies, and sales ballooned from $1.5 million to $120 million. His community service has covered many areas — he was chairman of the Minneapolis Park Foundation; worked in helping people with substance-abuse problems; worked as a fundraiser for the Twins community fund; and, with former teammate Harmon Killebrew, raised money for physically disabled youngsters. He also had a kidney transplant in 2012 and, as of 2014, was involved in raising awareness about organ donation.

On the personal front, Quilici married his second wife, Lila, in 2000. He had four children with his first wife, Penny.

Quilici's life came full circle in 2011. The man who grew up playing baseball in the Chicago parks system had a field named after him in north Minneapolis in August of that year. Frank Quilici Field is used by Major League Baseball's RBI (Reviving Baseball in Inner Cities) Program and, as of 2014, was the home park of the Grays of the Twin Cities Men's Baseball League.

SOURCES

Chicago Tribune

Minneapolis Star-Tribune

Pittsburgh Press

Traverse City (Michigan) *Record-Eagle*

Winona (Minnesota) *Daily News*

baseballbytheletters.blogspot.ca

coastalplain.com

Espn.go.com

milb.com

sabr.org/bioproj/person

Twinstrivia.com

Wilsontobs.com

NOTES

1 "Frank Makes 3 Points In His Talks to Kids," *The Sporting News* April 6, 1968.

2 Ibid.

3 At Class D-, the Appalachian League was below the Class D New York-Pennsylvania League

4 Tobs is short for Tobacconists. According to the team's website, the Tobacconists first played in the Eastern Carolina League from 1908 to 1910. The 2014 incarnation played in the Coastal Plain League, a summer league for collegiate players.

5 "Fenway Park? It Makes Those Minnesotans Mean," *Winona Daily News*, July 22, 1965.

6   Jeff Merron wrote in ESPN.com that Drysdale said to Alston, "I bet right now you wish I was Jewish, too." That quote appears in other articles as well.

7   This Associated Press article, entitled, "Grant Has First Outing Today," appeared in the *Daily Journal* (Fergus Falls, Minnesota), March 24, 1966.

8   The signature number of the Broadway musical *Gypsy*, based on the life of the famous stripper, was "Let Me Entertain You." In one of the lines from the song, Gypsy sings, "I'm very versatile."

9   Arno Goethel, "Quilici Is Swinging Quite a Bat; Twins Are Glad They Kept Him," *The Sporting News*, April 6, 1968.

10 Bob Fowler, "Quilici in Distressing Spot: Twins' Man Without a Job," *The Sporting News*, February 26, 1972.

11 The other coaches on the 1971 Twins were Morgan, Frank Crosetti, Marv Grissom, and Buck Rodgers.

12 Telephone interview conducted with Quilici by John Swol in May 2009 for twinstrivia.com

13 James Wilson, "Quilici, Twins' New Boss, Made Believer Out of Griffith," *Winona Daily News*, July 7, 1972.

14 John Swol telephone interview with Quilici, op. cit.

15 Bob Fowler, "Twin Fans Divided Into Two Camps Over Quilici," *The Sporting News*, September 14, 1974.

Rich Reese

BY CHIP GREENE

IF RICH REESE HAD AS MUCH SUCCESS in baseball as he later did in business, perhaps his major-league résumé would have been filled with All-Star appearances, batting titles, MVP awards, and World Series triumphs. As it was, his path to such acclaim was hindered by a succession of higher-profile players who kept him from a full-time job at his best position; a series of knee injuries; and an almost overnight diminution of his skills. By age 31, Reese's major-league career was over, and he began the second phase of his life, which ultimately took him to the top of his profession.

Richard Benjamin Reese was born on September 29, in Leipsic, Ohio. While it is of course customary to provide a birth year with any date of birth, in Reese's case there's a catch. According to Baseball-Reference.com and Retrosheet.org, Reese was born on that date in 1941. Yet delve into Reese's biography and that year is called into question. In March of 1963, as Reese was making a name for himself in the Class A minor leagues, he told a reporter from *The Sporting News* that he was actually born in 1942. Sometime around 1957, he explained, "when I attended a Tiger tryout camp, the minimum age was 16 and I was only 15, so I had to add a year."[1] Whether or not that statement is factual is difficult to corroborate, but it certainly says something about the savvy the young teenager must have possessed.

While Reese was born in Leipsic (in the northwestern part of the state), he grew up 12 miles north, in the town of Deshler, and it was there, at Deshler High School, that he became a schoolboy star. What influence his father, Howard, might have provided in Reese's athletic development, or to what degree he influenced his son's life at all, is unknown,[2] but in 1974 the press reported on Howard's untimely passing. On June 21 of that year, in Custar, Ohio, Howard, a 57-year old farmworker, was killed when a car in which he was a passenger crashed under the rear wheels of a tractor-trailer rig. The driver, who survived, was later charged with drunken driving. While in Howard's obituary the press made no mention of Reese's mother, Pauline, who died in 2006, it was reported that in addition to Rich, the elder Reese was also survived by son, James, one year older than Rich, and a daughter, Karen, a year younger.[3]

If Howard Reese's presence in his son's life is unclear, the ballplayer later credited another man with giving him a foundation in the game. Noting to the press in August 1969 that "I played Little League, Pony League, Babe Ruth League, American Legion, and summer league ball," Reese added that it was "my coach at Deshler High School, Gerold Parrett—who has won more than 1,000 games in 17 or 18 years—[who] really

Reese spent much of the 1965 season with the Double-A Charlotte Hornets. In limited action with the Twins, he managed two hits. The Twins starting first baseman in 1969 and 1970, Reese batted a career-high .322 in 1969. (Photo courtesy of Minnesota Twins Baseball Club).

got me started right in baseball. He was quite an influence at a critical time in my boyhood and I'll never forget him."[4]

Reese graduated from Deshler High School in 1959. Three years later, he began his professional baseball career. Accounts of his years in between are scarce, but by all appearances, once he graduated, Reese spent time working in Leipsic for the Christman Brothers Lumber Company.[5] At the same time, however, he probably continued in baseball, playing for an American Legion team; for in 1969, he explained, "Because I got a break in my age group, I played Legion ball for five years."[6]

Perhaps that's where the Tigers found him. If Reese made any impression on the Detroit organization during his tryout several years earlier, the team may have kept an eye on the teenager as he developed. The Tigers signed him before the 1962 season, and it didn't take him long to get noticed. A left-handed first baseman both in the field and at-bat, Reese split time that first season between the Thomasville (Georgia) Tigers, in the Class D Georgia-Florida League, and the Montgomery (Alabama) Rebels, also Class D, in the Alabama-Florida League. While he showed promise at the plate (.328/.441/.421 in 73 games at Thomasville), it was on defense that Reese stood out. For what would be the first of four consecutive minor-league seasons Reese led the Georgia-Florida League in fielding percentage. (In addition, he also led the Northern League, at Bismarck, in 1963; the Carolina League, at Wilson, in 1964; and the Southern League, at Charlotte, in 1965.) Indeed, it would primarily be his defense that propelled Reese to the major leagues; that and his workmanlike attitude and all-out hustle.

In November 1962 the 20-year-old Reese (assuming a 1942 birth date) was drafted from Detroit by the Minnesota Twins.[7] The following spring he began what became a five-year climb through the Twins' minor-league system. In 1967, his first full season with the Twins, managers Cal Ermer and Sam Mele commented on the traits that most impressed them about Reese. Mele called him an "outstanding first baseman, smooth with feet and glove—possibly better than Vic Power,"[8] who was then widely recognized as one of the premier glove men in the game. Further, noted coach Ermer, who later in the year took over for Mele, "Reese is so aggressive that he can help you in many ways. He can bunt to get on base when you need a run; he can steal a base for you; and he'll always hit the ball somewhere for you. … He hardly ever strikes out."[9] No doubt those attributes were part of what drew the Twins to Reese in the first place.

If Reese eventually became fond of the Twins organization, he was initially disillusioned with his new team. "I was disappointed at the time," he later recalled of the organizational change, "because I was raised in Deshler, Ohio, about 30 miles south of Toledo [which is only an hour south of Detroit], and had been a Detroit Tiger fan. But I've been very happy about my treatment here [in Minnesota], and of course, I've had a better opportunity. Norm Cash is pretty well set at Detroit's first base."[10]

As Reese opened his career with the Twins organization in 1963, the team was in the midst of a revolving logjam at first base that would have a direct impact on their young prospect's career. Beginning in 1961, the team's first year in the Twin Cities after relocating from Washington, and lasting throughout Reese's tenure with the team, Harmon Killebrew, Vic Power, Bob Allison, and Don Mincher all saw significant playing time at first base, with seemingly annual shuffling of the sluggers through first base, third base, and the three outfield positions. Throughout, Reese would find himself struggling to become management's everyday solution at the position, while also working hard to learn the nuances of left field—anything just to get and stay in the regular lineup.

First, though, he spent another three seasons in the minors. If 1963 with Bismarck-Mandan (North Dakota) in the Class A Northern League marked for Reese another successful performance on the field, off the diamond he experienced two other notable events. First, on September 15, at Leipsic's Methodist Church, he married Marinell Fretwell; the two honeymooned in Niagara Falls. Then, on October 1, Reese reported for six months of Army training, the beginning of what became a six-year military commitment that ended in July 1969.[11]

By 1964 the Twins were a veteran club. Coming off a 91-win third-place finish the previous season, they appeared poised for a World Series push. That year, while Allison and Mincher spent the lion's share of the season at first base in Minneapolis, Reese spent another season in Class A, this time with the Wilson (North Carolina) Tobs in the Carolina League. After a season in which he batted .301 and again fielded flawlessly, the Twins called up Reese for the final month of the regular season. On September 4, at home against the Boston Red Sox, he entered the game as a pinch-runner and remained in the game at first base, recording three putouts in three chances in his first major-league game. It was his only defensive appearance during a brief stay. In all, Reese came to the plate seven times in 10 games but failed to get a hit. It was an inauspicious debut. Nonetheless, Reese had made it to the major leagues.

That winter, for the first of two consecutive seasons, Reese played in the Florida Instructional League. The previous June, as part of a three-team trade, the Twins had traded Vic Power to the Los Angeles Angels, so the door was open for Reese to win a roster spot in spring training, which he did. With Power gone, Killebrew opened the season at first base, and he and Mincher eventually shared most of the first-base duties, as Allison took over in left field. In the end, there was little room for Reese. Between April 12 and May 7 he played in just 10 games and got just three at-bats, all as a pinch-hitter. In one of those at-bats, on April 23 at Detroit, he doubled for his first major-league hit. He played just six games at first base as a late-inning defensive replacement. On May 15, in a move the Twins made to reduce their roster, Reese was sent to the Charlotte Hornets, in the Double-A Southern League.

Manager Sam Mele agonized over the decision to send Reese down, telling the press, Reese is "always in the game, even when he's on the bench. ... He was helping to steal signals, yelling at baserunners. Sending a player like that down is hard for a manager."[12]

Understandably, the demotion was hard on Reese, too, and his performance showed it. Although he again led the league in fielding, his batting average in Double-A was a scant .226 and his OPS (On Base Plus Slugging) a dismal .630. Two years later, Reese hinted that conditions outside the game may have impacted his play, recalling, "It was hard for me when I was sent to the minors in 1965."[13] Beyond his poor hitting, "I had personal problems that no one knew about. I even had an ulcer over it."[14] (Reese's personal problems may have been a breakup with his first wife.) His spirits were surely dampened further when at the end of the season the Twins failed to protect him from the draft and sent him to their Triple-A affiliate in the Pacific Coast League, the Denver Bears. By all appearances, the slick-fielding first baseman's career with the Twins seemed in jeopardy.

Reese's 1966 season at Denver changed everything. Apparently free of his personal issues, Reese went on an unprecedented batting tear that lasted the whole season. Although the Twins took him to spring training under his Denver contract, he was one of the first players farmed out despite a .375 batting average. Yet Reese immediately proved he belonged at the higher level. In his first game, at Oklahoma City, Reese broke a 1-1 tie with an eighth-inning home run, one of 11 he hit that year. Moreover, batting second most of the year, Reese finished the season with a slash line of .327/.377/.485, and finished second in the league in batting, finishing just .003 behind league champion Walt Williams.

Beyond that, he also learned to play a new position. Whether by design or circumstance, with two power-hitting first basemen already on the Denver roster, Reese played 117 of his 138 games in left field, an "experiment"[15] that would soon be duplicated with the Twins.

It proved an invaluable season in Reese's maturation. The following spring, reflecting on his Denver stay, Reese credited not only the Bears' manager, Cal Ermer, but also another future Twins manager with helping him improve. At Denver, Reese said, "I learned to bunt, and I bunted for about 10 hits. ... I learned to sting an inside pitch and pull it toward the first baseman.... If you just hit it hard, you've got a chance for the ball to get through for a hit. Before, I always took the same even swing.... And I learned a lot about running bases—under Coach Billy Martin in the spring and also under Ermer. ... I'm not considered fast, but I'm a good baserunner now. ... I stole 14 bases in 18 attempts at Denver."[16]

Reese never played another season in the minor leagues.

By the spring of 1967, Reese's future with the Twins was seemingly restored. In the fall, two events had served to bring that future more clearly into focus. After the Denver season, Reese joined Twins infielders Zoilo Versailles and Ron Clark on the Aragua team of the Venezuelan League, where he split his time between first base and left field (he also played with the Boer Indians, in the Nicaraguan League); and in December the Twins traded first baseman Don Mincher to the California Angels. Of Reese's previous competition for first base, only Killebrew and Allison remained. But they weren't going anywhere.

Anxious for a full-time role, and feeling that left field was his best avenue to get there, Reese arrived early to spring training in 1967, reporting with the pitchers and catchers. That season the Twins would start Ted Uhlaender in center field and Tony Oliva in right, so Bob Allison became Reese's main competition in left field. "I'm going all out to win that job. Nothing else matters,"[17] Reese said.

At 6-feet-3-inches and 190 pounds, Reese was a big man, although never a classic power hitter. (Among his teammates, Reese was called PeeWee, a nod to the Dodgers Hall of Famer who bore the same last name.) Throughout the winter he had lifted weights, focusing primarily on his forearms and biceps, and now he appeared bigger physically, particularly in the arms, although he maintained a slim 34-inch waist. Early on, though, came signs of knee trouble. He had injured his right knee the previous season at Denver. Then a sprained ankle suffered during the first week of training camp exacerbated the knee trouble, as Reese accommodated his running to protect the very painful ankle. Still, he played through the injuries, determined to win a job.

In the end, the knee was not a distraction, for Reese spent most of the season as a pinch-hitter. In 95 games played, he made just 13 starts, nine in left field to spell Allison, and four at first base as Killebrew's backup. When Sam Mele was replaced in early June as manager by Cal Ermer, who promised to "use a lot of players,"[18] the feeling was that Reese's playing time might increase, given Ermer's knowledge of his abilities. But Reese was called for two weeks of Army Reserve training at Camp McCoy, Wisconsin, and when he returned he was largely forgotten. (During his service, the Twins flew Reese from camp to Metropolitan Stadium for several night games, and once to Cleveland for a weekend series. As he wasn't able to fly back to camp late at night after the games, Reese stayed at his apartment in Minneapolis for a few hours of sleep, arose at 3:00 a.m. for a 4:00 a.m. flight, then landed at an airfield near Tomah, Wisconsin, in time for 5:30 a.m. reveille. At camp he worked in the orderly room of Headquarters of the 367th Engineering Battalion.[19])

As the 1968 season dawned, Reese finally figured prominently in the Twins' plans. "Reese has to be given the opportunity," reasoned owner Calvin Griffith, "and the only spot I can think of for him is left field, where he could platoon with Allison,"[20] whose knees were giving him trouble. In October Reese had gone to the Mayo Clinic and addressed his own knee problems when he underwent surgery to repair torn ligaments that had affected cartilage in his right knee. According to Griffith, Reese was "sewn up good as new."[21]

One would never have known that by Reese's hitting, however. In a year during which the Twins would sink to seventh place, he got off to a miserable start. By July 1 he had started just 13 games in left field and produced a .176 batting average, with one home run. On May 8 in Oakland, he was called on to pinch-hit with two outs in the top of the ninth inning and was called out on strikes, the 11th strikeout and final out of Catfish Hunter's perfect game. Reese couldn't have sunk any lower.

Then, in an instant, his season turned around, although not exactly in the way he would have hoped. Despite a .204 average and just 13 home runs at the All-Star break, Killebrew was named the American League's starting first baseman for the All-Star Game, held on July 9 in Houston. In the third inning, while stretching to field a low throw from shortstop Jim Fregosi, Killebrew tore his left hamstring, an injury that appeared to be one that would sideline the slugger for the remainder of the season. So, despite battling a recurrence of his right knee problems (the knee had been acting up so much that he was considering asking for another operation during the season so he'd be ready for winter ball), Reese replaced Killebrew at first base. "With Harmon out," Reese said, "I've put that [another surgery] out of my mind now. ... I've been in and out of a Minnesota uniform since 1964, and to tell the truth I still haven't played enough to know whether I belong up here or not."[22] Over the remainder of the season, moved to second place in the batting order, Reese tallied a .285 average, to finish the season .259/.301/.352 in 126 games. Finally, after four years of finding his way blocked at first base, it appeared Reese's time had arrived.

Every major leaguer can usually point to a major-league mentor, someone who had faith in his abilities, tweaked his performance, and gave him the confidence to succeed. In Reese's case, that was Billy Martin. After 1961, his final season as a player, Martin joined the Twins as a roving minor-league scout. In Reese's first year in the organization, the two met. "In 1963," Reese later recalled, "when I was drafted by the Twins, a couple of guys didn't like the way I was swinging the bat. I didn't want to change, so I had Billy throw batting practice for an hour until his arm was just hanging. ... Billy was the one who told me when I was being used as a pinch-hitter to get my swings and be aggressive. He always believed I could hit";[23] "he talked with me about fundamentals. ... He was really great. He gave me a lot of time—and me, just a green kid. I really appreciated it."[24]

In 1969 Martin became the Twins' manager. He assured Reese that he'd see lots of action at first base. The previous October, Reese had returned to the Mayo Clinic for another procedure on his right knee, this one more complicated than the previous one. This time the surgeon had to shorten and attach ligaments, after which Reese spent six weeks in a cast and two more on crutches. Nevertheless, by spring training he was ready to start the season.

The 1969 season proved to be the pinnacle of Reese's career. After starting at first base on Opening Day (with Killebrew at third base), Reese played 132 games that season, 118 at first base. He hit brilliantly. In the early part of the season, Martin platooned him, batting him only against right-handers. By July, however, Martin put him in the lineup against left-handers, too, and Reese responded with the greatest performance of his career. At the All-Star break his average was .328, he had produced 23 multi-hit games, and also had smashed 10 of what would be a career-best 16 home runs. By season's end Reese's slash line read .322/.362/.513. Had he played a full season with that line, Reese would have finished second to teammate Rod Carew for the batting title, but with just 451 plate appearances, he fell short of the required 502. Still, never again would he approach that kind of production.

In a season of big hits, one of Reese's biggest took place on August 3, at home against the Baltimore Orioles. Baltimore lefty Dave McNally had won 15 consecutive games, and another victory would tie him with Smoky Joe Wood, Lefty Grove, Walter Johnson, and Schoolboy Rowe as the only American League pitchers to win 16 in a row. In the bottom of the seventh, with two outs and the bases loaded, Martin sent Reese to the plate as a pinch-hitter. It was the first time Reese had ever faced McNally. Asked after the game why Reese, a left-handed swinger, faced McNally, Martin replied, "It was Reese because he hits left-handers."[25] (Reese batted .322 against lefties for the season.) With the count 3-and-2, McNally threw a waist-high fastball, Reese turned on it and hit a home run to left-center field, the first grand slam of his career. McNally lost the game. It was that kind of magical season.

There wouldn't be another. For 1970, Bill Rigney replaced Billy Martin as the manager, hoping to repeat the Twins first-place finish of a year ago. He had high hopes for Reese, envisioning him as integral to the everyday lineup. "We need someone in that fifth spot who is so good pitchers won't be able to walk Killebrew and Oliva. I believe that man is Reese. With him there, Harmon and Tony will be seeing a lot of good pitches."[26]

Reese, though, struggled to repeat his singular performance. Finally the team's everyday first baseman, he pressed and got off to a terrible start, batting just .197 on May 1. Although he steadily improved as the season progressed, Reese was platooned through much of the early season as Rick Renick saw increased playing time at third base and Killebrew shifted back to first. In the end, despite almost 100 more at-bats than the previous season, Reese's .261/.332/.371 production was deemed a disappointment by the Twins front office, and they determined to return Killebrew to first base full-time in 1971. During the winter meetings, Griffith and Rigney tried unsuccessfully to trade Reese, and he was one of four players to receive a pay cut for 1971, from $30,000 to $25,000. That season, his performance declined even further, as his batting average plummeted to .219 and he managed just 329 at-bats in 120 games. His brief stay as the Twins' regular first baseman was over.

As his baseball career wound down, Reese positioned himself for life after the game. During the offseason he held a position in sales and public relations for the Hamm Brewing Company in Minneapolis. Also, for two years he served as chairman of Minnesota's Easter Seals Society, which honored him and Bob Allison for their volunteer work. Additionally, during spring training in 1971, Reese had his own radio show, sending daily reports back to Minneapolis, interviewing players, and updating listeners on the progress of the club.

The 1972 season was Reese's last with any significant playing time. He once again became primarily a pinch-hitter. On July 9 he set an American League record and tied a major-league mark when he blasted the third pinch-hit grand slam of his career, connecting against Lindy McDaniel of the Yankees.

Reese's final season, 1973, was a homecoming of sorts. After his awful 1972 performance, the Twins on November 30 sold his contract to the Tigers, where Billy Martin had assumed the managerial reins. If Martin thought Reese would be a wonderful reclamation project, Reese instead proved that he was through. Despite collecting his 500th hit on May 28, Reese sank to a .137 batting average in 102 at-bats. Admitting their mistake, the Tigers released Reese on August 17, and he was perhaps sentimentally re-signed by the Twins, just the second Minnesota player to return to a Twins uniform after being released. In 23 at-bats, Reese produced four hits, including his final home run. On September 27 Reese became Nolan Ryan's 383rd strikeout victim as he broke Sandy Koufax's season record. Reese retired at the end of the season.

Reese entered the business world, becoming the Northwest area sales manager for the James Beam Distilling Co., for which he covered Minnesota and North and South Dakota.

In 2003 Reese retired as CEO of Jim Beam Brands, headquartered in the Chicago suburb of Deerfield, Illinois.

SOURCES

In addition to the sources cited in the notes, the author consulted the Rich Reese player file at the National Baseball Hall of Fame Library, Cooperstown, New York, retrosheet.org, and baseball-reference.com.

The author expresses sincerest appreciation to SABR member Bill Mortell for his diligent genealogical research.

NOTES

1 *The Sporting News*, March 23, 1963, 16.

2 The author attempted to contact Rich Reese for an interview, but was unsuccessful.

3 *Toledo* (Ohio) *Blade*, June 23, 1963.

4 *Christian Science Monitor*, August 27, 1969.

5 *Lima* (Ohio) *News*, September 30, 1963.

6 *Christian Science Monitor*, August 27, 1969.

7   *The Sporting News*, July 28, 1968.
8   *The Sporting News*, March 18, 1967.
9   Ibid.
10 Christian Science Monitor, August 27, 1969.
11 It's unclear how long Reese's marriage to Marinell lasted. While the marriage produced no children, Reese later married Marit Anna Johnson, eight years his junior, and that union produced three children. In researching this biography, the author left a voicemail at the Reese residence in Arizona. The voicemail greeting was that of a female who announced "You've reached the Reeses. Please leave a message." Presumably, Reese's second marriage has endured to 2014.
12 *The Sporting News*, March 18, 1967.
13 Ibid.
14 Ibid.
15 *The Sporting News*, August 3, 1968.
16 *The Sporting News*, March 18, 1967.
17 Ibid.
18 *The Sporting News*, August 19, 1967.
19 *The Sporting News*, July 8, 1967.
20 *The Sporting News*, January 20, 1968.
21 *The Sporting News*, October 28, 1967.
22 *The Sporting News*, July 28, 1968.
23 *The Sporting News*, August 9, 1969.
24 *Christian Science Monitor*, August 27, 1969.
25 *The Sporting News*, August 16, 1969.
26 *The Sporting News*, January 9, 1971.

Garry Roggenburk

BY MARK ARMOUR

AN ACCOMPLISHED TWO-SPORT college athlete, Garry Roggenburk saw his baseball career ultimately shortened by an elbow injury suffered after his rookie major-league season. A tall, hard-throwing left-handed pitcher, he had one healthy and effective big-league year, and then six more trying to hang on with three different big-league teams. But even late in his career, with two surgeries behind him, Roggenburk remained upbeat about his job. "I have no regrets," he said. "Baseball has been good to me. I've been to Hawaii, Puerto Rico, the West Coast. I've been to just about every major city in the United States."[1] Once he stopped playing, he continued to find success in and out of baseball.

Garry Earl Roggenburk was born in Cleveland on April 16, 1940. He starred in basketball and baseball at St. Ignatius High School (where he played with Mike Hegan, a future big-league teammate), earning all-state honors in basketball in 1958. Moving on to the University of Dayton, he again played both sports, again earning more accolades on the hardwood. In three varsity seasons, the 6-foot-6, 195-pound forward led his team in scoring each year, hauled in a school-record 32 rebounds in a game against Miami of Ohio as a sophomore, and earned All-American honors as a senior while leading his club to the NIT title. "He has phenomenal timing and great spring," said coach Tom Blackburn. "When he jumps, his hands are always above the rim even though we play him out in the corner."[2] In baseball he set school records (that still stood as of 2014) for single season (0.33) and career (0.75) ERA.

After earning a B.S. in education, Roggenburk spurned an offer from the Philadelphia Warriors of the NBA (who had drafted him in the fourth round) and instead signed a contract with the Minnesota Twins, receiving a $12,000 bonus. "I had to make a decision," he recalled, "but I never really considered basketball. It seemed like I had my mind made up. It was really always set on baseball."[3]

Roggenburk began his career with Erie in 1962, and he proved more than up to the competition of the New York-Penn League, finishing 13-4 in 18 starts, with a 2.07 ERA. In his second professional game, he came within one out of a no-hitter when a groundball bounced over the third baseman's head. He was named the league's Player of the Month in July. After the season, he played for the Twins' Florida Instructional League club, winning three of four decisions.

"I like Roggenburk very much," said Twins executive Joe Haynes in spring training of 1963. "He has a live fastball and good curve and showed me a good change of pace in the Instructional League."[4] Nonetheless, the Twins spent time that spring revising Roggenburk's

The Twins called up left-handed reliever Garry Roggenburk in midseason in 1965. In his second of five seasons in the majors, he made 12 appearances and won once. (Photo courtesy of Minnesota Twins Baseball Club).

straight-up easy delivery and taught him to use his legs more, to push off the mound and strengthen his stride. He had four pitches — fastball, curve, slider, and sinker, and fielded his position well. "You don't have to worry about him on bunts," said manager Sam Mele. "He gets off that mound like a cat."[5]

Under the rules of the time, Roggenburk had to either make the Twins roster in 1963 or be subject to a first-year player draft at the end of the year. The club elected to put him on the big-league pitching staff. After starting the year as a situational left-hander, he got longer bullpen stints and even a couple of spot starts as the year went on. He pitched quite well — a 2.16 ERA in 50 innings — and especially well in relief, a role in which his ERA was 1.44.

After the season Roggenburk headed back to Florida to again pitch in the Instructional League, but he soon developed a bone chip in his pitching elbow and was sent home after a few weeks. He pitched in spring training in March 1964 but again came up lame, and underwent surgery in April. The team was optimistic that he would return in midseason, but other than a July exhibition game his injury and recovery cost him all of the 1964 season. He later admitted considering a return to basketball, but when his arm recovered he decided to stick it out.

Roggenburk returned in 1965, but the Twins sent him to Triple-A Denver to start the season. Working mostly out of the bullpen, he put up a 9-3 record with a 3.22 ERA in 81 innings. In late July he was recalled to the Twins, joining a first-place team on its way to the American League pennant. His best outing came on July 28, when he relieved an injured Camilo Pasqual and pitched 5⅓ innings of one-run ball to earn the win. Over the last 10 weeks of the season Roggenburk pitched 12 games in relief, and posted a 3.43 ERA over 21 innings. He did not pitch in the World Series, which the Twins lost in seven games to the Dodgers.

In 1966 Roggenburk divided the first four months of the season between Minnesota (where he pitched 12 times in relief) and Triple-A Denver (where 11 of his 12 appearances were starts). He struggled in both places, and on September 7 he was sold to the Boston Red Sox. "I feel fine," he told a reporter at the time of the deal. "There is nothing the matter with my arm. Haven't had a minute's trouble with it. Happy to be with the Red Sox."[6] On September 18 he got into his first game with his new club, pitching a third of an inning at Fenway Park and allowing a hit and a walk. The Red Sox were headed for a ninth-place finish, and the 26-year-old was no longer the hot prospect he had been a few years earlier.

As it happened, the 1967 Red Sox had an unexpectedly great season, capturing a surprising pennant on the final day of the season. Roggenburk, however, spent the entire season with the Red Sox' Triple-A affiliate in Toronto. In 21 games (17 starts), he finished 5-10 but with a 2.60 ERA in 121 innings. "They didn't score too many runs off me," he said. "It was the worst hitting team I've ever been on."[7] Though the Red Sox called up several pitchers during the season, Roggenburk stayed in the minors despite his strong pitching.

After an excellent spring, Roggenburk made the Red Sox to start the 1968 season. "He is faster than you think," said an impressed manager Dick Williams. "He's much faster this year than last spring."[8] After pitching in just four games (two runs in 8⅓ innings), once again Roggenburk underwent surgery on his left elbow. "It's hard when you're not playing," said the frustrated pitcher. "You have to contribute something to feel like you're part of the team."[9]

In mid-July Roggenburk began working out with the team again. "I'll run, throw, maybe pitch some batting practice," he said. "And I'll have some treatments on my arm. I'm really happy."[10] Nonetheless, when he was well enough to pitch he was sent to Louisville, where he finished the season with just four relief appearances.

Roggenburk married Karen Dorenkott on October 6, 1962, and the couple raised a daughter and two sons. "Sure it's tough moving around," he said in 1968, "especially when you have kids in school. But it's hard for me to visualize staying in one place. I've never really settled down. I know during the winter it gets to me. Around February you're ready to go down to spring training and get out of the snow. My wife looks forward to it, too. I know when I get out of baseball I'll miss that."[11]

He headed back to Louisville to start 1969, and he won five of his six starts before another recall to Boston on May 25. He pitched in seven games for the Red Sox (8.38 ERA in 9⅔ innings) before being sold to the expansion Seattle Pilots in late June. He pitched seven more games for Seattle, including four starts (his first in the majors since two starts as a rookie six years earlier). On July 8 Roggenburk pitched a complete-game five-hitter to beat the California Angels. After a few mediocre relief appearances at the end of the month, he abruptly retired and returned home to Cleveland. "I plan to either teach school or go into some kind of sales work," he said. He had no complaints about his pitching, or about the Pilots organization.[12]

Roggenburk's sudden departure from the Pilots led to an interesting observation in his teammate Jim Bouton's book *Ball Four*, a diary that largely chronicles Bouton's 1969 season pitching for Seattle. "I know Roggenburk has his four years in on the pension," wrote Bouton, "and has a college degree and planned to go into teaching this fall. The trouble is, when you're a marginal player and you walk out, you can't come back. No one runs after you. You get marked down as a nut and it's all over. I don't know if Garry fully appreciated that fact when he left. Sometimes it's better not to act. Sometimes it's better just to sit around and grouse."[13]

Still just 29, Roggenburk's baseball playing career was over.

After baseball Roggenburk resettled in Cleveland, where he worked as a real-estate appraiser. He also coached the baseball team at Cleveland State University from 1972 to 1978. He spent several seasons coaching in the Red Sox minor-league system, including six years (1978-1983) as the general manager of the Winter Haven Red Sox. As of 2014 he was living in Avon, a suburb of Cleveland.

Roggenburk was inducted into the University of Dayton's Athletics Hall of Fame in 1970 and was named to the school's All-Century Team in 2004. In 2012 he was inducted into the Ohio Basketball Hall of Fame.

NOTES

1. Bob Sales, "A Happy Time For Roggenburk," *Boston Globe*, July 11, 1968, 28.
2. Tom Fitzpatrick, "Dayton Fans Dance to New Victory Tune Over Flashy Flyers," *The Sporting News*, February 24, 1960, 5.
3. Sales, "A Happy Time For Roggenburk."
4. Arno Goethel, "Twins School Bonikowski, Stange to Solve Hill Puzzle," *The Sporting News*, March 2, 1963.
5. Max Nichols, "Mele Handing Tough Rescuer Missions to Fast-Learner Garry," *The Sporting News*, August 3, 1963.
6. Cliff Keane, "Lefty Roggenburk Purchased by Sox," *Boston Globe*, September 8, 1966, 45.
7. Ray Fitzgerald, "Lefty Roggenburk Impresses Williams, *Boston Globe*, March 8, 1968, 29.
8. Fitzgerald, "Lefty Roggenburk."
9. Sales, "A Happy Time For Roggenburk."
10. Sales, "A Happy Time For Roggenburk."
11. Sales, "A Happy Time For Roggenburk."
12. Hy Zimmerman, "Roggenburk Surprises Pilots by Quitting," *Seattle Times*, July 31, 1969, 65.
13. Jim Bouton with Leonard Shecter (ed.), *Ball Four — My Life and Hard Times Throwing the Knuckleball in the Big Leagues* (New York: World, 1970), 280-81.

Rich Rollins

BY RICK SCHABOWSKI

RICH ROLLINS' 10-YEAR CAREER in the major leagues included two All-Star Game appearances and playing in the 1965 World Series with the Minnesota Twins.

Richard John Rollins was born on April 16, 1938, in Mount Pleasant, Pennsylvania, near Pittsburgh. His father, a welder, was ambidextrous, and played baseball in coal mining leagues. The family later moved to the Cleveland area, where Rich played second base, third base and catcher for his Parma High School team, and playing second base for an American Legion team. He also sold popcorn at Cleveland Indians games. Commenting on his athletic ability, Rollins thought, "I knew I had to do something about my strength because I wasn't a natural. I wasn't a natural at all. We had a high school graduating class of 500 kids and I was the smallest kid in the class."[1]

After high school, Rollins enrolled to attend Ohio University, but then was offered a baseball scholarship to Kent State University. I had already enrolled at Ohio University when Matt Resnick, baseball coach at Kent, offered me the scholarship, even though he hadn't seen me play," Rollins once said. "I was recommended to him by Nobby Lewandowski, a pitcher in the Twins farm system who was attending Kent. Resnick and Moose Paskert, the frosh coach, helped me so much I could never repay them. They kept me going and told me I had a chance, in spite of scouting reports that I was too small (5-feet-10), couldn't hit the curveball, couldn't make the double play, and had a weak arm."[2]

At Kent State, Rollins was a three-time selection for the All-Mid-American Conference team at second base, and his career .383 batting average as of 2014 was bested only by Thurman Munson. Playing alongside Rollins at shortstop on the Kent State team was future major leaguer Gene Michael. After graduation Rollins planned to return to Parma High School to teach health and physical education, but things changed quickly.

There wasn't any amateur baseball draft at the time, and Rollins hadn't drawn any attention from any scout except Washington Senators scout Floyd Baker, who invited him to a tryout at Griffith Stadium in June 1960. Baker was impressed with Rollins, telling a sportswriter, "I liked his attitude. I knew he was willing to pay the price, to work hard."[3] Senators owner Calvin Griffith and his scouts offered Rollins an opportunity to play for the Senators' Class D team in Fort Walton Beach, Florida. Rollins, believing that at 22 he was too old to begin in Class D, wouldn't sign unless they sent him to Class B Wilson (North Carolina).[4] The scouts refused, so Rollins flew home. When he got home, a phone message from the Senators informed

Rollins enjoyed a career-year as a rookie third baseman for the Twins in 1962, batting .298 and knocked in 96 runs. After starting most of the season at third base and batting .249 in 1965, Rollins was replaced in late-September by Killebrew who returned from an injured elbow. (Photo courtesy of Minnesota Twins Baseball Club).

him that a plane would be leaving for North Carolina that evening, and he would receive a $6,000 bonus.

Rollins played under manager Jack McKeon and batted .341 in 62 games at second base for the Wilson Tobs. "And McKeon gave me a break." Rollins said. "When I reported, we had 30 players. Jack juggled the lineup by putting about 10 on the inactive list every night but kept me in there. He got a telegram telling him to send me to Fort Walton Beach but he did not want to let me go."[5]

Rollins spent the offseason serving six months in the Army, and his weight ballooned to almost 200 pounds. After beginning the 1961 season with Syracuse (International League) and after pinch-hitting once in three weeks, he was sent to Class A Charlotte (Sally League). Manager Ellis Clary got Rollins back in shape and improved his defense by hitting him 100 grounders a day for a week. Rollins batted .270, playing four games in the outfield before shifting to third base for the next 32 games.

The Twins called Rollins up, and he made his major-league debut on June 16, 1961, against the Chicago White Sox at Comiskey Park. In the second inning, facing Don Larsen, he flied out to right field. In the eighth inning he stroked his first major-league hit, a single off Early Wynn. Rollins got only 13 more at-bats the rest of the season, the highlight being a three-run double off the Angels' Ron Kline on July 6. "I sat on the bench most of the time, but it was a good experience because I got to learn the ropes and what these guys were going through," he said.[6]

Rollins' first season with the Twins was the final season for Twins infielder Billy Martin. Martin constantly criticized Rollins, telling him he couldn't go to his left and didn't belong on the field. Rollins said he was so incensed at Martin's comments that he was ready to punch him in the nose. "I got into more arguments with Billy Martin than anyone I ever met on the face of the earth, before or since, but the thing about Billy was the next day it was forgotten," he said.[7] Martin later told Rollins' father that he rode Rollins because he knew Rollins had the talent to play in the major leagues.

During spring training in 1962, three Twins shortstops were hampered by injuries, so manager Sam Mele inserted Rollins at shortstop. He made the most of the opportunity, leading the Twins with a .400 average. When the regular shortstop, Zoilo Versalles, returned to the lineup, Rollins was moved over to third base.

Rollins had a great season in 1962 for the Twins. He batted .298 with 96 RBIs, 23 doubles, and 16 home runs, and finished eighth in the American League MVP voting. He started at third base for the American League in both All-Star Games, receiving more votes than any other player. In the first game, played at D.C. Stadium on July 10, Rollins went 1-for-2, scored a run, and was hit by a pitch. In the second game, in Chicago's Wrigley Field on July 30, Rollins went 1-for-3. In a vote by his teammates, Rollins was voted the Twins' Most Valuable Player for the season.

The 1962 season was also memorable for Rollins outside of baseball. "I was rooming in Minneapolis in '62. One o'clock at night, I get this knock on the door. I'm up reading a book; I'm the only one in the apartment and this gal is at the door, in tears, and her father had just been killed in an automobile accident. She just needed someone to talk to. She knocked on the door, and we went out for coffee. We got back at 3 o'clock in the morning, and that was the first time I met her."[8] On February 9, 1963, Rollins and former United Airlines stewardess Lynn Maher of Newport Beach, California, were married. They had three sons and three daughters, who presented them with 11 grandchildren.

Expectations were high for Rollins for the 1963 season. Twins president Calvin Griffith predicted, "I think he'll have a better year in 1963 because he's intelligent and calm in every situation. He's not a flash in the pan."[9] Rollins had a setback before the season started when he was hit in the jaw by a pitch from the Tigers' Paul Foytack in an exhibition game in Knoxville, Tennessee. He was unable to eat solid food for a time, and didn't make his first start in a regular-season game until April 20 against the Chicago White Sox. Despite

Rich Rollins (Photo courtesy of Minnesota Twins Baseball Club).

the injury he played flawlessly in the infield through the end of the month. Because of his broken jaw, the Twins trainer, George Lentz, sat next to Rollins during team flights with wire cutters, to open Rollins' jaw if he became airsick.

Despite all the issues, Rollins finished the 1963 season with a .307 average, good for third place in the AL behind Carl Yastrzemski and Al Kaline. Before the 1964 season began, he went to the Mayo Clinic in Rochester, Minnesota, to get treated for a calcium deposit on his hip that had been bothering him. Rollins' batting average dropped to .270 in 1964, but he posted a .319 average with runners in scoring position and he led the AL in triples with 10. Rollins played in 140 games for the American League champion Twins in 1965, posting a .249 batting average. A prized possession that Rollins took home was his champagne-drenched, ripped uniform from the pennant-winning game. In the World Series, Rollins was limited to three pinch-hitting appearances, while Killebrew started all seven games in the hot corner.

Harmon Killebrew started the 1966 season as the Twins' third baseman, and Rollins didn't see much action the first month of the season, batting only twice.

He managed to break into the lineup in May, but slumped as a result of a virus. However, when he returned to the lineup in June, Rollins' play was so impressive that Killebrew was moved to left field. Rollins remarked, "I'm swinging as well as I ever have in my life, every time I go to the plate, I have that feeling I'm going to hit the ball hard," he said.[10] On June 9 Rollins, Zoilo Versalles, Mincher, Killebrew, and Tony Oliva made baseball history as each hit a home run in the seventh inning against the Kansas City Athletics. Rollins slumped in July, and finished the season appearing in just 90 games, batting .245.

During the offseason, Rollins and former teammate Bernie Allen, who were already partners in the insurance business, expanded their careers by going into the snowmobile business. Although Allen had been dealt to the Washington Senators, they maintained their friendship and their business endeavors.

With Don Mincher being traded and Harmon Killebrew being moved back to first base, Rollins had a chance to win back his starting job at third base in 1967. Overcoming an infected hand that sidelined him for a week of spring training, and a badly bruised knee and bruised foot, Rollins batted .333 with six homers and 12 RBIs in 17 games, and won the third-base job. But he suffered a knee injury in April that sidelined him for three weeks, and an arthritic hip condition forced him to play in great pain. Ron Clark and Cesar Tovar filled in at third base, but Rollins still had some big moments that season. On July 16 in the second game of a doubleheader against the California Angels, he blasted a game-winning home run in the ninth to give the Twins a 7-6 victory. He hit an eighth-inning home run to give the Twins a 3-2 victory over Washington on August 8, and he drove in all three runs in a 3-2 victory over the White Sox on August 13. Rollins played in 109 games, batting .245 in 339 at-bats.

The knee problems really frustrated Rollins. "Sometimes the pain was so bad it just didn't seem worth it to go out to the ballpark," he said.[11] After the season the injury led Rollins to inform Calvin Griffith that he was going to retire. Griffith talked him into going to the Mayo Clinic, where surgeons removed lateral cartilage from his right knee, and noticed that he had an earlier torn ligament that had repaired itself. After a period of rehab, he decided not to retire.

The starting third baseman's job in 1968 was between Rollins, Ron Clark, Tovar, Graig Nettles and Cesar Tovar. Rollins had a setback during spring training when he experienced a sleepless night due to knee pain. He went to the Twins trainer Doc Lentz, and had the knee aspirated to remove fluid from it. Rollins also had a bout with intestinal flu at the conclusion of the spring.

Rollins experienced more physical setbacks during the 1968 season. On June 2, while entering Comiskey Park, a vendor's 10-gallon coffee urn overturned, scalding Rollins' right leg. On June 4 a hard-hit, bad-hop grounder off the bat of the Yankees' Andy Kosco left Rollins with a 1½-inch wound that required four stitches. In 93 games, many of them off the bench, Rollins hit only .241.

On October 15, 1968, Rollins was selected by the Seattle Pilots in the American League expansion draft. Two days later, he sold his Savage, Minnesota, home and was hopeful about getting a fresh start in Seattle. "History shows that many players have benefited from a change. I'm sure I will," he said. "I've been in Minnesota more than seven years and sank some good roots, but anytime someone invests $175,000 in you, it has to give you confidence, and confidence is something I lacked there. I welcome a change, for I am only 30, and there doesn't seem to be room for me (on the Twins)."[12] Rollins, along with Chico Salmon and Don Mincher, helped promote their new team by participating in a goodwill tour caravan in the Pacific Northwest.

Rollins competed with former Yankee Mike Ferraro for the Pilots' third-base spot. He had a good spring training (9-for-10 in one three-game stretch) and started at third base in the Pilots' first ever game on April 8, 1969, against the Angels in Anaheim.

Despite the promising start, injuries plagued Rollins throughout the season. In May he had a bad back, and his knee problems persisted so frequently that he was sent home from a road trip. Rollins had surgery in July and was placed on the 60-day disabled list, effectively ending his season. He batted .225 in 187 at-bats, with 4 homers.

The Pilots moved to Milwaukee at the beginning of the 1970 season. Rollins played sparingly. After the Brewers moved Tommy Harper to third base and placed John Kennedy at second, Rollins was released on May 13. A week later the Indians signed Rollins with plans to use him as a pinch-hitter and a starter against left-handers. As it turned out, Rollins started only three games and batted .233 in 43 at-bats overall. He made his last major-league plate appearance on September 26, when he flied out against the Orioles' Pete Richert. He also helped out coaching the younger players.

The Indians released Rollins after the season. "I am not surprised to be released, but I am disappointed because I thought I would be offered another job in the organization," he said.[13] The Indians said they had no jobs available for Rollins at the time.[14]

Rollins stayed involved with baseball by running camps, and in 1972 by pitching batting practice along with Rocky Colavito for the Indians. Later in the season the Indians hired him as a minor league instructor and scout. At the end of the season Rollins resigned to return to his sales position with the Andrews, Bartlett & Associates, a Cleveland-based company that helped stage trade shows and conventions.

In 1973 Rollins opened a baseball school for boys aged 8 to 19 at the Minnesota Bible College located in Rochester, Minnesota. His staff included former major-league first baseman Dick Siebert, who was the baseball coach at the University of Minnesota. At the beginning of the 1974 season the Indians hired Rollins as an associate scout for the northeastern Ohio area, and at the end of the season, after growing tired of the constant travel and being away from his family, he took a job directing the Indians' group ticket sales.

In 1976 he was inducted into the Pennsylvania Sports Hall of Fame along with George Blanda and Arnold Palmer. He later joined the Cleveland Cavaliers of the NBA in an administrative role.

The Twins invited Rollins to Target Field for the 2014 All-Star Game and festivities. He said "I was shocked" when he saw a poster of his 1965 Topps baseball card on display outside Target Field for the festivities.[15]

NOTES

1. Seth Boster, "Rich Rollins :Minnesota Twins' Least Likely (and most grateful) All-Star." twincities.com/sports/ci_26102931/rich rollins July 10, 2014.
2. Arno Goethel, "Rollins Off and Rolling as Rookie Rage," *The Sporting News*, May 2, 1962.
3. Ibid.
4. *The Sporting News*, May 2, 1962.
5. Ibid.
6. Rich Rollins interview, twinstrivia.com/interview-archives rich rollins.
7. Jim Thielman, *Cool of the Evening* (Minneapolis.: Kirk House Publishing, 2005), 20.
8. Boster.
9. Arno Goethel, "Griffith Sees Even Richer Year for Kid Whiz Rollins," *The Sporting News*, February 16, 1963.
10. Max Nichols, "Twins Get Rich Dividends From Ever-Ready Rollins," *The Sporting News*, July 2, 1966.
11. Arno Goethel, "Twins' Rich Rarin' to Go; Knee Fine," *The Sporting News*, February 24, 1968.
12. Hy Zimmerman, "Draftees' Optimism Buoys Pilots' Hopes," *The Sporting News*, November 9, 1968.
13. Russell Schneider, "Hawk's Exit Likely With Chambliss' Arrival," *The Sporting News*, November 7, 1970.
14. Ibid.
15. Boster

John Sevcik

BY JOHN SWOL

JOHN JOSEPH SEVCIK MAY HAVE only 12 major-league games on his baseball résumé but those 12 games took place in 1965 when the Minnesota Twins won the American League pennant by winning a franchise-record 102 games and advanced to the World Series. The Twins lost to the Los Angeles Dodgers in seven games, and Sevcik did not get to play in any of them, but he witnessed history first-hand and has an American League championship ring to prove it.

John and his twin brother, Jim, were born in Oak Park, Illinois, a village about 15 minutes west of Chicago, on July 11, 1942, to hard-working parents Joseph and Helen Sevcik. Jim is technically John's older brother as he was born 20 minutes earlier. They also had a younger sister, Janet, who was born five years later.

Joseph Sevcik, of Czechoslovak heritage, worked for the Burton-Dixie Corporation, a bedding company, and attended law school at night. After earning his law degree, Sevcik entered politics and served in the Illinois legislature as a state representative from 1966 to 1977, when at the age of 61 he died suddenly of a heart attack while battling lung cancer. Helen (Urban) Sevcik, of Lithuanian ancestry, worked for Sears Roebuck until John and Jim were born and then she became a full-time homemaker. She died at 62 of pancreatic cancer a year after her husband died.

Although he was born in Oak Park, John and his family lived in Chicago. When he was about 7 or 8 the family of five moved from Chicago to the city of Berwyn, about 10 miles west of Chicago.

John spent his first two years of high school at Morton East High School in Cicero, and then attended Morton West High School in Berwyn when it opened in 1958. Morton West had an enrollment of more than 2,300 students, so its varsity athletic programs had plenty of good players to choose from. John became the starting catcher on the baseball team as a sophomore and was a starter at tackle on the football team his junior and senior years. Twin brother Jim was the starting shortstop as a sophomore on the baseball team and a starting end on the football team as a junior and senior. After his senior season, John was picked to the Illinois all-state team as a tackle and was a scholastic All-American.

John and Jim grew up in Big Ten country and the brothers knew that they wanted to play football and baseball together in the Big Ten. They were recruited to play football by Big Ten universities like Illinois, Wisconsin, Michigan, Minnesota, Northwestern, and Indiana as well as Arizona, Florida, Colorado, Missouri, and Vanderbilt. It was important to John and Jim that they stay fairly close to home so that their parents could watch them play. One of the problems they faced if they selected a Big Ten school was that the

In his only season in the big leagues, catcher John Sevcik appeared in 12 games for the Twins in 1965. (Photo courtesy of Minnesota Twins Baseball Club).

Big Ten had a grant-in-aid program meaning that how well off you were financially would determine how big a scholarship you would be given. Outside of the Big Ten it was pretty much a full-ride scholarship. After numerous trips the boys still had not made a choice on what school they would attend.

When the John and Jim went out on recruiting trips, the instructions from their father were always the same: Look, learn about the school, ask questions, but don't sign anything until you come home and we can discuss the trip. On a recruiting trip to Colorado the brothers were wined, dined, taken skiing, and set up with dates before meeting with coach Sonny Grandelius for the final pitch. Grandelius pressured them to sign with Colorado but John and Jim knew the rules they were operating under. However, when Grandelius promised them everything under the sun and told them that their parents would be provided transportation and lodging for all their games, the boys relented and agreed that Colorado was the place for them. Joseph Sevcik picked the boys up at the airport and as they drove home he asked them about the trip. After telling him about how great a school Colorado was and how well the Colorado program takes care of the parents, the boys blurted out that they had signed with Colorado. What happened next, according to John, went like this: Their father couldn't stop the car fast enough and he told them, "Geez! If they are going to do this for you guys, what do you think they are doing for the really good ballplayers, you dummies!"[1]

Joseph Sevcik was convinced that what Colorado was doing was illegal and he told the school that he would not co-sign the agreement. He could not have been more correct; shortly after Colorado lost the 1962 Orange Bowl, rumors started circulating that Grandelius used a slush fund to pay players and their families. The NCAA investigated Colorado and in April of 1962 the school was put on two years' probation and Grandelius was fired.

John and Jim ended up attending the University of Missouri from 1960 to 1964, and they both played baseball and football from 1962 to 1964. John took over as the starting catcher about midway through his sophomore year. (At the time, freshmen were not allowed to play.) The Missouri Tigers went to the College World Series each year John played. In 1964 they lost the championship game 5-1 to Minnesota after having beaten the Golden Gophers 4-1 earlier in the tournament. The Tigers have not been to a CWS since 1964.

Within days after the 1964 College World Series, seven players from the Missouri squad signed professional baseball contracts. Five of them, including John and Jim, were signed by scout Bill Messman of the Minnesota Twins. Messman scouted for the Twins from 1959 to 1984, signing players like Gary Gaetti, Graig Nettles, and Tim Laudner, before he died in 1984. John and Jim received $10,000 signing bonuses from Minnesota and were assigned to the rookie league in Cocoa Beach, Florida.

Before even appearing in a rookie-league game, John was sent to play for the Wisconsin Rapids Twins in the Class A Midwest League. There he appeared in 59 games and hit .284 with 14 doubles in 240 plate appearances. The team finished with a 50-71 record and the only other player on that team besides John who reached the major leagues was outfielder Pat Kelly, who played in the majors for 15 seasons with five different teams.

After Wisconsin Rapids ended its season, John and Glenda Lea Klipstein were married in Bismarck, North Dakota. They had met when he was attending Missouri and she was attending nearby Stephens College. Not too long after the wedding, Sevcik was off to play in the Florida Instructional League in the fall of 1964.

Because of the bonus signing rules at the time, players who got a bonus of $8,000 or more had to be placed on their team's 40-man roster or be exposed to waivers or the Rule 5 draft as a first-year minor-league player. After the 1964 draft, the club owners did away with the first-year draft, but it still applied to first-year players selected in 1964. Rather than expose Sevcik to waivers, the Twins kept him on the roster.[2] Manager

Sam Mele already had catchers Earl Battey and Jerry Zimmerman and had to find a spot for Sevcik.

It was almost two weeks into the 1965 season before Sevcik saw his first major-league action. The Twins started the season with a 6-1 record and were in Detroit on April 24. After eight innings the Twins were losing 3-2, but they pushed two runs across in the top of the ninth for a 4-3 lead. Mele brought in Jerry Fosnow to close out the game and Sevcik to catch. The first Tigers batter, Willie Horton, hit a home run to tie the game. Bill Freehan grounded out and Dick McAuliffe walked and stole second before Larry Sherry struck out for the second out of the inning. When Fosnow walked Jerry Lumpe, the Twins manager had seen enough and called for the veteran Al Worthington. The Tigers countered with Gates Brown to pinch-hit for Don Wert. Brown hit a walk-off three-run homer and Sevcik and the Twins were 7-4 losers.

Sevcik did not play in his next game until May 31, the second game of a doubleheader against the Orioles in Baltimore, game 42 on the Twins' schedule. He was the starting catcher and batted eighth in the Twins' power-laden lineup. In his first plate appearance in the big leagues, against future Hall of Famer Jim Palmer, Sevcik grounded out to the second baseman; in his second he coaxed a walk from Palmer and eventually scored what turned out to be the only run of his big-league career. In his third and final plate appearance in the game, he was struck out by Dick Hall. The Twins lost, 5-4, when Sam Bowens hit a walk-off home run in the bottom of the ninth inning.

As the Twins' march to the 1965 pennant continued, Sevcik spent most of his time in the bullpen, playing briefly in six games in June, one in July, and then none in August. Asked if he went to Mele to request more playing time, he said, "If an especially tough pitcher was slated to pitch against us that day like a Sam McDowell, Whitey Ford, or Dean Chance, I would ask Mele during batting practice if I was in the lineup that day because I knew we needed a win! He would just laugh and walk away."[3] In his book *Cool of the Evening*, Jim Thielman wrote, "In early August, 23-year-old John Sevcik sat in the bullpen under the scoreboard in right-center field at Met Stadium. He hadn't played in well over a month. The Twins-O-Gram, the portion of the electronic scoreboard that conveyed messages to fans, paid homage to the catcher with the lighted display: 'Sevcik is here, sittin' and a watchin' and a waitin'."[4]

When the calendar turned to September, the rookie Sevcik had played in only nine games, none since a brief appearance on July 10, and was 0-for-7. With the pennant wrapped up in late September, Sam Mele rested his regulars and Sevcik finally got his chance to play. He was the starting catcher against the Orioles on September 28 and on that day in Memorial Stadium got his only major-league base hit, a double to left field off Wally Bunker in the Twins' 158th game of the season. Pitcher Jim Perry followed with a hit to left but Sevcik was thrown out at the plate on a strong throw from Curt Blefary. On October 3 at Met Stadium the Twins played their final game of the regular season and beat the California Angels, 3-2. Sevcik pinch-hit for pitcher Dave Boswell in the fourth inning and stayed in to catch the rest of the game. He didn't get a hit in his final big-league game but he finally had a chance to walk off the field as a winner — in all his previous 11 games, the Twins had lost every time.

Sevcik did not get into any of the seven World Series games; as during most of the season, he witnessed Minnesota Twins history from the bullpen.

In 1966 Sevcik went to spring training with the Twins but did not make the team and spent the season gaining experience in the Double-A Southern League, starting at catcher for the Charlotte Hornets. He played in 94 games and hit .232 with three home runs.

In 1967 Sevcik once again was a Twins spring-training invitee but ended up getting farmed out to the Wilson Tobs of the Class A Carolina League, where he hit .286 with seven home runs in 262 at-bats as the starting catcher. Jim Sevcik was also on the Wilson team. This was the second time the Sevcik twins played on the same team in pro baseball; they were also teammates on the 1964 Wisconsin Rapids team.

John told a funny story about twins being twins.[5] One particularly hot day the Tobs were playing a doubleheader and John had caught the first game, switched into a clean, dry uniform and was in the bullpen for the second game. As the game progressed, Jim, who was playing left field, decided that, since he did not expect to hit, he would conserve some energy and just sit in the bullpen instead of running back to the dugout when the half-inning ended. Jim was complaining about how beastly hot it was when some of the players in the bullpen decided that the Twins should switch uniforms and that John should play left field for the next half-inning. Just go out there and stand around, no one will probably hit anything to you anyway, they said. So they did, and the second batter hit a single to left, but as John told the story, he turned the single into a triple. As he hustled after the ball the players bullpen were roaring and Tobs manager Vern Morgan didn't have a clue as to what was going on.

Later in 1967 John Sevcik was moved up to Triple-A Denver, where he hit .270 in 10 games. As it turned out, that was also the last time the Sevcik twins played together. After four seasons of pro ball and still in Class A, Jim decided that his dreams of reaching the major leagues were not going to materialize and that it was time to get a real job.

In 1968 John Sevcik was invited to spring training but had to miss a good portion of training camp because if his commitment to the US Army. He served in the Army Reserve from 1967 to 1973 and had to take time off from baseball each season to fulfill his active-duty commitments. He ended up getting sent back to Double-A Charlotte, where he again was the starting catcher, hitting a respectable .260.

Sevcik spent the 1969 season with Triple-A Denver, where he shared the catching duties and played in just 54 games, hitting .265. In 1970, still unable to find a catching spot on a very strong Twins team, Sevcik again was sent down to Triple-A after spring training. That season the Twins' Triple-A team was the American Association Evansville Triplets, where Sevcik again shared catching duties but hit a strong .281 with a very respectable .345 on-base percentage and earned a spot on the 1970 American Association all-star team.

The spring of 1971 found Sevcik with no invite to the Twins' spring training and another ticket to Triple-A, the fourth time he would play Triple-A baseball, this time in the Pacific Coast League with the Portland Beavers. Sevcik again was splitting catching duties when he was called into manager Ralph Rowe's office late in the season. When the office door closed the first thing that crossed his mind was "Here it is, time for the pink slip." It turned out not to be that at all. Rowe told Sevcik that he could keep on playing if he wished but his return to the big leagues was probably limited to backup catching and that maybe the best way to go would be to pursue managing. Rowe talked about how good a manager Sevcik would make with his temperament and catching experience and asked him to give it some thought. As the season wound down, Rowe kept after Sevcik about managing and told him to follow up with the Twins' front office after the season. Sevcik talked to George Brophy, and he offered him a job as a rookie-league manager. Sevcik called Rowe, who told him what to expect from owner Calvin Griffith's frugal Twins during salary discussions. Sevcik talked with Brophy again and the discussions went exactly as Rowe had told him they would. Sevcik turned down the offer. Brophy told him he was making a big mistake, but Sevcik stuck to his guns and walked away from baseball at the age of 28.

After baseball, John and Glenda stayed in the Minneapolis area. Glenda eventually opened an interior design and antiques business. John went into construction equipment sales and between 1972 and 1993 worked for a number of companies in the Twin Cities area, including George C. Ryan Companies, Valley Equipment Company, and Road Machinery & Supplies Company. In 1993, after a reorganization at the Road Machinery & Supplies Company, Sevcik found himself out of a job at the age of 50.

Sevcik reached out to an old baseball buddy, Rich Reese, who was an executive with Jim Beam Brands, and told him he was looking for a career change and wanted to get into the liquor industry. Reese hired

Sevcik and it wasn't long before John was responsible for sales in southern Minnesota and all of South Dakota. In 1997 the Texas region opened up and John and Glenda moved to San Antonio. Sevcik worked for Jim Beam Brands for about 13 years before retiring in July 2006.

As of 2014 John and Glenda were retired in Austin, Texas. John said he still followed the Twins and liked getting out to the local golf course a couple of days a week.

SOURCES

Baseball-Almanac.com

BaseballLibrary.com

Baseball-Reference.com

Jim Thielman, *Cool of the Evening* (Minneapolis: Kirk House Publishers, 2005).

The Sporting News

Twinstrivia.com

2012 Mizzou Football Records Book. grfx.cstv.com/photos/schools/miss/sports/m-footbl/auto_pdf/2012-13/misc_non_event/12-footbl-record-book.pdf"

2013 Mizzou Baseball Media Guide. mutigers.com/sports/m-basebl/archive/miss-m-basebl-archive.html

NOTES

1. Author's interviews with John Sevcik, conducted in August 2009 and June 2014.
2. Cliff Blau, "The Real First-Year Player Draft," SABR.org, sabr.org/research/real-first-year-player-draft.
3. Author's interviews with John Sevcik.
4. Jim Thielman, *Cool of the Evening* (Minneapolis: Kirk House Publishers, 2005), 86.
5. Author's interview with John Sevcik.

"Clinching a Tie is to Beer What Winning the Championship is to Champagne" —Harmon Killebrew

September 25, 1965: Minnesota Twins 5, Washington Senators 0 (Game One)
Minnesota Twins 5, Washington Senators 3 (Game Two)
at Griffith Stadium, Washington, D.C.

BY ALAN COHEN

THE MINNESOTA TWINS WERE fully aware of how, just one year before, the Philadelphia Phillies had blown a seemingly insurmountable lead with very little time remaining in the season. The Twins had been on the verge of clinching the pennant for about a week when they traveled to Washington in late September of 1965. They had an eight-game lead with eight games remaining in their season as they arrived at their former home for a series set to begin on Friday, September 24. Their magic number was three and Vice President Hubert Humphrey, a former mayor of Minneapolis and a US senator from Minnesota, was there to cheer his team on. Rain intervened, however, and Friday night's game was rescheduled as part of a doubleheader on Saturday.

Forty miles away in Baltimore, the Orioles kept the magic number at three on Friday, winning the first game of a scheduled doubleheader against the Angels, before the rains came. With their backs to the wall, the Orioles had won four consecutive games. In Baltimore, as in Washington, there would be a doubleheader on September 25. The Twins' lead over Baltimore, which had been 10 games on September 20, had been reduced to 7½ games. The Chicago White Sox were also barely alive. They were one loss or one Minnesota win away from elimination.

The Twins' best pitchers, Mudcat Grant, Camilo Pascual, and Jim Kaat, were set to go in the three-game set—and they were ready.

Jim "Mudcat" Grant (19-6) went into the opener on Saturday seeking his 20th win of the season. He was on the verge of becoming the first African American pitcher to win 20 games in the American League, as well as the AL's first 20-game-winner in 1965. He was opposed by Frank Kreutzer. Kreutzer had only a 2-5 record coming in but manager Gil Hodges chose the left-hander as the starter to keep the Twins' Tony Oliva and Don Mincher in check. The lefty pitcher also kept left-handed-hitting outfielders Jimmie Hall (.287) and Sandy Valdespino (.254) on the bench. Righties Joe Nossek (.234) and Bob Allison (.239) got the starts.

The game was scoreless for the first four innings and the closest Washington could get to a threat against Grant was in the third inning. An error by second baseman Frank Quilici allowed Washington's Jim French to get on base. The next two batters hit into force plays. Kreutzer stood at first with two outs as Don Blasingame strode to the plate. Blasingame's double moved Kreutzer to third, but Grant stranded the two runners as he induced Ken McMullen to ground out.

Zoilo Versalles helped his MVP credentials by hitting a home run with Grant aboard in the fifth inning to put the Twins in front, 2-0. It was his 18th homer of the season. Grant wouldn't need any more runs, but Versalles was not the least bit finished. The shortstop, who had four hits in the game after a first-inning strikeout, banged his 11th triple of the season in the seventh inning. It ignited a three-run rally that wrapped up the Twins' scoring. An RBI double by Oliva and a two-run pinch-hit single by Valdespino provided the additional three-run cushion for Grant.

Meanwhile Grant was rolling along. He walked Jim French with one out in the fifth inning, then proceeded to retire the final 14 batters to register the 5-0 win in 2:27. The third-inning double by Blasingame was the only hit he allowed.

A win in the nightcap would clinch a tie for the pennant.

The Twins sent veteran Camilo Pascual to the mound. His career with the team began when they were the original Washington Senators. The Cuban right-hander was 9-3 for the season after missing the entire month of August with arm problems that required surgery on August 2, performed by the Twins' team physician, Dr. George Resta. (The original diagnosis was a benign tumor towards the back of Pascual's shoulder, but surgery revealed that three frayed muscles had snapped, like severed rubber bands, and formed an egg-sized lump.[1]) The two-time 20-game-winner had gone without a win from June 9 through September 10.[2] Washington countered with right-hander Jim Duckworth. Duckworth, who had been inserted into Washington's starting rotation late in August, was 2-1 in six starts, and had two games in which he struck out 10 or more batters. In all, he had struck out 43 batters in 36 innings as a starter—and for Duckworth the best was yet to come.

In the bottom half of the first inning in the nightcap, Washington's Fred Valentine, on first base with a single, tried to steal second base. In the process, he collided with Versalles, as the throw from catcher Jerry Zimmerman was off-line. Valentine was called safe on the play and awarded a stolen base. But he sustained a cut over his right eye, left the game, and was taken to the hospital where he received two stitches to close the wound. Jim King came into the game for Valentine and was stranded at second base.

Versalles, somewhat bruised, remained in the game until the fourth inning, when he was replaced at shortstop by Jerry Kindall. Versalles was taken to the hospital, where he remained overnight.

The Senators took an early lead, scoring three runs in the second inning. The key hit was a double by Eddie Brinkman that scored Ken McMullen and Mike Brumley. Brinkman advanced to third on a throwing error by Versalles and scored on a first-pitch suicide squeeze bunt by Duckworth. Only one of the runs was earned as, prior to the Versalles error, Twins catcher Zimmerman, who was not having the best of days, misplayed a foul ball to extend Brumley's at-bat.

The Twins broke into the scoring column in the fourth inning. Singles by Tony Oliva and Harmon Killebrew put runners on first and third. Jimmie Hall delivered Oliva with a sacrifice fly. The single by Oliva was his second of the game and his third hit of the double-header. At the end of the day, his league-leading batting average stood at .322. The following day, he went 1-for-4 and wound up with a .321 batting average to earn his second consecutive batting title.

In the seventh inning, Don Mincher's 22nd homer of the season cut the Washington lead to 3-2.

Pascual was near perfect after the second inning, retiring 14 of the last 15 batters he faced, allowing only a fifth-inning walk to Jim King. Pascual was pulled for pinch-hitter Rich Reese in the top of the seventh and was replaced by Jim Merritt. Merritt shut down the home team with only one hit in three innings and didn't allow any further scoring.

Meanwhile, the Twins had some punch left in their bats. With one out in the eighth inning, Sandy Valdespino (2-for-4) singled, bringing up Oliva. Manager Hodges removed Duckworth, who had struck out 13 Twins in 7⅓ innings, and brought in lefty Mike McCormick, who had begun as a bonus baby with the New York Giants in 1956. McCormick got Oliva to fly out to center field, but walked Harmon Killebrew with the potential lead run. Twins manager Sam Mele sent the right-hand-hitting Joe Nossek up to pinch-hit for lefty Jimmie Hall and Hodges countered by bringing in right-hander Ron Kline to face Nossek. It was Kline's 74th appearance of the season. Nossek's double plated Valdespino with the tying run and put runners on second and third. An intentional walk to Mincher loaded the bases.

The stage was set for Frank Quilici. The utility infielder, who had joined the team in mid-July, had come into the game batting .211 and was hitless in six at-bats so far this day. He would never have a more important turn at the plate. He singled home two runs, giving the Twins a 5-3 lead. The RBIs were Quilici's sixth and seventh of the season. He would have no RBIs during the season's remaining games, but it mattered little. He had come through with the hit that clinched at least a tie for the pennant.

Merritt retired the Senators in order in the final two innings, striking out Don Lock for the game's final out, to put his record at 5-4 for the season. Only 9,373 fans had paid their way in to see the sweep of the single-admission doubleheader as the Twins finished their second game win in 2:53.

If Baltimore, the only team still with a chance to catch the Twins, lost either game in their twi-night doubleheader at Memorial Stadium against the Angels, the Twins would go to bed on Saturday night as American League champions. The Birds did not cooperate. While the Twins were completing their sweep of the Senators, the Orioles won the opener in dramatic fashion, scoring the winning run in the bottom of the ninth inning when Jerry Adair singled with one out and the bases loaded to drive in Russ Snyder.

It was now time for some good old-fashioned scoreboard watching. In this case, the Twins, in various stages of undress, elected to order in food and listen on transistor radios, to the broadcast of the second game of the Orioles-Angels doubleheader from Baltimore. At times the broadcast signal was weak and only Harmon Killebrew, with his ears glued to the radio for the entire nine innings, could hear Chuck Thompson describe the action. The Orioles won the nightcap, 2-0, behind the three-hit pitching of Milt Pappas, in his last win for the Orioles. Everyone dressed and rushed to the team bus. Sam Mele said, "We'll have to do it ourselves, tomorrow."[3]

The magic number remained at one.

SOURCES

Thielman, Jim, *Cool of the Evening: The 1965 Minnesota Twins* (Minneapolis: Kirk House Publishers, 2005).

Whittlesley, Merrill, "Twins Take 2, Clinch Flag Tie: Grant Wins 20th with 1-Hitter, 5-0," *Washington Sunday Star,* September 26, 1965, F-1.

Baseball-Reference.com

Daily Journal (Fergus Falls, Minnesota)

The Sporting News

Sunday Star (Washington)

Washington Post

Winona (Minnesota) *Sunday News*

NOTES

1   Thielman, 167.
2   *Fergus Falls* (Minnesota) *Daily Journal,* September 27, 1965, 10.
3   *Washington Sunday Star,* September 26, 1965, F-2.

Dwight Siebler

BY GREGORY H. WOLF

FATE CAN SOMETIMES BE CRUEL. After working his way through the Philadelphia Phillies farm system for three years, hard-throwing right-hander Dwight Siebler injured his elbow pitching to the first batter in his first major-league spring-training game, in 1962. Robbed of his heater, Siebler relied on ball movement, a hard curve, and command when he made it to the big leagues in July 1963 as a member of the Minnesota Twins. A three-hitter in his debut start suggested a bright future, but the tall Nebraskan spent all but one of his five seasons (1963-1967) with the Twins bouncing between Triple-A and the big leagues before retiring with a 4-3 record.

Dwight Leroy Siebler was born on August 5, 1937, in Columbus, Nebraska, the third of four children of William and Viola Siebler, whose parents had emigrated from Germany around the turn of the century. When Siebler was 3 years old and the Great Depression gradually gave way to the war years, the family moved from their farm to Omaha, about 85 miles to the east, where his father eventually opened a heating and air-conditioning company. The elder Siebler, a former semipro player, sponsored a team in a local Little League, where Siebler and his two brothers were introduced to the sport. "At that time, the distance between the bases and the mound was exactly like it was in pro ball," Siebler recalled. "I became a pitcher because I was one of the few 10-year-olds who could throw the 60 feet and 6 inches to home plate for strikes. My mom and dad were my biggest fans, and greatest influences in my life."[1]

Siebler came of age in Omaha as the city established itself as one of the hotbeds of amateur baseball by hosting the annual College World Series beginning in 1950. The tall, slender Midwesterner starred as a hard-throwing hurler at North High School, where he earned three letters each in baseball and basketball. His success in American Legion ball made him and his team, Storz, local celebrities when they won the state title in 1954 and advanced to the regional finals in Denver. Recruited by a number of college baseball programs, Siebler accepted a scholarship to attend the University of Nebraska, where he played for Tony Sharpe, the longest-tenured coach (1947-1977) in Husker baseball history.

Siebler played semipro ball for small towns like Columbus, Winside, and Genoa in the summers of 1955 to 1957, and pitched on the varsity squad at Nebraska in 1957 and 1958. "I pitched a no-hitter against Oklahoma, but lost 1-0," he said with a chuckle. "With a man on first base, the batter bunted, I fielded the ball and threw it into right field, and the runner scored." Big-league scouts took note of the All-Big Eight conference performer in 1958. "Tom Demark,

Right-hander Dwight Siebler spent most of the 1965 season with the Denver Bears of the PCL, and logged 15 innings over seven appearances with the Twins. The Nebraskan won four games and hurled in 48 games in parts of five seasons (1963-1967). (Photo courtesy of Minnesota Twins Baseball Club).

a scout for the Philadelphia Phillies, started showing up to my college and semipro games," Siebler said. "Scouts weren't supposed to approach us in college until after our junior year. But he kept it under cover and would casually run in to me when I'd go out to my car." Siebler passed up his senior year of eligibility to sign with the Phillies for a $20,000 bonus and a $400-a-month minor-league contract.

The chance to pursue his dream of a career in baseball was a big step for Siebler, who had gotten married in 1957. He and his wife, Pearl, had welcomed their first of four children to the world just weeks before he was to report to the Bakersfield (California) Bears in the Class C California League. "We just packed the baby into car and drove across the US," said Siebler, whose youthful enthusiasm could still be detected in his voice.

"The biggest challenge was playing every day," replied Siebler when asked about the transition to professional baseball. "The first half of the season I relieved. I was doing pretty good so manager Paul Owens moved me into the four-man rotation. I didn't know if I could do that. You were expected to go nine innings. In college I had just pitched once a week. But it worked out." Siebler tossed a four-hitter in his first professional start en route to an 11-7 record. His 190 strikeouts (in 179 innings) ranked second in the league while his 9.6 strikeouts per nine innings paced the circuit.

"I could throw the hell out of the ball when I was younger. In college and my first two years of pro ball I threw maybe 90 percent fastballs," said Siebler who cut an intimidating presence on the mound at 6-feet-2 and about 180 pounds. (He grew to 200 by the end of his career.) Relying on his heater with the Class A Williamsport (Pennsylvania) Grays in 1960, Siebler whiffed about a batter per inning, allowed just 6.9 hits per nine innings, and led the Eastern League in ERA (2.31) while splitting his time between starts and relief outings for the pennant winners.

Groomed by the Phillies to be a starter, Siebler was assigned to the Buffalo Bisons of the International League in 1961. "The team was independently owned and had a tremendous amount of ex-big leaguers who probably wouldn't make it back," he said. "It was difficult to break in as a starter." More concerned about wins and losses than player development, manager Kerby Farrell relied on veterans to lead the Bisons to their first Junior World Series title in 55 years. Siebler started only three times among his 30 appearances and earned praise from *The Sporting News* as the "ace of the … bullpen."[2] One of those starts was a stellar 14-strikeout performance against Toronto in July.

Despite his tossing only 73 innings (but striking out 87) for the Bisons, Siebler's third year in professional baseball was pivotal in his development as a pitcher. Al Widmar, the Phillies' roving pitching coach and instructor, had helped many prospects in the organization, and Siebler was no exception. "He taught me how to throw a curveball, and that pitch really developed in the next few years," explained Siebler. As with his fastball, he tossed his curve at a three-quarters angle. "It was a hard curve. I threw it to righties and lefties at exactly the same place. Low and away to righties and low and inside to lefties," said Siebler. The Nebraskan also fell under the tutelage of crafty veteran and former New York/San Francisco Giants starter, Ruben Gomez, who was trying to win his way back to the big show. "I learned to throw a screwball-change from Gomez," Siebler said. "It broke like a left-hander's curveball. I used it primarily against lefties, but was afraid to throw it to righties because it broke in to them. I was pretty effective in my career against left-handers." With his three-pitch arsenal, the hard-throwing "rescue artist" was added to the Phillies' 40-man roster in the offseason.[3]

Coming off a miserable 107-loss season, Phillies manager Gene Mauch looked forward to seeing Siebler in spring training in 1962. "His arm is as live as there is," said the young firebrand skipper.[4] Asked what he remembered about his first big-league camp, Siebler replied with vivid clarity. "It was an incredible feeling to be with all the big leaguers. But you learn the old saying, 'They put on their pants the same way you do.' I thought, these guys aren't really any better than I am. I could hold my own."

There was a tinge of doubt hovering over the highly touted prospect's quest to break into a staff that had ranked dead last in ERA in the previous season. "I had hurt my arm in Buffalo and didn't pitch the last month of season," explained Siebler. "Mauch told me 'I want you to show me that your arm is OK. If it is, you're our fourth starter.' I was in hog heaven after that."

Pitchers are always just one throw away from a career-altering or career-ending injury. Siebler's excitement soon transformed into bitter disappointment. "My arm wasn't hurting at all during camp. In the first exhibition game, I was scheduled to pitch the last three innings against, ironically, the Minnesota Twins," said Siebler. "Harmon Killebrew was the first batter up so I figured I'd blaze one by him. Well, I uncorked one and hurt my arm again." In excruciating pain, Siebler had reinjured muscles leading from his elbow to his wrist. Physicians determined that he had ripped a buildup of scar tissue, but they did not prescribe surgery.

After getting a taste of the life of a big leaguer in spring training, Siebler bounced around to three different Triple-A teams in 1962 (Buffalo, Dallas-Fort Worth Rangers, and Syracuse Chiefs). "I was dejected and depressed the whole year. I didn't have a good year and didn't feel strong,' said Siebler honestly about his 4.41 ERA in 100 innings. "It was frustrating because my arm was not hurting. But I had lost 3-4-5 miles off my fastball. I had to learn how to pitch and how to move the ball around. I never did get my 94-95-mile-an-hour fastball back."

Siebler was back at the Phillies camp in 1963, but the situation had changed drastically. Mauch had guided the team to its first winning season since 1953 while a core of young pitchers between 22 and 26 years old (Art Mahaffey, Chris Short, Jack Baldschun, and Dennis Bennett) anchored the staff. Siebler was optioned to the Arkansas Travelers of the International League, where he regained his form, appearing 30 times (10 starts) and posting a 3.06 ERA in 100 innings.

An unexpected phone call in late July 1963 gave Siebler a new lease on his big-league aspirations. "At about 10:30 or 11 at night I was in my room with [roommate] Danny Cater when [manager] Frank Lucchesi called me. He told me that I was sold to Minnesota. I'll never forget that," said Siebler. The previous season the Twins enjoyed a surprising second-place finish in their second season in Minneapolis after relocating from Washington, DC. "I was ecstatic about the trade. The Twins had all those hitters and I figured the pitchers didn't need to worry about getting any runs. But I didn't realize that Met Stadium was pretty small," said Siebler with a laugh. "And that other teams could hit 'em out of the park, too."

Siebler's lifelong dream was realized in the second game of a doubleheader against the Washington Senators in the nation's capital on August 26. "My debut was horrible," he said. "I was nervous. When I came in to relieve Jim Kaat, I couldn't get the ball over the plate. I hit Don Zimmer right in the middle of the back and walked two. I was so disgusted afterward." Despite permitting two inherited runners to score in two-thirds of an inning, Siebler's shot at redemption came quickly. "I didn't know anyone on the team except Don Mincher," he said. "I'm sitting in the hotel reading the paper and Sam Mele comes over and tells me that I'm starting the second game of a doubleheader. I was surprised." He shook off any butterflies and hurled a three-hit complete game to defeat the Senators, 10-1, on August 29. He also recorded his first hit and run batted in and accomplished something that he never repeated: He scored a run. On September 17 he tossed his second and final big-league complete game, a four-hitter to subdue the Detroit Tigers, 3-1. Siebler won two of three decisions for the third-place Twins, surrendering only 25 hits in 38⅔ innings, and carved out a sparkling 2.79 ERA.

In light of his impressive late-season performances, Siebler entered spring training as Minnesota's fourth starter. But like two years earlier with the Phillies, things didn't progress as he had envisioned. "We had a pitching coach—Gordon Maltzberger—and all I can say is that he was not good. Sam Mele didn't know anything about pitching. Maltzberger puts me in the bullpen and changes my delivery two different ways.

Dwight Siebler (Photo courtesy of Minnesota Twins Baseball Club).

First he didn't like my follow-through because I flopped clear to the left like Bob Gibson. That is how I generated my power, but I wasn't in ideal fielding position. Then he wanted me to throw a slow curve instead of my power curve. Well, I had been working on a slow curve for years and it never worked. By the time spring training was over, I couldn't get anyone out. I lost my fastball, my power curve, and my slow curve was not even average. I wasn't a good pitcher."

After five mostly ineffective relief appearances, the 26-year-old Siebler was optioned to the Atlanta Crackers of the International League. "Jack McKeon was an organizational manager," said Siebler respectfully about his skipper. "He wanted to develop players and didn't worry about winning the pennant. He pitched me every fourth day no matter what. I'd get my brains beat out because I was trying to go back to the way I had pitched. It took me a year to feel comfortable again." The good-natured right-hander posted a 7-12 record and carved out a 4.10 ERA in 156 innings. In a September call-up, he tossed hitless ball for five innings spread over four relief outings.

Siebler recalled that the general mood and attitude of the pitching staff change radically in spring training with the addition of Johnny Sain as the club's new pitching coach in 1965. "Sain showed us how to throw three different fastballs all at the same speed," said Siebler. "It all had to do with the placement of the fingers on the seams. One would rotate down like a sinker, the other broke away like a cutter, and the four-seamer looked like it would rise. He told us to throw only these fastballs in games until he said to mix in curves and change-ups." Siebler added that the pitchers were unsure at first about Sain's unorthodox methods but quickly accepted his philosophy. "Well, the staff really blossomed and I think that's what led us to the pennant." Mudcat Grant led the AL with 21 wins and six shutouts in his career year; Jim Kaat paced the circuit with 42 starts and lowered his ERA; and Jim Perry revived his career after being considered washed up.

Siebler spent the 1965 season on a proverbial yo-yo between the big-league club and its Triple-A affiliate in the Pacific Coast League, the Denver Bears. Starting out the season in Denver, Siebler was recalled in July to replace hard-throwing Dave Boswell who had been diagnosed with mononucleosis.[5] In six appearances (including one start), Siebler yielded seven runs and 11 hits and nine walks in 12 innings, and was ultimately sent back to Denver in August. "We were getting ready for an Eastern road trip (August 10) about a week after Killebrew dislocated his shoulder," said Siebler about his disappointing option in the middle of a pennant race. "We had a big lead, and Don Mincher did a great job filling in at first base. But I think Mele overthought the situation or panicked a little. He called up Andy Kosco, who was having a Triple Crown season for Denver. I had been the last person called up so I was sent down."

Siebler was recalled in mid-September, but unfortunately it was well after the deadline for determining postseason rosters, making him ineligible for the World Series. In his only appearance after his call-up, he hurled three scoreless innings of relief against the Baltimore Orioles on September 22. In stark contrast to the joy and excitement of his teammates, the up-and-down season between Minneapolis and Denver left Siebler with a sour taste. "[Club owner and general manager] Calvin Griffith told me that I could go with the team to Los Angeles, but could not suit up. I could sit on the end of the bench in civilian clothes," said Siebler. "I was so mad that I told him that I didn't want to go, though I wish now that I would have gone. My temper got the best of me. And then I told him that I really wanted to be traded."

Despite Siebler's request, Griffith did not trade him in the offseason. However, the team had to make a decision about the hurler's future because he was out of options. Mele described Siebler as the "most improved pitcher in … camp," and for the first time in two years Siebler went north to Minnesota with the team to kick off the regular season.[6] Siebler had a difficult time cracking a starting rotation consisting of six pitchers (Grant, Kaat, Perry, Boswell, Camilo Pascual, and Jim Merritt) who garnered all but three starts the entire season; while Al Worthington and 23-year-old power pitcher Pete Cimino were the first two right-handers out of the bullpen. Consequently, Siebler found himself as the as the tenth pitcher on a ten-man staff. Eight of his 23 appearances came in July, and he didn't pitch after August 28, finishing with a 3.44 ERA in 49⅔ innings. On August 17 he pitched 6⅓ innings of relief, surrendering four hits and one unearned run to the California Angels to earn what proved to be the last of his four wins in the big leagues.

"After the World Series and my trade demand, I don't think my career really developed right," said Siebler with a hint of melancholy. "I never got back in the groove of pitching. I pitched sparingly and not enough to stay sharp. I got stale. I did everything I could to stay in shape, but it's not the same as pitching in a game."

In 1967 Siebler made his final two appearances in the majors before he was sent outright to the Denver Bears prior to May 15, when rosters had to be trimmed from a maximum of 28 to 25 players. (This practice was eliminated the following season.) "I lost my interest and capability by not pitching much," said Siebler. "I just didn't have the zip anymore." He won only four of 14 decisions and posted a 4.56 ERA in 142 innings for the Bears.

Just 30 years old, Siebler made a big decision. "I quit at the end of the '67 season," said the pitcher bluntly. "I told Griffith that I didn't want to play anymore. They weren't happy about it because they had invested money in me. For two years I told them to trade me. Later I find out from Jim Rantz, a former teammate of mine who had moved into the front office, that several teams wanted to buy me in the previous years but the Twins refused to sell me. Of course there was no free agency at the time and I was stuck."

After pitching in parts of five big-league seasons, Siebler hung up his spikes. In 48 appearances, he logged 117⅓ innings and posted a 3.45 ERA. He also logged in excess of 1,000 innings over eight seasons in the minors.

Siebler returned to his family and home in Omaha, where he had spent almost all of his life. "I probably wouldn't have quit if I didn't have my family's business to fall back on," he said. But the hurler was far from retired. He successfully transitioned to his post-baseball career, taking over his family's heating and air-conditioning business. In his first year away from Twins, he managed a semipro team in nearby Ralston and pitched for them, too.

As of 2014, Dwight Siebler resided in Omaha with his second wife, Caryn, with whom he has two stepchildren. In 1994 he was inducted into the Nebraska Baseball Hall of Fame; and in 2011 was inducted to the Omaha Old-Timer's Baseball Association Hall of Fame.

ACKNOWLEDGEMENT:

The author expresses his sincere thanks to Dwight Siebler who was interviewed for this biography on February 17, 2014. He subsequently read the biography to ensure its accuracy.

SOURCES

The Sporting News

BaseballLibrary.com

Baseball-Reference.com

Retrosheet.com

SABR.org

NOTES

1 Author's interview with Dwight Siebler on February 17, 2014. All quotations from Siebler are from this interview unless otherwise stated.
2 *The Sporting News*, August 9, 1961, 29.
3 *The Sporting News*, December 20, 1961, 35.
4 *The Sporting News*, February 21, 1962, 26.
5 *The Sporting News*, July 31, 1965, 7.
6 *The Sporting News*, April 16, 1966, 22.

Dick Stigman

BY TOM TOMASHEK

AS A YOUNG BASEBALL PLAYER IN rural Minnesota, Dick Stigman picked the perfect day to pitch a perfect game. Cy Slapnicka, the man who signed Cleveland greats Bob Feller, Bob Lemon, and Herb Score, was watching.

In the spring of 1954, three days after graduating from Sebeka High School, Richard Lewis Stigman (born January 24, 1936, in Nimrod, Minnesota) was working in a lumber yard when he was called to the office. Slapnicka had come to sign the strapping left-hander, whom he had seen strike out 21 batters in Stigman's seven-inning perfect game.

"I came walking out of the yard in my overalls and there was his Cadillac with both my parents sitting in the car," Stigman said in an interview with the writer. "We drove to the Graystone Hotel in Detroit Lakes to discuss signing. I was very impressed that he respected my parents enough to include them so they would know that I wasn't getting involved in something that wasn't right.

"He offered me $200 a month and another 200 a month if I stayed. I was only making $185 at the lumber yard."

At the time the offer was the mother lode for the son of a working-class couple with three sons. As a youth, Dick and his older brother, Al, another left-hander and a star in Minnesota's town-team circuit, saved up their money to buy a left-handed catcher's mitt so they could pitch to one another. Al was considered a professional prospect, too, but lacked Dick's drive, and he pitched on town teams while watching his brother work his way through the ranks.

Stigman was a small-town boy with a healthy confidence. Al offered an example from their teenage days. "Dick was so much more confident than I was. I was always the nervous type. I remember when we were just kids, a Legion coach asked us to play for him," he said. "We were fairly young and I told him that I didn't know if we were good enough. But Dick just snapped, 'Yes we are.' That was the major difference between the two of us: confidence."

For both Stigmans, baseball was a sport for all seasons, even in the winter months. Their mother cleaned a large hall, large enough for the boys to play catch during any kind of weather.

So when Slapnicka made his offer, it wasn't simply the money that inspired Stigman to take the big step, to prove to Cleveland what he obviously proved to the former Legion baseball coach … and, who knows, even find his way into a larger, more revered Hall.

Stigman never attained the status or celebrity of Feller, Lemon, or Score, but the 6-foot-3, 200-pound lefty's

A starter for the Twins in 1963 and 1964, lefty Dick Stigman worked primarily out of the bullpen in 1965, appearing in 33 games and logging 70 innings. In his seven-year career (1960-1966), he went 46-54. (Photo courtesy of Minnesota Twins Baseball Club).

fastball and his variety of curves were stellar enough to earn him seven years in the major leagues with Cleveland, Minnesota, and Boston. And with a little luck and more offensive support, he might have stuck around longer instead of leaving professional ball at 31.

During Stigman's rookie year at Cleveland in 1960, Chicago manager Al Lopez selected him to the American League All-Star team, but in the years when they played two midseason classics a year, Stigman never got to throw a pitch. He played on the 1965 Minnesota Twins American League champions, winning four games during the regular season, but never got closer to the field than the bullpen during the World Series. Stigman pitched for Boston in 1966, the year before Boston won the American League pennant, but was sold at season's end and never pitched another game in the majors.

Even his finest moment in the minor leagues, 10⅔ innings of no-hit ball for Triple-A San Diego, was overshadowed by Pittsburgh's Harvey Haddix, who the same night (May 26, 1959) pitched 12 innings of perfect ball before Don Hoak's error in the 13th inning led to Milwaukee's 1-0 victory over the Pirates.

Good does not always mean lucky.

Stigman, however, had no major regrets. While some of his high-school peers were delighted to play in or for Detroit Lakes and New York Mills in central Minnesota town-team ball, he lived the childhood dream of a major-league career.

 "Some people say, 'Don't you wish you had pitched in another era?' but I figure that all and all I was blessed to play seven seasons in the major leagues," Stigman said, looking back on a career in which he pitched in 119 games, compiling a 46-54 won-lost record with a 4.03 earned-run average. "Just to have done that is an awesome feeling."

Stigman's major-league statistics belie a solid career as a starter and reliever. In a later era, when relief pitchers began to make millions, he might have stuck around much longer, but he appreciated his entire professional experience. He was particularly pleased to have survived a rocky minor-league start, let alone making it to the big leagues at age 24.

In 1954, after a brief stop at Fargo-Moorhead in the Class C Northern League, he was sent to Tifton (Georgia) in the Class D Georgia-Florida League, where he went 0-6, followed by a 5-12 full season with Olean (New York) in the PONY League. Stigman struggled with control early in his first professional season, becoming wild after five or six solid innings, and with Olean he played for a "terrible team." A collective 5-18 record in Class D might have caused many pitchers concern, but Stigman said he never feared being released.

"I think that naïveté carried me through it all. I loved everything about what I was doing. I was playing baseball and getting paid for it," he said. "But during spring training in Daytona Beach, Laddie Placek, Cleveland's director of scouts, came up to me and said, 'Dick, if you don't do something this season, I think you should go back home and look for a job.'

"That was kind of a wakeup call. If you look up my record you'll see I turned things around, one-eighty."

Assigned to Vidalia of the Class D Georgia State League for 1956, Stigman compiled a 17-9 record with a 1.44 ERA. He was second to Sandersville's 20-game winner Gil Bassetti in victories, and his ERA was not only best in the league but in the entire Cleveland farm system. Stigman spent two more seasons in the minors, splitting time between Double-A Mobile and Triple-A San Diego in 1958 and playing the entire 1959 season with San Diego. Too often a slow starter in his first six seasons, the left-hander played from October 1959 through January in Nicaragua and, after a solid spring training, was promoted to the Indians in 1960.

Stigman remembered little about his first professional game or victory, saying that pitchers did a little bit of everything from starting to relieving and even pinch-hitting, but he recalled his major-league debut, when he pitched 2⅓ perfect innings of relief against the Athletics in Kansas City.

"I wasn't in awe. ... I felt like I belonged there and was completely comfortable by midseason. It wasn't like I was jumping from Nimrod to Cleveland or New York," Stigman said, referring to his Minnesota home town, population 75. "It's a progressive thing in which the crowds get bigger and the pressure stronger as you make your way up. But when you consider that besides spring-training games, the first major-league game I ever saw I played in. ... Well, that was something."

Stigman finished his first major-league season with a 5-12 record in 41 appearances, not overwhelming, but Lopez, the American League All-Star Game manager, selected the rookie for his pitching staff. The major leagues played two All-Star games from 1959 through 1962, and though Stigman didn't throw a pitch in '60, he was thrilled to be "hanging around" a group of legends. "I don't know if I deserved to be on the team," Stigman said, "but I obviously did something to impress Lopez when I pitched against the White Sox."

Beset by arm problems, he pitched in only 22 games in 1961, finishing 2-5 with a career-low 48 strikeouts. The following April, in a preseason trade, he and Vic Power were sent to the Twins for pitcher Pedro Ramos. One might expect that Stigman was jubilant, but the Minnesota native was skeptical about going home and being placed in the spotlight.

"I really liked it in Cleveland and felt badly about leaving a bunch of friends behind," he said. "I thought that pitching at home would impose a lot of pressure because they expect you to be Superman and you're not. But the fans were fantastic. They treated me great. I never expected that type of reception.

"It made me proud to be from Minnesota. People recognized me everywhere. It was an exciting time to be a Twin. I felt almost as popular as [Harmon] Killebrew and the other big names."

Stigman wasn't Superman in his first Twins season, but he was extremely solid, finishing 12-5 with a 3.66 ERA. His first 25 games came in relief, but Sam Mele—in his first full season as manager—gave him his first start on July 18, 1962, against Cleveland. Stigman pitched a complete game, striking out the side in the first inning of a 14-3 victory, a memorable game for him as well as for Twins fans because Killebrew and Bob Allison both hit grand slams in the first inning.

Stigman's signature season came in 1963. He had 33 starts, going 15-15 with a 3.25 ERA in 241 innings. He lost seven one-run decisions in which the Twins scored four or fewer runs, and among his 15 losses the Twins were shut out four times and scored two or fewer runs in seven others. His prize victories included three shutouts and a 10-1 two-hitter against the Washington Senators.

"My best year was definitely 1963," Stigman said. "I had a lot of starts and that was good because I thrived on work. The more I worked, the better I felt. I could easily have won 20 games with a little more support, but over the seasons things have a way of evening out."

His best season was underscored by his marriage to Patti Degenhard, a United Airlines flight attendant. They had planned to marry in the offseason, but United closed its base in Minneapolis and she would have been transferred to Denver, so she resigned and they were married on a day off in Minneapolis with most of the Twins in attendance.

Parsimonious owner Calvin Griffith gave Stigman a raise to $18,000, his highest salary as a professional, and manager Sam Mele used him almost exclusively as a starter early in the 1964 season. In 29 games, all but two as a starter, he went 6-15 with a 4.03 ERA, a significant dropoff, but once again he received lackluster offensive support. The Twins were scoreless in five of his starts and scored two or fewer runs on 13 occasions (though he picked up wins in two of those).

The 1965 season was one of mixed emotions for Stigman. He had no-decisions in his first five starts before two innings of perfect relief earned him a 5-4 victory over Detroit. He was sidelined for more than two weeks with a foot injury midway through the

Dick Stigman (Photo courtesy of Minnesota Twins Baseball Club).

season and started only one game after a no-decision on July 21.

In what would be his final Twins appearance, Stigman pitched 2⅔ innings to earn the win in an 8-6 victory over Kansas City on September 6. Manager Mele used nine pitchers in the team's seven-game World Series loss to the Los Angeles Dodgers, but all Stigman had to show for the postseason was his $6,400 share of the losing team's purse. Stigman was disappointed, since he was a competitor who loved challenging baseball's best, but he also was philosophical. His only lament was that his friend, Jim Perry, a Twins stalwart through most of the season, didn't get a World Series start.

"I really hadn't pitched that well at the end of the season," Stigman said. "After a poor July, I only pitched about 20 innings, and the Dodgers had an entire infield of switch-hitters, which limited my opportunities. I warmed up a couple of times during the Series, but that was it."

What was a major disappointment came the next April as the Twins broke camp and headed to Houston for an exhibition game. Mele informed Stigman that Griffith wanted to see him, and the pitcher knew from previous spring trainings that the message meant one of two things, and neither was good.

"The last day is cutdown day, and that was the day players were released or traded," Stigman said. "So when you're called in, your heart is beating like a drum because you don't know what it's going to be." Minutes after Griffith released Jerry Kindall (another Minnesota native), he met with Stigman and told him that he had been traded to the Boston Red Sox.

The good news in Boston was that Stigman began as a starter, but after seven games in which he was 0-1 with six no-decisions, he was yanked from the rotation by manager Billy Herman and sent to the bullpen. He did receive three more starts, with the last, on July 3, being sadly memorable.

"Tommie Agee stole third base the day before when [the White Sox] had a four- or five-run lead ... a bush league play," Stigman said. "Herman told me before the game that I should knock him on his ass. Well, I never liked to throw at a hitter anyway and I was involved in a 1-0 game and surely didn't want to put a speedster like Agee on base. It just didn't make sense to jeopardize a game to make a point and I didn't throw at him."

The details don't match Stigman's recollection. In the game the day before (July 2) won by Chicago, 6-0, Agee's only stolen base was in the first inning when the game was scoreless. Also, Stigman's start on July 3 was in the second game of a doubleheader. If something had happened on July 2, it's more likely Herman would have sought retaliation by the first-game starter. It's possible that the offending behavior by Agee came in game one on July 3. However, it wouldn't have been a stolen base when the White Sox had a big lead because Boston won this game 5-2, and Agee did not steal a base. However, he broke a scoreless tie with a two-run homer in the sixth, and could have done or said something in his trot around the bases that offended the Red Sox. All of this is conjecture. As an undisputed fact, it's interesting that in his July 3 start Stigman was relieved after three innings even though he had given up only one run and one hit.

Whatever happened, Herman had made his point to Stigman. Although Stigman made 14 more relief appearances, adding up to 16⅔ innings, Herman virtually ignored him, and after the 1966 season Stigman was placed on a carousel that led him nowhere but toward retirement. He was sold to Cincinnati in the winter and sent to Buffalo, and then late in the 1967 season was sold to San Diego, where the Padres were in a Pacific Coast League playoff run. After the 1967 season, he was sold to Pittsburgh, which wanted him to sign a $9,500 contract and report to Columbus.

A 31-year-old bachelor might have taken a chance, but Stigman and his wife had begun a family, (which eventually grew to nine children, five biological and four adopted, and 22 grandchildren). They couldn't live on that salary, so he didn't report and instead became a Minneapolis businessman and one of the Twins' most avid fans.

Stigman spoke fondly about some of the people he met along the way. He liked the vast majority of his professional teammates and opponents and was grateful for the assistance he received from managers, coaches, and teammates like Mark Wylie, his manager in Vidalia in 1956, Johnny Sain, Jim Lemon, and Twins teammate Frank Sullivan, a close friend with whom he sought counsel when he struggled. He also developed a profound appreciation for former Brooklyn Dodgers great and 1960 Cleveland teammate Don Newcombe, who gave him tips on pitching and golf, the latter game being his extracurricular passion in retirement.

If he were granted one change in his career, Stigman said, he would alter the end. No, he still wouldn't have thrown at Tommie Agee. No, he didn't regret not having taken the final minor-league assignment, hoping to gain another shot at the big leagues. He simply would have preferred a more gratifying exit.

"A couple of years after I retired, I asked for my release so I could close my scrapbook," Stigman said. "[The Pirates] said no; it was as if 'If you don't play for us, you don't play for anyone.' That's a pretty sad way to end a 14-year professional career.

"They sent [the release] to me five or six years later. That's the kind of control the owners had back then."

Note

A version of this biography appeared in the book *Minnesotans in Baseball*, edited by Stew Thornley (Nodin, 2009).

SOURCES

The Baseball Encyclopedia, the Baseball Cube, and several other Google sites, Baseball Old-Timers Data Base, the Minnesota Twins media-relations office and website, and a two-hour one-on-one interview with Stigman in Minneapolis.

Cesar Tovar

BY RORY COSTELLO

IN THE LATE 1960S AND EARLY '70S, César Tovar was a fixture at the top of the Minnesota Twins lineup. The speedy, enthusiastic little Venezuelan (5-feet-9 and 150 pounds) came up as a second baseman, but he could handle just about any spot—he is perhaps best remembered today as one of the four players to play all nine positions during the course of a single big-league game.[1] Yet that game in 1968 was just one of 1,488 in a respectable 12-year major-league career. Tovar, who mainly played the outfield, hit .278 with 46 homers and 226 stolen bases. He was a great favorite of manager Billy Martin, another peppery little player, who loved all-out competitors.

Tovar played on after his final year in the majors, 1976. He was in Mexico during the summers of 1977 and '78; he also wound up playing in 26 seasons in the Venezuelan winter league, second only to Vic Davalillo's 30. Neither before nor since has Venezuela had a one-two table-setting duo to compare with "Pepa e Burra" and "Vítico," who were winter teammates for 19 straight years. (Tovar's raunchy nickname—it refers to the genitals of a she-donkey!—was cleaned up as "Pepito" or "Pepi."[2]) César started in 1959, after his first professional summer, and finally hung it up at the age of 45 after two final games in the winter of 1985-86. He was part of eight champion teams at home and ranks high among the lifetime leaders in various categories.

César Leonardo Tovar was born on July 3, 1940, in Caracas, the capital of Venezuela. His family name—which is properly pronounced "toe-VAR"[3]—is that of his mother, Justina Tovar. She and César's father, Francisco "Frank" Pérez, lived together but were never married. Frank, who worked in construction, and Justina had three children, all boys. César's older brother was named Pedro and his younger brother was Alfonzo. Neither of them was involved with sports—but their father was a ballplayer. As César said in 1967, he was "a good second baseman. In Caracas he played on the same amateur team with Chico Carrasquel. When my father quit playing, he gave me his glove. I used it for a long time."[4]

Young César came to baseball around the age of 8. As a lad he also helped the family's finances by shining shoes. "Sometimes I made around $10 or $12 a day. People would come and ask for me because I did a good job." César's earnings bought him a glove before he inherited his father's.[5]

Tovar attended Escuela Nacional Franklin Delano Roosevelt in Caracas. At 15, he became friends with

Venezuelan-born Cesar Tovar debuted for the Twins in 1965, collecting the first five of 1,546 hits over a 12-year career. Standing just 5-foot-9, the versatile "Pepito" batted .300 or better twice and led the AL with 204 hits in 1971. (Photo courtesy of Minnesota Twins Baseball Club).

another future Venezuelan big leaguer, Gustavo "Gus" Gil. They played sandlot ball together, and Gil noted, "César always played the game hard." On New Year's morning in 1959, Gabe Paul, general manager of the Cincinnati Redlegs, signed them both. Gil got a $2,000 bonus. Tovar got nothing.[6]

Gabe Paul told the story himself in 1968. "I went to see Gus Gil in a morning workout. He insisted on bringing Tovar along. Gil was the man we wanted. I thought he was a great one. He wanted his buddy Tovar signed, too. César showed nothing, but I signed him to get Gil."[7] The Reds' top farm team in those days was the Havana Sugar Kings. Havana owner Bobby Maduro had been friends with Paul since the early '50s and the Sugar Kings had a sizable following in Venezuela.

Tovar's first pro season, with Geneva of the New York-Penn League (Class D), was not that auspicious. He batted .252 in 87 games, with 3 homers and 41 RBIs. In the winter of 1959, he joined the Caracas Leones of La Liga Venezolana del Béisbol Profesional (LVBP). He became Rookie of the Year and spent 16 seasons with that club, winning championships in five of them.[8]

The young infielder's second summer in the US was more promising. With Missoula of the Pioneer League (Class C), he hit .304/12/68, including 10 triples. The local writers, sportscasters, scorers, managers, and umpires voted him to the league's 1960 All-Star team.[9] As a reward, he spent two games with Triple-A Seattle. On a personal level, César also married Beatriz Veitia on December 10, 1960.

Yet for reasons at present unknown, Tovar had to step back down to Geneva in 1961. He stole 88 bases in 100 attempts to lead the league, shattering the New York-Penn League record in the process. He batted .338 with 19 homers and 78 RBIs. He was named to both the league and Class D All-Star teams, a feat he repeated in 1962 with the Rocky Mount Leafs of the Carolina League (Class B). He led that league in batting at .329, to go with 10 homers and 78 RBIs.

Nonetheless, it appeared Tovar would have a hard time progressing through the Reds' system. In 1963 the big club in Cincinnati had a new second baseman: Pete Rose, who became National League Rookie of the Year. Future major leaguer Bobby Klaus was at Triple-A San Diego and Gus Gil was at Double-A Macon. The organization sent Tovar on loan to the Twins; he played for their Triple-A farm team, Dallas-Fort Worth. There too, manager Jack McKeon had veteran Jim Snyder at second base, so Tovar became a utilityman for the first time, playing shortstop and the outfield while hitting .297/11/49. "He has to be in the lineup and he has to be my leadoff man," McKeon worried, "but where do I play him?" After seeing him in the outfield, the skipper said, "It's amazing. He gets a great jump on the ball—as if he had always played out there."[10]

Tovar also made two good friends in the Twins organization in 1963. One was Billy Martin, who that year was a minor-league instructor in spring training and took César under his wing. Another was his roommate, Tony Oliva, from Cuba, who became his teammate for seven-plus seasons in Minnesota. That year César and Beatriz added twin boys Jhonny Gustavo (named for Gus Gil) and Edgar José to their family. César Augusto had been born in 1961.

Tovar returned to the Reds chain in 1964 and played for San Diego, which won the Pacific Coast League pennant. He hit .275/7/52 while playing third, short, second, and the outfield. During the pennant series against Eastern Division winner Arkansas, opposing manager Frank Lucchesi said, "Tovar killed us with his great plays in the field as well as his bat."[11]

On December 4, 1964, the Twins traded pitcher Gerry Arrigo (coming off his best big-league season) to Cincinnati to get Tovar. Minnesota owner Calvin Griffith had wanted Tommy Helms, but the Reds wouldn't part with him, and Griffith said the Twins "had to pay through the nose" for Tovar. Scouting reports at the time labeled César an "adequate" second baseman who was "not considered outstanding on the double-play pivot."[12] Minnesota was thinking about him at third base as well as second.

Manager Sam Mele gave Tovar a long look at second base during spring training 1965 in a competition with light-hitting Jerry Kindall. Martin, a former second baseman and by then the Twins' infield coach, became César's tutor again.[13] Tovar made the Twins roster to open the 1965 season, becoming just the ninth Venezuelan to reach the majors. It seems remarkable today, but at that time only two more of his countrymen were active at the top level, Luis Aparicio and Vic Davalillo. In his debut on Opening Day at Metropolitan Stadium, playing third base, Tovar went from goat to hero. He dropped a Joe Pepitone popup in the ninth inning, allowing the tying run to score — but in the 11th inning he came through with a two-out game-winning single.

César appeared in just nine games with just 13 at-bats through mid-May. Near the end of the month, the Twins sent him down to Triple-A Denver as they reached the 25-man roster limit. After he performed well (.328/11/50), the big club recalled him in September. He was not eligible for the postseason, but he never played in the minors again.

In April 1966 Tony Oliva said, "Tovar plays the game hard. He runs, he chases down groundballs, dives at the ball, steals bases. And he sure can hit."[14] Tony was right. The following seven summers with Minnesota, 1966 through 1972, were the heart of Tovar's big-league career. He averaged 153 games played and 653 plate appearances per season over this period — indeed, from 1967 to 1971 he never appeared in fewer than 157 games. As the table-setter for the likes of Tony Oliva and Harmon Killebrew, he averaged 166 hits and 92 runs scored a year. In 1970 he led the American League in doubles (36) and triples (13). Tovar followed up with a career-best 204 hits in 1971 — the best one-year total by any Venezuelan until Magglio Ordóñez got 216 in 2007.

Tovar received MVP votes in each year from 1967 to 1971. In fact, when Carl Yastrzemski finished one vote short of unanimous American League MVP honors during his Triple Crown season in 1967, the 20th first-place ballot went to Tovar (.267/6/47). Minnesota beat writer Max Nichols defended his choice, saying,

"He played six positions for the Twins and I saw him win games for them at all six positions. We didn't have the best of player relations on our club, but Tovar never got mixed up in any of the clubhouse politics. He kept plugging away, no matter where they put him, and to me he did a tremendous job. If I wanted to be a 'homer,' I would have voted for Harmon Killebrew. But Tovar was my choice and, if I had to do it all over again, I'd vote for him again."[15]

"I would've voted for him too," said Billy Martin, who became the Twins' manager in 1969.[16] In his 1981 book, *Number 1*, Billy said, "Tovar was my little leader. He was the guy who got everyone going. When I wanted him to push Leo [Cárdenas] a little bit or if Rod [Carew] was getting down and I needed someone to give him a boost, I'd get César to do it."[17]

Tovar was never known as an outstanding fielder at any of his positions, but thanks to his speed he covered a lot of ground wherever he played. "He can play center field as well as anyone," said Cal Ermer, who managed him at Denver in 1965 and with the Twins in 1967 and '68. In the infield, "He's too rigid with his hands in fielding groundballs," said Billy Martin, who spent a lot of time in practice with César. Tovar himself said he that he was very tense when he first came to the majors.[18] When Rod Carew arrived in 1967, however, the Twins had an outstanding young second baseman. Though Tovar played a lot of third base in 1967-68, his focus after that became the outfield.

Tovar did not walk as much as one would like in a leadoff hitter. His on-base percentage was .335 for his career, peaking at .356 in both 1970 and 1971. Yet despite his moderate walk totals (a high of 52 in 1970), he often got on base another way — he was hit by a pitch 88 times in his career. As new Twins manager Bill Rigney put it in 1970, "He does not mind sticking an elbow out."[19] A related anecdote came from 1974 and the Venezuelan Winter League. Umpire Armando Rodríguez (the first Latino ump in the majors) called each ball that hit Tovar's arm a strike because he knew what César was doing. Once Tovar got hit in the back and Rodríguez sent him to first base because he was truly hit. After the game, Tovar said, "I have to recognize that the guy has class."[20]

Although Tovar was small, he was muscular and tough-bodied. He was also a very good contact hitter who struck out in only 7 percent of his plate appearances in the majors. In this vein, Tovar holds a record along with Eddie Milner: They each had the only hit in five one-hitters. Tovar was the spoiler in gems by Barry Moore (April 30, 1967); Dave McNally (ninth inning, May 15, 1969); Mike Cuéllar (ninth inning, August 10, 1969); Dick Bosman (August 13, 1970); and Catfish Hunter (May 31, 1975).[21] There might have been a sixth, but he made the last out in Vida Blue's no-hitter (September 21, 1970).

Tovar's best season for stolen bases was 1969, with 45. Over his career he was successful 68 percent of the time when stealing, somewhat lower than ideal, especially in a leadoff hitter. Both he and Rod Carew had the skill and daring to steal home, though—in fact, they did it in the same inning against Mickey Lolich and Bill Freehan of the Detroit Tigers on May 18, 1969. On August 23 at Metropolitan Stadium, César also stole home on the front end of a triple steal. Billy Martin's club was remarkably aggressive on the basepaths that year, pulling off that feat four times.

The Twins won the AL West in both 1969 and 1970, but each time, the Baltimore Orioles swept them in three straight playoff games. Baltimore's superb pitchers kept Tovar off the basepaths in 1969, as he went 1-for-14 with one walk. He did better in 1970 (5-for-13) but scored just two runs.

Tovar played all nine positions on September 22, 1968. The Twins were trailing the league-leading Detroit Tigers by 26 games at the time, and Calvin Griffith thought it would be a good promotional stunt. (The game drew a modest crowd of 11,340 to Metropolitan Stadium). He started the game on the mound—his scoreless inning featured a strikeout of Reggie Jackson, plus a walk and a balk—then went behind the plate. He then moved counter-clockwise around the infield, followed by a trip across the outfield from left to right.[22]

On November 30, 1972, the Twins traded Tovar to the Philadelphia Phillies for outfielder Joe Lis and pitchers Ken Reynolds and Ken Sanders. The Twins were willing to let him go because "his figures slipped some in 1972, partly due to a shoulder injury when he was hit by a pitch."[23] The Phillies wanted César to play third base—a position he had not manned since 1968—because they had traded Don Money.[24] They weren't sure if young Mike Schmidt was ready, and indeed he did struggle in 1973, hitting just .196 before emerging as a star. General manager Paul Owens also wanted Tovar on hand in case Mike Anderson couldn't hold down the starting center-field job. "Tovar gives us all kinds of things," said Owens. "He's a team leader. He's an outstanding basestealer, which will help [shortstop] Larry Bowa in his learning process. But most important, he gives us maneuverability."[25]

Tovar played 97 games for the Phillies in 1973 (.268/1/21), missing most of July after knee surgery. That December the Texas Rangers purchased Pepi's contract, as his longtime backer had been clamoring to get him. "When Billy Martin became the Rangers' manager last September, he made one immediate request: 'Get me César Tovar.'" Billy added, "I didn't want him back just because I had him before. That'd be foolish sentiment. I wanted him because of his leadership and his hustle and his ability. He's always played for me—given 100 percent—and I know he will.

"The little guy can beat you so many ways—his bat, his feet, his brains, his hustle."[26]

Tovar rebounded nicely in 1974 (.292/4/58 in 138 games, with 629 plate appearances), playing mainly center field and left field. There was also an amusing footnote to that season. According to Mike Shropshire's 1996 book about the 1973-1975 Rangers, *Seasons in Hell*, there were rumors that Pepito had three wives in three different countries. In 1975 he played less in the field and served more as a designated hitter.

Billy Martin was fired in July 1975. On August 31 the Oakland A's purchased Tovar. Although they already had a healthy lead in the AL West, owner Charlie Finley still wanted a player to help in the final month of the season. Mike Shropshire wrote, "According to speculation, it would be Tovar's job to goad [Bert] Campaneris to get off his ass."[27] The A's placed Angel Mangual, who had been with Oakland since 1971, on irrevocable waivers.[28] Tovar was on the postseason roster and appeared in two playoff games against the Red Sox, going 1-for-2 with two runs scored.

In the winter of 1975-76, Tovar's career at home took a turn as the Caracas Leones merged with Tiburones de La Guaira. For one season, a franchise called "Tibuleones" de Portuguesa existed. When Tovar returned to Oakland in 1976, he was a little-used reserve, going 8-for-45 in 29 games. He broke his wrist making a diving catch on May 31 and was not reactivated until mid-August — it took a complaint to Players Association director Marvin Miller to make it happen.[29] On August 25 Finley — in a typical and quite possibly vengeful move — released the veteran.[30]

On September 1 Tovar signed as a free agent with the New York Yankees, becoming their first Venezuelan player. Again Billy Martin — who had landed with New York less than two weeks after Texas canned him — was behind the signing. The Yankees had been talking to the Rangers about acquiring Billy's old favorite the previous year.[31] He got into 13 games for the Bronx Bombers, going 6-for-39. He joined the club too late to be eligible for the postseason.

In December 1976 the Yankees released Tovar, and his big-league career came to an end. Of greater significance, though, was the development of the players' rights movement in Venezuela. The re-established Caracas Leones had traded both Vic Davalillo and Tovar to Tigres de Aragua before the 1976-77 season. They filed suit for severance pay. A reputable lawyer named Efraín Muñoz took the case to demonstrate to the Caracas front office and in the courts that his clients were workers and consequently deserved their benefits under national law. Muñoz won, setting a precedent.[32]

Tovar was by no means finished playing in the summers, though, as he joined Puebla in the Mexican League in 1977. During his first month, he batted .270, "but he said he was just 'studying the situation.'" He then went on a tear that lifted his average to .337.[33] He finished the year at .345/1/53 in 432 at-bats across 121 games — yet unlike his fellow Venezuelan vet, Davalillo, his performance south of the border didn't write his ticket back to the majors. Pepi returned to Mexico in 1978, playing with Tabasco, but though he hit well again (.336/1/17), it was in just 31 games. From mid-April to mid-June 1979, he also played with the Caracas Metropolitanos of Bobby Maduro's short-lived Inter-American League.

Tovar's winter career at home also continued. After two seasons with Aragua, he spent seven more with Águilas del Zulia. César, who was 39 when he joined Zulia as a player-coach, averaged just 22 games played per winter during his stretch there, the most being 49 in 1981-82. Zulia became league champion in 1983-84, and Tovar got into one game in the playoff finals. It was his eighth title at home, including the two he won as a playoff reinforcement with Tiburones de La Guaira (1965-66) and Navegantes del Magallanes (1969-70).

When Pepito finally decided to retire as a player, he had appeared in 1,116 games in La Liga Venezolana del Béisbol Profesional, tied for fourth in the league's history. He had 1,224 hits (also fourth lifetime) for a .286 average, along with 23 homers and 399 RBIs. As of 2014 he ranked second in runs scored (635) and steals (146), and third in doubles (191).

Tovar maintained his connection with baseball. He had long been known for his support of children in his homeland, for whom he collected uniforms and equipment. He worked as a softball coach for the INH (Instituto Nacional de Hipódromos, or Horse Racing Authority, which sponsored recreation for its workers and their families). He eventually recommended players to the professional teams. He also managed the Venezuelan national team in the 1990 Baseball World Cup, held in Edmonton. His squad won just one game and lost seven.

Mainly, though, Tovar continued to serve Águilas del Zulia as a coach. His special protégé was Carlos

Quintana, who played with the Boston Red Sox from 1988 to 1993. Red Sox bullpen coach John McLaren said in 1991, "I remember Cesar Tovar spent hours and hours with Carlos in winter ball." Quintana said, "He's my second father."[34]

Quintana was also worried when Tovar had to spend a month in the hospital with heart problems in 1991. "He smoked too much," said the first baseman. "I told him [to] stop. Maybe he will now."[35] It appears that Tovar traveled to Minnesota in May 1993 for a 1965 Twins reunion featuring more than 20 team members.[36] Not long after, though, Tovar was diagnosed with pancreatic cancer. This swift and deadly form of the disease ended his life on July 14, 1994. When the news reached Minnesota, the Twins called for a moment of silence before that night's game. Such was Tovar's stature in Venezuela that the nation's president, Rafael Caldera, attended the funeral.

César Tovar entered the Venezuelan Sports Hall of Fame in 1996 and the Venezuelan Baseball Hall of Fame as part of its first class in 2003. He is still remembered as one of the greatest players in the history of his nation's winter league. And as Tony Oliva said of their days with the Twins, "If we'd had nine players like him, we wouldn't have needed any others."[37]

Grateful acknowledgment to Jhonny Gustavo Tovar Veitia for providing information about his family (via a series of e-mails, August 2011). Continued thanks to SABR member Alfonso Tusa in Venezuela for his assistance.

SOURCES

baseball-reference.com

retrosheet.org

planeta-beisbol.com (Venezuelan statistics)

museodebeisbol.org (Hall of Fame/Museum of Baseball in Venezuela)

Treto Cisneros, Pedro, editor, *Enciclopedia del Béisbol Mexicano* (Mexico City: Revistas Deportivas, S.A. de C.V.: 11th edition, 2011)

Sporting News Baseball Register, 1965

NOTES

[1] The others: Bert Campaneris (1965), Scott Sheldon (2000), Shane Halter (2000).

[2] Online biographical sketch by Dr. Braulio Arteaga, *César Tovar: Pimienta Caraqueña*. (oocities.org/espanol/elpelotero_online/reportajes/cesar_tovar...). The origins are unclear.

[3] The *Sporting News Annual Register* for 1965 showed "TOH-var"—which is how people in the US often pronounced it. One notable exception was Twins P.A. announcer Bob Casey, who put the emphasis on the second syllable, in the Spanish way.

[4] Max Nichols, "Dad Delivers a Lecture When Cesar Strikes Out," *The Sporting News*, June 3, 1967, 11; Dick Gordon, "Letter Man at Minnesota," *Baseball Digest*, July 1967, 29.

[5] Gordon, "Letter Man at Minnesota," 30.

[6] Max Nichols, Sandlot Pals Tovar and Gil Meet Again—In Majors," *The Sporting News*, May 6, 1967, 11.

[7] Si Burick, "Blind Man's Buff," *Baseball Digest*, July 1968, 74. Originally published in the *Dayton Daily News*.

[8] They were 1961-62, 1963-64, 1966-67, 1967-68, and 1972-73.

[9] "Pioneer Names All-Star Team," *The Sporting News*, September 14, 1960, 46.

[10] Merle Heryford, " 'Little Cesar' Tovar Packing Big Wallop for Texas Rangers," *The Sporting News*, June 22, 1963, 33.

[11] Earl Keller, "Champ Padres Praise Bristol—Pilot Instilled Fighting Spirit," *The Sporting News*, October 3, 1964, 29.

[12] Max Nichols, "Cal Expects Swifty Tovar To Firm Up Twins' Infield," *The Sporting News*, December 19, 1964, 6.

[13] Max Nichols, "Kindall Duels Tovar At Twins' Keystone," *The Sporting News*, April 3, 1965, 8.

[14] Max Nichols, "Great Cesar's Ghost, Twins Find Zoilo's Sub in Wraith-Like Tovar," *The Sporting News*, April 16, 1966, 22.

[15] Joe Falls, "An Apology to Writer Who's True to Beliefs," *The Sporting News*, December 16, 1967, 2.

[16] George Vass, "Ninth Man in the Lineup," *Baseball Digest*, June 1968, 9.

[17] Billy Martin and Peter Golenbock, *Number 1* (New York: Dell Publishing, 1981), 268.

[18] Nichols, "Great Cesar's Ghost."

[19] Mike Lamey, "Little Cesar Tovar Becomes Twins' Mighty Triggerman," *The Sporting News*, May 16, 1970, 6.

[20] Alfonso Tusa, "El primer árbitro latinoamericano en ejercer en Grandes Ligas," Beisbol 007 blog, November 10, 2010 (beisbol007.blogia.com/temas/historia.php).

[21] Peter C. Bjarkman, *Diamonds Around the Globe* (Westport, Connecticut: Greenwood Press, 2005), 219.

[22] Emil Rothe, "The Day Cesar Tovar Played All 9 Positions," *Baseball Digest*, February 1973, 50-51; Bruce Markusen, "When

Cesar Tovar Played All Nine Positions in One Game," *Baseball Digest*, December 1998, 86-89.

23 Allen Lewis, "'Now Phillies Can Shoot For 2nd Place'—Ozark," *The Sporting News*, December 23, 1972, 45.

24 "Phils to Put Tovar at 3rd Base," *The Sporting News*, December 16, 1972, 59.

25 Lewis, "Now Phillies Can Shoot."

26 Merle Heryford, "Rangers Get Tovar … Martin Elated," *The Sporting News*, December 22, 1973, 47.

27 Mike Shropshire, *The Last Real Season* (New York: Grand Central Publishing, 2008).

28 Ron Bergman, "Mercury Matt Spurts Into Hearts of A's," *The Sporting News*, September 20, 1975, 7.

29 Ron Bergman, "Catcher Tenace Can Drive a Hard Bargain," *The Sporting News*, September 4, 1976, 7.

30 Ron Bergman, "A's More Flexible With Willie," *The Sporting News*, September 18, 1976, 34.

31 Randy Galloway, "Howell Fires Homer Barrage to Grab Ranger 3rd Base Job," *The Sporting News*, August 30, 1975, 16.

32 Adriana Cortés, *Montesinos: Su Derrota en Venezuela* (Caracas, Venezuela: Los Libros de El Nacional, 2001), 119. According to *The Sporting News* (July 30, 1977, 25), Tovar filed suit for severance pay in 1977 after the trade. The news may simply have been late getting to the United States.

33 "Mexican League," *The Sporting News*, July 9, 1977, 38.

34 Nick Cafardo, "Q. Who's the Red Sox' hit man? A. The Q," *Boston Globe*, May 29, 1991.

35 Cafardo, "Q. Who's."

36 Original announcement: Charley Walters, "Civic Center Officials Baffled That Green Rejected Their Offer," *St. Paul Pioneer Press*, March 4, 1993. Subsequent ads for the weekend of May 14-16 mentioned that more than 20 members would be at the shows in the Minneapolis suburb of Hopkins, but did not cite Tovar by name.

37 Arteaga, *César Tovar*.

Ted Uhlaender

BY JOSEPH WANCHO

THEODORE OTTO UHLAENDER WAS born on October 21, 1939. Although his birth took place in Chicago Heights, Illinois, he was raised in McAllen, Texas. He and his brother Mickey were the sons of Henry and Helen Uhlaender. Henry owned an electronics store. Ted Uhlaender was a superb all-around athlete, lettering in football, basketball, baseball, and track at McAllen High School.

After he graduated from high school, Uhlaender enrolled at Baylor University. Although he was on the small side for a catcher (5-feet-9, 130 pounds), Uhlaender starred for the Bears. He also excelled in the classroom, earning a bachelor's degree in statistics. Uhlaender also made a name for himself on the semipro circuit. He caught for the Texas State Champion McAllen Dons in 1959. The next year Uhlaender led the league in hitting and was named the MVP of the Kansas State League while playing for the Wichita Cessna Bobcats.

The 1961 major-league season was the first of the expansion era. The Washington Senators relocated to Minneapolis, and two cities were awarded expansion franchises: Los Angeles and a new club under new ownership in Washington. Minnesota Twins scout Morris "Buddy" Hancken signed Uhlaender to his first professional contract.

Uhlaender began his ascent through the Twins' minor-league chain in 1961, beginning with Class D (short season) Wytheville (Virginia) of the Appalachian League. He played in only five games because of a leg injury. "I was stealing second and in the middle of my slide, decided to stand up instead. I caught my spikes in the ground and broke my right leg," Uhlaender recalled.[1] Although the broken leg stalled his career before it even started, Uhlaender was faced with another obstacle. "I was always a catcher, but when the Twins sent me to Wytheville they had a catcher named Donny Hagen, a bonus baby who hit .376 that year."[2] Because he showed above-average speed, Uhlaender was shifted to the outfield. Also making his professional debut that year for Wytheville was Tony Oliva, whose .410 batting average showed that he was not long for the bush leagues.

Uhlaender went on to play for four teams in five leagues along his minor-league journey. The left-handed-batting Texan showed that he could hit the ol' rawhide. With the Erie Sailors of the Class D New York-Pennsylvania League in 1962, Uhlaender led the league in batting with a .342 average. But he found the going a little rougher the higher he went in the Twins chain. He struggled in back-to-back seasons at Double-A Charlotte, batting .228 in 1963 and .260 in 1964. The Twins front office was not pleased with his progress, or lack thereof, and a promotion to Triple-A Denver did not seem to be in the cards for the young outfielder. But Charlotte manager Al Evans assured Ermer that he believed Uhlaender would fill

Uhlaender made his major-league debut with the Twins as a September call-up in 1965. A sturdy contributor on the Twins divisional winner in 1969, batting .273 and scoring 93 runs, he was involved in the trade to the Cleveland Indians that brought Luis Tiant to Minnesota. (Photo courtesy of Minnesota Twins Baseball Club).

his need for an outfielder with some pop in the bat and sufficient speed.

Uhlaender began the 1965 season with an 11-game hitting streak on his way to winning the Pacific Coast League batting title with a .340 average. He drove in 57 runs and smacked 31 doubles for Ermer's Denver club. His fine season earned him a call-up to the Twins.

Uhlaender made his major-league debut against the Chicago White Sox on September 4, 1965, with the Twins in the hunt for their first pennant. Pinch-hitting, he was struck out by White Sox pitcher John Buzhardt. He got his first major-league hit the next day. Again pinch-hitting, he got an infield single off Joe Horlen. .Like many minor leaguers who are called up as the big-league rosters expand, Uhlaender was there to spell the regulars, who needed a break at the end of the long season. He played sparingly, but had a front seat to watch the action as the Twins outlasted the White Sox and Orioles to win the flag and punch their ticket to the World Series. Minnesota knocked the New York Yankees, who had won five straight pennants, from atop their perch in the American League.

The next season saw Uhlaender break spring training with the Twins, but in early May, with just two hits in 16 at-bats, he was sent back to Denver. After getting a taste of major-league life, it was gut-check time for Uhlaender to see how he would adjust to this latest impediment in his career. "Now we'll see what you're made of,"[3] Ermer told Uhlaender upon his return to the Mile High City.

Uhlaender had plenty to prove to himself and to the Twins organization. He responded with a .341 batting average in 43 games. The Twins recalled him and manager Sam Mele inserted him in center field on June 25, 1966. His minor-league days were in the rear-view mirror. "Uhlaender has shown me he can really go get those long drives," said Mele. "He lopes, but he makes the hard plays look easy. He's throwing much better than he did in the spring, and he gets a good jump on the ball. That's the best center-field play we've had since (Cesar) Tovar played there earlier this spring."[4]

Uhlaender hit 32 points higher in 1967 than in the previous season (up to .258 from .226). One of his highlights came on September 5, 1967, when he stroked two triples against Cleveland and scored both times in a 9-2 pasting of the Indians at Metropolitan Stadium. He led all center fielders in the American League with a .996 fielding percentage that season. "The way he plays center field, all Ted has to do is hit .250 or .260 to help us," said Twins owner Calvin Griffith.[5]

Cal Ermer replaced Mele 50 games (25-25 record) into the 1967 season, reuniting with Uhlaender. Under Ermer the Twins went 66-46. On September 26 they held a one-game lead with three games to play. But they dropped their last three games, including two to the Red Sox at Fenway Park. Boston squeaked by to grab the pennant.

Uhlaender's batting average continued to climb in 1968, as he hit .283 and posted a career high in doubles with 21. He tallied five hits, also a career high, against the New York Yankees on June 23, 1968, in a 6-3 Twins win. The 1968 season is commonly referred to as the Year of the Pitcher, when pitching dominated both leagues. While many batters had dismal seasons, Uhlaender flourished.

Uhlaender held out in spring training, feeling that he was entitled to a raise. "I made $10,000 in 1968, my fourth year in the league, and at the time the major-league minimum was $8,000," he recalled. "Calvin asked me how much I need for 1969 and I told him $14,000 and he laughed."[6] Uhlaender held out, and played baseball in the Mexican League to keep in shape. Billy Martin was the new Twins manager in 1969. "About the middle of March, Billy called me and said, 'Could you play tomorrow if we got it worked out?' I told him I could, so he said, 'Let me handle this, you just report tomorrow.'"[7] Uhlaender did as he promised Martin, and reported to spring training, signed his contract, and played the same day. "The next day, Billy said 'You look like you could use a day off.' So he didn't play me. I played one day, signed a contract, then got a day off. That drove Calvin crazy."[8]

In 1969 each major league expanded by two more teams and they each went to a two-division format. This created a round of playoffs before the World Series. No longer was the team with the best record guaranteed a spot in the fall classic.

The Twins won the newly formed American League West Division over the Oakland Athletics by nine games. They had a solid nucleus of players including Harmon Killebrew, Rod Carew, and Tony Oliva. Their pitching staff was led by Jim Kaat, Jim Perry, and Dave Boswell. Players like Leo Cardenas, Tovar, and Uhlaender helped to support the stars, and were integral parts of the team. Uhlaender hit .273, bolstered by a 20-game hitting streak from August 16 to September 7. He hit .307 during this span, stroked five doubles, and drove in 16 runs.

But in the inaugural American League championship Series, the Baltimore Orioles swept the Twins in three games. (Uhlaender started in left field in Game Three and went 0-for-5). Perhaps the knowledge that the Orioles had the better pitching caused the Twins to look for help. After the World Series they dealt Uhlaender to Cleveland, along with pitchers Dean Chance and Bob Miller, and third baseman Graig Nettles in exchange for pitchers Luis Tiant and Stan Williams.

Cleveland ace Sam McDowell was upbeat about the deal that brought Uhlaender to the Indians. "He's a fabulous center fielder and also one of the toughest batters around," McDowell said. "I'm counting on him to hit .300 and I know he'll walk plenty and steal a lot of bases."[9]

In 1970 Uhlaender struck a blow for players' rights. On behalf of professional baseball players, he sued Kent L. Henricksen and the Nemadji Game Company. The case sought to enjoin a manufacturer of a "scientific" baseball board game from using players' names and statistical records without payment of royalty or licensing fees to the players.[10]

A federal judge in Minneapolis agreed with the players, holding that a player's "name, likeness, statistics, and other personal characteristics, is the fruit of his labors and is a type of property" entitled to protection from unauthorized commercial use by others. The court rejected the claim of unlawful antitrust action by the players' union in demanding royalty fees for the use of the players' names and statistics. Once a ballplayer, always a ballplayer, in the eyes of the law.

Uhlaender may not have hit .300 for the Indians, as McDowell predicted, but he did reach a career high in homers (11) in 1970 and hit .288 in 1971. The Indians were not on the same plateau as the Twins, though, and were not considered a contender in the East Division. Uhlaender had a short "retirement" from the Indians in late June 1971. Upset at the lack of playing time, he jumped the team while it was en route from Detroit to New York. It was a curious move by Uhlaender, who achieved the second most at-bats in his career (500) that season. Although he and manager Al Dark worked out their differences, it did not sit well with the Cleveland front office. The Indians dealt him after the season to Cincinnati for pitcher Milt Wilcox.

Uhlaender was used in a reserve role with the Reds, playing mostly in right field and as a pinch-hitter. The Reds won their division and bested Pittsburgh in the NLCS. Their opponent in the World Series was Oakland. It was a tightly played series. With one exception, every game was decided by one run. The Athletics prevailed in seven games. Uhlaender was used as a left-handed batter off the bench. He got one hit, a double in Game Two.

At the age of 33, Uhlaender retired as a major league player after the 1971 season. For his career, he had a .263 batting average and fielded his position in center at a .991 clip. He did not stray far from the baseball diamond. He managed Rio Grande Valley in the Gulf States League in 1976. He joined former Twins teammate Charlie Manuel's coaching staff in 2000, when Manuel was named the Cleveland Indians manager. For two seasons he served as the club's first-base coach.

Uhlaender also was employed by various teams in their scouting departments, including the Yankees,

Arizona, and San Francisco. An avid outdoorsman, Ted hunted everything from rattlesnakes to elk to deer. He often went on excursions in the offseason with teammates. Uhlaender was also a licensed pilot, frequently flying from Texas to his new home in Kansas.

Uhlaender was diagnosed with multiple myeloma-bone marrow cancer in 2008. It was not a curable disease, although there was optimism if they could get in remission. Doctors appeared to have the condition under control by early the following year; the Giants even were hopeful he could get back to doing a little scouting for them. But on February 12, 2009, while chatting with his son at the family ranch in Kansas, Uhlaender had a heart attack and died. He was 69. He was survived by his second wife, Karen Uhlaender, and five children, Scott, Sheryl, Hank, William, and Katie.

At the time of her father's death, Katie Uhlaender was competing in a World Cup skeleton sliding race in Park City, Utah. She won the silver medal, and as the award was being presented, she was unaware that her father had died. She had wanted to be at home with her parents, but he encouraged her to compete.

"The only time I feel normal is when I slide, and that's because I feel like my dad is there with me," said Katie.[11]

SOURCES

Baseball-Reference.com

Retrosheet.org

Ted Uhlaender's player file, National Baseball Hall of Fame, Cooperstown, New York.

Author's interview with Karen Uhlaender, September 2, 2014.

NOTES

1. *Sports Collectors Digest*, July 18, 1997, 72.
2. Ibid.
3. *The Sporting News*, July 16, 1966, 34.
4. Ibid.
5. *Sporting News*, September 9, 1967, 20.
6. *Lorain* (Ohio) *Morning Journal*, February 6, 2000, B6.
7. Ibid.
8. Ibid.
9. *The Sporting News*, January 3, 1970, 38.
10. Marshall Tanick, "Play Ball—Minnesota Baseball Litigation Lore," *The National Pastime* (SABR, Phoenix, Arizona, 2012), 146.
11. *Cleveland Plain Dealer*, February 16, 2009.

Sandy Valdespino

BY ALAN COHEN

"Great catches are a lot like pretty girls. The last one you see is always the best one."

— Bob Sudyk of the *Cleveland Press*, after seeing a spectacular catch by Sandy Valdespino on June 18, 1967

IN 1967 SANDY VALDESPINO WAS A bench player for the Minnesota Twins. On June 18 the Twins were playing at Cleveland.

Valdespino was struggling that season, but on June 18, he most definitely was in the right place at the right time. In the bottom of the eighth inning the Indians had scored two runs, trailed the Twins 4-2 and had the bases loaded with two outs. Manager Cal Ermer replaced pitcher Jim Kaat with Ronnie Kline and moved left fielder Cesar Tovar to third base, in place of Rich Rollins, to shore up the infield defense. He inserted Valdespino into Kaat's place in the batting order, playing left field. The outfield switch paid a big dividend. Cleveland's Larry Brown banged a Kline delivery to deepest left field and it appeared that it was going to be a grand slam. Sandy Valdespino had other ideas.

Among those in Cleveland for the Old-Timers festivities that day was Joe DiMaggio. As Sandy said, "I wanted to bring back memories for Joe DiMaggio. I saw the DiMaggio catch in movies." Valdespino was referring to the catch made on DiMaggio by the Dodgers' Al Gionfriddo in the 1947 World Series.

Pitcher Kline thought it was a home run. Batter Brown thought it was a home run. But Sandy just ran. "When the ball was hit, I thought I could catch it," he said after the game. "I turned to my left and chased it. But when I got closer to the fence, I knew it was out of the park, over the screen. But I stayed with the ball, because the wind was bringing it back. When I got near the fence, I had the ball in range. I was watching it over my right shoulder. I took a couple of steps up the screen fence and caught (the ball) with my glove over the fence."[1]

It was the third out of the inning and preserved the Twins lead. The ninth inning was scoreless, and the Twins had a 4-2 win.

Ten years earlier, on May 23, 1957, 18-year-old Sandy Valdespino, in his first year in Organized Baseball, slammed a two-run-homer that got him a mention in *The Sporting News*. He was with Midland (Texas) in the Class B Southwestern League that season, and was en route to a .295 batting average with 11 homers, 62 RBIs, and a team-leading 12 triples.

Hilario (Borroto) Valdespino was born in San Jose de las Lajas, Cuba, on January 24, 1939, and was signed

Cuban-born, 5-foot-8 Sandy Valdespino was a unexpected rookie sparkplug on the Twins in 1965, starting 38 games in leftfield. In the most productive of his seven seasons in the majors, the 26-year-old Valdespino appeared in 108 games and batted .261. (Photo courtesy of Minnesota Twins Baseball Club).

• 272 •

by Joe Cambria of the Washington Senators before the 1957 season. Because he looked like Sandy Amoros of the Dodgers, his first minor-league manager, Johnny Welaj, rechristened him Sandy. Valdespino's ever-present smile was in contrast to a life that was at times hard. His father died when he was 9 years old, and Sandy went to work in an iron pipe factory.

"My brother worked as a shoemaker. My mother did washing. I went to school in the morning, worked in the afternoon, and played baseball after work," Valdespino said. "But I never felt bad about having to work. And my mother was always happy. So it is natural for me. I think I am so big in the shoulders [his 5-foot-5 body carried 170 pounds], because of that hard work. It was a good thing for me."[2]

In 1958 with the Fox Cities Foxes (Appleton, Wisconsin) in the Three-I League, Valdespino was batting just .143 when he was optioned to Missoula (Montana) in the Class C Pioneer League on June 4.[3] He caught fire and slugged 15 homers while posting a batting average of .312 in 87 games.

By 1959 Valdespino was with Charlotte in the Class A Sally League. The speedster led his team with 10 triples en route to a .270 batting average for the second-place Hornets. Batting leadoff, he knocked in 61 runs, including five in a game on June 10. He was chosen to play in the league's All-Star Game.

Valdespino's next stop, in 1960, was with the Charleston (West Virginia) Senators of the Triple-A American Association in 1960. Though he got off to a great start (seven hits in a four-game stretch from April 20 through April 24, including two doubles, a triple and a home run), his batting average for the season was .267, with 31 doubles, 10 triples, and 11 homers. Teammates Zoilo Versalles and Don Mincher were promoted to the Twins, but Valdespino remained in the minors.

He played in Cuba during the offseason, leading the Cuban league in batting with a .345 average while playing for Havana.[4] By this point Fidel Castro was in control and it was getting more difficult to leave the country. Valdespino along with other Cubans in the organization—Camilo Pascual, Pedro Ramos, Versailles, Dave Sanchez, and Marty Martinez—received clearances and made it back to the United States by way of Mexico.

In the spring of 1961 Valdespino was in spring training with the brand-new Minnesota Twins, but was sent down to Syracuse Chiefs of the International League. After breaking a bone in his left hand on April 23 and batting .237 in 51 games with Syracuse, he was sent to Indianapolis in the American Association on August 8. With Indianapolis, he returned to form, batting .302 in 28 games, as his team won the American Association pennant.

After the season Valdespino played in the Panama-Nicaragua league for Cinco Estrellas. His best performance came on January 11 when his two singles, a triple, and a homer propelled his team to a 7-0 win over Cerveza Balboa.

In the spring of 1962 Valdespino was again with the Twins during spring training. Despite a productive spring that included a game winning homer, he was optioned to Vancouver of the Pacific Coast League on March 28. He got off to the worst start of his career and was batting only .179 in 21 games when the Twins sent him to Dallas-Fort Worth of the American Association on May 25.

In Texas Valdespino's productivity improved immediately. He batted .278 in 81 games, but was sidelined when he injured his ankle on August 18. For the balance of the season, he was restricted to pinch-hitting.

During the offseason, he was married on February 19, 1963. In 1963 at Dallas-Fort Worth, he was reunited with Jack McKeon. Healthy for the first time in three years, he got into 114 games with the Rangers and batted .284.

Another year, making it eight in all, would elapse from the time Valdespino was signed until he made his major-league debut. In 1964 at Atlanta, he led the International League in batting with a .337 average and led his team in virtually every offensive category.

At Dallas-Fort Worth and Atlanta, Valdespino came under the tutelage of veteran third baseman Ray Jablonski, whom he credited with showing him how to handle pitches and hit to all fields.[5] However, the Twins had an outfield of Bob Allison, Jimmie Hall, and Tony Oliva. How would Sandy fit in at Minnesota in 1965?

As the season began, Valdespino was most often used as a pinch-hitter and defensive replacement. In his debut, on Opening Day against the New York Yankees at Minnesota, he was walked intentionally to load the bases with the scored tied at 4-4 in the bottom of the 11th inning. Cesar Tovar drove in the winning run later that inning.

After 13 pinch-hit appearances, in which he went 3-for-11 with a walk and a sacrifice fly, Valdespino got his first start on May 19 in a road game against the California Angels, playing left field in place of Allison. He went 3-for-6 with a double and his infield single in the 12th helped as the Twins won 3-1.

Valdespino went 9-for-20 in his May starts to bring his batting average up to .364. He saw even more action in June, starting 11 games, and on June 23 he hit his first of seven major-league homers as the Twins defeated Cleveland, 6-3. The win took the first place Twins' record to 39-24.

In July, Allison missed eight games after being hit by a pitch. Valdespino was inserted into the lineup against right-handed pitchers, starting six games and going 9-for-23 to bring his average to .281. Once Allison returned, Valdespino resumed his role as the team's premier pinch-hitter. On August 19 and 20, his pinch-singles helped win two games against the Tigers, and Minnesota's lead over its closest rivals stood at 8 games.

Valdespino's batting average fell off to .261 by the end of the season, but he led all Twins rookies in games played and at-bats.

Yet, for Valdespino and the other Cubans on the Twins, there was a certain sense of isolation. Versalles noted that, while the team celebrated its victory, "I stand in front of my locker with Tony (Oliva), Camilo (Pascual), and Sandy (Valdespino), and we don't say nothing. Tony cries. I think this is the biggest moment I ever have in my life and I can't go home and tell about it. I have nothing to do with politics. The trouble between Castro and the United States should not cause things like this."[6]

In the World Series the Twins faced the Los Angeles Dodgers, who were appearing in their second Series in three years. In the opener, Valdespino got the start in left field against the tough righty Don Drysdale and went 1-for-4. In the bottom of the third inning, his double was one of six hits as the Twins scored six times in the inning and went on to win 8-2. His next start came against Drysdale in Game Four. He again went 1-for-4 as the Dodgers won, 7-2. Valdespino's third hit of the Series came in Game Five, a pinch-single off Sandy Koufax in the ninth inning, but the Dodgers won to take a 3-2 edge in the Series. His last chance, again against Koufax, was in Game Seven when he fouled out in the eighth inning as the Twins lost 2-0.

At the beginning of the 1966 season, it appeared that Valdespino had beaten out Allison for the starting position in left field. He started each of the first seven games. On Opening Day he drove in both Twins runs with a pair of singles as they defeated Kansas City, 2-1, getting the winning blow off Catfish Hunter in the bottom of the ninth.[7] The Twins swept the opening series against the A's, and Sandy's average stood at .364, including a home run. But then he went 1-for-16 in the next four games, and Allison was back in left field. Over the rest of the season, Valdespino spent most of his time on the bench. His slump was so bad that he was sent to Denver on June 23. In 72 games there he batted .321 and was recalled in September, but for the season he played in only 52 games for the Twins and batted .176.

The following season, Valdespino was with the Twins for the entire season and was one of their first players off the bench. He appeared in 99 games but only started nine times. Early on, in limited opportunities, he produced. As a pinch-hitter, he doubled and homered, going 3-for-11 with two walks in 13 attempts through June 2. The homer helped win a game against the Yankees on May 3.

Valdespino got his first start at Anaheim on June 3. Playing in right field in place of the injured Tony Oliva, he came up big in the sixth inning. With the Twins' leading 6-5, Bobby Knoop tried to score from second with the tying run, but Valdespino gunned him down at home plate. The Twins went on to win 8-6.

Overall, though, the season was a disappointment and frustration for Valdespino. His batting average, which stood at .300 at the end of May, severely plummeted during the last four months of the season. In August, as the Twins made a charge and took the league lead, Sandy appeared in nine games between August 10 and August 19, but in each game he was just a late-inning defensive replacement. He finally got a few starts when Allison pulled his hamstring on August 24. With Valdespino in the lineup, the Twins won four of five games.

Valdespino was back on the bench during the September stretch drive, but got into 19 games, mostly as a defensive replacement. The Twins won 16 of the 19 games in which he played, but it wasn't enough, as the Boston Red Sox defeated the Twins in a two-game series on the season's final weekend to win the pennant by one game. For the season, Valdespino batted only .165.

In the offseason, Valdespino was sold to the Twins' Triple-A Denver affiliate and was subsequently drafted by the Atlanta Braves. For Sandy, it was a coming home. He had last played in Atlanta in 1964 as a minor leaguer, and it was hoped that he would show the flair that he had exhibited when he led the international League in batting. He had a good spring and figured to be a key player for the braves when Rico Carty was sidelined with tuberculosis. Valdespino started the season well and was batting .333 as April came to a close.

On April 19 at Cincinnati, Valdespino had his best day in a Braves uniform. He homered in the third inning as the Braves went on to win, 3-0. In the field, he excelled. In the bottom of the third inning, with a runner on first base and none out, Valdespino robbed John Tsitouris of an extra-base hit. On the very next play, he snatched a foul fly hit by Pete rose just as it was about to disappear into the stands.[8] By day's end, Valdespino's average stood at .364.

In April Valdespino played in 14 of his team's 17 games, but the Braves were in sixth place in the 10-team National League. After April Sandy's average began to slide and he provided no power. His playing time decreased. In all, he played in 36 games with the Braves, batting .233 before being sent to Triple-A Richmond at the end of June.

After the 1968 season, Atlanta traded the 29-year-old Valdespino to the Houston Astros for pitcher Paul Doyle. He began the season at Oklahoma City in the American Association and was brought up to the Astros on June 11. He batted .244 in 41 games with Houston. On August 17 he stole home against the Philadelphia Phillies. The Astros were at that point tied for third place, two games out of the division lead. At the end of August, the Astros, looking for help in the stretch run, traded Valdespino and Danny Walton to the Seattle Pilots for outfielder Tommy Davis. With the expansion Seattle team, Valdespino batted .211 in 20 games.

The Pilots moved to Milwaukee during the offseason and Valdespino began the 1970 season on the bench with the Brewers. After going hitless in nine at-bats he was farmed out to Portland of the Pacific Coast League, where he batted .280 in 59 games. On July 14 he was traded to Omaha, the Kansas City Royals affiliate in the American Association, where he was again reunited with manager Jack McKeon. With the Omaha Royals, Valdespino batted .300 in 54 games as they won the American Association pennant.

Valdespino was back with Omaha in 1971, batting .311 before getting a late-season call-up to Kansas City. In his major-league swan song, Valdespino batted .317 in 18 games with the Royals, hitting the last two of his seven major-league homers. On September 10 Sandy had his best day with the Royals as he singled, doubled, homered, and batted in four runs as Kansas City defeated Chicago 6-1. He was on the Royals' major-league roster from September 1 through September 29, leaving him just days short of eligibility for a pension. In 765 major-league at-bats (839 plate appearances), Valdespino batted .230 and had 67 RBIs.

Valdespino returned to Omaha in 1972. He finished his playing career in the Mexican League in 1974. He worked as a minor league coach in the New York Yankees organization, and as of 2014, he was living in Las Vegas, Nevada.

SOURCES

Hensler, Paul, *The American League in Transition, 1965-1975* (Jefferson, North Carolina: McFarland and Company, 2013).

Regalado, Samuel, *The Special Hunger: Latin Americans in American Professional Baseball, 1871-1970* (Doctoral dissertation, Washington State University, May 1987).

Associated Press, "Valdespino's Sensational Catch Saves Twins Victory," *Winona* (Minnesota) *Daily News*, June 19, 1967, 13.

Cartwright, Gary, "One Riot, One Ranger," *Dallas Morning News*, Feburary 7, 1963, 2-1.

Heryford, Merle, "Bridegroom Sandy Grins, Rangers Win Sixth Straight," *Dallas Morning News*, March 30, 1963, 2-1.

Minshew, Wayne, "Sandy a Real Dandy," *Atlanta Journal and Constitution*, April 21, 1968, 2-C.

Minshew, Wayne, "Smiling Sandy's Hot Bat Makes Braves Break Out in Big Grins," *The Sporting News*, May 11, 1968, 16.

Nichols, Max, "Bench Riders Click for Juggling Mele," *The Sporting News*, June 19 1965, 11.

Nichols, Max, "Mele Does Slick Patch Job on Twin Lineup," *The Sporting News*, July 10, 1965, 11.

Nichols, Max, "Valdy Rates Ohs, Ahs For Dazzling Catch," *The Sporting News*, July 8, 1967, 15.

Paustian, John L., "Meet Your Foxes: No Interpreter Needed When Sandy's in Box," *Appleton* (Wisconsin) *Post Crescent*, April 25, 1958, 22.

Gastonia (North Carolina) *Gazette*

New York Times

Baseball-Reference.com

GenealogyBank.com

NewspaperArchive.com

Newspapers.com

NOTES

1 *Winona Daily News*, June 19, 1967, 13.

2 Max Nichols, *The Sporting News*, July 10, 1965, 11.

3 *Appleton* (Wisconsin) *Post-Crescent*, June 5, 1958, 30.

4 *Appleton (Wisconsin) Post Crescent*, January 5, 1961, 13.

5 Lee Walburn, *The Sporting News*, September 5, 1964.

6 Samuel O. Regolado, *The Special Hunger: Latin Americans in American Professional Baseball, 1871-1970*, 174.

7 Lew Ferguson, "Sandy Valdespino Paces Twins Win: Singles Home Both Runs in 2-1 Win Over Athletics," *Appleton* (Wisconsin) *Post Crescent*, April 13, 1966, 27.

8 Wayne Minshew, *The Sporting News*, May 11, 1968, 16.

Zoilo Versalles

BY PETER C. BJARKMAN

A FAMILIAR BASEBALL STEREOtype of the mid-twentieth century was the "good field, no hit" Latino shortstop.[1] The prototype was captured by Willy Miranda—who many contend was the slickest Cuban glove man ever born but who ended his near-decade-long sojourn in the majors with a mere 70 extra base hits and a lightweight .221 batting average. Other Cuban imports like José Valdivielso, Humberto "Chico" Fernández, Juan Delis and Ossie Alvarez also fit the popular pattern perfectly.

Havana-born Zoilo Versalles (ZOY-lo vair-SY-yez) contributed heavily to overturning this image in the early 1960s by three times pacing the junior circuit in triples and reaching double figures for home runs on four consecutive occasions.[2] Then he obliterated the image altogether in 1965 with a breakout offensive campaign for the surprising American League champion Minnesota Twins. The wiry, at times bespectacled Cuban was the very first Latin American import—actually the first-ever non-USA-born athlete—to capture a big-league MVP award. That distinction, albeit much debated in later years, will always overshadow all the other peaks and valleys of an admittedly imbalanced and inconsistent career.

Some across the years have dismissed Versalles as one of baseball's true all-time flops. Analyst Steve Treder stated the case most forcefully in an article examining 20 of the game's most dramatic individual slides ("the Fades" in Treder's terminology) and 30 of the biggest overnight disappointments (Treder dubs them "the Flops"). Rubén Sierra is Treder's choice for all-time "Fade," defined as a player who slowly and gradually recedes from earlier career glory. Zoilo Versalles tops his longer list of "Flops"—the more dramatic type of slide where a one-time star "plummets with sudden alacrity." Treder interprets the Cuban's extraordinary 1965 summer as a lofty perch from which "Versalles' fall was immediate and sickening."[3]

Versalles has also been frequently dismissed simply as a one-year wonder, but this too is something of a misconception. Although the Cuban's rise was indeed striking, he had already enjoyed some notable successes before the Twins' championship summer. The two previous years he had already paced the junior circuit with double figures in triples; he slugged 20 homers in 1964 (one better than the total from his MVP season and also two better than another slugging shortstop named Felix Mantilla reached a year later in Boston). He also made the AL All-Star team in 1963, and as early as his rookie summer of 1961, he had demonstrated considerable offensive talent with a .280 batting

Shortstop "Zorro" Versalles was one of the catalysts on the pennant winners. The 1965 AL MVP led the league in runs (126), doubles (45), triples for the third consecutive season (12), extra base hits (76), and total bases (308). (Photo courtesy of Minnesota Twins Baseball Club).

average and 25 doubles. The cascade off the mountaintop may have been rapid after 1965, but the buildup was more gradual than rocket-like. And if the new Cuban Comet (a designation he may have better deserved than the highly consistent Minnie Miñoso) failed to sustain his peak performance, he nonetheless left a strong legacy.

Zoilo Versalles shared more than a single limited stereotype with his Cuban compatriots and other Latinos breaking into the big leagues in the 1950s and '60s. One commonality was the name by which he became known during his major league sojourn.[4] Just as Roberto Clemente became "Bob" on many U.S. sports pages of the era—while Orestes Miñoso became Minnie, Víctor Pove became Vic Power, and Octavio Rojas became Cookie—Zoilo would be colorfully known as Zorro (part mispronunciation and part clubhouse prank) to many big-league followers. Like Clemente, Cepeda and Felipe Alou, he was tagged with labels such as "moody" and "uncoachable"—largely because he was slow to grasp English and found it difficult to adjust to the cultural norms of a foreign land.

His career was also both shortened and robbed of its true potential by devastating injury—a fate shared with Cuban teammate Tony Oliva. Oliva was sabotaged at his peak by an inherited pair of bad knees; Versalles was stripped of continuing glory by a freak back injury that never properly healed—and also continued to plague him long after his retirement.

If Zoilo's MVP selection in 1965 was controversial at the time it seems hardly unreasonable in retrospect. Versalles was the first Latin recruit widely acknowledged by sportswriters (as reflected with their MVP ballots) to have spurred his club into a World Series. Cincinnati's Dolf Luque had been the first Cuban to star in the Fall Classic back in 1919, yet Luque was then still several years short of his peak seasons and was not at all a major factor in getting his team there.[5] Mexico's Roberto Ávila finished third in the AL MVP race in 1954 even though his Cleveland Indians captured the pennant. Clemente never wore his 1960 Series ring, "upset by his embarrassingly low [eighth-place] finish in the MVP tally" behind Pirates teammates Dick Groat and Don Hoak.[6] Felipe Alou and (to a lesser degree) Orlando Cepeda were important cogs for San Francisco in 1962, yet they placed just 13th and 15th, respectively, in the MVP lottery, behind teammates Willie Mays (#2) and Jack Sanford (#7). Some might argue that Tony Oliva was as much a factor in the Twins' success of 1965 as Versalles, but Oliva got just one first-place vote that year—Zoilo got the other 19.

Zoilo Casanova Versalles y Rodríguez was born on December 18, 1939 in the run-down Marianao section of Cuba's capital city, Havana. His father, also named Zoilo, struggled as an itinerant laborer seeking whatever manual tasks might be available to support a small and anything but prosperous family. Zoilo's mother, Ámparo, had three years earlier given birth to another son, Lázaro—Zoilo's constant childhood companion and the one family member who joined his successful ball-playing brother years later in Minneapolis. Writer James Terzian mistakenly gave Versalles' year of birth as 1940 in his 1967 young adult biography. The slight discrepancy seems to have arisen from a frequent practice by Latino ballplayers of that era—claiming somewhat later birthdates in order to appear younger and thus improve chances of making the grade.[7]

A childhood fan of the Almendares Scorpions club in Cuba's professional winter league, the scrawny teenager broke into organized league play as a raw 16-year-old with the Fortuna Sports Club team in the highly popular Cuban Amateur Athletic Union league. His dream, like that of so many of his playmates, was to pattern his game after that of flashy Almendares star shortstop and active major leaguer Willy Miranda (who epitomized the "good field, no hit" breed). Further encouragement and inspiration came from another neighborhood big-leaguer, Carlos Paula, who gave the young hopeful one of his tattered and discarded fielder's mitts.

A year after joining Fortuna, Versalles was already one of the club's top hitters during the winter 1957 season. Despite the attention later paid by baseball scholars to Havana's professional winter league of pre-revolution years, it was in truth the weekend amateur circuit of the 1930s, '40s and '50s that provided the most popular form of baseball across the island. Future big leaguer and '40s-era amateur national team pitching hero Conrado "Connie" Marrero — a true island icon during Zoilo's youth — had earlier launched his career in that league. Most of the better white-skinned Cuban players also performed on those amateur teams because the money was actually better than that offered by the professionals.[8]

After finally turning professional, Versalles also logged brief stints with two of the four clubs in the Havana-based and MLB-affiliated Cuban Winter League. The first two of those winter seasons involved only token appearances — six at-bats with Cienfuegos in 1957-58 and seven plate appearances for Marianao a year later. It was only in his fourth and final year, 1960-1961 (again with the Marianao Tigers), that he played regularly. That was also the swan song for Havana's pro league because Fidel Castro shut down professional sports of all types late in 1961. Marianao finished in the basement, though only four games behind champion Cienfuegos in one of the tightest races in league history. Zoilo's .214 batting mark in the pitcher-dominated competition might not have been quite as weak as it seems, since his 14 homers (almost 40 percent of his 37 total base hits) ranked second best on both his own club and in the entire league (Marianao teammate Julio Bécquer had 15).

The talented Cuban prospect was signed to a free agent contract by celebrated Washington Senators bird dog "Papa Joe" Cambria in the spring of 1958. He soon headed north to try his fortunes as a pro. It proved to be an exceedingly difficult trial; Versalles struggled with not only an obvious language barrier but also a host of additional adjustment issues away from the diamond. Over the next several summers the youngster would battle deep bouts of depression spawned largely by homesickness. As a result he repeatedly threatened to abandon the game in order to rejoin his sorely missed family — especially his teenaged girlfriend María Josefa Fransillo. The youngsters had become emotionally attached several years earlier while Zoilo was still playing for Fortuna.

The first spring camp with the Senators in Orlando proved particularly unsettling. The transition from his native island was eased somewhat only by the presence of a handful of other scared Cuban prospects and seasoned Cuban veterans (including Julio Bécquer) with whom he could at least communicate in a familiar tongue. One of those few companions was Hilario "Sandy" Valdespino, an eventual Twins teammate, who three years later also smoothed the same transition for another struggling rookie named Tony Oliva.

That initial spring in Florida also produced a novel nickname. As was so often the case with Latinos, it came via a rather commonplace linguistic misunderstanding. English-speaking ballplayers at the camp quickly dubbed Versalles "Zorro," referring to the then-popular western TV character. Apparently they first misheard his difficult-to-pronounce Spanish given name and then assumed he must have the same handle as the dashing Mexican bandit-hero.[9]

The first minor league assignment for the still-raw 18-year-old prospect was with the Elmira Pioneers in the Class D New York-Penn League for a meager paycheck of $175 a month. The timid rookie may have still struggled emotionally, but nevertheless his progress and performance on the field was solid enough at the start and his batting average soared to .340 by the end of the first month. But tragedy struck quickly: Zoilo's mother Ámparo had fallen ill and died unexpectedly back in Havana. This crushing blow almost scuttled a promising career before it ever got started. After a week-long furlough to attend his mother's funeral, Zoilo returned to Elmira seemingly stripped of all enthusiasm for baseball and more depressed than ever by separation from family and friends back in Cuba. Some timely pep-talks and emotional coaching from co-managers Packy Rogers and Mel Kerestes helped the distraught youngster to gradually regain both form and composure and finish the season on a notable upswing. Overall Versalles hit .292 (tenth best in the circuit) in 124 games, smacked 18 doubles and

7 triples, and walked off with league rookie-of-the-year honors.

After only a single summer of rookie league seasoning, the young Cuban enjoyed spring training the following year with the parent club. Calvin Griffith's Senators were talent-thin and in a continuous rebuilding mode, especially in the middle infield, where trial shortstops Rocky Bridges, Billy Consolo and José Valdivielso had all recently failed to impress. Spring training nonetheless ended in another mid-level minor league summer assignment, since neither the Cuban's bat nor glove seemed yet ready for the big league wars. A brief trial was soon in the offing, however, and Versalles made his American League debut on August 1, 1959 as the 79th Cuban-born athlete ever to reach the majors. In his first game in Chicago's Comiskey Park he struck out three times against White Sox hurler Ray Moore. Zoilo appeared in 29 late-season contests but was clearly overmatched, collecting only nine hits and a lone extra-base smash (a homer) in 59 chances at the plate (a .153 average).[10]

Versalles actually spent most of the 1959 summer season with the Fox City Foxes of the Class B Three-I (Illinois-Indiana-Iowa) League, where he batted a respectable .278 and even slugged 19 doubles, a pair of triples and nine homers — a pleasant offensive surprise for a shortstop and perhaps a strong signal of things to come. But another less-promising signal was the Cuban's league-high 34 errors. The hefty offense apparently seemed to outweigh defensive lapses and Zoilo was named a starting shortstop for the Three-I League's mid-season All-Star Game. He had also impressed Senators brass enough to merit the late-season call-up.

Zoilo's third pro season in the United States was divided between AAA Charleston (American Association) and another "cup of coffee" with the American League parent club. In Charleston Versalles continued to struggle with ongoing homesickness and an emerging image as a moody, overconfident player who repeatedly refused constructive coaching. He battled even more with his continued defensive shortcomings. The offensive side of his game continued its slow but notable progress: a solid .278 BA, 50 RBIs, 24 stolen bases, eight homers. But as a defender he struggled mightily and committed a whopping 42 errors, posting one of the league's worst fielding percentages.

Things did take a turn for the better on the personal side, despite a disquieting political upheaval on his native island that had unfolded in the aftermath of Fidel Castro's government takeover in January 1959. Zoilo was finally married to his longtime sweetheart María Josefa in Havana on February 2, 1961. While he had just turned 21 and she was only 18, Zoilo had been impatient for the union for several years; María Josefa had insisted on waiting, however, until she had completed her high school education. Their first six years of marriage produced four young daughters named Amparito, Ester, Angela and Luz María. Two of those daughters eventually enjoyed their own small celebrity. The elder, Ampy Versalles-Curtis, is currently pursuing a career as head chef at a prestigious Minneapolis restaurant, while Luz María sang the national anthem (April 2011, along with Tony Oliva's son Rick) at the second Opening Day Ceremonies in the Twins' new showcase ballpark, Target Field in downtown Minneapolis.

Baseball's big league map was reshaped from 1952 to 1962, and Washington was part of the shift. The Griffith family, longtime owners, moved the Senators franchise to Minneapolis-St. Paul for the 1961 season, remolding it as the Minnesota Twins. Several budding stars quickly blossomed in the new environment, especially pitcher Camilo Pascual (a consistent loser with basement-bound Washington but a two-time 20-game winner in the early '60s) and sluggers Harmon Killebrew and Bob Allison. Another star on the horizon was Versalles. He finally solidified himself as a big leaguer, getting a shot at regular duty as a replacement for fellow Cuban José Valdivielso.[11] He hit a solid .280 over 129 games — a mark he did not top in nine subsequent seasons. Zoilo's 1961 Topps "rookie" bubble gum card also featured his name as "Zorro" — further engraining a moniker that stuck for the rest of his big-league days.

Zoilo Versalles (Photo courtesy of Minnesota Twins Baseball Club).

During a second Minnesota season, Versalles exhibited signs that he might become a greater force in the offensive lineup as well as an infield anchor. Although his batting average dipped nearly 40 points, Zoilo smacked 17 homers, behind only fellow Cuban Chico Fernández of Detroit, Woodie Held of Cleveland, and Tom Tresh of the Yankees among AL shortstops. The slide in batting average may have disappointed, but the upside was a slight drop in errors, a 20-point surge in fielding percentage, and a top spot among the league's shortstops in assists. One reward for such progress was a smattering of American League MVP votes.

Improvement was even more dramatic during 1963. The batting average rose back to .261, he led the league in triples for the first of three straight years, and the glove work even showed improvement Versalles was voted to his first All-Star Game that year and earned a Gold Glove for his solid if not spectacular defense. The latter award broke the five-season streak of Venezuela's Luis Aparicio (then playing for the White Sox). During the Midsummer Classic in Cleveland, Zoilo relished six successful innings — singling, walking, and reaching as a hit batsman in his three plate appearances — before Aparicio replaced him in the seventh.

The rapid progress continued in 1964 — 20 homers, a stable batting average, and again more than 30 doubles. Zoilo's healthy home run total was surpassed by only one other shortstop — Detroit's Dick McAuliffe. The productive infielder once more led the league in triples, tying with teammate Rich Rollins at 10. In one single four-day stretch in September he twice spoiled no-hitters, first against Milt Pappas (September 2) and then Bill Monbouquette (September 6). On the second occasion, that lone hit was a game-winning two-run homer that cost Boston's Monbouquette not only his second no-no but also the victory. Playing only his fourth full season, Versalles might have been an even bigger Minneapolis hero that summer if Tony Oliva had not also remained on the local scene for his first full big-league season. The fellow Cuban was voted AL Rookie of the Year and won his first of three batting crowns.

The stage had now been set for true stardom. The MVP performance by Zoilo Versalles at the decade's midpoint ranked at the time as one of the best offensive years ever enjoyed by a major league shortstop. Tutored perhaps even more by third base coach Billy Martin than by manager Sam Mele, Versalles that summer made a hefty contribution to revolutionizing not only the popular view of Latino middle infielders but also of shortstops universally. Coach Martin's new protégé topped the American League in seven categories: plate appearances (728), at-bats (666), runs scored (126), doubles (45), triples (12), extra-base hits (76), and total bases (308). He also appeared (as a sixth-inning sub for starter Dick McAuliffe) in his second All-Star Game alongside five fellow Twins, on their home turf in Minnesota's Metropolitan Stadium.

On top of his offensive production, Versalles also claimed his second Gold Glove, even though he posted a career-high and league-leading 39 errors. Good offense apparently masks questionable defense, though more modern fielding metrics cast a better light on his play in the field.¹² Overall, Zoilo easily walked off with nearly unanimous MVP honors. There was one further catch to the award; in addition to the league lead in errors, Zoilo also produced a league and career high for strikeouts. It was a fine season, but featured some nagging negatives.

There has been much subsequent debate that Oliva (or perhaps others like Brooks Robinson or Rocco Colavito) and not Minnesota teammate Versalles was the more legitimate league MVP during the Twins' 1965 pennant run.¹³ Bill James eventually gave the matter a sabermetric spin by pointing out that during that peak season Versalles amassed the fewest "win shares" of any previous or subsequent league MVP.¹⁴ Tony Oliva's supporters would argue that he earned a second hitting title, becoming the first player ever to capture a batting crown in each of his first two full years. But a flip side to this argument is rarely stressed by revisionist historians. Tony Oliva's performance had been just as strong—in fact arguably even stronger—a year earlier (when his BA and totals for runs, hits and doubles were all higher). Yet the contribution of Versalles was both tangible, as seen in his offensive totals, and intangible—an aggressive style in the vein of Pepper Martin and Pete Rose. That, according to the voting writers, seemed more than anything to shift the ball club from a contender into a surprising league champion.

None other than Mickey Mantle agreed. So did Billy Martin, who said, "He does it all now. Fields, hits, thinks—and most important, runs. He's got to be the most fearsome runner in our league, regardless of the stolen base column." Martin pointed out how Versalles had scored from first base on singles several times that summer. Teammate Bob Allison added, "I don't think any one man carried this club this year. But if I had to pick one key man I'd pick Versalles."¹⁵

Minnesota's heralded MVP graced the cover of *Sports Illustrated* ahead of the 1965 Fall Classic, and that honor was only yet another example of the often discussed (if largely mythical) "*Sports Illustrated* cover curse."¹⁶ The Series matched Minnesota's vaunted offense (led by a quintet of Oliva, Versalles, Killebrew, Allison and catcher Earl Battey) against the remarkable pitching of Los Angeles (headlined by Sandy Koufax, Don Drysdale and Claude Osteen). As is so often the case, the pitching won out in the end. The Twins did take the first game; Versalles smacked his only homer as part of a six-run third-inning uprising that drove starter Drysdale to the showers. The success continued in Game 2 with Jim Kaat beating Koufax 5-1 behind a triple and two runs from Versalles. But the upstart Twins couldn't generate any further offense once the series moved on to spacious Dodger Stadium—the very park where the American League club had struggled against the Los Angeles Angels during regular season outings.¹⁷ On the coast the Twins were blanked twice (by Osteen and Koufax) and generated a mere 14 hits over the three-game set. The Series did stretch to a seventh and deciding contest, but then Sandy Koufax—on only two days of rest—slammed the door with a three-hit 2-0 shutout in the finale.

Versalles was part of an overall collapse of Minnesota offense during the Series—explained perhaps by the link between Dodger mound mastery and Chavez Ravine. Zoilo did hit a respectable .286 (tied with Killebrew for the club's best mark) but his only homer and all four of his runs batted in came as a single bunch during the opening contest. Batting champ Tony Oliva suffered an even worse slump (two extra-base hits and a hollow .192 BA), while Allison (.125), Battey (.120), and slugging outfielder Jimmie Hall (.143) all struggled mightily at the plate. The team that had paced the AL in both total average (.254) and base hits managed only an aggregate .195 mark with the world championship on the line.

The MVP season earned Versalles a substantial pay raise of $40,000—nearly double his 1965 paycheck and a hefty amount for an era long before multi-million dollar contracts became a big-league norm. But the monetary reward seemed to bring with it mixed blessings—Zoilo's performance slipped immediately afterward. Indeed, that pay boost and corresponding performance dip launched his reputation as flop. The raw statistics seemed to tell the surface story: the star shortstop's batting average dropped 24 points, and his other numbers sagged even more (only 7 homers and less than half the number of doubles).

There were nonetheless a couple of memorable moments in 1966, including an entry into the record books on June 9, when the Twins slugged five homers off Kansas City pitching in a single inning (Harmon Killebrew, Don Mincher, Tony Oliva, Rich Rollins and Versalles). But the season on the whole was a letdown for both the Minnesota club and especially for the former MVP. The club spent the first half of the summer buried in the second division while the Baltimore Orioles raced to an early lead that would never be surmounted. The Twins did eventually catch fire after Zoilo's return from a midseason stint on the disabled list. Down the stretch, they overhauled Detroit and Chicago for a disappointing second-place finish (a distant nine games behind Baltimore).

But statistics alone won't ever unlock the full story of Versalles's post-MVP comedown. An abnormally slow start in April and May resulted mainly from an extended bout with a severe case of the flu which kept the infielder in subpar condition—hovered around the Mendoza Line (sub-.200) for the first eight full weeks of the season. There was more bad news in early late June and early July in the form of a heel injury that also caused a painful hematoma (blood leakage and consequent tissue swelling) in the ballplayer's lower back. The immediate result was a brief stint on the disabled list. The long-term consequence was constant recurring back pain that not only sabotaged the remainder of Zoilo's playing career but also hampered his post-baseball life severely.

Versalles eventually logged 543 ABs (123 behind his previous total), scored 73 runs (down 53), and his extra-base hits were sliced by more than half. Things didn't get much better the next summer—both the constant back pain and resulting poor bat work continued across 1967. Playing 160 games (but at far less than full speed), Zoilo again produced embarrassingly little for a Minnesota club that—sparked by Rookie of the Year Rod Carew and the continued slugging of Tony Oliva—managed to hang in the pennant race until the final day of the season. Despite nearly 600 at-bats, the shortstop's batting average slid to an embarrassing .200 level and his doubles fell to a mere 16. Versalles also stole only five bases, 22 fewer than two seasons earlier.

To make matters worse still, a lead glove and poor mobility produced league-leading error totals at shortstop in both 1966 and 1967, continuing a three-year defensive lapse that had begun during the stellar 1965 season. Weak defense could be overlooked perhaps with a star bolstering the team's offense (as in 1965)—but not with a lineup liability who was now anticipating Mario Mendoza at the plate. Using such modern-era sabermetric measures as Win Shares and Isolated Power, Steve Treder argued in his 2004 article that if Zoilo's 1967 outing "wasn't the worst a full-time player has ever had, it was certainly one of the top contenders."[18]

The combination of injury and poor performance both offensively and in the field—along with the arrival of Rod Carew to shore up the Twins infield—meant that Versalles was no longer a valued commodity in the Twin Cities. Zoilo's Minnesota career came to an abrupt end when he was shipped off to the Los Angeles Dodgers on November 27, 1967. The headline deal also included Jim "Mudcat" Grant and brought catcher John Roseboro and relievers Bob Miller and Ron Perranoski to the Twins. The three Dodgers had all played major roles in the Los Angeles World Series triumph only two years earlier.

For the rapidly fading ex-star Versalles, a single summer on the West Coast brought only a further dip in performance. After committing the most errors in the AL in each of his last three campaigns, he finished only fourth in that department in the NL (as much as anything because he played in only 122 games), yet he also hit an anemic career-low .196. Washed up rapidly in L.A., Zoilo was left exposed by the Dodgers in the 1968 NL expansion lottery. The newborn and talent-desperate San Diego Padres took a chance on drafting Versalles, but he never played for them. They quickly traded him to Cleveland on December 2.

Worse yet, during the temporary stop in Los Angeles, Versalles once again severely aggravated his earlier back problems. The spinal hematoma first suffered in July 1966 flared up once again after he suffered further trauma while running out a routine ground ball during a midseason game. His only true Dodger highlight came on May 28, 1968, when a fifth-inning single proved to be the only hit against Cincinnati's Jim Maloney.

Back on friendly American League soil, Zippy Zee (as he was familiarly known by teammates during his glory years in Minnesota) enjoyed a slight revival. He boosted his hitting to .226 in 72 early and midseason games with the Indians. He also saw more duty at second base and third base than at shortstop in Cleveland. By now an obvious journeyman, Zoilo was soon purchased by another 1961 expansion club — the new version of the Washington Senators — on July 26, 1969. The second trade in seven months landed Versalles on a trivia list as one of only nine players to appear for both incarnations of the Senators AL team.[19] Back in the nation's capital, he held his own for the rest of 1969, hitting .267 in 31 games as an infield fill-in and earning a training camp invitation for the following spring. But this was only a brief reprieve: the former All-Star was released by Washington in April 1970, only four-plus years after his MVP honors.

Once the debilitating back problems arose in July 1966, Versalles was only a shadow of what he had once been. He never again hit as many as 20 doubles or reached above seven triples or homers in a single season; only once did he log as many as 160 games in a season. The injuries had more to do with the career collapse than any possible side effect from a bigger contract or any possible dip in motivation. It might well be debatable whether Versalles was actually one of the least legitimate MVPs ever selected, yet it is hard to deny that no other such honoree ever enjoyed so little success after winning the award. Other big names in the game (Greg Luzinski, Pete Incaviglia, Johnny Callison and Rubén Sierra come first to mind) may have fallen further, but few fell from their perch in quite so brief a span.

Pro baseball was not quite over for Versalles after his final departure from the AL. He latched on with Unión Laguna in the Mexican League for 1970. At what amounted to Class AAA baseball in Mexico, the 31 year-old veteran posted his career-best batting mark of .326 over a 103-game season. He had one final shot at the big time when the Atlanta Braves picked him up on May 31, 1971. During this last trial, he appeared in 66 games and again failed to climb above the Mendoza Line, hitting .191. Versalles returned briefly to Unión Laguna in both 1971 and 1972, logging 120 total games over two partial seasons. One final crack at rejuvenation came during a brief tour with the Hiroshima Toyo Carp of the Japanese Central League during the 1972 summer season. With that final Asian stopover, Zoilo joined countryman and ex-big-leaguer Tony González as the first pair of non-Japanese imports to play for the Hiroshima ball club.

Zoilo Versalles spent his post-baseball years in the Minneapolis area. It was not a very pretty picture. An inability to find consistent employment was in large part related to a lack of both English fluency and any practical non-baseball skills. Repeated economic failure was also attributable to deteriorating health, notably the lingering back injuries. The quarter-century following his active baseball days represented little more than a continuation of the downward spiral that had defined his athletic career. Several spells of unemployment resulted in the loss of his house to foreclosure and forced him to sell such valuable mementos as his cherished MVP trophy, Gold Glove awards, and All-Star Game rings. He eventually suffered two heart attacks and also underwent painful stomach surgery. Zoilo finally separated from his wife María Josefa and their six daughters and barely subsisted on meager disability and Social Security payments plus the modest big-league pension that he'd begun drawing in 1984.[20]

The ongoing tragedy finally ended when Versalles was found dead in his rented home on June 11, 1995.

Coroner's tests showed that he had apparently died two days earlier. The cause of death was not revealed at first but was eventually determined to be arteriosclerotic heart disease.

More than a decade after his death, Versalles was posthumously honored by induction into the Minnesota Twins Hall of Fame. Seven of the 10 previous honorees attended the ceremony on June 25, 2006, in the Hubert H. Humphrey Metrodome. It was a belated tribute that, despite its distinction, paled beside the numerous honors eventually bestowed on teammate Tony Oliva. In 2011, Oliva (to some, the more deserving 1965 league MVP) received a larger-than-life bronze statute outside Target Field in his honor. Yet when Versalles was (however briefly) in command of his physical powers and had mastered the mental demands of the game on and off the field, he was indeed a remarkable player—one of the better all-around shortstops of his era. Zoilo aptly described his own style, full of pent-up energy, in 1963: "Like a tiger in a cage."[21]

SOURCES

Books

Peter C. Bjarkman, *A History of Cuban Baseball, 1864-2006*. Jefferson, North Carolina: McFarland & Company Publishers, 2007.

Peter C. Bjarkman, *Baseball with a Latin Beat: A History of the Latin American Game*. Jefferson, North Carolina: McFarland & Company Publishers, 1994.

Bill James, *The New Bill James Historical Abstract*. New York: The Free Press, 2003.

Tony Oliva (with Bob Fowler), *Tony O! The Trials and Triumphs of Tony Oliva* (New York: Hawthorn Books, 1973).

James Terzian, *Zoilo Versalles—The Kid from Cuba*. Garden City, New York: Doubleday & Company, 1967.

Jim Thielman, *Cool of the Evening: The 1965 Minnesota Twins*. Minneapolis: Kirk House Publishers, 2005.

Newspaper articles

Robert McG. Thomas, "Zoilo Versalles, 55, Shortstop Who Was Mr. Baseball in 1965," *The New York Times*, June 12, 1995 (http://www.nytimes.com/1995/06/12/obituaries/)

Internet resources

Zeke Fuhrman, "Zoilo Versalles: The Forgotten MVP," *Bleacher Report*, Match 15, 2010 (http://bleacherreport.com/articles/362919-zoilo-versalles-the-forgotten-mvp/)

Carl Kolchak, "Zoilo Versalles—an MVP that Wasn't," *Yahoo! Voices*, August 10, 2006 (http://voices.yahoo.com/zoilo-versalles-mvp-wasnt-60728.html/)

Steve Treder, "Of Fades, and Flops, and Zoilo," *The Hardball Times*, November 23, 2004 (http://www.hardballtimes.com/main/article/of-fades-and-flops-and-zoilo/)

ACKNOWLEDGMENT

I am indebted to Rory Costello, whose considerable editorial skills both tightened and redirected this essay in several key areas and thus definitely improved upon the original version.

NOTES

1. It is one of baseball's great small ironies that this label held a double connection to Cuban ballplayers. It not only applied to the players themselves but also is widely attributed to a pioneering Cuban big leaguer of some note: Miguel Ángel (Mike) González, the journeyman big league catcher of the 1910s and 1920s, the third base coach who waved Enos Slaughter home in that famous wild 1946 World Series winning dash from first, and the first Latino native ever to manage a game in the big leagues. González reputedly used the term in a St. Louis Cardinals scouting report on another famous journeyman catcher, Moe Berg (whom others described as speaking a dozen languages and yet unable to hit in any of them).

2. Another factor in upsetting the stereotype was countryman Leo Cárdenas, who had a strong season with the bat for the Cincinnati Reds in 1962,

3. Treder's analysis is actually somewhat self-contradictory. He begins with the caveat that there are cases (he cites Chuck Klein, Hal Trosky and Don Mattingly) of "flops" or fast "faders" that don't actually fit the definition of the prototype, since debilitating injury or illness can be cited to explain and excuse why tremendous early careers petered out almost overnight. But Versalles would also seem to qualify for such exemption in view of his mid-career back injury.

4. The misnaming of Miñoso, Oliva, the Alous, Tany Perez and Vic Power among others is explained in some detail in the notes to my recent SABR Bio Project essay on Tony Oliva. Sometimes (as in the case of Oliva and Miñoso) the ballplayer himself was implicated, since Oliva himself used his brother's name and passport and Miñoso early-on went along in Cuba with the practice of using the last name of his stepbrothers. But in most cases the problems were linguistic and cultural and often tied to the stereotypes that always plagued Latino ballplayers. The name confusion with Versalles comes with the mispronunciation of his last name, which is not ver-SIGH, like the French city. It is ver-SIGH-yeas. The LL (single letter in Spanish) is not silent but carries a Y sound; the first syllable rhymes with fair, the second syllable rhymes with pie, and the last rhymes with yes. Stress falls on the middle syllable. Also in rapid native Cuban speech the final s is sometimes dropped (thus ver-SIGH-yea). The first

5. Facts about Adolfo Luque as a pioneering big league pitcher are provided in my SABR Bio Project essay on that near Hall of Famer. The Cuban was the first Latino pitcher both to appear in (1919) and win (1933) a World Series game. But the future star was still only a mop-up hurler in 1919 (10 wins) on a staff that featured Slim Sallee (21-7), Hod Eller (19-9), and Dutch Ruether (19-6).

6. Bruce Markusen, *Roberto Clemente: The Great One*, Champaign, Illinois: Sports Publishing LLC, 2001, 102.

7. The issue of Versalles's birthdate change is not as clearly documented as that for Oliva. But there is no evidence for the December 1940 date that is given for Versalles in Terzian's young adult biography. The 1959 Washington Senators yearbook (I have one in my collection) gave Versalles' birth year as 1940, as did his baseball cards.

8. Chapter 7 ("Havana as the Amateur Baseball Capital of the World") of my volume *A History of Cuban Baseball* (2007) details the role and the stature of the pre-revolution Cuban amateur league. Amateur Athletic Union clubs were sponsored by enterprises like the telephone and electric companies or by long-established social clubs like the Havana Yacht Club or Víbora Tennis Club. In order to retain their athletic skills, sponsoring firms offered ballplayers lucrative (and cushy) employment; players on these teams would perform on weekends only. But these preferred roster spots in the segregated amateur league were closed to blacks, who were left with no alternative but to join the lower-paying pros.

9. The tale of the colorful nickname is related by James Terzian in his young adult biography and presumably comes from Terzian's interview with the ballplayer himself. The Topps Company (in an era devoid of political correctness) had earlier labeled Roberto Clemente as "Bob" Clemente on their 1958 cardboard image—an Anglicization that the proud Puerto Rican always despised. American League 1954 batting champ and Mexico native Roberto Avila, whose nickname was "Beto" at home, was also redubbed as "Bob" or "Bobby" Avila on his Topps cardboard images.

10. Versalles got his first big league hit in his second game (August 2, 1959), off Chicago hurler Billy Pierce in Comiskey Park. His first and only rookie year homer came four days later in Griffith Stadium (August 5, 1959) off future Twins teammate Jim "Mudcat" Grant (at the time hurling for Cleveland).

11. Willy Miranda, the childhood hero of Versalles, also played his final pro season with the Twins' top farm club, Syracuse.

12. Versalles was 17 Total Fielding Runs above average in 1965, vs. a mere 1 run during his other Gold Glove season, 1963. His range factor was largely in line with the AL averages, suggesting that his higher error total was not at all a function of getting to more balls, as was true of Willy Miranda.

13. The argument is most concisely summarized by Carl Kolchak, who pointed out numerous negatives. Oliva hit almost 50 points higher and struck only half as much (Versalles led the league in Ks). Oliva was also tabbed by the seemingly more astute editors of *The Sporting News* as baseball's "Player of the Year." Zoilo ranked only fourth on his own club in batting average, and runs batted in and was fifth in homers. Teammate Mudcat Grant posted 21 wins on the mound, six more than he had ever had previously, and thus could boast his own breakout season. 1964 MVP Brooks Robinson also enjoyed another good year with the bat, plus earned another Gold Glove at third base. Cleveland's Rocco Colavito and Detroit's Willie Horton both knocked in better than 100 runs; etc.

14. Bill James first described his notion of "Win Shares" in a 2002 book of the same name co-authored with Jim Henzler. The exceedingly complicated formula (the explanation takes almost 80 pages of James' 2002 volume) attempts to assign single numbers to individual players as a measure of their contribution for that season. A given team is assigned a "win shares" total (3 times the team's actual number of victories), which is then divided between that club's offense and defense. The pitching, hitting and defensive contributions (in terms of statistics) are all considered and the figures are adjusted for ballpark, league and era. There have been numerous criticisms of the value of using such a metric, one of the main ones being that the metric rewards players whose teams win more games than expected and heavily penalizes those who don't have that same advantage.

15. Francis Stann, "Erstwhile Moody Versalles Finally Wins Acceptance," *Baseball Digest*, October 1965, 30.

16. It was the cover of the October 4, 1965 issue, and only Versalles' hands, arms and bat appear in the cover image.

17. In his own autobiography Tony Oliva commented on the Twins' difficulties while playing at Chavez Ravine, as the park was alternately known when the Angels played there. "It was a big park, a pitcher's park, and we had always had trouble in it. The Angels played there that season, and we won only four of nine games although they didn't have a very good team. We just couldn't get our offense going in that park. Teams, for some unknown reasons, don't play well in certain stadiums. Chavez Ravine was that way for us." Oliva and Fowler, 89.

18. Treder, 2004.

19. The others were position players Roy Sievers, Don Mincher, Johnny Schaive, and pitchers Camilo Pascual, Pedro Ramos, Hal Woodeshick, Hector Maestri, and Rudy Hernández.

20. Sparse details concerning Zoilo's pension are provided by Jim Thielman. Disabled to the degree that he could not find work after 1982 (when he was only 43) Versalles petitioned MLB for access to his earned pension—but was informed that a new collective bargaining agreement prevented a player from drawing on those funds before reaching the minimum age of 45. In 1984, after reaching the set qualification age, Zoilo began drawing the sum of $13,500 annually.

21. Francis Stann, "The New Mark of Zorro," *Baseball Digest*, June 1963, 42.

A Pennant for the Twins

September 26, 1965: Minnesota Twins 2, Washington Senators 1 at Griffith Stadium, Washington, D.C.

BY ALAN COHEN

THE MAGIC NUMBER WAS ONE. A Minnesota win or Baltimore loss would assure the Twins of the 1965 American League pennant. Baltimore was in no mood to cooperate. They had swept a doubleheader on Saturday night and they were looking for their seventh consecutive win as they took the field on Sunday, September 26, against the California Angels at just about the same time the Washington Senators took the field against the Twins.

The scene, ironically, was the nation's capital. Only seven of the 1965 Twins had been with the Senators when they departed Washington for the Twin Cities after the 1960 season. Griffith Stadium was history and the teams were playing at D. C. Stadium. In 1965 Washington had been a home away from home for the transplanted Twins. Going into this game they had won seven and lost only one in their old hometown, and had gone 14-3 overall against the Senators.

The assemblage was small; only 8,302 were on hand to witness history in a town where late September had far more to do with the beginning of the football season, and most folks stayed home to watch the Washington Redskins and Dallas Cowboys on television.

The irony was not lost on the *Boston Globe's* Harold Kaese, who wrote after the game, "The Washington Senators have won their first pennant since 1933, but nobody is dancing on the steps of the Capitol. There will be no pennant-raising next spring in District of Columbia Stadium. The Senators are now known as the Minnesota Twins. All the frolicking will be in Minneapolis, St, Paul and the land of sky blue waters. The pennant the Twins clinched Sunday should belong to the fans of Washington. For the Twins to clinch it in Washington—their original home—was the cruelest of ironies. Simply diabolical."[1]

Early in the year the Washington club had determined that a home-run-hitting contest before the opening game of the final series of the season between the Senators and the Twins was a good idea. With Friday night's rainout and Saturday afternoon's doubleheader, the contest was moved to Sunday afternoon. The Twins sluggers were somewhat preoccupied. Nevertheless, the event was held and Twins Jimmie Hall and Bob Allison tied the Senators' Don Lock.

The Sunday game's hero, Zoilo Versalles, one of the seven Twins who had been with the Senators in 1960, was wrapping up his 1965 MVP season as the Twins

The Twins celebrate after capturing the pennant. Killebrew and Mele in center; Lemon on far left. (Photo courtesy of Minnesota Twins Baseball Club).

took to the field for the clincher after sweeping a doubleheader and clinching a tie the day before. In the second game of that doubleheader, Versalles had collided with the Senators' Fred Valentine in a play at second base, and had been hospitalized overnight for observation.

Jim Kaat took a 16-11 record to the mound for the Twins. Washington manager Gil Hodges was not about to give the game away. He had set up his pitching for the series and scheduled his ace, Pete Richert (15-10), for the Sunday finale. It was hoped that the lefty would keep Tony Oliva in check.

The game was scoreless in the first two innings. Washington broke the ice by scoring a run in in the bottom of the third. Ken McMullen singled. Frank Howard followed with another hit. Oliva's throw trying to get McMullen at third got past third baseman Harmon Killebrew. Kaat fielded the overthrow poorly and was charged with an error as McMullen scored and Howard went to second base.[2] Richert was able to make the run stand up until the sixth inning. Through five innings, the only hit he allowed as an infield hit by Oliva in the first inning.

Versalles led off the sixth with a triple to left-center field. Don Zimmer was catching for the Senators that day. (The one-time Dodger shortstop of the future caught 33 games for the Senators in 1965 in a utility-player role.) With the right-handed hitting Joe Nossek at the plate, a pitch from Richert went off Zimmer's glove. The ball went just a short distance, but Versalles scampered home with the tying run.[3]

In the eighth inning Frank Quilici led off with a double and advanced to third base on a wild pitch. Versalles came to the plate with one out and launched a fly ball to center field that was deep enough to score Quilici with the deciding run. It capped a great campaign for Versalles who had been fined $300 by the club during spring training for insubordination. The fine was not rescinded.[4]

The Senators had two more at-bats but couldn't do any more scoring against Kaat. The Twins lefty stranded a runner in the eighth inning. Ed Brinkman led off the inning with a single but was erased on a double play. A single by Frank Howard proved harmless as Kaat struck out Woodie Held to end the inning.

Kaat set the Senators down in order in the ninth inning to earn his 17th win. The final batter was Zimmer, who struck out, becoming Kaat's 10th strikeout victim of the game. Richert, who allowed two tainted runs and gave up only three hits, was tagged with his 11th loss.

And when it was all over and the champagne was flowing, the telephone rang. On the other end, speaking with manager Sam Mele, was Vice President Hubert Humphrey, a former mayor of Minneapolis and US senator from Minnesota. "I just wanted to congratulate you, Sam, and tell you I'll be in a front-row seat when the World Series starts," said Humphrey.[5] Afterwards, Humphrey, accompanied by his Secret Service detail, visited the locker room of the victors.[6]

The clubhouse was rocking. The Twins were drinking champagne, throwing food, and tearing the uniforms off one another's backs. Amid the jubilation Mele exclaimed, "We're in, and we went right through the front door winning three straight. That's the way to do it."[7]

And Harmon Killebrew, who had first played with the Twins when they were the 1954 Washington Senators, reflected, "It's hard to get used to the taste."[8]

Not at the celebration in Washington was team owner Calvin Griffith. He dared not set foot in the city as there were subpoenas waiting for him and members of his family. They were being sued by H. Gabriel Murphy, a 40 percent shareholder in the team, who was still angered by the team's move to the Twin Cities in 1961.[9] Murphy made his way to the clubhouse for the celebration, stood in a corner, and mused, "It's a great day, isn't it?"[10]

Back in Minneapolis, the fans at the Minnesota Vikings game cheered the news of the win in Washington, but there was no champagne to flow in the Twin Cities — liquor sales were banned on Sunday in Minnesota.[11]

That night Mele went to his home in Quincy, Massachusetts, for yet another celebration. His daughter Cheryl, remembering how her dad's job had been in jeopardy at the end of the previous season, greeted him with a homemade sign stating for all to see — "We Eat Again Next Year!"[12]

SOURCES

Thielman, Jim, *Cool of the Evening: The 1965 Minnesota Twins* (Minneapolis: Kirk House Publishing, 2005).

Baseball-Reference.com

Boston Globe

Washington Evening Star

Washington Post

The Sporting News

Winona (Minnesota) *Daily News*

NOTES

1. Harold Kaese, "Twins' Pennant Belongs to D. C.," *Boston Globe*, September 27, 1965, 21.
2. Merrell Whittlesey, "Champion Twins Sweat Out the Result in NL: Kaat's Peak Game Opens Champagne," *Washington Evening Star,* September 27, 1965, B2.
3. Bob Addie, "Twins Edge Nats, Clinch Pennant," *Washington Post*, September 26, 1965, C5.
4. Shirley Povich, *Washington Post*, September 26, 1965, C1, C5.
5. Bob Addie, "Twins Shower in Champagne," *Washington Post*, September 27, 1965, C5.
6. Jim Thielman, *Cool of the Evening: The 1965 Minnesota Twins,* 203.
7. Max Nichols, "Twins Pull All Victory Stops, Stage Orgy of Grog and Grub," *The Sporting News*, October 9, 1965, 24.
8. Addie, "Twins Shower."
9. Bob Addie, "The People Who Boss the Twins Deserve Their Pennant," *The Sporting News*, October 9, 1965, 9.
10. Addie. "Twins Shower."
11. *Winona* (Minnesota) *Daily News*, September 27, 1965, 1.
12. Will McDonough, "Meles 'Will Eat Again Next Year,'" *Boston Globe*, September 27, 1965, 21.

Al Worthington

BY BILL NOWLIN

AL WORTHINGTON CAME FROM A large Alabama family, the seventh of ten children born to Walter B. Worthington, a newspaper compositor, and his wife, Lake Worthington. After four daughters, the Worthingtons welcomed Allan Fulton Worthington into the world on February 5, 1929, in Birmingham. Walter worked for the *Birmingham News* for his last ten years and also pitched in one of the local amateur leagues.[1] Al became a right-handed pitcher who worked 14 years in the major leagues. Over the course of his career, he hurled for both Chicago teams, both Sox teams, both the New York and San Francisco Giants, and—perhaps fittingly, given all those pairings—he finished his career with the Twins, pitching six seasons for Minnesota.

Al had two brothers who also played some ball. "My two older brothers signed professional baseball contracts, one with the Philadelphia Athletics and the other one was with the St. Louis Cardinals. One brother—Robert Oliver—came out of the Navy and he was 25 or 26. He was a little bit too old, but he played for a while with the Cardinals. He was the younger one. Walter played with the Athletics. In their farm system."[2] Walter was a catcher who played in 1939 and 1940 in the Athletics chain, while Robert played three years as a catcher (1946-48) in the Cardinals system.

Al attended Inglenook Elementary School, graduated from Phillips High School, and spent three years at the University of Alabama at Tuscaloosa. At 6-feet-2 and 195 pounds, Worthington also played end on the Crimson Tide's football team, though "Big Al" was considered "lanky" even for a pitcher in those days.[3] He didn't play much football, and quit the team in his sophomore year after injuring his left arm and shoulder and finding that it was not healing quickly.[4] At age 21, he married Shirley Reusse in December 1950.

"Nobody really wanted me in baseball. That was before they had agents. Dickey Martin worked for the railroad in Birmingham. I pitched against his local team. He called his friend [Nashville manager] Larry Gilbert. They gave me $1,500."[5] Martin signed him in June 1951 and Worthington started his career pitching for the Southern Association's Nashville Volunteers. His record that first year was 7-10 (4.57 ERA), but he showed some real promise, throwing a two-hitter against Chattanooga in early September.

Worthington struggled badly at the beginning of the 1952 season, still pitching for Nashville, now a Giants farm club. Manager Hugh Poland said he was "trying to throw too hard for his own good."[6] He righted himself, however, and on August 24 threw a one-run, six-hit, 14-inning game against Little Rock. He finished the season 13-13 (3.54).

"Red" Worthington was an undistinguished journeyman when the Twins acquired him in early 1964, but at age 35 the right-hander transformed into one of the AL's best relievers over a five-year stretch (1964-1968). In 1965 he won ten times, saved 21 games, and sported a nifty 2.13 ERA in 62 appearances. (Photo courtesy of Minnesota Twins Baseball Club).

On April 1, 1953, Worthington's contract was sold outright to the Giants, though they asked him to begin the year with their Triple-A club in Minneapolis. He was 9-5 with a 2.90 ERA when he was brought up to the big leagues in early July—and pitched back-to-back 6-0 shutouts. On July 6 at the Polo Grounds, he threw a two-hitter against the Phillies and on the 11th pitched a four-hitter at Ebbets Field against the Dodgers. Manager Leo Durocher referred to him as "this kid pitcher."[7] Worthington's consecutive shutouts in his first two appearances equaled a major-league record that only three other pitchers had achieved. Worthington was the first to achieve it in the National League since the modern era of baseball began.[8] It was the only time all year that Brooklyn would be shut out; Worthington held them to four singles.

Eight days later Al proved he was "not Superman after all," suffering his first loss, giving up just two runs (one earned) to the Milwaukee Braves in a five-inning, darkness-shortened game.[9] Then he lost his next seven decisions—all the way until September, when he won his final two games, giving up just one earned run over the two games on the 19th and 25th. The last loss was on September 10 and saw Worthington dole out 11 bases on balls to the St. Louis Cardinals. The two wins to close out the season left him 4-8 for the year, but with a decent 3.44 earned-run average, distinctly better than the fifth-place Giants' 4.25 team ERA.

In 1954 the Giants won the pennant. The team ERA dropped all the way to 3.09, with starter Johnny Antonelli (21-7, 2.30) and reliever Hoyt Wilhelm (12-4, 2.10) two standouts, while closer Marv Grissom's 2.35 ERA was superb as well. Worthington did not make the club out of spring training, but was brought up midway through the season and wound up 0-2 in ten games, working 18 innings, mostly in relief, from July 29 on. Worthington appeared on the postseason roster, but saw no action in the World Series; he got a one-third share of the World Series earnings.[10] He also recalled, "I had a real good seat for that Willie Mays catch! We beat Cleveland four in a row. I wouldn't have pitched anyway, but I had a great seat."[11]

Worthington spent all of 1955 back in the minors, with Minneapolis. He was 19-10 (3.58), and his three wins and one save were key in helping the Millers win the Junior World Series over Rochester. He played winter ball for Santurce in Puerto Rico, and was 9-2 for the pennant-winning team.

In 1956 Worthington made the Giants out of spring training. He lost his first start for new Giants manager Bill Rigney, 3-2, despite giving up only two runs in seven innings. The Giants finished in sixth place, and to some extent Worthington's 7-14 record reflected the team's. His 3.97 ERA was not much above the team's 3.78, while the club finished a disappointing 67-87. He did lose a full month—almost all of August—due to a sore arm. He was never much of a batter (.137 career average and .165 on-base percentage in 293 plate appearances), but he helped win the September 30 game against the Phillies with two RBIs, one of them coming on his only major-league home run. In 602 big-league games (69 starts), he drove in 15 runs.

In 1957, with the New York Giants still a losing team (sixth place, 69-85), Worthington was 8-11 with a 4.22 ERA (team ERA was 4.01). While in 1956 he had started 24 of his 28 games, he was used more as a reliever in 1957, appearing in 55 games but starting only 12 of them. One of the starts was a complete-game 1-0 shutout of the Phils. Five days later, he worked the first ten innings of a 16-inning win, allowing just two runs and keeping the Giants in the game.

The Giants franchise left the Polo Grounds behind and moved to the West Coast for the 1958 season, playing at Seals Stadium their first season in San Francisco and finishing in third place, with Rigney still at the helm. Worthington had his best season to date, 11-7 (3.63), again with 12 starts, this time in 54 games. He was said to have an "elegant slider."[12] It was good to have a versatile pitcher like Worthington—he could start, he could close (17 games finished, with six saves), and he could pitch in long relief (like the four innings of no-hit ball he threw against Cincinnati on June 7.) His sterling work didn't apply against the Milwaukee Braves, who kind of saw Worthington as their "cousin"—his record against them through the end of the 1958 season was 3-13.

In 1959 Worthington signed after a prolonged (and ultimately successful) contract holdout. He was used in 42 games, but with only three starts—and they were his last three starts in the majors. He finished 15 games but for the most part worked middle relief. He threw 73⅓ innings with a 3.68 ERA and a 2-3 won-loss record.

Worthington had to fight for a spot on the Giants' staff during spring training in 1960, and he didn't make it. Instead, on March 29, he was traded to the Boston Red Sox for first baseman/outfielder Jim Marshall. Red Sox pitching coach Sal Maglie knew Worthington well from their time together on the Giants. Maglie said he was "pretty quick and had a good sinker. We plan to use him as a relief pitcher here. He has developed a good slider and curve to go with his fast sinker, and I believe he will help us."[13] But Worthington spent most of the season (after five relief appearances in April and one in early May) in Triple-A with the Minneapolis Millers. He'd been hit hard with Boston, to the tune of a 7.71 earned-run average. Larry Claflin of the *Boston American* wrote that he was becoming known as Al "Worthless." Claflin asked manager Billy Jurges why he was using Worthington so often. "I had to find out about him," Jurges said, and added after a grimace, "I guess I found out."[14]

In Minneapolis, Worthington started 11 games and relieved in 26 with an excellent 2.04 ERA (he was 11-9). On August 29 the Chicago White Sox announced the purchase of Worthington's contract from the Red Sox. On September 8, having just pitched 5⅓ innings in four games, he left the team and went home. He'd won one and lost one, and had given up two earned runs. He said, "I'm home and I'd rather leave why I'm here a personal matter," though he did indicate he might enroll at Howard College.[15] It was later said that he left because "the club stole signals from the opposition."[16]

A nationally syndicated Jim Murray column provided more of the details. Worthington's objections were ascribed to his being "a man of deep religious convictions."[17] Worthington had followed evangelist Billy Graham since a 1958 faith meeting, and both Worthingtons were "born again" during the Billy Graham Crusade.[18] "I'd been going to church since I was six," he said, "and I'd always wanted to go to heaven, but I'd never understood how."[19] "I do not want to do anything that would displease the Lord," he explained.[20] Murray wrote that his biggest save was himself. Worthington was active in the Brotherhood of Christian Athletes.

Worthington also said, "As a Christian, I couldn't throw a spitter, and never would. It's an illegal pitch."[21]

He'd left the ballclub on principle, and it wasn't the first time he'd spoken up when he'd seen or heard something he thought was wrong. In September 1959, with the Giants holding a slim lead over the Dodgers in the National League pennant race, he heard that the Giants were using a spy in the grandstand, armed with a pair of binoculars. He went to manager Bill Rigney. "I told Bill that I had been talking to church groups, telling people you don't have to lie or cheat in this world if you trust Jesus Christ. How could I go on saying those things if I was winning games because my team was cheating?"[22] With the White Sox, manager Al Lopez would neither confirm nor deny the spying. Worthington told GM Hank Greenberg, "I can't play for a team that's cheating."[23]

Worthington wrote a newspaper column discussing his "stage fright" in becoming a closer in baseball, and how the pressure truly got to him. As it happened, Rev. Graham was holding a crusade in San Francisco. A few days, they went back again and this time he accepted Graham's challenge to "break with the old ego-centered life." He wrote that he learned "the more I centered on Him, the less problem I had with my ego and with pressure." The inner tension he had always felt, which often caused him to tighten up, was something he could control through his faith.[24]

Around 1961 or so, perhaps still troubled by the fact that he knew White Sox owner Bill Veeck condoned the cheating, Worthington was asked to complete a questionnaire for the Baseball Hall of Fame. Asked if he were to do it all over, would he play professional baseball again, he answered: "Maybe not."[25]

There was a gratifying moment for the family that April, when Al's wife saved the life of 3-year-old Bruce Whitaker in Birmingham. She'd heard screams from the boy's mother, found him lying in a drainage ditch, and applied artificial respiration.[26]

Worthington continued pitching, and worked 1961 and 1962 in the White Sox system, in Triple-A both years, for San Diego (9-10, 3.55) and then Indianapolis (15-4, 2.94). "We tried to sell him," GM Greenberg admitted, "but the word was out that he was some sort of cuckoo."[27] Though his record in San Diego may not seem that impressive, he did throw three consecutive shutouts in August, the third of which was a 5-0 no-hitter against Hawaii on the 26th. It was the first no-hitter in Padres history. Worthington walked four.

Worthington's work with Indianapolis was good enough to attract interest. The Mets were expected to select him as their first choice in the minor-league (Rule 5) draft that fall. The October 9 *New York Times* and the Associated Press reported, apparently prematurely, his purchase by the Mets prior to the draft, but he wound up instead with the Cincinnati Reds. The Mets thought they might get him in the second round, but the Reds claimed him for the $25,000 draft price.

Al had a strong 1963 season for Cincinnati, with an ERA of 2.99 over 50 appearances. He was 4-4 with ten saves; he finished 32 of the 50 games in which he appeared. It was almost as though he had been reborn as a pitcher. His teammates showed a good sense of humor. At a team party late in the season, Worthington's gift was a pair of binoculars.[28] Beginning in 1963, Worthington worked six seasons in a row in which he finished with an ERA under 3.00. Those earned-run averages were—beginning in 1963—2.99, 2.16, 2.13, 2.46, 2.84, and 2.32. It was quite a run.

Worthington began 1964 with Cincinnati but appeared in only six games (seven innings) at the beginning of the year, giving up runs to the tune of a 10.29 ERA, and got himself sent down. His explanation: "It always takes me a while to get going in the spring."[29] He found himself again with San Diego, then a Reds farm club, where he went 4-1 with a 3.18 ERA in ten games. Then the Minnesota Twins bought his contract on June 26 in a straight cash deal. Back in the majors once more, in the American League, Worthington pitched in 41 games for the Twins with a 1.37 ERA, not allowing even one earned run in his first 20 appearances. An AP story said that after 14 years of bouncing around he "finally has a steady job."[30] He earned 14 saves. Twins catcher Earl Battey said he had one of the biggest assortments of pitches in the league: "He gives you that big motion and keeps the ball down and throws at the corners … an amazing pitcher."[31]

Recalling his best stuff in a 2014 interview, Worthington said, "The best pitches I had? My fastball slid and sank. It was a natural slider that also sunk. I didn't have a thing to do with that. Just put my hand on it. God gave me that. It just sunk. Then I had a curveball. Those were my two pitches."[32]

The 1965 Twins won 102 games under manager Sam Mele, and won the pennant with ease. Ten of those wins were Worthington's. Pitching exclusively in relief, he worked in 62 games (finishing 38) and his 2.13 ERA was the best on a very good staff. Worthington was credited with 21 saves. Fellow Twins reliever Johnny Klippstein must be noted, too, with a 9-3 record and a 2.24 ERA in 56 games.

The World Series against the Dodgers went the full seven games. The Twins took the first two but lost four of the next five games. Worthington worked only four innings, in part because Mudcat Grant and Jim Kaat both went the route in the first two games, and Grant pitched another complete game in Game Six. Worthington threw two innings in Game Four and two in Game Seven. Though he wasn't charged with an earned run, he gave up singles to each of the first two batters he faced in Game Four and his own throwing error allowed one of the three runs that scored on his watch. Worthington got two votes (of 24 cast) for UPI's Comeback Player of the Year.

The Twins finished in second place in 1966, but nine games behind the Orioles. Worthington pitched in 65 games with a 2.46 ERA (and a 6-3 record). He was the team's principal reliever, most often the closer, from 1966 through 1968, and in 1968 led the league in saves with 18. He had losing records in 1967 (8-9) and 1968 (4-5) but excellent ERAs, as we have seen. In 1967 the Twins lost the pennant to the Red Sox in the final game of the regular season. Worthington came into the game in relief of starter (and 20-game winner) Dean Chance in the sixth inning with three runs already across the plate and two men on. He threw two wild pitches, allowing another run to score and putting the Red Sox up 4-2. A fifth run scored on an error by first baseman Harmon Killebrew. Both inherited runners had scored, but without a base hit. The Twins lost, 5-3.

At the end of the 1968 season, Worthington retired from the game. In May 1969, more than a month into the season, he decided to come out of retirement for one more year.[33] "Billy Martin got a sportswriter to call me. He asked me to come back," Worthington said. He added, "It was very nice to be wanted. . It wasn't easy. It took me a while to get back in shape."[34]

This time it was his final year—1969. He made his first appearance June 8. He went 4-1 in 46 games, with a 4.57 ERA in the year he turned 40. The Twins made it to the postseason again that year. There were now league playoffs to win the pennant and the Twins played the Orioles in the best-of-five American League Championship Series. The O's swept. Worthington appeared in just the third game. With the score Orioles 5, Twins 1, he pitched a 1-2-3 fourth inning but after retiring Jim Palmer in the fifth, gave up a double and two singles, and manager Billy Martin replaced him.

Worthington concluded his time in the majors with a career 3.39 ERA and 110 saves.

In 1970 and 1971, he worked "trying to sell life insurance—but I'm a Christian and when I got a call that someone was sick in a school somewhere, I had to go. So I didn't do very good selling life insurance." There was another call on his services. "Yes, it was. It was the biggest call."[35]

Worthington was the major-league pitching coach for Minnesota in both 1972 and 1973. He made the *New York Times* at one point in August 1973, when—in what might seem a reversal of roles—umpire Frank Umont apologized to him for the umpire's abusive language. Worthington thought that Umont was missing pitches and told him to "bear down," upon which Umont "came over to the dugout and started calling me every name in the book."[36]

In August 1973 Worthington announced he would take the position of head baseball coach (and, later, athletic director) at Lynchburg Baptist College (now Liberty University) in Lynchburg, Virginia, the university founded by Rev. Jerry Falwell. Bobby Richardson took over as baseball coach for him. Worthington retired in December 1989. Liberty's record under him was 343-189-1. Among the players he coached were four all-Americans, including future major leaguers Sid Bream and Lee Guetterman.

After retirement, "I came home [to Birmingham]." We have a Christian school called Briarwood. It's a big school. I became their pitching coach for a while."[37]

Al and Shirley had five children—three boys and two girls. His oldest son played at Alabama. He was a pretty good player, but not good enough to attract attention from scouts.

In 2010 Worthington was inducted into the Liberty University Athletics Hall of Fame. In 2012, he was inducted into the Alabama Sports Hall of Fame.

SOURCES

In addition to the sources noted in this biography, the author also accessed Worthington's player file and player questionnaire from the National Baseball Hall of Fame, the *Encyclopedia of Minor League Baseball*, Retrosheet.org, and Baseball-Reference.com. Thanks to Rod Nelson for scouts information.

NOTES

1. Interview with Al Worthington, May 4, 2014 (hereafter cited as Worthington interview).
2. Worthington interview and correspondence from Al Worthington, May 23, 2014.
3. *Baton Rouge Advocate*, April 9 and May 25, 1950.
4. Worthington correspondence.
5. Worthington interview.
6. *State Times Advocate* (Baton Rouge), May 30, 1952.
7. *Greensboro* (North Carolina) *Record*, July 16, 1953.
8. The three were Joe Doyle, 1906 New York Highlanders; Johnny Marcum, 1933 Philadelphia Athletics; and Dave "Boo" Ferriss, 1945 Boston Red Sox. In the 19th century, James Hughes of Baltimore did it in 1898.
9. *New York Times*, July 20, 1953.
10. The value of a one-third share was reported by the *Chicago Tribune*, October 8, 1954, as just over $3,715.
11. Worthington interview.
12. Associated Press, *Boston American*, April 18, 1958.
13. *Boston Globe*, March 30, 1960.
14. *Boston American*, April 28, 1960.
15. *Omaha World Herald*, September 9, 1960. Worthington graduated from Samford University, formerly Howard College.
16. *Chicago Tribune*, November 27, 1961.
17. *Trenton* (New Jersey) *Evening Times*, January 29, 1965. The *Chicago Tribune* of October 22, 1987, said he'd been asked to sit in the stands and send signals.
18. Worthington correspondence.
19. Jack Devaney, "A Bible in the Bullpen," *Saturday Evening Post*, May 2, 1964.
20. *Rockford* (Illinois) *Morning Star*, October 8, 1965.
21. *The Oregonian* (Portland), October 30, 1968.
22. Devaney, *Saturday Evening Post*, op. cit.
23. Ibid.
24. The article ran in several newspapers, including the March 7, 1967, *State Times Advocate*.
25. Interestingly, he did not recall writing this when interviewed in 2014.
26. *San Diego Union*, April 15, 1961.
27. Devaney, op. cit.
28. Ibid.
29. *Hartford Courant*, August 13, 1964.
30. *The Oregonian*, August 13, 1964.
31. *Hartford Courant*, August 13, 1964.
32. Worthington interview and correspondence.
33. *Washington Post*, May 24, 1969.
34. Worthington interview.
35. Worthington interview.
36. *New York Times*, August 30, 1973.
37. Worthington interview.

Jerry Zimmerman

BY NORM KING

AROUND THE TIME THAT ROBERT Zimmerman, a/k/a Bob Dylan, left Minnesota to start the world of music a-changin', Jerry Zimmerman arrived there to play for the Twins. And although Jerry could only hit a home run if the ball was blowing in the wind (three career homers), he provided steady defense and a relaxing clubhouse presence as a catcher for seven seasons with the Twins after one season with the Cincinnati Reds. Upon ending his playing career, he went on to serve as a major-league coach, scout, and, for part of one game, as an umpire.

Gerald Robert Zimmerman was born on September 21, 1934, in Omaha, Nebraska, the son of Leonard (L.P.) and Helen Zimmerman. L.P. was a motorman, who moved his family to Milwaukie, Oregon, just outside Portland, when Jerry was a boy.[1] Jerry was an excellent baseball player at Milwaukie High School, where his four-year batting average of .425 caught the attention of scouts, as did his .625 average during his senior year.

Zimmerman attracted attention from 14 of the 16 major-league clubs, and allowed them to conduct a bidding war while he played semipro ball the summer after he graduated.[2] The Boston Red Sox eventually won the auction, and West Coast scout Charley Wallgren signed Zimmerman on June 6, 1952, for a reported $80,000 signing bonus. The offers poured in until the day he signed.

"As late as yesterday afternoon, scouts from the New York Yankees and Chicago White Sox talked with Leonard Zimmerman, Jerry's father," reported the United Press.[3]

The 17-year-old Zimmerman's first stop was with the San Jose Red Sox of the Class C California League. His .625 high-school average soon became a memory as he adjusted to professional pitching; he hit .230 in 72 games with no home runs. His second stop was the altar, when he married Phyllis Ellen Turney on October 24, 1952. They went on to have four children, sons Jeff and Joe and daughters June and Karen.[4]

The Red Sox kept Zimmerman in San Jose in 1953. His numbers improved slightly; in 101 games, he had a .265 average with two home runs. His offensive improvement was offset by the 13 errors he committed behind the plate. Looking at the package as a whole, the Red Sox demoted him to the Corning Red Sox of the Class D Pennsylvania-Ontario-New York league for 1954.

Zimmerman responded well to the demotion, batting over .300 for the only time in his professional career (.302) and setting career highs in triples (4) and home runs (7). The Red Sox were pleased enough with his play to promote him to Class B, and his ping-ponging

Zimmerman was a dependable back-up catcher for the Twins in the 1960s. In 1965 he made 44 starts and was a late-inning replacement in 38 others. (Photo courtesy of Minnesota Twins Baseball Club).

across the country continued with the Greensboro Patriots of the Carolina League for 1955. Here he batted a respectable .275 with six home runs.

Beginning in 1956, Zimmerman's minor-league career was all "A's," as he began moving up the higher rungs of the minor-league ladder. That year he played for the Albany Senators of the Class A Eastern League. The following season saw the Red Sox promote him to Double-A, with the Oklahoma City Indians of the Texas League. In 1958 he advanced to Triple-A with the Minneapolis Millers of the American Association, the Red Sox' top farm team at the time. here he began a long association with Millers player-manager Gene Mauch.

The 1958 Millers had a successful if unremarkable season, but they followed it up with an incredible playoff run in which they won 11 straight games on their way to the Junior World Series title. They finished in third place with an 82-71 record and Zimmerman hit only .250 with two home runs and 16 RBIs in 57 games. But the top four teams in the league made the playoffs that year, and the Millers were pitted against the Wichita Braves. After falling behind two games to one against the Braves, the Millers roared back on the strength of their pitching to win three straight games and the series. They then swept the Denver Bears in four straight to win the American Association championship, and then repeated the feat against the International League champion Montreal Royals to take it all in the Junior World Series. Zimmerman contributed throughout the playoff run, including a .357 average in the final.

"The power hitting of big Art Schult, the catching of Jerry Zimmerman, the inspired defense and pitching and the stick work of newcomer Stu Locklin were the prime factors in the surge which astonished both leagues," wrote Halsey Hall.[5]

Zimmerman's glory was short-lived. The 1959 season was his eighth in the minors, and it was evident to the Red Sox that their one-time hot prospect had cooled off considerably, especially when he began the year hitting .186 after 20 games. They released him on July 16 but he wasn't unemployed for long as the Orioles signed him that same day. Once they got their man, the O's sent him to the Vancouver Mounties of the Pacific Coast League. In 44 games there, he hit a meager .176, but made only one error behind the plate. Not impressed by his numbers, the Orioles released him on September 25, 1959. He again avoided the unemployment line, because the Cincinnati Redlegs came calling, signed him the same day, and had him report to the PCL's Seattle Rainiers for the 1960 season.

Maybe it was because the move to Seattle from Vancouver wasn't very difficult, but whatever the reason, Zimmerman had a decent season in 1960, batting .279 with six home runs in 82 games. The Reds thought enough of those numbers to bring him up to the majors in 1961.[6]

After nine years of perseverance, Zimmerman finally got to experience the thrill and tension of appearing on a major-league field for the first time on April 14, 1961, when he put on the tools of ignorance for the bottom of the ninth in the Reds' 7-3 win over St. Louis. He got his first two major-league hits and scored his first runs on April 30.

The Reds employed enough catchers to form a chorus line in 1961 (six different men played the position during the season) with Zimmerman appearing in more games (76, with 64 starts) than the others.[7] The players were not known for their offense—the position produced only four home runs all season—but for whatever reason it worked.[8] The Reds won the National League pennant with a 93-61 record, four games ahead of the second-place Los Angeles Dodgers. Their pitching staff was third in the league in earned-run average (3.78), second in fewest earned runs allowed (576) and tied for first in shutouts (nine), in part because the catchers excelled at calling pitches.

The Reds faced the New York Yankees of Roger Maris (61 home runs) and Mickey Mantle (54 home runs) in the 1961 World Series. Even with Mantle appearing in only two games due to injury, the Reds were no match for the Bronx Bombers, who won the Series in five games. Reds manager Fred Hutchinson alternated Darrell Johnson and Johnny Edwards behind the plate, and Zimmerman appeared in only two games as a late-inning defensive replacement. He never had a plate appearance.

The Reds decided that too many catchers were spoiling the pot and traded Zimmerman to the Minnesota Twins on January 30, 1962, for reserve outfielder Dan Dobbek. Zimmerman got to practice his pine-riding during 1962 and 1963 in Minnesota because the team's regular catcher, Earl Battey, was an All-Star both those seasons. Zimmerman appeared in only 73 games over those two years and batted .254 with no home runs and a total of only 10 RBIs. However, low batting numbers aren't always an indication of a player's value to a team. In 1964 the Twins had an offyear, with a 79-83 record after back-to-back 91-win seasons, but they led the American League in runs scored (737) and home runs (221). They didn't need to look to Zimmerman for offense (he hit .200 in 63 games with 12 RBIs), but even as a backup player, he had a positive clubhouse influence. He was very popular with his teammates because of his sense of humor and his quiet acceptance of his backup role.

"His teammates have been visiting (his locker) in clusters for years," wrote Max Nichols in *The Sporting News*. "In fact, Zimmerman's corner has long been a place of rest and quiet conversation after games, possibly a retreat from writers who continually pump the stars for quotes."[9]

The Twins came back with a vengeance in 1965, going 102-60 and winning the American League pennant. Zimmerman proved to be a good-luck charm, as injuries to Battey gave him the chance to catch 43 of the team's first 75 games—and the Twins won 31 of them. Manager Sam Mele knew, though, that Zimmerman was more than a talisman.

"I've said before that Zimmerman is the best receiver in the American League," said Mele. "He doesn't hit for a high average, but he helps you in other ways with his bat, moving runners around."[10]

On June 6 Zimmerman hit a ball where no ball off his bat had gone before, as he smacked his first major-league home run, a two-run shot, in front of the hometown fans. He blasted another homer in 1966 and a third in 1967.

As in 1961, Zimmerman saw little action in the 1965 World Series, which the Twins lost to the Los Angeles Dodgers in seven games, appearing only as a late-inning defensive replacement in Games Three and Four. He did get to the plate once, grounding into a double play to end Game Three.

The 1966 season was more of the same for Zimmerman as he only played in 60 games and batted .252. However, things changed considerably for him in 1967, when he ended up with more work than he could handle. When the season began, Zimmerman had taken on the role of bullpen coach in addition to his duties as backup catcher; this meant a higher salary plus a single room on road trips. That situation became problematic when Battey ended up spending considerable time out of the lineup because of injuries and poor play. As a result, Zimmerman played in 104 games that year, by far the most in his career, but he spent a lot less time in the bullpen than was expected. Perhaps the extra workload was more than he was used to because his batting average plummeted to .167.

Battey retired after the 1967 season, but if Zimmerman had any hopes of becoming the regular catcher, they were dashed when the Twins traded for John Roseboro in November of that year. Zimmerman appeared in only 24 games in 1968, but was still busy on the field continuing in the part-time role of bullpen coach.

The Twins released Zimmerman after the 1968 season, and he was going to become manager of the brand-new Seattle Pilots' farm club in Billings, Montana, when an old friend came calling. Mauch, Zimmerman's manager when he played for the Minneapolis Millers, was piloting the expansion Montreal Expos and hired him as the team's first-ever bullpen coach. They worked together in Montreal until Mauch was fired after the 1975 season. The two continued on back to Zimmerman's old stamping grounds in Minnesota while Mauch was skipper there from 1976 to 1980.

Zimmerman got a taste of the manager's life for two games in August 1978 when Mauch was hospitalized with a foot infection. He went 1-1, beating the Seattle Mariners 10-2, then losing to them the next night, 4-1. That same month, he had an unusual experience for a coach; when the umpires went on strike on August 25, Zimmerman helped the two amateur umpires hired to call the game by donning the blue at third base for one inning in a game against the Blue Jays in Toronto. Just to keep things fair, Blue Jays coach Don Leppert manned second. The coaches returned to their respective benches when a third amateur umpire arrived in the second inning.

After leaving the Twins, Zimmerman went on to scout for the New York Yankees and the Baltimore Orioles. He had only recently retired when he died of a heart attack on September 9, 1998, in Neskowin, Oregon, at the age of 63.

SOURCES

Baseball-reference.com

1974topps-pennantfever.blogspot.ca/

Bend (Oregon) *Bulletin*

Wellsville (New York) *Daily Reporter*

The Sporting News

coolofttheevening.com

NOTES

1. A motorman is a streetcar operator.
2. Neither the Washington Senators nor the St. Louis Browns sent any scouts to evaluate Zimmerman.
3. United Press, "Red Sox Sign Up Oregon Prep For Estimated $80,000," *Bend Bulletin*, June 7, 1952.
4. Jerry's son Jeff is not related to the Jeff Zimmerman who played for the Texas Rangers.
5. Halsey Hall, "Millers Haul Away Playoff Loot With 11 Wins in Row," *The Sporting News*, October 8, 1958.
6. The team had changed its name from Reds to Redlegs in 1954 because of the association of the word "Reds" with communism during that era. In 1959 they resumed using the name Reds.
7. The other Reds catchers that year were Johnny Edwards (52 games), Darrell Johnson (20 games), Bob Schmidt (27 games), Ed Bailey (12 games), and Pete Whisenant (who played one inning of one game, but still managed to commit an error).
8. Johnny Edwards hit two home runs, while Darrell Johnson and Bob Schmidt hit one each.
9. Max Nichols, "Twins Sluggers Applaud As Zim Takes Rare Bow," *The Sporting News,* September 5, 1964.
10. Max Nichols, "Just a .217 Hitter, But Zim Puts Vim In Galloping Twins," *The Sporting News*, July 17, 1965.

Sam Mele

BY BILL NOWLIN

SAM MELE MANAGED THE MINNESOTA Twins to the American League pennant in 1965, but just a year and a half later was fired by the team. Subsequently, his former team rallied to finish the 1967 season tied with the Tigers, just one game out of first place in the American League.

The record books show Sam Mele was born on January 21, 1923, in Astoria, in the New York City Borough of Queens. He was really born a year earlier, in 1922. "I'll tell you why," he confided. "I had two uncles in the major leagues [Tony and Al Cuccinello]. They told me cheat a year on your age because you'll last a year longer in the big leagues. So I did." The tradition is a venerable one. The Cuccinellos were his only major-league relatives; Sam was well aware of Dutch Mele, but there was no relation. Sam's mother, Anna, was a Cuccinello and the two were her brothers; Anna herself was born in Avellino, Italy, as was Sam's father, Antonio. They met in America.

Antonio worked for Consolidated Edison but had an accident early on, and the utility company made him a maintenance man so he didn't have to do anything too strenuous. Anna Mele was enterprising and borrowed "something like $2,200 or $3,200—she bought an apartment house. What did she know about real estate, coming from Italy, you know? It was a thriving place; it was a six-family house and that was where I was born and lived almost all my life." She kept busy managing the house, and the couple's seven children.

The house was in the city, but there was a dirt road in front as young Sabath Anthony Mele[1] grew up. "Completely dirt. We used to play stickball with a rubber ball and a broom handle. We played all the time until they paved the road. We used to have to hide the goddam stick because the cops would come and break it. The neighbors, I guess, would complain. You could break some windows. Then we'd have to get another broom handle. If you could hit on a dirt road, you could hit in the damn major leagues, the way the ball bounced. Up and down, all directions."

Sam played high-school baseball his sophomore year, but Bryant High School stopped offering it after his first season. The story he heard at the time was that the principal's son had been hit and killed by a baseball, but he didn't know if that ever truly occurred. There was, however, a boy on the team that year who played for a team out on Long Island called Louona Park, in the Queens Alliance League. Sam and his brother played for them one Sunday, a doubleheader. His brother Al got about seven hits and Sam got six. "Oh Christ, I thought I was something. The following weekend I went out again, didn't get a base hit. Come home, threw my uniform on the floor, and my mother chewed my ass out. About being a quitter. Now of course, she tells her brothers, Tony and Al. Major

Following a ten-year big league playing career, Sam Mele guided the Twins to a 524-436 record in parts of seven seasons and to the club's first pennant since 1933 when they were located in Washington and called the Senators. (Photo courtesy of Minnesota Twins Baseball Club).

leaguers. And one by one, they chewed my ass out about you don't ever quit. And my uncle Tony, I'll never forget, he said he had gone, I forget, I think, 8-for-30 in the big leagues, but there's always another day, you're going to play again and again and again. As you went in our apartment, there's a transom. So I come home one day and there's a goddam noose hanging down, and they said, well, if you're going to quit, why don't you just hang yourself?" Tough love?

There was a lot of baseball talk around the house. Sam remembered Al Lopez in particular, who came by for years. "I used to listen to them talk baseball. Christ, it was amazing. When I went away to play ball, I knew more than the damn managers that I played for because of those guys. My uncle was very friendly with Babe Ruth. I'll never forget, I met him at Bayside Country Club, and he was so big — or maybe I was so small — I was looking up to him like he was God. I didn't realize how great a player he was. I was too damn young."

Growing up in New York at the time, one would think, Sam would have been a Dodgers fan or a Giants fan, or a Yankees fan with all the great Italian players they had. No, Sam was a Tigers fan. "When I played in '46, when I went to play for Cronin — I went to spring training with Cronin — he said, 'Did you ever see Lazzeri play?' I said no. 'He was one of the smartest and greatest ballplayers you'd ever meet in your life. Being Italian, you're Italian. Yankee Stadium wasn't that far from where you lived, and you never went to see him play?' Oh Christ, he told me off. I never did see Lazzeri. But he couldn't tell me enough about him."

Sam's oldest brother Dominick played first base for Erie, but was the only other one in the family to play baseball. Dominick also played for Bradford in the PONY League and Charleston in the Middle Atlantic League. "We had four boys and three of us would sleep in one bed, my older brother in the other because he had a job. My mother would want him to get his rest. So we three guys had to sleep in the one bed. He ended up as a mailman in the office."

Because both of his uncles played second base, Sam saw himself as a second baseman, too. That's not what his uncles saw. "When they saw me play they said, 'Get the hell in the outfield.'" In fact, basketball was more his sport than baseball and he attended New York University on a basketball scholarship. He'd played professionally when still a high-school student "and they caught me. They banned me for a year in high school. But then I went on a basketball scholarship." NYU's baseball coach, Bill McCarthy, was friendly with Red Sox scout Neil Mahoney. McCarthy drove Sam up to Fenway Park more than once and he had the opportunity to work out with the Red Sox before regular batting practice. He was batting against the likes of Herb Pennock and Bump Hadley.[2]

"I remember one day taking batting practice, and they said, 'Take five swings.' I had about three swings, and then I took a pitch. This voice behind the cage asks, 'Why'd you take that?' And I said, 'Well, I thought it was outside.' And the voice says, 'You're right, but it was high enough for a strike.' So when I got out, finished hitting, I walked around and this guy called me over and it was Ted Williams. He explained to me about batting, and from that day on, whenever I'd see him … he took a great liking to me for some reason. In spring training in '46, I'd take my batting practice and run to left field and talk to him about hitting.

"Then I asked him about fielding — one question — and he said, 'No. You go to center field. Ask that guy.' Which was Dom DiMaggio."

This was during his first year at NYU. The Red Sox were accommodating, putting Mele up at a "nice hotel" in Boston. After two or three visits, there was some real interest. The Washington Senators made him an offer, but for very little money. The Cubs offered him $1,000. Al Cuccinello acted more or less as his agent, and Neil Mahoney had told them, "Don't sign with anybody until I talk to you." Mahoney brought Sam and Uncle Al to the Hotel Commodore in New York and introduced him to Red Sox owner Tom Yawkey. Sam was about to go into military service, and Yawkey told him, "We'll give you $5,000. We'll give you $2,500 now and we'll give you the rest when you come out." That was too good a deal to pass up.

Mele entered the Navy's V-12 program, signing up as a Marine. He was sent to train at Yale, and played baseball there under Red Rolfe. He remembers the club having a 14-1 record, though one can't find such a record, but as far as going to classes … that wasn't his strong suit. "Finally the teachers said to me, 'Look, you're either going to play ball or you're going to go to class.' I was there about four months and they shipped me out to California, and I played on the Marine Corps team out there. We had no-name guys on the team, and we used to play against DiMaggio, Walter Judnich, and against the Navy with Barney McCosky, Rizzuto, all those big-name guys." He served from July 1943 to very early 1946.

Mele was formally signed by the Red Sox in 1946, watched their first homestand from the press box and was sent out to Louisville. "I think my first game in Minneapolis, I went 4-for-6, but being a young player in that league—Triple-A—I guess I had a lot to learn about the pitchers. [He hit .226 in 53 at-bats.] Then they sent me to Scranton, and I got the Most Valuable Player award in that league. I had a hell of a year down there. There must have been about seven of us that went to the big leagues that year." Mele hit .342 with Scranton, leading the league, ranking second with 154 hits, and with 226 total bases, including 18 triples.

In 1947 Mele made the Boston ballclub and played 123 games—119 as an outfielder, and one game at first base, with only two errors all year long. Playing for Joe Cronin in his last year as skipper, Sam hit for a very strong .302 average with 12 homers and 73 RBIs. His debut came on Opening Day; batting seventh, he was 2-for-2 at the plate. It was a very good first year. One of Sam's favorite memories came during his first game in Yankee Stadium. His parents had never seen him play ball, and he got them box seats. "And I hit a damn home run off of Floyd Bevens [April 22, 1947]. As I'm rounding second, I can see the box seats. And they're smiling. Never got up, never clapped or anything. Just smiling. As I'm rounding third, I take a look again over there. I'll never forget the look on their faces. Two Italian immigrants. Yankee Stadium. Never saw a game. Oh, brother!"

In December 1947 the Sox traded for left-handed batter Stan Spence and it was thought that he and Mele might platoon. Joe McCarthy took over as manager in 1948, and his relationship with Mele got off to a difficult beginning in spring training. "I'm taking batting practice and I had a style like Joe DiMaggio—not that I hit like him, but a wide stance, short stride … and this voice behind the cage—I'd never met McCarthy—says, 'How're you going to hit like that?' I'm saying to myself, well, shit, I just hit .302. I get out and he calls me over and says, 'You have to have your feet closer together, and take a long stride.' Well, you know, Joe McCarthy, with all those winning teams, he must know what he's saying. So I tried that and goddammit, I could never get back to my old style. I went to New York after that to play and Tommy Henrich—I'll never forget it—says, 'What the hell are you doing with your batting style?' And I told him what had happened. He says, 'Goddammit, you were a good-looking hitter. I don't know why the hell they would change you.'"

"McCarthy didn't play me, hardly. I don't know why and I'm thinking it could have been Opening Day in Fenway Park. I lost a ball in the sun and the Athletics beat us. I don't know if he ever held that against me, although he told a writer—a New York writer, and it's in a book—he said Henrich would have stuck that ball in his ass. Now I called that writer and then wrote him, and he never answered me. It was a line drive in right field. I had my glasses down, shielded my eyes, and the next thing I know, the ball went right by my head—pshooooo—and I said, that's the real story. Never mind about Henrich sticking it. … He couldn't have caught it either. If a ball is in the sun, you don't have a chance. Well, anyway, I'm not playing hardly at all in '48."

Mele found himself in the doghouse for another reason, too. In early July, on the train to Philadelphia, he and Ted Williams were playing around mock-sparring with each other. A few hours later it was discovered that Ted's cartilage had become separated from a rib; Williams missed two full weeks. Then, on September 17 in St. Louis, Mele tore up his foot trying

Sam Mele (Photo courtesy of Minnesota Twins Baseball Club).

to steal third in the fourth inning and was out for the rest of the year.

The story of Mele's injury requires a little delicacy. Joe McCarthy was known to have imbibed to excess. "He's riding the horse," folks would say. White Horse scotch. It got so bad that they locked him in his room and coach Del Baker managed the game. Mele doubled in three runs in the first inning, then got on base in the fourth. Birdie Tebbetts got a hit, too. By now McCarthy had appeared in the dugout and Baker was in the coach's box. Joe Dobson was up and Baker conveyed the sign for a double steal. Mele was hurt, badly, sliding into third base. Mickey Harris called for a stretcher, and when McCarthy came across the field, he looked down at Mele and said, "Since when do they have to take ballplayers off on a stretcher?" Mele, angered, fired back, "F—- you, you son of a bitch, I'll walk." McCarthy then blustered at Baker, "Why would you go for a double steal with a pitcher hitting?" and so forth. As Mele tells it, "Del Baker was good enough to say, 'Hey, you gave me the sign, whether you know it or not.'" The players insisted Mele take the stretcher, but he was out for the season. "I couldn't even put a shoe on."

Mele had far fewer plate appearances in 1948 and performed poorly, batting just .233. Stan Spence didn't do much better, batting .235. All the Red Sox needed was one more win that year and they wouldn't have had to face the Indians in the one-game playoff that cost them the pennant.

In 1949, two months into the season, Mele had been in just 18 games for Boston, batting just .196. On June 13 he was traded to Washington, with pitcher Mickey Harris for pitcher Walt Masterson. In 78 games for the Senators, Mele batted .242. He got in a fairly full year for Washington in 1950, accumulating 435 at-bats, and hit for a .274 average, driving in 86 runs. The 1951 season was equally good, with the very same .274 batting average, a league-leading 36 doubles, and 94 runs batted in. Early in 1952, despite batting .429 at the time (in 28 at-bats), he was traded to the White Sox (on May 3) for outfielder Jim Busby and infielder Mel Hoderlein. For the White Sox he hit .248 the rest of the year, driving in 59 runs. Six of those RBIs came in one inning of one game, when he hit a three-run homer and a three-run triple in the fourth inning on June 10 against Philadelphia.

Chicago had Sam Mele for a full year in 1953 and, for the third time in four years, he batted .274. He drove in another 82 runs. Shortly before spring training of 1954, the White Sox traded him to the Orioles (with infielder Neil Berry) for outfielder Johnny Groth and infielder Johnny Lipon. He was batting .239 in limited action, and finally was offered on waivers in late July. The Red Sox claimed him, and Mele rejoined his original team. Lou Boudreau was managing the Red Sox and found a role for Mele, who responded by hitting .318 over 132 at-bats in 42 games.

He had a hard time getting going in 1955, though, and was hitting only .129 in his first 31 at-bats. The Red Sox sold him to Cincinnati on June 23. For the Reds, he hit just .210. Released by them in mid-January 1956, he was signed a couple of months later by the Cleveland Indians. He appeared in 57 games (114 at-bats) and batted .254. He also drove in 20 runs, the last runs he would drive in as a major-league ballplayer. He was released by the Indians on Opening Day of 1957.

Sam spent a couple of years playing minor-league ball — .265 for Indianapolis in the American Association, in 370 at-bats, and more limited action in 1958 (.322 in 59 at-bats for Indianapolis, then .216 in 134 at-bats for the International League team in Buffalo).

After 1958 Mele turned to coaching, working for Washington in 1959 and 1960, and moved with the Senators to Minnesota beginning in 1961. On June 6 the Twins asked him to temporarily replace manager Cookie Lavagetto, who took a leave of absence and was ultimately fired 2½ weeks later. Mele became manager and served the Twins for six years. In his first full year managing the Twins, he had tremendous success, bringing the 1962 Twins to a second-place finish in the ten-team American League, just five games behind the New York Yankees. The Twins won 91 games in 1963—the same total as in 1962—but the Yankees won eight more games, so the third-place Twins finished 13 games out of first. After a significant dip to sixth place in 1964, the Twins took the American League pennant in 1965, winning 102 games and coming in seven games ahead of the second-place White Sox.

The "usually mild-mannered Mele" (Associated Press) was involved in one unfortunate incident during the '65 campaign. During a July 18 doubleheader with the Los Angeles Angels, he got into it with umpire Bill Valentine and his left hand connected—or nearly so—with Valentine's jaw. There was clearly some pushing and shoving. Mele said he didn't remember hitting the umpire, but news reports quoted him as saying, "He had his finger stuck in my face. I know that." He later said, with a wink, "I tripped, I stumbled into him. I guess I stumbled into him first." Mele was fined $500 and suspended for five days.

The 1965 World Series pitted the pitching and speed of the Los Angeles Dodgers against the pitching and power of the Minnesota Twins. On paper the Twins had the edge offensively and took the first two games at home, 8-2 and 5-1, defeating the Dodgers' duo of Don Drysdale and Sandy Koufax. Los Angeles took three games in a row in their home park, as Bob Allison, Harmon Killebrew, Tony Oliva, and AL MVP Zoilo Versalles arguably underproduced; the Dodgers pitched around Killebrew; he drove in only two runs. Ron Fairly drove in six runs in the Series for the Dodgers, but Mele was able to take the Twins all the way to Game Seven, in Minnesota. The final blow was Lou Johnson's solo home run off Jim Kaat, while Sandy Koufax threw a complete game, three-hit shutout.

The 1966 Twins won 89 games, good enough for second place, nine games behind Baltimore, but when the team seemed to struggle in the first part of 1967, Mele was fired and Cal Ermer was named manager. The Twins were an even 25-25 on June 9 when Mele was shown the door. They finished up in second place, just one game behind the Red Sox.

Boston owner Tom Yawkey had remained friendly with Mele over the years, and had often told him, "If anything happens to you in Minnesota, you call me, immediately." After returning to his home in Boston, he called on Yawkey, who hired him on the spot. Mele worked in the Red Sox system for 25 years.

"I was an instructor in the minor leagues, ran the minor-league camp, hitting instructor, baserunning, bunting, and then when the spring training was over, they sent me all over the damn country doublechecking players that the scouts had recommended. I did that for a long time. Then in the fall, they had like an instructional league, and I used to run that." Working as a cross-checker, he first met Jim Rice. Sox scout Mace Brown took him to Anderson, South Carolina, to look at Rice.

"Now there's a Detroit scout in the stands," Sam remembered, "and Rice didn't show up for three innings. So the scout said, 'Christ, he don't want to play'—so he left. Mace Brown and I talked to Rice after the game. He had worked at a variety store. His replacement didn't show up, so he stayed on to help the owner. We called the owner; he said, 'That's exactly true.' Houston was after Rice, too, but when they took a pitcher, the Red Sox pounced and signed up Jim Rice. He was a driven pupil in the instructional league. "You know how, as an instructor, you've got to get the kid and say, 'Let's go, we've got extra work to do'? He used to grab me, every day. Every day. I didn't get him; he got me. And we became great, great friends.

"He went to Winter Haven in that league. I'd go down to watch him. He had power to all fields. All fields. Now watching these few games, he's trying to pull everything. Pull everything. Pull everything. So I talked to him after the game. The general manager was a pitcher, who thought he was a hitter. He'd try to tell the kid, you've got to pull the ball for Fenway Park, the Wall. I told him after the game, I said, 'You don't have to worry. You're not a dead pull hitter. You can hit balls to right center, right field, center field, left center, left field. Your power is all over.' That's what he did his whole career."

Sam Mele's time with the Red Sox ended on a sour note, when GM Dan Duquette said he'd been telling Cleveland how to pitch to Boston's hitters. Far-fetched as that might seem, it apparently led to the Red Sox parting ways with a longtime scout. As of 2007, physical ailments began to afflict him. He's had his hip socket go out twice, suffered a ruptured disc in his back, and has macular degeneration in his right eye. The only contact he'd had with new ownership at the time was to have received a Red Sox watch after the team won the 2004 World Series. "What the hell. I gave it to one of my kids."

Note

An earlier version of this biography originally appeared in the book *Spahn, Sain, and Teddy Ballgame: Boston's (almost) Perfect Baseball Summer of 1948*, edited by Bill Nowlin and published by Rounder Books in 2008.

SOURCE

Interview with Sam Mele done April 15, 2006.

NOTES

1. His surname is pronounced MEE-lee.
2. Interview with Sam Mele, April 15, 2006.

Jim Lemon

BY GREGORY H. WOLF

ON AUGUST 31, 1956, PRESIDENT Dwight D. Eisenhower traveled approximately two miles from the White House to Griffith Stadium take in an afternoon of baseball featuring the Washington Senators and New York Yankees, whose star, Mickey Mantle, was in pursuit of Babe Ruth's home-run record. Mantle walloped his 47th round-tripper in the Yankees' 6-4 victory, but was upstaged by Washington's 28-year-old slugger, Jim Lemon, in his first full season. The hulking 6-foot-4, 200-pound Lemon stole the show by belting three consecutive home runs off starter Whitey Ford, accounting for all of Washington's runs and letting Lemon join the Yankees' Joe DiMaggio as the only players to clout three round-trippers in a game in the mammoth ballpark. An exuberant Lemon met an equally excited Eisenhower after the game, and sealed his reputation as the president's favorite player.

Like Joe Adcock, Rocky Colavito, Ted Kluszewski, and Dick Stuart, among many others, Lemon was the kind of big, lumbering slugger that many clubs had in an era defined by powerful hitters. "Every team approached the game with the same essential offensive strategy," wrote Bill James about big-league ball in the 1950s. "Get people on base and hit home runs."[1] Lemon averaged 28 round-trippers and 87 RBIs during his first five full seasons (1956-1960) with the lowly Senators. Plagued by injuries after the team relocated to Minnesota, Lemon retired after the 1963 season with 164 home runs to his credit in 1,010 games. A baseball lifer, Lemon served two different stints on the coaching staff of the Minnesota Twins (1965-1967 and 1981-1984) and piloted the Washington Senators in 1968.

James Robert Lemon was born on March 23, 1928, in Covington, a small town nestled in the Allegheny Mountains in north-central Virginia near the border with West Virginia. His parents, James G. and Elizabeth Lemon, raised six children (two daughters, followed by Jim, then three more sons) in the unforgiving times of the Great Depression. Like many men in the picturesque city surrounded by mountains and lush forests, the elder Jim was employed in the paper mill industry as a millwright. Young Jim (whom everyone called Bob) seemed to be a natural athlete. Always tall for his age, lanky, fast, and blessed with quick reflexes, Lemon could hit a baseball a country mile. After graduating from Covington High School in 1947, he was signed by the Cleveland Indians. Soon thereafter, he became known as Jim in order to avoid confusion with the team's other Lemon, star pitcher Bob Lemon.

In 1948 Jim began his professional baseball career and commenced an eight-year odyssey filled with disappointments and triumphs, promotions and demotions, and a trade before he finally landed a permanent spot on a big-league roster in 1956 at the age of 28. Initially assigned to the Pittsfield (Massachusetts) Electrics in the Class C Canadian-American League, Lemon lasted only seven games before he was dropped a class

A feared-slugger with the Washington Senators, Lemon moved with the club to Minnesota in 1961. He served as the Twins' batting coach from 1965 to 1967 and managed the Cleveland Indians the following season. (Photo courtesy of Minnesota Twins Baseball Club).

to the Bloomingdale (New Jersey) Troopers in the North Atlantic League. He batted .298 and displayed his speed and power by ranking in the top ten in triples and homers (11 each).

Over the next two seasons, Lemon emerged as one of the top sluggers in the minor leagues. As a member of the Harrisburg (Pennsylvania) Senators, Lemon led the Class B Interstate League with 27 round-trippers in 1949. The following season, his 39 clouts for the Double-A Oklahoma City Indians of the Texas League were the most in Double-A. He also led the league in RBIs (119), slugging percentage (.585), and total bases (275) in less than a full season.

In a fierce pennant race with the Detroit Tigers and New York Yankees, the Cleveland Indians called up Lemon on August 18, 1950.[2] According to sportswriter Hal Lebovitz, manager Lou Boudreau wanted the hot prospect even though his squad was filled with home-run threats (Al Rosen, Luke Easter, and Larry Doby), and clashed with GM Hank Greenberg, who considered Lemon still too green.[3] Batting third and playing left field, Lemon went 1-for-4 with two strikeouts in his debut on August 20. He struggled both at the plate, knocking in just one run (on his first home run) in 34 at-bats, and in the field.

Lemon served in the US Army in 1951 and 1952, and was stationed primarily at Fort Meade, Maryland. In addition to playing on his camp team, Lemon used his furlough to participate in his first spring training with the Indians in 1952. "I believe he is not only going to become a big leaguer," said Greenberg, impressed with Lemon's commitment to baseball, "he's going to become a star."[4]

Lemon was back with the Indians in 1953, but it was obvious that a two-year absence from Organized Baseball had taken a toll on the once-promising prospect. While playing Army ball, he had developed the habit of backing away from pitches because of wild throwers, and consequently lost his power stroke. "Greenberg told me to throw my shoulder toward the pitcher on every delivery," said Lemon in spring training.[5] Looking confused at the plate, Lemon went 8-for-46 (.174) with one home run through May before he was optioned to "regain his swing" with the Triple-A Indianapolis Indians in the American Association.[6]

Lemon's career seemed to reach a crossroad in 1954 after a poor season with Indianapolis, where he batted just .218. Despite a productive offseason playing for Gavilanes in the Venezuelan winter league, Lemon's spring training with the Indians was a bust. Still weak from a tonsillectomy before arriving in Tucson, Lemon was sent at his own request to Cleveland's minor-league camp in Daytona Beach in mid-March.[7] Not yet optioned, Lemon was working out with the Richmond Virginians of the International League when he was recalled to the Indians due to a technical oversight. Because Lemon had served two years in the service, he had to clear waivers before he could be optioned, and that was a risk the Indians were unwilling to take. Instead, they sold him for a reported $20,000 to the Washington Senators on May 12. After going 2-for-4 in his first start, on May 16, Lemon lined a walk-off, pinch-hit single to lead the Senators over the New York Yankees, 2-1, on May 26.

Despite his first big hit, Lemon was hitting just .212 (7-for-33) with no homers. His career reached its nadir when he cleared waivers and was optioned to the Charlotte (North Carolina) Hornets of the Class A South Atlantic League in mid-June. Surprisingly, Lemon resurrected his career, finishing second in batting (.346) and tying for the league lead in slugging percentage (.604). Called up in September, he started 24 consecutive games for the Senators, batting well enough (.242 with three triples and two homers) to rekindle Washington's interest in his career.

Lemon's rise to the big leagues hit another stumbling block in 1955. The previous year the Senators had given prospect Harmon Killebrew a hefty bonus to sign with the team; under rules established in 1947 to discourage large bonuses, Washington was obliged to keep the "bonus baby" on the team's roster for two years. The Senators thus had little flexibility with Lemon, whom they assigned to the Chattanooga Lookouts in the Double-A Southern Association. The 27-year-old slugger "smash[ed] record breaking drives all season," wrote *The Sporting News*, including a 450-foot blast over the center-field wall at Pelican Park in New Orleans.[8] He was the first right-hander to clear the 30-foot-tall right-field wall at the 317-foot mark at Chattanooga's Joe Engel Stadium (he did it four times). The highlight of Lemon's season came in July at the league's all-star game in Birmingham, Alabama, when he clouted four home runs and knocked in seven runs. At the subsequently staged "Jim Lemon Day" in Chattanooga in August, Lemon provided an encore by belting a grand slam in the Lookouts' 6-4 victory over the Birmingham Barons.[9] Lemon tied for the league lead in RBIs (109), paced the circuit in triples (12), and finished fourth in home runs (24). In a September call-up to Washington, he went 5-for-25 with a one home run.

Lemon arrived at spring training in 1956 with renewed confidence after leading the Mexican Pacific winter league in home runs while playing for Ciudad Obregón. According to *Washington Post* beat reporter Shirley Povich, Lemon was "rated roughly as outfielder number six"[10] before he raised eyebrows by belting a grand slam and driving in eight runs against the Cincinnati Reds in an exhibition game in Columbia, South Carolina.[11] In Washington's third game, Lemon made his first start of the season, going 3-for-4 with a double, home run, and two RBIs in a victory over the Yankees, and won a permanent job.

In his first 15 starts (all in right field), Lemon batted .396 (21-for 53), hit six home runs (surpassing his career total of five in 233 at-bats), and knocked in 18 runs. "I never expected to play regularly," said Lemon, astonished by his success. "I figured I'd be playing only when the opposition pitched a southpaw."[12] While the Senators were firmly ensconced in the second division all season long, and finished in seventh place, Lemon's seemingly meteoric rise gave fans something to celebrate. Lemon went from "merely part of the bench strength," wrote Povich, to the "biggest box office attraction in years.[13] His "bat thundering with … Wagnerian strokes," Lemon and teammate Roy Sievers assaulted Senators home-run records.[14] With 27 and 29 round-trippers respectively, both sluggers surpassed the team record of 25 home runs that Sievers had set the previous season, and were the AL's most potent long-ball combination after Mantle and Yogi Berra. En route to a team-record 112 home runs, Lemon and Sievers became just the third pair of Senators teammates to record at least 20 round-trippers in one season. Lemon batted a respectable .271, led the team in slugging percentage (.502), and paced the AL with 11 triples.

The power surge in Griffith Stadium, one of the largest in baseball, was the result of Calvin Griffith's decision to alter the outfield dimensions. After taking over the team upon the death of his uncle, Clark Griffith, the cash-strapped owner wanted sell more tickets by generating more offense. Consequently, the left-field foul pole was reduced from 388 feet from home plate to 350 feet, making it more attractive to right-handed sluggers, while the right-field power alley (with its famed 31-foot-tall concrete fence) remained at 373 feet. Despite the changes, the Senators ranked last among big-league clubs in attendance (431,647) in 1956.

Lemon had an erect and wide batting stance, often crowded the plate, and generated his power from a classic roundhouse swing. Baseball fans throughout the country had the chance to see Lemon's graceful stroke when he participated on Mark Scott's *Home Run Derby* television series, which aired in 1960.[15] Lemon's swing also produced a lot of strikeouts. He set a new AL record with 138 whiffs in 1956. At a time when strikeouts were frowned upon and much less frequent than in today's game (only four big-leaguers struck out 100 or more times in 1956, compared with 105 in 2013), Lemon's dubious record was national news. "I'm not swinging for singles," Lemon said defiantly. "When you take that big swing, you're bound to strike out."[16] Lemon constantly worked on his swing to cut down on his strikeouts, yet led the AL in whiffs again in 1957 (94) and 1958 (120), and finished second in 1960 (114). "There's no difference between a strikeout and a popup as far as I am concerned," he said unapologetically.[17]

Lemon capitalized on his new-found notoriety by participating in barnstorming tours in 1956, 1957, and

Jim Lemon and Harmon Killebrew at spring training. (Photo courtesy of Minnesota Twins Baseball Club).

1958. With the migration of big-league baseball westward and the rise of televised games, the lucrative and time-honored tradition of big leaguers barnstorming to augment their income was gradually coming to a close.

Named the "hardest working veteran in camp" by *The Sporting News*, Lemon took manager Chuck Dressen's advice in 1957 and began crouching more at the plate so that he would not miss the low pitch for a strike. The result was disastrous. Through his first 24 games, the big Virginian had connected for just one home run in 93 at-bats, and had knocked in only six runs. After Dressen was fired following a 4-16 start and replaced by Cookie Lavagetto, Lemon reverted to his open stance and went on a tear, belting 11 round-trippers, driving in 35 runs, and batting .345 over a 44-game stretch from May 13 to June 27. "I was striding into the ball too much," replied Lemon when asked about his success. "Now there's practically no stride."[18] Mired in a slump the last two months of the season (two homers and nine RBIs), Lemon finished with a career-high .284 batting average, but his 17 homers and 64 RBIs failed to meet expectations. More troubling to Lavagetto was Lemon's failure to develop as an outfielder.

Lemon's defensive liabilities were no secret, but they nonetheless frustrated managers. "From the moment he had left the Virginia Hills to sign with the Cleveland Indians," wrote sportswriter Sandy Grady, "Lemon could hit baseball where they couldn't find 'em ... [but] fly balls popped around him like hail stones. 'Lemon will hit .900' and 'field .300 for you,'" said one scout.[19] Lemon's fielding woes were puzzling given his exceptional speed for a big man and his strong, accurate arm. *The Sporting News* once rated him the fastest player on the team.[20] He was quick out of the batter's box, and his sprint to first base was timed at 3.7 seconds, just as fast as Dick Groat and Frank Robinson.[21] Yet, that speed did not transfer into the ability to cover large swaths of ground in the outfield—a necessity in Griffith Stadium. Lemon led all AL outfielders in errors as a rookie in 1956 (12), and in 1960 (11), finished second in 1959 and fourth in 1957. Lavagetto, irked that so many balls dropped in front of Lemon for base hits, moved him to first base in July 1957. The ill-fated experiment ended after the third game when Lemon committed three errors.

Judged by *The Sporting News* as "not an answer to [Lavagetto's] right field situation," Lemon overcame stiff competition from hot prospect Neil Chrisley, who had batted .343 in Indianapolis the previous year, to win the starting job in 1958.[22] On Opening Day Lemon belted a home run much to the excitement of President Eisenhower, who threw out the ceremonial first pitch. On a team that finished in last place for the third time in four years, Lemon and his roommate Sievers provided fans a reason to cheer. They clubbed 65 home runs, matching Rocky Colavito and Minnie Miñoso of the Cleveland Indians for the most of any pair of teammates in the AL. Lemon belted 26 of those (eighth most in the AL) and drove in 75 runs, but, batted a disappointing .246. His strikeouts and outfield play exasperated Lavagetto, who benched him at least five times during the course of the season.

Unsurprisingly, Lemon's name cropped up continually in offseason trade rumors.

Lemon's offseason knee surgery to repair cartilage ended trade rumors, but also put him behind in spring training. He lost his job in right field to 24-year-old hard-hitting rookie Bob Allison, and was relegated to the bench. Lemon might have remained there all season had left fielder Sievers not suffered an early-season injury. The gentle giant Lemon took over right field and was later shifted to left field, as Lavagetto shuffled his outfield. Even though Senators had a losing record every month of the season en route to their fourth last-place finish in five years, the club boasted three of the six AL sluggers with at least 30 home runs in what sportswriter Frederick G. Lieb tabbed the "New Murderer's Row."[23] The Senators set a team record with 163 home runs, trailing only the Cleveland Indians. Harmon Killebrew, in his first full season, tied the Tribe's Rocky Colavito for the league lead in home runs with 42; Rookie of the Year winner Allison, who ultimately settled in center field, belted 30; and Lemon clouted 33, third-best in the American League. In a career day, Lemon went 3-for-5 with seven RBIs in the Senators' blowout victory against the Boston Red Sox, 14-2, on September 5. In the third inning of that game, he tied two major-league records by belting two home runs (including the second of two career grand slams, both that season) and driving in six runs. Notwithstanding his limited mobility in the outfield, Lemon enjoyed his hitherto best season, led the team in batting (.279), and also knocked in 100 runs.

Throughout his career, Lemon was praised as a gentleman, a sportsman, and a "big leaguer with class."[24] Quiet and unpretentious, Lemon always played in shadows of a star—first Sievers, then Killebrew and Bob Allison—and was never considered the star of his team. He played in a "partial eclipse," wrote *The Sporting News*.[25] A man of few words, the sandy-haired Lemon rarely complained publicly, even when he could have (such as when Casey Stengel left him off the AL All-Star team in 1959), and was a consummate teammate with a reputation of helping younger players. He had a good voice, too. While a member of the Indians, he was part of a barbershop quartet with teammates Jim Hegan, Billy Joe Davidson, and Lou Brissie; and with Albie Pearson and Roy Sievers, he formed the "Singing Senators," who performed on the *Today Show* in 1958.

In 1960 the Senators did not have a fairy-tale, worst-to-first finish in their 59th and final season in Washington. With Killebrew and Allison failing to duplicate their seasons from 1959, and Sievers having been traded to the Chicago White Sox, Lemon emerged as the team's most consistent and dangerous slugger. By the All-Star break he was among the league leaders with 21 home runs and 50 RBIs, and it appeared he would be snubbed yet again. But when his teammate, right-handed pitcher Camilo Pascual, came down with an injury, Lemon took his place on the roster. He went 0-for-1 and drew a walk in the first All-Star game that season; and did not play in the second game. Lemon made national news on May 3 when he became the first big-league player to wear what the press described as a "Little League helmet," a protective cap with flaps over both ears.[26] (In 1953, the Pittsburgh Pirates became to first team to require its players to wear batting helmets; the NL mandated it beginning in 1956 and the AL in 1958; however, these helmets did not have ear flaps.) At 32 years of age, Lemon enjoyed his best season, belting a career-high 38 round-trippers, tying a career-high with 100 RBIs, and slugging .508. He finished tenth in MVP voting.

Lemon looked forward to the Senators' move to Minnesota and to an excited fan base. "They are enthusiastic about us … and that does a lot for a player who's not used to it."[27] However, Lemon's first season in the Twin Cities was as disappointing as his final campaign in the nation's capital was exciting. A bitter contract squabble with Calvin Griffith played out in the press, making a poor first impression on Lemon's new fans. Off to a slow start, he suffered a shoulder injury when he was hit by a pitch thrown by Don Larsen of the Kansas City Athletics on April 24. By midseason, he had trouble raising and extending his left arm, and consequently lost his power. In his last full season, Lemon clouted only 14 home runs and knocked in 52 runs.

With just 21 plate appearances, Lemon spent most of the 1962 on the disabled list because of his shoulder. He had offseason surgery to repair the damage, but at 35, the odds were stacked against a comeback. A shell of his former self, Lemon was sold twice during the 1963 season, and concluded his final year in Organized Baseball by playing for the Twins, Chicago White Sox, and Philadelphia Phillies, batting just .218 and hitting three home runs in 156 at-bats. He retired at the end of the season. In his 12-year big-league career, Lemon hit 164 round-trippers, drove in 529 runs, and batted .262; he clouted 129 home runs over six years in the minors.

Lemon transitioned to coaching immediately after the end of his playing career. After skippering the York (Pennsylvania) White Roses, the Senators' affiliate in the Double-A Eastern League, to a last-place finish in 1964, he accepted a job as hitting coach for the Minnesota Twins the following season. "I've seen Lemon work with hitters many times," said team owner Griffith. "I've known few players who have studied hitting so thoroughly."[28] Rejoining many of his former teammates, Lemon was a stickler for fundamentals and one of the earliest advocates of the use of film in teaching hitting.

The Twins won the pennant in Lemon's first season, leading the league in batting (.254) and runs scored (774). After three years with the Twins (1965-1967), Lemon signed a two-year contract to manage the Washington Senators, who had traded their skipper, Gil Hodges, to the New York Mets for pitcher Bill Denehy and $100,000. Lemon guided a talent-poor team to a last-place finish (65-96) in 1968, but was then unexpectedly fired when Minneapolis millionaire Bob Short, former owner of the Los Angeles Lakers basketball team, purchased the Senators. Short surprised the baseball world by luring Ted Williams out of retirement to manage the team.

In the 1970s Lemon directed his attention to his business pursuits, but occasionally served as a scout and hitting instructor in baseball camps. In 1981 he resumed his formal coaching career when he rejoined the Twins and served as the team's hitting instructor for four years (1981-1984). For the next decade he was a roving hitting instructor in the minor leagues and also the hitting coach for the Elizabethton (Tennessee) Twins in the Rookie Appalachian League. His last managerial position was with the rookie-level Gulf Coast Twins in 1992.

A baseball lifer whose passion for teaching the game never waned, Lemon was inducted into the Virginia Sports Hall of Fame in 1988. On May 14, 2006, he died at the age of 78 at his home in Brandon, Mississippi. He suffered from melanoma. Survived by his wife of 54 years, Ella, and their three children, Lemon was buried at the Emory United Methodist Church Cemetery, Alleghany County, Virginia.

SOURCES

Jim Lemon player file at the National Baseball Hall of Fame, Cooperstown, New York

Ancestry.com

BaseballLibrary.com

Baseball-Reference.com

Chicago Daily Tribune

New York Times

Retrosheet.com

SABR.org

The Sporting News

NOTES

1 Bill James, *The New Bill James Historical Baseball Abstract* (New York: Free Press, 2001), 223.

2 *The Sporting News*, August 30, 1950, 11.

3 *The Sporting News*, March 7, 1951, 18.

4 *The Sporting News*, April 2, 1952, 7.

5 *The Sporting News*, March 18, 1953, 21.

6 *The Sporting News*, June 17, 1953, 6.

7 *The Sporting News*, March 31, 1954, 08.

8 *The Sporting News*, July 27, 1955, 35.

9 Associated Press, "Chattanooga Stages 'Day' For Jim Lemon," *Fort Pierce* (Florida) *News Tribune*, August 15, 1955, 5.

10 *The Sporting News*, March 20, 1957, 8.

11 United Press, "Senators Outslug Red Legs 16-12," *Post Herald and Register* (Beckley, West Virginia), April 8, 1956, 14.

12 Frank Eck, "Big Jim Lemon Bends to Improve Slugging," (Associated Press), *North Adams* (Massachusetts) *Transcript*, April 13, 1957, 2.

13 *The Sporting News*, May 16, 1956, 18.

14 Ibid.

15 YouTube clips of Lemon facing Hank Aaron and Willie Mays in the Home Run Derby are available at youtube.com/watch?v=Ckb0LWrdNZs and youtube.com/watch?v=irsE3vOULuM . See Don Zminda, "Home Run Derby: A Tale of Baseball and Hollywood," SABR.org

16 International News Service, "Dressen Says Jim Lemon Has What It Takes, " *Kokomo* (Indiana) *Tribune*, April 6, 1957, 9.

17 *The Sporting News*, March 20, 1957, 8.

18 *The Sporting News*, June 19, 1957, 20.

19 Sandy Grady, "Jim Lemon Has His Own 'Late Show,'" Unattributed article, dated May 6, 1963. Lemon's Hall of Fame file.

20 *The Sporting News*, April 17, 1957, 15.

21 *The Sporting News*, November 7, 1956, 18.

22 *The Sporting News*, March 5, 1958, 22.

23 *The Sporting News*, July 22, 1959, 3.

24 *The Sporting News*, July 15, 1959, 12.

25 *The Sporting News*, September 16, 1959, 23.

26 United Press International, "Jim Lemon First to Wear Little League Helmet," *Weirton* (West Virginia) *Daily Times*, May 3, 1960, 14.

27 *The Sporting News*, March 1, 1961, 12.

28 *The Sporting News*, November 7, 1964, 2.

Billy Martin

BY JIMMY KEENAN AND FRANK RUSSO

AS A PLAYER ON THE GREAT NEW York Yankees teams of the 1950s and later as a manager with five different major-league clubs, Billy Martin was known to be brash, bold, and fearless. He played the game hard and made no excuses for the way he handled himself on or off the field. Many people, including his off-and-on boss, George Steinbrenner, considered Martin a baseball genius for the intuitive way he managed his teams.

Asked about Martin's prowess as a field general, former Yankees manager Casey Stengel, who had known Billy since his minor league days in Oakland, told *The Sporting News* in an interview printed on August 23, 1975: "He's a good manager. He might be a little selfish about some things he does and he may think he knows more about baseball than anybody else and it wouldn't surprise me if he was right." Asked why he thought so highly of Martin as a player, Stengel replied, "If liking a kid who never let you down in the clutch is favoritism, then I plead guilty."

As difficult, irascible, and pugnacious as he was, Martin commanded respect as a manager. In 1987, in a poll of 600 former players, he ranked eighth among some heavyweights—behind Stengel, Joe McCarthy, Walter Alston, John McGraw, Connie Mack, Earl Weaver, and Al Lopez, and ahead of Whitey Herzog, Sparky Anderson, and Tommy Lasorda.[1]

Alfred Manuel Pesano, Jr. was born in Berkeley, California, on May 16, 1928, to Alfred Manuel and Joan (Salvini) Pesano. Joan, who went by the nickname Jenny, was of Italian descent, and Alfred Sr. was born in the Azores. He abandoned the family when Billy was 8 months old, and Jenny later married a nightclub singer named Jack Downey. Alfred Jr.'s maternal Italian grandmother called him Belli or Bellitz when he was an infant and this name eventually evolved into Billy. Soon after, his mother changed the family name to Martin.[2]

Billy started out playing baseball on the sandlots around Berkeley, and while in high school joined up with the Oakland Junior Oaks, an amateur club sponsored by Oakland's Pacific Coast League team. Showing his proclivity for a good fight, Martin was spending his free time boxing in the amateur ranks in the San Francisco/Oakland area.

After graduating from high school in 1946, Martin signed with the Idaho Falls Russets of the Class D Pioneer League. He played 32 games at third base for the Russets, not hitting much but playing solid infield

Billy Martin played the final 108 games of his 10-year career with the Twins in 1961. He remained with the organization, serving as scout (1962-1964), coach (1965-1967) and minor-league manager (1968). In his first season as a big-league skipper, he guided the Twins to the AL West crown in 1969 before he was fired in the offseason. (National Baseball Hall of Fame, Cooperstown, New York).

defense. Even with his lackluster batting, Oakland Oaks owner Brick Laws saw something in the youngster and purchased his contract from Idaho Falls.

Martin struggled at the plate and in the field for the Oaks in 1947, causing manager Casey Stengel to farm him out to the Phoenix Senators of the Class C Arizona-Texas League. Once in Phoenix, he regained his confidence, hitting .392 in the hitter-happy league.

In his next two seasons with Oakland, Martin, moved to the middle infield, played well defensively and began to hit more consistently. During his early tenure with the Oaks, Martin complained to manager Casey Stengel about hitting eighth in the batting order. Stengel, who enjoyed a father/son relationship with the brash youngster, told him that he was actually the second cleanup hitter. Martin grudgingly accepted Casey's explanation and that night collected two hits and three RBIs.

In October 1949 Oakland sold Martin and outfielder Jackie Jenson to the New York Yankees for cash and a player to be named later.[3]

Martin, reunited with his former mentor Stengel,[4] made his major-league debut on April 18, 1950, against the Boston Red Sox. He banged out two hits in the eighth inning of a 15-10 New York victory. A short time later, Martin, Duane Pillette, and future Hall of Fame first baseman Johnny Mize were sent down to the Kansas City Blues of the American Association on 24-hour recall. The move was made just before the May 17 deadline, which required major-league teams to trim their rosters to 25 players.

A month later, Mize and Martin were recalled, Mize to fill in for injured first baseman Tommy Heinrich and Martin to replace second baseman Snuffy Stirnweiss, who had been traded to the St Louis Browns.

Martin batted .250 in his first big-league season and, aside from 1955, never hit over .267. His forte was his consistent defense and his ability to come up with big hits in crucial situations.

During the offseason, Martin and teammates Whitey Ford and Bob Brown were drafted into the military. Martin spent five months in the Army during the winter of 1950-51 before being discharged in the spring for hardship reasons (his financial responsibilities to his wife, sister, mother, and stepfather). Because of his military service, the Yankees had to keep him on the roster for a year, though he didn't count against the 25-man limit. Martin made one appearance as a pinch-runner in the 1951 World Series. The Yankees defeated the New York Giants in six games, Martin's first of four world championship teams as a player.

After the 1951 season, Martin and a group of major and minor leaguers traveled to Japan for a series of exhibition games. The Americans, managed by Lefty O'Doul, played 15 games against top players in Japan, winning 13. Near the end of the tour, Martin, Dom DiMaggio, Mel Parnell, Ferris Fain, and George Strickland flew to Korea and spent two days visiting the front lines.

The following March, Martin broke two bones in his right ankle demonstrating his sliding technique for a Joe DiMaggio television show. The injury caused him to miss the first few weeks of the 1952 campaign.

Shortly after he returned to the Yankees, Martin got into a fight with Boston's rookie shortstop Jim Piersall under the grandstands at Fenway Park. A few weeks later, he got into another scuffle with Browns catcher Clint Courtney. Around this time the national newspapers started referring to Martin as "One-Round."

The Yankees won the pennant in 1952 and faced their crosstown rival Brooklyn Dodgers in the World Series. The Yankees came out on top, and Martin's spectacular catch of a wind-blown popup by Jackie Robinson in the seventh inning of Game Seven with two outs and the bases loaded helped seal the win.

Martin and Courtney got into another scuffle during the 1953 season, and that same year he exchanged blows with Detroit Tigers catcher Matt Batts. Because of his growing reputation as a fighter, players on opposing teams were coming in hard at second base, trying to injure the 160-pound second baseman on nearly every close play around the bag. Stengel commented, "Billy's being hit with the hardest blocks this side of a professional football field."[5] Martin simply said, "They can slide as hard as they like, as long as they slide clean. When they don't slide clean they'll hear it from me. Otherwise, they'll get no complaints." Rough slides aside, Martin finished with the second highest fielding percentage of all American League second basemen.

The Yankees captured their fifth consecutive pennant in 1953 and again squared off against the Brooklyn Dodgers in the World Series. New York came out on top in the first two contests, but Dodgers ace Carl Erskine cooled off the Yankees' hot bats in Game Three with a 14-strikeout performance. After the game Erskine told the United Press, "It's hard to believe but players like Phil Rizzuto and Billy Martin give me a lot more trouble than hitters like Mickey Mantle and Yogi Berra. You just can't strike out Rizzuto and Martin. At least I can't anyway."

The two teams split Games Four and Five and the stage was set for Martin's heroics in Game Six. In the bottom of the ninth inning, he smacked a base hit off Clem Labine, plating Hank Bauer with the game-winning run. It was the Yankees' fifth consecutive world championship.

Martin's 23 total bases in the six-game series eclipsed the old record of 19 set by Babe Ruth 30 years earlier. Billy collected 12 hits, including two home runs, two triples, and a double. His 12 hits also tied the mark for a seven-game Series. His .500 batting average, five extra-base hits and two triples tied the record for a six-game Series. He received the Babe Ruth Memorial Award, given to the best player in the Series.

Asked about Martin by a United Press sportswriter, Stengel said, "Look at him. He doesn't look like a great player — but he is a helluva player. Try to find something he can't do. You can't."

Shortly after the birth of his daughter, Kelly Ann, in January 1954, Martin was reclassified 1-A by the Berkeley, California, draft board. He appealed the decision, claiming that he supported his estranged wife, Lois (whom he had married in 1950), his daughter, his sister, his mother, and his stepfather to support. Losing his appeal, he was drafted into the Army.

In late April Martin applied for a hardship discharge, but was turned down. An Associated Press article in late May said Martin claimed he was being treated unfairly by his commanding officers at Fort Ord, California. Congressman William E. Hess, chairman of a legislative committee that was investigating claims that the military was showing preferential treatment toward professional athletes, contacted Martin, who told him that not only was he not given preferential treatment, he was actually being discriminated against. Among his complaints were that he was not given as many weekend passes as his fellow trainees and was not allowed to play on the Fort Ord baseball team. Hess, after hearing Martin's allegations, asked Secretary of the Army Robert Stevens to look into the matter.[6]

After basic training, Martin was sent to Fort Carson, Colorado, where he eventually rose to the rank of corporal in the 61st Infantry Regiment and managed the post baseball team to a 15-2 record. He also played on the base basketball team.

Given a furlough, Martin rejoined the Yankees and worked his way back into the lineup, hitting .300 in 20 games. The Yankees edged out Cleveland for the pennant and once again drew the Brooklyn Dodgers in the Series. The Army extended Martin's furlough, which allowed him to play in the World Series. New York lost in seven games, but Martin performed well, finishing with a .320 batting average.

Billy the Kid, as he was now being called in the media, got into a shoving match with Dodgers catcher Roy Campanella after he was thrown out trying to steal home in Game One. Martin told the Associated Press, "I wasn't sore. I just don't like being pushed around. I might have punched him in the nose if it hadn't been the World Series."

Although he missed most of the season, the Yankees voted Martin a full $5,598 share of the losers' World Series bonus.

Finally discharged from the Army, Martin discovered that his reputation as a brawler and carouser was not ingratiating him with Yankee management and, most importantly, general manager George Weiss. After a much-publicized brawl at the Copacabana nightclub in New York, Martin was traded to the Kansas City A's in a seven-player deal. Martin initially accepted the deal as standard baseball business, but later stopped talking to Stengel over what he perceived to be his manager's not fighting hard enough to keep him on the team. He played the rest of the 1957 season with the A's and on November 20 was traded with five other players to the Detroit Tigers for five major leaguers and a minor leaguer. Martin was livid over the trade, telling the Associated Press, "They just can't throw us [players] around from one club to another without us having a say-so." His complaint fell on deaf ears; after the season he was traded to Cleveland, the third time the scrappy infielder had been traded in 17 months. And in December 1959 he was on the move again, this time traded to the Cincinnati Reds.

On August 6, 1960, Martin was suspended for five days and fined $500 by National League President Warren Giles for punching Chicago Cubs pitcher Jim Brewer in the face. The incident occurred after Brewer had thrown a pitch behind Martin, the ball caroming off the fiery second baseman's bat and hitting him in the head. On the next pitch, he swung and missed, letting the bat fly in the direction of the pitcher's mound. While Martin walked out to retrieve the Louisville Slugger, Brewer picked it up and took a few steps toward the Reds infielder. Feigning to reach for the bat, Billy unleashed a right-handed haymaker that landed squarely on Brewer's face, fracturing the orbital bone around the pitcher's eye. The *Montreal Gazette* of August 6, 1960, printed Martin's description of the incident, "Brewer threw at my head and nobody is going to do that. I was in the hospital last year when I got hit in the face and had seven fractures. Nobody is going to throw at my head again. That first pitch by Brewer was behind my head and Cub pitchers knocked me down three times on Wednesday." Both benches cleared during the incident, and Martin was ejected from the game.

The Cubs lost Brewer's services for the season, and the team sued Martin for $1 million in damages. After almost a decade of litigation, the lawsuit was finally settled for $10,000 in 1969. Informed that a settlement had been reached, Billy replied, "Do they want a check or cash?"

In December 1960 the Reds sold Martin to the Milwaukee Braves. He failed to win the second-base job from incumbent Frank Bolling, and in June of 1961 was traded to the Minnesota Twins for shortstop Billy Consolo. The Twins acquired Martin to take the place of Billy Gardner, who was at the end of his career.

In the spring of 1962, Martin lost the second-base job to rookie Bernie Allen and was released by the Twins. Although the Kansas City A's had expressed an interest, Billy decided it was time to retire as an active player and pursue other interests on and off the field. A fair hitter who always seemed to come through in the clutch, Martin finished his career with a .257 batting average. He made the All-Star team in 1956. Steady with the glove, he usually showed above-average range.

In his five World Series (28 games), Martin collected 33 hits, two doubles, three triples, five home runs, and 19 RBIs while posting a .333 batting average.

After he retired, the Twins hired Martin as a special scout. He also took a public-relations job with a local brewery. By 1965 he was back on the field, as the Twins' third-base coach. In June 1968 he was named manager of Minnesota's Triple-A affiliate in Denver.

Martin succeeded Cal Ermer as manager of the Twins in 1969. In his first year the team went 97-65 and finished in first place in the newly formed American League West division. The Twins' opponent in the first best-of-five American League playoffs was the Baltimore Orioles. Baltimore swept the Twins in three games, and Martin was criticized in the press for some

Billy Martin barking orders. (Photo courtesy of Minnesota Twins Baseball Club).

of his decisions during the series. For example, he started pitcher Bob Miller in the third game; Miller was knocked out of the box in the second inning. When Twins owner Calvin Griffith asked him why he started a pitcher who had a 5-5 record during the regular season, Martin told him, "Because I'm the manager, that's why." The rash comment led to Martin's firing a few days later.

The Twins owner said of Martin, "Billy is popular to a certain degree. You know Billy can go into a crowd and charm the hell out of you, but he ignored me. I asked him to come in and see me several times and he didn't. I think the Twins are just as much a part of me as they are of Billy Martin."[7]

Martin had been on shaky ground with the Minnesota front office all season for numerous reasons, including criticizing the Twins farm system in the press and for getting into a well-publicized fight with pitcher Dave Boswell, a 20-game winner, outside a Detroit bar in early August.

After being fired, Martin took a year off from baseball and went to work for radio station KDWB in Minneapolis. The following October, the Detroit Tigers hired him as their manager. In his first year with the club, Martin guided Detroit to 91 wins and a second-place finish in the American League East.

In 1972 Martin's Tigers edged out the Boston Red Sox by a half-game for the American League East pennant but lost to Oakland in the playoffs. The series was marred by a heated brawl in the seventh inning of Game Two. The donnybrook started when A's shortstop Bert Campaneris threw a bat at Tigers pitcher Lerrin LaGrow after being hit by a pitch. Martin was incensed and had to be restrained from going after Campaneris.

While the team was conducting spring training in 1973, Martin and Tigers rookie prospect Ike Blessitt were arrested outside a Lakeland, Florida, restaurant. Blessitt had a disagreement with a patron in the establishment; Martin, acting as peacemaker, took the young player outside to calm him down. The police arrived and, according to Martin, directed racist remarks toward Blessitt, who was African American. When the Tigers manager objected to the police comments, both men were arrested and charged with using profanity in a public place.

A few days later, Martin quit as manager of the Tigers over a disagreement with general manager Jim Campbell about a fine that Martin had levied on outfielder Willie Horton. Campbell increased the fine on Horton, making Martin so mad he resigned from the team. Reconsidering his rash decision, he returned the next day.

On September 2, 1973, the Tigers fired Martin, with one year left on a reported $65,000 annual contract. Martin was finishing up a three-day suspension for ordering his pitchers to throw spitballs when he learned of his release in a phone call from Jim Campbell.

The spitball incident occurred in a game against Cleveland Indians. Martin felt that Indians pitcher Gaylord Perry was doctoring the ball and in an effort to show him up ordered Tigers pitchers Jim Coleman and Fred Scherman to use saliva and Vaseline on their pitches. Martin blatantly told reporters after the game about his tactics, leading to his suspension from American League President Joe Cronin.

Asked by a reporter from United Press International about his firing, Martin replied, "They did what they thought was right and I did what I thought was right." Martin had been cautioned by Campbell not to make disparaging comments in the newspapers about Commissioner Bowie Kuhn, Joe Cronin, and various Tigers front-office personnel. Martin repeatedly disregarded the warnings, and the spitball incident was the final straw.

When Texas Rangers owner Bob Short heard Martin was available, he told Whitey Herzog, his current manager, that he would fire his grandmother for the chance to hire Billy. A few days later, Short fired Herzog and hired Martin, leading to the deposed Ranger manager's reply: "I'm fired, I'm the grandmother."[8]

The Rangers had lost 100 games or more in the previous two seasons, but under Martin they won 84 games and finished in second place in 1974, his first full year with the team. Texas signed a number of high-priced free agents The next year the team struggled during the first half of the season, and on July 20, 1975, the new owner, Brad Corbett, fired Martin.

On August 1 Billy was hired as the manager of the New York Yankees by owner George Steinbrenner, replacing Bill Virdon. The Yankees responded well to Martin, and the next season they led the American League East, defeated Kansas City in the American League Championship Series, and faced Cincinnati's Big Red Machine in the World Series. The New York bats fell silent in the Series; they scored only eight runs while losing four straight games. Martin wasn't around to see the final out of Game Four as he was ejected by first-base umpire Bruce Froemming in the ninth inning after throwing a baseball at home-plate umpire Bill Deegan. Talking to the Associated Press after the game, the manager explained: "Deegan threw three balls at me when he was changing baseballs. One hit me in the chest and another almost hit me in the mouth. I threw the ball at him in disgust because I thought he called a brutal game and I got tired of him throwing balls at me."

The 1977 campaign was tumultuous for the Yankees as Martin feuded with owner Steinbrenner and newly acquired superstar Reggie Jackson. Martin, in the first year of a $100,000 contract, was rumored to be on the chopping block for most of the season.

Despite the turmoil, the Yankees won the American League East and again defeated the Kansas City Royals in the ALCS. The Bronx Bombers went on to defeat the Los Angeles Dodgers in six games in Martin's only World Series championship as a manager.

In a show of support just before Game Six, Steinbrenner rewarded Billy's good work with a $50,000 bonus and a brand-new Lincoln Continental. Asked about the Yankee skipper's getting a bonus, Martin's major antagonist, said, "The club needed that. The timing was perfect. Obviously, it was planned that way. He has been through probably more than I have. I didn't know until I got to the park that Billy got his bonus. I could see in his face he was more relaxed. Maybe now he can look like 49 instead of 99."[9]

In 1978 Martin made disparaging comments about Steinbrenner and Jackson: "One is a born liar and the other convicted." Not surprisingly, he was forced to resign on July 24. But he was rehired in 1979 and then fired at the end of the year after the Yankees failed to reach the playoffs for the first time since 1975.

In 1980 Martin was hired to manage the Oakland A's by the team's eccentric owner, Charlie Finley. Martin instilled his aggressive style of inside baseball, eventually known as Billyball, with great success. The 1981 season was divided into two parts because of the players strike. The A's won the first half of the schedule and went on to sweep Kansas City in the initial round of the playoffs. But they were swept by the Yankees in the American League Championship Series. Oakland played poorly under Martin in 1982 and, amid criticism of his handling of the A's pitching staff, he was let go on October 20, 1982.

Steinbrenner brought Martin back as Yankees manager in 1983 and on July 24 he became embroiled in one of the most controversial plays in modern baseball history.

The incident occurred after Kansas City Royals third baseman George Brett clouted a two-run homer off Goose Gossage with two outs in the top of the ninth inning at Yankee Stadium that gave the Royals a one-run lead. Martin had been aware for a while that Brett used more pine tar on his bat than was allowed by league rules. Billy decided that this would be a good time to bring it to the attention of the umpires. They agreed with Martin, and the home run was disallowed, constituting the last out of the game. Kansas City protested the game, and American League President Lee MacPhail ruled in favor of the Royals. The game was scheduled to be resumed on August 18, 1983. The Yankees informed the public that they would have to pay full admission to see the rest of the game, which led to a lawsuit by group of fans. Eventually the Yankees relented, allowing fans who had stubs from the July 24 game to get in the ballpark free while charging bargain prices for those who wished to buy tickets. Only 1,200 people showed up to watch Hal McRae strike out to end the top of the ninth and the Yankees fail to score in the bottom half of the inning. The game officially ended with the Royals leading 5-4.

Martin was cut loose once again by Steinbrenner on December 16, 1983, and replaced by Yogi Berra. Martin went on to have two more managerial stints with the Yankees. In 1985 he took over for Berra 16 games into the season. The team went 91-54 under Martin and finished in second place. He was fired on October 27, 1985, and replaced by Lou Piniella. On October 19, 1987, he came back for the fifth time, succeeding Piniella. Martin lasted 68 games into the 1988 season before being ousted once again by Steinbrenner.

On August 10, 1986, the Yankees retired Martin's jersey number 1 and dedicate a plaque with his likeness at Monument Park in Yankee Stadium. The plaque read, "There has never been a greater competitor than Billy." Speaking at the dedication, Martin said with great emotion, "I may not have been the greatest Yankee to ever put on the uniform but I was the proudest."

During his tenure as a major-league manager, Martin's off-field exploits were legendary; he got into fights with team officials, bar patrons, a cab driver, a marshmallow salesman, various fans, and two of his pitchers.

After leaving the Yankees in 1988, he remained on the team's payroll as a special consultant. A short time later, rumors began to circulate that Billy would return to manage the Yankees in 1990.

In the early evening hours of December 25, 1989, Martin's pickup truck skidded off an icy road near his country home in Fenton, New York, and plummeted 300 feet down an embankment, flipping over and landing on its right side. The 61-year-old Martin was killed in the accident, and his good friend from his days in Detroit, Bill Reedy, was seriously injured. The two had been drinking at a local bar, and Martin allowed Reedy to drive his truck home that evening.

At Martin's viewing in a New York City funeral home, thousands filed in to pay their last respects. The funeral took place at St. Patrick's Cathedral, and Cardinal John O'Connor delivered the eulogy. More than 500 attended, including former President Richard Nixon, numerous baseball executives, and many players and ex-players.

Billy Martin was survived by his fourth wife, the former Jill Guiver; children Kelly Ann and Billy Joe; and one grandchild.[10] The self-proclaimed proudest Yankee was laid to rest at Gate of Heaven Cemetery in Hawthorne, New York, a stone's throw from the grave of Babe Ruth.

SOURCES

Nash, Bruce, and Allan Zullo, *The Baseball Hall of Shame* (New York: Pocket Books, 1985)

Pietrusza, David, Matthew Silverman, and Michael Gershman, eds., *Baseball: The Biographical Encyclopedia* (Kingston, New York, and New York City: Total Sports, 2000)

Russo, Frank, and Gene Racz, *Bury My Heart at Cooperstown, Salacious, Sad, and Surreal Deaths in the History of Baseball* (Chicago: Triumph Books, 2006)

TheDeadballEra.com

Baseball-Reference.com

Baseball Almanac

Wikipedia

Associated Press

Christian Science Monitor

Deseret News, Salt Lake City

Edmonton Journal

Eugene (Oregon) *Register-Guard*

Lewiston Daily Sun

Lodi (California) *News*

Madison (Indiana) *Courier*

Massillon (Ohio) *Evening Independent*

Miami News

Montreal Gazette

Meriden (Connecticut) *Journal*

Milwaukee Journal

Milwaukee Sentinel

New York Times

Pittsburgh Press

St. Petersburg (Florida) *Evening Independent*

St. Petersburg (Florida) *Times*

Pittsburgh Post Gazette

Pittsburgh Press

Rock Hill (South Carolina) *Herald*

Spokane Daily Chronicle

The Sporting News

Nashua (New Hampshire) *Telegraph*

Toledo Blade

United Press International

NOTES

1. "Billy Martin" in David Pietrusza, Matthew Silverman, and Michael Gershman, eds., *Baseball: The Biographical Encyclopedia*, 715.
2. William Kates (Associated Press), "Billy Martin dies in crash on icy road," *Madison* (Indiana) *Courier*, December 26, 1989, 6.
3. The deal was completed on July 5, 1950, when the Yankees sent catcher Eddie Malone to Oakland.
4. Stengel took over as the manager of the Yankees in 1949.
5. *Miami News,* August 3, 1953.
6. We were never able to locate information pertaining to any action Secretary of the Army Stevens may have taken in the Martin case. The situation may have settled itself as Martin was sent to Fort Carson and made no further complaints about his treatment.
7. *Miami News,* October 13, 1969.
8. Richard Sandomir, "Life According to Herzog" *New York Times,* July 25, 2012.
9. *Milwaukee Sentinel,* October 17, 1977.
10. Martin and Lois Berndt were married in 1950; she left him in 1954 and was the mother of Kelly Ann. Sources vary, but Martin and Gretchen Winkler were married in 1959 or 1961, and divorced in 1979; she was the mother of Billy Joe. Martin married Heather Ervolino in 1982; they divorced in 1984. He and Jillian Guiver married on January 25, 1989.

Hal Naragon

BY TRACY J.R. COLLINS

HAL NARAGON GAVE UP TWO years of his professional baseball career when he was drafted into the US Marines in 1951. Like many players of his era, he was proud to serve his country. His story is not unique in that respect. Yet, unlike many players, Naragon thought that he was lucky. With his atypical unselfish and positive personality he said his time in the Marines was "a good thing." Still, luck is nothing without talent and hard work. In fact, Naragon's story is one Horatio Alger could have written. Like Alger's characters, Naragon experienced success through hard work, courage, determination, and concern for others. He would say it was all luck, but it's a story any American would dream about: A boy grows up in small-town Ohio, dreams of playing professional baseball, marries his high-school sweetheart, and plays in a World Series. It is exactly this quietly effective personality that served Naragon well not only as a player but also later as a respected bullpen coach for the Minnesota Twins and the 1968 world champion Detroit Tigers.

Harold Richard Naragon was born on October 1, 1928, the third of four children, to Dwight and Dorothy Naragon in Zanesville, Ohio. When he was in the seventh grade, his parents moved to Barberton, Ohio, near Akron, "because there were more jobs there during the war," he said. Hal essentially never left Barberton again. Exceptionally proud of his hometown, he was quick to recite the city's proud sporting history, which includes Bo Schembechler, the University of Michigan football coach, who began his own sports career on the Barberton High School baseball team as a teammate of Naragon's, and Bob Addis, the first Barberton High School graduate to sign a contract with a major-league baseball team (Boston Braves, 1950).

While Hal was in high school, the Barberton Magics were not always successful. According to the 1944 Barberton High School yearbook, "The 1944 season was unsuccessful in wins and losses, but a green team gained valuable experience for another season." Naragon, a right-handed-throwing, left-handed-hitting freshman catcher, nonetheless earned his varsity letter. The 1946-1947 school year proved to be a good one for Haddie Naragon, as he was referred to in the yearbook. To begin with, Hal spent summer of 1946 playing on a baseball team in Akron that fielded former major leaguers as well as college players. One day a teammate told Hal that some players were driving to Cleveland to try out for "Mr. Veeck," the new owner of the Cleveland Indians. Bill Veeck was conducting open tryouts throughout Ohio to increase interest in the team. Naragon played well at the tryouts, earning a contract. But, as he told the story, "I was not supposed

A former big-league catcher, Naragon finished his ten-year career with the Twins in 1962. He was on the Twins' coaching staff from 1963-1966, serving as bullpen coach in 1965. (Photo courtesy of Minnesota Twins Baseball Club).

to be there. I wasn't going to graduate until next year and couldn't sign the contract until I graduated. I asked Mr. Veeck if I could let him know my decision tomorrow. My dad was going to kill me if he knew I was in Cleveland trying out for the Indians. So I came home and explained what happened to my dad, and he drove up to Cleveland with me the next day. Mr. Veeck explained his interest in me to my dad and my dad told him I had not yet graduated from high school, and so Mr. Veeck asked if I would give the Indians the opportunity to sign him the following spring. My dad asked, 'Will a handshake do?' Mr. Veeck said yes. The two men shook hands and that was that."

Back in Barberton, 1947 was declared the year of sports champions. In the winter Naragon helped the basketball team get its first Ohio State Athletic Association trophy for winning the district championship. The Magics lost to Ashtabula in the regional tournament. Then there was the baseball season. The 1947 team, described in *A Bicentennial Remembrance: Barberton, Ohio, the Magic City* as "the greatest group of athletes ever to play together on a single team in the City," won all of its games during the regular season with three shutouts and one no-hitter. The team was district and regional champion and lost the state championship game in extra innings. "The team's slugger was Hal Naragon, who could be counted on to hit one 'out of the park' every third game. People still speak of those 'Naragon shots.'" Early in the season the *Barberton Herald* referred to Naragon as "a fixture behind the plate" and "a good sticker as well as receiver." Naragon batted .444 in his senior year, and over .400 for his high-school career.

Naragon was ready to begin his career with the Indians. He signed in the spring of 1947 and in July headed off for the Pittsfield (Massachusetts) Electrics of the Class C Canadian-American League. It was his first time away from home, but "with a strong arm and good defensive catching skills," Hal was ready to be a professional baseball player, the only career he said he ever wanted.

By April 1948 he was the first-string catcher for Harrisburg (Pennsylvania) of the Class B Interstate League. His hometown *Herald* reported that Naragon "has been credited with having one of the best throwing arms ever seen in those parts working from behind the plate." In midseason he was sent down to Watertown (New York) of the Class C Border League to work on his hitting, and went back up to Harrisburg when it began to improve. That year was important for Naragon in at least two ways. First, Watertown manager Fred Gerken helped him improve his hitting; and second, in what Naragon called the most important and best decision he ever made, on October 10, 1948, he married his high-school sweetheart, Joanne Schake, in Barberton.

Naragon ended the 1948 season with a .224 batting average and was back in Harrisburg for 1949. Muddy Ruel, the Indians' assistant farm director, sang Naragon's praises, saying, "If anyone in this camp has a chance to become a solid major leaguer it's Hal Naragon. He has a very fine chance to become a good catcher. He has the physique and the natural aptitude of a catcher, and he has a sure pair of hands when he comes to catching foul flies," and was "willing to learn." That willingness to learn helped Naragon immensely as he worked his way up to playing for Oklahoma City in the Texas League in 1950; and by 1951 he was in spring training with the Indians. After spring training he was sent to San Diego of the Pacific Coast League, and earned a call-up to the Indians at the end of the season. He singled as a pinch-hitter in his first game, against Detroit, and then played in two more games before the season ended—enough to keep his name in the minds of his coaches as the Korean War then intervened.

After the 1951 season, Naragon was drafted into the Marines and was stationed at Quantico, Virginia. He was discharged in December 1953. Asked if he felt his career suffered during those years, he responded, "I didn't miss a thing. In fact, I got stronger physically during those years. I always thought everything I have done has been a positive experience. Frankly, when all those other guys weren't coming back I thought I was lucky." After his discharge, former Tigers great

Hank Greenberg, then the Indians' general manager, sent him to Panama to play winter ball.

Naragon started the 1954 season with the Indians and was part of the winningest team in American League history to that point (111 victories). He became friends with All-Star outfielder Dale Mitchell, who he says was the person who helped him the most in his baseball career: "He helped me a lot with my hitting." Most remarkably for Naragon, during that season he caught four future Hall of Fame pitchers, Bob Feller, Early Wynn, Hal Newhouser, and Bob Lemon. The Indians would have won the World Series had it started in Cleveland, Naragon maintained. They were instead swept by the New York Giants. Playing backup to Jim Hegan, Naragon finished the season with a .238 batting average and a perfect 1.000 fielding percentage in 45 games behind the plate. He returned to Panama to play winter ball after the season, and in 1955 played 57 games with a batting average of .323. In 1956 and 1957, still in a backup role, Naragon hit .287 and .256, playing in about 50 games each season. He was sent back to San Diego for 1958, coming back to the Indians for only nine plate appearances.

On May 25, 1959, Naragon was traded by Cleveland with pitcher Hal Woodeshick to the Washington Senators for catcher Ed Fitz Gerald. Of the Senators' lackluster record, Naragon said tactfully, "We had some good players there, but maybe we didn't all belong together on the same team." He moved to Minnesota in 1961 when Calvin Griffith relocated the franchise from Washington to become the Minnesota Twins. In his first year with the Twins when they returned to Washington to play the expansion Senators, Naragon hit the last sacrifice bunt in Griffith Stadium, on September 21, 1961, in the seventh inning. That first year in Minnesota was one of Naragon's better years hitting (.302 in 57 games as a backup to Earl Battey), but it was no roster guarantee. In 1962 he had only 35 at-bats, and played his last game on August 5 of that season. He was released by the Twins on October 19, having played his entire 10-year career in the American League. (Asked what he thought of not playing in the National League, he chuckled and replied, "I was glad to be playing in any league.")

During an era when players spent their offseasons working, Naragon was no exception, spending his winters working at the rubber factory in Barberton. However, when his playing career was over, Hal was not quite ready to return to the factory. The Twins named him their bullpen coach. As a coach, Naragon found another calling. In 1965 the Twins won the American League pennant in 1965 only to lose the World Series in seven games to the Los Angeles Dodgers. From 1965 to 1969, when he left baseball, Naragon was in tandem with pitching coach Johnny Sain, moving with Sain to Detroit after both were released by the Twins after the 1966 season.

According to Naragon, "There were some disagreements—we had a great time at Minnesota –but some people thought that John only got along with the pitchers, which was not true. John, in his career, he always seemed to have a run-in with the managers or different ideas than the managers." What it came down to was that Sain and manager Sam Mele could not work together any longer and, "because Naragon supported Sain strongly," Mele also asked for Naragon's release. *Sports Illustrated* quoted Twins pitcher Jim Kaat, who won 25 games for the Twins in 1965, as calling the firing of Sain and Naragon "the Great Mistake." Kaat added, "This is the worst thing that could happen to our club at this time. Every move John Sain and Hal Naragon made was in the best interest of the Minnesota Twins. … Hal Naragon was the last instrument of communication between Mr. Mele and the players. Now there is complete division."

The combination of Sain and Naragon proved just as effective in Detroit as in Minnesota. When they arrived for the 1967 season the Tigers had just finished in third place, but the 1967 season found them climbing. They finished second, only one game behind the Boston Red Sox. With pitchers like Denny McLain and Mickey Lolich, first baseman Norm Cash and Hall of Fame outfielder Al Kaline, the Tigers would not be denied in 1968. McLain won 31 games, and, in the World Series against the St. Louis Cardinals,

Lolich pitched three complete-game victories, allowing only five earned runs in 27 innings. Toward the end of that season Watson Spoelstra, a longtime Detroit sportswriter, wrote, "There's no question that Sain and his close friend and associate, coach Hal Naragon, know about as much as anyone on pitching. They are dedicated baseball men with a low-key selling job." After the season the Tigers signed Naragon for the 1969 season. Spoelstra quoted Lolich as saying, "Sain and Naragon are my boys. They know how to get a guy straightened out." The Tigers were not as successful in 1969; Naragon retired from professional baseball after the season. Writers had always said that "Naragon goes where Sain goes," but when Sain landed with the Chicago White Sox in 1971, Naragon decided to try something different. "Could I make a living outside of baseball was always at the back of my mind and when John went to Chicago I decided it was time to answer that question for myself," he said.

Naragon returned to Barberton, to live with his wife and daughter. He did indeed make a living outside of baseball. "I am proud to say that I owned the largest and best sporting-goods store in Barberton, Ohio. Of course, it was also the only sporting-goods store in Barberton." According to Barberton historian Phyllis Taylor, Naragon bought the local sporting-goods store in 1974. He sold the business and retired in 1990. He became active in charitable fundraising events through an association of major-league alumni. He also enjoyed playing golf with his two grandsons and his wife, and watching the Barberton High School Magics play baseball on Naragon Field, built in 2000 and named in his honor in April 2006.

Asked what he thought his best attributes were as a coach, Naragon laughed and said, "I had trouble with that question. I asked my wife and she said I was a good listener. I guess I was a positive thinker. I learned in pro ball that folks started off negatively because they were so used to hearing criticism, but I thought the power of positive suggestion was much stronger. At a 1965 Twins reunion in 2005 Jerry Kindall said I was very even-tempered and it was always a new day with me. John [Sain] was a very positive person too and we were a good team." Watson Spoelstra, in a June 22, 1968, article for *The Sporting News*, called Naragon "the quiet man who ran the bullpen."

"I have met some wonderful people playing baseball," Naragon said. "I don't think anything else I could have done would have put me in contact with as many good people." Such people include Naragon himself, by all accounts a truly good man among baseball's alumni.

SOURCES

A Bicentennial Remembrance: Barberton Ohio, the Magic City (Akron: Beaumarc Publications. 1975).

Taylor, Phyllis, *100 Years of Magic: The Story of Barberton, Ohio, 1891-1991* (Akron: Summit County Historical Press. 1991).

Thielman, Jim, *Cool of the Evening: The 1965 Minnesota Twins* (Minneapolis: Kirkhouse Publishers. 2005).

"B.H.S. Baseball Team Captures Three Contests," *Barberton Herald*, April 18, 1947.

"Barberton High Wins District Baseball Title," *Barberton Herald*, May 23, 1947.

"Barberton Wins First Tournament Game in Baseball," *Barberton Herald*, May 16, 1947.

"Baseball 1944," Barberton High School Yearbook, 1945.

"Baseball 1947," Barberton High School Yearbook, 1948.

Bradley, Pam Naragon, "Barberton Facts and History," 2004, barbertonmagics.com/history.htm. Accessed May 31, 2007.

"Hal Naragon," Baseball-Reference, May 30, 2007, baseball-reference.com/n/naraga01.shtml. Accessed May 31, 2007.

"Harold Naragon Begins New Baseball Season at Harrisburg," *Barberton Herald*, April 29, 1949.

"Hat Naragon Booked as Harrisburg Catcher," *Barberton Herald*, April 30, 1948.

"Johnny Sain, RIP," The Southpaw, November 8, 2006, .108mag.typepad.com/the_southpaw/2006/11/index.html. Accessed May 15, 2007.

"Kaat's Meow," *Sports Illustrated,* October 17, 1966, 24–25.

"Magics Play in State Baseball Tournament This Weekend," *Barberton Herald*, May 30, 1947.

"Naragon May Play in Indians Minors Game," *Barberton Herald*, September 23,. 1949.

Nichols, Max, "Dropped by Twins, Sain and Naragon Join Tigers," *The Sporting News*, October 15, 1966.

Spoelstra, Watson, "Price Is Right as No. 2 Backstop, Bengals Learn," *The Sporting News*, June 22, 1968.

—-, "Sain's Advice Huge Plus for Tiger Hurlers," *The Sporting News*, September 7, 1968, 9.

—-, "Sain, Naragon Give Tigers Early Line on '69," *The Sporting News,* November 2, 1968, 29.

Stann, Francis, "How Grant Takes Washington," *Baseball Digest,* September 1960, 18–19, 45-46.

"The Big Defeat," Barberton High School Yearbook, 1947.

All quotations from Hal Naragon come from several interviews the author had with him in June and July 2007.

Acknowledgements

The author would like to thank Lynn O'Neil and the Barberton Public Library Local History Room for assistance with finding yearbooks and other early material regarding Hal Naragon.

Note

This article originally appeared in *Sock It to 'Em Tigers — The Incredible Story of the 1968 Detroit Tigers,* published by Maple Street Press in 2008.

Johnny Sain

BY JAN FINKEL

*First we'll use Spahn, then we'll use Sain,
Then an off day, followed by rain.
Back will come Spahn, followed by Sain
And followed, we hope, by two days of rain.*

—Gerry Hern, *Boston Post*, September 14, 1948

NOBODY WOULD MISTAKE *POST* sportswriter Hern's famous lines for "Casey at the Bat" or even poetry except in the broadest sense, but it sums up most of what many people today know about Johnny Sain. That's unfortunate, because Sain was so much more than someone whose name, fortuitously for Hern, rhymed with "rain"—trainer of fighter pilots, ace pitcher, one of the great pitching coaches, and holder of a little-known but remarkable record attesting to his genius as a contact hitter.

He was born John Franklin Sain in the tiny town of Havana, Arkansas (population 375 in the 2010 census), on September 25, 1917, to Eva and John Sain. An automobile mechanic and a good left-handed pitcher at the amateur level, the elder Sain would profoundly affect his son's career, encouraging him early on and teaching him to throw a curve while varying his motions and speed.

No one showed much interest in young Johnny as a pitching prospect, and his journey to the majors became a six-year odyssey. According to author Al Hirshberg, Bill Dickey declined Johnny's father's request to talk to his son after watching him pitch in a high-school game because he didn't want to tell the boy he didn't have it. To make matters worse, Bill Terry tried soon after to talk him out of pursuing a baseball career.

Receiving little encouragement or interest, Sain began a long odyssey to the majors. After graduating from Havana High School in 1935, the 17-year-old Johnny reportedly signed a Class D contract from the Red Sox for $5. However, the Detroit Tigers signed him as an amateur free agent the next year. Whose property was he? It's a good question. He'd signed with the Red Sox first, but he was under age. He was of age when he signed with the Tigers, but he'd already signed a contract with Boston.

In any case, Sain wound up in the Red Sox' farm system. Memphis native James "Doc" Prothro, manager of the Red Sox farm club in Little Rock, part of the Class A Southern Association, sent him to Osceola in the Class D Northeast Arkansas League for the

Johnny Sain won 139 games as a big-leaguer, but left his mark on the sport as one of the most innovative, yet divisive pitching coaches in history. Widely admired by his players, he coached for six teams and no less than 15 of his pitchers won at least 20 games in a season. (Photo courtesy of Minnesota Twins Baseball Club).

1936 season. The 18-year-old gave up a home run to the first batter he faced in a pro game, but still managed to win the contest and go 5-3 with a 2.72 ERA. The Red Sox dropped whatever association they had with Osceola in 1937, and the team began an affiliation with the St. Louis Browns. Despite the change in affiliation, Sain remained with Osceola, the only player from the 1936 roster to do so. The Indians slipped from second place to fifth (out of six) in 1937, and Sain's 5-8, 4.13 slate reflected the decline. Osceola left the league after the season, and Sain landed with the unaffiliated Newport Cardinals of the same league.

Coming into his own in 1938, Sain finished up 16-4 with a 2.72 ERA for Newport, good for a spot on the league's all-star team. Foreshadowing another of his talents, he also batted .257 with a home run and 14 RBIs. Remaining at Newport, now affiliated with the Detroit Tigers, who had originally signed him, Johnny had another strong year in 1939, his 18-10 mark accompanied by a 3.27 ERA; in addition, he and teammate Ed Hughes each set the league record for complete games with 27. Sain, who worked hard to become a good hitter and occasionally played in the outfield when not pitching, topped off his fine season with a .315 average, a pair of homers, and 20 RBIs.

Two good years with Newport weren't enough to get Sain to the majors, but he was unwittingly approaching the turning point in his career. It started innocuously on December 9, 1939, when Detroit traded second baseman Benny McCoy to the Philadelphia Athletics for outfielder Wally Moses. Citing corruption and cover-ups in the Tiger organization, Commissioner Kenesaw Mountain Landis nullified the trade and on January 14, 1940, granted free agency to 91 Detroit players and farmhands.[1] Sain was among the fortunate new free agents and one of 23 released players who made it to the majors, although in his case it would take two more years.

Accordingly, 1940 found Sain with the Nashville Volunteers, a Dodgers affiliate in the Southern Association. His 8-4 mark and 4.45 ERA pale beside the Vols' 101-47 record, good for a .682 winning percentage. The 1941 Vols, no longer a Brooklyn farm club, fell off to 83-70, in second place, and Sain fell much further to 6-12 and a 4.60 ERA. At this point Johnny didn't seem to be going anywhere, but the woeful Boston Braves, possibly on the advice of Pat Monahan, a longtime scout who worked for many teams, or Prothro, and hungry for pitchers, purchased his contract from Nashville and signed him to a major-league contract in March 1942.

Sain made his debut in the Braves' home opener on April 17, 1942 — in relief — retiring all seven Giants batters he faced and striking out three in a 4-3 Boston win. For his efforts he was awarded (retroactively) the first save of his career. He picked up his first win on April 29 at Wrigley Field in relief of Al Javery. All told, he went 4-7 with a 3.90 ERA, mostly in relief, for Casey Stengel's last Boston team, a dismal unit that could manage only a 59-89 record and a seventh-place finish.

Even with World War II on, Sain was able to complete the season. Upon receiving his draft notice, he had enlisted for aviation training in the Navy on August 21. However, he didn't have to report until November 15, whereupon he was sent to Amherst College along with fellow big-league inductees Ted Williams, Johnny Pesky, Joe Coleman, and Buddy Gremp. Having completed preliminary ground training by May 1943, Sain was transferred to Chapel Hill, North Carolina, for preflight instruction. After a few months there, he moved on to Corpus Christi Naval Air Training Base and graduated as an ensign in August 1944. He wound up teaching flying at Corpus Christi through the end of the war, receiving his discharge on November 25, 1945.

The experience proved seminal for the young man, who noted, "I think learning to fly an airplane helped me as much as anything. I was twenty-five years old. Learning to fly helped me to concentrate and restimulated my ability to learn."[2] Shortly before his discharge, on October 1, Sain married Dallas native Doris May McBride. The couple had four children — John Jr., Sharyl, Rhonda, and Randy.

Service in the war benefited Sain in a variety of ways. For one thing, his arm got some rest. He threw whenever he could, though, and pitched on several teams against stiff competition that often included other major leaguers. He went 12-4 with the North Carolina Pre-Flight team, appropriately named the Cloudbusters, in 1943, but it was a war-relief game in Yankee Stadium on July 28 that stood out. The Cloudbusters were facing a team made up of reserves from the Yankees and Indians, whose regulars played a charity, regular-season doubleheader that same day. In the sixth inning, "Yank-Lands" third-base coach Babe Ruth left the box to pinch-hit. Seeing the game as a sort of audition in front of a number of big-league officials, Sain wanted to retire the 48-year-old Ruth, but catcher Al Sabo came out and told him not to throw Ruth any curves and risk embarrassing him. As Sain later said, "Taking away my curveball was like cutting off two of my fingers, but it was Babe Ruth in Yankee Stadium. Then, it became obvious that the home plate umpire wasn't going to call any strikes on him. So I threw five medium fastballs, almost batting practice pitches. Ruth took one, then hit a long foul ball and then walked on the last three pitches."[3] It was the Babe's last at-bat in an organized game.

Another benefit of the war years is that a maturing Sain came to realize and accept that although he was large for his era at 6-feet-2 and 180-200 pounds, he didn't have high-octane velocity. Accordingly, he'd have to rely on mechanics, finesse, and guile, letting batters hit the ball and letting his fielders do their jobs. Moreover, he changed his delivery. Through 1942 he constantly varied his arm action, even occasionally throwing from a crossfire motion. As Sain saw it, there were two problems with this approach: He risked hurting his arm, and it wasn't effective (63 walks in 97 innings with Boston in 1942 were ample proof). After the war he kept his windmill windup (he was one of the last pitchers to do so) and threw almost exclusively overhand, dropping down to side-arm on occasion if he was ahead of the hitter.

Finally, there was the curveball his father had taught Sain how to throw. Johnny had a good curve before the war, to be sure, but the knowledge of aerodynamics he'd absorbed as a pilot helped him turn his best pitch into so effective a weapon that he earned the nickname the Man of a Thousand Curves.

Showing no signs of rustiness after a three-year layoff, Sain became a star pitcher and Boston's staff ace in 1946. He turned in a 20-14 slate, a career-best 2.21 ERA, and a league-leading 24 complete games for the Braves, who took a big leap to 81-72 and fourth place under new manager Billy Southworth. Johnny also had the honor on May 11 of pitching the first night game in Boston big-league annals. Facing the Giants in a special "sateen" uniform designed to stand out under the lights, he lost to the Giants, 5-1, in front of 35,945 fans at Braves Field. The pitching highlight of Sain's year, however, came on July 12 at Cincinnati. In the first inning, Grady Hatton hit a pop fly that dropped among three Braves behind third base for a double. No other Red reached base as Johnny beat Ewell Blackwell, 1-0.

Life was improving for the Braves. Tommy Holmes was an effective contact hitter. Bob Elliott, a hustling, hard-hitting team player, was acquired from the Pirates over the winter and won the Most Valuable Player Award in 1947. And there was a decorated war hero, a southpaw who would be the perfect complement to Johnny Sain and a number of other pitchers over a long career—Warren Spahn.

Spahn and Sain became a factor in '47. Spahn had his first great year, going 21-10 with a 2.33 ERA, and Sain was close behind, turning in a 21-12 mark and 3.52 ERA (the relatively high ERA partially offset by an outstanding .346 batting average and only one strikeout in 107 at-bats). At 86-68, the Braves moved up another notch to third place. Sain even became a part of history on Opening Day, April 15, becoming the first major-league pitcher to face Jackie Robinson. Robinson went hitless in three trips to the plate as the Dodgers won, 5-3, at Ebbets Field.

Sain's reward for his fine early-season work was pitching in the All-Star Game at Wrigley Field. Replacing the Cardinals' Harry Brecheen in the seventh inning of a 1-1 contest, he contributed to his own undoing. He got George McQuinn to ground out. Bobby Doerr followed with a single, then stole second. Sain had Doerr picked off second but fired the ball into center field, sending Doerr to third. He struck out Buddy Rosar, but Stan Spence, batting for Spec Shea, singled, scoring Doerr with the go-ahead run. The American League held on for the 2-1 win, and Sain absorbed the loss. Nevertheless, it proved a good year, leaving the Braves and their fans reason to be optimistic.

The 1948 season *almost* brought baseball Nirvana to Boston and New England. The Red Sox finished 96-58, two games ahead of the hated Yankees. The bad news was that the Indians under the leadership of Lou Boudreau were also 96-58. The first playoff in American League history—a one-game affair—saw the Sox go down, 8-3, in Fenway Park as Boudreau put on a one-man show with two homers and four hits. However, the Braves, Boston's "other team" and a perennial poor cousin to the aristocratic Red Sox, took the National League flag with a 91-62 mark that would have been good only for fourth place in the American League.

The close pennant race gave rise to Gerry Hern's often quoted (and misquoted) lines about "Spahn and Sain." In a way Hern took advantage of a little poetic license. He got the Sain part right, but at 15-12 with a 3.71 ERA, Spahn actually had one of the least effective seasons of his brilliant career, a season more typical of a third or fourth starter than an ace. Vern Bickford (11-5, 3.27) and Bill Voiselle (13-13, 3.63) were a touch more effective.

As for Sain, he was in a class by himself, going 24-15 with a 2.60 ERA. He led the league in wins (24), games started (39), complete games (28), and innings pitched (314⅔). He pitched the Braves into first place on June 15, beating the Cubs, 6-3. It was a historic moment, as the game at Braves Field was the first to be televised in the Boston area. Appearing in the All-Star Game on July 13, he had three strikeouts (Vern Stephens, Bobby Doerr, and Hoot Evers, all in the fifth) over 1⅔ hitless innings. The year also included an extraordinary streak of personal endurance. From August 24 to September 21, Sain started and completed nine games, winning seven of them. Backed by Sain's efforts, and equally hot hurling from Spahn, the Braves took 21 of their final 27 games to coast to the National League pennant by 6½ games over St. Louis. *The Sporting News* rewarded Sain by naming him National League Pitcher of the Year, and he was runner-up to Stan Musial in voting for the NL Most Valuable Player Award.

The year wasn't all roses. During the season the Braves signed 18-year-old southpaw Johnny Antonelli for a sum reported to be at least $50,000. As a "bonus baby," Antonelli couldn't be sent to the minors for two years; but since he almost never pitched, he was taking a place on the roster that most players believed belonged to a proven veteran while pocketing more money than most could make in several seasons. Not surprisingly, the presence of Antonelli and other bonus babies made for tension in major-league clubhouses. All of the Braves were annoyed, none more so than Sain, who took his frustrations straight to owner Lou Perini in the front office. Mounting what he called the "Golden Staircase" that led to Perini's door, Sain told the boss that as a proven pitcher he deserved better treatment than an untried teenager. Perini listened, and before the All-Star Game the Braves gave Johnny a new contract for the remainder of the season—and 1949 as well.

The World Series opened in Boston on October 6, with Sain drawing the nod against the Indians' Bob Feller. It was all a Series contest should be, as both pitchers were at the top of their craft. With the game scoreless in the bottom of the eighth, Bill Salkeld led off with a walk. Phil Masi ran for him, and Mike McCormick sacrificed Masi to second. Feller then intentionally walked Eddie Stanky, with utility infielder Sibby Sisti going in to pinch-run for him. With Sain at bat, Feller turned and fired to shortstop Lou Boudreau in an attempt to pick Masi off second. As the story goes, everyone in Braves Field thought Masi was out—everyone, that is, except second-base umpire Bill Stewart, who had the majority vote and called him safe. Sain lined out, but Tommy Holmes singled past third to score Masi from second and put Boston up 1-0. Sain shut down the Indians in the ninth, and

Boston won. Sain had given up four hits on 95 pitches, Feller, two hits on 85 pitches in a game of exemplary efficiency.

After Cleveland won the next two contests, Johnny came back to face Steve Gromek in Game Four at Cleveland and pitched superbly in a 2-1 loss. The Braves staved off elimination in Game Five, but the Indians took Game Six back at Boston, and the Series. Sain was magnificent in defeat — two complete games, a shutout, a heartbreaking loss, nine strikeouts against no walks, nine hits allowed, and a 1.06 ERA.

All told, Sain was arguably the top pitcher in the National League from 1946 to 1948 with a 65-41 record and 2.77 ERA. Indeed, he fit in nicely with his American League counterparts Bob Feller (65-41, 2.75) and Hal Newhouser (64-38, 2.59). Johnny's decline, however, was swift and sudden. He was up and down — mostly down — from 1949 to 1951, going a combined 37-44 with an ugly 4.31 ERA. The kindest thing one can call the 1949 season is a disaster. Spent from his efforts of the year before and a sore shoulder that Sain blamed on his experimenting with a screwball during the spring, he suffered through a career-worst 17 losses (against just ten wins) with a horrendous 4.81 ERA. He had the dubious honor of leading the league in runs (150) and earned runs (130) allowed. For the only time in his career he walked more than he struck out (75 to 73), and he also surrendered more than a hit per inning (285 in 243 innings pitched), starting a pattern that would continue throughout the remainder of his career. True, he completed 16 of his 36 starts, but he was taking a beating most of the time. In short, there is no way to put the season in a positive light. The defending champs of the National League fell to fourth place with a 75-79 mark.

It wasn't just Sain's ailing shoulder at fault; almost everything went wrong for the Braves in 1949. Billy Southworth, whose demands were grudgingly accepted when his teams were winning, reportedly became intolerable during spring training. Claiming credit the players considered theirs and breaking rules that he set, Southworth put the defending National League champs through two-a-day sessions that totaled six hours and instituted a midnight curfew, complete with room checks by clubhouse attendant and watchdog Shorty Young. An early-to-bed, early-to-rise type, Sain usually retired by 9:30. Young checked on Sain just once, waking him out of a sound sleep. Furious, Sain said that if it ever happened again, he'd send the offender out the window. A rumor got out that Southworth had checked up on his star pitcher, that Sain had threatened to throw *him* out the window, and that Sain and Southworth weren't speaking. For his part, Sain said he never socialized with his managers.

Although Sain rebounded in 1950 with his fourth 20-win season (20-13), the won-lost record is deceptive. Even in a year replete with heavy hitters, his 3.94 ERA was well off the league pace. While he completed 25 of his 37 starts, he gave up 294 hits in 278⅓ innings. Particularly ominous was Sain's career-high and league-leading 34 home runs surrendered.[4] He was lucky to win more than he lost, largely because he was pitching for a team that went 83-71 in a nice recovery from the debacle of 1949.

All that kept Sain's 1951 season from being a repeat of 1949 was fewer innings pitched, because the figures were pretty proportional (195 hits in 160 innings and a 4.22 ERA with the Braves). It added up to a 5-13 slate when struggling Boston sold him to the Yankees for $50,000 and a young pitcher who would pay long-term dividends to the Braves and haunt the Yankees a few years hence — Lew Burdette. Sain appeared in seven games for New York, starting four and completing one, while posting a 2-1 mark. The Yanks won the pennant, and Johnny was brought in to relieve starter Vic Raschi in the seventh inning of Game Six of the World Series with two on and nobody out. He retired the Giants without allowing an inherited runner to score, and worked out of a bases-loaded jam in the eighth. The Giants loaded the bases on three singles in the ninth before Bob Kuzava came in and surrendered two runs (both charged to Sain) but saved the game, 4-3, and the Series for the Yankees. It was hardly an auspicious start for Sain with a new team, especially one that had come to consider World Series titles their birthright (this was their third straight).

Making matters worse, the shoulder injury that had ruined Johnny's 1949 season had never completely gone away. With nothing to lose, he underwent a new radiation therapy from a doctor in Dallas, and was so pleased that he recommended it to others. Teammate Eddie Lopat tried it and was happy. In later years Whitey Ford had it done five times, and Mel Stottlemyre went Ford one better.

One of many keys to the Yankees' phenomenal success from the late 1940s to the mid-1960s was a genius for resurrecting the careers of players thought to be finished. Johnny Mize and Enos Slaughter, for example, had several productive years added to their careers, and Johnny Sain was a chief beneficiary among the pitching fraternity. How the Yankees did it was brilliant in its simplicity, and one wonders why nobody else figured it out. They made him a spot starter and reliever so that a bit fewer than half of his appearances were starts—16 of 35 in 1952 and 19 of 40 in 1953. He completed half of his starts, eight in 1952 and ten in 1953, and relieved superbly the rest of the time. In 1954, his last full year in pinstripes, all 45 of his appearances were in relief, and he saved a league-leading 22 games to become just the second pitcher (after Ellis Kinder of the Red Sox turned the trick the year before) to win 20 games in one season and save 20 in another. As of 2013, Wilbur Wood, Dennis Eckersley, John Smoltz, and Derek Lowe were the only other pitchers to accomplish the feat.

Adapting to his new role, Sain began to pay dividends in 1952 as both starter and reliever. On May 20 he scattered six hits to beat the White Sox, 4-3. He rescued the Yankees twice at Fenway Park on September 24, coming on in the ninth with the game tied and earning a 3-2 win in the opener of a doubleheader, then saving an 8-6 win in the nightcap. Two days later he got the win in relief in the Yankees' 11-inning pennant-clinching 5-2 win in Philadelphia. For the year he was 11-6 with a decent 3.46 ERA and seven saves. He pitched capably but didn't fare well in the World Series against the Dodgers. Taking over in the sixth inning of Game Five for starter Ewell Blackwell with the Yankees leading 5-4, he gave up the tying run in the seventh and the winning run in the 11th to take the 6-5 loss. The Yankees didn't use him again in their hard-fought seven-game win over their subway rivals.

Now a vital part of the Yankee machine, Sain was outstanding in 1953. Again dividing his duties between starting and relieving, he posted a 14-7 mark with nine saves and a 3.00 ERA while earning a spot on the All-Star team. Once again, the Yankees and Dodgers squared off in the World Series. Relieving starter Allie Reynolds in Game One with one out in the sixth and the Dodgers threatening, Sain stopped the damage, pitched the final 3⅔ innings, and picked up the 9-5 win, even contributing a double and a run scored. He was not as effective in his other appearance, in Game Four, but the Yankees nonetheless captured their fifth straight world championship.

By 1954 Sain was a full-time reliever, going 6-6 with a 3.16 ERA and the aforementioned 22 saves. The Yankees had their best season under Casey Stengel with a 103-51 record, but it was only second-best to the Indians' 111-43 mark, the American League record at the time. Johnny wouldn't get a chance to pitch in his fifth World Series.

Shortly into the 1955 season, after three appearances and a 6.75 ERA, the Yankees determined that Sain was finished. On May 11 New York traded Johnny and future Hall of Famer Enos Slaughter (he was hitting .111 at the time) to the Kansas City Athletics for journeyman pitcher Sonny Dixon and cash. Sain appeared in 25 games for Kansas City, winning two and losing five while posting one save and an ERA of 5.44. He pitched his final game on July 15 and was released the next day.

For someone who toiled in the minors for six years, lost three more years to the war, and got started at an age when most players are entering their peak, Sain had a fine career: 139 wins against 116 losses,[5] a solid 3.49 ERA; an award as *The Sporting News* Pitcher of the Year; four 20-win seasons; three trips to the All-Star Game; four World Series; the league lead in wins once; the league lead in saves once; and league leads in other categories.

That's just the pitching side of the Sain ledger. An outstanding contact hitter, Johnny had always helped himself with the bat. He sported a .245 career average, led the league with 16 sacrifice hits in 1948 (the first pitcher to lead his league in an offensive category), led his league's pitchers in runs batted in five times, and struck out a mere 20 times in 774 lifetime at-bats. Those 20 strikeouts are extraordinary, the fewest for all hitters with between 500 and 800 at-bats from 1910 (when the National League began keeping strikeout records) and 1913 (when the American League followed suit) to the present.

While his playing days were over, Sain wasn't really through. He returned to Arkansas, to Walnut Ridge, and raised his children there. He'd had a prospering Chevrolet dealership in the town since 1952, but at heart he was a baseball man and was happy to get back into the game in 1959 as pitching coach for the Kansas City Athletics. Working with a veteran staff on a team that could do no better than 66-88, he got adequate seasons out of Ned Garver, Bud Daley, Ray Herbert, and Johnny Kucks. Sain resigned after the season to concentrate on business at home.

Catching on in the same capacity with the Yankees when Ralph Houk replaced the fired Casey Stengel for the 1961 season, Sain showed what he could do with good material. Persuading Houk to go with a four-man rotation, he transformed Whitey Ford from a perennially very good pitcher into a great one. Ford, who credited Sain with rejuvenating his career, posted a 25-4 mark and a 3.21 ERA in 1961, good enough to garner his only Cy Young Award; he followed that up with 17 wins in 1962 and 24 in 1963. Ralph Terry found his groove in 1962, leading the league with 23 wins. Jim Bouton, who called Sain "the greatest pitching coach who ever lived," had a career year in 1963 with a 21-7 slate and a 2.53 ERA.

Two contradictory versions exist as to why Sain and the Yankees parted company. Sain said in 1993 that he had heard that Houk was going to move into the Yankee front office, with Yogi Berra taking over as manager. Since Sain doubted that Berra would be effective managing recent teammates, he claimed he resigned. His misgivings were well-founded in that Berra was fired after one season despite leading the Yankees into the World Series.

The alternate version is that Houk showed his appreciation for Sain's helping him to three World Series appearances and two world championships in three years by firing him after the 1963 season. The move mystified many people, but Bouton offered a possible explanation: "What general—Houk started thinking of himself as a general—wants a lieutenant on his staff who's smarter than he is?"

After sitting out for a year, Sain joined the Minnesota Twins in 1965. Helping this club to its first pennant, he got Jim "Mudcat" Grant to achieve a 21-7 mark, good enough to lead the league in wins. Under Sain's tutelage, lefty Jim Kaat went 25-13 with a 2.75 ERA in 1966 to lead the American League in wins and help the Twins finish second. Twins manager Sam Mele was so happy with Sain's contribution that he fired him.

Sain moved from Minnesota to Detroit in 1967. Working with manager Mayo Smith's staff that year, he turned Earl Wilson into a 20-game winner for the first and only time in his career. In 1968, Sain crafted his masterpiece—Denny McLain, whose 31 wins were the most since Lefty Grove achieved the same total in 1931, and haven't been challenged since. With just six losses and a 1.96 ERA, McLain took home the Cy Young and Most Valuable Player awards. With lefty Mickey Lolich picking up three wins in the World Series, the Tigers beat the Cardinals and Bob Gibson. Sain kept McLain sufficiently focused in 1969 to go 24-9 and share the Cy Young Award with southpaw Mike Cuellar of the Orioles.

World Series victory aside, Sain and manager Mayo Smith were barely speaking. Sain's tenure with Detroit soured for good in 1969. One day Johnny took some time off to attend to some personal business. In his absence, Smith had the pitchers run, angering Sain, who asked Smith if he wanted to stick with what worked or with what hadn't worked for 25 years. Smith made his preferences clear on June 15, 1969, when he sold Sain favorite Dick Radatz to Montreal. By August 10, Sain was fired.

The rest of Sain's life was taking a bad turn as well. His marriage had fallen apart, as he later explained: "My first wife went back to college and got her degree at age 50 and it changed the tone of our relationship. My life in baseball seemed more and more trivial to her. The divorce was an enormous financial strain on me. I pretty much lost almost everything I had, to the point that I had to declare bankruptcy."

Attempting to dig out from under, Sain spent the 1970 season until late September as a roving minor-league pitching instructor for the California Angels, becoming friends with Angels minor-league manager Chuck Tanner. Next, Johnny was off to the White Sox, where he managed to stay for six years, in no small part because Tanner was manager the whole time and had the sense to let Sain go about his business. The approach produced incredible results. Wilbur Wood, who started out as a reliever, became a workhorse starter and won 20 games each year from 1971 to 1974. Wood's ERA in 1971 was a minuscule 1.91, and his work in 1972 earned him *The Sporting News* Pitcher of the Year Award. Reunited with Sain, Jim Kaat won 21 and 20 in 1974 and 1975, respectively. Stan Bahnsen, Rookie of the Year with the Yankees in 1968, reached his peak in 1972 with a 21-16 slate. Making Sain's achievement remarkable is that the White Sox usually were a middle-of-the-pack club during his tenure, while the Yankees, Twins, and Tigers had all been contenders or pennant winners.

The years on the South Side of Chicago paid an even greater dividend than all those 20-game winners. On July 3, 1972, now divorced, Sain was introduced to Mary Ann Zaremba, the 35-year-old widow of a Chicago policeman, at a club in the suburbs. Johnny was smitten. Mary Ann remembered, "He called me the next day and said, 'You have to marry me.'" That seemed a little impetuous, so they compromised on a date at Comiskey Park on the Fourth. The date must have gone well, for they were married on August 24.

Sain coached the Atlanta Braves pitchers in 1977, but on a miserable team that went 61-101, he had only one first-rate pitcher, future Hall of Famer Phil Niekro. Stints with several clubs in Atlanta's farm system followed, and he went back to the Braves for one final fling from 1985 to 1986, where he was reunited with Chuck Tanner on a pair of second-division teams.

Most of Sain's coaching career followed a pattern: Almost immediate success, the lifelong loyalty and devotion of his pitchers that he reciprocated, inevitable conflict with management (and managers), and the search for another job. Often it seems to have been insecurity and jealousy on the manager's part, knowing that the pitchers listened to and respected Sain more than they did him. Sometimes a manager simply thought he knew more or better than Sain, and didn't want to be challenged.

On the flip side, some of the difficulty was Johnny's fault. To begin with, he encouraged pitchers to demand to be paid what they were worth, to mount the "Golden Staircase," as he had done back in 1948. Naturally, this didn't sit well with management. In the second place, he was extremely protective of his charges and wouldn't tolerate interference from anybody, including the manager. His refusal to speak ill of any of his pitchers led Detroit skipper Mayo Smith to conclude that he could never get a straight answer from Sain on a pitcher's physical condition, state of mind, or anything else. Ironically, Houk, Mele, and Smith all won a *Sporting News* Manager of the Year Award with Sain as their pitching coach, then left town not long after Sain's departure.

Always willing to stick up for his pitchers, he further endeared himself to hurlers by not making them run. Some baseball people found this strange, but Sain had two reasons for the tactic, one practical and the other philosophical or pedagogical. On the practical side he noted, "You don't run the ball up to home plate." On the philosophical or pedagogical side, Sain said, "I've always felt that a lot of pitching coaches made a living out of running pitchers so they wouldn't have to spend that same time teaching them how to pitch." On the other hand, he believed that pitchers had to keep their arms strong, so he had them throw almost every day, even after a long stint on the mound the day or night before. To keep pitchers mentally focused, he had, as an example, Wednesday's pitcher chart pitches for Tuesday's game; that way, the pitcher could observe both his teammates and the opposing pitchers and hitters. It seems of obvious benefit, and most managers and pitching coaches now have their pitchers chart the game, but Sain seems to have been the first to make it a practice.

Finally, Sain brought his own brilliant creation to the table. Noted baseball author Roger Kahn described it in *The Head Game*:

The Yankees hired Sain in 1961 as pitching coach. He showed up with a briefcase full of inspirational books and tapes and a machine he was patenting as the "Baseball Pitching Educational Device," which everyone soon called "the Baseball Spinner." Baseballs were mounted on rotating axes—one axis per ball—and you could snap one in a variety of fastball spins and the other in rotations for sliders and curves. The baseballs were anchored. Except for rotating, they didn't move. Using John Sain's Baseball Pitching Educational Device, you could practice spinning your delivery at home or in a taxi or in a hotel room without endangering lamps, mirrors, or companions.

What Sain achieved as a pitching coach (sixteen 20-game winners in all or part of 17 seasons) is impressive, given the diversity of talents he worked with. Some, like Whitey Ford and Denny McLain, had experienced considerable success. On the other hand, Jim Bouton, Jim Kaat, Mudcat Grant, and Stan Bahnsen had yet to show how capable they were. Then there was Wilbur Wood, undergoing the transformation from reliever to starter.

The project that best epitomizes Sain at work has to be Denny McLain. The quintessential flake, McLain had all the tools to be a great pitcher except seriousness of purpose, sense, and maturity. Sain took Denny for what he was and worked his magic indirectly. Learning that McLain was working to obtain a pilot's license, Sain helped him prepare for the required tests, and even went up in the air with him. From that basis the two moved to McLain's pitching so smoothly that he was the best pitcher in the American League in 1968 and 1969, winning 55 games, a Most Valuable Player Award, and two Cy Youngs. At 25, he already had 114 wins under his belt and seemed on path for the Hall of Fame. What McLain's career might have been had he had Sain's guidance for a few more seasons is pure speculation, but the train wreck—erratic and criminal behavior; suspensions from baseball; prison for drug dealing, racketeering, and extortion; poor health in the form of obesity and heart trouble; and who knows what else—that has been McLain's life in the more than 40 years since is indisputable. Denny needed grounding, and Sain gave it to him for a magical couple of years.

Out of baseball, the Sains settled down to a quiet life in the Chicago suburb of Downers Grove, Illinois. John lectured and consulted with various teams and players, happy to talk with anybody who wanted to listen about the fine art of pitching. Mickey Lolich, a beneficiary of Sain's tutelage, could have been speaking for scores of pitchers when he described his mentor: "Johnny Sain loves pitchers. Maybe he doesn't love baseball so much, but he loves pitchers. Only he understands them."

Over the years there has been talk of enshrining coaches in the Hall of Fame. Writing of Sain in *Newsday*, Roger Kahn noted, "The Hall of Fame admits broadcasters, umpires, entrepreneurs, even newspaper writers. For goodness sake, let's enshrine a great coach."[6] Mike Shalin, Neil Shalin, and Brent Kelley, authors of books about players who were not in the Hall of Fame at the time of writing, have indicated support for the cause. Former White Sox GM Roland Hemond, Jim Bouton, Jim Kaat, and others have spoken up for Sain. There have been some letter-writing campaigns. Nevertheless, the movement has never gained sufficient traction.

Cooperstown notwithstanding, the Boston Braves Historical Association saw that Sain was honored for his years in their city. Sain, Warren Spahn, and Sibby Sisti were inducted into the Boston Braves Hall of

Fame on October 16, 1994. Four years later, on October 4, 1998, the Association sponsored a 50th-anniversary celebration of the Braves' championship season. Bob Feller came to town, and the two aces revisited their pitching duel and the pickoff play that "failed."

After suffering a stroke on March 31, 2002, Sain spent his remaining years in ill health. On August 31, 2002, he became the seventh player inducted into the Braves' franchise Hall of Fame at Turner Field. Mary Ann wrote an acceptance speech for him; they couldn't attend the induction, but Hank Aaron read the speech at the ceremony in Atlanta.

Johnny Sain died on November 7, 2006, in Resthaven West Nursing Home in Downers Grove. Surviving him were Mary Ann, his four children, 11 grandchildren, and two great-grandchildren. Returning to Havana, he was buried in Walker Cemetery after a ceremony attended by many of his former pitching "pupils" and other friends he had made in the game. Several teams sent gorgeous floral arrangements; in death, all the hard feelings were forgotten.

The last pitcher to face Babe Ruth and the first to face Jackie Robinson, Sain started the first night game in Boston and the first game televised in New England, unleashed the potential of pitchers like Mudcat Grant, Jim Kaat, Earl Wilson, and Mickey Lolich, and coached probably the last 30-game winner. In the words of baseball historian Maxwell Kates "a veritable Forrest Gump in baseball history," Johnny Sain left a rich legacy.[7]

Acknowledgments

Gabriel Schechter, former research associate at the Hall of Fame, provided me with copies of the National and American Leagues' daily sheets detailing each of Sain's games and files of pitchers who came under Sain's tutelage.

Bob Brady sent me copies of the articles by Ed Rumill, thoroughly and thoughtfully reviewed my work, and provided me with invaluable material that I had missed.

Jim Sandoval and Rod Nelson, co-chairmen of SABR's Scouts Committee, guided me through the intricacies of scouts, contracts, and franchises — all as they applied to Sain.

Saul Wisnia, James Forr, and Len Levin edited versions of this article. They made it better.

SOURCES

Allen, Thomas E., *If They Hadn't Gone: How World War II Affected Major League Baseball* (Springfield: Southwest Missouri State University, 2004).

Bailey, Jim, "Sain stood out as pitcher, excelled as coach." *Arkansas Democrat-Gazette*. November 16, 2006.

Eig, Jonathan, *Opening Day: The Story of Jackie Robinson's First Season* (New York: Simon & Schuster, 2007).

Fagen, Herb, "Johnny Sain Did It His Way … As a Pitcher and Coach," *Baseball Digest*. December 1993.

Gilbert, Bill, *They Also Served: Baseball and the Home Front: 1941-1945* (New York: Crown Publishers, 1992).

Hirshberg, Al, *The Braves: The Pick and The Shovel* (Boston: Waverly House, 1948).

_____, "What Really Happened to the Boston Braves?" *Sport*. January 1950.

James, Bill, and Rob Neyer, *The Neyer/James Guide to Pitchers: An Historical Compendium of Pitching, Pitchers, and Pitches* (New York, London, Toronto, and Sydney: Simon & Schuster, 2004).

Johnny Sain files at the National Baseball Hall of Fame and Museum in Cooperstown, New York.

Johnson, Lloyd, and Miles Wolff, eds. *The Encyclopedia of Minor League Baseball*. 3rd ed. (Durham, North Carolina: Baseball America, Inc., 2007).

Kaese, Harold, *The Boston Braves, 1871-1953* (Boston: Northeastern University Press, 2004). Reprint of 1948 original and 1954 reprint issued by Putnam.

Kahn, Roger, "A Slide Rule Can't Measure a Ballplayer," *New York Newsday*. July 29, 1994.

_____, *The Head Game: Baseball Seen From the Pitcher's Mound* (San Diego, New York, and London: Harcourt, Inc., 2001).

Kates, Maxwell, "Van Lingle Mungo." Baseball Analysts (baseballanalysts.com), November 13, 2006.

Kelley, Brent, *The Case For: Those Overlooked by the Baseball Hall of Fame* (Jefferson, North Carolina: McFarland, 1992).

McCann, Mike, "Mike McCann's Page of Minor League History," geocities.com/big_bunko/minor.html.

O'Donnell, Jim, "Mind over Batter: Ex-Major League Baseball Star and Coaching Legend Johnny Sain Never Was One to Do Things by the Book," *Chicago Tribune,* October 10, 1993. Reprint from *Chicago Tribune* archives at chicagotribune.com.

Peary, Danny, ed., *We Played the Game: 65 Players Remember Baseball's Greatest Era, 1947-1964* (New York: Hyperion, 1994).

Professional Baseball Players Database Version 6.0

Rumill, Ed, "Johnny Sain—Hero of the Hub," *Sport Pix,* February 1949.

_____, "Twenty for Sain, *Baseball Magazine,* January 1947.

Sandoval, Jim, and Bill Nowlin, eds., *Can He Play? A Look at Baseball Scouts and Their Profession* (Phoenix: Society for American Baseball Research, 2011), Electronic book.

Shalin, Mike, and Neil Shalin, *Out by a Step: The 100 Best Players NOT in the Baseball Hall of Fame* (London, South Bend, New York, and Oxford: Diamond Communications, 2002).

Siegel, Arthur, "Sain Is Product of Own Planning to Be Box Star," *Sports Parade.* October 13, 1948.

Thorn, John, and John Holway, *The Pitcher: The Ultimate Compendium of Pitching Lore: Featuring Flakes and Fruitcakes, Wildmen and Control Artists, Strategies, Deliveries, Statistics, and More* (New York, London, Toronto, Sydney, and Tokyo: Prentice Hall Press, 1988).

Tourangeau, Dixie, "Spahn, Sain, and the '48 Braves," *The National Pastime* 18 (1998), 17-20.

Vincent, David, Lyle Spatz, and David W. Smith, *The Midsummer Classic: The Complete History of Baseball's All-Star Game* (Lincoln and London: University of Nebraska Press, 2001).

Westcott, Rich, *Masters of the Diamond: Interviews with Players Who Began Their Careers More Than 50 Years Ago* (Jefferson, North Carolina: McFarland, 1994).

Wright, Craig R., and Tom House, *The Diamond Appraised* (New York and London: Fireside Books at Simon & Schuster, 1989).

sabr.org

baseballindex.org

baseball-reference.com

retrosheet.org

baseballlibrary.com

baseball-almanac.com

paperofrecord.com

proquest.com

Note

This article originally appeared in two different books: *Sock It To 'Em Tigers—The Incredible Story of the 1968 Detroit Tigers,* published by Maple Street Press in 2008; and *Spahn, Sain and Teddy Ballgame—Boston's Almost Perfect Baseball Summer of 1948,* published by Rounder Books in 2008.

NOTES

1 McCoy and Connie Mack made out nicely in the whole affair. Attracting bids from several clubs, McCoy signed with the Athletics for a $45,000 bonus and a two-year contract at $10,000 a year. Mack kept Moses and obtained the second baseman he wanted in the first place.

2 Thomas E. Allen, *If They Hadn't Gone: How World War II Affected Major League Baseball* (Springfield: Southwest Missouri State University, 2004), 136.

3 Jim O'Donnell, "Mind Over Batter: Ex-major League Baseball Star And Coaching Legend Johnny Sain Never Was One To Do Things By The Book," *Chicago Tribune* (October 10, 1993).

4 Sain, Ken Raffensberger of the Reds, and Preacher Roe of the Dodgers all gave up 34 homers in 1950. It was the third highest number of home runs surrendered up to the time. Murry Dickson of the Cardinals gave up 39 in 1948, and Larry Jansen of the Giants was tagged 36 times in 1949. Jansen also gave up 31 homers in 1950.

5 Allen, 139. Allen projects a 45-33 slate with a 3.21 ERA for the three seasons Sain missed due to the war, but such projections seem to be enjoyable speculations.

6 *New York Newsday.* July 29, 1994.

7 Maxwell Kates, "Van Lingle Mungo." Baseball Analysts (www.baseballanalysts.com), November 13, 2006.

Herb Carneal

BY STEW THORNLEY

"HI, EVERYBODY" WAS THE TRADEmark opening of Herb Carneal, who spent his career in sportscasting, most notably calling Minnesota Twins games from 1962 to 2006. "Baseball lends itself to radio," he wrote as the opening sentence of his 1995 autobiography, *Hi, Everybody!*, explaining, "People aren't hanging on every pitch. They don't have to keep their eyes glued to a television screen, and they don't have to keep their ears tuned in to a radio either. Baseball is played during the summer, when people are out doing other things. People enjoy radio broadcasts while sitting in a boat or working in a garden. During the summer they'd rather listen to the radio on the porch than watch television cooped up indoors."

Carneal was born on May 10, 1923, in Richmond, Virginia. His father, Charles, was not in good health and died when Carneal was 7 years old. His mother, Edith, worked as a milliner and was helped by her mother in raising Herb.

Carneal said he visited some Civil War battlefields in Virginia as a youth but was never a student of history. "Richmond was still a very segregated city when I was growing up, although I never gave the matter much thought. A black youngster around my age hung around with my friends and me all through elementary and junior high school, and played baseball and football with us just like anybody else."

Carneal said he developed his love of baseball from his mom. His high school, John Marshall in Richmond, didn't have a baseball team, but he played some American Legion baseball as a center fielder and pitcher, despite a "fastball that wouldn't have broken a pane of glass." Carneal had little time for sports when he got into high school because he worked for Imperial Tobacco Company every afternoon.

He and his mother attended semipro games on weekends and sometimes a game of the Richmond Colts of the Piedmont League. Carneal and his friends developed loyalties to the Washington Senators and went to Griffith Stadium to see them play in 1939, Herb's first major-league game. Carneal was also a fan of the St. Louis Cardinals during the time of the Gas House Gang, and had the chance to chat with Pepper Martin at an exhibition game that was rained out. In 1942 he saw the Cardinals in the World Series at Yankee Stadium, traveling with his friends to New York, where they attended the third game and the fifth and final game.

"As a kid, I was like most of my friends, crazy about baseball and other sports. Maybe I was a little crazier

A recipient of the Ford Frick Award from the Baseball Hall of Fame, Carneal broadcast Twins games from 1962 through 2006. (National Baseball Hall of Fame, Cooperstown, New York).

than most. By the time I graduated from high school, I had decided that I wanted to spend my life in sports, but I had realized early on that it wouldn't be as a player."

As was the case with a future Minnesota Twins colleague, Ray Christensen, Carneal played dice baseball games with his friends and announced the outcome dictated by the dice in a play-by-play manner.

After high school, Carneal began working at WMBG Radio in Richmond, doing mostly booth announcing. At night he tried to pick up baseball broadcasts from elsewhere, listening to the announcers and dreaming of getting such a job. He got his first shot at sportscasting at WMBG, filling in for another announcer at a boxing match.

In 1945 Carneal responded to an ad in *Broadcasting* magazine, sent an audition tape, and landed a job at WSYR Radio in Syracuse, New York. He initially broadcast football games for a high school in Watertown, about 70 miles away, and worked his way into basketball at Syracuse University. He also announced games of the Syracuse Nationals of the National Basketball League (a forerunner of the NBA) and did the public-address announcing at MacArthur Stadium for the Syracuse Chiefs of the International League. Occasionally Carneal did re-creation play-by-play of major-league baseball games.

While in Syracuse, Carneal became part of a school of announcers assembled by the Atlantic Refining Company and did college football games around the region. He recalled a humorous story from that time. "When I was assigned the Colgate-Bucknell game in Hamilton, New York, I arrived the night before the game, had a room at the Colgate Inn, and put together my spotting board of the numbers and names of the different players organized by their positions. I used India ink, which wouldn't run if it got wet. Back home in Syracuse, I couldn't find my bottle of India ink. The next year, I was assigned another Colgate game in Hamilton. I stayed in the same room at the Colgate Inn and there was my bottle of India ink, still on the desk."

After five years in Syracuse, Carneal moved to Springfield, Massachusetts, in 1950 and called the games –from the ballpark at home and through re-creations for road games—for the Springfield Cubs of the International League. His first broadcasts for the Cubs were from spring training in Haines City, Florida. "The Cubs' stadium was a few miles south of Highway 28 in a rather swampy area," Carneal recalled. "One day Ben Taylor, a young prospect trying to make the team, was running in the outfield and stumbled over an alligator. That's the fastest I've ever seen anyone run off the field."

Even more memorable to Carneal than an alligator in the outfield was his trip to spring training. On his way to Florida, he stopped in Richmond and met Katherine Meredith, a Richmond native who was living in Atlanta at the time and was back in her hometown visiting her aunt. Kathy and Herb had never met before, but once an introduction was made, they hit it off. Kathy visited Springfield that summer and was in the studio as Herb did a re-creation of a game. The crew always stood during the seventh-inning stretch, and as they did, Herb produced a ring and proposed. "Kathy and I were married on September 12 of that year, right after the Cubs' season ended. When I started broadcasting games in the majors, where the season extends longer than in the minors, I was never free on our anniversary. Years later, when I was with the Twins, someone asked what we did on our anniversary. I said, 'Every other year, when the Twins are at home on September 12, Kathy has a real treat. She gets to go to a ballgame.'"

While in Springfield, Carneal continued announcing college football for the Atlantic Refining Company. He also got his first shot at hockey, doing games for the Springfield Indians of the American Hockey League.

After the 1953 baseball season, Carneal landed a job with KYW in Philadelphia to announce different sports. Major-league baseball wasn't part of the plan, but when the Phillies and Athletics expanded their television coverage, they needed another announcer for radio and Carneal got his chance. He became the swing man, announcing home games on WIBG for the A's and WFIL for the Phillies. The arrangement ended after one season when the Athletics moved to Kansas City. Carneal said, "I still had a good sports job with KYW, but I was hooked on announcing baseball."

He stayed in Philadelphia through 1956, when a sponsor shift in Baltimore created an opening with the Orioles. During a time when sponsors called the shots on announcers, National Brewing Company switched its sponsorship from the Orioles to the Washington Senators. Chuck Thompson moved with the company to Washington, and Carneal was hired by the new sponsor, Gunther Brewing Company, to work with Ernie Harwell in Baltimore.

"When he [Harwell] took me under his wing in 1957, I learned a lot about baseball and other aspects of life. In Cleveland, on my first road trip with a baseball club, a night game was scheduled, but it rained all afternoon. At 4:30 Ernie phoned to tell me the game had been postponed, but at 5:00 he took me out to the stadium anyway for the pregame meal in the press room. 'No sense letting all that good food go to waste,' he said."

Another sponsor shakeup with the Orioles after the 1961 season left Carneal out of a job. Fortunately for him, an opportunity came up in Minnesota.

Actually, Carneal had two opportunities in Minnesota. He was hired by CBS Television to announce Minnesota Vikings games. (At the time, CBS assigned broadcast crews to each individual National Football League team.) He was also hired to join the Minnesota Twins broadcast crew for 1962.

Carneal worked with Ray Scott and Halsey Hall, and the three covered all the games on radio and television. Scott left the crew after the 1966 season and was replaced by Merle Harmon. The three continued on radio and television through 1969. After that, the Twins had separate broadcast crews to handle the duties. In 1970 Carneal still switched between the two media, but in 1971 he began working exclusively on radio.

He had a variety of partners through the years. Frank Quilici, after being fired as Twins manager, moved into the booth with Carneal in 1976. In the 1980s Joe Angel spent a few years with Carneal, who recalled his partner sometimes being too colorful. "Angel, who became my broadcast partner in 1984, liked to manage from the broadcasting booth, and some of his attempts at humor didn't go over well with Midwestern listeners," related Carneal in *Hi Everybody!* "Once at Yankee Stadium the message board announced that the next night would be Latin American Night. Joe read the message on the air and added, 'I wonder what they're going to give away for Latin American Night—hubcaps?' On another occasion he read some information on a pitcher from Jamaica, New York. Joe said, 'Jamaica? No, just shook hands.'"

Angel lasted three years with the Twins before moving on. In 1987 Carneal got a partner, John Gordon, who would be with him the rest of his career. Carneal remained the lead announcer, calling the beginnings and endings of games while Gordon covered the middle innings. Carneal ceded another inning, the seventh, after Kathy died in June 2000. At the Metrodome, Kathy had a seat below the broadcast booth. In keeping with his seventh-inning-stretch proposal to her 50 years earlier, Herb made a point of looking to her in the middle of the seventh inning, and they waved to one another. Carneal told the story at Kathy's funeral and, upon returning to the broadcast booth, found that he couldn't look down to her seat in the seventh inning. From that point on, he announced the first three innings of Twins games and didn't resume until the eighth inning.

In 1996 Carneal received the Ford Frick Award from the Baseball Hall of Fame. In 2001 he was inducted into the Minnesota Twins Hall of Fame.

"Announcers who cover games that are nationally broadcast should remain neutral, but since I'm the announcer for just one team, I think it's okay to indicate that I'm pulling for the Twins," Carneal wrote in his autobiography. "Although listeners can detect more excitement in my voice when the Twins are doing well, I'm not a cheerleader on the air."

Carneal's friendly and familiar delivery stayed a part of Twins baseball, although when he hit 70, he had to cut back at times. A heart-valve replacement in 1993 caused him to miss more than two months of the season. As he approached his 80s, Carneal scaled back and began working only a portion of home games.

"I think I'd have trouble giving up announcing completely," he said in 1995. "I want to keep going as long as the fans want to listen to me." The fans wanted to listen to him, and Carneal continued on the air for the rest of his life.

He was in the Twins' plans for the 2007 season, but he had health problems that winter and spent six weeks in the hospital with edema. On April 1, the day before the Twins' first game of the season, he died at the age of 83. He was survived by his daughter, Terri, and a grandson, Matthew.

Judd Zulgad, writing of his death in the *Minneapolis Star Tribune*, said Carneal could "never be called flashy or a character, but he combined his slight Southern drawl with a low-key approach that never made him seem bigger than the broadcast."

Zulgad's colleague at the newspaper, Patrick Reusse, concurred. "He left the happy screams to us. … What Herb Carneal did was describe precisely what was occurring in front of him and allow us to react. When you consider hysterical play-by-play is now often the norm, Herbie deserves lasting admiration for the trust he placed in all of us."

SOURCES

Much of the material in this article is derived from *Hi Everybody!* by Herb Carneal with Stew Thornley (Minneapolis: Nodin Press, 1996). Unless indicated otherwise, all quotations attributed to Carneal are from this book.

Reusse, Patrick, "Generations of Twins Fans Lose a Distinctive Voice of Summer," *Minneapolis Star Tribune*, April 2, 2007, 1C.

Zulgad, Judd, "Hello to a New Season, Goodbye to an Old Friend," *Minneapolis Star Tribune*, April 2, 2007, 1A.

Halsey Hall

BY STEW THORNLEY

HOLLER "HOLY COW!" IN THE Eastern United States and people might think of Phil Rizzuto, the New York Yankees' shortstop-turned-broadcaster, while a cry of "Holy Cow!" in Chicago brings Harry Caray to mind. In the Upper Midwest, though, "Holy Cow!" remains synonymous with Halsey Hall, who, if not the first to use the expression on a baseball broadcast, was at least using it before Rizzuto or Caray.

One of the most beloved sports and media personalities Minnesota has ever known, Hall was known to fans who grew up in the state in the 1960s as the color analyst on radio and television broadcasts for the Minnesota Twins.

However, Hall's career—as an announcer as well as a writer—went back well before the Twins came to Minnesota. He was a newspaperman first and later combined it with other sidelines, including writing, public speaking, and sports officiating.

Hall was a man of many trademarks. For many, a mention of his name conjures up images of green onions, cigars, and glasses full of scotch. Others, though, think of stories when they think of Halsey Hall—stories told about him and the tales told by him. He was the consummate raconteur.

For many fans in the 1960s, the best part of a Twins game was a rain delay. That's because Hall filled the time with stories of baseball from an earlier era and of the colorful characters who had played for the Minneapolis Millers and St. Paul Saints. During rain delays, 'Halsey was in demand from the opposing team's broadcast crew, as well. They put him on their stations and, as a result, Hall developed a following in other American League cities.

Just as Hall could tell stories, there were many stories told about him. Several revolve around his love of distilled beverages and the satchel full of liquor bottles that he lugged along on road trips. If asked about the contents of his bag, he would say it contained reference books. "If that was the case," said Dave Mona, who covered the Twins for the *Minneapolis Tribune* in the late 1960s, "they were the only reference books I ever knew of that clinked."

Another former colleague, Joe Soucheray, said Hall had so many bottles in his satchel that when he stepped off a plane he sounded like a glockenspiel. And then there was the time a cub reporter asked the venerable

A sports reporting and radio pioneer, Hall broadcast sports in the Twins Cities from the 1920s until the early 1970s. He was part of the Twins' original broadcast team in 1961 and remained with the crew until 1972. (Photo courtesy of WCCO Radio, Minneapolis).

Mr. Hall why he bothered carrying his own liquor; after all, every town they visited had a bar. "My boy," Hall replied, "you never know when you'll run into a local election."

Some Hall stories illustrate his irreverent nature, such as the manner in which he once described the arrival of the Michigan Wolverines onto the gridiron for a game against the Minnesota Gophers. "Michigan comes onto the field in blue jerseys and maize pants. And how they got into Mae's pants, I'll never know."

There was also his fear of flying. Hall spent a lot of time studying train schedules, hoping to find a way to reach his destination without leaving the ground. He never did warm up to the idea of flying, nor did he endear himself to airline agents when he would approach a ticket counter and ask for "One chance to Chicago." His friends didn't help to ease his anxieties, either. Once, prior to a flight, they arranged to have a pilot walk past Hall with a seeing-eye dog.

How did this captivating character get to be the way he was? Heredity may have played a part in the interests and aptitudes that Hall was to develop.

The Hall family tree is a fascinating one. Many of Halsey's ancestors were prominent citizens in their own right. His maternal grandfather was a distinguished Missouri judge and his mother, Mary Hall, a noted Shakespearean actress. In the 1920s Mary Hall was described as the "greatest stock actress alive today."

Halsey had little contact with his mother throughout his life. His parents were divorced when he was a baby, and he was raised by his father's side of the family. On his father's side was a long line of newspapermen. Halsey's father, Smith B. Hall, was a publicist and newspaper reporter who chronicled the growth of Minneapolis. His great-uncle, Harlan P. Hall, was a co-founder of the *St. Paul Dispatch*.

With this lineage, it's hardly surprising that Hall was born with ink in his veins. He entered the newspaper profession upon his discharge from the Navy in 1919. His first byline appeared in the *Minneapolis Tribune* in November of that year. Hall wrote for several newspapers in the Twin Cities on both sides of the Mississippi. He jumped to the *St. Paul Pioneer Press* in 1922; a few years later he came back to Minneapolis to join the sports staff of the *Journal*. After the *Journal* was purchased by the *Minneapolis Star*, Hall's byline appeared in both the *Star* and *Tribune*, which were operated by the same ownership group.

He had a variety of columns through the years; the two longest-running were "Here's How" and "It's a Fact." For many years he concluded his columns with the nostalgic "Do You Remember?" feature that was unrelated to sports. A couple of examples:

"Do you remember when kids went swimming in the raw in the creek where the Glenwood Chalet now stands?"

"Do you remember when you opened a bottle of pop by giving the cap a resounding smack to release it?"

Hall's descriptive and highly colorful writing style was enjoyed by fans not just in the Twin Cities but across the country. On several occasions, his articles were included in national publications that recognized the best sports stories of the year.

Hall definitely had a way with words. It was particularly evident when he wrote about his "Celestial All-Star Team," a group he would make reference to when writing about the passing of a baseball great. On August 16, 1948, Hall reported on the team's newest addition, Babe Ruth:

"There's a one-two cleanup punch on the Celestial All-Stars now. Once again George Herman (Babe) Ruth is hitting ahead of Lou Gehrig. With the passing of the Babe, this peerless tandem of batting torture is reunited in pastures where all infields are green and from where they may look down upon current mortals weakly trying to emulate their feats. ..."

At the same time Hall was writing for the newspaper, he was pursuing a full-time career in sports announcing. He started in 1923 with the Jack Dempsey-Tommy Gibbons heavyweight title fight in Shelby, Montana. Hall called the fight not from Shelby, but from a

The WCCO broadcasting team: Ray Scott, Halsey Hall, and Herb Carneal (Photo courtesy of WCCO Radio, Minneapolis).

second-floor window of the Pioneer Press building in St. Paul. Because Gibbons was from St. Paul (he later served as Ramsey County sheriff for 23 years), there was great local interest in the bout. Hall re-created the action from a Western Union wire and delivered a blow-by-blow account through a megaphone to the fight fans gathered on the street below.

Hall soon took to announcing in a more conventional manner — on radio instead of out a second-floor window — and his voice became familiar one to people throughout the Upper Midwest. His friendly delivery and contagious laugh was once described in a *Sports Illustrated* article as "redolent of happy days at Grandpa's house."

Hall had already established a following as a writer, but his popularity soared after he moved into broadcasting. In fact, his fame was so lasting that in 1979 he was voted as the top sportscaster of the 1970s in Minnesota — even though the poll was taken two years after his death.

Just as he had done with newspaper work, Hall jumped back and forth between radio stations. He started with WCCO and helped that station establish a national reputation it enjoys to this day as one of the giants of the industry.

In 1935 he jumped to crosstown rival KSTP but nine years later returned to WCCO and began a five-minute sports show that aired at 10:25 each evening. Hall shared a half-hour news block with Cedric Adams. So popular was the duo that when their segment ended every evening, airline pilots reported that they could see the lights in homes darken in droves throughout WCCO's listening area.

In addition to his sports show, Hall did a great deal of play-by-play announcing. In 1934 he hooked on with a pair of championship teams. One was Bernie Bierman's Minnesota Gopher football team, which was beginning a string of three straight national titles. He loved the Gophers, and it was Hall who came up with the now familiar nickname of Golden Gophers. He also started broadcasting games for the Minneapolis Millers, a minor-league baseball team that was in the midst of winning three American Association pennants in four years.

Hall called the play-by-play of the Millers' home games from his familiar perch in the press box at Nicollet Park. When the team went on the road, though, Hall broadcast the games from the radio studio, re-creating the action from a Western Union wire, just as he had done with the Dempsey-Gibbons fight.

"A recording of a stadium crowd would murmur in the background, its volume rising or fading to accommodate the changing action of play as Hall described it," recalled another longtime Minnesota broadcaster, Dave Moore, in his book, *A Member of the Family*.[1] Behind Halsey's voice, a makeshift sound effects gadget created the sound of bat meeting ball. In later years, first Dick Enroth and then Ray Christensen would hone and perfect the magic to an even more polished state than Halsey had.

"But Halsey was the only practitioner at the time and he was wondrous!" said Dave Moore. "He put you right there in that game!"

A full-time writing and broadcasting career would be more than enough to fill a person's time, but Hall was able to fit in a couple of other sidelines into his schedule. He was one of the area's most highly regarded referees of football and basketball games. He officiated primarily at the high-school and college level, although he also worked a handful of games in the National Football League on the two occasions that Minneapolis had a team in the NFL in the 1920s.

On some occasions Hall combined his roles as referee and reporter. After officiating a game, he'd bang out a story of the contest that would appear in the newspaper the next day.

Hall also stayed busy as a public speaker. He became the area's leading toastmaster, regaling hundreds of audiences throughout the region as a speaker and as a master of ceremonies. Hubert Humphrey, himself a prolific orator, once called Hall "one of the few men who has given more speeches in Minnesota than I have."

In 1961 Hall became a member of the original broadcast crew for the Minnesota Twins. For many years his partners on Twins broadcasts were Herb Carneal and Ray Scott. They both loved Hall even though they may not of been too fond of some of his habits — particularly his copious consumption of green onions and his cigars.

"Halsey always enjoyed a good cigar," Carneal once said. "Unfortunately, those weren't the kind he smoked."

Hall's cigar caused all kinds of discomfort for his broadcast partners. During a game in Chicago in 1968, his cigar ash ignited a large mass of ticker tape paper that had piled up on the press-box floor. Smoke drifted upward, and Hall turned to see his sport coat, which was draped over his chair, in flames. The fire was brought under control, but not before a large hole had been burned in his jacket.

News of the conflagration reached Minnesota and, when the Twins returned from their road trip, the 3M Company of St. Paul presented Hall with an asbestos sport coat. Twins catcher Jerry Zimmerman said, "Halsey's the only man I know who can turn a sports coat into a blazer."

His colleagues maintain that life with Halsey was always an adventure — both on and off the air. Many fans recall his mixed-up description of a promotion at the ballpark in which all those attending received a free pair of pantyhose. "In promotions here tonight," he announced, "it's pantywaist night."

Herb Carneal's favorite story of Hall is of the night the pair, along with Merle Harmon, who had replaced Ray Scott on the broadcast crew, went out to eat at a fancy restaurant in Baltimore. When the check was delivered to their table, Hall was taken aback by the total. He called the waiter over and asked him to re-add the figures. "What are you trying to do?" he said. "Put the chef on a pension?" The waiter pulled out his pencil, did a little addition, and said, "No, sir, this is the correct amount." If that wasn't enough, Hall then reached for his wallet and discovered it wasn't there. He probably had left it back at the hotel, but the combination of events was too much for Hall. Before Carneal or Harmon could stop him, Hall stood up and began tapping his water glass with his spoon.

"Ladies and gentlemen," he announced to the patrons. "I want you to know this is the biggest clip joint I've ever been in. Not only do they pad the check, but they also pick your pocket!"

Hall left the Twins broadcast crew after the 1972 season, but his name remained synonymous with baseball in the area thanks to Hal Greenwood, president of Midwest Federal Savings and Loan, the prime sponsor of Twins' broadcasts at that time. Greenwood hired Hall to be the Ambassador of Baseball with duties that included presiding over pregame ceremonies at Met Stadium.

Hall received numerous awards through the years, but his greatest may have come in 1966 with a testimonial dinner at which more than 1,700 people turned out to honor him. Bill Veeck, the former baseball executive, was one of the speakers on the program and commented on the size of the gathering. Veeck referred to his days as owner of the hapless St. Louis Browns and said, "With this kind of a crowd, we would have played a doubleheader!"[2]

Besides "Holy Cow!" another favorite saying of Hall's was "Same house, same wife, same suit –must be the gypsy in me!" This expression may well have summed up the simple approach to life he followed away from the public eye. While he may have owned more than one suit in his life, Halsey and his wife, Sula, did live in the same house on Alabama Avenue in St. Louis Park, Minnesota, for 55 years.

And for most of those years, Hall did not have an unlisted phone number. This did result in a certain amount of inconvenience for him, and Hall could count on an occasional post-midnight phone call from drunks trying to settle a sports bet before the bars closed. Hall would let the callers know how angry he was at their waking him up, but he'd also answer their question before hanging up.

Another passion of Hall's was poetry. His ability as a wordsmith manifested itself in many other manners and mediums than just through sports articles in the newspaper. "He thought words could solve anything," said his daughter, and Hall often used poetry as a way of dealing with problems, whether they were family difficulties or health problems.

The subjects of his poems could cover cheerier topics as well, such as sports and soap operas. Hall was an avid soap-opera fan and often said the greatest acting in the world could be seen on the daytime serials because, as he explained, "Every day is a brand-new performance for these people."

Hall went to great lengths to watch his soaps. When he and Sula drove to Florida for spring training each year, he brought along a battery-operated television set. It wasn't unusual for Halsey and Sula to pull off the road around 1 o'clock in the afternoon, hop in the back seat, and try to pull in a television signal.

After leaving the Twins broadcast crew in 1972, Hall continued to watch a lot of baseball. He was presented with a lifetime pass from the American League and still spent time at Met Stadium, watching the Twins.

In his autumn years, however, Hall's health began to fail. He had lengthy hospital stays in 1974 and 1975 because of heart troubles.

In January of 1976, his wife was injured in an accident at the Radisson Hotel. While ascending the stairs to the dais for a testimonial dinner for Hubert Humphrey, the Halls fell. Sula cracked her head on the floor and had to undergo brain surgery. She survived, but never fully recovered, and finally had to be put in a nursing home.

The final months for Hall were lonely ones as he rattled around in his house without Sula. On December 30, 1977, Halsey joined the Celestial All-Stars. He died of a heart attack at his home in St. Louis Park at the age of 79.

Halsey was gone, but his stories live on, as do the honors. In 1985 Minnesota members of the Society for American Baseball Research organized themselves into a regional chapter and named themselves after Hall.

In November of 1989, Hall was inducted into the Minnesota Sports Hall of Fame.

But the greatest encomiums are the memories that remain in the minds of those who knew him best. Upon Hall's death, Dick Cullum, his newspaper colleague and close friend, provided what may be the most fitting eulogy: "Halsey Hall laughed his way through life, and he kept the rest of us laughing, too."[3]

Note

A version of this biography appeared in the book *Minnesotans in Baseball*, edited by Stew Thornley (Nodin, 2009).

SOURCES

Newspaper accounts of Halsey Hall's columns and articles; interviews and correspondence with friends and family members, most notably his daughter, Sue Hall Kennedy, in February 1990.

Airline pilots seeing lights in homes darken throughout WCCO's listening area: "Halsey Hall Puffs Past Fifty-Yard Line" by Ron D. Johnson, *Minnesota Motorist*, January 1969.

1966 testimonial dinner and Hubert Humphrey quote: "Minnesotans Pack Hall, Raise Cheers In Salute to Halsey," by Max Nichols, *The Sporting News*, July 30, 1966.

Play-by-play description: *Sports Illustrated* quotation: "And Here, to Bring You the Play By Play," by Jerry Kirshenbaum, *Sports Illustrated*, September 13, 1971, 32.

Voted top sportscaster of the 1970s: "1970s TV Poll: Local Sportscaster," by John Carman, *Minneapolis Star*, October 15, 1979, 2C.

NOTES

1. Dave Moore, *A Member of the Family: Letters and Reflections* (Minneapolis-St. Paul: The Lazear Press, 1986), 87.
2. *Suburban Life*, July 17, 1966
3. *Minneapolis Tribune*, January 1, 1978, 2C

Ray Scott

BY STEW THORNLEY

"NOT ALL VETERAN FANS REMEMBER him. Credit it to the fact that he was simply too good at what he did, which was use his voice with the range and subtlety of a concert violinist," wrote *TV Guide* of Ray Scott. "CBS's National Football League coverage didn't make a move to any big game without him in the late 1950s and early sixties."[1]

Widely known as the voice of the Green Bay Packers for a decade and the play-by-play announcer for four Super Bowls, Scott brought his deliberate demeanor and the same cadence, clarity, and conciseness to baseball that had already become his trademark on football broadcasts. Longtime Minneapolis and St. Paul sports columnist and baseball observer Patrick Reusse said, "Everyone knows he was a great f***ing football announcer, but not everyone remembers he was a great f***ing baseball announcer."

Ray Scott was born on June 17, 1919, in Pennsylvania to William and Ada (Long) Scott. He had a younger brother, Hal, and at least one other sibling, a sister, Virginia.[2] He attended high school in Connellsville, Pennsylvania, graduating in 1936. Along the way he tried to follow the gridiron path of other western Pennsylvania young men. Connellsville became notable in football in part because of the Lujack brothers, including Johnny, who would later win the Heisman Trophy at Notre Dame. Though he tried, Scott wasn't up to the Lujack standards. "I tried to play," he told Reusse in 1996, "and was kindly told by several coaches that I was lacking speed, size, and ability. Thanks to those coaches, I became a sportscaster."

His first job in broadcasting, in Johnstown, Pennsylvania, included other duties, including writing copy and selling radio time to sponsors. He also got his first shot at sportscasting, calling high-school football and basketball games. After serving more than four years in the Army during World War II, Scott returned to Johnstown and resumed his radio career. Later he moved to Pittsburgh, where he did the play-by-play for Carnegie Tech and University of Pittsburgh football and then worked for an advertising agency while announcing sports on the side. Scott recognized the rise of television in sports and worked his way into broadcasting National Football League games for the DuMont Television Network starting in 1953.

In January 1956 Scott was assigned to work with Bill Stern on the ABC telecast of the Sugar Bowl between Pittsburgh and Georgia Tech. Stern, who was dealing with an addiction to painkillers, arrived at the stadium as the game was about to start. He was in no condition to be on the air, leaving Scott to handle the broadcast duties. "While it was a terribly dark day for Stern,"

Scott broadcast Twins games from 1961 to 1966, and called the 1965 World Series for NBC television. (Photo courtesy of WCCO Radio, Minneapolis).

wrote David J. Halberstam in *Sports on New York Radio: A Play-by-Play History*, "it was a sparkling start for Ray Scott, whose career rocketed after that Sugar Bowl performance."

That fall, CBS Television hired Scott. At the time, CBS designated a set of announcers for each of the teams, and Scott got the assignment to work the Green Bay Packers games. At the time the Packers were a poor team, but in 1959 Vince Lombardi arrived as coach, and the Packers became the dominant team in football through much of the 1960s. "Scott's deep-throated, concise descriptions of the Packer games were as much a trademark of the team to the television viewing public as [Bart] Starr, Paul Hornung, Jimmy Taylor, Jerry Kramer, and all the rest of the Packers," wrote Maury Allen in *Voices of Sport*.

Scott got his first shot at baseball in 1957. NBC was carrying the Cubs-Pirates game in Pittsburgh on June 15 and needed a fill-in for Lindsey Nelson, who was covering a golf tournament in Toledo, Ohio. Scott got the call and worked with Leo Durocher as his color sidekick on the game. It was his first experience announcing baseball, but he was a fan and hoped to do more. "I loved baseball," Scott said in a 1990 interview. "I probably attended more Pirate games than any other nonbroadcaster."

After the 1960 season, the Washington Senators moved to Minnesota and became the Twins. Bob Wolff was the only member of the Senators broadcast crew to come with the team. A Minneapolis writer and announcer, Halsey Hall, was hired to do the color on the broadcasts, and Scott was under consideration for the third and final spot. Scott had done some work for Sports Network Incorporated (later the Hughes Sports Network) and was recommended by people there for the Twins job. Hamm's Beer was one of the key sponsors of Twins broadcasts on WCCO Radio and WTCN Television. Art Lund of the Campbell-Mithun advertising agency handled the Hamm's account and had a relationship with people at Sports Network.

"Somehow my name came up," said Scott, "but to never have done baseball [except for the one game in 1957] turned out to be an insurmountable hurdle. [Twins owner] Calvin Griffith was involved in the decision and said, 'Let's hear a tape of him doing baseball.' I got the rosters of the players involved in a game between the Orioles and Senators and went to a friend who had a recording studio in Pittsburgh. With sound effects, I did two or three innings of an Orioles-Senators game. Apparently, it met Calvin's okay, because I was hired."

Scott settled in nicely with Hall, who was more than 20 years older. "I had a rapport from the very first," Scott said of Hall, describing him as "a kindly man," and adding, "It was obvious that he knew and loved the sport of baseball." In 1962 Wolff left the Twins broadcast team and was replaced by Herb Carneal. Scott, Hall, and Carneal became the familiar voices for a team that rose in the standings and reached the World Series within a few years.

The trio worked both television and radio. On the 50 telecasts each year, Scott and Carneal split up, each covering a portion of the game on WCCO and WTCN. Hall bounced back and forth between the booths on televised games. For the radio-only games, all were in the booth at the same time, but they never talked over one another. A radio clip of the final inning of Jack Kralick's no-hitter for the Twins in August 1962 provides a glimpse of the crew's style. With Scott handling the play-by-play at the time, Carneal sat nearby and helped provide information but did not lend his voice to the broadcast. Hall chimed in only on a few occasions, a contrast to the constant chatter now provided by color analysts.

The group stayed together through the 1966 season, when Scott left. "I left baseball and the Twins in 1966 to try and resolve a family situation," Scott explained. "Except for that I never would have left baseball. If I'd been forced to make a choice between football and baseball, my choice would have always been baseball."

For a time during the 1960s, both Scott and his younger brother, Hal, were sports announcers in the Twin

Cities. Hal had worked in radio in Johnstown and Pittsburgh and came to Minnesota for to visit Ray in 1962. He discovered that WCCO Television was looking for a sportscaster. By the time Hal's visit was over, he had the job. He was the main sports anchor for WCCO until 1980, when he injured his vocal cords in a fall on the stairs at the television station; he hit his throat on the end of the bannister.

After leaving the Twins, Scott continued announcing National Football League games and also golf tournaments. "I did basically four sports," he said of his career, with baseball and basketball being the other two.

After CBS discontinued the practice of assigning specific announcers to particular teams following the 1967 season, Scott became the network's lead announcer for its NFL broadcasts. Paul Christman teamed with Scott until his death in March 1970, and then Pat Summerall became Scott's partner.

Scott got back into baseball broadcasts with the Washington Senators (an expansion team that started when the previous Senators moved to Minnesota) and later came back and announced Twins games on television in 1973 and 1975. (By this time the Twins had separate announcing crews for television and radio.)

CBS and Scott parted in 1974. "Reasons for Scott's exit are difficult to put in focus. But reportedly neither side was sorry about the parting," wrote Jack Craig in *The Sporting News*. To author Curt Smith, Scott said the reason was "because I choose to speak out against the growing tendency to focus on the announcer, not the event, and because I'm not afraid to deplore 'show biz broadcasting' and athletes-turned-announcers who have no talent whatsoever."

Scott did local football broadcasts on radio, first for the Kansas City Chiefs and then for the expansion Tampa Bay Buccaneers, who lost their first 26 games in 1976 and 1977. He had his last stint as a baseball announcer in 1976 and 1977 for the Milwaukee Brewers, working with Bob Uecker and Merle Harmon. (Harmon had filled Scott's spot on Twins broadcasts and worked in Minnesota from 1967 to 1969.)

Scott eventually came back to Minnesota with his second wife, Bonnie. (Scott and his first wife, Eda, had five children: Sharon, Michael, Bill, Patrick, and Preston.) In a 1990 interview, Scott told a story that revealed the itinerant nature of his life, particularly in recent years. "I'm a jazz fan and have quite a collection — the only thing I saved from my first marriage," he said. "They've been in big cartons. We haven't unpacked them in our last four moves. They haven't been out of the carton in about six years. We're hoping our next move, probably in the next year, will be a permanent move to a house. We're going to stay here."

Scott remained what he always was, a sportscaster. He conducted a nightly radio sports talk show live from a restaurant he owned in downtown Minneapolis and continued the show from other venues after his establishment went out of business. Health problems, including prostate cancer and a leg infection that nearly caused an amputation, slowed him, but in 1996 he got involved in a nationally syndicated radio show. The talk show had rotating hosts, including Scott one night a week, on the SportsAmerica Radio Network.

SportsAmerica didn't last long, and, unfortunately, neither did Scott. Other health issues, including triple-bypass heart surgery, a kidney failure that resulted in a transplant, knee surgery, and hip replacements, had plagued him in the 1990s, and Scott died in Minneapolis on March 23, 1998, at the age of 78.

Scott was twice named National Sportscaster of the Year by the National Sportscasters and Sportswriters Association and was inducted into its Hall of Fame in 1982. After his death he was elected to the American Sportscasters Association Hall of Fame in 1998, was the recipient of the Pete Rozelle Radio-Television Award from the Pro Football Hall of Fame, and was inducted into the Green Bay Packers Hall of Fame.

In *Voices of the Game*, Smith wrote of Scott in the announcer's words: "I've never tried to draw all attention to myself. I never believed in trying to please the whims of a producer or director. I just considered myself a conduit to provide the fan with something he couldn't obtain himself. My primary concern was not making Ray Scott a household word,' as he became exactly that."

SOURCES

Allen, Maury, *Voices of Sport* (New York: Grosset & Dunlap, 1971), 207-209.

Halberstam, David J., *Sports on New York Radio: A Play-by-Play History* (Lincolnwood, Illinois: Masters Press, 1999), 59-61.

Smith, Curt, *Voices of the Game* (South Bend, Indiana: Diamond Communications, Inc., 1987), 318-321.

Adams, Jim, "Hal Scott, WCCO Sportscaster and Mentor," *Star Tribune,* Minneapolis, September 24, 2010, B6.

Craig, Jack, "Big Turnover in Telecast Teams," *The Sporting News,* September 21, 1974, 58.

Millea, John, "Legendary Sports Broadcaster Ray Scott Dies," *Star Tribune,* Minneapolis, March 24, 1998, B7.

Reusse, Patrick, "Ray Scott's Still Making the Calls," *Star Tribune,* Minneapolis, August 16, 1996, C2.

Shepherd, Don, "'Seens' & Sounds," *Augusta Chronicle,* June 15, 1957.

Author interview with Ray Scott, February 27, 1990.

Author conversation with Patrick Reusse, February 21, 2014.

Broadcast of ninth inning of Kansas City at Minnesota game, August 26, 1962, WCCO Radio.

NOTES

1   The date of the *TV Guide* issue with comments on Scott is not known, but it was referenced on page 319 of Curt Smith's *Voices of the Game*.

2   Scott's death certificate, which lists his name as Ray E. Scott and provides the source of his parents' names, has only Pennsylvania for his birthplace. Some sources list Johnstown, Pennsylvania, the location of his first job in radio, as Scott's birthplace, although he graduated from high school in Connellsville, Pennsylvania, about 60 miles southwest of Johnstown. Scott's obituary, written by John Millea, in the *Star Tribune* of March 24, 1998, lists Hal and Virginia as survivors but does not indicate if Scott had had any other sisters or brothers.

Dick Gordon

BY STEVE WEST

DICK GORDON GOT HIS START BY breaking a national story when he was in college, and parlayed that into a long career as a Minnesota sportswriter. His prodigious memory enabled him to recall facts long after the event happened, and his writing, while factual, contained enough embellishment to make it entertaining for the reader.

Charles Richards "Dick" Gordon was born on January 15, 1911, in St. Paul, Minnesota, the son of Charles William Gordon (1861-1939) and Charlotte (Bishop) Gordon (1874-1960). His grandfather, Richards Gordon (1829-1911), had immigrated from Ireland in the 1840s and co-founded Gordon & Ferguson, a well-known Minnesota fur trading company. Late in the 1800s the company began the manufacture of fur clothing using the Field & Stream trademark on its products, which continues. Dick's father, Charles, took over and was running the company by the time Dick was born. Dick had an older sister, Virginia, born in 1908, who died in 1923 at the age of 15.

Because of the success of their business, the family was wealthy by the time Dick was born. He grew up in his grandfather's home, where three generations of the family lived together, along with several servants. He attended the St. Paul Academy prep school, where he was editor of the school newspaper. The headmaster of the school said that Gordon was a better writer than F. Scott Fitzgerald, who had attended the school more than a decade earlier.[1]

While in high school Dick got a job as copy boy at the *St. Paul Dispatch*, supposedly by walking in and talking himself into the job.[2] When he went to Princeton University he wrote for the student newspaper, the *Daily Princetonian*. During the US Open golf tournament at Interlachen Country Club in suburban Minneapolis in 1930, he talked to professional golfer Bobby Jones, and was able to break the story of Jones's forthcoming retirement from the game.[3] This earned Gordon the nickname Scoop, and helped as an entry point into the world of sportswriting. While at Princeton Gordon even attended the 1929 World Series, where he saw the famous game in Philadelphia between the Athletics and the Chicago Cubs in which the A's scored 10 runs in an inning to come back from an 8-0 deficit and win.[4]

After graduating from Princeton, Gordon joined the *St. Paul Pioneer Press* as a sportswriter. After a few years there, where he met and worked with many local writers and sports celebrities, he moved to Chicago

Gordon was a sportswriter for the Minneapolis Star from 1946 to 1976, covering the University of Minnesota sports, the Vikings, and Twins. (Photo courtesy of the Minneapolis Star Tribune).

in 1939, where he began writing for the *Chicago Daily News*.

When the US entered World War II, Gordon enlisted in the Marine Corps, and served in the Pacific as a combat correspondent. One of his stories, about an Army baseball team on Guadalcanal, became his first published article in *The Sporting News*.[5] After two years in combat and promotion to sergeant, he returned to Minneapolis, where he worked as a recruiter for the Marines, and where he met his future wife, Adelaide Washburn, who had taught at the University of Minnesota and worked for the Red Cross during the war. The couple married in Minneapolis on April 26, 1945, just days before the victory over Germany.

The couple had three children: Charles was born in 1946, Robert in 1951, and Richards in 1953, and they lived in St. Paul all their lives. "I worked in Minneapolis, but I always lived in St. Paul," Dick said.[6] Adelaide kept the house together while Dick traveled for work, sometimes taking the family with him but often as not going by himself. He wrote letters to his sons all his life, whether they were away at camp or after they had become adults and moved away from Minnesota.[7]

Gordon regularly took his boys to sporting events, where they met many famous athletes. His son Charlie recalled that at one baseball game he was introduced to Willie Mays, Ted Williams, and golfer Sam Snead.[8]

"He would be the first to admit that he was not a great athlete, but he loved sports," Gordon's son Dick said.[9] Gordon was even able to poke fun at his own sporting ability in print: "Now, Pop, don't feel badly if your son's high school efforts, on gridiron, court, rink or diamond, top your own prior performances at that level. That would be par for the course, as the author's three male offspring will be the first to point out."[10]

While Dick was working, Adelaide looked after the family and occupied her time on numerous charity boards, with organizations as diverse as the Schubert Club (a performing-arts organization, where she started a music therapy program), the Junior League, her alma mater Smith College, and church groups.

The couple played various sports together including tennis and golf, and she attended all her children's sporting events, whether Dick was able to make it or not.

At the end of the war Gordon returned to his old job as a sports reporter for the *Chicago Daily News*. He soon left there, though, because during his time away at war, "Some 4-Fer (military reject) stole my job."[11] He returned home to Minnesota, joining the *Minneapolis Star* as a sportswriter. He stayed there from 1946 to 1976 and continued his side work writing for numerous national publications. Over the years Gordon wrote many articles for *The Sporting News* and *Baseball Digest*, starting in the 1940s and continuing through the 1970s. He also became one of the earliest writers for the new national weekly magazine *Sports Illustrated* in the 1950s.

Gordon covered local sports including the Minnesota Twins, the Vikings, and his favorite subject the University of Minnesota Golden Gophers football team. "He was a walking history of University of Minnesota sports," said fellow writer Will Shapira.[12] Before professional sports came to Minnesota, Gordon said, the Gophers were "the only game in town. From when practice started the day after Labor Day until the bowl games, Gopher football was the big sports story every day. We only took time out for the World Series."[13] He would regularly write about college football, including the history of the Little Brown Jug, the trophy fought over by the Gophers and the University of Michigan, which he called "an insignificant 35-cent crock from a Hennepin Avenue variety store."[14]

Gordon also covered national and international sports, including the 1960 Olympics in California. There he wrote about the US men's hockey team for *Sports Illustrated*. "He always considered that the true miracle on ice," Gordon's son Charlie said.[15] He presaged the modern era of sports reporting, all-access all-the-time, when he complained about not being able to talk to the athletes. "You couldn't go into the Village and you couldn't go into the locker room," he said.[16]

Gordon regularly covered baseball as a beat writer in Minneapolis, writing about the minor-league Minneapolis Millers and St. Paul Saints, and the efforts to bring a major-league team to the area, culminating in the arrival of the Minnesota Twins in 1961. He continued to write about the Twins for years afterward, and once noted that his favorite player was Harmon Killebrew. He never hid from you. If he had a bad day at the plate, he didn't try to duck the reporters after the game."[17]

Gordon's output was legendary, and his wide range of sports coverage was too. Even within a single sport he could write about many different topics. For example, with the Twins at their peak in 1964-65, he wrote several articles about the team and its players (Killebrew, Al Worthington, Tony Oliva), but also composed a profile of Walter Alston, a comparison of fathers and sons in the major leagues, a discussion of whether Luke Appling or Joe Cronin was the second-best shortstop of all time, and a look at shortstops in the majors and how their job had changed. This range of articles showing both statistical and historical knowledge was in many ways a precursor to the modern baseball researcher.

Gordon was elected vice chairman of the Twin Cities chapter of the Baseball Writers Association of America in 1969 and 1971 and chair in 1972, and in 1974 he was honored as Minnesota Sportswriter of the Year by the National Sportscasters and Sportswriters Association.

His greatest quality was his memory, and the ability to recall long-ago events. "I miss him terribly, but what I most miss is all the information he knew," son Richards Gordon said of his father. "He had an unbelievable memory."[18] He took this knowledge, added in great detail from his conversations with players and officials, and created well-rounded stories that involved the reader at every step. "Gordo's game stories were exemplary. He would featurize them — he was ingenious at digging up things," said Will Shapira.[19]

During the 1970s Gordon wrote about the possibility of a new stadium for the Vikings and Twins, one of several Minnesota writers who saw the need for the area to develop, and he also wrote about social issues involving sports, including a 1974 story about the implementation of Title IX at the University of Minnesota.[20]

After retiring in 1976, Gordon wrote special pieces for the *Minneapolis Star* until 1982 and continued writing for the *Highland Villager* in St. Paul in his retirement. He never stopped writing, although in his final column for the *Villager* he wrote, "This column may well be my last contribution to the *Villager*. Age 96 and 11 months seems an appropriate time to quit hitting - and missing — the keys (as in typewriter, not computer)."[21]

Adelaide died in January 2007, and after 61 years together Dick obviously missed her. "I hate being alone. I hate it!" he said.[22] He lived the last part of his life in an assisted-living center in St. Paul, and died on December 8, 2008, aged 97. He left a large family, and a long legacy of great writing that covered a wide range of Minnesota sports history.

NOTES

1 "Charles Richards Gordon," obituary, *Minneapolis Star Tribune*, April 19, 2009.

2 Don Boxmeyer, "At age 96, newsman finally stops his own press," *St. Paul Pioneer Press*, January 28, 2008.

3 "Bobby Jones Praises Professional Golf For Preventing Rise of False Amateurs," *The Daily Princetonian*, September 29, 1930.

4 Charley Walters, "Fans urge contract extension for Minnesota Gophers football coach Tim Brewster," *St. Paul Pioneer Press*, October 16, 2008.

5 Dick Gordon, "Long Pacific Win Streak Wrecked by Leathernecks," *The Sporting News*, November 12, 1943: 12.

6 Boxmeyer.

7 "Charles Richards Gordon," obituary, *Minneapolis Star Tribune*, April 19, 2009.

8 Joe Christensen, "Dick Gordon, longtime Twin Cities sportswriter, dies at 97," *Minneapolis Star Tribune*, December 8, 2008.

9 John Brewer, "Twin Cities' sportswriter was 'a walking history,' mentor," *St. Paul Pioneer Press*, December 13, 2008.

10 Dick Gordon, "The Second Generation Doesn't Take First Honors," *Baseball Digest*, March 1964, 35.

11 Boxmeyer.

12 Brewer.

13 Boxmeyer.

14 Boxmeyer.

15 Christensen.

16 Seamus O'Coughlin, *Squaw Valley Gold: American Hockey's Olympic Odyssey* (Lincoln, Nebraska: iUniverse, 2001).

17 Boxmeyer.

18 Brewer.

19 Brewer.

20 Dick Gordon, "U Plans No Women's Sports Scholarships," *Minneapolis Star*, November 14, 1974.

21 Boxmeyer.

22 Boxmeyer.

Max Nichols

BY STEVE WEST

MAX NICHOLS KNELT IN AN on-deck circle beside Jackie Robinson, had his picture taken with Pee Wee Reese, and watched Satchel Paige throw strikes over a matchbook—and all that by the age of 15. As a sportswriter he would meet hundreds of players, write thousands of columns about them, cast the worst vote in MVP history, and preside over induction day at the Baseball Hall of Fame. And all with the honesty and integrity that would bring him many rewards.

Max Joseph Nichols was born on March 5, 1934, in Oklahoma City, to Dale and Margaret Nichols. His father was an apartment manager and his mother a housewife. Max had two brothers: Gordon, three years older, and Larry, three years younger. One of Max's earliest memories was riding the streetcar with his father to Texas League Park in Oklahoma City and sitting in the bleachers to watch a game in 1941. He loved baseball, but as a teenager he hurt his arm playing shortstop, an injury that ended his dream of being a professional ballplayer. He could still write about the game, though, and that became his entry point into a lifetime of involvement in sports.

At 15, Max won an essay contest, with the prize being the job of batboy for teams visiting the Oklahoma City Indians. His first day was April 5, 1949, an exhibition game with the visiting Brooklyn Dodgers, and Max got to kneel in the on-deck circle with the subject of his essay, Jackie Robinson. The next day it was Satchel Paige and the Cleveland Indians coming to town, and during the season Max would meet former and future major leaguers. For the next four years he worked in the press box as a gofer for the writers, and watched and learned all he could about sportswriting.

While at the University of Oklahoma, where he got a BA in journalism in 1956, Nichols worked at the *Daily Oklahoman* as a sportswriter. Moving on to Columbia University in New York City, he added a master's in journalism in 1957, this time working as sports publicity director for the college. After graduation he worked for the Associated Press in New York, covering everything from tennis to horse racing to baseball, including a story about the Giants and Dodgers and their plans to move to the West Coast. After just a few months at the AP, he was drafted into the US Army, and following basic training he married his girlfriend from Oklahoma, Mary "Mickey" Conroy, before they moved to Germany for the two years he was stationed there. During his service Nichols spent his time as sports editor of the 3rd Infantry Division newspaper, and the couple had their first child, Karl,

Nichols was beat writer for the Twins throughout the 1960s and 1970s, and also covered professional football, basketball and hockey. (Photo courtesy of the Minneapolis Star Tribune).

in 1958. They had three more children back in the United States: Renata in 1960, Kelley in 1961, and Kevin in 1966.

After he got out of the service in 1959, Nichols joined the *Minneapolis Star*, which was awaiting the imminent arrival of major-league baseball to the city. When the Washington Senators moved to Minnesota in 1961, Nichols stepped into the baseball beat with the Twins. The early days with the new team were a struggle to establish their new identity, but as the team showed improvement on the field, so did Nichols in his reporting. He added correspondent for *The Sporting News* to his résumé in 1962, and eventually wrote dozens of articles for the newspaper over the years. This helped raise Nichols' profile as a writer, as did articles he wrote in 1965 for *Sport* magazine, and the appearance of the Twins in the 1965 World Series.

In 1967 Nichols took up a new position, and faced the worst time of his career. In early September he stopped being the baseball beat writer and switched over to the assistant city editor job on the *Star*, the *Tribune's* sister paper. At the end of the season he was one of the two Minnesota voters for the American League MVP, and his vote for the Twins' Cesar Tovar (.267/6/47) made him the only person not to vote for Triple Crown winner Carl Yastrzemski (.326/44/121). The outrage at this vote was immediate, and before his identity was revealed, writers across the baseball world attacked him for not voting for Yastrzemski. One of Nichols' own outlets, *The Sporting News*, wrote "[W]e believe that the BBWAA, within its own ranks, should take some action to penalize the writer for his unwise vote by banning him from ever serving again on a selection committee."[1] The paper quoted several writers as saying it was a hometown vote, and since the other voter from the Twin Cities, Arno Goethal of St. Paul, specifically noted that he had voted for Yastrzemski and put Tovar seventh, little doubt was left as to who it could be.

In November Nichols acknowledged that he had voted for Tovar and gave his reasoning, as summarized in a newspaper article. " 'It was not a hometown vote,' says Nichols. 'In my opinion, the basic idea is who is the most valuable to a team. Tovar won games at six positions. … [H]is arm, his catches and his play in both infield and outfield made him most valuable. He played in a record 164 games. My vote was not a knock at Yastrzemski. … I suppose it's a matter of the meaning of most valuable.' "[2] In a further interview, Nichols wondered about the process of voting and why people would see the need to attack him: " 'I don't know why it had to be unanimous. If that's democracy — that I had to vote the same way everyone else voted — then we're living in two different democracies.' "[3]

Almost immediately after Nichols was named, a number of writers rallied to Nichols' side. Some who had attacked him when he was anonymous suddenly changed their tune, saying that it was his vote and his right to make it how he felt. *The Sporting News's* attitude changed to say, "Nichols' vote for Tovar did not reflect discredit on himself as much as it did on the Baseball Writers' Association, which has been in hot water all too often for unwise, thoughtless and even capricious voting by its committee members."[4] Other writers praised Nichols' character. "He is one of the most sincere, honest, open-minded baseball writers I have ever met," said one.[5]

Still, there continued to be attacks. Nichols had switched jobs at the beginning of September and missed the last month of the baseball season when Yastrzemski made his push for glory. Some thought he should have given up his MVP vote since he wasn't there for the full season, and Nichols partly concurred: "If I did anything wrong, it may have been that."[6] Later writers, with the remove of history and context, took a much harsher view. "That's the worst individual vote in Baseball Writers history," suggested Joe Posnanski. "Max Nichols went on to have a long and admirable career in journalism, by the way. That was, however, the last year he covered baseball."[7]

A final word on the subject must go to Nichols himself. He spent a month going through the media storm, something he would spend much time on the other side of over the years, and he did not enjoy the experience at all: "But what hurt the most was that my own colleagues turned on me. It has not been any fun for me."[8]

Nichols took some time away from the *Star* in 1968 when he was hired as public-relations director for the Minnesota Pipers of the American Basketball Association. The Pipers had moved from Pittsburgh that summer, and spent one disastrous season in Minneapolis before moving back to Pittsburgh the following year. Max didn't even last that long, starting in July 1968 but leaving at the end of the year to return to the *Star*, becoming sports editor in February 1969.

Back at the *Star*, Nichols was now free to write about anything involving sports. Over the years he would cover golf (the U.S. Open was held at Hazeltine, Minnesota, in 1970), fishing (for many years he went to Bemidji in northern Minnesota at the opening of the fishing season, often taking son Karl with him), and football with both the University of Minnesota Golden Gophers and the Minnesota Vikings. But baseball was Nichols' first love, and he would write about it again and again.

Nichols was also moving up in the world of writers, and the Yastrzemski firestorm seemingly did not hurt him at all. In October 1970 he was elected vice president of the Baseball Writers Association of America, and a year later became president, something he called the greatest honor of his life. Among his duties as president in 1972, he was an official scorer at both the All-Star Game and the World Series, and in midsummer he was the master of ceremonies at the Hall of Fame induction ceremony. There he mixed with the stars, introduced Commissioner Bowie Kuhn, and was there for the induction of eight players into the Hall of Fame, among them Sandy Koufax, Yogi Berra, and Josh Gibson.

In 1974 Nichols accepted a new job when Kuhn appointed him director of information for Major League Baseball. "We are fortunate to secure the services of a man of the professional stature and ability of Max Nichols," Kuhn said. "His addition to our staff will add significantly to our capacity to keep the public fully and accurately informed about our game."[9]

However, Nichols lasted only two days on the job. "The job was quite satisfactory," he said, "but I was under a great deal of emotional strain for personal reasons and I didn't want to bring my family into the situation."[10] He said later that the commute back and forth from Minnesota to New York was too difficult to deal with for his family.

Nichols returned to the *Star* as a daily columnist, again covering various sports, but now also different aspects of civic life. He reported, for example, on the Minneapolis school board and on changes to downtown, and spent much time writing about the Metrodome. He believed in the possibilities that the Metrodome would bring to Minneapolis, wrote columns about how it would help the city, and had much influence in the civic and political machinations that eventually resulted in the dome being built.

In 1980 Nichols and his wife moved back to his hometown, as he accepted a job as editor of the *Oklahoma City Journal Record*, a daily business and legal newspaper. He wrote deep articles about the local business scene and community, and received numerous awards over the years for his writing. "Max clearly has a vision for the community," the judges for an AP award said. "Although some readers may disagree with his opinions, they are at least exposed to an intelligent discussion of the issues."[11]

From his reporting Nichols wrote two books, one a history of Oklahoma's First Interstate Bank, the other a biography of John and Eleanor Kirkpatrick, two Oklahoma philanthropists. His interest in history led him to take a position in 1990 as public-relations director at the Oklahoma Historical Society, for whom he wrote a monthly column, "One for the Oklahoma History Book," which appeared in newspapers across the state. He continued to write a column for the *Journal Record*.

More awards followed. Nichols received a Distinguished Alumni award from the University of Oklahoma in 1986; he was inducted into the Oklahoma Journalism Hall of Fame in 1995; and was inducted into the Oklahoma Historians Hall of Fame in 2013.

In 2005 Nichols wrote a much more personal book, *Every Single Good Day*. This was the story of his wife's battle with Alzheimer's disease and the response his family had to it. Mickey had died of the disease in 2002 and Max hoped the book would be used by other families going through the same problems that he and his family had. It provided many lessons about the disease, and also much personal information about their lives.

After Mickey's death, Max moved to New York City to join his partner, Carol Rosenwald, a longtime friend, and he continued to write his columns for both the Oklahoma City Historical Society and the *Journal Record*. Now he covered items of interest to Oklahoma in New York, whether it was Oklahomans showing up on the stage in New York, or a discussion of Southern-style barbecue in New York City. Perhaps taking a dig at the writers who had turned on him those many years ago, he wrote about how much New Yorkers know baseball, and said, "[M]y doorman Joe knows more baseball than some writers I knew during my years of covering the Minnesota Twins for the *Minneapolis Star* from 1961 through 1979."[12]

Max Nichols has experienced everything in his profession from the heights to the depths, but always in an honest and intelligent way. He wrote the truth, whether for good or bad, and ultimately he believed that to serve his readers properly was the only way he could do his job. One quote may serve to sum up his writing career: "He gave up the job of official scoring because he found the squabbles he was getting into with the players were interfering with his responsibility to report the true picture of the Twins to his readers."[13]

SOURCES

Nichols, Max, *Every Single Good Day* (Mustang, Oklahoma: Tate Publishing, 2005).

Nichols, Max, *Batboy for Jackie Robinson and The Brooklyn Dodgers!*

NOTES

1. C.C. Johnson Spink, "Who Voted For Cesar Tovar?" *The Sporting News*, December 2, 1967, 16.
2. Rick Talley, "Keyes Nears One-Mile Mark," *Rockford* (Illinois) *Register-Star*, November 23, 1967, D2.
3. Joe Falls, "An Apology to Writer Who's True to his Beliefs," *The Sporting News*, December 16, 1967, 2.
4. C.C. Johnson Spink, "Tovar in Jensen's Class," *The Sporting News*, December 16, 1967, 14.
5. Falls.
6. Ibid.
7. Joe Posnanski, "Pitchers and the MVP Award," Joe Blogs, joeposnanski.com/joeblogs/pitchers-and-the-mvp-award/, accessed July 5, 2014.
8. Jim Bell, "A fellow makes a point," *Alton* (Illinois) *Evening Telegraph*, June 15, 1968, B2.
9. "Nichols Joins Kuhn as Director of Information," *The Sporting News*, August 24, 1974, 11.
10. "Nichols Resigns From Commissioner's Staff," *The Sporting News*, October 12, 1974, 24.
11. "The Journal Record Wins Five Firsts in AP Contest," *Oklahoma Journal Record*, April 2, 1993.
12. Max Nichols, "No Amount of Mudslinging Disheartens Big Apple Baseball Fans," *Oklahoma City Journal Record*, February 28, 2005
13. Falls.

The 1965 Los Angeles Dodgers

BY GREG ERION

WHILE MEMBERS OF THE Baseball Writers' Association of America picked Minnesota to finish fifth in 1965, their eventual opponents in the World Series, the Los Angeles Dodgers, were not selected to do much better.[1] After finishing sixth in 1964, in part because of Sandy Koufax's season-ending arm injury in mid-August and an anemic offense that ranked eighth in the league in runs scored, Los Angeles was picked for fourth place by baseball's prognosticators. Koufax's health going into the 1965 season was of major concern. His injury in 1964 was his second in three years. (Koufax was shut down for two months during the 1962 season because of a circulatory ailment in his fingers, an absence that undoubtedly cost Los Angeles the pennant.) Concern about the offense was exacerbated when outfielder Frank Howard, the team leader in home runs, was traded during the offseason. Had the writers known that scarcely three weeks into the season the Dodgers would lose their best offensive player for the year, their assessment of the team's destiny would have been even gloomier.[2]

If Koufax could stay healthy, however, he combined with Don Drysdale, Johnny Podres, and newcomer Claude Osteen to make up what was considered the best starting rotation in the league. That preseason observation was confirmed when Los Angeles won seven of its first nine games, giving up just 15 runs in the process. Over the next several weeks the Dodgers jockeyed for the lead, taking it on May 5 and not relinquishing their hold until early July, fending off various challenges by the Cincinnati Reds and the Braves (who were playing a lame-duck season in Milwaukee before moving on to Atlanta in 1966).

The Dodgers would hold that lead without the services of left fielder Tommy Davis. Davis, who had led the league in batting in 1962 and 1963, was considered the team's most potent hitter. On May 1 in a game against the San Francisco Giants, he led off the fourth inning with a single. Then disaster struck. Ron Fairly hit a groundball that the Giants would turn into a double play. Davis explained what happened on the play. "I was running on the inside of the baseline expecting (Orlando) Cepeda to throw to (Jose) Pagan. As I approached the bag I did a crossover step with my left leg and the back spike caught in the clay and turned my foot completely around."[3] Davis broke his ankle and was done for the season. Although Davis would stay in the majors through 1976 as a solid outfielder, then a designated hitter, he never again reached the level of play he had previously shown. Of immediate concern to the Dodgers, however: who would replace him?

Los Angeles quickly summoned Lou Johnson from its Spokane farm club in the Pacific Coast League to fill Davis's spot on the roster. Johnson, a 13-year minor-league veteran, had not impressed in previous trials with the Chicago Cubs, Los Angeles Angels, and Milwaukee Braves. He would with the Dodgers. Less than two weeks after Johnson joined the team, he became the regular left fielder, batting fifth in the lineup and hitting well over .300 for the next several weeks. His fierce competitiveness and natural enthusiasm proved a solid replacement for Davis. Louis Brown Johnson soon had fans in the left-field bleachers riffing on President Lyndon Johnson's campaign slogan of the previous year, chanting, "All the way with LBJ."[4] Through the season and in the World Series Johnson proved an integral part of the Dodgers' success — success not well measured by a season batting average of .259 with 12 home runs. Twelve home runs for an outfielder is a modest number — but it tied him with second baseman Jim Lefebvre for the team lead.

With Johnson's contributions aiding their effort, Los Angeles built a five-game lead in early June. It would be the Dodgers' largest lead of the year. Toward the end of the month they went into a slump, losing 11 of 17 games, and they relinquished first place to the Reds in July. Cincinnati had on paper a more balanced team than Los Angeles. While the Dodgers' starting rotation was considered peerless, many felt the Reds' solid front-line pitchers and deep bullpen made them strong contenders. Frank Robinson, Vada Pinson, Deron Johnson (who led the majors in RBIs with 130), and Pete Rose (enjoying his first .300 season) headed an offense Los Angeles could only dream about. The Reds held the lead through the All-Star break. After the break, Los Angeles reeled off six straight victories to regain the lead, which held into August. At this point Koufax (17-3) and Drysdale (15-8) were 1-2 in the league in wins and accounted for over half of the Dodgers' 57 victories.

Koufax's performance was remarkable, all the more so because of the constant pain he endured. Pulled muscles and hemorrhaging experienced during spring training caused his doctor to warn him that if he kept pitching he was certain to become permanently disabled. The possibility that he could extend his career a few years starting once a week seemed the most prudent option. With the aid of drugs and salves, Koufax's arm recovered and, spurning his physician's advice, he pitched every fourth day. He ended the season starting 41 games as well as relieving twice.[5]

By August 1 the pennant race had turned into a four-team affair as the Braves and Giants drew close. San Francisco was fourth behind the Dodgers, Cincinnati, and the Braves but only four games out. Los Angeles gave way to the Braves for several days in mid-August, with Milwaukee surging into the lead on the strength of 11 wins in 13 games. The Braves' hold on first would be fleeting, however. They lost nine of 11 and dropped out of the race, eventually finishing fifth.

Injuries played a part in Milwaukee's middling performance. Outfielders Hank Aaron and Rico Carty lost playing time– Carty almost half the schedule. Shortstop Denis Menke injured his knee early on and missed much of the season; Felipe Alou was sorely missed during the critical part of the season; Denny Lemaster (17-11 in 1964), saddled with a sore arm, fell off to 7-13.[6] Perhaps more than injuries, though, was a pall cast over the club by the knowledge that they were playing their last season in Milwaukee; they were destined to move to Atlanta the following year. Hank Aaron recalled, "We actually had a contending team in 1965, although nobody in Milwaukee seemed to care."[7] Milwaukee's attendance, at a little over 555,000, was lowest in the league.

As Milwaukee began to slip out of the race, Los Angeles opened a four-game series in San Francisco against the Giants, who would prove their most daunting challenger in the pennant race. San Francisco had solid hitting. Willie Mays, who won the Most Valuable Player award that season, hit .317 and a personal-best 52 home runs. Another future Hall of Famer, Willie McCovey, had 39 home runs. Third baseman Jim Ray Hart had 23 home runs and a .299 average. Juan Marichal, the staff ace, went 22-13, backed up by Bob Shaw (16-9) and Bob Bolin (14-6). Frank Linzy provided a solid effort in the bullpen, going 9-3 with 21 saves. Masanori Murakami, who in 1964 became the first Japanese player to play in the major leagues, saved eight and went 4-1 to help solidify the bullpen. Like Los Angeles and Milwaukee, however, the Giants also experienced a major injury — the loss of Orlando Cepeda, who had averaged 32 home runs and 107 RBIs the prior seven seasons. He appeared in just 33 games during the season.

Los Angeles won the first game of the San Francisco series as reliever Ron Perranoski shut the Giants down for four innings in relief of Drysdale; Johnson's homer in the top of the 15th provided the go-ahead runs. Perranoski would prove a key support to the Dodgers' starting staff the last two months of the season, winning three games and saving 10 on a 0.85 ERA. The Dodgers' win gave them a half-game lead over Milwaukee and a 1½-game edge over the Giants. The Dodgers and Giants split the next two games before entering the final contest on Sunday, August 22. That game would prove the most memorable of the season — so controversial that it was still being talked about a half-century years later.

The four-game series was accompanied by an atmosphere of great tension between the two teams. The Dodgers and Giants carried a long history of intense rivalry, quite possibly born out of Giants manager Bill Terry's infamously asking, "Is Brooklyn still in the league?" after the 1933 season and Brooklyn then knocking the Giants out of the pennant race in 1934 on the final weekend of the season. The enmity intensified during the late 1940s and early 1950s through a series of brawls, knockdown wars, and exchanges of brutal taunts as the two teams battled through a series of tight pennant races. It lessened somewhat when the teams moved to California in 1958 but was definitely a presence over the ensuing years, especially in the 1962 pennant race, won by San Francisco in a three-game playoff against Los Angeles.

As the 1965 season began, tensions arose almost immediately when Drysdale beat the Giants 2-1 in late April, a game punctuated by a series of knockdown pitches. Juan Marichal warned, "If Drysdale ever comes close to one of our batters again, he better watch out." Drysdale responded, warning that Marichal had better get him good "or I'll take four players with me, and I don't mean .220 hitters.[8]

As the four-game series played out, additional incidents further exacerbated the hostility between the two rivals. By Sunday August 22, the last game of the series, a breaking point was reached. Nearly 43,000 fans were in attendance to watch arguably the two best pitchers in baseball square off, Koufax (21-4) and Marichal (19-9).

In the third inning catcher John Roseboro buzzed a return throw to Koufax mere inches from Marichal's ear. A full-scale riot erupted on the field, the incident memorialized by a picture of Marichal swinging his bat at Roseboro. Once order was restored, Marichal was ejected from the game, which the Giants won on Mays's three-run homer off Koufax later in that inning. The victory was costly for the Giants, though. Marichal was immediately suspended and missed one, possibly two crucial starts. When he returned to play, the incident seemed to have affected his performance. He went just 3-4 in September.

Tumult aside, the series ended with Los Angeles a half-game up on Milwaukee and San Francisco. Over the next few weeks, Los Angeles maintained its precarious hold on first. By the morning of September 4, the Dodgers were one game ahead of Cincinnati and two ahead of Milwaukee and San Francisco. That day the Giants began a 14-game winning streak. After the last victory in that streak, on September 16, San Francisco was 4½ games up on the Dodgers and Reds. Los Angeles won six of 11 during the Giants' run, one of which saw Koufax throw a 1-0 perfect game against the Chicago Cubs. The lone run scored on a run manufactured by Johnson's walk, a sacrifice, a stolen base, and an error — typical of so many Dodger rallies that year.

On September 16, as the Giants won their 14th straight, Los Angeles beat Chicago 2-0. Claude Osteen shut down the Cubs for eight innings, Koufax came in to save the game in the ninth. All season long Los Angeles had played fairly consistently, never winning more than six in a row and only once losing as many as four consecutive games. Their consistency gave way to excellence as, starting with their defeat of Chicago, they won 13 in a row. San Francisco had peaked too early. When Los Angeles finally lost—a 2-0 defeat by Milwaukee on October 1, they had pulled ahead of San Francisco by two games. The lead held as both the Giants and Los Angeles won their final two games of the year.

In the final analysis, pitching carried the day for the Dodgers. Their team ERA of 2.81 was the best in the league; they gave up 59 fewer runs than any other team. Koufax ended with a record of 26-8, a league leading 2.04 ERA and a season record for strikeouts with 382. Drysdale at 23-12; Osteen at 15-15; and Perranoski (17 saves in the season and phenomenal down the stretch) proved key members of the staff.

The offense was anemic as the Dodgers outscored only the 9th- and 10th-place Houston Astros and New York Mets. Maury Wills led the team in hitting with a powerless .286; however, he stole 94 bases to lead the majors. It was a remarkable achievement considering that a badly damaged knee slowed him down for several weeks. Jim Gilliam began the season as a coach, was activated as a player at the end of May, and provided several clutch hits on his way to a .280 average. That Johnson's and Lefebvre's 12 home runs led the team truly epitomized Los Angeles's offensive liabilities.

The Dodgers could not dwell on how they came to capture the franchise's 12th league title, however. Just three days after winning the pennant they had an appointment in Minnesota.

NOTES

1 Oscar Kahan, "Yanks, Phils Picked By Writers, Fans," *The Sporting News*, April 17, 1965, 1.

2 Clifford Kachline, *Official Baseball Guide for 1966* (St. Louis: The Sporting News Pub. Co.), 12.

3 Mark Stewart and Paul Hirsch, *Tommy Davis*, SABR Bioproject, sabr.org/bioproj/person/664f669f.

4 Jane Leavy, *Sandy Koufax, A Lefty's Legacy* (New York: HarperCollins Publishers, 2002), 108-110.

5 Leavy, 156-160,

6 Kachline, 27-28.

7 Hank Aaron with Lonnie Wheeler, *I Had a Hammer; The Hank Aaron Story* (New York: HarperCollins*Publisher*s, 1991), 175.

8 James S. Hirsch, *Willie Mays: The Life, The Legend* (New York: Scribner, 2010), 433.

Koufax's Famous Refusal to Play

1965 World Series Game One
Minnesota Twins 8, Los Angeles Dodgers 2
October 6, 1965, at Metropolitan Stadium, Bloomington, Minnesota

BY NORM KING

GAME ONE OF THE 1965 WORLD Series between the Los Angeles Dodgers and the Minnesota Twins was as noteworthy for who didn't play as it was for who did.

New York Yankee pinstripes were nowhere to be found in the fall classic for the first time in six years. The Bombers finished sixth in 1965 with a 77-85 record, the first time since 1925 that they had finished below .500. This season marked the end of a dynasty that had accounted for 29 American League pennants and 20 World Series titles since 1921.

Also missing from Game One was Dodgers ace Sandy Koufax, who led the National League with a 26-8 record and a 2.04 earned-run average. Game One fell on October 6, the same date as Yom Kippur, the Day of Atonement in the Jewish calendar. Jewish law forbids anyone working on that day, and Koufax, as a Jewish player, refused to pitch.

"It was a reflexive decision to do what was right in deference to his own family, in deference to his own tradition and in deference to recognition that, as a public figure, setting an example mattered," said Jane Leavy, author of a biography on Koufax.[1]

Fortunately for the Dodgers, pitching was the team's strength; they led the National League in team ERA (2.81), complete games (58), and shutouts (17). Therefore Dodgers manager Walter Alston had no qualms about starting the team's second best pitcher, Don Drysdale, in the first game. Drysdale's 23-12 record and 2.77 ERA would have made him a staff ace on any team that did not have a Koufax in the rotation. He was also in a groove, having pitched complete-game shutouts in his last two starts of the season.

The Twins countered with their best pitcher, Jim "Mudcat" Grant, who led the American League in wins with 21 (the only 20-win season of his career) and shutouts, with six.

Naturally, with this being the first game of the Series and a battle looming between two 20-game winners, everyone expected a pitching duel; but in the grand tradition of great expectations gone awry everywhere, this game had 20 hits, a bat-around inning, a rare hitting feat from an unlikely source, a heroic stroke from Zorro, and, possibly, one manager wishing his pitcher would change religions.

Anyone who has watched NFL films of Minnesota Vikings playoff games in the 1970s may be excused in thinking that the Dodgers and Twins played in a blizzard. Such was not the case in Game One, as the

Versalles steals second base in Game One. (Photo courtesy of Minnesota Twins Baseball Club).

temperature reached 68 degrees that afternoon (yes, afternoon). The pitchers copycatted each other in the first two innings; both retired the side in order in the first, while striking out the leadoff hitter (Grant struck out Dodgers shortstop Maury Wills while Drysdale returned the favor with Twins shortstop Zoilo Versalles). In the second, both pitchers gave up solo home runs. Dodgers right fielder Ron Fairly smacked one to deep right field off Grant, while Twins first baseman Don Mincher tied the game in the bottom of the inning.

Grant retired the side in order in the top of the third and then the Twins reached down inside themselves for their inner disc jockey because the hits just kept on coming during their turn at bat. The team's number-eight hitter, second baseman Frank Quilici, started the fun with a double. Grant reached on an error while trying to sacrifice Quilici to third (second baseman Jim Lefebvre dropped Drysdale's throw to first), and with two on, Versalles, nicknamed Zorro, swung his rapier-like bat and belted a three-run homer to left field. Another double followed, this time by left fielder Sandy Valdespino, before Tony Oliva grounded out. Drysdale then loaded the bases by giving up a single to third baseman Harmon Killebrew and walking Mincher (with a strikeout of center fielder Jimmie Hall sandwiched in between). Catcher Earl Battey singled to score Valdespino and Killebrew. Coming up for the second time in the inning, Quilici, who hit only .208 during the regular season, performed the rare feat of getting two hits in one frame during the World Series. His single scored Mincher, making the score 7-1.

After Quilici's hit, manager Alston came to the mound to take Drysdale out of the game. As he was leaving, Drysdale is reported to have said, "I bet right now you wish I was Jewish, too."[2]

The six-run, six-hit inning buried the Dodgers. Versalles drove Grant in with the Twins' eighth run in the sixth, and Wills' bunt single scored second baseman Lefebvre with a too-little, too-late run in the ninth. The 8-2 final allowed the Twins to take a 1-0 lead in the Series.

Even though he pitched a complete game and scattered ten hits — nine of them singles — Grant wasn't happy with his performance. He even went over to the box where US Senator Hubert Humphrey of Minnesota was sitting, and told the senator that he (Grant) was not pitching well because he didn't have his curveball. Humphrey told him to stick with the fastball.

"I didn't have as good a fastball [today] as I had during the season," Grant said after the game. "Most of the game I had control trouble. I was 2-and-2 and 3-and-2 on most of the hitters."[3]

Alston, of course, put on as positive a spin on the loss as he could. "We got 10 hits, they got 10 hits, but theirs came in a bunch and scored runs. Ours didn't," he said.[4] He also pointed out that the Dodgers lost the first game of the 1959 World Series to the White Sox, 11-0, and came back to win the championship.

SOURCES

sportsillustrated.cnn.com/

almanac.com/weather/

NOTES

1 "Q & A" with Jane Leavy: Author speaks on how Koufax overcame bias, pain," SI.com, posted September 3, 2002.

2 Jeff Merron wrote Drysdale's remark in ESPN.com. That quote appears in other articles as well.

3 Lew Ferguson, "Twins 'Have to Keep Going'" *Oneonta* (New York) *Star*, October 7, 1965.

4 Bob Myers, "Dodgers Haven't Given Up Hope," *Oneonta* (New York) *Star*, October 7, 1965.

Twins Beat Dodgers at Their Own Game to Take Commanding Series Lead

1965 World Series Game Two
Minnesota Twins 5, Los Angeles Dodgers 1
October 7, 1965 at Metropolitan Stadium, Bloomington, Minnesota

BY NORM KING

NATIONAL LEAGUE PRESIDENT Warren Giles would have been excused if he had thought that somebody in his office screwed up and sent the 1962 New York Mets to play Game Two of the World Series instead of the National League champion LA Dodgers. By committing three errors and allowing poor relief pitching to let a winnable game get away from them, the Dodgers looked more like those Mets, who lost 120 games, than the team that won 97.

The weather was cool and wet—the high reached only 58 and it drizzled throughout the game. Despite the conditions, fans expected a pitcher's duel between Dodgers ace Sandy Koufax and 18-game winner Jim Kaat. And for the first 4½ innings, that's exactly what they got. Then came the top of the fifth and a play that changed the course of the game.

Dodgers right fielder Ron Fairly led off the frame with a single to right. Second baseman Jim Lefebvre followed with a liner to left that was drifting away from left fielder Bob Allison and looked like a sure double. But Allison ran a long way to the foul line and made a spectacular diving catch that left the Dodgers with one out and a runner on first instead of two runners in scoring position with nobody out. Good thing, too, because first baseman Wes Parker then grounded a single into right field that would probably have scored two runs. Instead, Kaat got the next two batters on foul pop-ups and the game remained scoreless.

"I don't know when I've seen a catch like that," said Twins manager Sam Mele. "It was a tremendous catch. It could have meant something big for the Dodgers if the ball had dropped in there."[1]

The game then proceeded from Allison's sublime to Dodger third baseman Jim Gilliam's ridiculous.

Anyone who ever did something because it seemed like a good idea at the time, only to regret it afterward, would know how Gilliam felt after the sixth. Gilliam started the 1965 season as a Dodger coach, but then went back on the active roster in May. He may have wished he was back in the coaching ranks after Zoilo Versalles's grounder bounced off him for a two-base error to lead off the inning. After center fielder Joe Nossek sacrificed Versalles to third, the Twins shortstop scored on Tony Oliva's double to give Minnesota a 1-0 lead. Killebrew's single then drove in Oliva, and the Twins led 2-0.

It was still anybody's game in the top of the seventh, when Fairly and Lefebvre singled to open the inning. After the runners advanced on a sacrifice by Parker, catcher John Roseboro singled to score Fairly; Lefebvre and Roseboro moved up on the throw to the plate. Dodgers manager Walter Alston then made a move that said a lot about his team's lack of scoring punch. Koufax was the next scheduled batter, and Alston made the standard move by pinch-hitting for him because his team was behind in the late innings. The Twins were probably surprised when Don Drysdale, the loser of Game One, came out of the dugout swinging a bat. On the surface it seemed a bizarre move, but Drysdale was, in fact, an excellent hitting pitcher. His .300 batting average was the highest on the team that season. Drysdale also hit seven homers, an astounding total for a pitcher, in just 130 at-bats. By comparison, Lefebvre and left fielder Lou Johnson tied for the team lead in home runs with 12. The gamble didn't pay off, however, as mighty Drysdale struck out. Wills followed and flied to center to end the threat.

Reliever Ron Perranoski replaced Koufax on the mound in the bottom of the seventh and started off well enough by getting the first two batters out. Leadoff hitter Versalles then tripled to right and while he was on third, he began dancing up and down the line in the tradition of Jackie Robinson. This rattled Perranoski, who threw a wild pitch with Joe Nossek at the plate, allowing Versalles to score. Nossek reached first on another error by poor Gilliam, but was stranded.

The Twins put the game away in the eighth. Killebrew walked and advanced to third on an Allison double. Killebrew was tagged out at the plate on a fielder's choice by first baseman Don Mincher. Allison advanced to third and Mincher to second on a balk by Perranoski. The Dodgers walked number-eight hitter Frank Quilici to load the bases and bring Kaat to the plate, and while Kaat was no Drysdale at the plate, his numbers weren't that bad (.247 average, one home run). His single brought two runners home and put the game away. Los Angeles threatened in the ninth with two runners on and one out, but didn't score.

The Dodgers were 7-5 favorites going into the Series and there had been some talk of a sweep. That talk continued, except that now the wags were speculating on the possibility of the Twins getting the brooms out. Suffice it to say that the Twins surprised everyone by beating both Drysdale and Koufax.

However, Alston knew from experience that being down 2-0 doesn't mean the Series is over. In 1955 his Brooklyn Dodgers were in this situation and won it all. The following year they were up 2-zip on the Yankees and lost. He was also the manager of a veteran team whose players knew what it took to get the ring.

As for Gilliam, it was simply one of those days. He had committed only one error in his previous 108 World Series chances, and didn't make any miscues the rest of this Series.

Now it was on to Los Angeles for Game Three.

SOURCES

wunderground.com

Winona (Minnesota) *Daily News*

San Bernardino (California) *Sun*

NOTES

1   Lew Ferguson, "Allison's Roll-Over Catch Snuffs Dodgers," *San Bernardino* (California) *Sun.* October 8, 1965.

'Well Golllly': Gomer Gets Dodgers Back in the Series

1965 World Series Game Three
Los Angeles Dodgers 4, Minnesota Twins 0
October 9, 1965 at Dodger Stadium, Los Angeles, California

BY NORM KING

People of a certain age may remember a television show from the 1960s called *Gomer Pyle, USMC*, about a country hick who joins the Marines and drives his sergeant crazy. It's a good bet, though, that people didn't know that Gomer also pitched for the Los Angeles Dodgers.

"Gomer" was the nickname bestowed on Claude Osteen, the Dodgers' starter in Game Three of the 1965 World Series, because of his (rather unfortunate) resemblance to the television character. And while the television Gomer was a goof, the real live one was anything but. Osteen was a solid major-league pitcher, a three-time All-Star in an 18-year major-league career, who went 15-15 with a 2.79 ERA in 1965. His won-loss record is misleading, as the Dodgers scored only 28 runs in his 15 defeats.

The Dodgers' star pitchers, Sandy Koufax and Don Drysdale, overshadowed Osteen in the media. But on this day he didn't take a back seat to anyone, shutting down the powerful Twins with a 4-0 complete-game victory, giving the Dodgers new life in the fall classic.

This was a typical Dodger win, with speed and pitching complementing their ten-hit attack. Shortstop Maury Wills, who led the world in stolen bases in 1965 with 94, stole his first sack of the Series, as did first baseman Wes Parker (who stole third), and even catcher John Roseboro. (Parker and Roseboro combined on a double steal in the fourth.) Five of the Dodgers' hits were doubles.

The Twins' starter, Camilo Pascual, was no slouch either. He had a 9-3 record during the season with a 3.35 ERA. During his career he was a five-time All-Star and led the American League three times each in complete games and shutouts.

The game got off to a bad start for the Twins in general and catcher Earl Battey in particular. Shortstop Zoilo Versalles led off the first inning with a ground-rule double to left. Center fielder Joe Nossek grounded to the right side, allowing Versalles to reach third with one out. After a groundout by right fielder Tony Oliva and a walk to third baseman Harmon Killebrew, Battey came to the plate. Twins third-base coach Billy Martin flashed the hit-and-run sign, but Battey missed it.

What followed was the pivotal play of the game and, perhaps, the Series. Killebrew was supposed to head for second and draw a throw from Roseboro, at which point Versalles would take off for home. Killebrew was supposed to run to second but stopped. Wills saw Versalles breaking for the plate and threw back to Roseboro, who threw to third baseman Jim Gilliam, who applied the tag; 6-2-5 for you who score.

"That was the big play," said Osteen. "If they score they have a big advantage. Getting a run early makes a team confident and more aggressive. They would have been tougher to pitch to."[1]

"Earl missed the sign," said Martin. "He usually protects the runner pretty good."[2]

The game remained scoreless until the fourth inning. Right fielder Ron Fairly led off the Dodgers' half with a double to left and moved to third on a sacrifice by left fielder Lou Johnson. Second baseman Jim Lefebvre got an infield hit, but Fairly had to stay at third. Pascual then did what he didn't want to do; he walked Parker to load the bases. Up came number-eight hitter John Roseboro and he didn't disappoint, driving in two runs with a single to right. The Dodgers had broken through and went into the fifth ahead 2-0. The only downside to the inning came when Lefebvre bruised his heel crossing the plate. Dick Tracewski replaced him for the rest of the Series.

The Dodgers added to their lead in the fifth. Fleet-footed center fielder Willie Davis singled to center and went to second on a Fairly groundout. Johnson came up again and smacked a double to left-center field, scoring Davis.

With the Twins down by three and the pitcher's spot due up first in the top of the sixth, Twins manager Sam Mele chose to pinch-hit for Pascual with Rich Rollins, who was the Twins' regular third baseman during the season but saw duty only as a pinch-hitter in the Series. Rollins grounded back to Osteen, but had he gotten on base, the Twins may have gotten back into the game, because Versalles and center fielder Joe Nossek followed with singles. However, with runners on first and third, Osteen induced right fielder Tony Oliva to hit into a double play to end the Twins' last serious threat of the game.

Jim Merritt replaced Pascual on the mound and Parker greeted him with a base hit to center. Roseboro flied to right, and then Dodgers manager Walter Alston ordered the next batter, Osteen, to attempt a sacrifice with one out. The move worked, as Osteen successfully bunted over Parker, who then scored on a double by Maury Wills. Merritt got a measure of revenge by picking Wills off second to end the inning.

Battey's horrid day continued in the bottom of the seventh. While chasing a foul pop off Jim Gilliam, he smashed into the fence next to the Twins' dugout, bruising his neck and jaw. Jerry Zimmerman replaced Battey behind the plate. The doctor who examined Battey after the game would not allow him to talk unnecessarily, which was fine with him after the bad day he had.

"Gomer," who got the nickname from Tracewski, piled up the zeroes the rest of the way and earned a 4-0 complete-game win. The victory was impressive because the power-laden Twins had been shut out only three times all season, but at the same time Osteen seemed to have their number, having compiled a 5-0 record against them when he pitched for the Washington Senators from 1961 to 1964.

"I just feel I know how to pitch to them," he said. "Except for Zoilo Versalles, all the hits they got off me were on bad pitches. "When I got the ball where I was supposed to, they didn't hit me."[3]

SOURCES

Baseball-reference.com

San Bernardino (California) *Sun*

Kingsport (Tennessee) *Times-News*

Sports Illustrated

dodgers.mlblogs.com

NOTES

1 Jack Mann, "Dodgers Down—and Up," *Sports Illustrated*, October 18, 1965.

2 Lew Ferguson, "Missed Hit-and-Run Sign Throttles Minnesota," *San Bernardino* (California) *Sun*, October 10, 1965.

3 Joe Reichler, "Gomer's Luck Finally Changes," *San Bernardino* (California) *Sun*, October 10, 1965.

Dodger Small Ball and Twins Forgetting Fundamentals Tie the Series

1965 World Series Game Four
Los Angeles Dodgers 7, Minnesota Twins 2
October 10, 1965 at Dodger Stadium, Los Angeles, California

BY NORM KING

THE FAMOUS LINE IN THE MOVIE *A League of Their Own*, "There's no crying in baseball," came about because Tom Hanks' character, Jimmy Dugan, brought tears to the eyes of outfielder Evelyn Gardner by screaming at her for missing the cutoff man. It's a good thing there's no crying in baseball because judging by the way the Minnesota Twins played in Game Four of the 1965 World Series, when two outfielders missed the cutoff man and infielders and pitcher threw the baseball all over the field, the locker room would have been a veritable waterworks after the game.

It must have been frustrating for the Twins because in addition to their fielding miscues, they were matched home run for home run by the Dodgers, even though the Minnesotans hit almost twice as many homers as Los Angeles during the season (150 to 78), and the Dodgers evened the World Series at two games apiece with a convincing 7-2 trouncing.

Game Four saw a rematch between Game One starters Don Drysdale and Jim "Mudcat" Grant. Unlike Game One, in which Drysdale was lifted in the third inning, this time he went all the way, giving up five hits and striking out 11 while walking only two. On the other hand, if this Grant were at Appomattox, he would have signed the surrender papers instead of Robert E. Lee. He pitched five innings (plus two batters in the sixth), gave up five runs (four earned) on six hits, struck out two, and walked one.

The Dodgers made it clear very early that they were going to use every weapon in their offensive arsenal to win this one. The Twins also made it clear that they needed some practice in the fundamentals that make for a winning ballclub. Shortstop Maury Wills led off the bottom of the first with an infield single that would have been an out, but first baseman Don Mincher, having both Grant and second baseman Frank Quilici to throw to, ended up tossing it between them. Wills collided with Quilici on the play. After stealing second, Wills went to third when Grant failed to cover first on a groundball by center fielder Willie Davis. With Davis at first, Wills scored on a groundout to second by right fielder Ron Fairly that would have been an inning-ending double play, but shortstop Zoilo Versalles was late in getting to the ball.

"My spikes stuck like I stepped on a piece of gum," explained Versailles.[1]

Dodger small ball succeeded again in the bottom of the second. First baseman Wes Parker reached first on a bunt single and then stole second and continued to third when Grant uncorked a wild pitch. Then Parker scored on an error by second baseman Frank Quilici.

Drysdale was cruising along, allowing only two hits through the first three innings. But in the fourth, Harmon Killebrew, the Twins' leading home-run hitter during the season with 25, belted a solo home run to bring the Twins to within one.[2] The Dodgers got that one back in the bottom of the inning with some power of their own, as Parker parked one into the right-field seats, making the score 3-1. It was Parker's fifth hit in nine at-bats against the Twins, and the ninth time he had reached base in 14 plate appearances.

The Twins made it interesting in the top of the sixth when right fielder Tony Oliva, to that point just 2-for-14 in the Series, hit a shot into the right-field seats. It was his first dinger in nearly two months. But any chance of a Minnesota comeback ended in the bottom of the inning when they completely fell apart. Grant prepared for a trip to the showers by walking third baseman Jim Gilliam and allowing a single to right by Davis. Davis advanced into scoring position when Oliva overshot the cutoff man and threw to third in an ill-advised attempt to cut down Gilliam. After Al Worthington replaced Grant, Fairly singled to center through a drawn-in infield, scoring Gilliam and Davis, and Fairly made it to second when center fielder Jimmie Hall did what Oliva had done—bypassed the cutoff man and threw directly to the plate. Feeling left out of the mistake-fest, Worthington allowed Fairly to score when he made a throwing error on a bunt single by left fielder Lou Johnson. Johnson, who was credited with a hit, made it to second on the miscue, overran the bag and was tagged out by Quilici after a rundown. Overall, the Dodgers scored three runs in the inning on three singles and poor defense by the Twins.

It was all over except the shouting by this point, and the fans no doubt shouted themselves hoarse when Johnson put the exclamation point on the Dodgers' victory with a solo shot in the eighth.

After the game, Twins manager Sam Mele stated the obvious when he admitted that his team played poorly: "We didn't make the plays. We didn't play our best ball—missing cutoff men and not playing the grounders right," he said. "I'll talk to my players … and keep reminding them to do the things they've got to do."[3]

Despite allowing only two harmless singles and a walk through the first three innings, Drysdale didn't feel in complete command of his pitches until the fourth: "My fastball began to come on after about two innings and I'd say my curve around the third or fourth," he said. "This time I pitched my game. I didn't do that in Minnesota."[4]

Wills told reporters that the Dodgers' use of speed and one-base-at-a-time-type baseball was difficult for other teams to adapt to: "A type of game like ours will force players to rely on fundamentals," he said. "Players who have been around a long time have forgotten fundamentals and find it hard to go back."[5]

The Series was now tied 2-2, and the Twins had to go up against Dodgers ace Sandy Koufax in Game Five.

SOURCES

imdb.com

baseball-reference.com

Mason City (Iowa) *Globe-Gazette*

Modesto (California) *Bee and News-Herald*

San Bernardino (California) *Sun*

Sports Illustrated

NOTES

1. Jack Mann, "Dodgers Down—and Up," *Sports Illustrated*, October 18, 1965.
2. Killebrew's 25 home runs were more than the two leading Dodgers homer hitters combined. Jim Lefebvre and Lou Johnson tied for the team lead with 12 each.
3. Associated Press, Koufax Needs Win to Put LA In Front," *Modesto* (California) *Bee and News-Herald*, October 11, 1965.
4. Bob Myers, " 'Bad Stuff' Won for Don," *San Bernardino* (California) *Sun*, October 11, 1965.
5. Mike Rathet, "Dodgers Forcing Twins Back to Fundamentals," *San Bernardino* (California) *Sun*, October 11, 1965.

Koufax's Clutch Hitting (!) Gives Dodgers the Series Lead

1965 World Series Game Five
Los Angeles Dodgers 7, Minnesota Twins 0
October 11, 1965 at Dodger Stadium, Los Angeles, California

BY NORM KING

THIS EDITION OF THE FALL CLASSIC had so many bizarre twists and turns that they might as well have had Rod Serling do the pregame show. First there were the Twins beating both of the Dodgers' best pitchers, Don Drysdale and Sandy Koufax. Then the punchless Dodgers turned around and won the next two games by a combined score of 11-2, hitting as many home runs in the victories (two) as the powerful Twins. The strange twists continued in Game Five, which the Dodgers won by a touchdown, 7-0. Cue the music.

Koufax started Game Five. He had lost Game Two, but was so dominant a pitcher in 1965, winning the pitching triple crown with 26 wins, a 2.04 ERA, and a then-record 382 strikeouts, that even Serling's vivid imagination couldn't see him losing two games in a row. He didn't, pitching a four-hitter and striking out ten. The Dodgers offense helped with 14 hits off three Twins pitchers, and by driving Twins catcher Earl Battey ... well, batty, with four stolen bases, three by center fielder Willie Davis and one by shortstop Maury Wills. The Dodgers raised their team batting average for the Series to .302, 60 points higher than their regular-season average.

Jim Kaat once again started for the Twins, but unlike his start in Game Two, when he went all the way in a 5-1 Twins victory, this was not to be his day, as he pitched only 2⅓ innings, giving up four runs (three earned) on six hits. The carnage started with the leadoff hitter, Wills, who led off the bottom of the first with a ground-rule double to right. Third baseman Jim Gilliam followed with a single that scored Wills. Davis followed that with a bunt attempt. Twins third baseman Harmon Killebrew handled it cleanly, but second baseman Frank Quilici, who was covering first, lost sight of Killebrew's throw. The ball ended up in the outfield, allowing Gilliam to score and Davis to reach third. It was Quilici's second error of the Series.

Davis stole his first base of the game in the third after singling to right with one out. Left fielder Lou Johnson singled to center, scoring Davis. Right fielder Ron Fairly then doubled to left-center. Fairly's hit ended Kaat's day much earlier than Jim had anticipated.

By the fourth inning, knowing that it was Koufax who had the 4-0 lead, the Dodgers began messin' with the Twins' heads. Wills beat out an infield hit and with Gilliam up, pitcher Dave Boswell threw to first six straight times in an effort to keep Wills close to the bag. He should have known that wasn't going to work, because Wills, on his way to a four-hit day, stole second anyway, and scored when Gilliam singled to right-center field, making it 5-0.

"I didn't know [Boswell] before the game, so I had no line on him," said Wills. "But it became a challenge. I just wanted to make sure I got a good jump because I was determined to steal the first time he threw home."[1]

Meanwhile, ho-hum, Koufax was perfect through four. Killebrew broke up the perfecto with a single to center in the fifth that, according to newspaper accounts, Davis should have caught but lost in the background of fans' white shirts. Koufax still ended up facing the minimum that inning as the next batter, Battey, grounded into a double play and left fielder Bob Allison struck out.

"In the fifth, Harmon Killebrew looped a hit into center field," wrote Ted Smits. "Willie Davis … misjudged it. When he finally ran in, it was too late. He managed to catch the ball momentarily in his glove but dropped it in a sliding fall."[2]

The perfect illustration of what kind of day it was for the Twins came in the seventh. Fairly hit a ball to deep short off pitcher Jim Perry that resulted in an infield hit. He advanced to second on first baseman Wes Parker's sacrifice. With first base open and facing the number-eight hitter, catcher John Roseboro, the Twins made the standard move of walking him to face the pitcher. Koufax, with an .097 lifetime batting average, singled to center to drive in Fairly. Wills singled to drive in Roseboro for the final run of the game.

The Twins got two meaningless singles in the ninth, but the game ended when center fielder Joe Nossek hit a liner to Wills, who capped a great day by catching the ball, then throwing to second for a game-ending double play.

Although Koufax put in a magnificent performance, he wasn't entirely happy with the way he pitched that day: "I'm not disappointed with the way I pitched, but I have pitched better," he said. "I was behind the hitters too much and I became awfully tired after the seventh inning."[3]

This modest self-assessment was of little comfort to the Twins, who came into Los Angeles with a 2-0 Series lead but headed back to Minneapolis down 3-2.

Twins third-base coach Billy Martin griped before Game Five about the hardness of the Dodger Stadium infield, saying balls traveled faster as a result.

"This infield is hard as a rock and the sun bakes it down," he said. "And they use a 1,200-pound roller on it. That makes the infield exceptionally hard. Balls will go through this infield that wouldn't go through in other ballparks."[4]

The Twins were happy to leave Dodger Stadium, but it's not as if they were unfamiliar with the locale. They played the California Angels there nine times that season (the Angels moved to Anaheim in 1966).

Anyway, the Twins flew back to Minneapolis after the game and were greeted into the warm bosoms of more than 1,000 fans upon their return. At least the bosoms would have been warm if the temperature weren't 37 degrees.

SOURCES

Appleton (Wisconsin) *Post-Crescent*

San Bernardino (California) *Daily Sun*

Sports Illustrated

Baseball-reference.com

NOTES

1 Mike Rathet (Associated Press), "Koufax Fans Too Many, Wills Says," *Appleton* (Wisconsin) *Post-Crescent,* October 12, 1965.

2 Ted Smits (Associated Press), "Only Second Guessing Was How Twins Got Four Hits." *Appleton* (Wisconsin) *Post-Crescent,* October 12, 1965.

3 Joe Reichler (Associated Press), "Modest Sandy Wasn't Angry," *San Bernardino* (California) *Daily Sun,* October 12, 1965.

4 "Dodger Infield 'Too Hard,' Twins Complain" (Associated Press), *San Bernardino* (California) *Daily Sun,* October 12, 1965.

Mudcat Ties the Series with His Pitching and Hitting

1965 World Series Game Six
Minnesota Twins 5, Los Angeles Dodgers 1
October 13, 1965 at Metropolitan Stadium, Bloomington, Minnesota

BY NORM KING

IT SOUNDS LIKE A CORNY HOLLYWOOD movie. The home team has its back against the wall. It calls on its best pitcher, who bravely goes to the mound despite being sick. He not only wins the game, but hits a home run to boot. And if that's not enough cornball for you, a friend had asked the pitcher to win a game for the man's wife, who recently died in an automobile accident.

Welcome to Game Six of the 1965 World Series, where everything described above really happened. The Twins had their backs against the wall, having dropped three straight to the Dodgers in Los Angeles after winning the first two games in Minneapolis. Twins manager Sam Mele gave the ball to Jim "Mudcat" Grant, who had a 1-1 record in the Series and who only had two days' rest after giving up five runs (four earned) in five-plus innings in a 7-2 Twins loss. The pressure on Grant was compounded by the fact that he had a bad cold and sore knees.

"My head feels like a balloon, my cold's no better and my knees are bothering me," said Grant. "Otherwise, I'm all right."[1]

Claude Osteen started Game Six for the Dodgers. Osteen was the Twins' nemesis, having accumulated a 5-0 won-lost record against them when he pitched for the Washington Senators, plus a 4-0 shutout win in Game Three of this World Series.

So far, this had been a homer's Series, with each team winning in its home park. After taking the first two games at Metropolitan Stadium, the Twins lost all three games in Los Angeles, were shut out twice, and were outscored 18-2.

"In losing the three games in LA, the all-round play of the Twins was like that of disorganized sandlotters," wrote sportswriter George Raubacher. "Little Leaguers generally function better than did the Twins in three reverses away from home."[2]

Ouch.

Perhaps that critique didn't motivate Grant, but the need to win certainly did, and his pitching showed it, as he was almost perfect through four innings. Dodgers catcher John Roseboro reached safely in the third on an error by third baseman Harmon Killebrew, but was thrown out trying to steal second on a "strike 'em out, throw 'em out" double play with second baseman Dick Tracewski at the plate. Osteen started off well enough, giving up three hits and two walks through the first three frames, but keeping the Dodgers off the scoreboard. That all changed in the fourth.

Twins catcher Earl Battey led off the inning with a groundball to second base but Tracewski, playing in place of the injured Jim Lefebvre, booted the ball and Battey was safe. Left fielder Bob Allison, who was 1-for-10 at this point in the Series, sent Osteen's third pitch on a long ride into the lower left-field pavilion, giving the Twins a 2-0 lead.

Grant gave up his first hit in the fifth, a harmless single by Dodgers right fielder Ron Fairly. Grant experienced his only tough spot of the game in the next inning. Tracewski singled and then, after Willie Crawford struck out while pinch-hitting for Osteen, moved to second on a base hit by shortstop Maury Wills. With two on and one out, Grant induced third baseman Junior Gilliam to pop to short and got center fielder Willie Davis to fly to center.

When managers make the standard move in a game, such as removing a pitcher for a pinch-hitter or walking the number-eight hitter to get to the pitcher's spot in the batting order, they know that sometimes these moves won't work. It's when both moves backfire in the same inning that the gray hair comes in. Dodgers manager Walter Alston would have bought a truckload of "Just For Men" if it had existed back then after the Twins' half of the sixth because his moves failed spectacularly.

Howie Reed replaced Osteen on the mound and, with one out, walked Allison, who then stole second while first baseman Don Mincher struck out looking. Alston then ordered Reed to walk second baseman Frank Quilici, who was hitting .188 for the Series, to get to Grant, who hit .155 during the season with no home runs. The same move blew up in the Twins' face in Game Five, when Dodgers pitcher Sandy Koufax got a single to drive in a run; and on this day Grant got a hit, too, except in this case it was a three-run homer to left-center, making the score 5-0.

It's a tradition in baseball that any pitcher who hits a home run can suddenly talk about hitting as if he's Ted Williams.

"I said to myself, 'He's going to throw me a curve. He can't afford to give me a fastball in a situation like this,'" said Grant. "Sure enough, he threw the curve. I knew it was gone the moment I hit it."[3]

The Dodgers didn't mount any further threats. Fairly belted a solo home run to right-center leading off the seventh, but otherwise Grant breezed through the rest of the game. He pitched masterfully, allowing only six hits and striking out five while not walking anyone. He stayed ahead of the hitters the whole game — of the 33 batters he faced, he threw first-pitch strikes to 28.

The fact that it was a win-or-go-home situation no doubt motivated Grant, but he had a deeper, more personal incentive as well. Before the game, he received a telegram from a friend that said: "Win the next one for Scotty. ... Your friend, Howdy Doody."[4] Grant explained to a reporter that "Howdy Doody" was a friend of his in Kansas City and that Scotty, the friend's wife, had died in a car accident a week and a half before, and that they were married for less than a year.

"I thought about her when I went out to the mound," said Grant. "I'm glad I made my friend a little happier."[5]

On to Game Seven.

SOURCES

Janesville (Wisconsin) *Daily Gazette*

Ellensburg (Washington) *Daily Record*

Sports Illustrated

San Bernardino (California) *Daily Sun*

NOTES

1 Associated Press, "Minnesota's Hopes Ride on Tired, Sick Pitcher," *Ellensburg* (Washington) *Daily Record*, October 13, 1965.

2 George Raubacher (Associated Press), "Twins Alive by Coming Alive," *Janesville* (Wisconsin) *Daily Gazette*, October 14, 1965.

3 Joe Reichler (Associated Press), "Twins Hero Inspired by Letter," *San Bernardino* (California) *Daily Sun*, October 14, 1965.

4 Reichler.

5 Reicher.

Koufax Has Nothing to Atone for with Classic Game Seven Performance

1965 World Series Game Seven
Los Angeles Dodgers 2, Minnesota Twins 0
October 14, 1965, at Metropolitan Stadium, Bloomington, Minnesota

BY NORM KING

UNFORTUNATELY FOR THE Minnesota Twins, there were no Jewish holidays that would prevent Sandy Koufax from pitching for the Los Angeles Dodgers in Game Seven of the 1965 World Series. As a result, he came. He pitched. He shut the Twins out, 2-0. That's really all you need to know.

Actually, there's a little bit more to Game Seven than that. Dodgers manager Walter Alston elected to start Koufax on two days' rest, rather than Don Drysdale, who hadn't pitched in four days. Alston made it clear during a pregame meeting that Drysdale would take over if Koufax faltered.

Jim Kaat started for the Twins, also on two days' rest, and Twins manager Sam Mele was not afraid to change pitchers at the first sign of trouble. He ended up using five pitchers in the game, all of whom shut the Dodgers out after Kaat gave up two runs in the fourth.

"You hate to lose but we didn't disgrace ourselves," said Mele. "We were beaten by the best pitcher that there is anywhere."[1]

Oddly enough, Koufax didn't breeze through the early innings. Some luck, plus good defense, kept the Twins off the scoreboard until he found his rhythm in the middle frames. He walked right fielder Tony Oliva and third baseman Harmon Killebrew back-to-back in the first inning with two out, prompting Alston to get Drysdale up in the bullpen. But Koufax struck out catcher Earl Battey to escape any damage. In the third, Drysdale began warming again after shortstop Zoilo Versalles singled with one out. Versalles stole second, but had to return to first when center fielder Joe Nossek was called out for batter interference. Koufax then struck out Oliva for the third out.

(National Baseball Hall of Fame, Cooperstown, New York)

Lou Johnson opened the fourth with a home run to deep left, giving the Dodgers a 1-0 lead. Ron Fairly followed that with a double and scored on a single by first baseman Wes Parker. That was the end of the season for Kaat, who was replaced on the mound by Al Worthington.

The Twins' most serious threat came in the fifth. With one out, second baseman Frank Quilici doubled to left. Koufax walked the next batter, Rich Rollins, who was pinch-hitting for Worthington. Versalles was up next and he hit a scorcher toward third base that could have scored one, possibly two runs. However, third baseman Jim Gilliam made an outstanding backhanded stab and touched the bag for the force on Quilici. Nossek then grounded into a force play at second and the inning, and the Twins, were done.

"I didn't even have time to think about (the play)," said Gilliam. "It was about a foot from the bag and as I grabbed it, I slipped to one knee. But I saw the runner and knew I had time so I got up and stepped on the bag."[2]

"Gilliam's play could have been the turning point," said Mele. "Rollins has a chance to score from first, depending on what happens in the left-field corner. It was a great play, no doubt about it."[3]

Minnesota went three-up-three-down in the sixth, seventh, and eighth. Killebrew got a base hit with one out in the ninth, but—stop me if you've heard this one—Koufax struck out the next two batters to win the game with a flourish.

The game capped a remarkable World Series for Koufax, who was chosen Series MVP for the second time (he also earned the honor in 1963 when the Dodgers swept the New York Yankees). He went 2-1 and gave up only one earned run in 24 innings pitched (a 0.38 ERA), struck out 29, and threw two shutouts. He even had a hit and an RBI.

While Koufax deserved the award, he wasn't the only suitable candidate. Ron Fairly had 11 hits in the Series, for a .379 batting average, with two home runs, three doubles, and a 1.069 OPS. Wills also had 11 hits, for a .367 average. If they had an unsung-hero award, Lou Johnson would have won easily. Johnson was a 31-year-old career minor leaguer with only 96 games of major-league experience prior to the 1965 season. After playing for six different organizations in such far-flung outposts as St. Jean, Quebec, and Ponca City, Oklahoma, he got his big break in 1965 when regular left fielder Tommy Davis broke his ankle on May 1. Johnson proved to be a sparkplug for the Dodgers, helped carry them to the pennant, and batted .296 with two home runs in the fall classic, one of which was the Series-winning hit.

Associated Press sportswriter Joe Reichler summed up the reasons for the Dodgers' victory quite succinctly: "In the final essence, it was Dodger pitching with the shutouts and the ability of Los Angeles' supposedly weak hitters to all but match the Twins in home run power that swung the balance to the Dodgers."[4]

As for Mele, if he didn't have enough on his plate during the Series, his wife, Connie, was several days overdue with the couple's fifth child. In fact, Sam was told during Game Five that she had gone into labor, but that turned out to be a false alarm. Connie gave birth to their fifth child, Scott, four days after the Series ended.

SOURCES

Milwaukee Journal

San Bernardino (California) *Daily Sun*

Sports Illustrated

Janesville (Wisconsin) *Daily Gazette*

NOTES

1 William Leggett, "The Final Strength Was Sandy," *Sports Illustrated*, October 25, 1965.

2 Jack Hand, "Shutout Sandy Stymies Twins to Give Dodgers World Series," *San Bernardino* (California) *Daily Sun*, October 15, 1965.

3 Ibid.

4 Joe Reichler, "Koufax Dominant Figure of World Series Champions," *Janesville* (Wisconsin) *Daily Gazette*, October 15, 1965.

By the Numbers: Major League Baseball in 1965

BY DAN FIELDS

1ST

Black pitcher in AL history to win 20 games in a season: Mudcat Grant, on September 25. Grant tossed a one-hit shutout against the Washington Senators in the first game of a doubleheader to reach the milestone.

1-2

Rank of two Cuban-born Twins—shortstop Zoilo Versalles and right fielder Tony Oliva—in voting for the AL Most Valuable Player Award. Versalles became the first Latin American-born player to be named MVP. He led the AL in plate appearances (728), at-bats (666), runs scored (126), total bases (308), and extra-base hits (76); tied for first in doubles (45) and triples (12); finished second in hits (182); and was third in stolen bases (27). He also won his second Gold Glove Award, even though he led all major leaguers with 39 errors. Oliva led the AL in both batting average (.321) and hits (185) for the second consecutive year. He was second in runs scored (107); third in doubles (40), RBIs (98), total bases (283), and on-base percentage plus slugging average, or OPS (.870); and tied for third in extra-base hits (61). Oliva was named the AL Player of the Year by *The Sporting News*.

3RD

Consecutive year in which Zoilo Versalles led the AL or tied for the league lead in triples.

4TH

Gold Glove Award won by pitcher Jim Kaat. He won 16 consecutive Gold Gloves from 1962 through 1977.

5

RBIs by pitcher Camilo Pascual on April 27 against the Cleveland Indians. He hit a first-inning grand slam and also drove in catcher Earl Battey with a fifth-inning single. The Twins won, 11-1.

5

Hits by Tony Oliva in a July 21 game against the Boston Red Sox (first game of a doubleheader) and on July 28 against the Senators.

6

Twins who played in the All-Star Game before 46,706 fans at Minnesota's Metropolitan Stadium on July 13. Harmon Killebrew, the AL's starting first baseman, hit a two-run homer in the fifth inning. Earl Battey was the starting catcher. Other Twins who appeared were Mudcat Grant, Jimmie Hall, Tony Oliva, and Zoilo Versalles. Willie Mays of the San Francisco Giants led off the game with a home run; Juan Marichal of the Giants, the NL's starting pitcher, tossed three scoreless innings and was named the game's MVP. The NL won, 6-5.

7

Players on the 1965 Twins who had played with the Washington Senators before the team moved to Minnesota: Bob Allison, Earl Battey, Jim Kaat, Harmon Killebrew, Don Mincher, Camilo Pascual, and Zoilo Versalles.

15

Runs scored by the Twins in the fourth through seventh innings, against the Red Sox on May 25. During the fifth through the seventh innings, Mudcat Grant gave up a total of four home runs. The Twins had 20 hits for the game and won, 17-5.

17-1

Record of the 1965 Twins against the Red Sox. The Twins were 15-3 against the Senators and 13-5 against the New York Yankees.

21

Wins by Mudcat Grant, most in the AL, against seven losses. He also led the league in winning percentage (.750) and shutouts (6), finished second in games started (39), tied for second in complete games (14), and was third in innings pitched (270⅓). Grant also topped the league in home runs allowed, with 34. He was named the AL Pitcher of the Year by *The Sporting News*.

22-9

Record of the Twins in July. They outscored their opponents by 50 runs (168 to 118).

25

Home runs by Harmon Killebrew, most on the team, despite missing 48 games owing to a dislocated elbow.

32

Years since the Washington Senators/Minnesota Twins franchise had won the AL pennant, in 1933. The team played in Washington from 1901 to 1960 and moved to Minnesota in 1961.

42

Games started by Jim Kaat, tied (with Don Drysdale of the Los Angeles Dodgers) for most in the majors and tied (with Walter Johnson in 1910) for most in a single season in Senators/Twins franchise history as of 2014.

48.1

Caught-stealing percentage of catcher Earl Battey, best in the AL. He led the league in runners thrown out while attempting to steal, with 26.

93

Double plays grounded into by the Twins, fewest in the AL.

102

Wins by the Twins, against 60 losses. The team had a 51-30 record both at home and on the road. (In 1964 the Twins won only 79 games and lost 83.) As of 2014, the 102 wins were still the most in a single season in for the Senators/Twins franchise.

105

Double plays turned as shortstop by Zoilo Versalles, most in the majors.

166

Home runs given up by the Twins, most in the AL and tied for most in the majors.

172

Errors by the Twins, most in the majors. Their fielding percentage of .973 was lowest in the majors.

.254

Batting average of the Twins, highest in the AL.

257

Doubles by the Twins, most in the AL.

774
Runs scored by the Twins, most in the AL.

.997
Fielding percentage as catcher by Jerry Zimmerman, highest in the majors.

1,463,258
Attendance at Minnesota home games, highest in the AL and a Senators/Twins franchise record at the time.

1965 WORLD SERIES

0.38
Series ERA of Series MVP Sandy Koufax of the Dodgers. After giving up two runs (one earned) in six innings in Game Two and taking the loss, he shut out the Twins in Game Five and Game Seven.

2
Wins by Mudcat Grant (Game One and Game Six). He helped his own cause by hitting a three-run homer in Game Six. Grant also took the loss in Game Four. He had an ERA of 2.74 in 23 innings.

2
Losses by Jim Kaat (Game Five and Game Seven). He also got the win in Game Two. Kaat had an ERA of 3.77 in 14⅓ innings.

2.10
ERA of the Dodgers in the Series.

3
Number of times the Twins were shut out in the Series. In addition to the two shutouts by Koufax, Claude Osteen blanked Minnesota in Game Three. During the entire regular season, the Twins were shut out three times.

3.15
ERA of the Twins.

8
Hits by Zoilo Versalles, most on the Twins.

11
Hits each by Los Angeles right fielder Ron Fairly and shortstop Maury Wills. Fairly had at least one hit in all seven games (Wills was hitless in Game Seven). In Game Five, Wills had four hits and Fairly had three.

29
Strikeouts in 24 innings pitched by Sandy Koufax.

.195
Batting average of the Twins in the Series.

.274
Batting average of the Dodgers.

AROUND THE MAJORS IN 1965

0
Hits allowed by Dave Morehead of the Red Sox in a 2-0 blanking of the Indians on September 16. He walked only one batter. Morehead had a record of 10-18 for the year. After the no-hitter, Morehead threw only five more complete games and two shutouts before he retired in 1970.

0

Errors by Cleveland outfielder Rocky Colavito in 162 games. He handled 274 chances.

0

Home runs by Maury Wills during 1965 in 650 at-bats.

1ST

Career home run by Tony Perez of Cincinnati Reds, on April 13. The 22-year-old first baseman hit a grand slam off Denny Lemaster of the Milwaukee Braves. Perez hit his 379th and final home run more than 20 years later, on October 4, 1986.

1ST

Win as manager of the St. Louis Cardinals by Red Schoendienst, on April 17 against the Reds. The skipper would go on to win 1,041 games with the team.

1ST

Career win by Phil Niekro of the Braves, on May 13 against the Pittsburgh Pirates. The knuckleballer would win 318 games during his 24-year career.

1ST

Amateur Free Agent Draft, on June 8. Arizona State sophomore Rick Monday, selected by the Kansas City Athletics, was the first player chosen. Johnny Bench (17 years old) was selected in the second round by the Reds, and Nolan Ryan (18 years old) was selected in the 12th round by the New York Mets.

1ST

Major-league pitch faced by Brant Alyea of the Senators, on which he hit a three-run home run against Rudy May of the California Angels on September 12. Alyea would hit a total of 38 homers during his six-year career.

1ST

Gold Glove award won by pitcher Bob Gibson of the Cardinals, who took the prize nine consecutive years through 1973.

2

Home runs by Curt Blefary of the Baltimore Orioles in his first full major-league game, on April 17 against the Red Sox. He hit 20 more home runs in 1965 and finished in the top three in the AL in on-base percentage (.381) and walks (88) and in the top 10 in slugging average (.470), on-base percentage plus slugging average (.851), and at-bats per home run (21.0). He won the AL Rookie of the Year Award.

2

Consecutive games in which Willie Horton of the Detroit Tigers had two home runs and five RBIs, on May 13 against the Senators and May 14 against the Red Sox.

2

Consecutive games in which Felipe Alou of the Braves hit a leadoff home run, on July 26 and 27 against the Houston Astros.

2

Games in which Jim Maloney of the Reds held opponents hitless for 10 innings. On June 14, he lost a no-hit bid in the 11th inning against the Mets while striking out 18 batters. On August 19 (first game of a doubleheader), he won a 10-inning no-hitter against the Chicago Cubs despite issuing 10 walks.

2ND

NL MVP Award won by Willie Mays, who led the majors in home runs (52), total bases (360), on-base percentage (.398), slugging average (.645), and on-base percentage plus slugging average (1.043). He was second in the NL in runs scored (118) and extra-base hits (76) and third in batting average (.317) and RBIs (112). And he won his ninth consecutive Gold Glove Award.

2ND

Unanimous Cy Young Award won by Sandy Koufax, who struck out 382 batters (a modern-day record until 1973) while leading the major leagues in wins (26), ERA (2.04), winning percentage (.765), innings pitched (335⅔), complete games (27), walks and hits per inning pitched (0.855, the lowest in the majors since 1915), and ratio of strikeouts to walks (5.38, the highest in the majors since 1913).

2.18

ERA of Sam McDowell of the Indians, lowest in the AL.

4

Home runs by the Braves (Joe Torre, Felipe Alou, Hank Aaron, and Gene Oliver) in the 10th inning against the Cubs on June 8. The Braves won, 8-2.

4

Runs driven in by Mel Stottlemyre of the Yankees with a fifth-inning fly ball to deep center field at Yankee Stadium on July 20, against Bill Monbouquette of the Red Sox. It was the first inside-the-park grand slam by a pitcher since 1910.

4

Future Hall of Fame pitchers who debuted in 1965: Steve Carlton (on April 12 with the Cardinals), Catfish Hunter (on May 13 with the Athletics), Fergie Jenkins (September 10 with the Philadelphia Phillies), and Jim Palmer (April 17 with the Orioles). The foursome would combine for nine Cy Young Awards, 1,105 wins, 11,552 strikeouts, and 199 shutouts.

4TH

No-hitter (in four consecutive years) thrown by Sandy Koufax, on September 9 against the Cubs. In his only perfect game, Koufax struck out 14 batters, including the last six he faced. Opposing pitcher Bob Hendley allowed only one hit and one walk as the Dodgers won, 1-0.

6

Hits, including two home runs, in six at-bats by 21-year-old Joe Morgan of the Astros, on July 8 against the Braves. Despite Morgan's accomplishments, the Braves won 9-8 in 12 innings.

6

Milwaukee players with at least 20 home runs: Hank Aaron (32), Eddie Mathews (32), Mack Jones (31), Joe Torre (27), Felipe Alou (23), and Gene Oliver (21). The Braves led the majors with 196 home runs.

7

Consecutive batters struck out by Denny McLain of the Tigers, against the Red Sox on June 15. After starter Dave Wickersham gave up three runs in a third of an inning, McLain replaced him and struck out the first seven batters he faced. He totaled 14 strikeouts in only 6⅔ innings of work.

8

RBIs by catcher Ed Bailey of the Cubs on July 22 against the Phillies. He hit a three-run homer in the second inning and a grand slam in the fifth inning. In 90 games with the Giants and the Cubs in 1965, Bailey had five home runs and 26 RBIs.

9

Positions played by Bert Campaneris of the Athletics on September 8 against the Angels. He played a different position in each of the first nine innings of a

12-inning game and gave up only one run while on the mound (eighth inning).

10

Shutouts thrown by Juan Marichal, most in the majors.

10.7

Strikeouts per nine innings pitched by Sam McDowell, best in the majors and an AL record that lasted until 1989.

15

Wins as a relief pitcher by Eddie Fisher of the Chicago White Sox. He also had 24 saves. Fisher and Hoyt Wilhelm (20 saves) became the first teammates with at least 20 saves in a season.

16

Triples by Johnny Callison of the Phillies, most in the majors.

17

Home runs by Willie Mays in August, setting an NL record for the most in any month. From August 16 through 22, he homered in six consecutive games in which he played.

17

Runs allowed by the Dodgers during their final 16 games. The team won 15 of the 16 games and shut out opponents eight times.

18

Innings in a scoreless tie between the Mets and the Phillies on October 2, in the second game of a doubleheader. Philadelphia southpaw Chris Short had 18 strikeouts in 15 innings. The Phillies won the first game, 6-0. For the day, the Mets scored 0 runs and struck out 31 times in 27 innings.

18

Complete games by Mel Stottlemyre, most in the AL.

22

Wild pitches by Tony Cloninger of the Braves, most in the majors. Sam McDowell led the AL, with 17.

24

Losses by Jack Fisher of the Mets, most in the majors, against eight wins. Teammate Al Jackson lost 20 games and won eight.

27

Consecutive games with a hit by Vada Pinson of the Reds, from September 3 through October 3 (the end of the season). Pinson also had a hit in his first four games in 1966, running the streak to 31 games.

30

Saves in 1965 by Ted Abernathy of the Cubs, after he held the Mets hitless for 1⅔ innings on September 18. He became the first major-league pitcher to reach this mark, and he finished the season with 31 saves. Ron Kline of the Senators tied the AL record with 29 saves.

31 2/3

Consecutive scoreless innings pitched by reliever Stu Miller of the Orioles, from April 24 to June 8. Bob Veale of the Pirates tossed 29⅓ scoreless innings (including two shutouts) from May 28 to June 10.

32

Home runs by Tony Conigliaro of the Red Sox, most in the AL. At 20 years old, he became the youngest player to win a home-run crown.

33
Passed balls by J.C. Martin of the White Sox, an AL record until 1987.

35 1/3
Consecutive innings without scoring a run by the Indians, from July 9 (first game of a doubleheader) to July 14.

36 1/3
Consecutive scoreless innings pitched by the White Sox from June 23 (first game of a doubleheader) to June 26.

40
Doubles by Hank Aaron, most in the NL.

42.7
At-bats per strikeout by Nellie Fox during his 19-year career, which ended in 1965 with the Astros. As of 2014, the ratio was the fifth highest in major-league history.

49
Wins by Sandy Koufax (26) and Don Drysdale (23) of the Dodgers. By comparison, the Mets won 50 games in 1965.

59 YEARS, 2 MONTHS
Age of Satchel Paige on September 25, when he pitched the first three innings for the Athletics against the Red Sox. In his first major-league appearance in 12 years, Paige allowed just one hit, a double by Carl Yastrzemski, and struck out opposing pitcher Bill Monbouquette.

69
RBIs by NL Rookie of the Year Jim Lefebvre of the Dodgers. He hit 12 home runs and batted .250.

79
Extra-base hits by Billy Williams of the Cubs, the most in the majors.

84
Games played by Ted Abernathy, a major-league record at the time for pitchers. He did not commit an error all season. Eddie Fisher played in 82 games, an AL record at the time.

91
Home runs by San Francisco's Willie Mays (52) and Willie McCovey (39). By comparison, the Dodgers hit only 78 home runs in 1965.

94
Stolen bases by Maury Wills, the most in the majors. It was his sixth consecutive year as the NL leader. Bert Campaneris topped the AL, with 51 steals. It was the first of five consecutive years in which Campaneris had at least 50 steals and the first of 10 consecutive years in which he had at least 30 steals.

97
Walks drawn by Joe Morgan, the most in the majors. Rocky Colavito led the AL, with 93 walks.

126
Runs scored by Tommy Harper of the Reds, the most in the NL.

130

RBIs by Deron Johnson of the Reds, the most in the majors. Teammate Frank Robinson was second, with 113. Rocky Colavito led the AL with 108 RBIs.

150

Strikeouts by Dick Allen of the Phillies, the most in the majors.

175-404

Record of Casey Stengel as manager of the Mets. The 75-year-old Stengel announced his retirement on August 30. He won seven World Series titles and 10 pennants as manager of the Yankees from 1949 through 1960.

.185

Batting average of Ed Brinkman of the Senators, with only 82 hits in 444 at-bats.

209

Hits by Pete Rose of the Red, the most in the majors. Teammate Vada Pinson was second, with 204.

291

Innings pitched by Mel Stottlemyre, the most in the AL.

.300

Batting average of Don Drysdale, who had 39 hits (including seven home runs) in 130 at-bats.

317

Wins as teammates by Bob Friend (176) and Vern Law (141) of the Pirates during 13 seasons (1951, 1954-1965).

325

Strikeouts thrown by Sam McDowell, the most in the AL. He was the first pitcher in the junior circuit with at least 300 strikeouts in a season since Bob Feller had 348 in 1946.

.329

Batting average of Roberto Clemente of the Pirates, the highest in the majors. He also led the majors in 1964, with a .339 average.

363

Career wins by Warren Spahn when he retired after the 1965 season. During his final year, he had a 4-12 record with the Mets and a 3-4 record with the Giants. His other 356 wins were with the Boston/Milwaukee Braves. As of 2014, Spahn still held the record for the most career wins by a left-handed pitcher.

.395/.536/.932

On-base percentage, slugging average, and on-base percentage plus slugging average of Carl Yastrzemski, all tops in the AL.

.475

Winning percentage of the Yankees, with a 77-85 record. It was the team's first losing season in 40 years.

500

Career home runs by Willie Mays after his homer against Houston on September 13. He was 34 years and 4 months old. At the time, only Jimmie Foxx had reached the milestone at a younger age.

670

At-bats by Pete Rose, the most in the majors. Teammate Vada Pinson was second, with 669.

773

Home runs as teammates by Hank Aaron and Eddie Mathews, on August 20. When Mathews hit his 28th home run of the year, he and Aaron passed Babe Ruth and Lou Gehrig as the most prolific home-run tandem in major-league history.

.994

Career fielding percentage as a first baseman by Vic Power, who retired after the 1965 season. He won seven consecutive Gold Gloves from 1958 through 1964. He was the last active player who had been a member of the Philadelphia Athletics.

1,000

Career RBIs by Al Kaline (all with the Tigers) on June 20 and by Frank Robinson (all with the Reds) on September 21. Robinson accomplished the feat in his 10th year and Kaline in his 13th.

1,699

Career games as catcher by Yogi Berra, who was behind the plate for two games with the Mets in 1965. He appeared in two other games as a pinch-hitter during his final year as a player.

1,750

Dollars that Juan Marichal was fined for hitting Los Angeles catcher John Roseboro on the head with a bat on August 22, sparking a melee that lasted some 15 minutes. Marichal took offense when Roseboro returned a pitch to the mound close to the Dominican ace's head. The fine was an NL record at the time. Marichal was also suspended for eight games.

2,000

Career games by Mickey Mantle, on September 18. A crowd of more than 50,000 turned out for Mickey Mantle Day at Yankee Stadium. He was given a barbecue grill in the shape of a prairie schooner and a six-foot kosher salami weighing 100 pounds.

2,230

Plate appearances by teammates Pete Rose (757), Tommy Harper (745), and Vada Pinson (728), who finished 1-2-3 in the NL.

12,577

Attendance at the last game the Braves played in Milwaukee's County Stadium, on September 22 against the Dodgers. The Braves lost 7-6 in 11 innings. The team relocated in Atlanta in 1966.

47,876

Attendance at the opening of Harris County Domed Stadium (the Astrodome) on April 9. The Astros beat the Yankees 2-1 in an exhibition game that went 12 innings. President Lyndon B. Johnson and Texas Governor John Connally were among the attendees.

SOURCES

Nemec, David (editor), *The Baseball Chronicle: Year-by-Year History of Major League Baseball* (Lincolnwood, Illinois: Publications International, 2003).

Society for American Baseball Research, *The SABR Baseball List and Record Book* (New York: Scribner, 2007).

Solomon, Burt, *The Baseball Timeline* (New York: DK Publishing, 2001).

Sugar, Burt Randolph (editor), *The Baseball Maniac's Almanac*, third edition (New York: Skyhorse Publishing, 2012).

baseball-almanac.com

baseballlibrary.com/chronology

baseball-reference.com

retrosheet.org

thisgreatgame.com/1965-baseball-history.html

A Surprising Disappointment: The Minnesota Twins of the Late 1960s

BY DANIEL R. LEVITT

ON OCTOBER 14, 1965, THE Minnesota Twins lost a heartbreaking World Series Game Seven to Sandy Koufax and the Los Angeles Dodgers, 2-0. While the disappointment was palpable, there was every reason to believe the Twins would soon be back in the Series. The team had won the pennant convincingly with a record of 102-60, seven games ahead of the second-place Chicago White Sox. Owner Calvin Griffith, acting as his own general manager, had built a deep and talented club. And the once mighty New York Yankees dynasty that had dominated the American League over the previous four decades appeared to have run its course.

In Harmon Killebrew and Tony Oliva, the Twins had two of the top hitters in the league. Shortstop Zoilo Versalles led the league in total bases and runs scored, won a Gold Glove, and was named the league's Most Valuable Player. Along with Versalles, among the team's position players *The Sporting News* named Oliva, center fielder Jimmie Hall and catcher Earl Battey to its year-end American League all-star team. Left fielder Bob Allison was only one season removed from finishing second in the league in on-base percentage and fourth in slugging.

Led by these and other stars, the team had dominated the American League offensively with 774 runs; Detroit finished a distant second with 680. In 1963 and 1964 the team had hit 225 and 221 home runs respectively, the second and third highest single-season totals of all time up to that point. In 1965 manager Sam Mele chose to emphasize the team's speed and the club stole 92 bases — fourth in the league — while being caught only 33 times. The Twins featured a terrific blend of power and speed.

The team also sported an excellent and deep pitching staff. Minnesota finished third in the league in ERA despite pitching in one of the league's better hitters' parks. Six pitchers started at least nine games, and every one could boast an ERA below the league average. Between 1963 and 1970 each of the six would win 20 games in a season at least once.

Rotation anchor Jim Kaat won 283 games over the course of his 25-year career. One of the league's best left-handers in the mid-1960s, in 1965 Kaat went 18-11 with a 2.83 ERA while leading the league in games started. Teammate Jim "Mudcat" Grant led the league with 21 wins and a .750 winning percentage. At that time only one Cy Young Award winner was named for the major leagues; in 1965 it went to the National League's Sandy Koufax. *The Sporting News*, however, named a Pitcher of the Year for each league and awarded the American League honor to Grant.

Curveball pitcher Camilo Pascual was the third Twin with more than 20 starts in 1965. He led the league in strikeouts from 1961 to 1963 and finished second in 1964, winning 20 games in both 1962 and 1963. Unfortunately, after a great start to the 1965 season that included winning his first eight decisions, he tore a muscle in his back near his shoulder. Pascual made it back by early September and started Game Three of the World Series. Although he pitched with less than stellar success after his return, Pascual was only 31, and the Twins had every reason to believe he would bounce back in 1966.

The other three hurlers who started at least nine games consisted of two youngsters, 20-year-old Dave Boswell and 21-year-old Jim Merritt, along with swingman Jim Perry. Boswell and Merritt both turned in an ERA below the league average and struck out more than seven batters per nine innings. Fourth starter Perry finished ninth in the league in ERA. Al Worthington, with 21 saves and a 2.13 ERA, anchored a good bullpen.

The Twins were not only talented but young. No player with more than 150 at-bats was yet on the wrong side of 30; of the starting pitchers, only Pascual was older than 30. With good reason, the Twins and their fans looked forward to a promising future.

But it was not to be. The Twins would not again win the pennant for more than 20 years, behind a completely different generation of players. The club came agonizingly close in 1967 when no dominant team emerged, and after some retooling won division titles in 1969 and 1970. Nevertheless, with a boatload of young talent that had already proved it could win at the highest level, Minnesota averaged only 86 wins from 1966 through 1968. This was not going to win a pennant in the 10-team American League.

So what happened? Why did the Twins, who showed so much promise in 1965, fail to capture another flag? Like many complex questions, one can identify several causes for the failure to repeat. Most significant was the unexpected and dramatic falloff in production from the top position players. The table below highlights the players' performance before and after their pennant-winning season. Every single player batted worse over the remainder of his career than he had through 1965. And not just a little bit worse; several simply collapsed below the level of a major-league-caliber baseball player.

Change in Twins Player Batting Statistics After 1965

Player	Age in 1965	Through 1965 AVG/OBP/SLG	OPS	After 1965 AVG/OBP/SLG	OPS	dOPS
Zoilo Versalles	25	259/303/408	711	217/270/304	573	-138
Tony Oliva	26	324/371/526	897	299/349/464	813	-84
Jimmie Hall	27	276/342/488	830	229/296/371	667	-163
Bob Allison	30	259/364/482	846	243/340/443	784	-63
Rich Rollins	27	283/347/405	752	239/289/353	642	-110
H Killebrew	29	261/368/534	902	252/382/486	868	-34
Earl Battey	30	276/353/425	778	235/318/300	619	-160
Don Mincher	27	242/340/501	842	252/352/429	781	-61

Jimmie Hall played for several years after 1965, but never again as a more than a stopgap. Some of his decline may be attributed to a beaning, but in any case his dramatic falloff left the Twins with a gaping hole in center field. Catcher Earl Battey suffered from chronically sore knees, exacerbated by goiter and weight gain that likely led to a premature end to his career. But the suddenness with which he fell from being one of the league's top catchers to being out of the league in just two years would have surprised almost any organization. Third baseman Rich Rollins had regressed since breaking in as a regular in 1962, when he actually led all American League players in votes for the All-Star Game. The next year he hit .307 to finish third in the batting race, and in 1964 he led the league in triples. Nevertheless, despite his still young age, Rollins would never again be a quality major-league regular after 1965. In 1966 Bob Allison suffered a broken bone in his hand and turned in only two more quality seasons. Tony Oliva's recurring problems with his right knee and a shoulder separation in 1968 left him a star but well below the level he had established during his first two years as a regular.

Zoilo Versalles, though, may have been the saddest case of all. Uncovered by legendary scout Joe Cambria, in the summer of 1957 Versalles had arrived in Key West as a 17-year-old: hopeful, scared, unable to communicate in English, and thrown into a segregated society he didn't understand. Versalles covered much of his anxiety with a cocky swagger and a reputation as a hot dog. The talented youngster quickly worked his way through the Twins system and by 1961 was the team's regular shortstop as a 21-year-old.

After his 1965 MVP season, however, Versalles completely lost his ability to play baseball. By 1967 he was one of the worst starting regulars in the league; both his on-base and slugging percentages fell below .285. Sportswriter Doug Grow once asked Griffith what had happened. Griffith told him, "drugs." Versalles had been prescribed pain killers for a chronically bad back. Unfamiliar with the culture and the language, Versalles often ignored the correct dosage, taking well over the prescribed amount.[1]

How exactly leadership of a baseball team affects performance on the field has long been debated. The Oakland A's of the 1970s fought each other and owner Charles Finley to three World Series victories. In many other instances, however, turmoil and dissension have often been used to explain the failure of otherwise talented clubs. The Twins of the late 1960s were fractured into several distinct cliques, and unlike the A's with a strong, skilled manager in Dick Williams, they had no one with a firm hand on the reins.

Twins owner Calvin Griffith grew up in baseball and by the early 1960s directed a truly family operation. Brothers Sherry, Jimmy, and Billy Robertson along with brother-in-law Joe Haynes all held down key executive positions within the organization. By the time Griffith moved the franchise to Minnesota, he had become an astute judge of baseball talent and was ably assisted by his family and scouts. Moreover, prior to the death of Haynes in 1967 and Sherry Robertson in 1970 and the changing baseball economics that Griffith never really understood, the Twins organization should be regarded as one of the league's more successful, both on the field and in the stands. Over their first decade after moving from Washington to Minnesota in 1961, the Twins led the American League in attendance.

Despite his success, Griffith represented the last of the family owners; by the late 1960s baseball teams were owned by men who had made their fortunes in other lines of work and bought into baseball. Because Griffith operated as his own general manager and was not particularly skilled at leadership, he often micromanaged and rankled those who worked for him, somewhat akin to the problems George Steinbrenner experienced in the 1980s when not buffered by a solid general manager. His desire for hands-on involvement also occasionally hindered his hiring judgment.

After a disappointing 1964 season in which the Twins won only 79 games, Griffith cut manager Sam Mele's salary by $3,000 and publicly criticized his manager for being "too nice a guy" and managing a team that played sloppy baseball. Mele's managing philosophy of offering criticism and encouragement in private and highlighting what he wanted each player to practice, but not providing a lot of specific instruction, played into Griffith's concerns.[2]

To remedy the situation, Griffith foisted two brilliant but strong-willed coaches on Mele: pitching coach Johnny Sain and third-base coach Billy Martin. Much of the hullabaloo surrounding Sain derived from his tendency to separate the pitchers from the position players. Many pitchers he coached were his ardent students and in particular on the Twins, Jim Kaat. Martin was a ferocious competitor and helped enormously in relating to the Latino players. He was also a short-tempered, paranoid bully.

After winning the pennant, the beleaguered Mele became a hot commodity, and the White Sox tried to lure him away by offering him a raise. Mele remained loyal to Griffith, though, and settled for a raise from the Twins without pushing his salary demands. He still had his two strong-willed, independent minded coaches to deal with, however.[3]

By 1966 Martin and Sain hated each other, and Mele was at odds with his pitching coach as well. The antagonism flared in midseason in Kansas City when Sain confronted Martin after the third-base coach had cussed out a pitcher over a squeeze play. Martin and Sain were both angry and neither felt that Mele sufficiently took control of the situation. Moreover, in the aftermath of the altercation, players began to take sides, always a dangerous situation. After that season, in which the Twins finished 89-73, nine games behind the Orioles, Griffith jettisoned Sain. In response, Kaat, who went 25-13 and surely would have won the American League Cy Young Award had the award been bestowed in both leagues, sent a widely-circulated open letter defending Sain and criticizing the decision to fire him, and took over Sain's locker.

Finally, after a 25-25 start to the 1967 season, Griffith fired Mele and promoted Cal Ermer from the Twins' Triple-A farm team in Denver. Ermer found himself in an almost impossible situation: a man with little major-league experience as either a player or coach thrust into a team fractured into cliques, both racial and otherwise, made up of stars who had tasted a pennant, and with a hands-on owner breathing over his shoulder.

To Calvin Griffith's credit, he had assembled one of baseball's more racially mixed teams. Many of the team's stars were African-Americans and Cubans who would have been banned for being too dark-skinned before 1947. But race relations in America in the 1960s were in flux, and baseball was not exempt. Just 12 days into his tenure, Ermer was faced with a difficult situation on the team bus in Detroit, a city teeming with racial tension.

White pitcher Dave Boswell was playing with a gun, when Grant, who is black, told him to put it away. When Boswell ignored him, Oliva also told Boswell to knock it off. "You Cubans play with guns down there," Boswell reportedly replied. "We got a right to play with guns up here."[4] Sandy Valdespino and Ted Uhlaender nearly came to blows, before cooler heads held them back. Ermer went to the back of the bus to calm things down and later held a meeting at the hotel to simmer down the tensions. Many of the black players remained unconvinced, but there can be no doubt that the team responded on the field. "Cal Ermer was a great guy," Kaat remembered. "I don't know if he ever had control over big-league players, but he was a different presence than Sam and it worked for the rest of that season."[5] And for his first 112 games the team responded: the Twins went 66-44 (with two ties), taking a slim lead in the pennant race into the final weekend.

But the Twins could not seem to shake their controversies. Holding onto a one-game lead, the team once again faced off against itself on September 29. In a contentious players-only meeting to divvy up the World Series money (a small portion was also allotted to high-finishing teams that did not win the pennant), many of the players argued against giving Mele a share. Once this had been pushed through, five members of the pro-Mele faction symbolically voted not to give Ermer a share either. More substantively, 11 players agreed to pool their own shares to give Mele a portion. Even the commissioner's office felt the need to weigh in and castigate the players but otherwise took no action. In the aftermath of this dramatic meeting, the Twins lost the final two games of the season, and the pennant, in Boston.

Sportswriter Jeff Miller suggested that the Twins players were frustrated that the club made no moves during the year to bolster the team while their competitors improved throughout the season. he Red Sox picked up Jerry Adair, Gary Bell and Elston Howard, all quality veterans who played a large role in the team's pennant drive, and then signed Ken Harrelson as a reaction to Tony Conigliaro's eye injury. The White Sox acquired Don McMahon, Ken Boyer, and Rocky Colavito and all were given important roles. The Tigers obtained veteran Eddie Mathews and he played a key role down the stretch at both third base and first base. The Twins made no major in-season moves. One regular grumbled, "We got a $35,000 bench."[6]

The team's success under Ermer over the last half of 1967 did not translate into 1968. In addition to the players' dropoff noted earlier, Killebrew suffered a brutal hamstring injury that contributed to a 79-83 record. "It has been quite apparent to me that Ermer has lost control over the club," Griffith complained late in the season.[7] Moreover, this was not a lone sentiment. "Cal Ermer was a weak man," wrote catcher John Roseboro. "He was quiet like [Los Angeles Dodgers manager Walter] Alston, but he didn't have Walt's firmness and he didn't have the respect Walter had."[8] Griffith, a lifelong baseball man with strong opinions of his own, too often exacerbated the situation by criticizing Ermer, making it hard for him to exercise the necessary managerial authority.

With the firing of Ermer, for 1969 Griffith finally relented and hired fan favorite and domineering personality Billy Martin. In this first year of two divisions, Martin brought the Twins home first in the West. With young star Rod Carew and several other quality newcomers having joined the aging nucleus of 1965, the Twins could still perform at a fairly high level. But it was too little, too late. The Orioles had built a superior team in Baltimore, ranked by some as one of the greatest of all time. The Twins' window of opportunity had closed.

The Twins also had two players changing positions so often that it must have contributed to the difficulty of addressing the team's needs and slumping players. Although defensive versatility is valuable in the abstract, the Twins' continual changes inhibited making sound long-term decisions based on which positions needed improvement. As the table below indicates, Harmon Killebrew changed positions among first base, third base, and the outfield on what seemed an annual basis depending on the Twins' personnel situation. For example, to start the 1965 season the Twins moved Killebrew to first base and returned Allison to the outfield—after his one-year experiment playing first. Then toward the end the season, the Twins entered into a complex platoon in which Killebrew played third against right-handed pitchers with Don Mincher at first base and first against lefties with Rollins at third.

Killebrew Games by Position

Year	1B	3B	LF
1959	0	150	4
1960	71	65	0
1961	119	45	2
1962	4	0	151
1963	0	0	137
1964	0	0	157
1965	72	44	2
1966	42	107	18
1967	160	3	0
1968	77	11	0
1969	80	105	0
1970	28	138	0

The Twins never really knew whether they needed a third baseman or a first baseman. In 1967, after trading Don Mincher, the Twins moved Killebrew back to first. After Killebrew ruptured a hamstring muscle stretching for a throw in the 1968 All-Star Game, the Twins installed perennial prospect Rich Reese, then 26 years old, at first. Reese hit no more than adequately over the second half of the season, but the Twins kept Killebrew at third and Reese as the starting first baseman against right-handed pitching for 1969 (Killebrew still played in 80 games at first, Reese 117). Reese actually had a very strong 1969 season but never again hit above .261 or topped 10 home runs.

As strange as Killebrew's odyssey around the diamond appears, that of Cesar Tovar was even more bizarre. Tovar first appeared regularly in 1966 as a candidate to fill the second-base hole, but played at least 20 games at third and in the outfield as well. The table below summarizes Tovar's first five years as a regular.

Tovar Games by Position

Year	2B	3B	SS	OF
1966	76	0	31	24
1967	36	70	9	74
1968	18	75	35	78
1969	41	20	0	113
1970	8	4	0	151

In 1967 Tovar led the league in at-bats while appearing at no defensive position more than 74 times. At the end of the season one Minneapolis sportswriter cast a vote for Tovar as MVP, thus preventing Triple Crown winner Carl Yastrzemski from a unanimous election.

One year of Tovar-like versatility can be extremely valuable to a team filling in-season holes due to injuries or slumps, but when it shows up over an extended period of time, it more likely signifies a team unable or unwilling to make decisive player personnel decisions.

Whether because of the constant position shifts or simply due to the club's preference for sluggers, the Twins never really exhibited the fielding prowess often demonstrated by top teams. The table below summarizes the club's fielding percentage and Defensive Efficiency Ratio (the fraction of balls in play that the team turns into outs—a good proxy for overall team defense).

Minnesota Twins Fielding Statistics

Year	Fld%	Rank	DER	Rank
1964	.977	9	.712	7
1965	.973	10	.724	3
1966	.977	7	.722	2
1967	.978	6	.704	10
1968	.973	10	.715	8
1969	.977	8	.709	8
1970	.980	4	.714	6

Over the four-year period 1966 through 1969, the Twins finished in the top half of the league in either statistic only once. One cannot help but feel that Griffith and his managers could have crafted a better team defense without sacrificing much on offense.

In one of the odder mistakes, the Twins had a potentially great pitcher whom they simply didn't use. Early in 1963 season the Twins traded for Cleveland's Jim Perry, a good pitcher who had been struggling recently. During Perry's first two years in the majors, 1959 and 1960, he had won 30 games while leading the league in wins, starts, and shutouts in 1960. He fell off over the next couple of years, but with the help of Twins pitching coach Johnny Sain and a new curveball, he rejuvenated his career in Minnesota. For some reason, however, the Twins relegated Perry to the periphery of the rotation, essentially keeping him as a swing man from 1965 to 1968. Only once during those four years did Perry start more than 20 games despite having an ERA better than any rotation regular in three of them. When Martin finally put Perry into the rotation in 1969, he went 20-6. The next year he won the Cy Young Award with a 24-12 record. Perry as of 2014 held the Twins' career record for lowest ERA (minimum 750 IP) at 3.15 and finished with a career total of 215 wins.

By 1965 Calvin Griffith had built a terrific young team in Minnesota. The team won the American League pennant by a comfortable margin and came within a Sandy Koufax three-hitter of winning Game Seven of the World Series. Griffith, a lifelong baseball man, had built a solid organization manned primarily by baseball-savvy family members and close friends. The team drew well at the gate, and Griffith paid his players well by the standards of the time. But this group of Twins players could not repeat. Too many of the stars suffered unexpected rapid and severe declines, and in fairness to Griffith, it is almost impossible to know when a star is truly declining and when it is simply a one-year aberration, especially at the young age of many of his players. Furthermore, Griffith did continue to add talent over the next couple of years, most notably second baseman Rod Carew.

Griffith also seemed to lose control over the team. The team bickered and fought with itself in nearly every possible permutation: coach versus coach, coach versus management, and player versus player. Until hiring Martin in 1969 Griffith was unwilling to vest in his managers the sort of authority necessary to truly manage a diverse group of stars with strong personalities. In the years after 1965, a combination of bad luck and ill-defined manager control thwarted the Twins from reprising their success.

SOURCES

Anderson, Dr. Wayne J., *Harmon Killebrew: Baseball's Superstar* (Salt Lake City: Deseret Book, 1971).

Armour, Mark L., and Daniel R. Levitt, *Paths to Glory* (Washington D.C.: Brassey's, 2003).

Carew, Rod, with Ira Berkow, *Carew* (New York: Simon and Schuster, 1979).

Golenbock, Peter, *Wild, High and Tight: The Life and Death of Billy Martin* (New York: St. Martin's Press, 1994).

Kerr, Jon, *Calvin: Baseball's Last Dinosaur* (Dubuque, Iowa: Wm. C. Brown, 1990).

Miller, Jeff, *Down to the Wire* (Dallas: Taylor Publishing, 1992).

Roseboro, John, with Bill Libby, *Glory Days With the Dodgers and Other Days With Others* (New York: Atheneum, 1978).

Sporting News Baseball Guides. 1965 through 1970.

Urdahl, Dean, *Touching Base With Our Memories* (St. Cloud, Minnesota: North Star Press of St. Cloud, 2001).

Zanger, Jack, *Major League Baseball*, 1965 through 1970.

Furlong, Bill, "The Feuding Twins: Inside a Team in Turmoil," *Sport*, April, 1968.

Jordan, Pat, "In a World of Windmills," *Sports Illustrated*, May 8, 1972.

Leggett, William, "A Wild Finale—and It's Boston," *Sports Illustrated*, October 9, 1967.

Nichols, Max, "The Kaat Organization," *Sport*, December, 1966.

———, "Sam Mele: A Study in Pressure," *Sport*, April, 1966.

Smith, Gary, "A Lingering Vestige of Yesterday," *Sports Illustrated*, April 4, 1983.

Williams, Jim, "Which Is the Real Jim Kaat," *All Star Sports*, August 1968.

"Minnesota Twins," *Sports Illustrated*, April 18, 1966.

NOTES

1 Doug Grow, Phone Interview, February 21, 2011.
2 Nichols, *Sam Mele*, 81.
3 Miller, 71.
4 Furlong, 24.
5 *Minneapolis Star Tribune*, July 21, 2007, C8.
6 Miller, 146-147.
7 Kerr, 78.
8 Roseboro, 230.

Contributors

MARC Z. AARON is a Certified Public Accountant and Certified Valuation Analyst with a tax practice in Randolph, Vermont. He is also an adjunct professor of economics at Vermont Technical College and the Anglo American University in Prague and an adjunct professor of accounting at Norwich University and the University of New York in Prague. A born and bred Yankees fan, Marc has four sons, coached little league for six seasons, and like Tony La Russa, retired after his team (sadly named Red Sox) won the league championship. Marc a tournament tennis player, has been a ranked singles player by the New England United States Tennis Association (USTA) and has captained several USTA league teams.

MARK ARMOUR is the co-author of *In Pursuit of Pennants—Baseball Operations from Deadball to Moneyball* (Nebraska, 2015) and the director a SABR's Baseball Biography Project. He lives in Oregon's Willamette Valley.

PETER C. BJARKMAN is Senior Writer for www.BaseballdeCuba.com.

ALAN COHEN is a retired insurance underwriter who has been a member of SABR since 2011. He has written 20 biographies for the SABR bio-project. A native of Long Island, he now resides in West Hartford, Connecticut with his wife Frances, two cats and two dogs. He graduated from Franklin and Marshall College in 1968. His article about the Hearst Sandlot Classic, which launched the careers of 88 major leaguers, appeared in the Fall, 2013 edition of the Baseball research Journal. During the baseball season, he serves as datacaster (stringer) for the New Britain Rock Cats of the Eastern League.

TRACY J.R. COLLINS is a native of Ludington, Michigan, and has a Ph.D. from Purdue University. When she is not teaching Wuthering Heights and other "baggy monsters," she plays softball, reads and writes about baseball literature and plays catch in her backyard with her husband and daughter.

RORY COSTELLO has written biographies of players from numerous different countries but has a special fondness for Latin Americans. Conducting research in Spanish adds an extra dimension. César Tovar was always at the top of the Twins' box scores when Rory first became a fan. He lives in Brooklyn, New York with his wife Noriko and son Kai.

JEFF ENGLISH is a graduate of Florida State University and resides in Tallahassee, Florida with his wife Allison and twin sons, Elliott and Oscar. He is a lifelong Cubs fan and serves as secretary of the North Florida/Buck O'Neil SABR chapter.

GREG ERION is retired from the railroad industry and currently teaches history part time at Skyline Community College in San Bruno, California. He has written several biographies for SABR's BioProject and is currently working on a book about the 1959 season. He and his wife Barbara live in South San Francisco, California.

DAN FIELDS is a manuscript editor at the New England Journal of Medicine. He loves baseball trivia, and he regularly attends Boston Red Sox and Pawtucket (RI) Red Sox games with this teenage son. Dan lives in Framingham, Massachusetts, and can be reached at dfields820@gmail.com.

A retired English professor, **JAN FINKEL** has been a member of SABR since 1994, and serves as Chief Editor of the Biography Project, to which he has contributed several articles. He readily admits to frequently confusing his twin passions of great books and baseball, sometimes to strange effect. He lives on Deep Creek Lake in western Maryland with his wife Judy.

JAMES FORR is a past winner of the McFarland-SABR Baseball Research Award, and co-author (with David Proctor) of Pie Traynor: A Baseball Biography. He lives in Scottsdale, Arizona. He was a fact-checker for a number of pieces in several BioProject books, and for all of the items in this book. He is one of the leaders of SABR's Games Project.

CHIP GREENE has been a SABR member since 2006. A lifelong Orioles fan, he is a frequent contributor to SABR's Biography Project and is currently editing an upcoming BioProject book about the three-time World Champion Oakland A's. Chip's grandfather, Nelson Greene, pitched eleven games for the Brooklyn Dodgers during the 1924-25 seasons. A management consultant, Chip lives in Waynesboro, PA, with his wife, Elaine, and two daughters, Anna and Haley.

KEVIN HENNESSY is the Bioenergy Manager for the State of Minnesota. In his younger days he had a 17-year career as a secondary math and science teacher, with 16 of those years in the Minneapolis Public School system. He resides with his wife in St. Paul, Minnesota.

JACK HERRMANN is an attorney and Catholic deacon who lives and works in the Chicago area. He is a former member of the Emil Rothe chapter of SABR. He is originally from Ohio and a lifelong Cleveland Indians fan, but his niece is a 2013 graduate of the University of Minnesota and he has attended games at both the Metrodome and Target Field.

JIMMY KEENAN has been a SABR member since 2001. His grandfather Jimmy Lyston, along with his great-grandfather John M. Lyston and John's two brothers Marty and Bill were all professional baseball players. He is the author of the book, "The Lystons- A Story of One Baltimore Family and Our National Pastime." Jimmy has contributed articles to the 2009 and 2013 editions of SABR's annual publication "The National Pastime." In addition, he was the writer and historian for the original Forgotten Birds Documentary that chronicles the fifty-year history of the minor league Baltimore Orioles. Jimmy is a 2010 inductee into the Oldtimers Baseball Association of Maryland's Hall of Fame and a 2012 inductee into the Baltimore's Boys of Summer Hall of Fame.

NORM KING lives in Ottawa, Ontario and has been a SABR member since 2010. His interests focus on baseball history and writing player biographies. He focuses particularly on players and events in the history of the Montreal Expos. He has contributed to a number of SABR books including, *Thar's Joy in Braveland: the 1957 Milwaukee Braves*, *Winning on the North Side: The 1929 Chicago Cubs*, and *VanLingle Mungo: The Man, The Song, The Players*, as well as other publications. He is currently serving as editor for a book on the 50 greatest games in the history of the Expos. He still misses them dearly.

BEN KLEIN grew up in Southern California, but moved to Washington, D.C. to attend college and law school. Now in Rockville, Maryland, Ben enjoys cheering for the Nationals, a pastime that he shares with his wife, Jen, and their newborn daughter, Abby. In the offseason, Ben and his dog, Charlie, turn their attention to college hoops and the Georgetown Hoyas.

PATRICK LETHERT is CMO for an electronic payments company, author of a book on parenting, and a contributor to Total Hockey, the Official Encyclopedia of the NHL. Patrick is a lifelong Twins fan. He shares a home with his wife Jennifer, a daughter who likes Michael Cuddyer, a two left-handed power hitting sons who favor Mike Trout and Denard Span respectively, 900 baseball books and 150 bobbleheads.

LEN LEVIN, a resident of Providence, Rhode Island, has been a copyeditor for most of SABR's recent books and a Red Sox fan long before that. He is a retired newspaper editor, and currently works part-time editing the decisions of the Rhode Island Supreme Court.

DAN LEVITT is the author (with Mark Armour) of *In Pursuit of Pennants: Baseball Operations from Deadball to Moneyball*, a spring 2015 publication from the University of Nebraska Press. He is also the author of several other notable baseball books including *The Battle that Forged Modern Baseball: The Federal League Challenge and Its Legacy*, *Ed Barrow: The Bulldog Who Built the Yankees' First Dynasty*, and *Paths to Glory: How Great Baseball Teams Got That Way*. He lives in Minneapolis with his wife and two boys.

BILL NOWLIN is vice president of SABR and author or editor of close to 50 books, mostly on baseball. A former university professor, he co-founded Rounder Records in 1970 and helped build the company into what became probably America's most active independent music label. One of the recent books he edited for SABR was the book *Van Lingle Mungo: The Man, The Song, The Players*.

J.G. PRESTON is a freelance writer in Benicia, California and has extensive experience as a radio and television host, play-by-play broadcaster and media relations professional. He edited the Minnesota Twins' program and monthly magazine from 1988-90 and contributed to the Twins' program and yearbook for more than a decade after that. He also wrote the script for a video biography of Kirby Puckett that was narrated by Bob Costas. Other biographies he has written have appeared in SABR books about the 1934 Cardinals, 1972-74 A's and wartime replacement players. He writes about baseball history at http://prestonjg.wordpress.com

JOEL RIPPEL is the author or co-author of seven books on Minnesota sports history. He has contributed to several SABR publications including *The National Pastime and The Emerald Guide to Baseball*.

A resident of East Brunswick, New Jersey, **FRANK RUSSO** is a nationally known Baseball Researcher/Baseball Necrologist who has been researching deceased major leaguers for over 45 years. He is the owner/webmaster of TheDeadballEra.com website, the first website dedicated to deceased major league players and personalities. A rabid New York Yankees fan, he is also a fan of the New York Football Giants and the New York Islanders, although he hopes you won't hold that against him. A member of the Society for American Baseball Research (SABR), he is also a former radio announcer and former blogger for Mike Silva's NYbaseballdigest.com, where he covered the Yankees.

RICK SCHABOWSKI, a retired machinist from the Harley-Davidson Company, is currently an instructor at Wisconsin Regional Training Partnership in the Manufacturing program, and is a certified Manufacturing Skills Standards Council instructor. He is also President of the Ken Keltner Badger State Chapter of SABR, Treasurer of the Milwaukee Braves Historical Association, President of the Wisconsin Oldtime Ballplayers Association, and is a member of the Hoops Historians and Pro Football Research Association.

STEVEN D. SCHMITT was born and raised and now lives in Madison, Wisconsin. A lifelong Chicago Cubs fan, Steven pulled for the Twins in the 1965 World Series while in the first grade and remembers Mudcat Grant hitting a home run, Earl Battey colliding with the dugout railing, and Sandy Koufax winning Game 7. Steven has written a book on the history of University of Wisconsin baseball and is a master's graduate of the UW - Madison School of Journalism and Mass Communication. His daughter, Natalie, is a psychology major and a swimmer at UW - Stevens Point.

DOUG SKIPPER has contributed to a number of SABR publications, presented research at national and regional conventions, and profiled more than a dozen players and managers for the SABR Baseball Biographical Project. A SABR member since 1982, he is serving as president of the Halsey Hall (Minneapolis) Chapter in 2014-2015, and a member of the Deadball Era Committee, and is interested in the history of Connie Mack's Philadelphia Athletics, the Boston Red Sox, the Minnesota Twins, and old ballparks. A market research consultant residing in Apple Valley, Minnesota, Doug is also a veteran of father-daughter dancing. Doug and his wife have two daughters, MacKenzie and Shannon.

JOHN SWOL, has followed baseball since 1957 and the Minnesota Twins since they started play in 1961.

Published a book called *Twins Trivia* back in 1997. John has owned and maintained a Minnesota Twins historical web site called www.twinstrivia.com for over ten years.

THOMAS TOMASHEK originally wrote bios on Jerry Kindall and Dick Stigman for the book *Minnesotans in Baseball*.

STEW THORNLEY grew up in Minnesota and attended his first Twins game at Metropolitan Stadium in 1962. He worked in radio broadcasting as a sportscaster/sports director at radio stations in Missouri and central Minnesota in the 1970s before going to college at the University of Minnesota. In the 1980s he worked in sales and also began writing books. His first, *On to Nicollet: The Glory and Fame of the Minneapolis Millers*, received a baseball research award from Macmillan Publishing and the Society for American Baseball Research. He has since written more than 40 other books for adults and young readers. He has worked in training, communications, and media relations for the drinking-water program for the Minnesota Department of Health since 1993 while continuing to write and work in sports. He does official scoring for the Minnesota Timberwolves of the National Basketball Association and is an official scorer for Minnesota Twins home games for Major League Baseball. He is also a member of the MLB Official Scoring Advisory Commmittee. Stew lives in the Twin Cities with his wife, Brenda Himrich.

JOSEPH WANCHO lives in Westlake, Ohio and is a lifelong Cleveland Indians fan. He has been a SABR member since 2005 and serves as Chair of the Minor League Research Committee. He edited a Bio Project Book on the 1954 Cleveland Indians, *Pitching to the Pennant*, (Nebraska Press, 2014)

STEVE WEST'S love of math attracted him to baseball when it arrived in his native New Zealand via ESPN in 1990. He married a Texan and moved to Dallas in 1998, and has not missed an Opening Day since. Steve (a SABR member since 2006), his wife Marian and son Joshua are Rangers season ticket holders, and he will forever hold a grudge against Nelson Cruz for not standing two steps deeper in 2011.

A lifelong Pirates fan, **GREGORY H. WOLF** was born in Pittsburgh, but now resides in the Chicagoland area with his wife, Margaret, and daughter, Gabriela. A Professor of German Studies and holder of the Dennis and Jean Bauman Endowed Chair in the Humanities at North Central College in Naperville, Illinois, he edited the SABR book *"Thar's Joy in Braveland." The 1957 Milwaukee Braves* (2014) and *Winning on the North Side. The 1929 Chicago Cubs* (2015). He is working on a project about the County Stadium in Milwaukee.

Join SABR today!

If you're interested in baseball — writing about it, reading about it, talking about it — there's a place for you in the Society for American Baseball Research.

SABR was formed in 1971 in Cooperstown, New York, with the mission of fostering the research and dissemination of the history and record of the game. Our members include everyone from academics to professional sportswriters to amateur historians and statisticians to students and casual fans who merely enjoy reading about baseball history and occasionally gathering with other members to talk baseball.

SABR members have a variety of interests, and this is reflected in the diversity of its research committees. There are more than two dozen groups devoted to the study of a specific area related to the game — from Baseball and the Arts to Statistical Analysis to the Deadball Era to Women in Baseball. In addition, many SABR members meet formally and informally in regional chapters throughout the year and hundreds come together for the annual national convention, the organization's premier event. These meetings often include panel discussions with former major league players and research presentations by members. Most of all, SABR members love talking baseball with like-minded friends. What unites them all is an interest in the game and joy in learning more about it.

Why join SABR? Here are some benefits of membership:

- Two issues (spring and fall) of the *Baseball Research Journal*, which includes articles on history, biography, statistics, personalities, book reviews, and other aspects of the game.
- One expanded e-book edition of *The National Pastime*, which focuses on baseball in the region where that year's SABR national convention is held (in 2015, it's Chicago)
- 8-10 new and classic e-books published each year by the SABR Digital Library, which are all free for members to download
- *This Week in SABR* newsletter in your e-mail every Friday, which highlights SABR members' research and latest news
- Regional chapter meetings, which can include guest speakers, presentations and trips to ballgames
- Online access to back issues of *The Sporting News* and other periodicals through Paper of Record
- Access to SABR's lending library and other research resources
- Online member directory to connect you with an international network of SABR baseball experts and fans
- Discounts on registration for our annual events, including SABR Analytics Conference & Jerry Malloy Negro League Conference
- Access to SABR-L, an e-mail discussion list of baseball questions & answers that many feel is worth the cost of membership itself
- The opportunity to be part of a passionate international community of baseball fans

SABR membership is on a "rolling" calendar system; that means your membership lasts 365 days no matter when you sign up! Enjoy all the benefits of SABR membership by signing up today at SABR.org/join or by clipping out the form below and mailing it to SABR, Cronkite School at ASU, 555 N. Central Ave. #416, Phoenix, AZ 85004.

SABR MEMBERSHIP FORM

	Annual	3-year	Senior	3-yr Sr.	Under 30
U.S.:	❑ $65	❑ $175	❑ $45	❑ $129	❑ $45
Canada/Mexico:	❑ $75	❑ $205	❑ $55	❑ $159	❑ $55
Overseas:	❑ $84	❑ $232	❑ $64	❑ $186	❑ $55

Add a Family Member: $15 for each family member at same address (list on back)
Senior: 65 or older before 12/31/2015
All dues amounts in U.S. dollars or equivalent

Participate in Our Donor Program!
I'd like to designate my gift to be used toward:
❑General Fund   ❑Endowment Fund   ❑Research Resources   ❑_____
❑ I want to maximize the impact of my gift; do not send any donor premiums
❑ I would like this gift to remain anonymous.

Note: Any donation not designated will be placed in the General Fund.
SABR is a 501 (c) (3) not-for-profit organization & donations are tax-deductible to the extent allowed by law.

Name _____

Address _____

City _____ ST_____ ZIP_____

Phone _____ Birthday _____

E-mail: _____
(Your e-mail address on file ensures you will receive the most recent SABR news.)

Dues $_____
Donation $_____
Amount Enclosed $_____

Do you work for a matching grant corporation? Call (602) 496-1460 for details.

If you wish to pay by credit card, please contact the SABR office at (602) 496-1460 or visit the SABR Store online at SABR.org/join. We accept Visa, Mastercard & Discover.

Do you wish to receive the *Baseball Research Journal* electronically?: ❑ Yes   ❑ No
Our e-books are available in PDF, Kindle, or EPUB (iBooks, iPad, Nook) formats.

Mail to: SABR, Cronkite School at ASU, 555 N. Central Ave. #416, Phoenix, AZ 85004

www.ingramcontent.com/pod-product-compliance
Lightning Source LLC
Chambersburg PA
CBHW081342080526

44588CB00016B/2357